Conflict in the Classroom:

The Education of Emotionally Disturbed Children

Third Edition

Conflict in the Classroom:

The Education of Emotionally Disturbed Children

Third Edition

Nicholas J. Long
American University

William C. Morse
University of Michigan

Ruth G. Newman
*Washington School
of Psychiatry*

*Wadsworth Publishing Company, Inc.
Belmont, California*

ISBN 0-534-00400-8
L.C. Cat. Card No. 75-23506
Printed in the United States of America

4 5 6 7 8 9 10—80 79

CONTENTS

4 What Kinds of Schools and Programs Are Provided?

5 How Do You Teach These Children?

Conceptual Models of Emotional Disturbance

The Psychoeducational Approach

6 Hygienic Management

7 The Evolution of Practice: Evaluation and Innovation

Preface

Never has there been more upheaval in special education. The area of education for the emotionally disturbed is more subject to change than other areas of special education because approaches to this particular field reflect what is happening both in special education and in mental health.

It is interesting to look back over the 1960s and recall the predictions we made in the first edition of *Conflict in the Classroom* (1965) about the future treatment of emotionally disturbed children. For example, we predicted that new programs would not be as committed to psychiatric supervision and direction as those of the past; that the United States Office of Education, Bureau of the Handicapped, would play a major role in funding new and different teacher-training models; that the Council of Children with Behavioral Disorders would grow to new dimensions and assure new leadership in the field; that school administrations and teachers, faced with conflicting theories, practices, and opinions, would search for a simple, economic solution to the complex problem of educating the emotionally disturbed; and that public school programs for children with behavioral problems would expand.

But we did not envision the full impact of a cultural revolution. In June 1969, the Joint Commission on the Mental Health of Children and Youth reported the findings of a three-year national study. The results and recommendations of the comprehensive study were in sharp contrast to the values we espouse. The report documented violence, frustration, and discontent among our youth, the vast numbers of unserved

handicapped pupils, the thousands of children excluded from school, and the inexcusable existence of malnutrition among children. The *myth* that we are a child-centered society was exploded. In addition, the report described the existence of ten million people under 25 who need immediate mental health services, but who will go untreated because the needed services do not exist, because services are fragmented, or because color, class, or cost barriers stand in their way. There has been much verbal response and even some actual change in special education for the emotionally disturbed. We see-saw between brave new concepts and partial fulfillment. Mandatory special education laws have been passed, but seldom have the needed resources been appropriated. Labeling has been decried, yet in most states labeling is still required to obtain special education services. We are in the midst of mainstreaming the special pupil but have not insured the quality of service in the new setting. Rights of children are being recognized in legal decisions, and we can hope the psychological aspects which are the real basis of rights will catch up. In some instances, the needs of the child are still made subservient to set ideas of cures, and there are even prescriptions for the disturbed child which ignore the affective components completely. But we have evolved new ways to help disturbed children by adding to the old methodologies, and the educational component has come to be central in the treatment. The distinction between formal therapy and doing therapeutic things has been erased. We have assumed the lofty goal of programs for all special children reflected mandatory legislation. Parents are being given their right to participate in decisions and to undertake partnership in helping the disturbed youngsters. So we are on the move even in face of the current social stress, which puts children in increasing jeopardy as Escolana says in a recent issue of the *American Journal of Orthopsychiatry*. Children's violence, aggression, alienation, confusion, and discouragement, resulting from the breakdown of social institutions, are everyday news. Fortunately, there are many professionals, new and old, who are pursuing with vigor a new alignment in special education for the disturbed.

This book is about the problems these professionals face. It is a book in sharp contrast to the pop culture special education which offers miracle solutions today that die tomorrow. There are no simple answers. Neither are there any cheap answers. At this point in time one would hope that the profession of special education could leave its adolescence behind. This book is put together for those who want other than simplistic pap, who want positions made clear, who want the most profound issues made explicit by leaders in the field. This is a resource book for teachers in any classroom as well as the special education classroom, who live endless hours with children, sometimes singly, but most often in groups. Some articles are aimed at practice tomorrow and others for basic understanding which also suggest practice potentials for the creative reader. The challenge is here, and it is all but overwhelming. But the challenge is what is now attracting new young professionals as well as those with experience to work with the emotionally disturbed. Because emotional disturbance is as often an accompaniment to other special education conditions as it is an entity in its own right, these matters are of concern to all special education teachers.

The selections have been sifted from a vast literature: there were many more we wished to include had there been space. As in previous editions, recent and original articles have been included to provide the reader with a relevant study of old and new topics. Most important, we not only indicate our personal psychoeducational bias in the teaching of children with problems, but we provide the reader an opportunity to examine different approaches to re-educating pupils found in the psychodynamic, behavioral, educational, social competence, and ecological models.

Finally, the chapter introduction and continuity sections have been expanded. Although each of the articles carries its own story, the significance of a selection must be considered in context. This is the purpose of the continuity sections. In fact, one might say this results in a new kind of professional resource book.

It is helpful for those readers who use it on their own. For other students working with an able teacher and a class of colleagues, *Conflict* provides the basis of a new and exciting learning adventure. It aims not in a methodbound indoctrination but in expansion of understanding with faith in the integrity of those who work with disturbed children and youth.

Nicholas J. Long
William C. Morse
Ruth G. Newman

1

How Does It Feel to Be Emotionally Disturbed?

How It Feels Inside Looking Out

Emotional disturbance in childhood is not a new problem, but only recently has it been recognized as a condition that can be alleviated through early diagnosis and careful treatment. Although scientists battle over the causes of emotional disturbance and the relative importance of genetic, constitutional, and environmental factors, everyone agrees that its form is in some degree dependent on the cultural and social values of the times.

Each of us contains the whole range of emotional health and disease within himself. Our nightmares, if they serve no other purpose, enable us to share the ways in which many psychotics experience life. If our legs "go to sleep" and refuse to behave as they should, we can briefly experience the helpless and often outraged feelings of the organic spastic. The sudden loss of temper nearly all of us have experienced gives a momentary empathy with the feelings of uncontrollable rage, helplessness, confusion, guilt, and self-hate felt by the child with no impulse control. Most of us have shared a variety of neurotic symptoms: the terrifying fear of something that we know rationally should not in itself cause fear; the magical, protective cloak of knocking on wood, crossing fingers, counting to ten, holding our breath; the compulsive need to get one thing done, no matter how inane or how inconvenient, before we can do something else; the piece of work that can never be finished because it is never good enough; the headaches, stomach pains, or shortness of breath (unexplainable in the doctor's office) that often occur at a family reunion, at exam time, or at the appearance of a certain person; the need to eat greedily though we are not hungry, or the reverse—being unable to swallow a mouthful; the uncontrollable blush or stutter; the immobilizing lapse of memory; or the urge to take something, to break something, to say the very thing that will get us into trouble, or to be silent when speaking up might simplify our lives and reduce the hostility of others.

Such illogical behavior does not mean that most of us are neurotic—only that some emotional disorder is as much a part of everyone's life as the common cold. It is not surprising, therefore, that emotional disturbance should play so great a role in childhood—a period of dependency and change, in which the world and its demands are new and often confusing, conflicting, and frustrating. When the case histories of severely disturbed children are examined, we often are amazed that more disturbance has not occurred or, indeed, that they have survived at all.

Many literary artists have chronicled the actions of disturbed children or of adults with disturbances rooted in their childhood. Writers were describing these people long before Freud; and since good writers are skilled in conveying pictures and feelings, their descriptions often have greater impact on us than the clinical descriptions in textbooks. For this reason, we present in this chapter excerpts from a variety of fictional and autobiographical works to illustrate the kinds of mental illness and disturbance that beset children. Mostly, the stories are about children of various ages, but there are also some descriptions of adult behavior that show clearly the final development of a childhood disturbance. There are examples of behavior problems and of delinquency in various forms and degrees. There are accounts of trauma, anxiety, and panic. There are decriptions of the workings of several kinds of neuroses, from mild to severe, as well as some psychotic behavior. You will find here the withdrawn child and the acting-out child; the culturally or emotionally disadvantaged and the physically or mentally handicapped; the social rebel and the autistic child, who lives in a world of his own making; and even the child murderer and the child suicide. You will also find portrayals of the feelings and experiences of both young and old people living in today's society and reacting to it, its paraphernalia, its values, and its real or philosophical restrictions in ways that are often destructive to the person himself and to others. Though destructive reactions to the circumstances of life occur in all social and ethnic groups, certain forms of destructive behavior are often found more prominently among members of one or another particular economic class. For example, ghetto or poverty society—white, black, brown, yellow, or red—breeds certain kinds of hate, virulence, and acting out against others or oneself. The affluent middle class with its high priority on material things and achievement often breeds another kind of reaction, one which is frequently brought forcibly to our attention in the person of the middle-class drug user and addict. In both environments—poverty and the middle class—the reaction, against despair and misery on the one hand and against phony values on the other, may be a healthy one: it may result in the need to do something about the unsatisfactory environmental conditions. It is the reaction which signals passive helplessness and ends in greater inadequacy and despair that encourages emotional disturbance. Emotional upset in most people results in behavior that is ultimately both intelligent and useful. But when a person's initial feeling of rage or apathy becomes destructive of

himself or of others, his behavior can legitimately be called disturbed.

This chapter is divided into three parts: the first pictures basic intrapsychic difficulties that can be found anywhere, anytime; the second presents certain aspects of society, its deprivations, restrictions, and human devaluations, which breed disturbed behavior, or, in conflict with inner needs, cause some people to react destructively. Some people react by withdrawing into themselves; some separate feeling from thought; some resort to body language, get headaches or ulcers, or become psychologically deaf or paralyzed; others eat compulsively to build a wall of fat between themselves and others. And others drink to numb their pain. The third part discusses drug use. Many of our young people take drugs, some to such excess they delude themselves into a state of "nonfeeling" or believe they have grasped the import of their lives or expanded their awareness of the world; others take drugs to do what they might otherwise never be able to countenance.

The selections in this chapter portray some of these basic emotional states, caused either by internal dynamics or by external forces, or a combination of both. Of course, we cannot cover every circumstance—the selections chosen are particularly insightful or descriptive samples.

With most readings (except where the author himself does so), we give a description of how a teacher might recognize in his own classroom the kind of child described. Also, to familiarize the teacher with the language of psychiatric or psychological reports, we give the clinical terms which would be used in diagnosing the children in these readings. These terms are shortcut descriptions which imply a general pattern of personality or behavior. They have limited meaning and with glib use lose even that. In most cases diagnostic terms are as unmeaningful to laymen as Latin terms for medicines. The words are given here simply to remove their aura of mystery, so we may look deeper, as William James says, "like a child staring a fact in the face."

The fundamental purpose of this chapter, however, is to offer the reader an intense experience of *how it feels* to be emotionally disturbed, a victim of psychological forces which control and sometimes choke off one's sense of acceptance, adequacy, and love.

The Use of Force
William Carlos Williams

They were new patients to me, all I had was the name, Olson. Please come down as soon as you can, my daughter's very sick.

When I arrived I was met by the mother, a big startled looking woman, very clean and apologetic who merely said, Is this the doctor? and let me in. In the back, she added, You must excuse us, doctor, we have her in the kitchen where it is warm. It is very damp here sometimes.

The child was fully dressed and sitting on her father's lap near the kitchen table. He tried to get up, but I motioned for him not to bother, took off my overcoat and started to look things over. I could see that they were all very nervous, eyeing me up and down distrustfully. As often, in such cases, they weren't telling me more than they had to, it was up to me to tell them; that's why they were spending three dollars on me.

The child was fairly eating me up with her cold, steady eyes, and no expression to her face whatever. She did not move and seemed, inwardly, quiet; an unusually attractive little thing, and as strong as a heifer in appearance. But her face was flushed, she was breathing rapidly, and I realized that she had a high fever. She had magnificent blonde hair, in profusion. One of those picture children often reproduced in advertising leaflets and the photogravure sections of the Sunday papers.

She's had a fever for three days, began the father, and we don't know what it comes from. My wife has given her things, you know, like people do, but it don't do no good. And there's been a lot of sickness around. So we tho't you'd better look her over and tell us what is the matter.

As doctors often do I took a trial shot at it as a point of departure. Has she had a sore throat?

Both parents answered me together, No . . . No, she says her throat don't hurt her.

Does your throat hurt you? added the mother to the child. But the little girl's expression didn't change nor did she move her eyes from my face.

Have you looked?

I tried to, said the mother, but I couldn't see.

As it happens we had been having a number of cases of diphtheria in the school to which this child went during that month and we were all, quite apparently, thinking of that, though no one had as yet spoken of the thing.

Well, I said, suppose we take a look at the throat first. I smiled in my best professional manner and asking for the child's first name I said, come on, Mathilda, open your mouth and let's take a look at your throat.

Nothing doing.

Aw, come on, I coaxed, just open your mouth wide and let me take a look. Look, I said opening both hands wide, I haven't anything in my hands. Just open up and let me see.

Such a nice man, put in the mother. Look how kind he is to you. Come on, do what he tells you to. He won't hurt you.

At that I ground my teeth in disgust. If only they wouldn't use the word "hurt" I might be able to get somewhere. But I did not allow myself to be hurried or disturbed but speaking quietly and slowly I approached the child again.

As I moved my chair a little nearer suddenly with one cat-like movement both her hands clawed instinctively for my eyes and she almost reached them too. In fact she knocked my glasses flying and they fell, though unbroken, several feet away from me on the kitchen floor.

Both the mother and father almost turned themselves inside out in embarrassment and apology. You bad girl, said the mother, taking her and shaking her by one arm. Look what you've done. The nice man . . .

For heaven's sake, I broke in. Don't call me a nice man to her. I'm here to look at her throat on the chance that she might have diphtheria and possibly die of it. But that's nothing to her. Look here, I said to the child, we're going to look at your throat. You're old enough to understand what I'm saying. Will you open it now by yourself or shall we have to open it for you?

Not a move. Even her expression hadn't changed. Her breaths however were coming faster and faster. Then the battle began. I had to do it. I had to have a throat culture for her own protection.

But first I told the parents that it was entirely up to them. I explained the danger but said that I would not insist on a throat examination so long as they would take the responsibility.

If you don't do what the doctor says you'll have to go to the hospital, the mother admonished her severely.

Oh yeah? I had to smile to myself. After all, I had already fallen in love with the savage brat, the parents were contemptible to me. In the ensuing struggle they grew more and more abject, crushed, exhausted while she surely rose to magnificent heights of insane fury of effort bred of her terror of me.

The father tried his best, and he was a big man but the fact that she was his daughter, his shame at her behavior and his dread of hurting her made him release her just at the critical moment several times when I had almost achieved success, till I wanted to kill him. But his dread also that she might have diphtheria made him tell me to go on, go on though he himself was almost fainting, while the mother moved back and forth behind us raising and lowering her hands in an agony of apprehension.

Put her in front of you on your lap, I ordered, and hold both her wrists.

But as soon as he did the child let out a scream. Don't you're hurting me. Let go of my hands. Let them go I tell you. She shrieked terrifyingly, hysterically. Stop it! Stop it! You're killing me!

Do you think she can stand it, doctor? said the mother.

You get out, said the husband to his wife. Do you want her to die of diphtheria?

Come on now, hold her, I said.

Then I grasped the child's head with my left hand and tried to get the wooden tongue depressor between her teeth. She fought, with clenched teeth, desperately! But now I also had grown furious—at a child. I tried to hold myself down but I couldn't. I know how to expose a throat for inspection. And I did my best. When finally I got the wooden spatula behind the last teeth and just the point of it into the mouth cavity, she opened up for an instant but before I could see anything she came down again and gripping the wooden blade between her molars she reduced it to splinters before I could get it out again.

Aren't you ashamed, the mother yelled at her. Aren't you ashamed to act like that in front of the doctor?

Get me a smooth-handled spoon of some sort, I told the mother. We're going through with this. The child's mouth was already bleeding. Her tongue was cut and she was screaming in wild hysterical shrieks. Perhaps I should have desisted and come back in an hour or more. No doubt it would have been better. But I have seen at least two children lying dead in bed of neglect in such cases, and feeling that I must get a diagnosis now or never I went at it again. But the worst of it was that I too had got beyond reason. I could have torn the child apart in my own fury and enjoyed it. It was a pleasure to attack her. My face was burning with it.

The damned little brat must be protected against her own idiocy, one says to one's self at such times. Others must be protected against her. It is social necessity. And all these things are true. But a blind fury, a feeling of adult shame, bred of a longing for muscular release are the operatives. One goes on to the end.

In a final unreasoning assault I overpowered the child's neck and jaws. I forced the heavy silver spoon back of her teeth and down her throat till she gagged. And there it was—both tonsils covered with membrane. She had fought valiantly to keep me from knowing her secret. She had been hiding that sore throat for three days at least and lying to her parents in order to escape just such an outcome as this.

Now truly she *was* furious. She had been on the defensive before but now she attacked. Tried to get off her father's lap and fly at me while tears of defeat blinded her eyes.

Diagnosis

Behavior problem—resistance to adult authority, hostility, aggressiveness; might be the beginning signs of a "character" neurosis.

The story shows a power struggle—a sick, frightened, but powerful child who is accustomed to defeating adults and who will try to do so even when one adult is there to save her life. Confronted with incompetent grown-ups, she renders them more incompetent, testing their power with her own. In so doing, she alienates herself from others, refusing to accept the help she so badly needs. The ingredient of trust (which Erikson's developmental scale postulates as basic to growth) has been distorted, and her growth inevitably will be distorted also unless she and her parents can change. She needs adults who care and who can show they care by setting limits and providing consistent care.

An Incident
Anton Chekhov

Morning. Brilliant sunshine is piercing through the frozen lacework on the window-panes into the nursery. Vanya, a boy of six, with a cropped head and a nose like a button, and his sister Nina, a short, chubby, curly-headed girl of four, wake up and look crossly at each other through the bars of their cots.

"Oo-oo-oo! naughty children!" grumbles their nurse. "Good people have had their breakfast already, while you can't get your eyes open."

The sunbeams frolic over the rugs, the walls, and nurse's skirts, and seem inviting the children to join in their play, but they take no notice. They have woken up in a bad humour. Nina pouts, makes a grimace, and begins to whine:

"Brea-eakfast, nurse, breakfast!"

Vanya knits his brows and ponders what to pitch upon to howl over. He has already begun screwing up his eyes and opening his mouth, but at that instant the voice of mamma reaches them from the drawing-room, saying: "Don't forget to give the cat her milk, she has a family now!"

The children's puckered countenances grow smooth again as they look at each other in astonishment. Then both at once begin shouting, jump out of their cots, and filling the air with piercing shrieks, run barefoot, in their nightgowns, to the kitchen.

"The cat has puppies!" they cry. "The cat has got puppies!"

Under the bench in the kitchen there stands a small box, the one in which Stepan brings coal when he lights the fire. The cat is peeping out of the box. There is an expression of extreme exhaustion on her grey face; her green eyes, with their narrow black pupils, have a languid, sentimental look. . . . From her face it is clear that the only thing lacking to complete her happiness is the presence in the box of "him," the father of her children, to whom she had abandoned herself so recklessly! She wants to mew, and opens her mouth wide, but nothing but a hiss comes from her throat; the squealing of the kittens is audible.

The children squat on their heels before the box, and, motionless, holding their breath, gaze at the cat. . . . They are surprised, impressed, and do not hear nurse grumbling as she pursues them. The most genuine delight shines in the eyes of both.

Domestic animals play a scarcely noticed but undoubtedly beneficial part in the education and life of children. Which of us does not remember powerful but magnanimous dogs, lazy lapdogs, birds dying in captivity, dull-witted but haughty turkeys, mild old tabby cats, who forgave us when we trod on their tails for fun and caused them agonising pain? I even fancy, sometimes, that the patience, the fidelity, the readiness to forgive, and the sincerity which are characteristic of our domestic animals have a far stronger and more definite effect on the mind of a child than the long exhortations of some dry, pale Karl Karlovitch, or the misty expositions of a governess, trying to prove to children that water is made up of hydrogen and oxygen.

"What little things!" says Nina, opening her eyes wide and going off into a joyous laugh. "They are like mice!"

"One, two, three," Vanya counts. "Three kittens. So there is one for you, one for me, and one for somebody else, too."

"Murrm . . . murrm . . ." purrs the mother, flattered by their attention. "Murrm."

After gazing at the kittens, the children take them from under the cat, and begin squeezing them in their hands, then, not satisfied with this, they put them in the skirts of their nightgowns, and run into the other rooms.

"Mamma, the cat has got pups!" they shout.

Mamma is sitting in the drawing-room with some unknown gentleman. Seeing the children unwashed, undressed, with their nightgowns held up high, she is embarrassed, and looks at them severely.

"Let your nightgowns down, disgraceful children," she says. "Go out of the room, or I will punish you."

But the children do not notice either mamma's threats or the presence of a stranger. They put the kittens down on the carpet, and go off into deafening squeals. The mother walks round them, mew-

Reprinted with permission of The Macmillan Company and Chatto & Windus, Ltd. from *The Cook's Wedding and Other Stories* by Anton Chekhov, translated from Russian by Constance Garnett. Copyright 1922 by The Macmillan Company, renewed 1950 by David Garnett.

ing imploringly. When, a little afterwards, the children are dragged off to the nursery, dressed, made to say their prayers, and given their breakfast, they are full of a passionate desire to get away from these prosaic duties as quickly as possible, and to run to the kitchen again.

Their habitual pursuits and games are thrown completely into the background.

The kittens throw everything into the shade by making their appearance in the world, and supply the great sensation of the day. If Nina or Vanya had been offered forty pounds of sweets or ten thousand kopecks for each kitten, they would have rejected such a barter without the slightest hesitation. In spite of the heated protests of the nurse and the cook, the children persist in sitting by the cat's box in the kitchen, busy with the kittens till dinner-time. Their faces are earnest and concentrated and express anxiety. They are worried not so much by the present as by the future of the kittens. They decide that one kitten shall remain at home with the old cat to be a comfort to her mother, while the second shall go to their summer villa, and the third shall live in the cellar, where there are ever so many rats.

"But why don't they look at us?" Nina wondered. "Their eyes are blind like the beggars'."

Vanya, too, is perturbed by this question. He tries to open one kitten's eyes, and spends a long time puffing and breathing hard over it, but his operation is unsuccessful. They are a good deal troubled, too, by the circumstance that the kittens obstinately refuse the milk and the meat that is offered to them. Everything that is put before their little noses is eaten by their grey mamma.

"Let's build the kittens little houses," Vanya suggests. "They shall live in different houses, and the cat shall come and pay them visits. . . ."

Cardboard hat-boxes are put in the different corners of the kitchen and the kittens are installed in them. But this division turns out to be premature; the cat, still wearing an imploring and sentimental expression on her face, goes the round of all the hat-boxes, and carries off her children to their original position.

"The cat's their mother," observed Vanya, "but who is their father?"

"Yes, who is their father?" repeats Nina.

"They must have a father."

Vanya and Nina are a long time deciding who is to be the kittens' father, and, in the end, their choice falls on a big dark-red horse without a tail, which is lying in the store-cupboard under the stairs, together with other relics of toys that have

outlived their day. They drag him up out of the store-cupboard and stand him by the box.

"Mind now!" they admonish him, "stand here and see they behave themselves properly."

All this is said and done in the gravest way, with an expression of anxiety on their faces. Vanya and Nina refuse to recognise the existence of any world but the box of kittens. Their joy knows no bounds. But they have to pass through bitter, agonising moments, too.

Just before dinner, Vanya is sitting in his father's study, gazing dreamily at the table. A kitten is moving about by the lamp, on stamped note paper. Vanya is watching its movements, and thrusting first a pencil, then a match into its little mouth. . . . All at once, as though he has sprung out of the floor, his father is beside the table.

"What's this?" Vanya hears, in an angry voice.

"It's . . . it's the kitty, papa. . . ."

"I'll give it you; look what you have done, you naughty boy! You've dirtied all my paper!"

To Vanya's great surprise his papa does not share his partiality for the kittens, and, instead of being moved to enthusiasm and delight, he pulls Vanya's ear and shouts:

"Stepan, take away this horrid thing."

At dinner, too, there is a scene. . . . During the second course there is suddenly the sound of a shrill mew. They begin to investigate its origin, and discover a kitten under Nina's pinafore.

"Nina, leave the table!" cries her father angrily. "Throw the kittens in the cesspool! I won't have the nasty things in the house! . . ."

Vanya and Nina are horrified. Death in the cesspool, apart from its cruelty, threatens to rob the cat and the wooden horse of their children, to lay waste the cat's box, to destroy their plans for the future, that fair future in which one cat will be a comfort to its old mother, another will live in the country, while the third will catch rats in the cellar. The children begin to cry and entreat that the kittens may be spared. Their father consents, but on the condition that the children do not go into the kitchen and touch the kittens.

After dinner Vanya and Nina slouch about the rooms, feeling depressed. The prohibition of visits to the kitchen has reduced them to dejection. They refuse sweets, are naughty, and are rude to their mother. When their uncle Petrusha comes in the evening, they draw him aside, and complain to him of their father, who wanted to throw the kittens into the cesspool.

"Uncle Petrusha, tell mamma to have the kittens taken to the nursery," the children beg their uncle, "do-o tell her."

"There, there . . . very well," says their uncle, waving them off. "All right."

Uncle Petrusha does not usually come alone. He is accompanied by Nero, a big black dog of Danish breed, with drooping ears, and a tail as hard as a stick. The dog is silent, morose, and full of a sense of his own dignity. He takes not the slightest notice of the children, and when he passes them hits them with his tail as though they were chairs. The children hate him from the bottom of their hearts, but on this occasion, practical considerations override sentiment.

"I say, Nina," says Vanya, opening his eyes wide. "Let Nero be their father, instead of the horse! The horse is dead and he is alive, you see."

They are waiting the whole evening for the moment when papa will sit down to his cards and it will be possible to take Nero to the kitchen without being observed. . . . At last, papa sits down to cards, mamma is busy with the samovar and not noticing the children. . . .

The happy moment arrives.

"Come along!" Vanya whispers to his sister.

But, at that moment, Stepan comes in and, with a snigger, announces:

"Nero has eaten the kittens, madam."

Nina and Vanya turn pale and look at Stepan with horror.

"He really has . . ." laughs the footman, "he went to the box and gobbled them up."

The children expect that all the people in the house will be aghast and fall upon the miscreant Nero. But they all sit calmly in their seats, and only express surprise at the appetite of the huge dog. Papa and mamma laugh. Nero walks about by the table, wags his tail, and licks his lips complacently . . . the cat is the only one who is uneasy. With her tail in the air she walks about the rooms, looking suspiciously at people and mewing plaintively.

"Children, it's past nine," cries mamma, "it's bedtime."

Vanya and Nina go to bed, shed tears, and spend a long time thinking about the injured cat, and the cruel, insolent, and unpunished Nero.

Diagnosis

Childhood trauma caused by parental insensitivity to children's feelings, identifications, and projections.

Sometimes this story is entitled "A Trivial Incident." On the continuum of disturbance, these two children as we see them are quite normal: fighting with each other, irritable when thwarted, quickly diverted, and deeply involved when the matter at hand (the kittens) interests them. From such a trivial incident, however, the children can grasp, sometimes with only half-awareness, the real attitudes of the significant adults in their world. The parents' callousness and lack of concern for important issues of life, death, or designs for the future shake the very foundations of the children's belief in adults. These two children have had the door opened on adult cruelty, evil, and unconcern; on the lack of imagination or ability to project feelings, characteristic of self-centered people. The children's natural sympathies have been shocked by recognition that others feel, see, and act in quite a different way. From such an event defenses are built. Whether these take the form of hiding vulnerability, of cloaking feelings with cruelty, or of rebellion against the world, will depend on the children's own genetic constitutions and the amount of love they have already received, as well as on the strength and humanness they are able to feed each other.

Children can be shocked into disillusion by crudity and lack of concern from teachers as well as from parents. Since school is the child's initial major sojourn into the world at large, teachers represent the world he is to cope with for good or ill. If both home and teachers affirm the evil, hypocrisy, and carelessness in the world, the problem of adjustment to injustice or of rebellion against injustice can become major and provide the soil in which pathology can grow. Likewise the school can mitigate the difficulty by providing experiences with kind adults who are sensitive to children's feelings.

The Runaway

Anton Chekhov

The doctor began seeing the patients. He sat in his little room, and called up the patients in turn. Sounds were continually coming from the little room, piercing wails, a child's crying, or the doctor's angry words:

"Come, why are you bawling? Am I murdering you, or what? Sit quiet!"

Pashka's turn came.

"Pavel Galaktionov!" shouted the doctor.

His mother was aghast, as though she had not expected this summons, and taking Pashka by the hand, she led him into the room.

The doctor was sitting at the table, mechanically tapping on a thick book with a little hammer.

"What's wrong?" he asked, without looking at them.

"The little lad has an ulcer on his elbow, sir," answered his mother, and her face assumed an expression as though she really were terribly grieved at Pashka's ulcer.

"Undress him!"

Pashka, panting, unwound the kerchief from his neck, then wiped his nose on his sleeve, and began deliberately pulling off his sheepskin.

"Woman, you have not come here on a visit!" said the doctor angrily. "Why are you dawdling? You are not the only one here."

Pashka hurriedly flung the sheepskin on the floor, and with his mother's help took off his shirt. . . . The doctor looked at him lazily, and patted him on his bare stomach.

"You have grown quite a respectable corporation, brother Pashka," he said, and heaved a sigh. "Come, show me your elbow."

Pashka looked sideways at the basin full of bloodstained slops, looked at the doctor's apron, and began to cry.

"May-ay!" the doctor mimicked him. "Nearly old enough to be married, spoilt boy, and here he is blubbering! For shame!"

Pashka, trying not to cry, looked at his mother, and in that look could be read the entreaty: "Don't tell them at home that I cried at the hospital."

The doctor examined his elbow, pressed it, heaved a sigh, clicked with his lips, then pressed it again.

"You ought to be beaten, woman, but there is no one to do it," he said. "Why didn't you bring him before? Why, the whole arm is done for. Look, foolish woman. You see, the joint is diseased!"

"You know best, kind sir . . ." sighed the woman.

"Kind sir. . . . She's let the boy's arm rot, and now it is 'kind sir.' What kind of workman will he be without an arm? You'll be nursing him and looking after him for ages. I bet if you had had a pimple on your nose, you'd have run to the hospital quick enough, but you have left your boy to rot for six months. You are all like that."

The doctor lighted a cigarette. While the cigarette smoked, he scolded the woman, and shook his head in time to the song he was humming inwardly, while he thought of something else. Pashka stood naked before him, listening and looking at the smoke. When the cigarette went out, the doctor started, and said in a lower tone:

"Well, listen, woman. You can do nothing with ointments and drops in this case. You must leave him in the hospital."

"If necessary, sir, why not?"

"We must operate on him. You stop with me, Pashka," said the doctor, slapping Pashka on the shoulder. "Let mother go home, and you and I will stop here, old man. It's nice with me, old boy, it's first-rate here. I'll tell you what we'll do, Pashka, we will go catching finches together. I will show you a fox! We will go visiting together! Shall we? And mother will come for you tomorrow! Eh?"

Pashka looked inquiringly at his mother.

"You stay, child!" she said.

"He'll stay, he'll stay!" cried the doctor gleefully. "And there is no need to discuss it. I'll show him a live fox! We will go to the fair together to buy candy! Marya Denisovna, take him upstairs!"

The doctor, apparently a light-hearted and

Reprinted with permission of The Macmillan Company and Chatto & Windus, Ltd. from *The Cook's Wedding and Other Stories* by Anton Chekhov, translated from Russian by Constance Garnett. Copyright 1922 by The Macmillan Company, renewed 1950 by David Garnett.

friendly fellow, seemed glad to have company; Pashka wanted to oblige him, especially as he had never in his life been to a fair, and would have been glad to have a look at a live fox, but how could he do without his mother? . . .

A long time passed, but the doctor still did not appear. The nurse brought in tea, and scolded Pashka for not having saved any bread for his tea; the assistant came once more and set to work to wake Mihailo. It turned blue outside the windows, the wards were lighted up, but the doctor did not appear. It was too late now to go to the fair and catch finches; Pashka stretched himself on his bed and began thinking. He remembered the candy promised him by the doctor, the face and voice of his mother, the darkness in his hut at home, the stove, peevish granny Yegorovna . . . and he suddenly felt sad and dreary. He remembered that his mother was coming for him next day, smiled, and shut his eyes.

He was awakened by a rustling. In the next ward someone was stepping about and speaking in a whisper. Three figures were moving about Mihailo's bed in the dim light of the night-light and the ikon lamp.

"Shall we take him, bed and all, or without?" asked one of them.

"Without. You won't get through the door with the bed."

"He's died at the wrong time, the Kingdom of Heaven be his!"

One took Mihailo by his shoulders, another by his legs and lifted him up: Mihailo's arms and the skirt of his dressing-gown hung limply to the ground. A third—it was the peasant who looked like a woman—crossed himself, and all three tramping clumsily with their feet and stepping on Mihailo's skirts, went out of the ward.

There came the whistle and humming on different notes from the chest of the old man who was asleep. Pashka listened, peeped at the dark windows, and jumped out of bed in terror.

"Ma-a-mka!" he moaned in a deep bass.

And without waiting for an answer, he rushed into the next ward. There the darkness was dimly lighted up by a night-light and the ikon lamp; the patients, upset by the death of Mihailo, were sitting on their bedsteads: their dishevelled figures, mixed up with the shadows, looked broader, taller, and seemed to be growing bigger and bigger; on the furthest bedstead in the corner, where it was darkest, there sat the peasant moving his head and his hand.

Pashka, without noticing the doors, rushed into the smallpox ward, from there into the corridor, from the corridor he flew into a big room where monsters, with long hair and the faces of old women, were lying and sitting on the beds. Running through the women's wing he found himself again in the corridor, saw the banisters of the staircase he knew already, and ran downstairs. There he recognised the waiting-room in which he had sat that morning, and began looking for the door into the open air.

The latch creaked, there was a whiff of cold wind, and Pashka, stumbling, ran out into the yard. He had only one thought—to run, to run! He did not know the way, but felt convinced that if he ran he would be sure to find himself at home with his mother. The sky was overcast, but there was a moon behind the clouds. Pashka ran from the steps straight forward, went round the barn and stumbled into some thick bushes; after stopping for a minute and thinking, he dashed back again to the hospital, ran round it, and stopped again undecided; behind the hospital there were white crosses.

"Ma-a-mka!" he cried, and dashed back.

Running by the dark sinister buildings, he saw one lighted window.

The bright red patch looked dreadful in the darkness, but Pashka, frantic with terror, not knowing where to run, turned towards it. Beside the window was a porch with steps, and a front door with a white board on it; Pashka ran up the steps, looked in at the window, and was at once possessed by intense overwhelming joy. Through the window he saw the merry affable doctor sitting at the table reading a book. Laughing with happiness, Pashka stretched out his hands to the person he knew and tried to call out, but some unseen force choked him and struck at his legs; he staggered and fell down on the steps unconscious.

When he came to himself it was daylight, and a voice he knew very well, that had promised him a fair, finches, and a fox, was saying beside him:

"Well, you are an idiot, Pashka! Aren't you an idiot? You ought to be beaten, but there's no one to do it."

Diagnosis

Panic—anxiety caused by adults' lies to avoid child's tears or anger.

This is the story of a child's terror, induced by adult mishandling. The child, ignorant and afraid, is brought by his ignorant mother to a clinic-hospital, where she, his protector, is cowed, scolded, and dominated by the doctor, who treats his cases in an utterly routine, impersonal manner. The child is left to the doctor and the hospital. He has never been left before, and the circumstances are not explained to him. Moreover, the doctor lies to him, promises him candy and a jaunt to a fair. He is put in a room with adults who are sick and in pain. His bewilderment increased by the terrifying atmosphere, he seeks out his "friend," the lying doctor, only to find himself once again helpless in the hands of adults, betrayed by the doctor, deserted by his helpless mother, and living in a nightmare of pain and uncertainty.

Thus are sown the seeds of distrust, suspicion, and the pervasive terror of helplessness.

Chekhov, who himself was a doctor, understood how the bewilderment and helplessness of children could lead to cruelty in adults or to ineffective, cowed adults. Here is a traumatic incident that could well affect a child's entire life, for his trust in his mother and in other adults who were supposed to take care of him was shattered.

Such adult lack of understanding happens daily, and not only in hospitals, clinics, and doctors' offices—though a child's physical helplessness in the hands of doctors and nurses makes him particularly vulnerable in such places. It can also happen the first day of school in a classroom, or whenever a ridiculing or sarcastic teacher holds a child up for shame or makes a false promise to the child simply to get himself over a potentially unpleasant situation.

The Day of the Last Rock Fight
Joseph Whitehill

Fallbrook Academy

May 16, 195–

Dear Dad,

I expect this will be a very long letter, so I am sending it to your office marked *Personal.* I know you don't like to do family business at the office, but I wanted you to have a chance to read this all by yourself, and I didn't want Mother or Sue reading it before you did.

Thank you for sending my allowance, and also for the subscription to the home paper. Thank you also for the nice new wallet for my birthday. I really needed it, as my old one was afflicted with rot and falling apart.

I apologize for not having written sooner. As you said in your last letter, "*Something* must have happened in the last two months worth writing down." I have been very busy with things here at school, but mainly I haven't written because I didn't know how to say what I wanted to say. I hope this letter will make up for the long delay.

You keep asking me what I think of Fallbrook Academy and if I'm happy here, and so on. Well, I don't like it here, and I want to come home. That's what this letter is for—to tell you that now it's all right for me to come back home. I guess I know why you sent me here, and I admit that I wanted very much to come when I did. It's not that the people here aren't nice or anything. They are. They're so nice it's phony. In all the catalogues of the school

they call it a *Special School,* but the boys here call it *Goodbar.* (Mr. Goodbar is a chocolate bar full of nuts.) They all kid about it, and pretend they don't care about being put in a school for misfits and boys with emotional problems. I guess most of them like it here. Most of them say they hate their parents, one or both, and are really glad to get away from them. All the faculty are so sweet and kind and sympathetic that a lot of the boys get away with murder. (That last word was sort of a poor choice, I suppose, but I'll leave it there anyway.) But I don't feel like I belong here any more.

It is going to be very complicated to explain everything in just one letter, because there are lots of different ways of looking at that mess that happened there at home, and I suppose I am the only one who knows the whole story. I guess you sent me here because you thought I was terribly upset by Gene Hanlon getting killed out there at Manning Day School at home, and seeing his body lying in the creek, and so on. Well, that was part of it, but only a little part. The rest of it I couldn't tell anybody until Detective Sergeant Gorman put the story in the paper last week. I got that paper in the mail yesterday and I have been reading the story over and over, and feeling relieved and awful at the same time.

I'm sure you read the same story, so you al-

From *Able Baker and Others* by Joseph Whitehill (Boston: Little, Brown and Co., 1957). Reprinted by permission of Candida Donadio & Associates, Inc. Copyright © 1954, 1955, 1956, 1957 by Joseph Whitehill.

ready know that Gene Hanlon was murdered, instead of getting killed accidentally as they said at first. But neither you nor anybody else knows that I saw the murder done, and knew all the time who did it. I guess if I acted upset afterwards it was from knowing all this and not being able to tell anyone about it. I'm going to work on this letter all night, if it takes that long, because I have to get all this out of my system. (When you stay up after curfew around here they don't actually *make* you go to bed, but the doctor who is on duty looks in on you every half hour or so to see what you're doing, and to try to make you *want* to go to bed.)

I suppose the beginning is the best place to start, so I will tell you first about Gene Hanlon, the boy who got killed. He came to Manning Day School last fall as a senior. They said he was fired from his last school, but I don't know about that. I didn't like him just from looking at him. I know you hate judgments that way on first impressions, but I couldn't help it. I wouldn't ever bring him over to our house, but if I had, you might have seen what I was talking about. He was big and beefy, and he played on the first string last fall. He was also blond, and the girls thought he was cute and from what I heard they fought over him for dates. But he was a bully, and he cheated in the classroom and he borrowed your stuff without asking you and then left it some place where you had to go hunt it up for yourself.

In a school like Manning Day there are always a number of tight little groups—cliques, I guess you call them—that move around independently and generally stay out of the way of the others. I mean there is a football group, and a group of boys who drink beer, and a group who studies hard, and a group who loafs and tries to avoid everything that looks like work, and a group that meets in the locker room to talk about sex and tell dirty jokes. It was probably the same way when you yourself went to school, but you may have forgotten. When you go to a school like that, you pretty soon find the group that suits you best, and you stay there and don't try to mix with any of the others, because if you do you won't be let in.

What I am getting at in this long explanation is that Gene Hanlon was the Big Man in all the groups I wouldn't be seen dead in. He was tops among the football players and their fans. He could tell filthier stories and, he said, hold more liquor than anybody else. And he told stories about the things he had done to girls that you wouldn't believe if anybody else had told them, but with him telling them, you

knew they were all possible. I guess he was feared more than he was liked, but one thing sure, he never went anywhere alone. There was always a loud bunch along with him horse-laughing and beating him on the shoulders.

I stayed out of his way. There is something about me that brings out the worst in bullies. That's what Peter Irish used to say. I guess it's because I'm slightly built, and because of those glasses I have to wear. Once, I was going upstairs to lab, and Gene Hanlon was coming down and we met halfway, and for no reason I could see, he belted me as hard as he could on my shoulder. My glasses flew off and bounced halfway down the stairs along with a whole armload of books and papers. I had to grab the banister to keep from following them down myself. Two other guys with him saw him do it and didn't say anything at first, but then they looked at Gene and knew they'd better laugh, so they did. So I sat there on the stairs all confused inside, holding my shoulder to make it stop hurting. Gene Hanlon and the others went on down the stairs laughing to beat all at how I looked there with everything scattered around me. On the way down, Gene kicked my physics book ahead of him, bouncing it all the way to the bottom. When I could stand up all right I went down and got it. When I picked it up it fell apart in my hands with its binding broken and I guess I started to cry. I hate to see books treated that way.

When I had about got everything picked up, Peter Irish came up to where I was and wanted to know what had happened. Peter being my best friend, I told him all about it. Probably there were still tears in my eyes about the physics book because Peter said, "Do you want me to get him for you?"

I thought for a minute how swell that would be, but then I said no. It was almost yes because Peter was the only one in school who could have whipped Gene under any rules, and it was a very satisfying thing to think about. But then I thought about afterwards, when Gene would have gotten over his beating and would begin to wonder why Peter had done it, and he would remember that Peter was my best friend. Then he would put one and one together and start out after me seriously. So I said no.

Peter Irish was a good friend to have. I suppose he was the strongest kid in school, but he didn't ever use his strength to bully people, but just for things that were fun, like squashing a beer can in one hand. You knew him pretty well because of all the times he came over to the house to study with me. I remember the time he beat you at Indian hand wrestling on the dining-room table, and you were a real good sport about it because Mother was watching and laughing at your expression. But anyway, you know how strong Peter was, and you can feature what he would have done to Gene if I'd told him to. Peter always stayed out of fights unless they were for fun, and if they ever got serious he'd quit because he didn't want to hurt anybody. But he would have torn Gene Hanlon apart if I had asked him to.

That was something I don't think you understood—Peter and me, I mean, and why we hung around together. The simplest way to say it is that we swapped talents. I used to write a lot of his themes for him, and help him in labs so he'd finish when the rest of us did, and he'd show me judo holds and how to skin a squirrel, and such things. You would call it a good working agreement.

Now, there are just two more things you have to know about to see the whole picture. The first one is Peter Irish and Angela Pine. Peter and Angela went together all last year and the year before, and neither of them wanted anybody else. Both their folks made them date other kids because they didn't like to see them going steady, but everybody knew that Angela belonged to Peter, and Peter belonged to Angela, and that's all there was to it. He used to talk to me a lot about her, and how they were going to get married and run a riding stable together. And he told me that he would never touch her that way until they were married. They used to kiss good night and that was all, because Peter said that when the great thing happened, he wanted it to happen just right, and it could never be really right while they were both kids in high school. A lot of the fellows thought that more went on between them than I know did, but that's because they didn't understand Peter really. He had a simple set of rules he operated under, and they suited him very well. He was good to Angela and good to animals, and all he asked was to be let alone to do things his own way.

The other thing you have to know about is the noontime rock fights. From the papers and the inquest and all, you know something about them, but not everything. I guess most of the parents were pretty shocked to learn that their little Johnny was in a mob rock fight every day at school, but that's the way it was. The fights started over a year ago, as near as I can recollect, and went on all that time without the faculty ever finding out. The papers made a big scandal out of them and conducted what

they called an "exposé of vicious practices at select Manning Day School." It was comical, actually, the way everybody got all steamed up over the things we knew went on all the time, not only at Manning but in all the other schools in town. Of course, we all knew the rock fights were wrong, but they were more fun than they seemed wrong, so we kept them up. (That time I came home with the mouse under my eye, I didn't get it by falling in the locker room. I just forgot to duck.)

We had a strict set of rules in the fights so that nobody would really get hurt or anything, and so the little guys could get into them too without fear of being killed. All sixty of us, the whole school, were divided into two teams, the Union Army and the Confederates, and after lunch in the cafeteria we'd all get our blue or gray caps and head out into the woods behind the school. The faculty thought we played Kick the Can and never followed us out to check up on us.

Each team had a fort we'd built out of sapling logs—really just pens about waist high. The forts were about two hundred yards apart, invisible to each other through the trees and scrub. You weren't allowed to use rocks any bigger than a hazelnut, and before you pegged one at a guy in the opposite army, you had to go *chk*, *chk* with your mouth so the guy would have a chance to find where it was coming from and duck in time. We had scouting parties and assault teams and patrols, and all the rest of the military things we could think up. The object was to storm the enemy's fort and take it before recess was up and we had to quit.

These rock fights weren't like the papers said at all. I remember the *Morning Star* called them "pitched battles of unrelenting fury, where injuries were frequent." That was silly. If the injuries had been frequent, it wouldn't have been fun any more, and nobody would have wanted to keep doing it. You *could* get hurt, of course, but you could get hurt a lot worse in a football game with the grandstand full of newspaper reporters and faculty and parents all cheering you on.

Now I guess you know everything that was important before the day Gene Hanlon got killed, and I can tell you how it happened so that you'll know why.

After our last morning class, Peter Irish and I went down to the washroom in the basement to clean up for lunch. All morning Peter had acted funny—silent and sort of tied up inside—and it was worrying me some. At first I thought I had done something he didn't like, but if I had, he'd have told me. He'd hardly said two words all morning, and he had missed two recitations in English that I had coached him on myself. But you couldn't pry trouble out of Peter, so I just kept quiet and waited for him to let me in on it.

While he was washing his hands I had to go into one of the stalls. I went in and shut the door and was hanging up my jacket when I heard somebody else come into the washroom. I don't know why, but I sat down—being real careful not to make any noise.

Somebody said, "Hi, Pete, boy." It was Gene Hanlon, and he was alone for once.

"Hi, Gene." That was Peter. (I am trying to put this down as near as I can just the way they said it.)

"Oh, man!" Gene said. "Today I am exhaust pipe!"

"Tired?"

"You said the word, man. Real beat under."

"Why so?"

"Big date last night. Friend of yours, Angela Pine." Just as if that stall door hadn't been there, I could see Gene grinning at Peter and waiting for a rise out of him. Peter didn't say anything, so Gene tried again. "You're pretty sly, Pete."

"What do you mean?"

"I mean about Angela. You've done a real fine job of keeping her in drydock all this time."

"She dates other guys," Peter said, sounding like he ought to clear his throat.

"Aaaah. She goes out with those meatballs and then comes home and shakes hands at the door. What kind of a date is that?"

"Well, that's *her* business."

Gene said, giggling, "I don't know what her business is, but I got a few suggestions for her if she ever asks me."

"What are you getting at?"

"Real coy, boy. She's crazy for it. Just crazy. Real crazy hungry chick, yeah."

"Are you through?"

"What? . . . Oh, sure. *Hey!* You sore or something?"

Peter said, "It's time for you to go eat lunch."

"All right already. Jesus! You don't have to get *that* way about it. A guy gives you a compliment and you go and get sore. You *are* an odd ball. You and your screwy horses too. See you around." And Gene went out scuffing his feet along the floor.

When I came out of the stall Peter was hunched stiff-armed over the wash-basin. He didn't even know I was around. I wished right then that I could have gone back and unlived the last five min-

utes. I wished they had never happened, and that everything was back just the way it was before. I was hurt and mad, and my mind was whirling around full of all the stuff Gene Hanlon had said. Just to be doing something, I got busy combing my hair, wetting and shaking the comb and all, trying to find a way to say what I was feeling. Peter was very busy turning both faucets on and off again in a kind of splashy rhythm.

Finally I said, "If you believe all that crap, you're pretty silly. That guy's a bragging liar and you know it."

Peter looked up at me as though he had just noticed I was there. "I've got to believe it," he said.

I jumped on him for that. "Oh, come on," I said. "Give Angela a little credit. She wouldn't give that pile of you-know-what the right time."

Peter was looking down the basin drain. "I called her this morning to say hello. She wouldn't talk to me, Ronnie. She wouldn't even come to the phone."

Now I knew what had been eating him all morning. There wasn't any more a friend could say to Peter, so I made him let go of the faucets and come with me to eat lunch in the cafeteria. All through lunch he just pushed dishes around on his tray and didn't say anything. As we scraped our plates I asked him if he was going out to the fight in the woods, and he surprised me by saying yes, so we got our caps and hiked out to the Confederate fort.

Almost everybody, Gene Hanlon too, was there before us, and they'd already chosen today's generals. Smitty Rice was General of the Armies of the Confederacy, and Gene Hanlon was the Union Commander. Gene took all his boys off to the Union fort to wait for the starting whistle, and Smitty outlined his strategy to us.

There was to be a feint at the south side of the Union fort, and then a noisy second feint from the north to pull the defenders out of position. Then Smitty and Peter Irish were to lead the real massed assault from the south, under the lip of the hill where the first feint had come from. When five minutes had gone by on my watch, we all got up and Smitty blew the starting whistle and we piled out of the fort, leaving only five inside as a garrison, and a couple of alarm guards a little way out on each side of the fort.

I got the job I usually got—advance observation post. I was to note enemy movements and remember concentrations and directions and elapsed times between sightings. Even though you couldn't see more than a hundred feet through the woods, you could always get a fair idea of the enemy strategy by the way they moved their troops around. So all I had to do was stay in one place and watch and listen and remember, and every so often Smitty would send a runner over from field headquarters to check up on what had happened lately. I had three or four good posts picked out where I could hide and not be seen, and I never used the same one twice running.

Today's was my favorite—Baker Post, we called it. It was a dense thicket of young blackjack oak on a low hill on the inside of a bend in the creek, and because nothing grew on the gravel bars of the creek, you could see a long way to each side. The creek ran generally south, cutting the fighting area between the forts right in two, and it made a good defense line because there were only a few places you could cross it in one jump and not get your shoes wet. The east bank of the creek, directly across from Baker Post, is a vertical bluff about ten feet high so that the ground up there is right on eye level with Baker, and the creek and the gravel bars are spread out between you and the bluff bank. I always knew that Baker Post was good, because every time I took it up I had to flush out a covey of quail or a cottontail.

It was always quiet in the woods during the first few minutes of those fights. Even the birds shut up, it seemed like, waiting for the first troop contacts. Out of the corner of my eye I saw somebody jump the creek at the North Ford, and I rolled over to watch. Because of the brush up there I couldn't see who it was, but I knew he was there because once in a while a bush would stir, or his foot would slide a little on the gravel. Pretty soon he came out to the edge of the underbrush and crouched there looking around and listening. It was Gene Hanlon. His eyes crossed right over me, without finding me, and after a minute he came out and ran low along the creek. When he got even with Baker Post, he went down to his knees and began filling his cap with rocks. I had to laugh to myself at how stupid that was. He should have collected his ammunition earlier, when he and his army were on their way over to their fort. He was wasting maneuvering time and exposing himself for no good reason. It makes you feel good when a guy you hate does something dumb like that.

I got ready to go *chk*, *chk* with my mouth just to scare him and see him run. But then I looked up at the bluff above him and my heart flopped over inside me. Peter Irish was there, down on one knee,

looking over at Gene Hanlon. Gene never looked up. Peter moves like that—floating in and out of the brush as quietly as if he didn't weigh anything. Peter was a good woods fighter.

So instead of going *chk*, *chk* I hunkered down lower in my thicket and thought to myself that now it wasn't a game any more. Peter looked a long time over at where I was hiding, then he looked up and down the creek bed, and then he moved back a little from the edge of the bluff. He put all his weight pulling on a half-buried boulder beside him until it turned over in its socket and he could get a good grip on it. Even from where I was I could see the cords come out in his neck when he raised it up in his arms and stood up. I hadn't heard a sound except the creek gurgling a little, and Gene Hanlon scratching around in the gravel. And also the blood roaring in my own ears. Watching this was like being in a movie and seeing the story happen on the screen. Nothing you can do or say will change what is going to happen because it's all there in the unwinding reel.

Peter held the heavy stone like a medicine ball and walked to the edge of the bluff and looked down at Gene Hanlon. Gene had moved a few feet south along the creek, so Peter above him moved south too, until he was even with Gene. Peter made a little grunt when he pushed the rock out and away and it fell. Gene heard the grunt and lifted his head to look up, and the rock hit him full in the face and bent his head away back and made his arms fly out. He sat right down in the water with his red and dirty face turned up to the sky and his hands holding him up behind. Then he got himself up with his head still twisted back like that, so he was looking straight up, and he wandered a little way downstream with the water up to his knees, and then he fell out on a gravel bar on his stomach. His legs and arms spread out like he was asleep, but his head was up rigid and his mouth was open. I couldn't look any more.

Peter hadn't made a sound leaving, but when I looked up, the bluff above was empty. As soon as I could move without getting sick I faded out of there and went up north a ways to Able Post and lay down in the foxhole there and held myself around the knees and just shook. I couldn't have felt more upset if I had dropped that rock myself. Just like a movie reel had the ends tied together, the whole scene kept rolling over and over in front of my eyes, and I couldn't stop the film or even turn off the light in the projector.

I lay there with my head down waiting for

someone to find the body and start hollering. It was little Marvin Herold, Smitty's courier, who started screaming in his high voice, "Safety! . . . Oh, God! . . . Safety safety safety! . . . Help! . . . Help!" "Safety" was the call we used to stop the fights if anyone saw a master coming or somebody got hurt. I lay there for several minutes listening to guys running past me through the brush heading for Baker Post, then I got up and followed them. I couldn't move very fast because my knees kept trying to bend the wrong way.

When I came out of the brush onto the gravel bank, I was surprised that everything looked so different. When I had left just five minutes before, the whole clearing and the creek were empty and lying bright in the sun, and Gene Hanlon was there all alone on the gravel bar. Now, with all the guys standing around and talking at once with their backs to the body, the whole place was different, and it wasn't so bad being there. I saw little Marvin Herold go over and try to take the pulse of Gene Hanlon's body. Marvin is a Boy Scout with lots of merit badges, and I expected him to try artificial respiration or a tourniquet, but he didn't find any pulse so he stood up and shook his head and wobbled over to where we were. He looked terribly blank, as though the *Scout Manual* had let him down.

The assumption going around was that Gene had run off the bluff and landed on his head and broken his neck. I couldn't see Peter anywhere, so I finally had to ask Smitty where he was. Smitty said he had sent Peter in to the school to tell somebody what had happened, and to get the ambulance. Smitty was still being the General, I guess, because there was nothing less for him to do. I tried to think to myself what Peter must be feeling like now, sent off to do an errand like that, but I couldn't get anywhere. My head was too full of what *I* was feeling like, standing with the fellows on the gravel bar looking at Gene Hanlon spread out half in the water like a dropped doll, knowing just how he had gotten there, and not being able to say anything.

Then Smitty got an idea, and he said, "Ronnie, weren't you here at Baker Post all the time?"

I made myself look at him, and then I said, "No, damn it, I got to thinking their army might try a crossing up by Able Post, so I went up there instead."

He said, "Oh," and forgot it.

Not long after, we heard a siren. We all knew what it was, and everybody stopped talking to listen to it as it got nearer. It was the first time I ever heard a siren and knew while hearing it why it had

been called, and where it was going. It was sort of creepy, like it was saying to us over the trees, "Wait right there, boys. Don't anybody leave. I'll be there in a minute, and then we'll see just what's going on." I wanted to run and keep on running, until I got away from all the things swarming around inside me. You always wish afterward you had never joggled the wasp ball.

Pretty soon we heard somebody moving in the woods on the bluff and then two big men in white pants, carrying a folded-up stretcher, and another man in a suit, carrying a black bag, came out to the lip of the bluff. They stood there looking at us a minute without saying anything until one of the stretcher-bearers saw Gene Hanlon lying there all alone on the gravel bar. The man said something to the other two, and they all three looked where he pointed. Then the doctor looked at us all bunched up where we were and said, "Well, how do we get down?" He sounded sore. None of us moved or said anything, and in a minute the doctor got tired of waiting and blasted us. "Wake up over there! How do we go to get down?" Smitty came unstuck and gave them directions, and they went back into the brush heading north.

From then on things got pretty crowded in the woods. Two uniformed policemen and a photographer and a plain-clothes man showed up, and then Peter Irish came back leading almost the whole school faculty, and later a reporter and another photographer arrived. Nobody paid any attention to us for a while, so we just sat there in a clump, not moving or saying much. I managed to get right in the middle, and I kept down, hiding behind the guys around me and looking between them to see what was going on. After the police photographer was through taking pictures of Gene Hanlon from all sides, the two ambulance men raised him onto the stretcher and covered him with a piece of canvas or something and carried him away. The photographer took pictures all around by the creek and then went up onto the bluff and took pictures of the ground up there too. The plain-clothes man poking around on the gravel bar found Gene Hanlon's blue cap half full of rocks and gave it, with the rocks still in it, to one of the policemen to save.

I finally got up nerve enough to look for Peter Irish. He was standing with Smitty and Mr. Kelly, the math teacher, and they were talking. Peter didn't look any different. I didn't see how he could do it. I mean, stand right out there in plain sight of everyone, looking natural, with all that in his head. He looked around slowly as though he felt me watching him, and he found me there in the middle of the bunch. I couldn't have looked away if I had tried. He gave me a little smile, and I nodded my head to show him I'd seen it, then he went back to his talking with the other two.

Then the plain-clothes man went over to the three of them, and I got all wild inside and wanted to jump up and say that Peter couldn't possibly have done it, so please go away and let him alone. I could see the plain-clothes man doing most of the talking, and Peter and Smitty saying something once in a while, as though they were answering questions. After a little the plain-clothes man stopped talking and nodded, and the other three nodded back, and then he led them over to where the rest of us were. Smitty and Peter sat down with us and Mr. Kelly collected all the other faculty men and brought them over.

The plain-clothes man tipped his hat back and put his hands in his pockets and said, "My name is Gorman. Sergeant Gorman. We know all about the rock fight now, so don't get nervous that you'll let on something that'll get you into trouble. You're already *in* trouble, but that's not my business. You can settle that with your instructors and your parents. Uh . . . you might think some about this, though. It's my feeling that every one of you here has a share in the responsibility for this boy's death. You all know rock fighting is dangerous, but you went ahead and did it anyway. But that's not what I'm after right now. I want to know if any of you boys actually saw this (what's his name?), this Hanlon boy run over the bluff." I was looking straight at Sergeant Gorman, but in the side of my eye I saw Peter Irish turn his head around and look at me. I didn't peep.

Then Sergeant Gorman said, "Which one of you is Ronnie Quiller?"

I almost fainted.

Somebody poked me and I said, "Me." It didn't sound like my voice at all.

Sergeant Gorman said, "Which?"

I said, "Me," again.

This time he found me and said, "Weren't you supposed to be lying there in this thicket all the time?"

"Yes," I said. All the kids were looking at me. "But there wasn't anything doing here so I moved up there a ways."

"I see," he said. "Do you always disobey orders?"

"No," I said, "but after all, it was only a game."

"Some game," said Sergeant Gorman. "Good clean fun."

Then he let me alone. There was only one person there who knew I would never have deserted the post assigned to me. That was Peter Irish. I guess, Dad, that's when I began to get really scared. The worst of it was not knowing how much Peter knew, and not daring to ask. He might have been waiting out of sight in the brush after he dropped that rock, and seen me take out for Able Post. I had always been his friend, but what was I now to him? I wanted to tell him everything was okay and I wouldn't for the world squeal on him, but that would have told him I knew he did it. Maybe he knew without my telling him. I didn't know what to do.

Sergeant Gorman finished up, "Let's all go back to the school now. I want to talk to each of you alone." We all got up and started back through the woods in a bunch. I figured Peter would think it was funny if I avoided him, so I walked with him.

I said, "Lousy damn day."

He said, "Real lousy."

I said, "It seems like a hundred years since lunch."

We didn't say any more all the way back.

It took all afternoon to get the individual interviews over. They took us from Assembly Hall in alphabetical order, and we had to go in and sit across from Sergeant Gorman while he asked the questions. He must have asked us all the same questions because by the time he got to me he was saying the words like they were tired. A girl stenographer sat by him and took down the answers.

"Name?"

"Ronnie Quiller." I had to spell it.

"Were you at the rock fight this afternoon?"

"Yes, I was."

"What side were you on?"

"The Confederates."

"What were you supposed to do?"

"Watch the guys on the other side."

"After this whistle, did you see anyone?"

"No."

"You sure?"

"No, I didn't. That's why I moved from Baker Post up to Able Post. There wasn't anything doing where I was hiding."

"In rock fights before, have you ever changed position without telling somebody?"

"Sure, I guess. You can't run clear back to the field headquarters to tell anyone anything. It's up to them to find *you*."

Sergeant Gorman squinted at me with his eyebrows pulled down. "You know that if you had stayed where you were supposed to be you would have seen him fall over that bluff there?"

"Yes," I said.

"I wish you had."

Afterwards I ran into Smitty out in the hall and I asked him why all this fuss with the police and all. I asked him who called them.

"It was Peter, I think. He told Mr. Kelly to, and Mr. Kelly did."

"What do you suppose they're after?" I asked Smitty.

"Oh, I guess they're trying to get a straight story to tell Gene's parents and the newspapers. From what I get from Mr. Kelly, the school is all for it. They want everybody to know they weren't responsible."

"Do *you* think Gene fell over that bluff?" I couldn't help asking that one.

"I don't know. I suppose so." He cocked his head to one side and grinned a little at me. "Like they say in the papers, 'fell or was pushed,' huh?"

I said, "I guess nobody'd have nerve enough to do that to Gene—push him, I mean." All of a sudden I was thinking about something I had seen. Going back in my mind I remembered seeing Sergeant Gorman pick up Gene's cap half full of rocks. Gravel rocks taken from the low bank of the creek. Now, I figured that Sergeant Gorman wouldn't have been a sergeant if he was stupid, and unless he was stupid he wouldn't go on for long thinking that Gene had fallen from above—*when the cap half full of rocks said he'd been down below all the time!*

I got my bike and rode home the long way to give me time to think about Peter and what he had done, and what I should do. You were real swell that night, and I guess I should have told you the whole story right then, but I just couldn't. I put myself in Peter's place, and I knew he would never had told on me. That's the way he was. He hated squealers. I couldn't think about his ever learning I had squealed on him. That would put me right alongside Angela Pine in his book. To him, I would have been the second person he trusted who let him down.

I felt like a rat in a cage with no place to go and no way out. When you kept me home nights after that, I didn't mind, because I wouldn't have gone out after dark if I'd been paid to. I don't blame you and Mother for thinking I had gone loony over the whole thing. Every noon recess for two whole weeks they pulled us into Assembly Hall and one of the masters would give a speech about group responsibility or public conscience or something awful like that, and then, worst of all, they made us bow our heads for five minutes in memory of Gene Hanlon. And there I'd be, sitting next to Peter Irish on the Assembly Hall bench, thinking back to the day of the last rock fight, and how Peter had looked

up there on the bluff with the cords of his neck pulled tight, holding that big rock like it was a medicine ball. I had the crawliest feeling that if anybody in the hall had raised up his head and looked over at us together there on the bench, he would have seen two great fiery arrows pointing down at us. I was always afraid even to look up myself for fear I would have seen my own arrow and passed out on the spot.

It was my nightmares that got you worried, I guess. They always started out with Peter and me on a hike on a dusty country road. It was so hot you could hardly breathe. We would walk along without saying anything, with me lagging a little behind Peter so I could always keep an eye on him. And then the road would come out on the football field there at school, and he would go over to the woodpile and pick up a thin log and hold it in one hand, beckoning to me with the other and smiling. "Let's go over to the drugstore," he'd say, and then I'd start running.

I would follow the quarter-mile track around the football field and I'd know that everything would be all right if I could only get around it four times for a full mile. Every time I turned around to look, there he'd be right behind me, carrying that log and running easily, just like he used to pace me when I was out for the 880. I would make the first quarter mile all right, but then my wind would give out and my throat would dry up and my legs would get heavy, and I'd know that Peter was about to catch me, and I'd never make that full mile.

Then I would jar awake and be sweating and hanging on tight to the mattress, and in a minute you'd come in to see why I'd screamed. Your face was always kind of sad over me, and there in my bed in the dark, with you standing beside, I would *almost* let go and tell you why things were so bad with me. But then as I'd come awake, and the hammering in my heart would slow up, and the sweat would begin to dry, all the things I owed Peter Irish would stand out again and look at me, and I would know that I could never tell you about it until my telling could no longer get Peter Irish into trouble.

I'm tired now, Dad—tired in so many ways and in so many places that I don't know where to begin resting. This letter took all night, as I thought it would. It's beginning to get light outside and the birds are starting up. I just reread the story in the paper where it says that Sergeant Gorman knew all along that Gene Hanlon had been murdered. I told you he wasn't stupid. He knew what that cap half full of rocks meant, and he knew what it meant to find a big damp socket in the earth on top of the bluff, and the rock which had been *in* the socket down below in the creek. And after he had talked to each of us alphabetically there in the school office, he knew the name of the only boy in school strong enough to lift up a seventy-pound rock and throw it like a medicine ball. He knew all of these things before the sun went down on the day of the last rock fight, but he was two months putting the rest of the story together so he could use it in his business.

As I read it in the paper, Sergeant Gorman went over to Peter's house last Monday and talked to him about the things he had learned, and Peter listened respectfully, and then, when Sergeant Gorman was through and was ready to take Peter along with him, Peter excused himself to go upstairs and get his toilet articles. He got his four-ten shotgun instead and shot himself. I suppose it was the same four-ten he and I hunted squirrels with.

There's only one good thing about this whole stinking lousy mess, Dad. Because Sergeant Gorman talked to Peter and Peter listened, there in the living room; when Peter Irish climbed up those stairs he did it knowing that I, Ronnie Quiller, had not squealed on him. That may have made it easier. I don't know.

Now please, Dad—please may I come home again?

RONNIE

Diagnosis

Traumatic or situational neurosis—severe anxiety reaction.

This story deals with a neurosis brought about by conflict between guilt and loyalty. Ronnie was fully aware of the guilt he shared with Peter by concealment. His conscience or superego immobilized him. He was torn between society's demand to report homicide to the authorities and his own love for and loyalty to his friend. Peter had many times protected Ronnie from the cruelty or bullying of other boys, particularly the star bully, Gene Hanlon. Ronnie's guilt was not only that of concealment but also that of shared hostility. He too hated Gene Hanlon and at times may have fantasied the aggression that Peter acted out.

In the adolescent struggle for identity, Peter and Ronnie made up one whole person, each compensating for the other's weaknesses and using the other's strength. "We swapped talents," Ronnie says—Ronnie being the intellectual performer. He considered himself a natural scapegoat and thus regarded Peter, the physical performer, with gratitude and respect. Ronnie sensed he must not under any circumstance betray his friend. His emotions were complicated by partial hostility and jealousy toward Angela (he also had trouble trusting his own mother, as indicated in the first paragraph of his letter); but, as the physically more passive of the two boys, he was taking the feminine role, which made him feel superior to Angela.

As a sensitive boy, Ronnie was aware that Peter must be protected not only from the police or another betrayer, but even from knowing that he, Ronnie, knew of the crime. Thus, Ronnie felt trapped—"like a rat in a cage"—by the necessity for silence and the projection of guilt. His overt symptoms were deep depression, nightmares, sweat, and inability to be with his friends.

The *fact* of his letter, written to a trusted parent as soon as the crime was exposed, without his having participated in its exposure, released him from his anxiety reaction. He was able to see his own part in the drama and also to evaluate realistically and without blame the part of the adults. His trust in his father's ability to listen to him sympathetically indicates he had a basically sound relationship and therefore the capacity to grow out of this incident.

If father listens, good! Ronnie should come home, resume normal life, and receive individual psychotherapy for catharsis of trauma, for his identity problems (including sexual identity), and for his scapegoat feelings. Obviously the boy has great capacity for awareness, introspection, and meaningful relationships.

Between the lines of this story runs an undercurrent of a homosexual relationship between Ronnie and Peter. Such a relationship, as Sullivan states in his theory of interpersonal development, is a normal aspect of growth and a primer for teaching about nonfamilial love. When the culture surrounds such development with opprobrium, dismay, and punitive or horrified responses, this normal tide may be turned to self-doubt, guilt, and immobilization. These factors may have contributed, along with the murder, to Ronnie's severe distress.

Paul's Case
Willa Cather

It was Paul's afternoon to appear before the faculty of the Pittsburgh High School to account for his various misdemeanors. He had been suspended a week ago, and his father had called at the Principal's office and confessed his perplexity about his son. Paul entered the faculty room suave and smiling. His clothes were a trifle outgrown, and the tan velvet on the collar of his open overcoat was frayed and worn; but for all that there was something of the dandy about him, and he wore an opal pin in his neatly knotted black four-in-hand, and a red carnation in his buttonhole. This latter adornment the faculty somehow felt was not properly significant of the contrite spirit befitting a boy under the ban of suspension.

Paul was tall for his age and very thin, with high, cramped shoulders and a narrow chest. His eyes were remarkable for a certain hysterical brilliancy, and he continually used them in a conscious, theatrical sort of way, peculiarly offensive in a boy. The pupils were abnormally large, as though he were addicted to belladonna, but there was a glassy glitter about them which that drug does not produce.

When questioned by the Principal as to why he was there, Paul stated, politely enough, that he wanted to come back to school. This was a lie, but Paul was quite accustomed to lying; found it, indeed, indispensable for overcoming friction. His teachers were asked to state their respective charges against him, which they did with such a rancor and aggrievedness as evinced that this was not a usual case. Disorder and impertinence were among the offenses named, yet each of his instructors felt that it was scarcely possible to put into words the real cause of the trouble, which lay in a sort of hysterically defiant manner of the boy's; in the contempt which they all knew he felt for them, and which he seemingly made not the least effort to conceal. Once, when he had been making a synopsis of a paragraph at the blackboard, his English teacher had stepped to his side and attempted to guide his hand. Paul had started back with a shudder and thrust his hands violently behind him. The astonished woman could scarcely have been more hurt and embarrassed had he struck at her. The insult was so involuntary and definitely personal as to be unforgettable. In one way and another, he had made all his teachers, men and women alike, conscious of the same feeling of physical aversion. In one class he habitually sat with his hand shading his eyes; in another he always looked out of the window during the recitation; in another he made a running commentary on the lecture, with humorous intent.

His teachers felt this afternoon that his whole attitude was symbolized by his shrug and his flippantly red carnation flower, and they fell upon him without mercy, his English teacher leading the pack. He stood through it smiling, his pale lips parted over his white teeth. (His lips were continually twitching, and he had a habit of raising his eyebrows that was contemptuous and irritating to the last degree.) Older boys than Paul had broken down and shed tears under that ordeal, but his set smile did not once desert him, and his only sign of discomfort was the nervous trembling of the fingers that toyed with the buttons of his overcoat, and an occasional jerking of the other hand which held his hat. Paul was always smiling, always glancing about him, seeming to feel that people might be watching him and trying to detect something. This conscious expression, since it was as far as possible from boyish mirthfulness, was usually attributed to insolence or "smartness."

As the inquisition proceeded, one of his instructors repeated an impertinent remark of the boy's, and the Principal asked him whether he thought that a courteous speech to make to a woman. Paul shrugged his shoulders slightly and his eyebrows twitched.

"I don't know," he replied. "I didn't mean to be polite or impolite, either. I guess it's a sort of way I have, of saying things regardless."

The Principal asked him whether he didn't think that a way it would be well to get rid of. Paul grinned and said he guessed so. When he was told that he could go, he bowed gracefully and went out. His bow was like a repetition of the scandalous red carnation.

His teachers were in despair, and his drawing

Reprinted from *Youth and the Bright Medusa.*

master voiced the feeling of them all when he declared there was something about the boy which none of them understood. He added: "I don't really believe that smile of his comes altogether from insolence; there's something sort of haunted about it. The boy is not strong, for one thing. . . . There is something wrong about the fellow."

The drawing master had come to realize that, in looking at Paul, one saw only his white teeth and the forced animation of his eyes. One warm afternoon the boy had gone to sleep at his drawing board, and his master had noted with amazement what a white, blue-veined face it was; drawn and wrinkled like an old man's about the eyes, the lips twitching even in his sleep. . . .

His teachers left the building dissatisfied and unhappy; humiliated to have felt so vindictive toward a mere boy, to have uttered this feeling in cutting terms, and to have set each other on, as it were, in the gruesome game of intemperate reproach. One of them remembered having seen a miserable street cat set at bay by a ring of tormentors.

As for Paul, he ran down the hill whistling the Soldiers' Chorus from *Faust*, looking wildly behind him now and then to see whether some of his teachers were not there to witness his light-heartedness. As it was now late in the afternoon and Paul was on duty that evening as usher at Carnegie Hall, he decided that he would not go home to supper. . . .

After a concert was over, Paul was often irritable and wretched until he got to sleep,—and tonight he was even more than usually restless. He had the feeling of not being able to let down; of its being impossible to give up this delicious excitement which was the only thing that could be called living at all. During the last number he withdrew and, after hastily changing his clothes in the dressing-room, slipped out to the side door where the singer's carriage stood. Here he began pacing rapidly up and down the walk, waiting to see her come out.

Over yonder the Schenley, in its vacant stretch, loomed big and square through the fine rain, the windows of its twelve stories glowing like those of a lighted cardboard house under a Christmas tree. All the actors and singers of any importance stayed there when they were in the city, and a number of the big manufacturers of the place lived there in the winter. Paul had often hung about the hotel, watching the people go in and out, longing to enter and leave schoolmasters and dull care behind him forever.

At last the singer came out, accompanied by the conductor, who helped her into her carriage and closed the door with a cordial *auf wiedersehen*,—which set Paul to wondering whether she were not an old sweetheart of his. Paul followed the carriage over to the hotel, walking so rapidly as not to be far from the entrance when the singer alighted and disappeared behind the swinging glass doors which were opened by a Negro in a tall hat and a long coat. In the moment that the door was ajar, it seemed to Paul that he, too, entered. He seemed to feel himself go after her up the steps, into the warm, lighted building, into an exotic, tropical world of shiny, glistening surfaces and basking ease. He reflected upon the mysterious dishes that were brought into the dining-room, the green bottles in buckets of ice, as he had seen them in the supper party pictures of the Sunday supplement. A quick gust of wind brought the rain down with sudden vehemence, and Paul was startled to find that he was still outside in the slush of the gravel driveway; that his boots were letting in the water and his scanty overcoat was clinging wet about him; that the lights in front of the concert hall were out; and that the rain was driving in sheets between him and the orange glow of the windows above him. There it was, what he wanted—tangibly before him, like the fairy world of a Christmas pantomime; as the rain beat in his face, Paul wondered whether he was destined always to shiver in the black night outside, looking up at it.

He turned and walked reluctantly toward the car tracks. The end had to come some time; his father in his night-clothes at the top of the stairs, explanations that did not explain, hastily improvised fictions that were forever tripping him up, his upstairs room and its horrible yellow wall paper, the creaking bureau with the greasy plush collar-box, and over his painted wooden bed the pictures of George Washington and John Calvin, and the framed motto, "Feed my Lambs," which had been worked in red worsted by his mother [*whom Paul could not remember*]. . . .

The leading juvenile of the permanent stock company which played at one of the downtown theaters was an acquaintance of Paul's, and the boy had been invited to drop in at the Sunday night rehearsals whenever he could. For more than a year Paul had spent every available moment loitering about Charley Edwards's dressing-room. He had won a place among Edwards's following not only because the young actor, who could not afford to employ a dresser, often found him useful, but because he recognized in Paul something akin to what churchmen term "vocation."

It was at the theater and at Carnegie Hall that Paul really lived; the rest was but a sleep and a forgetting. This was Paul's fairy tale, and it had for him all the allurement of a secret love. The moment he inhaled the gassy, painty, dusty odor behind the scenes, he breathed like a prisoner set free, and felt within him the possibility of doing or saying splendid, brilliant things. The moment the cracked orchestra beat out the overture from *Martha*, or jerked at the serenade from *Rigoletto*, all stupid and ugly things slid from him, and his senses were deliciously, yet delicately fired.

Perhaps it was because, in Paul's world, the natural nearly always wore the guise of ugliness, that a certain element of artificiality seemed to him necessary in beauty. Perhaps it was because his experience of life elsewhere was so full of Sabbath-school picnics, petty economies, wholesome advice as to how to succeed in life, and the unescapable odors of cooking, that he found this existence so alluring, these smartly-clad men and women so attractive, that he was so moved by these starry apple orchards that bloomed perennially under the limelight.

It would be difficult to put it strongly enough how convincingly the stage entrance of that theater was for Paul the actual portal of Romance. Certainly none of the company ever suspected it, least of all Charley Edwards. It was very like the old stories that used to float about London of fabulously rich Jews, who had subterranean halls, with palms, and fountains, and soft lamps and richly apparelled women who never saw the disenchanting light of London day. So, in the midst of that smoke-palled city, enamored of figures and grimy toil, Paul had his secret temple, his wishing-carpet, his bit of blue-and-white Mediterranean shore bathed in perpetual sunshine.

Several of Paul's teachers had a theory that his imagination had been perverted by garish fiction; but the truth was, he scarcely ever read at all. The books at home were not such as would either tempt or corrupt a youthful mind, and as for reading the novels that some of his friends urged upon him—well, he got what he wanted much more quickly from music; any sort of music, from an orchestra to a barrel organ. He needed only the spark, the indescribable thrill that made his imagination master of his senses, and he could make plots and pictures enough of his own. It was equally true that he was not stage-struck—not, at any rate, in the usual acceptation of that expression. He had no desire to become an actor, any more than he had to become a musician. He felt no necessity to do any of these things; what he wanted was to see, to be in the atmosphere, float on the wave of it, to be carried out, blue league after blue league, away from everything.

After a night behind the scenes, Paul found the school-room more than ever repulsive; the bare floors and naked walls; the prosy men who never wore frock coats, or violets in their buttonholes; the women with their dull gowns, shrill voices, and pitiful seriousness about prepositions that govern the dative. He could not bear to have the other pupils think, for a moment, that he took these people seriously; he must convey to them that he considered it all trivial, and was there only by way of a joke, anyway. He had autograph pictures of all the members of the stock company which he showed his classmates, telling them the most incredible stories of his familiarity with these people, of his acquaintance with the soloists who came to Carnegie Hall, his suppers with them and the flowers he sent them. When these stories lost their effect, and his audience grew listless, he would bid all the boys good-by, announcing that he was going to travel for a while; going to Naples, to California, to Egypt. Then, next Monday, he would slip back, conscious and nervously smiling; his sister was ill, and he would have to defer his voyage until spring.

Matters went steadily worse with Paul at school. In the itch to let his instructors know how heartily he despised them, and how thoroughly he was appreciated elsewhere, he mentioned once or twice that he had no time to fool with theorems; adding—with a twitch of the eyebrows and a touch of that nervous bravado which so perplexed them—that he was helping the people down at the stock company; they were old friends of his.

The upshot of the matter was, that the Principal went to Paul's father, and Paul was taken out of school and put to work. The manager at Carnegie Hall was told to get another usher in his stead; the doorkeeper at the theater was warned not to admit him to the house; and Charley Edwards remorsefully promised the boy's father not to see him again.

The members of the stock company were vastly amused when some of Paul's stories reached them—especially the women. They were hard-working women, most of them supporting indolent husbands or brothers, and they laughed rather bitterly at having stirred the boy to such fervid and florid inventions. They agreed with the faculty and with his father, that Paul's was a bad case. . . . .

[Paul steals money from the office where he works and takes a train to New York, where he buys himself some expensive clothes and, claiming that he is waiting for his parents to arrive from Europe, installs himself in an elegant hotel.]

On the part of the hotel management, Paul excited no suspicion. There was this to be said for him, that he wore his spoils with dignity and in no way made himself conspicuous. His chief greediness lay in his ears and eyes, and his excesses were not offensive ones. His dearest pleasures were the gray winter twilights in his sitting room; his quiet enjoyment of his flowers, his clothes, his wide divan, his cigarette and his sense of power. He could not remember a time when he had felt so at peace with himself. The mere release from the necessity of petty lying, lying every day and every day, restored his self-respect. He had never lied for pleasure, even at school; but to make himself noticed and admired, to assert his difference from other Cordelia Street boys; and he felt a good deal more manly, more honest, even, now that he had no need for boastful pretensions, now that he could, as his actor friends used to say, "dress the part." It was characteristic that remorse did not occur to him. His golden days went by without a shadow, and he made each as perfect as he could. . . .

[Paul has been in New York for eight days. His money is running out, and he had too much wine the night before.]

He rose and moved about with a painful effort, succumbing now and again to attacks of nausea. It was the old depression exaggerated; all the world had become Cordelia Street. Yet somehow he was not afraid of anything, was absolutely calm; perhaps because he had looked into the dark corner at last, and knew. It was bad enough, what he saw there; but somehow not so bad as his long fear of it had been. He saw everything clearly now. He had a feeling that he had made the best of it, that he had lived the sort of life he was meant to live, and for half an hour he sat staring at the revolver. But he told himself that was not the way, so he went downstairs and took a cab to the ferry.

When Paul arrived at Newark, he got off the train and took another cab, directing the driver to follow the Pennsylvania tracks out of the town. The snow lay heavy on the roadways and had drifted deep in the open fields. Only here and there the dead grass or dried weed stalks projected, singularly

black, above it. Once well into the country, Paul dismissed the carriage and walked, floundering along the tracks, his mind a medley of irrelevant things. He seemed to hold in his brain an actual picture of everything he had seen that morning. He remembered every feature of both his drivers, the toothless old woman from whom he had bought the red flowers in his coat, the agent from whom he had got his ticket, and all of his fellow-passengers on the ferry. His mind, unable to cope with vital matters near at hand, worked feverishly and deftly at sorting and grouping these images. They made for him a part of the ugliness of the world, of the ache in his head, and the bitter burning on his tongue. He stooped and put a handful of snow into his mouth as he walked, but that, too, seemed hot. When he reached a little hillside, where the tracks ran through a cut some twenty feet below him, he stopped and sat down.

The carnations in his coat were drooping with the cold, he noticed; all their red glory over. It occurred to him that all the flowers he had seen in the show windows that first night must have gone the same way, long before this. It was only one splendid breath they had, in spite of their brave mockery at the winter outside the glass. It was a losing game in the end, it seemed, this revolt against the homilies by which the world is run. Paul took one of the blossoms carefully from his coat and scooped a little hole in the snow, where he covered it up. Then he dozed a while, from his weak condition, seeming insensible to cold.

The sound of an approaching train woke him, and he started to his feet, remembering only his resolution, and afraid lest he should be too late. He stood watching the approaching locomotive, his teeth chattering, his lips drawn away from them in a frightened smile; once or twice he glanced nervously sidewise, as though he were being watched. When the right moment came, he jumped. As he fell, the folly of his haste occurred to him with merciless clearness, the vastness of what he had left undone. There flashed through his brain, clearer than ever before, the blue of Adriatic water, the yellow of Algerian sands.

He felt something strike his chest,—his body was being thrown swiftly through the air, on and on, immeasurably far and fast, while his limbs gently relaxed. Then, because the picture-making mechanism was crushed, the disturbing visions flashed into black, and Paul dropped back into the immense design of things.

Diagnosis

Severe neurosis bordering on psychosis—hysteria, narcissism—leading to suicide out of desperation.

The number of youthful suicides has increased in recent years. This story, though written many years ago, illustrates beautifully one of the syndromes leading to such an end.

The faculty meeting, which is held to rule on Paul's dismissal from school, demonstrates the amount of anxiety, hostility, and aggression such a child may evoke. Paul's arrogance—his contempt for the mundane world and its mundane teachers, values, and subjects—so enrages those who must try to teach him that they react punitively and hostilely (see "The Use of Force"). They become ashamed of themselves for allowing a child to get under their skin and thus build up guilt, which, when they meet with no success in further encounters with the child, spirals to further anger and guilt and so on.

The child, meanwhile, has developed a poor opinion of the people about him and conceals his lack of trust behind a strong wall of contempt. His suspicious or contemptuous ways bring out the worst reactions of people, thus alienating them still further.

Paul, in his hatred for his real life, his home, neighborhood, school, and teachers, takes refuge in a made-up world of theater, glamour, and make-believe. Only this world of showmanship has any meaning to him. He seeks beauty from outside, smooth and unruffled by reality, to make up for the lack of beauty and warmth inside him. Love and understanding have been so far lost in his young life that these values seem to exist only in the wealthy, the glamorous, the dramatic life. His hysterical nature arises from his feeling that if one poses enough, the pose may become reality. He steals money to buy himself a substitute for love. When the money runs out, the meaning of life runs out for him and he commits suicide.

To handle and reach such a child would require a great deal of security and self-esteem on the teacher's part—so that he would not be thrown by the child's false wall of arrogance and contempt, or repelled by the child's narcissistic manner. He would have to share some of this child's love of the unreal world, encouraging his taste for the drama in a useful way, offering him esthetic outlets and rewards for honest work. The ultimate despair leading to suicide might be averted in such a case if the child were given psychodynamic group or individual treatment and a sympathetic school atmosphere, especially if he were allowed to work out his feelings of emptiness and despair by identifying with someone of his own sex. The child who cannot care deeply (not necessarily sexually) for someone of his own sex is unlikely to move on to loving someone of the opposite sex. This explains the necessary pre-adolescent stage of development where girls are interested only in girls, and boys in boys—the clique, the group, the gang, the pal, the chum.

Lie Down in Darkness
William Styron

[The family members: Helen, the mother; Milton or Loftis, the father, whom the daughter, Peyton, calls Bunny.]

... He heard Edward's laughter somewhere, Edward who was already tight, with whom he had, for Helen's sake, enacted the most strained and touchy friendship, and for some reason the desire for a drink became hot and powerful. There were other footsteps in the hall, and he started, but they faded away; how silly to have this nervous, quarrelsome conscience, that resentment—yes, he had had it, just for a moment, at Edward's laughter which, in turn, had made him think of Helen and of the ridiculousness of her demands on him, demands he had

paradoxically brought on himself—all in all, how silly to have to pussyfoot about like this on Peyton's wedding day, dredging up such ugly conflicts. Or was it silly? Well, my God, just one. He found two glasses, got the bottle out of the dresser and went back to Peyton's room, closing the door behind him.

"Oh, Bunny, you're so clever," she said, "all in such a cunning little bottle."

Loftis looked at her sharply. "Baby," he murmured, sitting down beside her, "do you really want a drink? Why don't we wait until afterwards? There's champagne——"

"Don't be a spoilsport. Make me a drink. This is just for my nerves." Obediently he poured an ounce or so into a glass.

"Aren't you going to have one?" she asked.

Why had he suddenly become so depressed? It was unfair of Peyton to seduce him like this, and he found himself saying, "You know, baby, I've found that when everything is going along all right you don't need anything to drink. When you're happy——"

But she broke in with a laugh, her face rosy with some sudden excitement, "Don't be so solemn, Bunny, this is for my nerves, buck up, sweetie. . . ."

He poured himself a drink and with the first swallow, his dark mood fading, he gazed at her, then past her—avoiding those eyes—to say, while the whisky taste began to seem unfamiliarly sweet and strong, "So anyway, honey, you're here and you're going to get married to a swell guy and that's all that counts. Isn't it wonderful?"

"Yes. I'm here. Thanks to you."

"It's not my doing," he said, "thank your mother."

"I've thanked her," she said wryly, looking away.

"Now don't——" he began, for it was wrong, unbearably wrong for her to bring up, on this day of all, the faintest suggestion of regrettable memories; those memories had indeed made this day poignantly perfect, childish in its brazen delight, like the day long ago of the circus or the fair, sweet from its apocalyptic dawning to the last, exhausted, bedtime end; all the near-ruined moments in the family had made this particular day even sweeter, but it was absolutely unfair of Peyton to suggest now that anything had ever been wrong one bit. The illusion of serenity would be swept away like so many dew-drenched spider webs leaving only the unsightly façade, the dusty plaster and all the bricks with their weathered holes. So *quit, quit* it, he was trying to say, softly but forcibly. . . .

"Don't you see, Bunny, I've got my own reasons for coming home. I've wanted to be normal. I've wanted to be like everybody else. These old folks wouldn't believe that there are children who'd just throw back their heads and howl, who'd just *die* to be able to say, 'Well now my rebellion's over, home is where I want to be, home is where Daddy and Mother want me.' Not with a sort of take-me-back-I've-been-so-wrong attitude—because, Bunny, you can believe me, most kids these days are not wrong or wrongdoers, they're just aimless and lost, more aimless than you all ever thought of being—not with that attitude, but just with the kind of momentary, brief love recognizing those who fed your little baby mouth and changed your didy and

paid your fare all the way. Does that sound silly, Bunny? That's all they want to do, that's what I've wanted to do and I've tried, but somehow today it all seems phony. I don't know why. I lied. I'm really not excited at all. Maybe I've got too many sour memories." She paused and looked at him, her eyes enormously sad, and he approached her, with the day in its crumbling promise going before his vision, tried to put his arms around her. "Baby——"

"Don't," she said, "don't, Bunny. I'm sorry." She held him off without even a look, for she was gazing down at the lawn, at the guests moving toward the house, all together, silent, but with a sort of giddy haste, like picnickers before the storm —holding him off as much by her silence as if she had finished erecting between them a curtain of stone, then said gently: "I'm sorry, Bunny." She looked up at him. "I can't figure where the trouble starts. Mother. She's such a faker. Look at this circus. Flaunting the blissful family. Oh, I feel so sorry for us all. If just she'd had a soul and you'd had some guts . . . Come on now," she said, grabbing his sleeve, "let's go downstairs, sweetie. I'll put up a real good front for you."

He stood rooted to the rug, wishing to faint there forever. He had been bludgeoned half to death, not so much by these truths, he told himself while he drained the sedative glass, as by necessity.

"O.K., baby," he said. . . .

And this day had really been a triumph for her. No one would ever know. No one would ever know what electric fulfillment she felt, beneath the soft, tender dignity of her manner, behind the wrinkled, rather sad, but gracefully aging serenity of her brow. No one would ever know the struggle, either. The struggle to accomplish just this casual, collected air of the proud mother: the woman who has sacrificed, whose suffering is known to the community, but who, on the day of her daughter's marriage, presents only the face of humility and courage and gentle good will. It had been cruelly difficult to put on this act, and how she had connived, how she had falsified her true feelings! But she knew that any means justified *this* end, *this* day, and after she had murmured into Milton's ear, "Oh, darling, I do want Peyton to come home," she had rejoiced at the sincere and grateful look in his eyes; she could tell he didn't doubt her honesty.

Her honesty. Oh, what was honesty, anyway? After so much suffering, did a woman really have to be honest to fulfill herself? She felt that her marriage had been such a nightmare, she had endured so many insults—the weight of so many outrages had pressed so heavily upon her spirit—that she could discard honest intentions in order to make this one day come true. *Anything, anything,* she had said to herself these past months, *anything at all.* Anything that Peyton should come home. Anything that people should know Helen Loftis was a good mother, a successful mother. Anything that people should know: it was Helen Loftis, that suffering woman, who had brought together the broken family.

Now, in sheer, rash courtliness, Carey bent down and kissed her hand. She knew how Carey saw her: poised, gentle, smiling brightly. Who could tell, she asked herself—and certainly it wasn't Carey who could tell, in his dense, well-meaning charity —that this genteel sprightliness masked the most villainous intentions? Well they *were* villainous. Here a shadow passed over her mind, just briefly, but long enough for Carey to murmur, "What's wrong, Helen?"

"Why, nothing, Carey!"

They were cruel intentions, cruel feelings, and perhaps unnatural, but what could she do? She had suffered too much and too long not to feel them. Or it. This profound and unalterable *loathing* of Peyton. Poor Peyton. Dishonorable, sinful. Her own flesh and blood. . . .

Loftis was aware of the noise but for a solitary instant he felt—looking at Peyton and Helen and Harry—islanded in silence. And during this moment he again tried vainly to recall what he had said or done to bring on such a tense and obvious, such a mutual sense of uneasiness. *Ah, those smiles, those smiles.* Was it the kiss he gave Peyton?

Then all at once he had a flicker of insight and during this moment—so brief that it lasted, literally, one blink of Peyton's eyes—he knew what the smiles were about and he had a crushing, chilling premonition of disaster. Harry smiled politely, but he faded before his sight, for Loftis was watching Peyton. She held her glass in the air, touched it to her lips. But along with her smile there was something else he was conscious of, too: she had already drunk too much. Her face rubbed pink as if by a scrubbing brush, she glowed with a fever, and in the way her eyes sparkled, her lips moist and parted, he knew somehow, with a plummeting heart, that she was beyond recovery. It was a moment of understanding that came sharp and terrible. He felt that he had waited all his life for this moment, this flash of insight to come about. He had just said crazy,

unthinking, harmless words, but he had said words like "fickle" and "love" and "death," and they, in their various ways, had sent a secret corrosion through these two women's hearts. God help him, hadn't he known all along that they hated and despised each other? Had he had to spend twenty years deceiving himself, piling false hope upon false hope—only to discover on this day, of all days, the shattering, unadorned, bitter truth? Those smiles . . . of course . . . how Peyton and Helen had always smiled at each other like that! There had been words, too, attitudes, small female gestures which it had been beyond him to divine, or even faintly to understand.

And he had gone on for years deceiving himself—too proud, too self-conscious, maybe just too stupid to realize that it had always been he himself who had been at the focus of these appalling, baffling female emotions. Not anything he had done or had failed to do had made them hate each other. Not even Dolly. None of his actions, whether right or wrong, had caused this tragedy, so much as the pure fact of himself, his very existence, interposed weaponless and defenseless in a no-man's-land between two desperate, warring female machines. Now he had kissed Peyton, said the wrong words, and he had somehow hurt her. And the smile she wore concealed her hurt—to everyone else, at least—just as Helen's smile, echoing Peyton's, concealed only the wild, envenomed jealousy which stirred at her breast. What had she done? Why had Helen deceived him like this? Those smiles. He was chilled with a sudden horror. Those smiles. They had fluttered across the web of his life like deceptive, lovely butterflies, always leading him on, always making him believe that, in spite of everything, these two women really did love each other. That, deep down, there was motherly, daughterly affection. But no. Now he saw the smiles in a split moment for what they were: women smiles—Great God, so treacherous, so false, displayed here —himself between them—like the hateful wings of bats. . . .

"You just go straight to hell, Edward," Loftis muttered, shoving him away. He plodded on upstairs. In the hallway it was dark and silent. The sounds from below came up muted and indistinct. For a moment he stood at the head of the stairs with his nose in the air, sniffing, reconnoitering. He couldn't see a thing but in the darkness shapes and shadows reeled indiscriminately, and he had to steady himself against the wall. He felt his heart pounding, and a cold dread. He pulled himself together some and moved down the hall on precarious tiptoe, trying to avoid knocking things over. Finally from Helen's room he heard voices. A voice, rather: Helen's. He stole near the door. It was closed but not locked, and a thin wedge of light fell onto the hallway floor. He heard Peyton say, "Words, words, words—why don't you get to the point?" Later he was unable to recollect, because of the fog in his mind, just what came next, but it went something like this:

Helen's voice, unemotional, polite, but direct: "That's what I'm trying to tell *you*, my dear. No, I didn't expect you not to drink some. Do you think I'm a member of the W.C.T.U.? Certainly not. But my dear girl, it's this other thing that matters to me. Really, Peyton, after all we've done to plan this affair for you, do you think——"

Peyton's voice cut in angrily: "Do I think what? What? Will you please explain?"

"This business with your father. Do you really think you have any right to treat him like you have? After all he's done for you? I saw what happened just now. Really, Peyton, you needn't pretend that it didn't happen or no one saw it. Because I saw it. I *saw* it, I tell you."

"*What?*"

"Just this." Her tone grew short and harsh. "Just this. Lashing out at him like that. In front of everybody. I wasn't the only one who saw it. Chess Hegerty saw it, and the Braunsteins. Everybody. After all I've planned. After everything I've tried—not tried but *had* to forget about you, in order to make this whole affair come off right. I said to myself, 'Well, I'll forget everything that she's done.' For the sake of morality, for the sake of Christian principles. For the sake of everything decent I'll overlook the things you've done——"

"What things?"

"Never mind. I said I'd overlook them for the sake of everything decent. So you could be married properly, in your own home. The home you forsook easily, too. That was the irony. Anyway, for all these decent things, for their sake, I said I'd make this wedding a success. If it killed me. For your father's sake, too. Now see what you've done. Everyone knows you hate me. That doesn't matter. But for them to know you hate him, too! After all these years of your faking and your flattery and your seductions——"

There was a sudden thump, a creak of springs, as if someone had fallen abruptly back upon a bed. There was laughter, too, Peyton's, tense and somewhat hysterical but also muffled, the laughter of someone lying horizontal: "Oh, God, really. If that isn't the limit. Poor Helen, you've really suffered, haven't you? Poor Helen. You're a sad case, you know, and I really shouldn't be talking like this. I really should be silent and forbearing, charitable, really, but I just can't. You're such a wretched case I can't even feel pity——"

"You shut up. You respect your elders. Your parents who——"

"You can't even suffer properly," Peyton broke in, her voice solemn now; "You're like all the rest of the sad neurotics everywhere who huddle over their misery and take their vile, mean little hatreds out on anybody they envy. You know, I suspect you've always hated me for one thing or another, but lately I've become a symbol to you you couldn't stand. Do you think I'm stupid or something, that I haven't got you figured out? You hate men, you've hated Daddy for years, and the sad thing is that he hasn't known it. And the terrible thing is that you hate yourself so much that you just don't hate men or Daddy but you hate everything, animal, vegetable and mineral. Especially you hate me. Because I've become that symbol. I *know* I'm not perfect but I'm free and young and if I'm not happy I at least know that someday I *can* be happy if I work at it long enough. I'm free. If I'd hung around in Port Warwick and married some simple-minded little boy who worked in the shipyard and lived in a little bungalow somewhere and came to see you and Daddy every Sunday, you'd be perfectly content. You'd have your claws in me then. I'd be obeying your precious code of Christian morality, which is phony anyway. But it's not that way. I'm free and you can't stand it——"

"You hate——"

Peyton's feet hit the floor; Loftis could hear them, the snapping, outraged heels. "I know what you're going to say! You're going to say I hate Port Warwick, Daddy, everything. Well, it's not true! I don't hate anything that you haven't forced me to hate and, damn you, you've forced me to hate you——"

Helen's voice rose on a high, hysterical wail. "You *tell* me these things and you don't know . . . you don't *know*," she cried wildly, "and you come here and make a mockery—with your—airs . . . and after all your sleeping around . . . you don't know . . . and your filthy little Jew . . ."

Loftis moved toward the door, but it was too late. The moment of silence which lasted between Helen's final word and what came next seemed to possess at once brevity and infinite length; this silence, so brief and so timeless, had, in its sense of awfulness, all the quality of a loud noise. Then Loftis heard it, a scuffling sound and a single, agonized moan, but he was still too late; he threw open the door. Peyton rushed sobbing past him into the hallway, down the stairs. He reached out for her, but she had gone like air, and he stood wobbling in the doorway, watching Helen. With her hands at her face she was moaning, but through her fingers ran trickles of blood and he looked at these, with a sort of remote and objective fascination, and paid no attention to her moans. He never remembered how long he stood there—perhaps half a minute, perhaps more—but when, sensing his presence, she removed her hands and looked at him, her lips moving soundlessly and her cheeks so dead and white beneath the raw, deep slits gouged out by Peyton's fingernails, he only said—making a bad job of it because of his perverse, whisky-thick tongue: "God help you, you monster."

Then he went downstairs.

Diagnosis

Family neurosis—alcoholic father, with poorly repressed incestuous feelings toward daughter, embittered mother who has been completely involved with a severely handicapped older daughter—guilt on both sides and increasingly destructive family relationships.

William Styron's book, *Lie Down in Darkness,* describes a family neurosis in which the unhappiness of the parents, their frailties, their unmet needs, and their immaturity are played out on their healthy daughter so that she comes to reflect and incorporate in herself the misery of the entire family and cannot separate herself from it except by suicide. Space limitations permit us to give in this excerpt only a glimpse of these complex intertwinings. To fully appreciate this situation, it is strongly recommended that the reader read the book in its entirety.

One learns in the first chapter of this long novel that the focal character, Peyton, committed suicide at the age of 22. Her father is a weak, kind, charming alcoholic, deeply involved and overidentified with his daughter. Her mother, Helen, a borderline psychotic, is deeply resentful and jealous of the relationship of these two. She had given all her attention and affection to the older daughter, Maudie, a feebleminded cripple who died before Peyton's suicide. Time and again in the novel the author demonstrates how the beautiful, bright, and miserable Petyon is caught in the crossfire of the parents and is used as a weapon to fight their fight. Finally she learns how to use their hatred and hostile dependency, as a way of turning them further against each other.

Family neurosis is a phenomenon too often seen today. Indeed, most neurosis can be said to be a "family" illness. This story illustrates the common tragedy of an interwoven misery, where the illness of one member causes the illnesses of the other family members and, in turn, is fed by their sickness. No one can seem to disengage himself. Each one chooses an escape that is no escape: the father, alcohol; the mother, withdrawn, delusionary brooding; the daughter, suicide; even the feebleminded sister found comfort in her helplessness and, finally, in death.

This is not so unusual a history as one would like to think. You will see Peytons in your classroom. They will be bright, pretty, social successes, sporadically brilliant and careless. They will demand special privileges and special hours and turn in overdue reports and superficial papers. They frequently flunk out but more often get by through charm, manipulation, and cleverness.

You will see the father in the classroom as a charming boy—easily led, kindly, weak, unable to stick the hard subjects out, good at those he can bluff at, glib, seductive with his teachers and often successful in his seduction, infantile, passive, too eager to please, and lacking a secure sense of himself.

You can also see Helens in your classroom, strong-willed, stubborn, aggressive, dominating the other girls and belittling the weak members of the class, and attempting to thoroughly possess and control the lives of those around them.

For the Peytons and the Loftis-Miltons, the teacher must set firm limits. He must show full and hearty acceptance of their warmth and responsiveness but refuse to be manipulated or fooled by them. He must show them that they are acceptable and worthy, that bluff and pretense are unnecessary and unrewarding.

The Helens need more love and lower standards of perfection. Their standards for themselves are inhumanly rigid and high. They need to learn to accept their own fallibility and, thus, make room for the human foibles of others. Above all, they should not be allowed to cultivate their own sufferings or use them as a weapon against classmates or teachers.

In the case of Peyton's family, all of them needed some form of well-designed treatment. Perhaps everybody would not have been cured, or even reached, but some members of the family might have been. At least, Peyton's suicide might have been averted. The most desirable form of therapy in this case would be family therapy, in which the family is treated as a group. Though individual family members might be treated separately, their growth and even survival as individuals are so intimately dependent on their relationships to one another that unless this group problem is faced as a group problem it might be insoluble and their fate inescapable.

Notes from the Underground
Fyodor Dostoyevsky

But, in the beginning, what agonies I went through in this inner struggle! I didn't believe that there were others who went through all that, so I've kept it a secret all my life. I was ashamed (perhaps even now, I am still ashamed). I reached a point where I felt a secret, unhealthy, base little pleasure in creeping back into my hole after some disgusting night in Petersburg and forcing myself to think that I had again done something filthy, that what was done couldn't be undone. And I inwardly gnawed at myself for it, tore at myself and ate myself away, until the bitterness turned into some shameful, accursed sweetishness and, finally, into a great, unquestionable pleasure. Yes, yes, definitely a pleasure! I mean it! . . .

I, for instance, am horribly sensitive. I'm suspicious and easily offended, like a dwarf or a hunchback. But I believe there have been moments when I'd have liked to have my face slapped. I say that in all seriousness—I'd have derived pleasure from this too. Naturally it would be the pleasure of despair. But then, it is in despair that we find the most acute pleasure, especially when we are aware of the hopelessness of the situation. And when one's face is slapped—why, one is bound to be crushed by one's awareness of the pulp into which one has been ground. But the main point is that, whichever way you look at it, I was always guilty in the first place, and what is moxt vexing is that I was guilty without guilt, by virtue of the laws of nature. Thus, to start with, I'm guilty of being more intelligent than all those around me. (I've always felt that and, believe me, it's weighed on my conscience sometimes. All my life, I have never been able to look people straight in the eye—I always feel a need to avert my face.) And then, I'm also guilty because, even if there had been any forgiveness in me, it would only have increased my torment, because I would have been conscious of its uselessness. I surely would have been unable to do anything with my forgiveness: I wouldn't have been able to forgive because

the offender would simply have been obeying the laws of nature in slapping me, and it makes no sense to forgive the laws of nature—but neither could I have forgotten it, because it is humiliating, after all. Finally, even if I hadn't wanted to be forgiving at all, but on the contrary, had wished to avenge myself on the offender, I couldn't have done it, for the chances are I'd never have dared to do anything about it even if there had been something I could do. Why wouldn't I have dared? Well, I'd especially like to say a few words about that. . . .

And there, in its repulsive, evil-smelling nest, the downtrodden, ridiculed mouse plunges immediately into a cold, poisonous, and—most important—never-ending hatred. For forty years, it will remember the humiliation in all its ignominious details, each time adding some new point, more abject still, endlessly taunting and tormenting itself. Although ashamed of its own thoughts, the mouse will remember everything, go over it again and again, then think up possible additional humiliations. It may even try to avenge itself, but then it will do so in spurts, pettily, from behind the stove, anonymously, doubting that its vengeance is right, that it will succeed, and feeling that, as a result, it will hurt itself a hundred times more than it will hurt the one against whom its revenge is directed, who probably won't even feel enough of an itch to scratch himself. . . .

How can one, after all, have the slightest respect for a man who tries to find pleasure in the feeling of humiliation itself? I'm not saying that out of any mawkish sense of repentance. In general, I couldn't stand saying "Sorry, Papa, I'll never do it again."

And it wasn't at all because I was incapable of

From Dostoyevsky's *Notes from the Underground* translated by Andrew R. MacAndrew. Copyright © 1961 by Andrew R. MacAndrew. Reprinted by arrangement with The New American Library, Inc., New York.

saying it. On the contrary, perhaps it was just because I was only too prone to say it. And you should've seen under what circumstances too! *I'd get myself blamed, almost purposely, for something with which I'd had nothing to do even in thought or dream.* [Italics added.] That's what was most disgusting. But, even so, I was always deeply moved, repented my wickedness, and cried; in this, of course, I was deceiving myself, although I never did so deliberately. It was my heart that let me down here. In this case, I can't even blame the laws of nature, although those laws have oppressed me all my life. It makes me sick to remember all this, but then I was sick at the time too. It took me only a minute or so to recognize that it was all a pack of lies; all that repentance, those emotional outbursts and promises of reform—nothing but pretentious, nauseating lies. I was furious. And if you ask me now why I tortured and tormented myself like that, I'll tell you: I was bored just sitting with my arms folded, so I went in for all those tricks. Believe me, it's true. Just watch yourself carefully and you'll understand that that's the way it works. I made up whole stories about myself and put myself through all sorts of adventures to satisfy, at any price, my need to live. How many times did I convince myself that I was offended, just like that, for no reason at all. And although I knew that I had nothing to be offended about, that I was putting it all on, I'd put myself into such a state that in the end I'd really feel terribly offended. I was so strongly tempted to play tricks of this sort that, in the end, I lost all restraint. . . .

But I can't see any justice or virtue in vengeance, so if I indulge in it, it is only out of spite and anger. Anger, of course, overcomes all hesitations and can thus replace the primary reason precisely because it is no reason at all. But what can I do if I don't even have anger (that's where I started from, remember)? In me, anger disintegrates chemically like everything else, because of those damned laws of nature. As I think, the anger vanishes, the reasons for it evaporate, the responsible person is never found, the insult becomes an insult no longer but a stroke of fate, just like a toothache, for which no one can be held responsible. And so I find that all I can do is take another whack at the stone wall, then shrug the whole thing off because of my failure to find the primary cause of the evil. . . .

[Behind the veil of masochism and anger are dreams of glory and grandiose fantasies.]

But how much love—ah, how much—I experienced in my dreams, when I escaped to "the sublime and the beautiful." Perhaps it was an imaginary love and maybe it was never directed toward another human being, but it was such an overflowing love that there was no need to direct it—that would've been an unnecessary luxury. Everything always ended safely in a leisurely, rapturous sliding into the domain of art, that is, into the beautiful lives of heroes stolen from the authors of novels and poems and adapted to the demands of the moment, whatever they might be. I, for instance, triumph over everyone, and they, of course, are strewn in the dust, acknowledging my superiority; I'm all-forgiving; I'm a great poet and court chamberlain; I fall in love; I inherit millions and donate them to human causes and take advantage of this opportunity to publicly confess my backslidings and disgrace which, of course, is no ordinary disgrace but contains much that is "sublime and beautiful" in it, something in the Manfred style. Everyone is weeping and kissing me (they could hardly be so thickskinned as not to); then I leave, hungry and barefoot, to preach new ideas and rout the reactionaries at Austerlitz. Then, a triumphal march is played, an amnesty is declared, the Pope agrees to leave Rome for Brazil, there's a ball for all of Italy at the Villa Borghese on the shores of Lake Como, which lake, for this occasion, is moved to the vicinity of Rome. Then there's a scene in the bushes, and so on and so forth; see what I mean? . . .

Diagnosis

Masochist solution—repressed or concealed rage, impotent anger covering fantasies of grandeur, glory, and supremacy, which are never risked by being acted upon.

These "notes from underground" reflect the very core of the masochistic solution, demonstrating great self-imposed suffering. They indicate the unending hostility and rage behind the abject *mea culpa* attitude, anger which can never be expressed directly, for if it is the masochistic structure falls. Should the structure fall, the lurking, secret contempt and grandiose fantasies would have to be tested in the light of the real world, where they are bound to fail. Failure, though devastating, is less upsetting to the masochist than success. Strange? Think of the children who continually get hurt, always appear put upon, are always the scapegoats. At first one sides with them. Later, one observes, it is always the same little Johnny or Jane who gets in the way of the flung ball or book or rock; who sometimes by his very posture provokes Bill to bullying. It is the same Johnny or Jane whose paper gets torn just as it is to be passed in, or who always has obstacles in the way of completing the assignment that would assure the expected A or B. This Johnny or Jane always—whether academically, physically, or socially—falls short and looks sad and beaten. Sadness and indirectness can cover up the fantasy that it is outward circumstances that are keeping one from success, though the person who feels this way is often unwilling to give circumstances a chance because it would mean risking failure.

Why? There are many possible causes. The answer may lie in a mother who "suffers" all the time, so that joy is not in the child's perception of life and seems somehow wrong. A too-successful and proud parent or sibling may leave no room for Johnny or Jane to be anything special except a special failure. His parents may transmit to him, consciously or unconsciously, a feeling that he is alive only for the purpose of erasing their troubles or complementing their lives. Because these are impossible tasks, there is nothing left for Johnny or Jane but to live out an apology; to say, "I can't, I can't, I can't, I'm sorry, I'm sorry, I'm sorry." And "I hate you for asking this of me, for then I feel I must, but it is too much for me." This last is never said aloud and is often not consciously felt, but it is at the root of many a miserable life dedicated to masochistic suffering and failure.

Of Human Bondage
W. Somerset Maugham

. . . But meanwhile he had grown horribly sensitive. He never ran if he could help it, because he knew it made his limp more conspicuous, and he adopted a peculiar walk. He stood still as much as he could, with his club-foot behind the other, so that it should not attract notice, and he was constantly on the lookout for any reference to it. Because he could not join in the games which other boys played, their life remained strange to him; he only interested himself from the outside in their doings; and it seemed to him that there was a barrier between them and him. Sometimes they seemed to think that it was his fault if he could not play football, and he was unable to make them understand. He was left a good deal to himself. He had been inclined to talkativeness, but gradually he became silent. He began to think of the difference between himself and others.

Two years passed, and Philip was nearly twelve. He was in the first form, within two or three places of the top, and after Christmas when several boys would be leaving for the senior school he would be head boy. He had already quite a collection of prizes, worthless books on bad paper, but in gorgeous bindings decorated with the arms of the school: his position had freed him from bullying, and he was not unhappy. His fellows forgave him his success because of his deformity.

"After all, it's jolly easy for him to get prizes," the said, "there's nothing he *can* do but swat."

He had lost his early terror of Mr. Watson. He had grown used to the loud voice, and when the headmaster's heavy hand was laid on his shoulder Philip discerned vaguely the intention of a caress. He had the good memory which is more useful for scholastic achievements than mental power, and he knew Mr. Watson expected him to leave the preparatory school with a scholarship.

But he had grown very self-conscious. The new-born child does not realise that his body is more a part of himself than surrounding objects, and will play with his toes without any feeling that they belong to him more than the rattle by his side; and it is only by degrees, through pain, that he understands the fact of the body. And experiences of the same kind are necessary for the individual to become conscious of himself; but here there is the difference that, although everyone becomes equally conscious of his body as a separate and complete organism, everyone does not become equally conscious of himself as a complete and separate personality. The feeling of apartness from others comes to most with puberty, but it is not always developed to such a degree as to make the difference between the individual and his fellows noticeable to the individual. It is such as he, as little conscious of himself as the bee in a hive, who are the lucky in life, for they have the best chance of happiness: their activities are shared by all, and their pleasures are only pleasures because they are enjoyed in common; you will see them on Whitmonday dancing

From *Of Human Bondage* by W. Somerset Maugham. Copyright 1915 by Doubleday & Company, Inc. Reprinted by permission of Doubleday & Company, Inc., A. P. Watt & Son (Literary Executor of the late W. Somerset Maugham), and William Heinemann Limited.

on Hampstead Heath, shouting at a football match, or from club windows in Pall Mall cheering a royal procession. It is because of them that man has been called a social animal.

Philip passed from the innocence of childhood to bitter consciousness of himself by the ridicule which his club-foot had excited. The circumstances of his case were so peculiar that he could not apply to them the ready-made rules which acted well enough in ordinary affairs, and he was forced to think for himself. The many books he had read filled his mind with ideas which, because he only half understood them, gave more scope to his imagination. Beneath his painful shyness something was growing up within him, and obscurely he realised his personality. But at times it gave him odd surprises; he did things, he knew not why, and afterwards when he thought of them found himself all at sea. . . .

The King's School at Tercanbury, to which Philip went when he was thirteen, prided itself on its antiquity. The masters had no patience with modern ideas of education, which they read of sometimes in *The Times* or *The Guardian*, and hoped fervently that King's School would remain true to its old traditions. The dead languages were taught with such thoroughness that an old boy seldom thought of Homer or Virgil in after life without a qualm of boredom; and though in the common room at dinner one or two bolder spirits suggested that mathematics were of increasing importance, the general feeling was that they were a less noble study than the classics. Neither German nor chemistry was taught, and French only by the form-masters; they could keep order better than a foreigner, and, since they knew the grammar as well as any Frenchman, it seemed unimportant that none of them could have got a cup of coffee in the restaurant at Boulogne unless the waiter had known a little English. Geography was taught chiefly by making boys draw maps, and this was a favourite occupation, especially when the country dealt with was mountainous: it was possible to waste a great deal of time in drawing the Andes or the Apennines. . . .

[A new headmaster, Mr. Perkins, disturbs the older masters by occasionally taking their classes.]

The results were curious. Mr. Turner, who was the first victim, broke the news to his form that the headmaster would take them for Latin that day, and on the pretence that they might like to ask him a question or two so that they should not make per-fect fools of themselves, spent the last quarter of an hour of the history lesson in construing for them the passage of Livy which had been set for the day; but when he rejoined his class and looked at the paper on which Mr. Perkins had written the marks, a surprise awaited him; for the two boys at the top of the form seemed to have done very ill, while others who had never distinguished themselves before were given full marks. When he asked Eldridge, his cleverest boy, what was the meaning of this the answer came sullenly:

"Mr. Perkins never gave us any construing to do. He asked me what I knew about General Gordon."

Mr. Turner looked at him in astonishment. The boys evidently felt they had been hardly used, and he could not help agreeing with their silent dissatisfaction. He could not see either what General Gordon had to do with Livy. He hazarded an enquiry afterwards.

"Eldridge was dreadfully put out because you asked him what he knew about General Gordon," he said to the headmaster, with an attempt at a chuckle.

Mr. Perkins laughed.

"I saw they'd got to the agrarian laws of Caius Gracchus, and I wondered if they knew anything about the agrarian troubles in Ireland. But all they knew about Ireland was that Dublin was on the Liffey. So I wondered if they'd ever heard of General Gordon."

Then the horrid fact was disclosed that the new head had a mania for general information. He had doubts about the utility of examinations on subjects which had been crammed for the occasion. He wanted common sense.

Sighs grew more worried every month; and he hated the attitude the head adopted towards classical literature. And Squirts, the master of the middle-third, grew more ill-tempered every day.

It was in his form that Philip was put on entering the school. The Rev. B. B. Gordon was a man by nature ill-suited to be a schoolmaster: he was impatient and choleric. No master could have been more unfitted to teach things to so shy a boy as Philip. He had come to the school with fewer terrors than he had when first he went to Mr. Watson's. He knew a good many boys who had been with him at the preparatory school. He felt more grown-up, and instinctively realised that among the larger numbers his deformity would be less noticeable. But from the first day Mr. Gordon struck terror in his heart; and the master, quick to discern the boys who were frightened of him, seemed on that account to take a peculiar dislike to him. Philip had enjoyed his work, but now he began to look upon the hours passed in school with horror. Rather than risk an answer which might be wrong and excite a storm of abuse from the master, he would sit stupidly silent, and when it came towards his turn to stand up and construe he grew sick and white with apprehension. His happy moments were those when Mr. Perkins took the form. He was able to gratify the passion for general knowledge which beset the headmaster; he had read all sorts of strange books beyond his years, and often Mr. Perkins, when a question was going round the room, would stop at Philip with a smile that filled the boy with rapture, and say:

"Now, Carey, you tell them."

The good marks he got on these occasions increased Mr. Gordon's indignation. One day it came to Philip's turn to translate, and the master sat there glaring at him and furiously biting his thumb. He was in a ferocious mood. Philip began to speak in a low voice.

"Don't mumble," shouted the master.

Something seemed to stick in Philip's throat.

"Go on. Go on. Go on."

Each time the words were screamed more loudly. The effect was to drive all he knew out of Philip's head, and he looked at the printed page vacantly. Mr. Gordon began to breathe heavily.

"If you don't know why don't you say so? Do you know it or not? Did you hear all this construed last time or not? Why don't you speak? Speak, you blockhead, speak!"

The master seized the arms of his chair and grasped them as though to prevent himself from falling upon Philip. They knew that in past days he often used to seize boys by the throat till they almost choked. The veins in his forehead stood out and his face grew dark and threatening. He was a man insane.

Philip had known the passage perfectly the day before, but now he could remember nothing.

"I don't know it," he gasped.

"Why don't you know it? Let's take the words one by one. We'll soon see if you don't know it."

Philip stood silent, very white, trembling a little, with his head bent down on the book. The master's breathing grew almost stertorous.

"The headmaster says you're clever. I don't know how he sees it. General information." He laughed savagely. "I don't know what they put you in his form for. Blockhead."

He was pleased with the word, and he repeated it at the top of his voice.

"Blockhead! Blockhead! Club-footed blockhead!"

That relieved him a little. He saw Philip redden suddenly. He told him to fetch the Black Book. Philip put down his Caesar and went silently out. The Black Book was a sombre volume in which the names of boys were written with their misdeeds, and when a name was down three times it meant a caning. Philip went to the headmaster's house and knocked at his study-door. Mr. Perkins was seated at his table.

"May I have the Black Book, please, sir?"

"There it is," answered Mr. Perkins, indicating its place by a nod of his head. "What have you been doing that you shouldn't?"

"I don't know, sir."

Mr. Perkins gave him a quick look, but without answering went on with his work. Philip took the book and went out. When the hour was up, a few minutes later, he brought it back.

"Let me have a look at it," said the headmaster. "I see Mr. Gordon has black-booked you for gross impertinence.' What was it?"

"I don't know, sir. Mr. Gordon said I was a club-footed blockhead."

Mr. Perkins looked at him again. He wondered whether there was sarcasm behind the boy's reply, but he was still much too shaken. His face was white and his eyes had a look of terrified distress. Mr. Perkins got up and put the book down. As he did so he took up some photographs.

"A friend of mine sent me some pictures of Athens this morning," he said casually. "Look here, there's the Acropolis."

He began explaining to Philip what he saw. The ruin grew vivid with his words. He showed him the theatre of Dionysus and explained in what order the people sat, and how beyond they could see the blue Aegean. And then suddenly he said:

"I remember Mr. Gordon used to call me a gipsy counter-jumper when I was in his form."

And before Philip, his mind fixed on the photographs, had time to gather the meaning of the remark, Mr. Perkins was showing him a picture of Salamis, and with his finger, a finger of which the nail had a little black edge to it, was pointing out how the Greek ships were placed and how the Persian. . . .

Diagnosis

Withdrawal because of physical handicap—use of handicap to foster neurosis, masochism.

The question of emotional disturbance of children with physical handicaps is the problem of "Which came first, the chicken or the egg?" There is no question that some children with severe, even multiple physical handicaps have no more than an ordinary dose of emotional problems. These children generally have excellent physical health along with their disability, and they have warm, accepting, unpitying relationships at home, where reasonable expectations are blended with acceptance of limitations.

It is equally certain that many children who have physical handicaps also suffer from emotional disorders. Being different is hard for children; restriction by edict of fate breeds resentment and is hard on the ego. When parents cannot accept the disability, or when they use it as a means of tying their children to them, damage ensues. When, further, schoolmates and teachers ridicule or set the child apart by too little or too much sympathy, difficulties mount.

Philip's case is a good example. A lonely child, bereft of warmth and understanding, he feels different and unaccepted by his peers. He turns inward to reading and fantasy and removes himself from friendship. Here good teachers could come to the rescue. He looks toward religion—or, in his adolescent view, magic or miracle—to solve his problem. When this fails, he turns further inward and escapes to compulsive reading. Bad teachers underline his troubles. His school work falls off, and a pattern of failure follows through early manhood until he finds a way out for himself via projection, or identity with the sufferings of others.

You have seen this child—whether he be a Philip with a club foot, a stutterer like Maugham himself, or a child with a disability that makes it impossible for him to read. He needs careful watching, sympathy but not pity, understanding without overindulgence, acceptance but not resignation. At a further extreme, the brain-damaged child, the epileptic, the blind, and the deaf child (who feels the most isolated) bear similar marks. Special skills and teaching techniques are needed for various severely handicapped children; for the severer the handicap and the greater the difference this child feels between himself and others, the greater the chance for emotional disturbance.

Silent Snow, Secret Snow
Conrad Aiken

Just why it should have happened, or why it should have happened just when it did, he could not, of course, possibly have said; nor perhaps could it even have occurred to him to ask. The thing was above all a secret, something to be preciously concealed from Mother and Father; and to that very fact it owed an enormous part of its deliciousness. It was like a peculiarly beautiful trinket to be carried unmentioned in one's trouser-pocket—a rare stamp, an old coin, a few tiny gold links found trodden out of shape on the path in the park, a pebble of carnelian, a sea shell distinguishable from all others by an unusual spot or stripe—and, as if it were anyone of these, he carried around with him everywhere a warm and persistent and increasingly beautiful sense of possession. Nor was it only a sense of possession—it was also a sense of protection. It was as if, in some delightful way, his secret gave him a fortress, a wall behind which he could retreat into heavenly seclusion. This was almost the first thing he had noticed about it—apart from the oddness of the thing itself—and it was this that now again, for the fiftieth time, occurred to him, as he sat in the little schoolroom. It was the half hour for geography. Miss Buell was revolving with one finger, slowly, a huge terrestrial globe which had been placed on her desk. The green and yellow continents passed and repassed, questions were asked and answered, and now the little girl in front of him, Deirdre, who had a funny little constellation of freckles on the back of her neck, exactly like the Big Dipper, was standing up and telling Miss Buell that the equator was the line that ran round the middle.

Miss Buell's face, which was old and grayish and kindly, with gray stiff curls beside the cheeks, and eyes that swam very brightly, like little minnows, behind thick glasses, wrinkled itself into a complication of amusements.

"Ah! I see. The earth is wearing a belt, or a sash. Or someone drew a line round it!"

"Oh, no—not that—I mean—"

In the general laughter, he did not share, or only a very little. He was thinking about the Arctic

Reprinted by permission of The World Publishing Company from *The Collected Short Stories of Conrad Aiken* by Conrad Aiken. Copyright 1922, 1923, 1924, 1925, 1927, 1928, 1929, 1930, 1931, 1932, 1933, 1934, 1935, 1941, 1950, 1952, 1953, 1955, 1956, 1957, 1958, 1959, 1960 by Conrad Aiken.

and Antarctic regions, which of course, on the globe, were white. Miss Buell was now telling them about the tropics, the jungles, the steamy heat of equatorial swamps, where the birds and butterflies, and even the snakes, were like living jewels. As he listened to these things, he was already, with a pleasant sense of half-effort, putting his secret between himself and the words. Was it really an effort at all? For effort implied something voluntary, and perhaps even something one did not especially want; whereas this was distinctly pleasant, and came almost of its own accord. All he needed to do was to think of that morning, the first one, and then of all the others—

But it was all so absurdly simple! It had amounted to so little. It was nothing, just an idea—and just why it should have become so wonderful, so permanent, was a mystery—a very pleasant one, to be sure, but also, in an amusing way, foolish. However, without ceasing to listen to Miss Buell, who had now moved up to the north temperate zones, he deliberately invited his memory of the first morning. It was only a moment or two after he had waked up—or perhaps the moment itself. But was there, to be exact, an exact moment? Was one awake all at once? or was it gradual? Anyway, it was after he had stretched a lazy hand up towards the headrail, and yawned, and then relaxed again among his warm covers, all the more grateful on a December morning, that the thing had happened. Suddenly, for no reason, he had thought of the postman, he remembered the postman. Perhaps there was nothing so odd in that. After all, he heard the postman almost every morning in his life—his heavy boots could be heard clumping round the corner at the top of the little cobbled hill-street, and then, progressively nearer, progressively louder, the double knock at each door, the crossings and re-crossings of the street, till finally the clumsy steps came stumbling across to the very door, and the tremendous knock came which shook the house itself.

(Miss Buell was saying "Vast wheat-growing areas in North America and Siberia."

Dierdre had for the moment placed her left hand across the back of her neck.)

But on this particular morning, the first morning, as he lay there with his eyes closed, he had for some reason *waited* for the postman. He wanted to hear him come round the corner. And that was precisely the joke—he never did. He never came. He never had come—*round the corner*—again. For when at last the steps *were* heard, they had already, he was quite sure, come a little down the hill, to the first house; and even so, the steps were curiously different—they were softer, they had a new secrecy about

them, they were muffled and indistinct; and while the rhythm of them was the same, it now said a new thing—it said peace, it said remoteness, it said cold, it said sleep. And he had understood the situation at once—nothing could have seemed simpler—there had been snow in the night, such as all winter he had been longing for; and it was this which had rendered the postman's first footsteps inaudible, and the later ones faint. Of course! How lovely! And even now it must be snowing—it was going to be a snowy day—the long white ragged lines were drifting and sifting across the street, across the faces of the old houses, whispering and hushing, making little triangles of white in the corners between cobblestones, seething a little when the wind blew them over the ground to a drifted corner; and so it would be all day, getting deeper and deeper and silenter and silenter.

(Miss Buell was saying "Land of perpetual snow.")

All this time, of course (while he lay in bed), he had kept his eyes closed, listening to the nearer progress of the postman, the muffled footsteps thumping and slipping on the snow-sheathed cobbles; and all the other sounds—the double knocks, a frosty far-off voice or two, a bell ringing thinly and softly as if under a sheet of ice—had the same slightly abstracted quality, as if removed by one degree from actuality—as if everything in the world had been insulated by snow. But when at last, pleased, he opened his eyes, and turned them towards the window, to see for himself this long-desired and now so clearly imagined miracle—what he saw instead was brilliant sunlight on a roof; and when, astonished, he jumped out of bed and stared down into the street, expecting to see the cobbles obliterated by the snow, he saw nothing but the bare bright cobbles themselves.

Queer, the effect this extraordinary surprise had had upon him—all the following morning he had kept with him a sense as of snow falling about him, a secret screen of new snow between himself and the world. If he had not dreamed such a thing—and how could he have dreamed it while awake?—how else could one explain it? In any case, the delusion had been so vivid as to affect his entire behavior. He could not now remember whether it was on the first or the second morning—or was it even the third?—that his mother had drawn attention to some oddness in his manner.

"But my darling—" she had said at the breakfast table—"what has come over you? You don't seem to be listening. . . ."

And how often that very thing had happened since!

(Miss Buell was now asking if anyone knew the difference between the North Pole and the Magnetic Pole. Deirdre was holding up her flickering brown hand, and he could see the four white dimples that marked the knuckles.) . . .

"Now Paul—I would like very much to ask you a question or two. You will answer them, won't you—you know I'm an old, old friend of yours, eh? That's right! . . ."

His back was thumped twice by the doctor's fat fist,—then the doctor was grinning at him with false amiability, while with one finger-nail he was scratching the top button of his waistcoat. Beyond the doctor's shoulder was the fire, the fingers of flame making light prestidigitation against the sooty fireback, the soft sound of their random flutter the only sound.

"I would like to know—is there anything that worries you?"

The doctor was again smiling, his eyelids low against the little black pupils, in each of which was a tiny white bead of light. Why answer him? why answer him at all? "At whatever pain to others"—but it was all a nuisance, this necessity for resistance, this necessity for attention: it was as if one had been stood up on a brilliantly lighted stage, under a great round blaze of spotlight; as if one were merely a trained seal, or a performing dog, or a fish, dipped out of an aquarium and held up by the tail. It would serve them right if he were merely to bark or growl. And meanwhile, to miss these last few precious hours, these hours of which every minute was more beautiful than the last, more menacing—? He still looked, as if from a great distance, at the beads of light in the doctor's eyes, at the fixed false smile, and then, beyond, once more at his mother's slippers, his father's slippers, the soft flutter of the fire. Even here, even amongst these hostile presences, and in this arranged light, he could see the snow, he could hear it—it was in the corners of the room, where the shadow was deepest, under the sofa, behind the half-opened door which led to the dining room. It was gentler here, softer, its seethe the quietest of whispers, as if, in deference to a drawing room, it had quite deliberately put on its "manners"; it kept itself out of sight, obliterated itself, but distinctly with an air of saying, "Ah, but just wait! Wait till we are alone together! Then I will begin to tell you something new! Something white! something cold! something sleepy! something of cease, and peace, and the long bright curve of space! Tell them to go away. Banish them. Refuse to speak. Leave them, go upstairs to your room, turn out the light and get into bed—I will go with you, I will be waiting for you, I will tell you a better story than Little Kay of the Skates, or The Snow Ghost—I will surround your bed, I will close the windows, pile a deep drift against the door, so that none will ever again be able to enter. Speak to them! . . ." It seemed as if the little hissing voice came from a slow white spiral of falling flakes in the corner by the front window—but he could not be sure. He felt himself smiling, then, and said to the doctor, but without looking at him, looking beyond him still—

"Oh, no, I think not—"

"But are you sure, my boy?"

His father's voice came softly and coldly then—the familiar voice of silken warning.

"You needn't answer at once, Paul—remember we're trying to help you—think it over and be quite sure, won't you?"

He felt himself smiling again, at the notion of being quite sure. What a joke! As if he weren't so sure that reassurance was no longer necessary, and all this cross-examination a ridiculous farce, a grotesque parody! What could they know about it? These gross intelligences, these humdrum minds so bound to the usual, the ordinary? Impossible to tell them about it! Why, even now, even now, with the proof so abundant, so formidable, so imminent, so appallingly present here in this very room, could they believe it?—could even his mother believe it? No—it was only too plain that if anything were said about it, the merest hint given, they would be incredulous—they would laugh—They would say "Absurd!"—think things about him which weren't true. . . .

"Why no, I'm not worried—why should I be?"

He looked then straight at the doctor's low-lidded eyes, looked from one of them to the other, from one bead of light to the other, and gave a little laugh.

The doctor seemed to be disconcerted by this. He drew back in his chair, resting a fat white hand on either knee. The smile faded slowly from his face.

"Well, Paul!" he said, and paused gravely, "I'm afraid you don't take this quite seriously enough. I think you perhaps don't quite realize—don't quite realize—" He took a deep quick breath, and turned, as if helplessly, at a loss for words, to the others. But Mother and Father were both silent—no help was forthcoming.

"You must surely know, be aware, that you have not been quite yourself, of late? don't you know that? . . ."

It was amusing to watch the doctor's renewed attempt at a smile, a queer disorganized look, as of confidential embarrassment.

"I feel all right, sir," he said, and again gave the little laugh.

"And we're trying to help you." The doctor's tone sharpened.

"Yes, sir, I know. But why? I'm all right. I'm just *thinking*, that's all."

His mother made a quick movement forward, resting a hand on the back of the doctor's chair.

"Thinking?" she said. "But my dear, about what?"

This was a direct challenge—and would have to be directly met. But before he met it, he looked again into the corner by the door, as if for reassurance. He smiled again at what he saw, at what he heard. The little spiral was still there, still softly whirling, like the ghost of a white kitten chasing the ghost of a white tail, and making as it did so the faintest of whispers. It was all right! If only he could remain firm, everything was going to be all right.

"Oh, about anything about nothing,—*you* know the way you do!"

"You mean—day-dreaming?"

"Oh, no—thinking!"

"But thinking about *what?*"

"Anything."

He laughed a third time—but this time, happening to glance upward towards his mother's face, he was appalled at the effect his laughter seemed to have upon her. Her mouth had opened in an expression of horror. . . . This was too bad! Unfortunate! He had known it would cause pain, of course—but he hadn't expected it to be quite so bad as this. Perhaps—perhaps if he just gave them a tiny gleaming hint—?

"About the snow," he said.

"What on earth!" This was his father's voice. The brown slippers came a step nearer on the hearth-rug.

"But my dear, what do you mean!" This was his mother's voice.

The doctor merely stared.

"Just *snow*, that's all. I like to think about it."

"Tell us about it, my boy."

"But that's all it is. There's nothing to tell. *You* know what snow is?"

This he said almost angrily, for he felt that they were trying to corner him. He turned sideways so as no longer to face the doctor, and the better to see the inch of blackness between the window-sill and the lowered curtain,—the cold inch of beckoning and delicious night. At once he felt better, more assured.

"Mother—can I go to bed, now, please? I've got a headache."

"But I thought you said—"

"It's just come. It's all these questions—! Can I, mother?"

"You can go as soon as the doctor has finished."

"Don't you think this thing ought to be gone into thoroughly, and *now?*" This was Father's voice. The brown slippers again came a step nearer, the voice was the well-known "punishment" voice, resonant and cruel.

"Oh, what's the use, Norman—"

Quite suddenly, everyone was silent. And without precisely facing them, nevertheless he was aware that all three of them were watching him with an extraordinary intensity—staring hard at him—as if he had done something monstrous, or was himself some kind of monster. He could hear the soft irregular flutter of the flames; the cluck-click-cluck-click of the clock; far and faint, two sudden spurts of laughter from the kitchen, as quickly cut off as begun; a murmur of water in the pipes; and then, the silence seemed to deepen, to spread out, to become world-long and worldwide, to become timeless and shapeless, and to center inevitably and rightly, with a slow and sleepy but enormous concentration of all power, on the beginning of a new sound. What this new sound was going to be, he knew perfectly well. It might begin with a hiss, but it would end with a roar—there was no time to lose—he must escape. It mustn't happen here—

Without another word, he turned and ran up the stairs.

Not a moment too soon. The darkness was coming in long white waves. A prolonged sibilance filled the night—a great seamless seethe of wild influence went abruptly across it—a cold low humming shook the windows. He shut the door and flung off his clothes in the dark. The bare black floor was like a little raft tossed in waves of snow, almost overwhelmed, washed under whitely, up again, smothered in curled billows of feather. The snow was laughing: it spoke from all sides at once: it pressed closer to him as he ran and jumped exulting into his bed.

"Listen to us!" it said. "Listen! We have come to tell you the story we told you about. You remember? Lie down. Shut your eyes, now—you will no longer see much—in this white darkness who could see, or want to see? We will take the place of everything. . . . Listen—"

A beautiful varying dance of snow began at the front of the room, came forward and then retreated, flattened out toward the floor, then rose fountain-like to the ceiling, swayed, recruited itself from a new stream of flakes which poured laughing in through the humming window, advanced again, lifted long white arms. It said peace, it said remoteness, it said cold—it said—

But then a gash of horrible light fell brutally across the room from the opening door—the snow drew back hissing—something alien had come into the room—something hostile. This thing rushed at him, clutched at him, shook him—and he was not merely horrified, he was filled with such a loathing as he had never known. What was this? this cruel disturbance? this act of anger and hate? It was as if he had to reach up a hand toward another world for any understanding of it,—an effort of which he was only barely capable. But of that other world he still remembered just enough to know the exorcising words. They tore themselves from his other life suddenly—

"Mother! Mother! Go away! I hate you!"

And with that effort, everything was solved, everything became all right: the seamless hiss advanced once more, the long white wavering lines rose and fell like enormous whispering sea-waves, the whisper becoming louder, the laughter more numerous.

"Listen!" it said. "We'll tell you the last, the most beautiful and secret story—shut your eyes—it is a very small story—a story that gets smaller and smaller—it comes inward instead of opening like a flower—it is a flower becoming a seed—a little cold seed—do you hear? we are leaning closer to you—"

The hiss was now becoming a roar—the whole world was a vast moving screen of snow—but even now it said peace, it said remoteness, it said cold, it said sleep.

Diagnosis

Schizophrenic breakdown—delusions and hallucinations, both visual and auditory; gradual withdrawal from world of reality into autistic or fantasy world.

This secret world of snow is unbearably tempting or beckoning to Paul, like the Sirens to Ulysses, until this twelve-year-old boy is magnetized away from the world of home and school. Exactly what, in his middle-class home and daily life, was so painful for him that he needed to retreat? It could have been the clinging to mother or over-identification and unconscious hostility of one of the parents, so frequently found in schizophrenic breakdowns. We are told only how his delusionary cocoon spread from home to school. Mother, father, and teacher become aware of the increasing withdrawal of this boy, of his "not-thereness." The ways the doctor mishandles the child and the father's understandable irritation under the strain of anxiety are typical reactions to the frightening phenomenon of watching a child disappear into another world before one's eyes, unable to stop him, and probably even unconsciously encouraging that very withdrawal.

The story indicates well the kind of child this is. In a classroom, he is shy, quiet, withdrawn—no behavior problem except that more and more often he is miles away when a question is asked. Sometimes his answers are puzzlingly inappropriate, rooted in the question but winding off into outer space. He is the kind of child Miss Buell would describe in a conference as being very adequate sometimes, but just not there most of the time. The seemingly sudden onset of the illness is misleading. A keen and sensitive teacher could have recognized signs of increasing withdrawal if prepared to see them. An adequately prepared teacher would consult the psychological department of the school before actual breakdown occurred.

The transfer from fiction to reality occurs in the classroom every day. The following paper was written by an 11-year-old girl who was sent to the principal's office because of sullen behavior and passive refusal to complete assigned schoolwork. The principal, a warm, supportive woman, had been helpful to her on several occasions. After spending half an hour encouraging her to talk, the principal suggested that the girl might find it easier to express her troubles in writing. She responded slowly and quietly wrote the following statements.

May 18/1964

1. I don't like to be around many people.
2. I dislike some of people in my class.
3. I don't like boy.
4. I don't dream about boys.
~~8.~~
5. I'm always doing the wrong things.
6. I wish people didn't ask about my family.
7. I always have to tell where I'm going when I go out to play.
8. I don't like to talk about me.
~~9.~~
~~10.~~
8. People always calling me names.
10. I don't like the people on the street I live on.
11. I'm always getting in fight.
12. And I would want any wishes.
13. People always comparing me with my sister.
14. I don't cry at night.
15. I sometimes have nightmare.
16.

Notice the crossed-out sentences and the feelings of personal worthlessness that are expressed. How does it feel to be emotionally disturbed, whether temporarily or severely? How does it feel to be unhappy? It hurts!

**Some Reasons Why It Feels the
Way It Does (Poverty; Slums;
and Racial, Ethnic, Class,
and Economic Differences)**

E. R. Braithwaite is an Oxford-trained black engineer, who, unable to find a job that made use of his professional training and experience, took a teaching job at an experimental day school in the poorest white slums of London. The school, run by an inspired educator, takes on the obstreperous rejects from other schools. The entire book would be valuable reading for anyone working with disturbed or deprived children. The excerpt included here invites comparison with the selections from Malcolm X and Piri Thomas which follow.

To Sir, with Love
E. R. Braithwaite

Just about this time a new supply teacher, Mr. Bell, was sent to our school as supernumerary to the Staff for a few weeks. He was about forty years old, a tall, wiry man, who had had some previous experience with the Army Education Service. It was arranged that he should act as relief teacher for some lessons, including two periods of P.T. with the senior boys. One of Mr. Bell's hobbies was fencing: he was something of a perfectionist and impatient of anyone whose co-ordination was not as smooth and controlled as his own. He would repeat a P.T. movement or exercise over and over again until it was executed with clockwork precision, and though the boys grumbled against his discipline they seemed eager to prove to him that they were quite capable of doing any exercise he could devise, and with a skill that very nearly matched his own.

This was especially true in the cases of Ingham, Fernman and Seales, who would always place themselves at the head of the line as an example and encouragement to the others. The least athletic of these was Richard Buckley, a short, fat boy, amiable and rather dim, who could read and write after a fashion, and could never be provoked to any semblance of anger or heat. He was pleasant and jolly and a favorite with the others, who, though they themselves chivvied him unmercifully, were ever ready in his defense against outsiders.

Buckley was no good at P.T. or games; he just was not built for such pursuits. Yet, such is the perversity of human nature, he strenuously resisted any efforts to leave him out or overlook him when games were being arranged. His attempts at accomplishing such simple gymnastic performances as the "forward roll" and "star jump" reduced the rest of the P.T. class to helpless hilarity, but he persisted with a singleness of purpose which, though unproductive, was nothing short of heroic.

Buckley was Bell's special whipping boy. Fully aware of the lad's physical limitations, he would encourage him to try other and more difficult exercises, with apparently the sole purpose of obtaining some amusement from the pitiably ridiculous results. Sometimes the rest of the class would protest; and then Bell would turn on them the full flood of his invective. The boys mentioned this in their "Weekly Review," and Mr. Florian decided to discuss it at a Staff Meeting.

"The boys seem to be a bit bothered by remarks you make to them during P.T., Mr. Bell."

"To which remarks do you refer, Mr. Florian?" Bell never used the term "Sir," seeming to think it "infra dig." Even when he granted him the "Mr. Florian," he gave to this form of address the suggestion of a sneer.

"From their review it would seem that you are unnecessarily critical of their persons."

"Do you mean their smell?"

"Well, yes, that and the state of their clothing."

"I've advised them to wash."

"These are the words which appear in one review." The Headmaster produced a notebook, Fernman's, and read:

"'Some of you stink like old garbage.'"

His tone was cool, detached, judicial.

From the book *To Sir, with Love* by E. R. Braithwaite. © 1959 by E. R. Braithwaite, published by Prentice-Hall, Inc., Englewood Cliffs, New Jersey, and David Higham Associates, Ltd. Used by permission.

"I was referring to their feet. Many of them never seem to wash their feet, and when they take their shoes off the stink is dreadful."

"Many of them live in homes where there are very few facilities for washing, Mr. Bell."

"Surely enough water is available for washing their feet if they really wanted to."

"Then they'd put on the same smelly socks and shoes to which you also object."

"I've got to be in contact with them and it isn't very pleasant."

"Have you ever lived in this area, Mr. Bell?"

"No fear."

"Then you know nothing about the conditions prevailing. The water you so casually speak of is more often to be found in the walls and on the floors than in the convenient wash basin or bath to which you are accustomed. I've visited homes of some of these children where water for a family in an upstairs flat had to be fetched by bucket or pail from the single back-yard tap which served five or six families. You may see, therefore, that so elementary a function as washing the feet might present many difficulties."

Bell was silent at this.

"I've no wish to interfere, or tell you how to do your work; you're an experienced teacher and know more about P.T. than I ever will,"—the Old Man was again patient, encouraging—"but try to be a little more understanding about their difficulties." He then turned to other matters, but it was clear that Bell was considerably put out by the rebuke.

Matters came to a head that Monday afternoon. I was not present in the gym, but was able to reconstruct the sequence of events with reasonable accuracy from the boys' reports and Bell's subsequent admissions.

During the P.T. session he had been putting them through their paces in the "astride vault" over the buck, all except Buckley, who was somewhat under the weather and wisely stood down from attempting the rather difficult jump, but without reference to or permission from Bell, who was not long in discovering the absence of his favorite diversion.

"Buckley," he roared.

"Yes, Sir."

"Come on, boy, I'm waiting." He was standing in his usual position beside the buck in readiness to arrest the fall of any lad who might be thrown off balance by an awkward approach or incorrect execution of the movement. But the boy did not move, and the master stared at him amazed and angry at this unexpected show of defiance by the one generally considered to be the most timid and tractable in the whole class.

"Fatty can't do it, Sir, it's too high for him," Denham interposed.

"Shut up, Denham," Bell roared. "If I want your opinion I will ask for it." He left his station by the buck and walked to where Buckley was standing. The boy watched his threatening approach, fear apparent in his eyes.

"Well, Buckley," Bell towered over the unhappy youth, "are you going to do as you're told?"

"Yes, Sir," Buckley's capitulation was as sudden as his refusal.

The others stopped to watch as he stood looking at the buck, licking his lips nervously while waiting for the instructor to resume his position. It may have been fear or determination or a combination of both, but Buckley launched himself at the buck in furious assault, and in spite of Bell's restraining arms, boy and buck crashed on the floor with a sickening sound as one leg of the buck snapped off with the sound of a pistol shot. The class stood in shocked silence watching Buckley, who remained as he fell, inert and pale; then they rushed to his assistance. All except Potter; big, good-natured Potter seemed to have lost his reason. He snatched up the broken metal-bound leg and advanced on Bell, screaming:

"You bloody bastard, you fucking bloody bastard."

"Put that thing down, Potter, don't be a fool," Bell spluttered, backing away from the hysterical boy.

"You made him do it; he didn't want to and you made him," Potter yelled.

"Don't be a fool, Potter, put it down," Bell appealed.

"I'll do you in, you bloody murderer." Bell was big, but in his anger Potter seemed bigger, his improvised club a fearsome extension of his thick forearm.

That was where I rushed in. Tich Jackson, frightened by the sight of Buckley, limp and white on the floor, and the enraged Potter, slobbering at the instructor in murderous fury, had dashed upstairs to my classroom shouting: "Sir, quick, they're fighting in the gym." I followed his disappearing figure in time to see Bell backed against a wall, with Potter advancing on him.

"Hold it, Potter," I called. He turned at the sound of my voice and I quickly placed myself between them. "Let's have that, Potter." I held out my hand towards the boy, but he stared past me at Bell, whimpering in his emotion. Anger had completely taken hold of him, and he looked very dangerous.

"Come on, Potter," I repeated, "hand it over and go lend a hand with Buckley."

He turned to look towards his prostrate friend and I quickly moved up to him and seized the improvised club; he released it to me without any resistance and went back to join the group around Buckley. Bell then walked away and out of the room, and I went up to the boys. Denham rose and faced me, his face white with rage.

"Potts should have done the bastard like he did Fatty, just 'cos he wouldn't do the bloody jump."

I let that pass; they were angry and at such times quickly reverted to the old things, the words, the discourtesies. I stooped down beside Buckley, who was now sitting weakly on the floor, supported by Sapiano and Seales, and smiling up at them as if ashamed of himself for having been the cause of so much fuss.

"How do you feel, old man?" I inquired.

"Cor, Sir," he cried, smiling, "me tum does hurt."

"He fell on the buck. You should have seen 'im, Sir."

"Gosh, you should've heard the noise when the leg smashed."

"Mr. Bell couldn't catch Fatty, Sir, you should've seen him."

Most of them were trying to talk all at once, eager to give me all the details.

"Bleeding bully, always picking on Fats." This from Sapiano, whose volatile Maltese temperament was inclined to flare up very easily.

"If I'd had the wood I'd have done the fucker in and no bleeding body would have stopped me." Denham was aching for trouble and didn't care who knew it. Bell had slipped away unharmed after hurting his friend, and Denham wanted a substitute. But I would not look at him, or even hear the things he said. Besides, I liked Denham; in spite of his rough manner and speech he was an honest, dependable person with a strong sense of independence.

"Can you stand up, Buckley?"

With some assistance from Seales and Sapiano the boy got to his feet; he looked very pale and unsteady. I turned to Denham: "Will you help the others take Buckley up to Mrs. Dale-Evans and ask her to give him some sweet tea; leave him there and I'll meet you all in the classroom in a few minutes."

Without waiting for his reply I hurried off to the staffroom in search of Bell.

I was in something of a quandry. I knew that it was quite possible Buckley was all right, but there was no knowing whether he had sustained any internal injury not yet apparent. The Council's rules required that all accidents be reported and logged; the Headmaster should be informed forthwith, and in the light of what he had said to Bell so very recently, there would most certainly be a row.

I went up to the staffroom and found Bell washing his face at the sink.

"I've sent Buckley upstairs for a cup of tea," I said. "I suppose he'll be all right, anyway he was walking under his own steam."

"What happens now?" His voice was querulous.

"You should know as well as I do," I replied. "Shouldn't you see the Old Man and make some kind of report?"

"Yes, I suppose I'd better get over to his office right away. I should have attended to the Buckley boy, but the other one rushed me. Thanks for helping out."

"Oh, that's all right," I replied. "But why did you insist on the boy doing the vault?"

"I had to, don't you see; he just stood there refusing to obey and the others were watching me; I just had to do something." His whole attitude now was defensive.

"I'm not criticizing you, Mr. Bell, just asking. Buckley's a bit of a mascot with the others, you know, and I suppose that is why Potter got out of hand."

"I guess it was the way he jumped or something, but I couldn't grab him. He hit the buck too low and sent it flying."

"He's a bit awkward, isn't he; anyway I'm sure the Old Man will understand how it happened."

"He might be a bit difficult, especially after what he said the other day."

"Not necessarily. After all, it was an accident and thank Heaven it's not very serious."

He dried his hands and moved towards the door. "I suppose they'll really go to town on this in their weekly reviews," he remarked.

"I'll ask the boys to say nothing about it. I don't suppose Potter is now feeling any too pleased with himself at his conduct."

As he left Clinty came into the staffroom.

"What's happening, Rick?" she asked. "I just saw some of your boys taking Fatty Buckley upstairs. What's happened to him?"

I told her about the incident and added: "Bell has just gone to the Old Man's office to report the matter."

"Well, what do you know?" she chuckled. "Fancy Potter going for Bell like that. I always thought that boy a bit of a softie, but you never know with those quiet ones, do you?"

"He was not the only one. Sapiano and Denham were just as wild, I think, but they were too busy fussing over Buckley to bother with Bell."

"He is a bit of a tyro, isn't he. This might make him take it a bit easier."

"I don't think the boys mind his being strict during P.T. It's just that Buckley's a bit of a fool and they resented his being hurt. If it had been Denham or someone like that, I'm sure they would have done nothing."

"Yes, I guess you're right. Bell is a good teacher. I wonder how long the Divisional Office will let him stay here. I hope he hasn't had too much of a fright."

"Oh, he'll get over that. Now I must go and have a word with my boys."

I left her. For some inexplicable reason I felt nervous about being alone with Clinty; I felt that there was something she wanted to say to me, and for my part I did not want to hear it.

In the classroom the boys were sitting closely grouped together, looking rather sheepish. I knew they were feeling aggrieved and, according to their lights, justifiably so; but nevertheless the matter of Potter's behavior had to be dealt with.

"How's Buckley?" I asked.

"We left him upstairs with Mrs. Dale-Evans, Sir. He didn't want to stay, he kept saying he was all right. But she told him if he wasn't quiet she'd give him some castor oil, Sir. Ugh!" They all managed a smile at Seales' remark.

"Good," I replied, "I expect he'll be quite all right. But there is something I want to say to you about this unfortunate incident." I sat down on the edge of Fernman's desk.

"Potter, there is nothing I can think of which can excuse your shocking conduct in the gym."

Potter's mouth fell open; he looked at me in surprise, gulped a few times and stammered:

"But it was him, Sir, Mr. Bell, making Fatty fall and that." His voice was shrill with outrage at my remark.

"Mr. Bell was the master there, Potter, and anything that happened in the gym was his responsibility. Buckley's mishap was no excuse for you to make such an attack on your teacher."

"But Fatty told him he couldn't do it, Sir, and he made him, he made him, Sir."

Potter was very near tears. His distress was greater because of what he believed was the further injustice of my censure. The others, too, were looking at me with the same expression.

"That may be, Potter. I am not now concerned with Mr. Bell's conduct, but with yours. You came very near to getting yourself into very serious trouble because you were unable to control your temper. Not only was your language foul and disgusting, but you armed yourself with a weapon big enough and heavy enough to cause very serious harm. What do you think would have happened if everyone had behaved like you and had all turned on Mr. Bell like a pack of mad wolves?" I waited for this to sink in a bit, but Potter interjected:

"I thought he had done Fatty in, Sir, he looked all huddled up like, Sir."

"I see. So you didn't wait to find out but rushed in with your club like a hoodlum to smash and kill, is that it? Your friend was hurt and you wanted to hurt back; suppose instead of a piece of wood it had been a knife, or a gun, what then?" Potter was pale, and he was not the only one.

"Potts didn't think. He was narked, we was all narked, seeing Fatty on the deck. I wasn't half bleeding wild myself."

"You're missing the point, Denham. I think you're all missing the point. We sit in this classroom day after day and talk of things, and you all know what's expected of you; but at the first sign of bother you forget it all. In two weeks you'll all be at work and lots of things will happen which will annoy you, make you wild. Are you going to resort to clubs and knives every time you're upset or angered?" I stood up. "You'll meet foremen or supervisors or workmates who'll do things to upset you, sometimes deliberately. What then, Denham? What about that, Potter? Your Headmaster is under fire from many quarters because he believes in you—because he really believes that by the time you leave here you will leave learned to exercise a little self-control at the times when it is most needed. His success or failure will be reflected in the way you conduct yourselves after you leave him. If today's effort is an example of your future behavior I hold out very little hope for you."

At this moment Buckley walked in, smiling broadly and seemingly none the worse for wear. I waited until he was seated then went on:

"I've no wish to belabor this matter, but it cannot be left like this. Potter, you were very discourteous to your P.T. instructor, and it is my opinion that you owe him an apology." Potter stared at me, his mouth open in amazement at my remark;

but before he could speak Denham leapt to his feet.

"Apologize?" His voice was loud in anger. "Why should Potts apologize? He didn't do him any harm. Why should he apologize to him just because he's a bleeding teacher?" He stood there, legs slightly apart, heavy-shouldered and truculent, glaring at me. The others were watching us, but agreeing with him; I could feel their resentment hardening.

"Please sit down Denham, and remember that in this class we are always able to discuss things, no matter how difficult or unpleasant, without shouting at each other."

I waited, fearful of this unexpected threat to our pleasant relationship; he looked around at his colleagues indecisively, then abruptly sat down. I continued, in a very friendly tone:

"That was a fair question, Denham, although you will agree it was put a little, shall we say, indelicately?"

I smiled as I said this, and, in spite of his anger, Denham smiled briefly too. I went on:

"Potter, are you quite pleased and satisfied with the way you behaved to your P.T. teacher?"

Potter looked at me for a moment, then murmured, "No, Sir."

"But he couldn't help it," Denham interjected.

"That may be so, Denham, but Potter agrees that his own actions were unsatisfactory; upon reflection he himself is not pleased with what he did."

"How's about Mr. Bell then: How's about him apologizing to Buckley?" Denham was not to be dissuaded from his attitude.

"Yes, how about him?" echoed Sapiano.

"My business is with you, not with Mr. Bell," I replied.

This was not going to be easy, I thought. Denham was getting a bit nasty; the usual "Sir" had disappeared from his remarks, and Sapiano was following suit.

"It's easy for you to talk, Sir, nobody tries to push you around." Seales' voice was clear and calm, and the others turned to look at him, to support him. His question touched something deep inside of me, something which had been dormant for months, but now awoke to quick, painful remembering. Without realizing what I was doing I got up and walked to where he sat and stood beside his desk.

"I've been pushed around, Seales," I said quietly, "in a way I cannot explain to you. I've been pushed around until I began to hate people so much

that I wanted to hurt them, really hurt them. I know how it feels, believe me, and one thing I learned, Seales, is to try always to be a bit bigger than the people who hurt me. It is easy to reach for a knife or a gun; but then you become merely a tool and the knife or gun takes over, thereby creating new and bigger problems without solving a thing. So what happens when there is no weapon handy?"

I felt suddenly annoyed with myself for giving way to my emotion, and abruptly walked back to my desk. The class seemed to feel that something had touched me deeply and were immediately sympathetic in their manner.

"The point I want to make, Potter," I continued, "is whether you are really growing up and learning to stand squarely on your own feet. When you begin work at Covent Garden you might some day have cause to be very angry; what will you do then? The whole idea of this school is to teach you to discipline yourself. In this instance you lost your temper and behaved badly to your teacher. Do you think you are big enough to make an apology to him?"

Potter fidgeted in his seat and looked uncertainly at me, then replied: "Yes, Sir."

"It's always difficult to apologize, Potter, especially to someone you feel justified in disliking. But remember that you are not doing it for Mr. Bell's sake, but your own."

I sat down. They were silent, but I realized that they understood what I meant. Potter stood up:

"Is he in the staffroom, Sir?"

"I think he should be there now, Potter."

Denham and Seales stood and joined Potter and together they went to find Bell. I called Buckley.

"How are you feeling, Buckley?"

"Okay, Sir," he replied, as jovial as ever.

"What will your parents say about all this, Buckley?" I was being devious but, I thought, necessarily so.

"I shan't tell 'em, Sir. Must I, Sir?"

"It's up to you, Buckley. If you feel fine there's no need to bother; but if in the next few days or weeks you feel any pain, it would be best to mention it so that they'd know what to do."

In a few minutes the boys were back, Potter looking red and embarrassed; behind them came Mr. Bell.

"May I speak to your boys for a moment, Mr. Braithwaite?" He came in and stood beside my desk and I nodded to him.

"I want to say to all of you," he began, "that I'm sorry about what happened in the gym a little while ago. I think that one way or another we were all a bit silly, but the sooner we forget the whole thing, the better.

"How're you feeling now, boy?" He addressed himself to Buckley.

"Okay, Sir," the boy replied.

"Fine. Well, I suppose we'll see each other as usual next week." And with that he was gone, having made as friendly a gesture as his evident nervousness would allow.

The boys seemed not unwilling to let the matter drop, so we turned our attention to the discussion of other things.

Diagnosis

Impulse breakthrough—acting-out children—the syndrome of the socially and economically deprived child.

In this case the behavior of Potter was clearly provoked. However, the reason for losing control, as Potter did, is frequently neither so visible nor so apparently justified to the outsider. In very disturbed cases the provocation may come from inner fantasies, such as distorted images of the people around the child, which evoke tortured memories or half-memories. It may come from a tone of voice, a seemingly harmless phrase, a frustration that makes the child feel foolish, helpless, inept. Here, Potter's anger was aroused by injustice; and children, even disturbed ones, are happily committed to justice—even though their definitions may not coincide with society's. The crucial factor in Potter's case was not his anger but the way he handled it. Rage is an overwhelming experience. Inability to handle it in an acceptable fashion leads to tragedy.

Braithwaite is careful to make this point to the boys themselves as he details the precarious life ahead for one who is at the mercy of rage instead of its master. His handling of the problem in the group of children, where all could hear and express themselves, displays the kind of skill that comes from human understanding.

This selection also highlights the contagion of rage among children. It indicates, too, that the teacher's revelation of his own deep personal feeling communicated real, emotional understanding far more powerfully than intellectual reasoning. This, more than the proper words, got across to the boys. Children, even badly disturbed ones, respond to genuineness. In many cases the more troubled the child, the more therapeutic can a teacher's genuine feelings be, provided they are not overexploited or used to gain sympathy for the teacher.

Doctor Jack-O'-Lantern
Richard Yates

All Miss Price had been told about the new boy was that he'd spent most of his life in some kind of orphanage, and that the gray-haired "aunt and uncle" with whom he now lived were really foster parents, paid by the Welfare Department of the City of New York. A less dedicated or less imaginative teacher might have pressed for more details, but Miss Price was content with the rough outline. It was enough, in fact, to fill her with a sense of mission that shone from her eyes, as plain as love, from the first morning he joined the fourth grade.

He arrived early and sat in the back row—his spine very straight, his ankles crossed precisely under the desk and his hands folded on the very center of its top, as if symmetry might make him less conspicuous—and while the other children were filing in and settling down, he received a long, expressionless stare from each of them.

"We have a new classmate this morning," Miss Price said, laboring the obvious in a way that made everybody want to giggle. "His name is Vincent Sabella and he comes from New York City. I know we'll all do our best to make him feel at home."

This time they all swung around to stare at once, which caused him to duck his head slightly and shift his weight from one buttock to the other. Ordinarily, the fact of someone's coming from New York might have held a certain prestige, for to most of the children the city was an awesome, adult place that swallowed up their fathers every day, and which they themselves were permitted to visit only rarely, in their best clothes, as a treat. But anyone could see at a glance that Vincent Sabella had nothing whatever to do with skyscrapers. Even if you could ignore his tangled black hair and gray skin,

From *Eleven Kinds of Loneliness* by Richard Yates. Reprinted by permission of Monica McCall—International Famous Agency. Copyright © 1961 by Richard Yates.

his clothes would have given him away: absurdly new corduroys, absurdly old sneakers and a yellow sweatshirt, much too small, with the shredded remains of a Mickey Mouse design stamped on its chest. Clearly, he was from the part of New York that you had to pass through on the train to Grand Central—the part where people hung bedding over their windowsills and leaned out on it all day in a trance of boredom, and where you got vistas of straight, deep streets, one after another, all alike in the clutter of their sidewalks and all swarming with gray boys at play in some desperate kind of ball game.

The girls decided that he wasn't very nice and turned away, but the boys lingered in their scrutiny, looking him up and down with faint smiles. This was the kind of kid they were accustomed to thinking of as "tough," the kind whose stares had made all of them uncomfortable at one time or another in unfamiliar neighborhoods; here was a unique chance for retaliation.

"What would you like us to call you, Vincent?" Miss Price inquired. "I mean, do you prefer Vincent, or Vince, or—or what?" (It was purely an academic question; even Miss Price knew that the boys would call him "Sabella" and that the girls wouldn't call him anything at all.)

"Vinny's okay," he said in a strange, croaking voice that had evidently yelled itself hoarse down the ugly streets of his home.

"I'm afraid I didn't hear you," she said, craning her pretty head forward and to one side so that a heavy lock of hair swung free of one shoulder. "Did you say 'Vince'?"

"Vinny, I said," he said again, squirming.

"Vincent, is it? All right then, Vincent." A few of the class giggled, but nobody bothered to correct her; it would be more fun to let the mistake continue.

"I won't take time to introduce you to everyone by name, Vincent," Miss Price went on, "Because I think it would be simpler just to let you learn the names as we go along, don't you? Now, we won't expect you to take any real part in the work for the first day or so; just take your time, and if there's anything you don't understand, why, don't be afraid to ask."

He made an unintelligible croak and smiled fleetingly, just enough to show that the roots of his teeth were green.

"Now then," Miss Price said, getting down to business. "This is Monday morning, and so the first thing on the program is reports. Who'd like to start off?"

Vincent Sabella was momentarily forgotten as six or seven hands went up, and Miss Price drew back in mock confusion. "Goodness, we do have a lot of reports this morning," she said. The idea of the reports—a fifteen-minute period every Monday in which the children were encouraged to relate their experiences over the weekend—was Miss Price's own, and she took a pardonable pride in it. The principal had commended her on it at a recent staff meeting, pointing out that it made a splendid bridge between the worlds of school and home, and that it was a fine way for children to learn poise and assurance. It called for intelligent supervision—the shy children had to be drawn out and the show-offs curbed—but in general, as Miss Price had assured the principal, it was fun for everyone. She particularly hoped it would be fun today, to help put Vincent Sabella at ease, and that was why she chose Nancy Parker to start off; there was nobody like Nancy for holding an audience.

The others fell silent as Nancy moved gracefully to the head of the room; even the two or three girls who secretly despised her had to feign enthrallment when she spoke (she was that popular), and every boy in the class, who at recess liked nothing better than to push her shrieking into the mud, was unable to watch her without an idiotically tremulous smile.

"Well—" she began, and then she clapped a hand over her mouth while everyone laughed.

"Oh, *Nancy*," Miss Price said. "You *know* the rule about starting a report with 'well.'"

Nancy knew the rule; she had only broken it to get the laugh. Now she let her fit of giggles subside, ran her fragile forefingers down the side seams of her skirt, and began again in the proper way. "On Friday my whole family went for a ride in my brother's new car. My brother bought this new Pontiac last week, and he wanted to take us all for a ride—you know, to try it out and everything? So we went into White Plains and had dinner in a restaurant there, and then we all wanted to go see this movie, 'Doctor Jekyll and Mr. Hyde,' but my brother said it was too horrible and everything, and I wasn't old enough to enjoy it—oh, he made me so mad! And then, let's see. On Saturday I stayed home all day and helped my mother make my sister's wedding dress. My sister's engaged to be married you see, and my mother's making this wedding dress for her? So we did that, and then on Sunday this friend of my brother's came over for dinner, and then they both had to get back to college that night, and I was allowed to stay up late and say goodbye to them and everything, and I guess that's all." She always had a sure instinct for keeping her performance brief—or rather, for making it seem briefer than it really was.

"Very good, Nancy," Miss Price said. "Now, who's next?"

Warren Berg was next, elaborately hitching up his pants as he made his way down the aisle. "On Saturday I went over to Bill Stringer's house for lunch," he began in his direct, man-to-man style, and Bill Stringer wriggled bashfully in the front row. Warren Berg and Bill Stringer were great friends, and their reports often overlapped. "And then after lunch we went into White Plains, on our bikes. Only we *saw* 'Doctor Jekyll and Mr. Hyde.' " Here he nodded his head in Nancy's direction, and Nancy got another laugh by making a little whimper of envy. "It was real good, too," he went on, with mounting exictement. "It's all about this guy who—"

"About *a man who*," Miss Price corrected.

"About a man who mixes up this chemical, like, that he drinks? And whenever he drinks this chemical, he changes into this real monster, like? You see him drink this chemical, and then you see his hands start to get all scales all over them, like a reptile and everything, and then you see his face start to change into this real horrible-looking face—with fangs and all? Sticking out of his mouth?"

All the girls shuddered in pleasure. "Well," Miss Price said, "I think Nancy's brother was probably wise in not wanting her to see it. What did you do *after* the movie, Warren?"

There was a general "*Aw-w-w!*" of disappointment—everyone wanted to hear more about the scales and fangs—but Miss Price never liked to let the reports degenerate into accounts of movies. Warren continued without much enthusiasm: all they had done after the movie was fool around Bill Stringer's yard until suppertime. "And then on Sunday," he said, brightening again, "Bill Stringer came over to *my* house, and my dad helped us rig up this old tire on this long rope? From a tree? There's this steep hill down behind my house, you see—this ravine, like?—and we hung this tire so that what you do is, you take the tire and run a little ways and then lift your feet, and you go swinging way, way out over the ravine and back again."

"That sounds like fun," Miss Price said, glancing at her watch.

"Oh, it's *fun* all right," Warren conceded. But then he hitched up his pants again and added, with a puckering of his forehead, " 'Course, it's pretty

dangerous. You let go of that tire or anything, you'd get a bad fall. Hit a rock or anything, you'd probably break your leg, or your spine. But my dad said he trusted us both to look out for our own safety."

"Well, I'm afraid that's all we'll have time for, Warren," Miss Price said. "Now, there's just time for one more report. Who's ready? Arthur Cross?"

There was a soft groan, because Arthur Cross was the biggest dope in class and his reports were always a bore. This time it turned out to be something tedious about going to visit his uncle on Long Island. At one point he made a slip—he said "botormoat" instead of "motorboat"—and everyone laughed with the particular edge of scorn they reserved for Arthur Cross. But the laughter died abruptly when it was joined by a harsh, dry croaking from the back of the room. Vincent Sabella was laughing too, green teeth and all, and they all had to glare at him until he stopped.

When the reports were over, everyone settled down for school. It was recess time before any of the children thought much about Vincent Sabella again, and then they thought of him only to make sure he was left out of everything. He wasn't in the group of boys that clustered around the horizontal bar to take turns at skinning-the-cat, or the group that whispered in a far corner of the playground, hatching a plot to push Nancy Parker in the mud. Nor was he in the larger group, of which even Arthur Cross was a member, that chased itself in circles in a frantic variation of the game of tag. He couldn't join the girls, of course, or the boys from other classes, and so he joined nobody. He stayed on the apron of the playground, close to school, and for the first part of the recess he pretended to be very busy with the laces of his sneakers. He would squat to undo and retie them, straighten up and take a few experimental steps in a springy, athletic way, and then get down and go to work on them again. After five minutes of this he gave it up, picked up a handful of pebbles and began shying them at an invisible target several yards away. That was good for another five minutes, but then there was still five minutes left, and he could think of nothing to do but stand there, first with his hands in his pockets, then with his hands on his hips, and then with his arms folded in a manly way across his chest.

Miss Price stood watching all this from the doorway, and she spent the full recess wondering if she ought to go out and do something about it. She guessed it would be better not to.

She managed to control the same impulse at recess the next day, and every other day that week, though every day it grew more difficult. But one thing she could not control was a tendency to let her anxiety show in class. All Vincent Sabella's errors in schoolwork were publicly excused, even those having nothing to do with his newness, and all his accomplishments were singled out for special mention. Her campaign to build him up was painfully obvious, and never more so than when she tried to make it subtle; once, for instance, in explaining an arithmetic problem, she said, "Now, suppose Warren Berg and Vincent Sabella went to the store with fifteen cents each, and candy bars cost ten cents. How many candy bars would each boy have?" By the end of the week he was well on the way to becoming the worst possible kind of teacher's pet, a victim of the teacher's pity.

On Friday she decided the best thing to do would be to speak to him privately, and try to draw him out. She could say something about the pictures he had painted in art class—that would do for an opening—and she decided to do it at lunchtime.

The only trouble was that lunchtime, next to recess, was the most trying part of Vincent Sabella's day. Instead of going home for an hour as the other children did, he brought his lunch to school in a wrinkled paper bag and ate it in the classroom, which always made for a certain amount of awkwardness. The last children to leave would see him still seated apologetically at his desk, holding his paper bag, and anyone who happened to straggle back later for a forgotten hat or sweater would surprise him in the middle of his meal —perhaps shielding a hard-boiled egg from view or wiping mayonnaise from his mouth with a furtive hand. It was a situation that Miss Price did not improve by walking up to him while the room was still half full of children and sitting prettily on the edge of the desk beside his, making it clear that she was cutting her own lunch hour short in order to be with him.

"Vincent," she began, "I've been meaning to tell you how much I enjoyed those pictures of yours. They're really very good."

He mumbled something and shifted his eyes to the cluster of departing children at the door. She went right on talking and smiling, elaborating on her praise of the pictures; and finally, after the door had closed behind the last child, he was able to give her his attention. He did so tentatively at first; but the more she talked, the more he seemed to relax, until she realized she was putting him at ease. It was as simple and as gratifying as stroking a cat. She

had finished with the pictures now and moved on, triumphantly, to broader fields of praise. "It's never easy," she was saying, "to come to a new school and adjust yourself to the—well, the new work, and new working methods, and I think you've done a splendid job so far. I really do. But tell me, do you think you're going to like it here?"

He looked at the floor just long enough to make his reply—"It's awright"—and then his eyes stared into hers again.

"I'm so glad. Please don't let me interfere with your lunch, Vincent. Do go ahead and eat, that is, if you don't mind my sitting here with you." But it was now abundantly clear that he didn't mind at all, and he began to unwrap a bologna sandwich with what she felt sure was the best appetite he'd had all week. It wouldn't even have mattered very much now if someone from the class had come in and watched, though it was probably just as well that no one did.

Miss Price sat back more comfortably on the desk top, crossed her legs and allowed one slim stockinged foot to slip part of the way out of its moccasin. "Of course," she went on, "it always does take a little time to sort of get your bearings in a new school. For one thing, well, it's never too easy for the new member of the class to make friends with the other members. What I mean is, you mustn't mind if the others seem a little rude to you at first. Actually, they're just as anxious to make friends as you are, but they're shy. All it takes is a little time, and a little effort on your part as well as theirs. Not too much, of course, but a little. Now for instance, these reports we have Monday mornings—they're a fine way for people to get to know one another. A person never feels he has to make a report; it's just a thing he can do if he wants to. And that's only one way of helping others to know the kind of person you are; there are lots and lots of ways. The main thing to remember is that making friends is the most natural thing in the world, and it's only a question of time until you have all the friends you want. And in the meantime, Vincent, I hope you'll consider *me* your friend, and feel free to call on me for whatever advice or anything you might need. Will you do· that?"

He nodded, swallowing.

"Good." She stood up and smoothed her skirt over her long thighs. "Now I must go or I'll be late for *my* lunch. But I'm glad we had this little talk, Vincent, and I hope we'll have others."

It was probably a lucky thing that she stood up when she did, for if she'd stayed on that desk a minute longer Vincent Sabella would have thrown his arms around her and buried his face in the warm gray flannel of her lap, and that might have been enough to confuse the most dedicated and imaginative of teachers.

At report time on Monday morning, nobody was more surprised than Miss Price when Vincent Sabella's smudged hand was among the first and most eager to rise. Apprehensively she considered letting someone else start off, but then, for fear of hurting his feelings, she said, "All right, Vincent," in as matter-of-fact a way as she could manage.

There was a suggestion of muffled titters from the class as he walked confidently to the head of the room and turned to face his audience. He looked, if anything, too confident: there were signs, in the way he held his shoulders and the way his eyes shone, of the terrible poise of panic.

"Saturday I seen that pitcha," he announced.

"Saw, Vincent," Miss Price corrected gently.

"That's what I mean," he said; "I sore that pitcha. 'Doctor Jack-o'-lantern and Mr. Hide.' "

There was a burst of wild, delighted laughter and a chorus of correction: "Doctor *Jekyll!*"

He was unable to speak over the noise. Miss Price was on her feet, furious. "It's a *perfectly natural mistake!*" she was saying. "There's no reason for any of you to be so rude. Go on, Vincent, and please excuse this very silly interruption." The laughter subsided, but the class continued to shake their heads derisively from side to side. It hadn't, of course, been a perfectly natural mistake at all; for one thing it proved that he was a hopeless dope, and for another it proved that he was lying.

"That's what I mean," he continued. " 'Doctor Jackal and Mr. Hide.' I got it a little mixed up. Anyways, I seen all about where his teet' start comin' outa his mout' and all like that, and I thought it was very good. And then on Sunday my mudda and fodda come out to see me in this car they got. This Buick. My fodda siz, 'Vinny, wanna go for a little ride?' I siz, 'Sure, where yiz goin'?' He siz, 'Anyplace ya like.' So I siz, 'Let's go out in the country a ways, get on one of them big roads and make some time.' So we go out—oh, I guess fifty, sixty miles—and we're cruisin' along this highway, when this cop starts tailin' us? My fodda siz, 'Don't worry, we'll shake him,' and he steps on it, see? My mudda's gettin' pretty scared, but my fodda siz, 'Don't worry, dear.' He's tryin' to make this turn, see, so he can get off the highway and shake the cop? But just when he's makin' the turn, the cop opens up and starts shootin', see?"

By this time the few members of the class who could bear to look at him at all were doing so with heads on one side and mouths partly open, the way you look at a broken arm or a circus freak.

"We just barely made it," Vincent went on, his eyes gleaming, "and this one bullet got my fodda in the shoulder. Didn't hurt him bad—just grazed him, like—so my mudda bandaged it up for him and all, but he couldn't do no more drivin' after that, and we had to get him to a doctor, see? So my fodda siz, 'Vinny, think you can drive a ways?' I siz, 'Sure, if you show me how.' So he showed me how to work the gas and the brake, and all like that, and I drove to the doctor. My mudda siz, 'I'm prouda you, Vinny, drivin' all by yourself.' So anyways, we got to the doctor, got my fodda fixed up and all, and then he drove us back home." He was breathless. After an uncertain pause he said, "And that's all." Then he walked quickly back to his desk, his stiff new corduroy pants whistling faintly with each step.

"Well, that was very—entertaining, Vincent," Miss Price said, trying to act as if nothing had happened. "Now, who's next?" But nobody raised a hand.

Recess was worse than usual for him that day; at least it was until he found a place to hide—a narrow concrete alley, blind except for several closed fire-exit doors, that cut between two sections of the school building. It was reassuringly dismal and cool in there—he could stand with his back to the wall and his eyes guarding the entrance, and the noises of recess were as remote as the sunshine. But when the bell rang he had to go back to class, and in another hour it was lunchtime.

Miss Price left him alone until her own meal was finished. Then, after standing with one hand on the doorknob for a full minute to gather courage, she went in and sat beside him for another little talk, just as he was trying to swallow the last of a pimento-cheese sandwich.

"Vincent," she began, "we all enjoyed your report this morning, but I think we would have enjoyed it more—a great deal more—if you'd told us something about your real life instead. I mean," she hurried on, "For instance, I noticed you were wearing a nice new windbreaker this morning. It *is* new, isn't it? And did your aunt buy it for you over the weekend?"

He did not deny it.

"Well then, why couldn't you have told us about going to the store with your aunt, and buying the windbreaker, and whatever you did afterwards. That would have made a perfectly good report." She paused, and for the first time looked steadily into his eyes. "You do understand what I'm trying to say, don't you, Vincent?"

He wiped crumbs of bread from his lips, looked at the floor, and nodded.

"And you'll remember next time, won't you?"

He nodded again. "Please may I be excused, Miss Price?"

"Of course you may."

He went to the boys' lavatory and vomited. Afterwards he washed his face and drank a little water, and then he returned to the classroom. Miss Price was busy at her desk now, and didn't look up. To avoid getting involved with her again, he wandered out to the cloakroom and sat on one of the long benches, where he picked up someone's discarded overshoe and turned it over and over in his hands. In a little while he heard the chatter of returning children, and to avoid being discovered there, he got up and went to the fire-exit door. Pushing it open, he found that it gave onto the alley he had hidden in that morning, and he slipped outside. For a minute or two he just stood there, looking at the blankness of the concrete wall: then he found a piece of chalk in his pocket and wrote out all the dirty words he could think of, in block letters a foot high. He had put down four words and was trying to remember a fifth when he heard a shuffling at the door behind him. Arthur Cross was there, holding the door open and reading the words with wide eyes. "Boy," he said in an awed half-whisper. "Boy, you're gonna get it. You're really gonna *get* it."

Startled, and then suddenly calm, Vincent Sabella palmed his chalk, hooked his thumbs in his belt and turned on Arthur Cross with a menacing look. "Yeah?" he inquired. "Who's gonna squeal on me?"

"Well, nobody's gonna *squeal* on you," Arthur Cross said uneasily, "but you shouldn't go around writing—"

"Arright," Vincent said, advancing a step. His shoulders were slumped, his head thrust forward and his eyes narrowed, like Edward G. Robinson. "Arright. That's all I wanna know. I don't like squealers, unnastand?"

While he was saying this, Warren Berg and Bill Stringer appeared in the doorway—just in time to hear it and to see the words on the wall before Vincent turned on them. "And that goes fa you too, unnastand?" he said. "Both a yiz."

And the remarkable thing was that both their faces fell into the same foolish, defensive smile that Arthur Cross was wearing. It wasn't until they had glanced at each other that they were able to meet his eyes with the proper degree of contempt, and by

then it was too late. "Think you're pretty smart, don'tcha, Sabella?" Bill Stringer said.

"Never mind what I think," Vincent told him. "You heard what I said. Now let's get back inside."

And they could do nothing but move aside to make way for him, and follow him dumfounded into the cloakroom.

It was Nancy Parker who squealed—although, of course, with someone like Nancy Parker you didn't think of it as squealing. She had heard everything from the cloakroom; as soon as the boys came in she peeked into the alley, saw the words and, setting her face in a prim frown, went straight to Miss Price. Miss Price was just about to call the class to order for the afternoon when Nancy came up and whispered in her ear. They both disappeared into the cloakroom—from which, after a moment, came the sound of the fire-exit door being abruptly slammed—and when they returned to class Nancy was flushed with righteousness, Miss Price very pale. No announcement was made. Classes proceeded in the ordinary way all afternoon, though it was clear that Miss Price was upset, and it wasn't until she was dismissing the children at three o'clock that she brought the thing into the open. "Will Vincent Sabella please remain seated?" She nodded at the rest of the class. "That's all."

While the room was clearing out she sat at her desk, closed her eyes and massaged the frail bridge of her nose with thumb and forefinger, sorting out half-remembered fragments of a book she had once read on the subject of seriously disturbed children. Perhaps, after all, she should never have undertaken the responsibility of Vincent Sabella's loneliness. Perhaps the whole thing called for the attention of a specialist. She took a deep breath.

"Come over here and sit beside me, Vincent," she said, and when he had settled himself, she looked at him. "I want you to tell me the truth. Did you write those words on the wall outside?"

He stared at the floor.

"Look at me," she said, and he looked at her. She had never looked prettier: her cheeks slightly flushed, her eyes shining and her sweet mouth pressed into a self-conscious frown. "First of all," she said, handing him a small enameled basin streaked with poster paint, "I want you to take this to the boys' room and fill it with hot water and soap."

He did as he was told, and when he came back, carrying the basin carefully to keep the suds from spilling, she was sorting out some old rags in the bottom drawer of her desk. "Here," she said, selecting one and shutting the drawer in a businesslike way. "This will do. Soak this up." She led him back to the fire exit and stood in the alley watching him, silently, while he washed off all the words.

When the job had been done, and the rag and basin put away, they sat down at Miss Price's desk again. "I suppose you think I'm angry with you, Vincent," she said. "Well, I'm not. I almost wish I could be angry—that would make it much easier—but instead I'm hurt. I've tried to be a good friend to you, and I thought you wanted to be my friend too. But this kind of thing—well, it's very hard to be friendly with a person who'd do a thing like that."

She saw, gratefully, that there were tears in his eyes. "Vincent, perhaps I understand some things better than you think. Perhaps I understand that sometimes, when a person does a thing like that, it isn't really because he wants to hurt anyone, but only because he's unhappy. He knows it isn't a good thing to do, and he even knows it isn't going to make him any happier afterwards, but he goes ahead and does it anyway. Then when he finds he's lost a friend, he's terribly sorry, but it's too late. The thing is done."

She allowed this somber note to reverberate in the silence of the room for a little while before she spoke again. "I won't be able to forget this, Vincent. But perhaps, just this once, we can still be friends —as long as I understand that you didn't mean to hurt me. But you must promise me that you won't forget it either. Never forget that when you do a thing like that, you're going to hurt people who want very much to like you, and in that way you're going to hurt yourself. Will you promise me to remember that, dear?"

The "dear" was as involuntary as the slender hand that reached out and held the shoulder of his sweatshirt; both made his head hang lower than before.

"All right," she said. "You may go now."

He got his windbreaker out of the cloakroom and left, avoiding the tired uncertainty of her eyes. The corridors were deserted, and dead silent except for the hollow, rhythmic knocking of a janitor's push-broom against some distant wall. His own rubber-soled tread only added to the silence; so did the lonely little noise made by the zipping-up of his windbreaker, and so did the faint mechanical sigh of the heavy front door. The silence made it all the more startling when he found, several yards down the concrete walk outside, that two boys were walking beside him: Warren Berg and Bill Stringer.

They were both smiling at him in an eager, almost friendly way.

"What'd she do to ya, anyway?" Bill Stringer asked.

Caught off guard, Vincent barely managed to put on his Edward G. Robinson face in time. "Nunnya business," he said, and walked faster.

"No, listen—wait up, hey," Warren Berg said, as they trotted to keep up with him. "What'd she do, anyway? She bawl ya out, or what? Wait up, hey, Vinny."

The name made him tremble all over. He had to jam his hands in his windbreaker pockets and force himself to keep on walking; he had to force his voice to be steady when he said "Nunnya *business*, I told ya. Lea' me alone."

But they were right in step with him now. "Boy, she must of given you the works," Warren Berg persisted. "What'd she say, anyway? C'mon, tell us, Vinny."

This time the name was too much for him. It overwhelmed his resistance and made his softening knees slow down to a slack, conversational stroll. "She din say nothin' " he said at last; and then after a dramatic pause he added, "She let the ruler do her talkin' for her."

"The *ruler*? Ya mean she used a *ruler* on ya?" Their faces were stunned, either with disbelief or admiration, and it began to look more and more like admiration as they listened.

"On the knuckles," Vincent said through tightening lips. "Five times on each hand. She siz, 'Make a fist. Lay it out here on the desk.' Then she takes the ruler and *Whop! Whop! Whop!* Five times. Ya think that don't hurt, you're crazy."

Miss Price, buttoning her polo coat as the front door whispered shut behind her, could scarcely believe her eyes. This couldn't be Vincent Sabella—this perfectly normal, perfectly happy boy on the sidewalk ahead of her, flanked by attentive friends. But it was, and the scene made her want to laugh aloud with pleasure and relief. He was going to be all right, after all. For all her well-intentioned groping in the shadows she could never have predicted a scene like this, and certainly could never have caused it to happen. But it was happening, and it just proved, once again, that she would never understand the ways of children.

She quickened her graceful stride and overtook them, turning to smile down at them as she passed. "Goodnight, boys," she called, intending it as a kind of cheerful benediction; and then, embarrassed by their three startled faces, she smiled even wider and said, "Goodness, it *is* getting colder, isn't it? That windbreaker of yours looks nice and warm, Vincent. I envy you." Finally they nodded bashfully at her; she called goodnight again, turned, and continued on her way to the bus stop.

She left a profound silence in her wake. Staring after her, Warren Berg and Bill Stringer waited until she had disappeared around the corner before they turned on Vincent Sabella.

"Ruler, my eye!" Bill Stringer said. "Ruler, my eye!" He gave Vincent a disgusted shove that sent him stumbling against Warren Berg, who shoved him back.

"Jeez, you lie about *everything*, don'tcha, Sabella? You lie about *everything!*"

Jostled off balance, keeping his hands tight in the windbreaker pockets, Vincent tried in vain to retain his dignity. "Think *I* care if yiz believe me?" he said, and then because he couldn't think of anything else to say, he said it again. "Think *I* care if yiz believe me?"

But he was walking alone. Warren Berg and Bill Stringer were drifting away across the street, walking backwards in order to look back on him with furious contempt. "Just like the lies you told about the policeman shooting your father," Bill Stringer called.

"Even *movies* he lies about," Warren Berg put in; and suddenly doubling up with artificial laughter he cupped both hands to his mouth and yelled, "Hey, Doctor Jack-o'-lantern!"

It wasn't a very good nickname, but it had an authentic ring to it—the kind of a name that might spread around, catch on quickly, and stick. Nudging each other, they both took up the cry:

"What's the matter, Doctor Jack-o'-lantern?"

"Why don'tcha run on home with Miss Price, Doctor Jack-o'-lantern?"

"So long, Doctor Jack-o'-lantern!"

Vincent Sabella went on walking, ignoring them, waiting until they were out of sight. Then he turned and retraced his steps all the way back to school, around through the playground and back to the alley, where the wall was still dark in spots from the circular scrubbing of his wet rag.

Choosing a dry place, he got out his chalk and began to draw a head with great care, in profile, making the hair long and rich and taking his time over the face, erasing it with moist fingers and reworking it until it was the most beautiful face he had ever drawn: a delicate nose, slightly parted lips,

an eye with lashes that curved as gracefully as a bird's wing. He paused to admire it with a lover's solemnity; then from the lips he drew a line that connected with a big speech balloon, and in the balloon he wrote, so angrily that the chalk kept breaking in his fingers, every one of the words he had written that noon. Returning to the head, he gave it a slender neck and gently sloping shoulders, and then, with bold strikes, he gave it the body of a naked woman: great breasts with hard little nipples, a trim waist, a dot for a navel, wide hips and thighs that flared around a triangle of fiercely scribbled pubic hair. Beneath the picture he printed its title: "Miss Price."

He stood there looking at it for a little while, breathing hard, and then he went home.

Diagnosis

Culturally and affectionally deprived child in a middle-class environment.

The story is a realistic description of how a new child in a strange environment tries to find his way. His clothes, manner, and speech make him a stranger. His difference is felt keenly by classmates, the teacher, and himself. His attempt to be like the others by lying or make-believe is understandable enough. Equally understandable is his well-intentioned teacher's overinvolvement with him. Her behavior, although well-meaning and sympathetic, singles him out and further alienates him from the class. Teacher's pet is at best a hard role, particularly when a child is starving for attention and expression.

Vincent's reaction to the teacher's moralistic, middle-class approach to him is confused. In despair, anger, loneliness, and a sense of isolation, he uses the very tools that shock middle-class society most—bad language and lewd pictures.

Overinvolvement often results in a teacher's withdrawal and disappointment. The danger of the teacher's pet role is clear. A gradual welcome which would give the little boy a chance to be different, and an understanding that a week-end report from him is bound to be a fiasco, one way or another, is what was needed. Sadly, even teachers who come from the same ethnic groups as their students tend not to be trained in an awareness of their middle-class myopia. Though this condition is improving it is still much too familiar.

Ciske, the Rat
Piet Bakker

Thus the talk with Ciske's father produced no practical results and I was too busy to let it worry me too much. For twenty-six hours in the week I had Ciske under my care, but in a week there are 168 hours altogether, and during school time I had forty-seven other children who needed looking after. Moreover, what was involved was not only Ciske's soul but his mind, which had to be trained and stuffed with fractions and historical dates. Ciske's acquired knowledge seemed to be nil. Even Betty Van Gemert, the stupidest child in my class, did not make such fantastic spelling mistakes. It obviously wouldn't be easy to push him into the fifth form. But I wanted to achieve this at all cost, otherwise he would fall the following year into the hands of Maatsuyker. And one thing was quite clear: it would be easier for a hippopotamus to repair a wrist watch than for that professional lion tamer Maatsuyker to take the Rat!

Ciske was not stupid, but his education had been completely neglected. The redhaired schoolmistress at his old school had probably never given him a chance to learn, because she had not liked him. This was a great pity, because Ciske was not slow-witted. His math, for instance, was quite good by then. It seemed that he should be quite capable of competing with the best boy, Gerard Jonker, in this field.

While the others were trying to solve simple equations, I used to squat beside Ciske and try to explain fractions to him. He made quite good progress. At first he was anything but pleased, and would slowly edge his way to the other end of the bench, as if he thought that there was really no need for such close contact between us. Also, he seemed to take the view that one can sail quite happily through life without being able to add one-half and three-fourths.

I resorted to an undignified trick in order to get the Rat to cooperate. For quite a long time I had had the suspicion that Johnny Verkerk was Ciske's confirmed adversary, that there had been a mutual enmity at first sight. Johnny was of course jealous because he noticed that I gave more of my time to Ciske than to him.

"Well, Ciske," I said one day, "we will now wring the necks of these fractions. If you really try, you will soon know as much as Verkerk."

The Rat did not seem particularly interested, but Johnny himself proved to be of great assistance to me in my plan, as that was too much for his pride. "He will never do that!" he said. "He is much too stupid."

I should of course have rebuked him, but instead I turned to the Rat. "Did you hear that? Will you stand for it? Come and sit next to me and we'll show Verkerk how wrong he is!"

Grimly he slid closer to me, and we began diligently to cut apples in four and cakes into three parts. The Rat was a picture of concentration. After fifteen minutes, I left him to himself, but he continued to work away like mad, while I went around the class, praising the industrious and scolding the others.

Five minutes later, Ciske sat back—I thought he had given up already. "What now," I asked him, "are you taking a rest?"

He pushed his exercise book toward me without a word. He had finished!

"You see; it was quite simple really, Ciske."

"They weren't very difficult," said Johnny contemptuously, but I could see that he was mortified.

From then on the Rat worked doggedly at his fractions. I couldn't boast that I had solved the problem with any particular intelligence, but the result was satisfactory, and this seemed to me to be the important thing.

When it came to singing, the Rat was a dead loss. I could imagine the boy as almost anything—as the strangler of Johnny, as a burglar, as the best at math in the class but not as somebody who could intone with feeling, "Softly rustles the wind . . ." When the class sang sentimental part songs, Ciske sat there with tightly compressed lips. He hardly ever spoke, so how could one expect him to sing? But I felt I must make him do it. Only when I'd got him to open his mouth and start singing with the others, no matter how badly he did it, would I have reached my second objective. Only then would

From *Ciske, the Rat* by Piet Bakker (New York: Doubleday & Company, Inc., 1958). Reprinted by permission of Mrs. H. Bakker-Prager.

he really become a boy like the others, an integral part of the class.

Once, before class began, I saw him staring, mouth wide open, at the goldfish bowl on the window sill, quite engrossed in the small world of water plants and goldfish and sticklebacks swimming here and there. He drew back as if he had been caught misbehaving when I came up beside him.

"You could clean the bowl if you felt like it," I said.

He looked at me with astonishment, then laughed rather shame-facedly. If I dared, I would stroke your fat head, I thought to myself. A child that could laugh so naturally could not be unreceptive to a little happiness. This miserable little Rat, who was kicked around by everybody, was capable of deriving pleasure from something beautiful. My God! How many blighted and crippled lives there are around us which can be made happy by some small trifle! Short moments of happiness can mean so much to a human being. Why must one always pursue some big goal, out of one's reach? . . .

When the long vacation rolls around, the children are happy. When it is over, they are also happy. They used to strike me forcibly every year. When you asked them, "Are you pleased to be back at school?" they would exclaim in chorus, "Oh, yes!" and "No-oo." They feel somehow obliged to find school horrible and vacation wonderful. But how can one explain that most of them, on the first day of school, run, smiling and happy, to their teacher, as soon as they see him coming around the corner? Why is it always just the first school day that is so particularly nice and happy? And why is one personally so displeased? When everything is back to normal again, with the children sitting at their desks, the geraniums again on the window sill, and the fish in their aquarium, back in place, there is no class and no teacher who are not longing for the Christmas break.

When I looked at my class on that first morning of the new term, I could not discover much evidence of blooming health. Indeed the schools had been closed for a few weeks, but who cared whether the children really enjoyed their vacation or not? Sip Eisma was one of the very few who looked better than they did a month before. He had been staying with his uncle in Ernewouden, on the most lovely part of the coast in Friesland. Full of pride he showed his arms and legs. None of the others was as brown as he. Even Cornel Verstaveren, whose parents had a summer bungalow, seemed pale beside him.

And the Rat?

I didn't like the look of the Rat. It seemed to me that he was even grayer than before. He seemed somehow distrait. During the reading class he could not even find the place.

What could be the matter? Were things going wrong at home?

No, the vacation had done the child no good. When his eyes began to roam aimlessly around the class and I could at last catch his eye, he smiled shyly at me. For a whole five minutes after that the Rat concentrated gallantly, but then his thoughts again escaped somewhere else.

At four o'clock I kept the Rat in as he had to correct a few sums. "Why were you so inattentive today?" I asked him. "Is there anything the matter with you?"

"No, sir."

"How did you enjoy your vacation?"

"Very much, sir."

"So you had a nice time?"

"Yes, sir."

He answered all my questions mechanically. It was quite obvious that he was putting on an act. Children do it frequently without being conscious of it. Even if Ciske had wanted to tell the truth, he would not have been able to. Grownups and children often speak a different language. A child who does not tell the truth is not necessarily always lying!

Only when I asked the Rat whether he was pleased to be back at school did he say with real conviction, "Oh, yes, sir!"

That was genuine enough. School was Ciske's refuge, the place where he felt safe. The Rat, I was sure, had not had any pleasure during the vacation.

The class was set to write an essay about their vacation, and I read in the Rat's book, "And then I was asked to run a few errands for our neighbor. She gave me five cents, and I bought myself some candy. That was lovely!"

Apart from this, there was nothing "lovely" to be found in Ciske's essay. Only at the end he wrote again, "And then we went back to school, which is lovely!"

That afternoon I went again to visit Mrs. Freimuth. In the "best room" there was a smell of cigars. In the ash tray lay a heap of ashes. This did not necessarily mean anything, but in this case I had a definite feeling that when I appeared a man had been hastily shoved into the kitchen. The lady had obviously had a visitor.

She pretended to be extremely pleased to see me and she even congratulated me belatedly on my marriage. Nothing further had happened about the divorce. Her lawyer had advised her to insist on getting forty guilders a month at any rate.

"Then indeed nothing will come of it," I said. "It is rather silly, really, because not only do you lose twenty guilders, but you must also look after Ciske." I had to suppress a desire to comment on the cigar ashes and hint at the possibility of a new life for Mrs. Freimuth, but I was too shy to be so outspoken. "How did Ciske behave during his vacation?" I asked instead.

She shrugged her shoulders. "How should he behave?" she answered harshly. "He has been around the place pestering his mother. One should thank God when children go back to school."

The boy had not been at home much, she continued. Mostly just for his meals and at night. He had sat a lot with Dorus at his house and had, whenever possible, slipped off in the evenings to see his father's woman.

"What, don't you know? His father has got himself a mistress. Too funny for words—a common washerwoman. And after that he wants to tell me what to do! He should be pleased that I don't divorce him for adultery. Then he would have to pay up! Pay through the nose until the day of his death!"

One thing Ciske's mother made quite clear: Ciske would never be able to see that sluttish woman with her blessing—"Auntie Jane," as Ciske called her. (He called her that, of course, only to irritate his mother.) But she knew perfectly well that he was visiting her behind her back. She couldn't keep an eye on such a boy all the time, especially as she was so busy herself. Once she had followed him when he had said he was going to Dorus. But where did he go? Straight to the washerwoman! Well, she had shown him then where he got off. And at night she had been locking him in.

Now I could see quite clearly why the Rat had been so pleased to see the end of the vacation.

Something was in the air. I could not explain why I felt it, but I did. I was worried that the Rat fell silent whenever I mentioned home to him.

Maatsuyker asked me during the break one day, "How are things going with the Rat now?"

"Excellent! He is a changed boy, quite different from the child who came here some months ago"—I did not need to exaggerate.

"True enough," admitted Maatsuyker, "we have not had any trouble with him for quite some time. But let's wait and see if things remain that way. I don't trust the boy an inch."

Earlier I would have been very angry at this lack of confidence. Now I felt that the doubts expressed by my headmaster were not quite so unjustified. Just because I was so pleased with the Rat, I could not suppress a certain fear of the future. Why did the child stare so grimly into space when the moment before he had been so gay? Why was he suddenly, in the middle of an arithmetic problem, so far away in his thoughts? Why did he start when I called his name? What was going on in his mind?

For Dorus, Ciske would still walk through fire and for Betty and Sip he would run until his feet bled if necessary. I also knew that he was fond of animals. He was even fond of the fish in the tank and was very unhappy whenever one of them died a peaceful death.

If the Rat had only been my pupil and nothing more, I could have been reassured in every respect. But fate had decreed that I be concerned with his welfare outside school. How could I, though, be responsible for a child who spent a great part of his day outside my field of vision?

It became quite obvious to me that the Rat was hiding something from me. Something new and unknown had crept into our relationship. This did not mean that we didn't understand each other any more—quite the contrary. Only recently I had chased Ciske around the desks after class and shoved his head into a wastepaper basket. He had stuck out his tongue at me in reply. A boy does not do that when he does not like you. When he does it, as a joke and not to be naughty, it proves a certain inner bond. If Johnny had done it, he would have been sharply rebuked. The fact that I was prepared to take it from Ciske proved that our relationship was now capable of withstanding a knock or two.

Ciske was never resentful when sometimes he had to be punished, but he could not bear to be humiliated. In that case he was quickly offended and ready to seek revenge.

Piet Steeman, who sat just behind him, could best testify to this. One day during class I saw Ciske turn suddenly and give Piet a well-aimed blow in the eye. I took him by the collar and put him in the corner. Piet sat in his place with the face of a martyr.

"Piet shouldn't tease him," said Sip, springing to his defense. "Piet said that the Rat has to eat from the garbage pail at his mother's."

Ciske was very good at binding books, and did it very willingly. With Piet and Johnny I asked him once to stay on a little after school break. Piet wanted to go home after a little while because he had been asked to a birthday party, and Johnny went too because he wanted to meet his father's train. I stayed on alone with the Rat and we had a little chat.

"And when is your father coming back?" I asked.

Without looking at me, Ciske answered, "He went yesterday to Aalborg and Stettin, to the Baltic."

"Oh dear." I was most surprised. "And how long was he here then?"

"Five days."

"Did your mother object to your going to see him?"

"I didn't ask her; I just left her," said Ciske and again he did not look at me.

"And have you since then been to see . . . ?" I wondered how I should refer to "Aunt Jane."

No reaction at all from the Rat!

Something was wrong. I had a definite impression of this. Was it normal for Freimuth not to have come to see me when he was in town for five days? Or was I imagining things?

I felt at times that the Rat was now playing an active part in the Freimuth marriage tragedy. Ciske's temperament did not allow him to be a silent witness of the horrible quarrel between his parents. He would intervene—and leave nothing undone to help his father. When it came to the point, he would again be the old fighting Rat! And I racked my brains to think how to cope with the dangerous traits in the boy, the cold cruelty which could suddenly swamp all his good qualities.

It seemed to me as if invisible demons were hovering around the child but I could not let myself become a prey to my imagination. Was Maatsuyker by any chance right when he spoke about the "critical clash of personalities"?

Good God, how difficult it all was! . . .

"The father!" exclaimed Mrs. Freimuth in a fury. "The father! He doesn't give a damn for his children. He doesn't even want to support them."

"He wants to, but you prevent him from doing it," I put in. "You should not make these exaggerated claims."

"It's all quite clear," continued the headmaster. "When we get a written request from Ciske's father, the child can be taken away from this school, but not before. And if he does not come to school this afternoon, you will have the police at your house, do you understand?"

Mrs. Freimuth behaved like an offended queen. She cast a poisonous glance at me. "This is just in your line, isn't it?" she shouted. "Two men against a defenseless woman! You bastards!"

"Please get out of here," ordered Maatsuyker.

"You can open your mouth as wide as you like at home but not here."

"I believe that you have been handling the lady with kid gloves, Bruis," said Maatsuyker after she had gone. "She is the one who must be treated rough . . ."

In the afternoon the Rat was back in school. He looked pale and tired.

"So here you are again," I greeted him. "Are you pleased?"

He nodded vigorously. I noticed that his eyes were sad. What must the poor child have suffered when his mother forbade him to go to school! Kept away from Dorus, from Betty and Sip! Ciske must have been dragged straight down from seventh heaven when he got home yesterday, overjoyed about *Pieter Marits*, proud of the trust shown by Dorus in lending him his most wonderful book.

"Tell me what happened," I said gently. God, how sorry I was for my little Rat!

"Well, yesterday Mother told me I could not go to school any more. When I wanted to run here in the morning, she locked me up in the attic. I hammered on the door so hard that she came back and dragged me into the coal cellar. And then today at midday she said suddenly, 'Go to school now!' "

That was Ciske's unadorned report. The boy told his story without emphasis. His fingers drummed nervously on the desk. Something had again been broken in the Rat.

The other children obviously felt that something out of the ordinary was going on. This was not their normal Ciske! It was a quiet, sad little boy who could only understand with difficulty that he was again sitting in his old place.

I purposely didn't call on him. He must first find his feet again. He was staring at his reading book, but his thoughts were goodness knows where. From time to time I gave him a wink, but the Rat behaved like a sick person for whom normal life had become strange.

The last lesson of the day should have been singing, but I didn't feel up to it. "Drawing instead," I ordered, and there were several shouts of "Wonderful!"

The Rat remained apathetic. He tried to draw a horse, but it turned into a dog. I was glad when the bell rang and the class could be dismissed. I would like to have given Ciske a word of encouragement on his way home, but thought better of it. What was the use of words? The child surely felt anyway that I was on his side.

"Go on reading your *Pieter Marits*," was all I said to him. He nodded, and Dorus smiled at him from his chair.

That evening I was more uneasy than ever before. I had not liked the Rat's manner that day at all. What should I do? In despair I paced up and down my room. Susan looked at me quizzically but did not ask me any questions. Ciske, now you are between the four walls which are called your home! Ciske, boy, don't hang your head! Hold out! Ciske, Ciske, Ciske! The thoughts were running around and around in my head. I had to keep wiping the perspiration from my forehead.

At half-past nine, Muysken of the juvenile police knocked at my front door. I let him in. He told me that Ciske had killed his mother. Ciske! My Rat!

I felt the ground slipping away from under my feet. I was so shaken that I could only stare at Muysken without saying a word.

He nodded gravely. Yes, Mrs. Freimuth had ordered Ciske to bed early and tried to take his book away from him, the book he had borrowed from Dorus. She had torn it out of his hand, thrown it on the floor, and, in a senseless rage, trampled it under her feet. The Rat had become mad with rage. He had grabbed a knife which was lying on the table and had thrown it blindly in his mother's direction. It had penetrated Mrs. Freimuth's jugular vein; she had died within a few minutes.

"And the child?"

Ciske had fled instinctively to his Aunt Jane. She had taken him to the police. . . .

When I entered the quiet building of the psychiatric department at the remand school (the detention home where Ciske was being held until his trial), I was overcome by a feeling of uneasiness. From the street the noise of everyday activities penetrated into the prison, the sounds of life itself. Had the Rat irrevocably forfeited this life? Would he never be able to return to the company of happy children?

The head of the department showed me a door, and looking through the small window in it I saw Ciske sitting on a wooden bench. He was swinging his legs, exactly like a boy who is momentarily bored during vacation. Here he was, the Rat, my pupil. I had given my whole heart to the boy and yet I had been unable to prevent fate from striking him down.

Ciske jumped when I went into the cell. So, he was not as unconcerned as he had appeared. At once he hung his head and began to bite his knuckles nervously. He wouldn't look at me.

I couldn't feel anything but a deep, painful sympathy for the cowering child, for this sad little bundle of humanity which—without understanding it completely—had taken upon his conscience a mortal sin.

I felt, not for the first time, how relative guilt can be. A fraction further to the right or to the left and the knife would not have killed the woman, only wounded her. In Ciske's defense, mitigating circumstances would certainly have been found. But because Ciske happened to hit precisely the fatal place, he would be stigmatized for the rest of his life.

I put my hand on his head and stroked his hair. I could find no words. The boy was trembling like a captive, frightened bird. All of a sudden he began to cry, although he tried to keep back his tears. But when I pressed his head lovingly against me, he broke down completely—Ciske was now no more than an unhappy child.

If only I could have taken him home with me! But I had to leave him here, in this bare cheerless building, in which the Rat was a serious, perhaps even an interesting, case. What could I do to lighten for the child the burden of his tragic fate?

"Dorus sends his love," I said finally. "He wants me to tell you that he does not mind at all about the book. He will always remain your friend, he has assured me. Isn't that wonderful?"

The Rat continued to sob.

"Betty and Sip also send their love," I lied.

The boy pressed his wet face against my hand. Wordlessly he begged for my protection, which I was unable to extend to him any more.

Through the little window in the door, the head of the department made a sign that my time was up.

"Listen, my dear boy," I said to the Rat, "we won't discuss now what you have done. It was a terrible misfortune. But you must remember that I won't abandon you because of this—all right? Nor will the others, Ciske!" After a moment I said quietly, "And now I must go, Ciske."

He clung desperately to my arm with both hands. I could feel his loneliness, his utter misery. Gently I freed my arms, and Ciske lifted his pale face to me. The Rat's eyes imploring me to help him were the last thing I saw as I left. . . .

Meerstra reflectively chewed on the butt of his cigar. "I would like for five minutes to borrow the robes of the judge of the juvenile court," he said slowly, "and sentence the boy to be taken into a decent family, to people who have some love to spare for such a little fellow and who would not continuously talk of 'guilt and expiation.' I hate all this useless, juristic mumbojumbo. Why complicate matters so? It is a lot of dangerous twaddle; to repay evil with evil. Under certain circumstances one can do this with an adult, with a thoroughly depraved character, but not with a child. If you pronounce a vindictive sentence on the boy, you lightly commit spiritual infanticide in the name of the law, too. . . . Do you understand?''

Diagnosis

Affectional and cultural deprivation— learning difficulties.

This is a story of a Dutch teacher and a child of spirit whose experience of the world has been altogether negative up to the time he arrives in this class. The teacher is skillful and sensitive—skillful enough to keep from becoming overinvolved, sensitive enough to care, and perceptive enough to group his class in such a way that Ciske, the Rat, begins to find areas of success, joy, a sense of beauty, friendship, and relatedness. School becomes Ciske's heaven. At home is a hating, complaining mother and a weak, amoral father. Necessities are minimal, and Ciske gets less than the love, understanding, or privacy a child needs. At school he finds a dying, crippled child whom he protects and who gives him love and value. He becomes part of a group and finds a reliable adult and a world of intellect. When thwarted from reaching toward these values, he loses control of his impulses and fights back. The teacher uses himself and the peer group as therapeutic agents.

This story shows the buildup of tension. The teacher, social worker, and police officer admire Ciske's rebellion and spirit. The teacher turns this energy to useful channels. After the murder, however, he recognizes defeat in the trap that Ciske's life has set for him.

Unloved, spunky fighters and despairing, silent haters often sit in classrooms with much reason to hate and little to love, much reason to fight. Some, like Ciske, learn the meaning of love and beauty through a teacher with love and humor in his heart and skillful teaching techniques. Often, as in Ciske's case, there is little we can do to give lasting help, but there is more that society needs to do to create a world where parents need not be so destructive and where, if they are, children can find other positive helpers—enough to see them through. Ciske nearly had enough.

The waste of life portrayed in Ciske's story occurs in all kinds of poverty settings—European or American, black or white. A teacher's intervention can sometimes save such a life, but not always.

The Autobiography of Malcolm X

. . . My restlessness with Mason—and for the first time in my life a restlessness with being around white people—began as soon as I got back home and entered eighth grade.

I continued to think constantly about all that I had seen in Boston, and about the way I had felt there. I know now that it was the sense of being a real part of a mass of my own kind, for the first time.

The white people—classmates, the Swerlins, the people at the restaurant where I worked —noticed the change. They said, "You're acting so strange. You don't seem like yourself, Malcolm. What's the matter?"

I kept close to the top of the class, though. The topmost scholastic standing, I remember, kept shifting between me, a girl named Audrey Slaugh, and a boy named Jimmy Cotton.

It went on that way, as I became increasingly restless and disturbed through the first semester. And then one day, just about when those of us who had passed were about to move up to 8-A, from which we would enter high school the next year, something happened which was to become the first major turning point of my life.

Somehow, I happened to be alone in the classroom with Mr. Ostrowski, my English teacher. He was a tall, rather reddish white man and he had a thick mustache. I had gotten some of my best marks under him, and he had always made me feel that he liked me. He was, as I have mentioned, a natural-born "advisor," about what you ought to read, to do, or think—about any and everything. We used to make unkind jokes about him: why was he teaching in Mason instead of somewhere else, getting for himself some of the "success in life" that he kept telling us how to get?

I know that he probably meant well in what he happened to advise me that day. I doubt that he meant any harm. It was just in his nature as an

American white man. I was one of his top students, one of the school's top students—but all he could see for me was the kind of future "in your place" that almost all white people see for black people.

He told me, "Malcolm, you ought to be thinking about a career. Have you been giving it thought?"

The truth is, I hadn't. I never have figured out why I told him, "Well, yes, sir, I've been thinking I'd like to be a lawyer." Lansing certainly had no Negro lawyers—or doctors either—in those days, to hold up an image I might have aspired to. All I really knew for certain was that a lawyer didn't wash dishes, as I was doing.

Mr. Ostrowski looked surprised, I remember, and leaned back in his chair and clasped his hands behind his head. He kind of half-smiled and said, "Malcolm, one of life's first needs is for us to be realistic. Don't misunderstand me, now. We all here like you, you know that. But you've got to be realistic about being a nigger. A lawyer—that's no realistic goal for a nigger. You need to think about something you *can* be. You're good with your hands—making things. Everybody admires your carpentry shop work. Why don't you plan on carpentry? People like you as a person—you'd get all kinds of work."

The more I thought afterwards about what he said, the more uneasy it made me. It just kept treading around in my mind.

What made it really begin to disturb me was Mr. Ostrowski's advice to others in my class—all of them white. Most of them had told him they were planning to become farmers. But those who wanted to strike out on their own, to try something new, he had encouraged. Some, mostly girls, wanted to be teachers. A few wanted other professions, such as one boy who wanted to become a county agent; another, a veterinarian; and one girl wanted to be a nurse. They all reported that Mr. Ostrowski had encouraged what they had wanted. Yet nearly none of them had earned marks equal to mine.

It was a surprising thing that I had never thought of it that way before, but I realized that whatever I wasn't, I *was* smarter than nearly all of those white kids. But apparently I was still not intelligent enough, in their eyes, to become whatever *I* wanted to be.

It was then that I began to change—inside.

I drew away from white people. I came to class, and I answered when called upon. It became a physical strain simply to sit in Mr. Ostrowski's class.

Where "nigger" had slipped off my back before, wherever I heard it now, I stopped and looked at whoever said it. And they looked surprised that I did.

I quit hearing so much "nigger" and "What's wrong?"—which was the way I wanted it. Nobody, including the teachers, could decide what had come over me. I knew I was being discussed. . . .

In this year, 1965, I am certain that more—and worse—riots are going to erupt, in yet more cities, in spite of the conscience-salving Civil Rights Bill. The reason is that the *cause* of these riots, the racist malignancy in America, has been too long unattended.

I believe that it would be almost impossible to find anywhere in America a black man who has lived further down in the mud of human society than I have; or a black man who has been any more ignorant than I have been; or a black man who has suffered more anguish during his life than I have. But it is only after the deepest darkness that the greatest joy can come; it is only after slavery and prison that the sweetest appreciation of freedom can come.

For the freedom of my 22 million black brothers and sisters here in America, I do believe that I have fought the best that I know how, and the best that I could, with the shortcomings that I have had. I know that my shortcomings are many.

My greatest lack has been, I believe, that I don't have the kind of academic education I wish I had been able to get—to have been a lawyer, perhaps. I do believe that I might have made a good lawyer. I have always loved verbal battle, and challenge. You can believe me that if I had the time, right now, I would not be one bit ashamed to go back into any New York City public school and start where I left off at the ninth grade, and go on through a degree. Because I don't begin to be academically equipped for so many of the interests that I have. For instance, I love languages. I wish I were an accomplished linguist. I don't know anything more frustrating than to be around people talking something you can't understand. Especially when they are people who look just like you. In Africa, I heard original mother tongues, such as Hausa, and Swahili, being spoken, and there I was standing like some little boy, waiting for someone to tell me what had been said; I never will forget how ignorant I felt.

Aside from the basic African dialects, I would try to learn Chinese, because it looks as if Chinese will be the most powerful political language of the future. And already I have begun studying Arabic, which I think is going to be the most powerful spiritual language of the future.

I would just like to *study,*. I mean ranging study, because I have a wide-open mind. I'm interested in almost any subject you can mention. I know this is the reason I have come to really like, as individuals, some of the hosts of radio or television panel programs I have been on, and to respect their minds—because even if they have been almost steadily in disagreement with me on the race issue, they still have kept their minds open and objective about the truths of things happening in the world. Irv Kupcinet in Chicago, and Barry Farber, Barry Gray and Mike Wallace in New York—people like them. They also let me see that they respected my mind—in a way I know they never realized. The way I knew was that often they would invite my opinion on subjects off the race issue. Sometimes, after the programs, we would sit around and talk about all kinds of things, current events and other things, for an hour or more. You see, most whites, even when they credit a Negro with some intelligence, will still feel that all he can talk about is the race issue; most whites never feel that Negroes can contribute anything to other areas of thought, and ideas. You just notice how rarely you will ever hear whites asking any Negroes what they think about the problem of world health, or the space race to land men on the moon. . . .

Diagnosis

Intelligence and motivation thwarted by an environment of cultural bigotry and ignorance.

The *Autobiography of Malcolm X* is the story of a man who grew to responsible leadership from a background that offered almost no encouragement. Malcolm X grew up to fulfill much of his exceptional ability in an environment of poverty and racial discrimination and with an education that ended at the ninth grade. The despair and bitterness he felt as a young man led him from virulent self-hatred to hatred of others, delinquencies, and crimes which resulted in his imprisonment. In prison he found a protective therapeutic agent in the form of the prison library and a channel towards growth in the form of the Black Muslim organization, a group which he later left as he matured into a less sectarian view of the need for social change. Prison and poverty are miserable schools to have to learn in, but the public school system didn't help much. The less motivated and less gifted residents of racial ghettos are frequently trapped in the despair from which Malcolm X emerged.

The excerpts reprinted here describe one painful incident with a teacher and the lifelong despair and regret which had some of their source in the thoughtless words of that unknowing, unconsciously prejudiced teacher. The schools should be a source of hope and fulfillment for students, but for many—especially for members of racial minorties—they are the agents of despair, in convincing students that their personal goals are unreachable.

Most of the residents of New York's East Harlem, Spanish Harlem, are immigrants from Puerto Rico, a racially mixed population. Piri Thomas, the son of a black father and a white mother, is black, but all of his brothers and sisters are white. The combination of alien language, alien culture, poverty, and racial mixture in his own family made his adolescence, some of which he describes in these selections, unusually difficult.

Down These Mean Streets
Piri Thomas

. . . We were moving—our new pad was back in Spanish Harlem—to 104th Street between Lex and Park Avenue.

Moving into a new block is a big jump for a Harlem kid. You're torn up from your hard-won turf and brought into an "I don't know you" block where every kid is some kind of enemy. Even when the block belongs to your own people, you are still

an outsider who has to prove himself a down stud with heart.

As the moving van rolled to a stop in front of our new building, number 109, we were all standing there, waiting for it—Momma, Poppa, Sis, Paulie, James, José, and myself. I made out like I didn't notice the cats looking us over, especially me—I was gang age. I read their faces and found no trust, plenty of suspicion, and a glint of rising hate. I said to myself, *These cats don't mean nothin'.*

They're just nosy. But I remembered what had happened to me in my old block, and that it had ended with me in the hospital.

This was a tough-looking block. That was good, that was cool; but my old turf had been tough, too. *I'm tough,* a voice within said. *I hope I'm tough enough. I am tough enough. I've got* mucho corazón, *I'm king wherever I go. I'm a killer to my heart. I not only* can *live, I will* live, *no punk out, no die out, walk bad; be down, cool breeze, smooth.* My mind raced, and thoughts crashed against each other, trying to reassemble themselves into a patter of rep. I turned slowly and with eyelids half-closed I looked at the rulers of this new world and with a cool shrug of my shoulders I followed the movers into the hallway of number 109 and dismissed the coming war from my mind.

The next morning I went to my new school, called Patrick Henry, and strange, mean eyes followed me.

"Say, pops," said a voice belonging to a guy I later came to know as Waneko, "where's your territory?"

In the same tone of voice Waneko had used, I answered, "I'm on it, dad, what's shaking?"

"Bad, huh?" He half-smiled.

"No, not all the way. Good when I'm cool breeze and bad when I'm down."

"What's your name, kid?"

"That depends. 'Piri' when I'm smooth and Johnny Gringo' when stomping time's around."

"What's your name now?" he pushed.

"You name me, man," I answered, playing my role like a champ.

He looked around, and with no kind of words, his boys cruised in. Guys I would come to know, to fight, to hate, to love, to take care of. Little Red, Waneko, Little Louie, Indio, Carlito, Alfredo, Crip, and plenty more. I stiffened and said to myself, *Stomping time, Piri boy, go with heart.*

I fingered the garbage-can handle in my pocket—my homemade brass knuckles. They were great for breaking down large odds into small, chopped-up ones.

Waneko, secure in his grandstand, said, "We'll name you later, *panín.*"

I didn't answer. Scared, yeah, but wooden-faced to the end, I thought, *Chevere, panín.*

It wasn't long in coming. Three days later, at about 6 P.M., Waneko and his boys were sitting around the stoop at number 115. I was cut off from my number 109. For an instant I thought, *Make a break for it down the basement steps and through the back yards—get away in one piece!* Then I

thought, *Caramba! Live punk, dead hero. I'm no punk kid. I'm not copping any pleas.* I kept walking, hell's a-burning, hell's a-churning, rolling with cheer. *Walk on, baby man, roll on without fear. What's he going to call?*

"Whatta ya say, Mr. Johnny Gringo?" drawled Waneko.

Think, man, I told myself, *think your way out of a stomping. Make it good.* "I hear you 104th Street coolies are supposed to have heart," I said. "I don't know this for sure. You know there's a lot of streets where a whole 'click' is made out of punks who can't fight one guy unless they all jump him for the stomp." I hoped this would push Waneko into giving me a fair one. His expression didn't change.

"Maybe we don't look at it that way."

Crazy, man. I cheer inwardly, the cabrón *is falling into my setup. We'll see who gets messed up first, baby!* "I wasn't talking to you," I said. "Where I come from, the pres is president 'cause he got heart when it comes to dealing."

Waneko was starting to look uneasy. He had bit on my worm and felt like a sucker fish. His boys were now light on me. They were no longer so much interested in stomping me as in seeing the outcome between Waneko and me. "Yeah," was his reply.

I smiled at him. "You trying to dig where I'm at and now you got me interested in you. I'd like to see where you're at."

Waneko hesitated a tiny little second before replying, "Yeah."

I knew I'd won. Sure, I'd have to fight; but one guy, not ten or fifteen. If I lost I might still get stomped, and if I won I might get stomped. I took care of this with my next sentence. "I don't know you or your boys," I said, "but they look cool to me. They don't feature as punks."

I had left him out purposely when I said "they." Now his boys were in a separate class. I had cut him off. He would have to fight me on his own, to prove his heart to himself, to his boys, and most important, to his turf. He got away from the stoop and asked, "Fair one, Gringo?"

"Uh-uh," I said, "roll all the way—anything goes." I thought, *I've got to beat him bad and yet not bad enough to take his prestige all away.* He had corazón. He came on me. *Let him draw first blood,* I thought, *it's his block.* Smish, my nose began to bleed. His boys cheered, his heart cheered, his turf cheered. "Waste this chump," somebody shouted.

Okay, baby, now it's my turn. He swung. I grabbed innocently, and my forehead smashed into his nose. His eyes crossed. His fingernails went for my eye and landed in my mouth—crunch, I bit hard. I punched him in the mouth as he pulled away from me, and he slammed his foot into my chest.

We broke, my nose running red, my chest throbbing, his finger—well, that was his worry. I tied up with body punching and slugging. We rolled onto the street. I wrestled for acceptance, he for rejection or, worse yet, acceptance on his terms. It was time to start peace talks. I smiled at him. "You got heart, baby," I said.

He answered with a punch to my head. I grunted and hit back, harder now. I had to back up my overtures of peace with strength. I hit him in the ribs, I rubbed my knuckles in his ear as we clinched. I tried again. "You deal good," I said.

"You too," he muttered, pressuring out. And just like that, the fight was over. No more words. We just separated, hands half up, half down. My heart pumped out, *You've established your rep. Move over, 104th Street. Lift your wings, I'm one of your baby chicks now.*

Five seconds later my spurs were given to me in the form of introductions to streetdom's elite. There were no looks of blankness now; I was accepted by heart.

"What's your other name, Johnny Gringo?"

"Piri."

"Okay, Pete, you wanna join my fellows?"

"Sure, why not?"

But I knew I had first joined their gang when I cool-looked them on moving day. *I was cool, man,* I thought. *I could've wasted Waneko any time. I'm good, I'm damned good, pure* corazón. *Viva me!* Shit, I had been scared, but that was over. I was in; it was *my* block now.

Not that I could relax. In Harlem you always lived on the edge of losing rep. All it takes is a one-time loss of heart. . . .

When you're a kid, everything has some kind of special meaning. I always could find something to do, even if it was doing nothing. But going to school was something else. School stunk. I hated school and all its teachers. I hated the crispy look of the teachers and the draggy-long hours they took out of my life from nine to three-thirty. I dug being outside no matter what kind of weather. Only chumps worked and studied.

Every day began with a fight to get me out of bed for school. Momma played the same record over an' over every day: "Piri, get up, it's time to go to school." And I played mine: "Aw, Moms, I don't feel so good. I think I got a fever or something."

Always it ended up the same old way: I got up

and went to school. But I didn't always stay there. Sometimes, I reported for class, let my teacher see me and then began the game of sneaking out of the room. It was like escaping from some kind of prison. I waited for the teacher to turn her back, then I slipped out of my seat and, hugging the floor, crawled on my belly toward the door. The other kids knew what I was doing; they were trying not to burst out laughing. Sometimes a wise guy near me made a noise to bring the teacher's attention my way. When this happened, I lay still between the row of desks until the teacher returned to whatever he or she had been doing.

I sneaked my way to the door, eased it open and—swoom!—I was on my way. It was a great-o game, slipping past the other classes and ducking the other teachers or monitors.

One class I didn't dig at all was the so-called "Open Air Class" for skinny, "underweight" kids. We had to sleep a couple of half hours every day, and we got extra milk and jelly and peanut butter on brown bread. The teacher, Miss Shepard, was like a dried-up grape. One day I raised my hand to go to the toilet, but she paid me no mind. After a while, the pain was getting bad, so I called out, "Miss Shepard, may I leave the room?"

She looked up and just shook her head, no.

"But I gotta go, Miss Shepard."

"You just went a little while ago," she said.

"I know, Miss Shepard, but I gotta go again."

"I think it's sheer nonsense," said the old bitch. "You just want an excuse to play around in the hallways."

"No, ma'am, I just wanna take a piss."

"Well, you can't go."

I had to go so badly that I felt the tears forming in the corners of my eyes to match the drops that were already making a wet scene down my leg. "I'm goin' anyway," I said and started toward the door.

Miss Shepard got up and screamed at me to get back to my seat. I ignored her.

"Get back to your seat, young man," she screamed. "Do you hear me? Get right back—"

"Fuck you," I mumbled. I reached the door and felt her hands grab out at me and her fingers hook on to the back of my shirt collar. My clean, washed-a-million-times shirt came apart in her hand.

I couldn't see her face clearly when I turned around. All I could think about was my torn shirt and how this left me with only two others. All I could see was her being the cause of the dampness of my pants and hot pee running down my leg. All I could hear was the kids making laughing sounds and the anger of my being ashamed. I didn't think of her as a woman, but as something that had to be hit. I hit it.

"Ohhhhhh, you *struck* me," she cried, in surprise as much as pain.

I thought, *I did not, you fuckin' liar. I just hit you.*

"You struck me! You *struck* me! Oh, help, help!" she cried.

I cut out. Man, I ran like hell into the hallway, and she came right after me, yelling, "Help, help!" I was scared now and all I could think about was getting back to my Moms, my home, my block, where no one could hurt me. I ran toward the stairway and found it blocked off by a man, the principal. I cut back toward the back stairs.

"Stop him! Stop him!" dear Miss Shepard yelled, pointing her finger at me. "He struck me, he struck me."

I looked over my shoulder and saw the principal talk to her for a hot second and then take off after me, yelling: "Stop! Stop!" I hit the stairs and went swooming down like it was all one big step. The principal was fast and I could hear him swearing right behind me. I slammed through the main-floor door that led to the lunchroom and jumped over benches and tables, trying like hell to make the principal trip and break a leg. Then I heard a muted cry of pain as a bench caught him in the shin. I looked over my shoulder and I dug his face. The look said that he was gonna hit me; that he wasn't gonna listen to my side of the story; that I had no side. I figured I better not get caught.

I busted my legs running toward the door that led to the outside and freedom, and with both hands out in front of me I hit the brass bar that opens the door. Behind me I heard a thump as the principal smacked into it. I ran down the block, sneaking a look behind me. The principal was right behind me, his face redder and meaner. People were looking at the uneven contest.

I tore into my hallway, screaming as loud as I could for help. The apartment doors opened up, one right after another. Heads of all colors popped out. "*Qué pasa?*" asked a Puerto Rican woman. "Wha's happenin'?" said a colored lady.

"They wanna beat me up in school and that's one of them," I puffed, pointing at the principal, who was just coming into view.

"Hooo, ain't nobody gonna hurt you, sonny," said the colored lady, whose name was Miss Washington. She gently pushed me behind her with one hand and with the other held it out toward the principal roaring down at us.

The principal, blocked by Miss Washington's 280 pounds and a look of "Don't you touch that boy," stopped short and puffed out, "That —that—kid—he—punched a teacher and—he's got to be chastised for it. After all, school disci—"

"Now hol' on, white man," Miss Washington interrupted. "There ain't nobody gonna chaz —whatever it is—this boy. I knows him an' he's a good boy—at least good for what comes outta this heah trashy neighborhood—an' you ain't gonna do nuttin' to him, unless you-all wan's to walk over me."

Miss Washington was talking real bad-like. I peeked out from behind that great behind.

"Madam, I assure you," the principal said, "I didn't mean harming him in a bodily manner. And if you knew the whole issue, you would agree with me that he deserves being chastised. As principal of his school, I have his best interest at heart. Ha, ha, ha," he added, "you know the old saying, madam, 'A stitch in time saves nine.' Ha, ha, ha—*ahurmph.*"

I could see him putting that stitch in my head.

"I assure you, madam," he continued, smiling pretty, "we have no intention of doing him bodily harm."

Once again I peeked out from behind Miss Washington's behind. "Yeah, that's what you say," I said. "How about alla time you take kids down to your office for some crap and ya start poking 'em with that big finger of yours until they can't take it any more?"

There were a lot of people in the hall by this time. They were all listening, and I knew it. "Yeah, ask any of the kids," I added. "They'll tell ya." I looked sorry-like at the crowd of people, who were now murmuring mean-like and looking at the principal like he didn't have long on this earth.

Smelling a Harlem lynch party in the making, I said, "An'—you—ain't—gonna—do—it—to—me. I'll get me a forty-five an'—"

"Hush your mouth, boy," Miss Washington said; "don't be talkin' like that. We grownups will get this all straightened out. An' nobody's gonna poke no finger in your chest"—she looked dead at the principal—"is they?"

The principal smiled the weakest smile in this smiling world. "I—I—I—er, assure you, madam, this young man is gifted with the most wonderful talent for prevarication I've ever seen."

"What's that mean?" Miss Washington asked suspiciously.

"Er, it means a good imagination, madam. A-ha-ha—yes, *a-hurmph.*"

"That's a lie, Miss Washington," I said. "He's

always telling the kids that. We asked Mrs. Wagner, the history teacher, and she said it means to lie. Like he means I'm a liar."

The look in the principal's eye said, "Oh, you smarty pants bastard," but he just smiled and said nothing.

Miss Washington said, "Iffen thar's any pokin' ta be done, we all heah is gonna do it," and she looked hard at the principal. The crowd looked hard at the principal. Hard sounds were taking forms, like, "So this is the way they treat our kids in school?" and "What you-all expect? These heah white people doan give a damn," and "If they evah treats mah boy like that, I'd . . ."

The principal, smiling softly, began backing up.

I heard Momma's voice: "Piri, Piri, qué pasa?"

"Everything all right, Mis' Thomas," Miss Washington assured her. "This heah man was tryin' to hit your son, but ain't, 'cause I'll break his damn head wide open." Miss Washington shifted her weight forward. "Damn, Ah got a good mind to do it right now," she added. . . .

I'd turn and head back to my block, noticing the overflow wash strung out on front fire escapes and thinking about the people who complain that clothes on front-side fire escapes make the block look cheap, that people who do that have no sense of values and destroy the worth of the neighborhood. But I liked it; I thought it gave class to the front fire escapes to be dressed up with underwear, panties, and scrubbed work clothes.

I'd meet my boys, and all the other hearing and seeing suddenly became unimportant. Only my boys were the important kick, and for good reasons—if I had boys, I had respect and no other clique would make me open game. Besides, they gave me a feeling of belonging, of prestige, of accomplishment; I felt *grande* and bad. Sometimes the thoughts would start flapping around inside me about the three worlds I lived in—the world of home, the world of school (no more of that, though), and the world of street. The street was the best damn one. It was like all the guys shouting out, "Hey, man, this is our kick."

The worlds of home and school were made up of rules laid down by adults who had forgotten the feeling of what it means to be a kid but expected a kid to remember to be an adult—something he hadn't gotten to yet. The world of street belonged to the kid alone. There he could earn his own rights, prestige, his good-o stick of living. It was like being a knight of old, like being ten feet tall. . . .

These selections from Thomas's book illustrate a number of significant points. One impressive element is the high degree of sophistication of the bright boys of the street in terms of group behavior: leadership is established, challenged without being overthrown, enhanced, and maintained; a new member enters the group, participates in the appropriate verbal and nonverbal rituals, and finds a place in the pecking order. If teachers studied group behavior with such sophistication, their lives would be easier. The boys know when to be tough, when to ignore, and when to barge in, and with whom.[1] The teacher's lack of sensitivity is by no means an uncommon characteristic. She fails to recognize the boy's needs for the obvious purpose of humiliating him and asserting her power by imposing a formal rule. The neighborhood loyalty to its own against the alien establishment as represented by the principal is significant. The fact is that the privacy of the principal's office often sees physical mistreatment of children, and when it does the neighborhood knows it. As a defender, Miss Washington is careful both to protect the boy and to quash his fantasy of shooting the principal. She speaks as an adult—"We grownups will get this all straightened out"—and she does so both to Piri and to the principal.

These are selections from the transcript of an interview before the Senate Subcommittee on Indian Education which took place in December 1968 in Blackfoot, Idaho. LaNada Means is a young woman who has taken a leading role in the growing national effort to advance the long-neglected interests of American Indians. Here she describes some of her own experiences in the schools and the jobs to which she, as an Indian, was consigned.

Interview with LaNada Means

LM: As a student I went to Fort Hall schools, and I would like to say something about Indian education.

Bill Anderson, a staffmember of the subcommittee: Would you give your name?

LM: Yes. LaNada Means. I am from this reservation, Route 3, Blackfoot, Idaho. At the present, I am attending school at the University of California and residing at Albany, which is outside of Berkeley. I found that in my attempt to try to get a scholarship from the Bureau of Indian Affairs that it seems like I have just been put off. . . . Not only myself, but other students as well. . . .

I know that this is one of the biggest things as far as education is concerned, and that is the fact that they don't want us to go into higher education. They seem to push vocational training at all the Indian kids, and I guess this comes from boarding schools. By sending them to boarding schools, they proceed to acculturate the Indians, or the Indian children, and try to make duplicate copies of, you know, make us like white children. From there they send us to relocation in the cities, and then push us into vocational training. It's not like they're trying to get us to be able to take over our own affairs by putting us into higher education. It seems that they want to perpetuate their own jobs and the Bureau of Indian Affairs itself, by not helping us, or not letting us go into higher education. . . .

BA: How did you finally wind up at the University of California?

LM: Well, I was sent out on relocation in 1965 through the Bureau of Indian Affairs and dropped.

BA: Dropped where?

LM: In the city. It's like they transfer you from one pocket of poverty to another—from the reservation to the urban ghetto . . . in order to get us away from our reservations, because it's the only land that we're supposedly controlling, even though it's held in trust by the government. It seems that they're trying to get us away from our land so that they could have better access to our property. They've somewhat succeeded in that through the Bureau of Indian Affairs and through the Tribal Council, by using the council as puppets. . . .

BA: How did you survive?

LM: Well, this goes into my personal history a little bit, but it was bare existence . . .

BA: Describe it, and don't hold back. It's very useful for the Subcommittee to know this—we need personal testimony. . . .

LM: I knew I was going to commit suicide myself, but after I had my children, I wanted to try to think of them. They were the only reason why I kept on. At that point, I tried to contact welfare to see if they could help me, and because I wanted to go on to school. They thought I was out of my mind for ever suggesting going back to school at that point.

BA: Had you completed high school?

LM: No. . . . [She tells of being expelled from several Indian schools.] From that point, I just continued in school. I came out one of the ten top students in the school, and I made it through that school year.

BA: How did you do that, I mean, what drove, what motivated you to come out on top?

LM: It was so easy, because they looked down at you. They said, now all you little Indian children, do that. They look on you as children, that you don't have minds, and with that type of attitude, you know, well, I caught on to that. I knew all I had to do was just fake it. Grades were very easy, because I really wasn't actually producing. As a matter of fact, I was writing home and telling my parents I was doing terrible. I was more surprised than anyone that I was one of the ten top students. That's because they think you're so stupid that anything you do must really be good or exceptional. I was sent on the summer home program in the summertime from the school. At the end of school I had a nervous breakdown, and I stayed at the school, and from there I was sent to Minneapolis, Minnesota, on a summer home program. They send you out as indentured servants to work in white homes, and in this way, they can try to make you into being white, or not Indian. . . .

I went to Nevada, and by that time, my reputation was so bad that they expelled me within half a day.

BA: Within half a day at Nevada?

LM: Yes. (Laughter.)

Reprinted by permission of LaNada Means.

BA: Was it a processing in and out? How did it happen?

LM: Well, I'm still trying to figure it out. I never could figure out why I was always . . .

BA: Did you get in the building?

LM: Yes, I went to morning classes and registered. Then in the afternoon I wasn't feeling well from my bus trip. I was a little shaken because I get car sick. In the afternoon I tried to go back home, but Stewart is located several miles from Carson City and I just had to wait till it was time to go. I waited for the bus, and then I went on home. The next morning when I went to classes they called me into the office, and I didn't get through finishing registering for the second half of the day. I registered for the first half already, and I got called in the office and they told me I'd have to see the Chief of Police and the judge. I went down there and the judge, or the Chief of Police, started telling me that I was bad, and that I had a bad record, that no one could control me, that I was just bad . . .

BA: No charges?

LM: No, no charges. I was fifteen then. I started as a junior. They said they'd have to send me to reform school in Nevada, and I said, what did I do? I just got here, and I came here to go to school. I felt so bad, I mean, I was too emotionally shaken at that time. I felt so bad, and thinking they were going to send me to reform school, I told them, well, I still have parents, I'm going to go back to Idaho. So they told my guardian to just make arrangements for me to go back to Idaho. He knows the story. They said okay, and they sent me back to Idaho. . . .

I tried to get a job, but nobody wanted me because I didn't have enough education, plus they were so racist, really racist about it. They don't want Indian business. If I worked in the cafe, I would attract Indian customers, and they wouldn't want *that*, because it would ruin the class of the cafe or store or whatever else. I couldn't get a job, and my other alternative was to work for the Bureau, which I would *never, never, never* do in a million years. At this point I was forced to leave. I and my girlfriend started to take off, and we went to California, and got stranded, didn't have the clothes or anything to get a nice job. Nor the education . . .

BA: How did you survive?

LM: Oh, if you can call it survival . . . Well, it's really hard. What I did was I went to the places where I'd be most accepted, which were the worst places in the so-called ghetto. I was accepted there. The Mexican people took me in, and I worked as a

bar maid. I was underage and everything. I think I was about seventeen, and I worked as a bar maid.

BA: Did you have to hustle there?

LM: No.

BA: It was not that type of place?

LM: It was a different kind of a scene, because I was drunk most of the time. That was about it. I was just drunk most of the time.

BA: Did you get a salary or did you just get it in drinks?

LM: No, I got a dollar an hour. This way it wouldn't have to be reported to income tax and I could work any time I wanted, whenever I was sober. I finally decided that I really had to go back to school because I wasn't getting anywhere. Things were just too tough. It was too late. I was already pregnant; I had my child in San Francisco. . . .

BA: What do you want to do after college?

LM: Well, let's put it this way. While I'm in college, I want to learn as much as I can about the white man, so I can go back and know how to fight him back here on the reservation. Not only this reservation, but other reservations as well because Indians need legal advice. . . .

Diagnosis

Despair brought about largely by the clash between a spirited temperament and a setting in which cultural and personal aspirations receive little encouragement or support.

Many observers, Indian and non-Indian, have attested to the deplorable conditions of the Indian boarding schools that LaNada Means describes. The boarding school life; the separation from home, family, culture, language, and customs; the handling of the children in their non-school time; the absence of communication between child-care workers, school staff, and parents—these and other factors have had tragic consequences for hundreds and hundreds of Indian children. In most cases, staff and children alike come to look on the future of an Indian child with despair, thus destroying whatever natural motivation there might have been. The particular combination of spirit, stamina, guts, and determination shown by LaNada Means is a rare phenomenon. There is hope for the future in the Indians' increasing sense of independence and self-esteem, in their desire to work out their own problems with the counsel, not the patronage, of other Americans.

Drugs: What Some People Do about Their Feelings and What That Does to Them

Anxiety is hard to bear. Yet none of us can live without learning to tolerate a certain amount of it. Anxiety arises from the self-preserving instinct of fear, to which all animals react with either fleeing or fighting mechanisms; anxiety's basic purpose is to send us alarms and warnings, to alert us to whatever threatens so that we can do something about it. There is a good bit of evidence to support the theories of the biophysiologist John Cannon and the psychiatrist Harry Stack Sullivan which hold that without some degree of anxiety man would not learn to learn, and as a result his very survival would be endangered.

Yet as human society grows increasingly complex, man-generated anxieties haunt us. Competition, anger, feelings of inadequacy and unworthiness, guilt, loneliness, confusion, problems of sexual identity and dependency—to name a few—are the lot of men who live together and are by nature dependent on each other. When anxiety rises to too high a level, it is sometimes more than a person can handle. Immobilized, he may revert to the crudest, most primitive forms of combating danger and acute discomfort. In the moment of anxiety, everything a person knows can be forgotten, and everything he has repressed, often at great cost, may come pouring in: he may give way to overwhelming bursts of anger and violence, or he may take flight. Anxiety is often the reason for teenage runaways or for the apathetic lack of effort in a student who has ability. Over the years, we all learn certain defenses, and sometimes they serve us worse than the anxiety they are combating. The particular defense we choose is determined by our temperament and by our environment, past and present. Some of us have developed pusillanimous abjectness, some combativeness and irritability. For some, psychosomatic ills such as headaches, stomach upsets, and hives are the outward signs of the terror underneath. Many of us choose escape: some find escape in books, some in TV (which many people, especially preadolescents, use as a kind of drug), and some in alcohol (which can cause disabilities as damaging to human relationships, job-effectiveness, and physical or mental health as any of the hard drugs).

It is in an effort to escape anxiety and society's deficiencies and onslaughts that many young people today have turned to drugs, just as many in earlier generations turned to alcohol. Some drugs, such as marihuana, are not in themselves harmful physiologically to most people, though any drug, aspirin included, can be harmful to some. The overuse of some drugs, such as the amphetamines (which are stimulants) or barbiturates (downers), or glue-sniffing can cause long-term physical damage. Also, some inconclusive evidence suggests that the popular hallucinogen LSD may do permanent physical harm. Other drugs are so addictive they become the controlling force in a person's life. For the addictive drugs the craving is both physical and psychological. Those addicted to alcohol, the barbiturates, or the opiates (such as heroin, opium, and morphine) suffer not only an overwhelming desire for the drug but also extreme physical discomfort upon withdrawal—shaking, stomach cramps, and wracking pain—and a great risk of death as a result of unknown mixtures or an overdose. Addiction brings helplessness, abject dependency, misery to oneself and others, and self-loathing.

More and more young people are using addictive drugs, and increasing numbers of them are very young indeed. In New York City there were three reported heroin-caused deaths of children under ten years old in 1970. Some of the children on drugs get into it because bucking the crowd or being called square is too much for their essentially conforming, infantile, and dependent social natures. Some young people take a hard drug once or twice and leave it alone. But others have become addicted with few exposures. Some young people may turn to drugs out of frustration at their inability to tell their parents about their unhappiness, which may be the normal unhappiness of any adolescent growing up, but which sometimes seems especially acute in a world where so much is demanded, a world whose values often appear phony and hypocritical, a world whose problems seem nearly insoluble. Given a sufficient sense of powerlessness, a young person in today's culture is often tempted to give up. Sometimes he chooses a life of whose terrors and consequences he knows little.

Some of the drug takers have been disturbed for a long time, but because their parents were insensitive or unprepared or simply didn't want to see, or because their teachers were afraid of alarming someone or of "overstepping boundaries," things were left to go on until it was too late. These youngsters found no way to tell someone they were in trouble inside except through actions that will seriously limit, if not end, their futures. The disturbances were always there; drugs made them manifest. Of course drugs often make matters worse—at times irremediably worse. A familiar type of drug abuser is the gifted child of the middle- and upper-middle-class parent: sensitive to the ills of his environment, unable to reach his family, he sometimes shares with his family a tendency to avoid looking facts in the face. The drug abuser of the poor ghetto, like his wealthier counterpart, is dependent, frightened, and unwilling to grow up. Both may be disturbed in a psychiatric sense as well as for social causes. Both have little sense of self, and both share an inability to be direct or to communicate feelings; they have little ability to tolerate anxiety or to foresee that the future will largely derive from their present choices—for good or bad. The younger the child (and some are only nine to twelve years old), the more the will is affected, and training for coping with life is sacrificed.

Most adults are not nearly as learned as are their children in the varieties of pills, serums, powders, and plants that will take you up, out, or down. But there is a terrifying ignorance of the actual effects of drugs among many young users themselves as well as among adults who ought to know better, including many so-called experts. So little is known that there is still a great deal of work to be done in the field by people in medicine, physiology, psychiatry, psychology, social work, sociology, and anthropology, as well as by educators. The realistic handling of drug abuse by young people requires the active engagement of physicians, psychologists, researchers, lawyers, educators, and law enforcement officers in evaluating, preventing, and treating drug abuse—not simply in punishing it. Whatever other needs drug use may fill, the issue of its legality or illegality has given it among young people the added attraction of being another channel for the common adolescent rebellion against authority. It is altogether a very complicated issue and cannot begin to be understood without a differentiation of the drugs, their effects, and the individuals and groups who use them.

A sensible approach by teachers and school officials to student drug use will probably share at least one principle with their handling of other, less emotionally loaded subjects: certain things are appropriate to do in school, during work hours, and others are not; some things are appropriate to bring to school, and others are not. A person doesn't drink in school or at work or come drunk to school or work without consequences. Likewise, a person does not get high on drugs in school. But when this principle is ignored, as it frequently is, it should be a major concern of the school to assist the drug abuser in coping with the sources of his problem in anxiety, frustration, and the painful process of growing up.

Though heavy drug takers often fantasize great creations, they seldom act on them; the act of creation itself seems to require too much effort, to make too great a demand on the infantile orientation of the drug user. The addictive drugs reduce the appetite, so that undernourishment and the consequent lack of energy make productivity the exception rather than the rule among addicted users.

Although our literature is increasing on drug use among the young, remarkably little has been written that accurately conveys the experience and helps adults to recognize and deal with the problem. However, teachers are now aware of certain signals of student drug use: large pupils and heavy eyelids, leaden or slack bodies, atypical or inappropriate speech, excessive giggling or tears, or reports of fantasies. (Of course, these may be caused by other things besides drugs.)

Marihuana, hashish, and peyote are in a different category from synthetic drugs, hallucinogens, and hard drugs, because they are, according to most reports, *not in themselves* any more addictive than tobacco, except for certain people who have psychologically addictable personalities or are allergic to specific chemicals. The hallucinogens are well-described in a passage below by Alan Watts, and also in *The Electric Kool-Aid Acid Test* by Tom Wolfe.[2] His account of Ken Kesey's crew is strongly recommended for anyone interested in reading about a total drug life-style.

The hard drugs are represented in William Burroughs's *Deposition: Testimony Concerning a Sickness* (cocaine) and Piri Thomas's *Down These Mean Streets* (heroin). The serious problem of "downers" is thoroughly explored in *Richie,* a true account of a family tragedy in which downers were central. An excerpt from this book is included because it typifies family involvement, the total takeover of life by drugs, not only Richie's but his friends' as well. The book should be read by all educators, for so much that could have been done by the school was not done.

Although student drunkenness is increasing, the major alcohol problem (and it is major) is not with children but with parents. The school constantly has to deal with this problem (the teacher's dread in dealing with a drunk parent is an added hazard to the usual agony), and an excerpt has been included from a patient's diary to illustrate this all too common phenomenon and its effects on the child.

Marihuana, Hashish, and Peyote

These three natural hallucinogens are extracted from plants; LSD, the amphetamines, and the barbiturates are made synthetically. Most evidence indicates that moderate use of natural hallucinogens is not dangerous for most people.

Yet, as with aspirin or with any drug, some people are allergic or sensitive to them and for such people they can have destructive physiological and psychological effects. The desired effects can range from relaxation to intense excitement, from social pleasure to spiritual experience of an occult or mystical nature. Their use is worldwide and has a long, long history. With overuse or use by young people, hallucinogens appear to affect the will and abilities to concentrate and persevere. They become an escape from hard or unpleasant tasks often necessary for the achievement of ultimate goals. Their illegality has caused some of the serious psychological and perhaps moral damage to our young. The fact that so many very young children from eight or nine up use them is frightening; the younger the user, the more these drugs appear to affect the will or energy level and thus interfere with concentration on a work task, motivation, and acquisition of necessary skills.

These drugs have always been (and still are) used to induce altered dimensions of time, space, sound, and visual experience. For some, their use represents a lifestyle; to others, such as Mezz Mezzrow, the jazz musician, marihuana is seen as a way to enhance his art. To Charles Baudelaire, hashish was a way to induce his poetic imagery and allowed him to feel apart from and above the crowd, able to be or do anything. You will see, however, that he found this damaging and isolating as well as pleasurable.

Really the Blues
Mezz Mezzrow
Bernard Wolfe

It's a funny thing about marihuana—when you first begin smoking it you see things in a wonderful soothing, easygoing new light. All of a sudden the world is stripped of its dirty gray shrouds and becomes one big bellyful of giggles, a spherical laugh, bathed in brilliant, sparkling colors that hit you like a heatwave. Nothing leaves you cold anymore; there's a humorous tickle and great meaning in the least little thing, the twitch of somebody's little finger or the click of a beer glass. All your pores open like funnels, your nerve-ends stretch their mouths wide, hungry and thirsty for new sights and sounds and sensations; and every sensation, when it comes, is the most exciting one you've ever had. You can't get enough of anything—you want to gobble up the whole goddamned universe just for an appetizer. Them first kicks are a killer, Jim.

From *Really the Blues* by Mezz Mezzrow and Bernard Wolfe. Copyright 1946 by Milton Mezzrow & Bernard Wolfe; reprinted by permission of the Harold Matson Company, Inc.

The Poem of Hashish
Charles Baudelaire

"What does one experience? What does one see? Wonderful things, eh? Amazing sights? Is it very beautiful? Very terrible? Very dangerous?"...

The intoxication of hashish ... will not bring us beyond the bounds of the natural dream. It is true that throughout its whole period the intoxication will be in the nature of a vast dream—by reason of the intensity of its colors and its rapid flow of mental images; but it will always retain the private tonality of the individual. The man wanted the dream, now the dream will govern the man; but this dream will certainly be the son of its father. ...

It is right then, that sophisticated persons, and also ignorant persons who are eager to make acquaintance with unusual delights, should be clearly told that they will find in hashish nothing miraculous, absolutely nothing but an exaggeration of the natural. The brain and organism on which hashish operates will produce only the normal phenomena peculiar to that individual—increased, admittedly, in number and force, but always faithful to their origin. A man will never escape

Reprinted by permission of The World Publishing Company from *The Essence of Laughter and Other Essays, Journals and Letters* by Charles Baudelaire, edited by Peter Quennell. Copyright © 1956 by Meridian Books, Inc.

from his destined physical and moral temperament: hashish will be a mirror of his impressions and private thoughts—a magnifying mirror, it is true, but only a mirror.

Let me now revert to the normal development of the intoxication. After the first phase of childish mirth comes a sort of momentary lull. But soon new adventures are heralded by a sensation of chilliness in the extremities (for some people this becomes an intense cold), and a great weakness in all the members. In your head, and throughout your being, you feel an embarrassing stupor and stupefaction. Your eyes bulge, as if under the pull, both physical and spiritual, of an implacable ecstasy. Your face is flooded with pallor. Your lips shrink and are sucked back into your mouth by that panting movement that characterizes the ambition of a man who is a prey to great projects, overwhelmed by vast thoughts, or gaining breath for some violent effort. The sides of the gullet cleave together, so to speak. The palate is parched with a thirst that it would be infinitely pleasant to satisfy, if only the delights of idleness were not still more agreeable, and did they not forbid the slightest disarrangement of the body's posture. Hoarse, deep sighs burst forth from your chest, as if your *old* body could not endure the desires and activity of your *new* soul. Now and then a jolt passes through you, making you twitch involuntarily. It is like one of those sharp sensations of falling that you experience at the end of a day's work, or on a stormy night just before finally falling asleep. . . .

Notes of music turn into numbers; and, if you are endowed with some aptitude for mathematics, the melody or harmony you hear, whilst retaining its pleasurable and sensuous character, transforms itself into a huge arithmetical process, in which numbers beget numbers, whilst you follow the successive stages of reproduction with inexplicable ease and an agility equal to that of the performer. . . .

Let us suppose that you are sitting and smoking. Your gaze rests a moment too long on the bluish clouds emerging from your pipe. The notion of a slow, steady, eternal evaporation will take hold of your mind, and soon you will apply this notion to your own thoughts and your own thinking substance. By a singular transposition of ideas, or mental play upon words, you will feel that you yourself are evaporating, and that your pipe (in which you are huddled and pressed down like the tobacco) has the strange *power to smoke you.*

Luckily this apparently interminable fancy has lasted only for a single minute—for a lucid interval, gained with a great effort, has enabled you to glance at the clock. But a new stream of ideas carries you away: it will hurl you along in its living vortex for a further minute; and this minute, too, will be an eternity, for the normal relation between time and the individual has been completely upset by the multitude and intensity of sensations and ideas. You seem to live several men's lives in the space of an hour. You resemble, do you not? a fantastic novel that is being lived instead of being written. There is no longer any fixed connection between your organs and their powers; and this fact, above all, is what makes this dangerous exercise, in which you lose your freedom, so very blameworthy. . . .

So by this time my hypothetical man, this soul of my choosing, has reached the pitch of joy and serenity at which he is *compelled* to admire himself. Every contradiction effaces itself, all the problems of philosophy become crystal-clear, or at least appear to be so. Everything is a matter for rejoicing. The fullness of his life at this moment inspires him with a disproportionate pride. A voice speaks within him (alas! it is his own), saying to him: "You are now entitled to consider yourself superior to all men; nobody knows, or could understand, all that you think and feel; men would be incapable even of appreciating the benevolence with which they inspire you. You are a king unrecognized by the passersby, a king who lives in the solitude of his own certainty. But what do you care? Do you not possess that sovereign pride which so ennobles the soul?". . .

Stronger Hallucinogens

The synthetic hallucinogens, such as LSD, are best described by Alan Watts (excerpted below) and by Tom Wolfe in his remarkable book *The Electric Kool-Aid Acid Test.*

In the mid-sixties the so-called psychedelic drugs, particularly the synthetic LSD, were very popular, especially among middle-class high school and college students. After a great deal of publicity on the ill effects of LSD, the scientific evidence for any statements is still uncertain. Yet its use has diminished partly because of its severely bad effects on some people, because the impurities in its manufacture cause physical and emotional damage, and because of its gross misuse by some people on unsuspecting others. It has been claimed that LSD sometimes causes permanent psychological damage (actually producing psychosis and sometimes leading to suicide) and physical damage (leading to birth defects and chromosome breakdown), but there is much less reliable scientific information about the effects of LSD than about those of most other drugs. It is possible that lingering psychological reactions to LSD are occasioned not by the drug itself but by the attempts of a user who is more or less unstable to cope with the profound changes he experiences during the relatively long (eight to ten hours) period of the drug's action. Likewise, there is no proof that LSD has any permanent physical effect on people. Under controlled therapeutic conditions, LSD has for some time been useful in treating various psychological disorders. It has, of course, played a disastrous part in the experiences of a number of emotionally disturbed adolescents. Though LSD is not addictive, the practice of taking the drug has become a way of life for some and a way of avoiding life for others; and though for some it has long-range effects, often terrifying, there is so far no way of knowing whether or not any individual will be susceptible to "bad trips" or recurring effects. Because of its considerable impact among young people, the following selections on various aspects of the psychedelic experience should be of interest to readers of this book.

A Psychedelic Experience: Fact or Fantasy?
Alan Watts

To come . . . to an effective evaluation of these [psychedelic] chemicals and the changed states of consciousness and perception which they induce, we must begin with a highly detailed and accurate description of what they do, both from the standpoint of the subject and of the neutral observer, despite the fact that in experiments of this kind it becomes startlingly obvious that the observer cannot be neutral, and that the posture of "objectivity" is itself one of the determinants of the outcome. As the physicist well knows, to observe a process is to change it. But the importance of careful description is that it may help us to understand the kind or level of reality upon which these changes in consciousness are taking place.

For undoubtedly they are happening. The dancing, kaleidoscopic arabesques which appear before closed eyes are surely an observation of *some* reality, though not, perhaps, in the physical world outside the skin. But are they rearranged memories? Structures in the nervous system? Archetypes of the collective unconscious? Electronic patterns such as often dance on the TV screen? What, too, are the fernlike structures which are so often seen—the infinitude of branches upon branches upon branches, or analogous shapes? Are these a glimpse of some kind of analytical process in the brain, similar to the wiring patterns in a computer? We really have no idea, but the more carefully observers can record verbal descriptions and visual pictures of these phenomena, the more likely that neurologists or physicists or even mathematicians will turn up the physical processes to which they correspond. The point is that these visions are not *mere* imagination, as if there had ever been anything mere about imagination! The human mind does not just perversely invent utterly useless images out of nowhere at all. Every image tells us something about the mind or the brain or the organism in which it is found.

The effects of the psychedelics vary so much from person to person and from situation to situation that it is well nigh impossible to say with any exactitude that they create certain particular and invariable changes of consciousness. I would not go so far as to say that the chemical effects are simply featureless, providing no more than a vivid mirror to reflect the fantasies and unconscious dispositions of the individuals involved. For there are certain types of change which are usual enough to be considered characteristic of psychedelics: the sense of slowed or arrested time, and the alteration of "ego boundary"—that is, of the sensation of one's own identity.

The feeling that time has relaxed its pace may, to some extent, be the result of having set aside the better part of a day just to observe one's own consciousness, and to watch for interesting changes in one's perception of such ordinary things as reflected

"A Psychedelic Experience—Fact or Fantasy?" by Alan Watts from *LSD: The Consciousness-Expanding Drug* edited by David Solomon. Copyright © 1964 by David Solomon. Reprinted by permission of G.P. Putnam's Sons.

sunlight on the floor, the grain in wood, the texture of linen, or the sound of voices across the street. My own experience has never been of a distortion of these perceptions, as in looking at oneself in a concave mirror. It is rather that every perception becomes—to use a metaphor—more resonant. The chemical seems to provide consciousness with a sounding box, or its equivalent, for all the senses, so that sight, touch, taste, smell, and imagination are intensified like the voice of someone singing in the bathtub.

The change of ego boundary sometimes begins from this very resonance of the senses. The intensification and deepening of color, sound and texture lends them a peculiar transparency. One seems to be aware of them more than ever as vibration, electronic and luminous. As this feeling develops it appears that these vibrations are continuous with one's own consciousness and that the external world is in some odd way inside the mind-brain. It appears, too, with overwhelming obviousness, that the inside and the outside do not exclude one another and are not actually separate. They go together; they imply one another, like front and back, in such a way that they become polarized. As, therefore, the poles of a magnet are the extremities of a single body, it appears that the inside and the outside, the subject and the object, the self and the world, the voluntary and the involuntary, are the poles of a single process which is my real and hitherto unknown self. This new self has no location. It is not something like a traditional soul, using the body as a temporary house. To ask *where* it is, is like asking where the universe is. Things in space have a where, but the thing that space is in doesn't need to be anywhere. It is simply what there is, just plain basic isness!

How easily, then, an unsophisticated person might exclaim, "I have just discovered that I am God!" Yet if, during such an experience, one retains any critical faculties at all, it will be clear that anyone else in the same state of consciousness will also be God. It will be clear, too, that the "God" in question is not the God of popular theology, the Master Technician who controls, creates, and understands everything in the universe. Were it so, a person in this state should be able to give correct answers to all questions of fact. He would know the exact height of Mount Whitney in millimeters. On the other hand, this awareness of a deeper and universal self would correspond exactly with that other type of God which mystics have called the "divine ground" of the universe, a sort of intelligent and super-conscious space containing the whole cosmos as a mirror contains images. . . . though the analogy fails

in so far as it suggests something immense: we cannot picture sizelessness.

Anyone moving into completely unfamiliar territory may at first misunderstand and misinterpret what he sees, as is so evident from the first impressions of visitors to foreign lands where patterns of culture differ radically from their own. When Europeans depicted their first impressions of China, they made the roofs of houses exaggeratedly curly and people's eyes slanted at least 45 degrees from the horizontal. Contrariwise, the Japanese saw all Europeans as red-haired, sunken-eyed goblins with immensely long noses. But the unfamiliarities of foreign cultures are nothing to those of one's own inner workings. What is there in the experience of clear blue sky to suggest the structure of the optical nerves? Comparably, what is there in the sound of a human voice on the radio to suggest the formations of tubes and transistors? I raise this question because it is obvious that any chemically induced alteration of the nervous system must draw the attention of that system to itself. I am not normally aware that the sensation of blue sky is a state of the eyes and brain, but if I see wandering spots that are neither birds nor flying saucers, I know that these are an abnormality within the optical system itself. In other words, I am enabled, by virtue of this abnormality, to become conscious of one of the instruments of consciousness. But this is most unfamiliar territory.

White Rabbit

Grace Slick

One pill makes you larger
And one pill makes you small
And the ones that mother gives you
Don't do anything at all.
Go ask Alice
When she's ten feet tall.

And if you go chasing rabbits
And you know you're going to fall,
Tell them all who got silken colored hair
Has given you the call,
Call Alice
When she was just small.

The following excerpt from *Richie* describes the facts about barbiturates. It is an accurate account of a family tragedy that centers around addiction to drugs.

Richie

Thomas Thompson

Barbiturate is the family name given to drugs whose ingredients include barbituric acid and whose purpose is to depress the central nervous system. This family has two branches, sedative-hypnotics and tranquilizers. . . . The branch of the barbiturate family most favored on the street is the kind known as short- or intermediate-acting. The three most popular in this group, their trade names as familiar as breakfast cereals to a good percentage of America's young, are secobarbital, which Eli Lilly and Co. manufactures under the brand name Seconal; pentobarbital, which Abbott makes under the brand name Nembutal; and amobarbital, which Lilly puts out under the name Amytal. . . .

Barbiturates rarely have sinister parentage. They are, in fact, usually pure, carefully produced products of great American industry. They are enormous profit items for distinguished pharmaceutical houses. They account for 20 percent of all prescriptions written in the United States in 1971. They are supposed to be obtained only by doctor's prescription, sold only by pharmacists, kept under lock and key until dispensed.

But somewhere, somehow, something went awry because in 1970 the drug houses of America, according to President Nixon in a speech before the AMA, churned out *five billion* barbiturate pills, of these almost half, enough to put the entire country to sleep forever, were unaccounted for and were presumably distributed in the street. . . .

But somehow the barbiturate story did not get around. Rather like a tumor growing quietly and unnoticed in the leg bone while doctors worked on something else at the neck, barbiturate use and abuse multiplied in the late 1960s and early 1970s until the malignancy metastasized throughout the body of America. "There are supposed to be 500,000 heroin addicts in this country," says a Nassau County narcotics officer. "Then there have to be a million barb freaks." A Los Angeles psychiatrist, testifying before a Senate Committee, reported in 1972 that barbiturates were the number-one drug problem among the young of this country, surpassing marijuana, heroin, and LSD. He predicted that 1972 would be "the year of the Barb."

"Why is this so?" asked this psychiatrist, Dr. Sidney Cohen, Chief of UCLA's Center for Study of Mind-Altering Drugs and among the nation's more sophisticated minds in the field of youth and pills. He was testifying before Senator Birch Bayh's Senate Subcommittee on Juvenile Delinquency, which held hearings on barbiturates in late 1971 and early 1972. "For the youngster, barbiturates are a more reliable 'high' and less detectable than marihuana. They are less strenuous than LSD, less 'freaky' than amphetamines (speed), less expensive than heroin.

"A schoolboy can 'drop a red' and spend the day in a dreamy, floating state of awareness untroubled by reality. It is drunkenness without the odor of alcohol. It is escape for the price of one's lunch money."

[The following excerpts give the flavor of the drug and its effects on an all-too-typical schoolboy and his family.]

Richie's interest in animals started to wane. He gave away his snakes and hamsters, or let them go. When Boots, the family's second Boston bull terrier, died, Richie had neither grief, nor attention for the large gray poodle, Bridget, that Carol bought as replacement. The squirrels still waited for Richie to come home and feed them, but more and more he ignored them or told Russell to do it. His room for so many years a naturalist's lair, underwent a dramatic change of character.

The extensive library of nature books went onto the top shelf of his closet and began to gather dust. Once they had been all over his room, open on his desk, on his bed, their pages thumbed and underlined. In their place came the decor of the youth culture: posters of rock stars, ticket stubs from pop concerts, a display of drawings from an underground artist whose work seemed drenched in drug-induced horror. Specializing in monstrous creatures, he drew modern half-man, half-animal grotesqueries with electrified hair, claws for hands, and violence as avocation. One such apparition was drawn seated in a bathtub with daggers and blood about him; the impression was that he had disemboweled himself.

Richie carefully stapled these drawings on the paneled wall directly in front of his bed. As he lay there, he could look at them without moving his head on his pillow. After attending one of his mother's charity dances, Richie delightedly collected the white styrofoam balls that had been used for decorations. Splashing them with Day-Glo paints, he hung them from the ceiling of his room. Somehow he found money to buy a black light, which, switched on, transformed his chamber into a sanctum of psychedelia. Everything was precise. The mementos were not thrown helter-skelter on the wall. Richie placed them with almost geometrical care. His decorative labors produced the desired effect. One friend told Richie, "You have the best room of anybody." They began to come, as Carol always said they would.

To only a few of these, his new friends, did Richie show the prize attraction of his quarters—a small storage chamber at the back of his closet that he had discovered one day by accident while putting his shoes in a neat row. There was an opening about eighteen inches square covered with a nailed piece of plywood. Removing the plywood, Richie was elated. Within was a small secret area, perhaps an architectural blunder, a place big enough for him to lie in—six feet long by three feet wide by four feet high. To improve it, Richie lined the walls with crinkled aluminum foil. On the ceiling he placed rock posters. On the floor went a cast-off single mattress. The opening to the private place he disguised with his shoe rack.

He took to entering his hideaway and lying on the mattress, with only an eerie crack of light from the closet and the glow of his pot pipe to illumine him. There he could escape his parents' calls. Often Carol would announce dinner, knowing that Richie was in the house, hearing the rock music from his room that announced his presence, but puzzled when he did not respond. When she went to his room, he would not be there.

Finally George discovered the place and dismantled it, annoyed that Richie would crawl inside a wall to hide from his parents. Pulling down the aluminum-foil walls, he found a small cache and, in it, a piece of hardened substance in a plastic sandwich bag.

"What is this?" George demanded, suspecting it was important because of the elaborate method by which it had been hidden.

"I don't know," the boy replied. "Mud, I guess."

"I'd guess it's more than that," said George. "Or you wouldn't take such pains to hide it."

"It's hash," Richie finally said, explaining that it was hashish he was keeping for a friend. "It isn't mine," said Richie, "I swear."

Whatever, George angrily threw it out, despite Richie's protestations that he had no right to destroy someone else's property. And he nailed up the secret place. . . .

During this autumn of 1969 there developed a shortage of marihuana not only in East Meadow, but in much of America. It was probably due to Operation Intercept, the attempt by President Nixon to close the Mexican border to marihuana smuggling. With a flurry of headlines, television lights, and regular press releases, the project promised—with the cooperation of the Mexican government—to seal off the principal avenue of marihuana into the United States. While Nixon earned the politically attractive reputation of a foe to marihuana—a few arrests were indeed made and several thousand kilos of grass discovered and confiscated—an ironical development occurred.

During the brief American marihuana famine —it would take two or three months before illegal traffickers could develop alternate lines of supply from Colombia, Jamaica, several African countries, and by new routes from Mexico—some of the drug's regular users looked for a substitute. This flies in the face of those advocates who contend that using marihuana absolutely does not lead to the desire for something else, something more potent. In the majority of cases, this is no doubt true. In Richie's case it was not.[1]

Brick encountered the grass shortage of 1969 when he met with his regular dealer, a youth named Corley who worked now and then as a roofer. Later Corley would become a heroin addict and, while trying to work with a head full of the narcotic, would fall off a house and land squarely on his head, causing permanent brain damage. After that the kids called him Zombie.

At the time of their meeting, Corley had no marijuana to sell.

"Wanna try some ups instead?" suggested Corley.

Brick shook his head. He had bought some amphetamines a few months earlier and they had done nothing for him. "I can't get off on ups," he said.

"You can on these," said Corley. "These are Dexedrines, real pharmaceuticals." He showed Brick the capsules, brown on one end, clear on the other. "You know they're real when they have SKF printed on them."

Brick bought twenty. At the time they cost five for one dollar. On his way home, he popped five into his mouth and, when no more than ten minutes had passed, was startled at how rapidly the rush had come. "It's far out," he told Richie that night. "Faster than grass and a helluva lot better."

But Richie declined to take any. It was the pattern of his drug experimentation that he always declined, vigorously, any new plateau.

However, as his pattern also went, a few days later he weakened under Brick's salesmanship. The two boys were at the home of a girl Brick knew, sitting on stools in her kitchen.

While the girl watched with interest, Brick pulled five Dexedrines from his jeans and ate them with ceremony. Then he offered three to Richie. His outstretched palm was clearly a dare.

Brick later related the story to a friend:

"Richie grabs the ups and eats them quick. Then we sat there looking at each other. The chick was waiting for something to happen, like maybe our hair was supposed to stand on end, or our eyes would turn red and spin like a merry-go-round. Pretty soon the chick's mother comes into the kitchen, and, about that time, Richie and me got off. Pow! We were getting paranoid quick. I could see Richie was scared, but I couldn't stop talking. About everything and nothing. You do that on ups. You rattle on like crazy. This old mother was staring at us, like she knew something was happening. Something was, man. We were in outer space.

"Richie flashes me a signal he wants to get out of there fast. We go over to my house, and my mother insists on both of us having dinner. She always fixes a big meal. Richie stares at this heaping plate, and he gets one tiny piece of lettuce and a little bit of meat down when he pulls his chair back and runs out of the room. I follow him, and he's upstairs white as a sheet. He's trembling. He throws up all over my room. Jeez, he'd only taken three. Then he starts crying and I don't know what to do."

Richie was frightened. The next day he told Brick he did not like "the feeling of ups" and that he would never take them again. "I don't dig being hyperactive and paranoid," he said. "Grass is better."

His attitude towards ups was reinforced when Brick, unaffected by Richie's disavowal, went on a two-week binge. Taking an astonishing fifty amphetamines a day, Brick whipped about the neighborhood as if shot from a cannon. He told Richie he felt like a rubber band stretched so tightly it might break. "When it breaks," Brick said, "I'll come down." But deep into his two-week trip, Brick began to hallucinate. After forty-eight hours of no sleep, he telephoned Richie in panic. "I get in bed," he said, "and I turn off the lights, and I close my eyes, and I try to push out all my thoughts to get my mind totally blank—only then I suddenly think to myself, 'I'd like to see a monster,' and I think on this, and sure enough, the monster appears on my wall. In color, too!"

At the end of the binge, during which he lost thirty pounds (amphetamines are sometimes used as diet pills), Brick swore off them. But a few weeks later, Corley the roofer offered his good client some "downs," street slang for barbiturates. Other names are "reds," "rainbows," "blue devils," "peanuts," "yellow jackets," "goofballs," "double trouble," and "nimbies."

"These are Seconals," said Corley proudly. "The best." He pointed out the tiny word *Lilly* printed on the bright red, bullet-shaped capsules. Seconals, a brand name for secobarbital, are made by Eli Lilly & Co. They are powerful pills with various reputable medical uses, chiefly to induce sleep. One can usually not only knock out an adult for a full night of hard, deep slumber, but give him a slightly groggy head the next morning. In the late 1960s the drug culture discovered that a unique, albeit frightening alteration of the mental state could be obtained from using secobarbitals, often heightened by washing them down with whiskey or wine. But the rite was perilous; one too many of the capsules and the celebrant could sleep forever. The combination of barbs and alcohol could also be fatal.

"You must be lame," said Richie, when once again tempted by Brick. The two were walking from Richie's house to an enormous discount house in a shopping center one mile away.

"You're the one who's lame if you don't try these," said Brick. He walked over to an ice-water fountain at a service station, filled his mouth with water, and waited until he was a block away to take five Seconals. He had three left, but Richie remained adamant.

"I'm scared of downs," he said frankly. "I don't wanna OD or something."

"You're not gonna OD, dummy," said Brick. "I'm with you. You'd have to take twenty to OD, anyway."

Richie shook his head once more. "I'll stick to grass."

"Grass is good," Brick agreed. "Great grass is fantastic. But you can't depend on it. You can always get downs. They're around. And there's less hassle. You told me yourself you still hate the smoke when you do grass. Downs are cool. You see a cop walking toward us and you've got a joint in your pocket, what are you gonna do? Eat it? you'd vomit. But you got downs on you and you *can* eat 'em. Fast. If the cop saw you, he couldn't prove anything. You could say they were M&M's."

Brick's proselytizing was typical. He was not trying to seduce his friend into becoming addicted to pills and thus dependent on him for supply. He was not a pusher in the classic sense, for the sallow man in the overcoat lurking outside school fences had disappeared, if indeed he ever existed. Kids turned one another on in East Meadow in 1969, for little reason other than social reinforcement. Brick needed an ally for his adventure, as any man does when venturing into an unknown.

A Nassau County narcotics officer once said that the thing that puzzled him most about the drug culture was "the glamour attached to it." How, wondered the cop, did drug-taking cease being a dark affair and suddenly transform into "a phenomenon of teen-age status"?[2]

Brick Pavall's testimonial and the dare contained in it were effective, as they always were with Richie. The younger boy suddenly stopped on the road and faced his friend. "Gimme those mothers," he said. He put the three red capsules into his mouth, one by one, swallowing them without water.

Twenty minutes later, Richie and Brick were, to use their favorite word of behavioral description, "wasted." The two staggered down the street in swerves and arcs. Later that night Brick telephoned Richie to see if the downs had worn off. Richie said they had, but not before he had difficulty getting through dinner with his parents. "They kept looking at me like I was a freak show," said Richie. "All the time I was afraid my head would fall in my plate."

"They shoulda seen you on Hempstead Turnpike about four o'clock," said Brick. "You couldn't walk, much less talk good. You were like some old drunk. Doing downs is the same as being drunk, you know. You either get in a rowdy mood, or a nice, mellow mood. Me, I get courage and I can talk

to any chick in Ryan's bar and try to make it with her."

Richie yawned. It was only a few minutes past nine, but, he said, he could hardly keep his eyes open.

"You'll sleep well tonight, that's for sure," said Brick. "Me, I'm gonna take some more downs. I like to take about five around this time and stay up till one. I'll wake up tomorrow morning early and take two more—only I get off better and quicker the next morning on only two than on five the night before."

"It was really a weird thing that happened this afternoon," said Richie. He started to begin another sentence, but he yawned once more, said good-bye, and hung up. Barbs are, after all, sleeping pills. . . .

Psychiatrists believe that in most human beings there is a repository of violence and aggressive behavior, but the brain throws up a barrier, a fence to keep such in check under normal conditions. Secobarbital acts quickly upon the central nervous system to depress it. The drug will, of course, induce drowsiness and finally sleep. But it can also, through overdosage, rip down this mental fence and permit hostility, even violence to rush forth. In hospital operating rooms, personnel often must cope with the patient who, having received sedation for surgery, suddenly rouses from his half-sleep and tries to attack a nurse, or climb off the table with a torrent of curses. In his normal life, the patient could not conceive of such behavior.

In the first few months he used downs, Richie rarely took them before occasions when he would have to face his parents. Usually it was before going out with Brick, or on the rare evening when Carol and George were out. Thus the parents did not witness the sudden flames that leaped up within their son. Richie used barbiturates for more than a year before George and Carol became aware of them. There were no needle marks on his arms for a mother to spot, only troubling changes in his attitude and behavior. But were these different from any adolescent's? wondered the parents. That communication with Richie was becoming more and more difficult George passed off as the generation gap he read about and saw dramatized so often on his color TV. . . .

Now the police were gone, and the young people went away, and Richie and his father were alone. George prepared to leave the house, but Richie began to taunt him. He draped himself against the kitchen door and stopped George from passing.

"Someday," said Richie, "I'm really gonna kick the shit out of you."

George lowered his head and attempted to go through the door. Richie shot out a hand to stop him. "You hear me? Someday you're gonna get it."

Seizing his son's hand, George pushed it away, his face white. He backed up and took a stand. "OK," snapped George. "Let's get it on right now. Man to man. Come on." George raised his fists.

Richie was not sure how to react. He seemed stunned. George flattened the palm of his hand and slapped his son. "Now you've got a reason to fight back," said George.

On the end table next to the couch rested a pair of Carol's mending scissors. Richie seized them and held them up. They were golden scissors that Carol had once used to create the masquerades for Richie when he was young.

George felt fear. Richie came at him, grabbed his arms, pinned one behind him, put the scissors to his father's throat. "Motherfucker, when you and me fight," he hissed, "it ain't gonna be fair. Some night when you least expect it, these scissors'll come at your throat. Only next time . . ."

George broke free. He dropped his hands to indicate he wanted no more fight. "Richie! Sit down! We've got to talk."

"I'm fuckin'-A tired of talking! I've had enough of this shit. I'm tired of everything!" Richie threw the scissors onto the end table. George watched as they gouged out a small chunk of wood and fell clattering to the floor.

"Please, son. We're killing each other."

Richie glanced at the fallen scissors. "I don't know if I should do you in now, or let my friends do it later."

This time George fled the house. Richie sank to the floor and began to cry as he heard his father drive away.

George drove blindly through the streets of his town, playing the scene over and over again in his mind. He drove past the precinct police station, almost stopping, then pressing the accelerator. Finally he saw a candy store and stopped and dialed his home. He wanted to try, once more, to talk to Richie. But the number was busy. He stayed in the telephone booth fifteen minutes, trying to get through.

Hanging up in frustration, he began to drive to the junior high where Carol was working. Maybe she would know what to do. He glanced at his speedometer. He was doing seventy in a thirty-mile-per-hour zone.

Richie first called Fritz and began to brag of the incident. "My old man was scared shitless. He thought he was dead . . ." Then his words began to tumble out, dipping and diving like a radio fading in and out. When George heard them late that night, Richie seemed incoherent on the tape: "I kicked the shit out of some kid in the cafeteria today . . . because I heard he gave my name to the cops. . . . I said something to him . . . I wouldn't hurt him . . . but I grabbed him by the neck. . . . He wouldn't answer me! They've got to listen to me, man! . . . I said, 'Hey, motherfucker, you gonna answer me?' He was like scared, man. I popped him in the eye to make him look at me . . . and he didn't do nothing so I popped him again. And he started fighting and a bunch of people broke it up . . . some fuckin' Jews. . . . I was holding my coat over my shoulders and one of them knocked it off and I said, 'Can't you say you're sorry, you little cocksucker?' and he said, 'I am sorry, Richie.' and I said, 'Watch it,' and . . . Did you ever pull a knife on your old lady? That's the same thing as what I did. . . ."

Fritz was trying to interrupt the rambling monologue, but Richie gave him no entry.

"I know you wouldn't hurt your old lady," plunged on Richie. "But that's what I did today. I swear I couldn't help it man." Richie paused briefly; his voice broke and his words were sobs. "He called me names in front of my friends. He called me a dope addict . . . I couldn't help it . . . I was stoned on Amytals . . . I only took one, but I was stoned from last night. . . . All of a sudden he smacked me in the face . . . I can't take that from him . . . so I picked up those scissors . . . 'If we're gonna fight,' I say, 'it ain't gonna be clean . . .' O God, O Godgodgodgod godgod. . . ."

The line went dead. Richie kept holding the phone in his hand. He sobbed for several moments—on the tape—before he dialed another number.

Still sniffling, he waited for Carol to dry her hands and come to his aid.

"Ma?"

"Yes. Who is this?"

"Ma. This is RICHARD." His voice was full out, like a man shouting across an overseas cable from East Meadow to Moscow. "Ma . . . I got KICKED out of school today."

"Yes? How come?" Carol's voice tensed.

"Cause I wised off to a teacher. They can't do that . . . just because I'm failing. Ma, I'm a senior. I'm supposed to graduate." Richie could not keep his voice in check; it began to crawl sideways. "Then Daddy came home with two cops."

"Why, Richard?"

"Cause he thought we were having a POT party. And they came bustin' in, and . . ."

"And?"

"And we were just drinking. I'm at home now, and he smacked me in the face and I pulled the scissors on him. I didn't . . . I didn't *touch* him with it. . . . I just punched him in the face."

"*Where* are you?" The line crackled with static. Carol wanted to ask her son to hang up and get a new connection, but she feared she would lose him. She strained to hear his voice.

"I'm right here. At home. This is where it happened. This is where it started. Two girls and two other guys. Daddy started getting loud, calling me names in front of these people. So I told him to shut up . . ."

"Richard . . . are you . . . *on* anything?"

"What?" It took him a moment to absorb his mother's meaning. "No . . ." Once more his voice went out of control. It cracked. A sob caught his throat and dragged its way into the phone. "I think I'm crazy, Ma . . ."

"Who's crazy?"

"I'm crazy!"

"No, you're not." Carol's voice trembled even as she denied her son's diagnosis of himself. But she feared it was true. Richie was going mad on the telephone, and Carol was having to listen to it.

"Young white male was discovered lying in supine position at foot of basement steps, clad in dark blue dungarees and dark blue turtleneck cotton shirt. Shirt was stained with blood over left chest. Blood smears over left upper arm. Upon lifting shirt, there was an oval penetrating wound in left chest representing entrance wound. An apparent exit wound on posterior chest below left scapula."

[How did it happen that a father whose son was the most important part of his life ended by shooting his son?]

In detail, George took the detectives over the story of his life, and of his years with Richie. He told everything he could remember leading up to the moment when Richie stood at the top of the stairs. He said he was certain that drugs had altered his son's personality and turned him mad.

Q.   Was your son high today when he came down the stairs?

A.   Today he was definitely high. He told his mother—when I came up the first time and heard the crash, he was high. He said he

had been down into his room, where he took a few Seconals.

Q.   Did he appear wobbly as he came down the stairs?

A.   I guess, I would say slightly wobbly, swaying.

Q.   Do you feel that you could have disarmed him?

A.   I was scared to death of him.

Q.   Well, wasn't he in such a condition when he had the ice pick that the ice pick flew out of his hand?

A.   Yes.

Q.   Then what about the knife? What did you feel?

A.   I don't know. If I thought I could have disarmed him . . . I definitely didn't think I could disarm him, because if I thought I could have disarmed him, I would have tried without shooting him. But the thought of my dying and leaving him to be the head of my household and telling my wife and other son what to do was something I really couldn't—

Q.   But when you fired, you fired right at his chest?

A.   Yes. I didn't shoot to wound him. All these things went through my mind, such as, if you shoot to wound him, what happens if you cripple him? Then you've got a mad animal on your hands. I felt I had to do what I did.

Q.   Is there anything else you want to put on the record?

A.   If there was any way in the world around what I did, I would have taken it.

A.   Okay. Thanks very much, Mr. Diener.

Carol was not permitted to see her husband until almost midnight, after the detective had finished questioning him. She had spent the hours at her home after George was taken away, making coffee for the investigating officers. Then she went to the police station and sat on a hard bench outside the homicide office. June Marck took a detective aside and warned that Carol had had a heart condition since childhood, that she must be treated gently or face the possibility of an attack.

When George was led out, Carol went to him. They embraced. George held her tightly. "I'm sorry," he said. "There was no other way."

Carol bit her lip. She wanted to be strong at this moment in support of her husband. "I know . . . If I hadn't been home when it happened, I might have blamed you," she said. "I would have hated you. I would have taken Richard's side, like I usually did."

Article Footnotes

---

1. Dr. Victoria Sears, a psychiatrist who had worked with youngsters at the Nassau County Drug Abuse Council since 1966, noticed something of alarm in the autumn of 1969.

"During those several weeks when marijuana was scarce, and expensive," she says, "a lot of kids out here turned to amphetamines, barbiturates, and even heroin. These were solid middle-class youngsters, not delinquent blue-collar gang members. The fact of the matter is that a lot of addicts I am treating today, in 1972, date their use of harder drugs from Operation Intercept."

2. In a 1972 magazine article called "The Suburban Hustlers," writer Jack Shepherd interviewed a teen-age drug salesman who lived not far from Richie Diener. The quotes he elicited from the youngster were chilling: "When I first started getting high in Freeport, there were maybe fifteen people in town who also got high. It was really a new thing. Now, in all these towns everybody's getting high. It's all over. Seven years ago (in 1965) out here, it was like the real suburbs. Kids were still into surfing and beer drinking. Drugs were unheard of. In fact, kids who used drugs were put down by other kids: 'Ah, he's a junkie.'

"Now, it's the opposite. Kids say, 'Don't worry about him; he's cool, he's got good connections.' It's the complete reverse. Now kids say. 'Ah, he don't get high. Don't hang around him. He's lame. He don't know what's happening'."

"Everything's inside out. The suburbs are the city now."

Hard Drugs

The hard drugs, all obtained from the opium poppy, are opium, morphine, and heroin. They are extremely addictive both physiologically and psychologically. That is, the body learns to tolerate the drug, so that greater and greater doses are required at decreasing intervals of time in order to experience its effects. Withdrawal is exceedingly painful for most people: among the reactions are stomach cramps, vomiting, diarrhea, muscle pains, dizziness, and nausea.

Drug addiction is illegal and very expensive. Drug sellers are often part of a vast network of underworld crime. The hard drug user lives with the constant fear not only of arrest but of the criminals he is forced to deal with. There is also the constant fear of being forced into crime himself in order to support his addiction.

Hard drug use was largely a phenomenon of the poorest classes until recently, when the middle class, black and white, began more and more to turn to drugs. Recent years have also seen the young, in colleges, high schools, and junior high schools, become involved. Last year in New York there were a number of deaths from heroin of children below ten years of age.

Because the dangers of hard drug use are very widely known today, most of the adolescents and adults who turn to hard drugs do so out of pressure from seemingly unbearable circumstances, out of an overwhelming need to conform with a hard-drug-taking group, or out of the illusion that they somehow have the omnipotence to escape addition. All of these reasons in-

dicate disturbance. And addiction is bound to make the disturbance much more severe. If the factors that led to drug use have not been ameliorated or adjusted to by the person who has quit using drugs, it is extremely likely that he will go on drugs again. There are people who have lived most of their short lives as hard drug users and whose entire outlook centers around how to get the next "fix." This need frequently leads them to crime—theft, burglary, sometimes murder—and lying is an essential component of the drug taker's life, as it is of the alcoholic's. Early deaths are commonplace among hard drug users. As the average age level of hard drug users has gone down, the death rate among users has gone up sharply. Overdoses, inadequate supply, faulty needles, adulterated drugs, and dirty suppliers are some of the causes of the rise in deaths.

The typical hard drug user is withdrawn and very shy. His sense of identity is tenuous at best, and his infantile needs were never sufficiently satisfied to permit him to cope with adolescent or adult life. He is desperately lonely, unable to communicate, and requires immediate gratification—either, like many poverty cases, because he has never had enough or, like many from a more privileged background, because he has never learned how to deal with the frustration of doing without or waiting. Drugs relieve him for the moment of his pains, fears, and self-doubts; he revels in a brief period of euphoria, until the drug wears off and he has to take himself as he was and with the added knowledge that he will in a short time be driven to take another dose, that he may have to beg, borrow, or steal to get it, that he is even less in command of his destiny than he was before, and that he is becoming increasingly dangerous to himself and others. Resolutions to stop, however bravely made, disintegrate when the need for the next fix becomes strong, and he is aware that he lies not only to others but to himself in order to live with himself at all. The despair he felt before taking the drug is thus compounded, and only more of the drug seems to offer an escape. What can be done to break the cycle?

One method that has been successful, especially with adult addicts, employs a synthetic narcotic called methadone as a substitute for heroin. It relieves the user's craving for the drug and prevents withdrawal symptoms. It does not produce the highs that heroin produces and allows the user to participate in everyday activities during withdrawal. It is in itself addictive, however, and many therapists maintain that unless the user's dependency needs are themselves overcome, unless he learns to live with a certain amount of deprivation, methadone treatment is merely substituting one form of slavery for another. The supporters of methadone feel that it is by far the least of the possible evils, that because cures of hard drug use are discouragingly few and slow, methadone treatment saves many lives and buys time for rehabilitation.

The best treatment results so far seem to have come out of small therapeutic communities which, whether run by ex-addicts themselves or by nonaddicted professionals, are group-centered and organized on a system of increasing the individual addict's responsibilities to the group and to himself as he becomes capable of accepting them. Housekeeping, school or work attendance, and other forms of responsibility to the group and to oneself are the criteria which determine a person's status in the therapeutic community. At first the addict spends all his time in the community. He gradually comes to spend less and less time in the protected setting, though it seems to be important, even many years after being cured, for ex-addicts to continue to involve themselves in helping other addicts—through educational work in the therapeutic communities, assistance to addicts in finding jobs, or work as group leaders or as housemothers or housefathers in the communities. An important element of the work of these communities involves representatives of the larger community (school, court, and police officials) and the families of the addicts, in an effort to prevent ex-addicts from returning to the same situations that sent them to drugs in the first place. There is a need for skilled teachers to work with adolescents and with uneducated adults in these programs: addicts are often people who have not had the will to follow their studies, though they may be quite able and even gifted. The opportunity to return to an education can be an effective element of treatment, especially with young people. But even in well-organized therapeutic communities the chances of an addict's finding a lasting cure are uncertain, though the possibilities are greater there than elsewhere.

The following selections describe the individual experiences of two drug users, one of them on morphine, the other on heroin—both of them miserable.

Deposition: Testimony Concerning a Sickness
William Burroughs

I lived in one room in the Native Quarter of Tangier. I had not taken a bath in a year nor changed my clothes or removed them except to stick a needle every hour in the fibrous grey wooden flesh of terminal addiction. I never cleaned or dusted the room. Empty ampule boxes and garbage piled to the ceiling. Light and water long since turned off for non-payment. I did absolutely nothing. I could look at the end of my shoe for eight hours. I was only roused to action when the hourglass of junk ran out.

If a friend came to visit—and they rarely did since who or what was left to visit—I sat there not caring that he had entered my field of vision—a grey screen always blanker and fainter—and not caring when he walked out of it. If he had died on the spot I would have sat there looking at my shoe waiting to go through his pockets. Wouldn't you? Because I never had enough junk—no one ever does. Thirty grains of morphine a day and it still was not enough. And long waits in front of the drugstore. Delay is a rule in the junk business. The Man is never on time. This is no accident. There are no accidents in the junk world. The addict is taught again and again exactly what will happen if he does not score for his junk ration. Get up that money or else. And suddenly my habit began to jump and jump. Forty, sixty grains a day. And it still was not enough. And I could not pay.

Down These Mean Streets
Piri Thomas

"Hey Waneko, hey man, wait up."

Waneko waited and I crossed the street. He saw me like I was and said, "What's happening?"

"I'm sick, man."

"Yeah, you've been looking like real shit warmed over for a couple of days."

"Yeah, that *tecata's* got to me. Jesus Christ, man, I'm hooked and I've been trying to get off but I can't, like if I'm in love with this bitch."

I sniffed and thought how I wasn't gonna get hooked. How I was gonna control it. Why the hell did I have to start playing with stuff? Who wants to be a man at that rate? Hell! All for the feeling of belonging, for the price of being called "one of us." Isn't there a better way to make the scene and be accepted on the street without having to go through hell?

I wiped my nose. The water kept oozing out and my eyes were blurred. My guts were getting wilder all the damn time.

"Man, Waneko, I gotta quit. I just gotta quit."

"Look, man, don't be a jerk and try to kick the habit all at once."

My mind went back and his voice blended into the background of my thoughts. I thought of all the hustling I had gone through for the sake of getting drugs, selling pot, pushing stuff, beating my girl for money. Man, I was sick all over, inside and outside.

"Like all you gotta do is get off the habit a little at the time. Get a piece of stuff and break it up. Each time take less and less and bang, you've kicked, cause trying to kick it cold-turkey is a bitch. Do it this way and—"

"You sure?"

"Yeah, I'm sure."

"I'm gonna try it, but I gotta get some bread so I can cop some stuff. You got anything?"

"Yeah."

"How about it?" I was trying to act cool. I wanted the stuff bad, but no matter how hard I fought it, everything in me was crying out for that shit's personal attention.

Waneko's hand went into his pocket and I dug the stuff in his hand. I felt my throat blend in and out with the yen. The taste that takes place even before you get the junk into your system. All of a sudden, I felt like nothing mattered, like if all the promises in the world didn't mean a damn, like all that mattered was that the stuff is there, the needle is there, the yen is there, and your veins have always been there.

I went up to the roof of number 109, running up those stairs like God was on that roof, like everything would be lost if I didn't get up there on time. I felt the night air and my eyes made out the shadows of others like me. Cats I knew and yet never really seen before. Their forms made word noises.

"Got any shit, Piri?"

"Yeah, but I need it all, man. I've been fighting a fever. I'd really like to split with you all, but I'm really strung out like I'm swingin' between hell and the street."

"Yeah, baby, we understand, it's okay."

But I knew they didn't really understand. But it's got to be okay; if it was them, it would be the same.

A little later I felt well, like normal. I was looking at the Triborough Bridge and all its lights and thinking about when I was a little kid and how I used to stand up there on the roof and make believe and there I was, almost twenty years old, and I was still going to that roof and still making believe.

I looked toward Madison Avenue and thought of how close it was to Christmas. I thought about shipping out as soon as I could.

"Funny," I said half aloud, "it's like I've been kinda hanging around waiting for Brew to show up. Hope that Negro's okay."

I felt good about something else—me and Trina was making a steady scene; we really dug each other. My eyes crossed Park Avenue and got nearer Trina's house. I thought about being hung up on *tecata* and Trina kind of noticing that I was acting way out. *Coño*, like the time at the flick. I was goofing so bad, I couldn't hold my head up and just kept going into my nod.

"*Qué te pasa*, Piri?" she asked.

"Nothing, girl, just sleepy—tha's all."

I saw Trina come out and stand on the stoop. I felt mad at me for not being satisfied to just snort or a "just once in a while skin-pop." Naw, I hadda be hitting the main vein.

Man, a thought jumped into my mind, *mainline is the best time.* I pushed that thought outta my mind, except for the part of the way out feeling when that good-o smack was making it with you, that nothing in the whole *mundo* world made no difference, nothing—neither paddies nor Poppa and strange other people.

My mind fell back on my pushing stuff to keep my veins happy, and how I was on a certain cat's shit list for taking some stuff from him to sell, and instead, I shot up for as long as it lasted. I mean, like down people know a cat can't help it when *embalao*, like strung out every which way when you need it—that's it, you just need it. But that's a bad bit, cause them people that give you the stuff to push gotta have some kind of trust in you. Even a junky gotta have some kind of dependable, he gotta have some kinda word.

I sat down on the edge of the roof ledge. My mind refused to get off its kick of reminiscing. Man, like how many times some cat's come up to me with his old man's watch or sister's coat and swap for a three-cent bag. Heh, a three-cent bag—like a grain of rice crushed to powder, that's how much it is for a cost of three dollars, and you couldn't beat down that hell-like look as the begging took place in exchange for that super-tranquilizing ca-ca powder. I sniffed back a tear that came out of my nose. And how about the time I plowed through that falling snow with no pride at all in my Buster Brown shoes—like brown on top and bustered on the bottoms—knowing without a doubt in the world that the only thing that would get me warm again so I could care about being cold was the connecting—the blending of my vein's blood and dogie drug.

Shit, man, how far can pride go down? I knew that all the help in the world could get that stuff out of my system, but only some kind of god would be able to get it out of my swinging soul and mind. What a sick mudder scene! If you didn't get gypped outta your stuff, you'd get beat on some weak, cut-down shit. If you didn't get dead on an overdose, you'd get deader on a long strung-out kick. Everything in the world depended on heroin. You'd go to bed thinking about stuff and wake up in the morning thinking about it. Love and life took second place to it and nothing mattered except where, and how soon. It was like my whole puking system had copped a mind bigger than the one in my head.

I walked toward the roof landing. I was thinking. I was gonna kick for good. "I can do it. I swear ta God and the Virgin. Gonna get me li'l shit and cut down good. *I ain't no fuckin' junkie.*"

I went looking for Waneko. I found him in *El Viejo's* candy store. I put my want to him in fast words.

"Help me kick, man?" It was a question. Waneko knew how it was. Even though he was pushing now, he wasn't using, but he'd been through that kicking road *mucho* times. Waneko nodded, "Sure, *panin*—sure I will." We walked into Waneko's place. He explained to his moms what was shaking. She smiled nice-like and said everything was gonna be all right. Waneko followed that assurance up with, "Moms helps most of the cats that want to kick and even some of the chicks. She should be some kind of church worker or something." He laughed. I tried a weak smile.

They put me in a room that just had a bed and chair and a window that had a metal gate across it to keep the crooks out and kicking junkies in. I laid down, and after a while Waneko brought in a small radio so I could dig some music, to take my mind off what was coming. Both he and I knew that the li'l taste of stuff I had shot up on the roof a while ago was gonna wear off and then World War III was gonna break out inside of me. Billie was wailing some sad song. I wailed along with her in a soft hum. Then some kinda time started to go by and my system was better than a clock. And then Judgment Day set in . . .

Man, talk about wantin' to die—everything started off as it should. First like always, the uncomfortable feeling as you knew your system wanted its baby bottle. And nose running ever so gently at first and the slow kind of pain building up not so gently. I tried hard to listen to some wailin' on the radio, but all I could hear was my own. I got up and went to the door. It was locked from the outside. "Hey, Waneko, open the door," I yelled.

"*Qué es?*"

"I feel real bad, like in bad, man."

"Man, lay down, you ain't been in there long enough to work up any kind of sweat. I'll tell you when, and only then I'll give you a li'l taste to ease you off. So cool it, *panín*."

I don't know how many hours ran crawling by. I just knew I couldn't make it. *But I hadda. I just hadda.*

"Lemme out, Waneko—lemme out, you mother-fucker." I swam to the door and hit at it.

"Waneko is not home right now." It was Waneko's moms.

"Let me out, *señora*. I kicked already."

"He said not to let you come out until he comes back, *hijo*."

"Did he leave something for me?" My voice sounded like tears. I went back to bed and just rolled and moaned all alone.

I don't know how many hours ran crawling by. It was a lot of them. At one time I heard the lock being taken off the door and heard it fall from some one's hand. I felt Waneko's mom's voice—I felt her cool hand on my face and felt her wipe my cold sweating face. I heard sounds of comfort coming from her.

"*No te apures, hijo*, you weel soon be fine."

I tried to get up and make it, but she was faster. I felt the iron gates on the window. I shook them. I turned and flopped back on the bed. I was shaking. I was in bad pain. I was cold and I couldn't stop my snots from flowing. I was all in cramps and my guts wouldn't obey me. My eyes were overflowing real fast.

"Lemme out, Waneko—lemme out, you mother-fucker." Shit, I was like screaming out of veins.

Nobody answered and I just lay there and moaned and groaned all alone and turned that mattress into one big soaking mopful of my sweat.

I don't know how many hours went crawling by. Millions maybe. And then a real scared thought hit me. Waneko wasn't coming back. He was gonna let me make it—cold-turkey—*a la canona*. I kept trembling and my whole swinging soul full of pain would make my body lurch up and tie itself up into one big knot and then ease itself almost straight and then retie itself. I felt like a puke coming afar. I thought, didn't I puke before? I felt it come out of my mouth like a green river of yellow-blue bile. I couldn't control nothing, and all the strength I had was enough just to turn my head away. I think I made some soft ca-ca on myself. I think I made some hard ones too.

Sometimes I think I heard Waneko telling me, "It's almost over, baby, it's almost over—we got it beat." But I couldn't answer. I'd just hold myself together with my arms holding me tight and rockaby baby myself to some kind of vague comfort. In a dream I'd eat mountains and mountains of sweet, sweet candy. I opened my eyes and Waneko had me sitting in a chair and I saw Moms cleaning the toilet I had made out of the room—and then I was back in the bed. I still had all the pain, all the cramps. I still had the whole bad bit, but I knew I was gonna make it. I rocked myself to and fro.

I don't know how many hours ran crawling by. Jillions maybe. At last the pain cut itself down. I felt all dried out. Waneko came into the room and rubbed my body down, like trying to work all the knots to straighten out. Waneko and his moms kept me with them for a week or so putting me into shape with hot pigeon soup, liquids, and later heavier stuff like I mean, rice and beans. They were great, Waneko and Moms. My body was kicked free from H—gone was dogie. They said it takes seventy or so hours to kick a habit. I think it seemed like seventy years. Now all I had to do was kick it outta my mind.

I left Waneko's house after really thanking them from way down. I hit the street thinking, "Wow, dying is easier than this has been. Never — never—*nunca más*."

Alcohol

Although alcohol has once again become popular among high school and college students, it is not a new problem for the school. Alcohol is a problem for the schools primarily because it has such a profound effect on the lives of children of alcoholic parents. The parents' secrecy, their lies, their loss of jobs, status, and self-respect soon reflect themselves in the children, who are often enlisted to protect or take care of the family—to be the adults in a family where the actual adults have become like dependent children. Such a child is often left with a lost childhood because he has had to carry the burdens of adulthood. His pride and his shame make it difficult for him to communicate his sense of loss, and he is often unaware of what he is missing.

Therefore, it is in work with alcoholic parents that schools have the most to do with alcohol, and it is not easy to deal with the alcoholic. He is often the last person among all of his friends, relatives, and acquaintances to admit that he has a problem. Perhaps because so much less opprobrium attaches to the misuse of alcohol than to the misuse of other drugs, the alcoholic is frequently able to manipulate the people around him, to persuade them that his addiction is milder than it in fact is, and to obtain their forgiveness and pity rather than their efforts to help him change. Because he lies so consistently to himself and others, the alcoholic suffers deep feelings of guilt. The shame and worry of his children are intensified by their awareness that most of what their alcoholic parent says is not true. This affects the children's willingness to trust or believe any adults. It is important for a teacher to be very careful in saying precisely what he means to the child of an alcoholic, and it is important that such a child be offered plenty of opportunities where he may legitimately indulge in being a child.

Handling conferences with drunken parents is a dreadful undertaking. One cannot talk with a drunken parent because one will not be heard. Excusing the parent from the interview, if done tactfully, will save her or his pride and one's own sanity. A skilled social worker or psychologist can help the teacher with interview techniques. Home visits are sometimes necessary. When sober, the same parents are often charming and helpful, but when they are drunk, these qualities vanish.

Patient's Reminiscence

I never told anyone, you see, that my mother was mostly drunk when I came home from school. Sometimes, she was very drunk and had fallen down in the house or even outside and, though I was little, I had to pull her into the bedroom so no one would find out—not my friends, or the neighbors or the teachers who passed by. So, of course, I couldn't have friends over. I didn't have many friends. I tried to buy them things so they'd like me and make me feel like other people, but I couldn't invite them in. They would have seen my mother like that.

It was worse when she yelled or ranted. She wanted me with her all the time. The first time I stayed out overnight was in high school at a friend's. My mother got drunk and came and got me, yelling curses at my friend's family. My father left us when I was two, and there was never a man around I could count on. Oh, she'd bring drunk dates home from time to time, but no one lasted and in between she'd rave and rant about men and my father and how awful he was—so I grew up hating men. I still don't trust them. I always felt her drunkenness was his fault for leaving. But now I wonder if he left her because she was a drunk.

The worst was graduation day from the parochial eighth grade school I went to. For weeks, the nuns asked us to get dresses or have them made.

My mother promised and promised—weeks went by and nothing happened. I had no money but I took little jobs and saved up and bought the material and my mother promised to sew it. When she was sober she could sew. Dress rehearsal came and went; the Sister was furious at me because I had no dress. I promised I would have it on graduation day and pleaded with my mother to get it done. She began working on it the night before graduation, but then she got very drunk and as usual yelled and screamed at me because I wanted something. In her rage and drunkenness, she tore the dress in ribbons, and threw them at me.

All the long day of graduation the phone rang. My mother passed out and I knew it was one of the Sisters from school. I couldn't answer. I just cried and cried, and I never got to graduation. The one Sister in charge of my class was furious with me because I had spoiled her processional line, and called me to come in. She said I couldn't graduate because I'd been so unreliable. I went myself to see the head Sister—the Mother Superior—and burst into tears and, for the first time ever, told the truth about my mother. She was nice and put her arm around me, and I wept with shame and hurt. My mother couldn't come to explain. She got upset about what she had done, so she went out to a bar and got drunk.

I never could think at school since I was busy worrying about what was happening to her—and my worst thoughts always happened.

Alienation of Today's Youth
Ruth G. Newman

Closely related to the use of drugs—sometimes the cause and sometimes the effect—is the basic problem of alienation among young people. The problem is particularly prevalent among the economically privileged, but it is also found among the very poor. Here, the sensitive child indirectly experiences his parents' struggle against the steel-like bonds of the system; to the parents (and thus the child), there seems no hope of escaping from squalor and poverty. The child often gives up in early adolescence and sinks into apathy, numbness, or antisocial behavior. Each of these states is a kind of personal protest against society, but quite a different protest from the organized, politically oriented youth rebellions. Rather, it is a withdrawal of feeling and energy from anything society represents.

For less obvious reasons, the economically privileged exhibit alienation more frequently. Usually, it emerges in adolescence. Young people look at their parents' lives and judge them empty of meaning or destructive to others. They answer their parents' pleas for achievement, industry, ambition, and competition with "For what?" meaning, "Why? To be like you?" The young alienated see their parents' often hard-earned material prizes as false gods. They view the impersonal, automated society as sick. They respond to social problems by despair, by resigning from the fray. By not persevering in the external world, they are forced to enter the solo arena within themselves, subjectively exploring their own inner worlds. The search for life's meaning attracts many to Eastern religions, whose practices of meditation, retreat, and diet enrich their lives by yielding a more universal answer than any they have found in their inherited religions. Thus, the modern popularity of forms of Buddhism and the rise of "Jesus Freaks," whose simplification of Christian principles and rituals attempts to suit more basic human values.

Some youngsters "drop out" while accepting money from their families, whose money-making goals they deplore. Such action probably indicates that underneath the talk of love, spiritual values, care for the land and nature, crafts, etc., there lies a deep, unconfessed (perhaps unconscious) dependency and hostility—although they cannot relate to their parents, neither can they leave the nest.

Because adolescents have traditionally viewed their elders critically, today's revolution is not extraordinary when compared to other generations, but the means, style, and results are different. Alienation is probably an indication of where our complex society is at the moment—its coldness, lack of personal individual communication, opportunistic values, and corruption in high places. The result is that millions of young people have banded together (as adolescents have in the past) even if now their common bond is unrelated to work or achievement. Instead, they congregate on the street, or in communes, coffeehouses, and church basements, searching for leadership in charismatic leaders or gurus.

Understanding and relating to these young people is difficult for adults, particularly privileged parents who often try to force their children into what they consider "the good life"—education and training for professions. For a time, these benefits are rejected and scorned, for few tasks undertaken through coercion or cajolement are completed. So instead of attending college, some drop out of high school, take jobs as dishwashers, construction workers, waiters or waitresses, service-station helpers, and quit when they tire of the routine or don't like their bosses. Parents look in horror at nonperseverance, loss of valuable time, their child's appearance or behavior, their sexually open experiments in living, their lack of interests outside their own minds and desires. They become stymied by the weapon of aggressive passivity by which their children fight by not fighting. What does it all mean and why?

Although the alienation phenomenon stems from the adolescent search for identity, it is also a commentary on the older generation's lack of personal joy, on the computerized, mechanized takeover of a society where loneliness abounds and self-realization has been lost in the service of externals. The gains in self-knowledge that come from communal living and the attempt to establish a sound personal base are considerable for the young. There are many admirable values in such a lifestyle, especially those concerned with the importance of human beings being more human. Society needs such a commentary. But it also needs skilled people who can work within society as well as within themselves. It is the chasm between the two that is most worrisome.

Given time, however, the less disturbed come back to the fold. They find that they are ready to adapt to life in society, go back to school, learn a skill or profession, or bring up a family. Some return having profited by their time out and hold stronger values and more certainty than their elders.

Some, however, cannot or do not wish to return. Others have been burned out by drugs and are unable to attempt the tasks they would once have found easy. It is these young people who concern us when we find them, lost, often sickly, and lacking motivation, back in high school or college classrooms unable to get "with it" again. Or in hospitals and clinics, trying to separate reality from delusion, struggling to live. Adults worry about these young people who seem lost to society, and they worry about the future of society itself, a society which, with its myriad complexities, needs special skills to accomplish its work and ameliorate its ills.

In the meantime, alienated youth have taught us a great deal about the society from which they have turned away.

1.   They have taught us about the rigidity and sterility of our sexual patterns, based on outmoded needs of societies when many children, not few, were needed, when homosexuality was societally wasteful, when the penalty of sexual contact between the sexes was often unwanted babies and disgrace. True, the philosophy of the young has often

been seriously flawed, but nonetheless society is now forced to come to grips with its present needs and ways to establish more meaningful family relationships.

2.   They have pointed out the real failures in our society: inhumaneness, phony values, lack of ability to listen, loneliness, and waste of spiritual values. Adolescent exposure of society's corruption and phoniness is expressed by "streaking," a quicker and more direct message to society and parents than a long and painful course of alienation.

3.   They have shown the worth of simple skills, arts and crafts, and the necessity of conserving our land and resources.

4.   They have revealed that in our great efforts to gain the "good life" we have lost much of the good in life. The goals of achievement and success have become so important we have forgotten just what it is we are trying to achieve.

The amount of damage to the alienated generation—and to society because of it—is still to be measured. Literature in this field abounds. Keniston[1] and Friedenberg[2] have made important contributions in the social sciences, and in fiction, the problem has been illuminated by Samuel Beckett among others.

Article Footnotes

1.   Kenneth Keniston, *The Uncommitted— Alienated Youth in American Society* (New York: Harcourt, Brace and World, 1965).

2.   Edgar Z. Friedenberg, *The Vanishing Adolescent* (New York: Dell, 1962).

Chapter 1 Footnotes

1.   An exciting and informative description of the power focus games in this subculture can be found in **Herbert L. Foster,** *Ribbin', Jivin', and Playin' the Dozens* (Cambridge, Mass.: Ballinger Publishing, 1974).

2.   **Tom Wolfe,** *The Electric Kool-Aid Acid Test* (New York: Farrar, Straus, & Giroux, 1968).

2

Identification and Diagnosis
of the Disturbed Child

The mental health "business" is in a state of flux. Hersch[1] has pointed out the abundance of diametrically opposed theories; there no longer is agreement on who is disturbed, who are the helpers, how one helps, or even how one evaluates change. Certainly the complex problems involved in mental health screening and identification of disturbed pupils have yet to be satisfactorily resolved. The difficulty starts with the lack of a standard criterion—no universally accepted, succinct definition of "disturbance."

The Joint Commission on the Mental Health of Children and Youth has stated that an emotionally disturbed child is one who has (a) impairment of age-relevant capacity to realistically perceive the external environment, (b) inadequate impulse control, (c) a lack of rewarding interpersonal relationships, and (d) failed to achieve appropriate learning levels. Studies of American children in the Commission reports estimate that less than 0.2 percent of all children are psychotic, 2 to 3 percent are severely disturbed, and an additional 8 to 10 percent have emotional problems needing specialized services. Thus, approximately 10 million people age 24 or under need professional help. Yet, less than seven percent of them receive that help. Eighty-five percent of the total who need care can be treated by school personnel, clergy, general practitioners, social workers, and paraprofessionals who have been oriented in mental health work—the vast responsibility of the public schools is obvious. The Commission indicates that the percentage of institutionalized children is increasing at twice the rate of the child population.

Rhodes[2] points out that a valid definition of "disturbance" should explicate a system in distress, a "disrupted pattern of human-environment exchanges." Too often, only one part of this pattern is examined. Has the child, as a consequence of biological limitation and/or prior learning developed a repertoire of deviant behaviors which assert themselves even in a "normal" nonprovoking environment? Or is the youngster's behavior a "normal" or reasonable response to a deviant, overstressful life milieu?

In the pendulum swings of argument and rebuttal, the tendency has been to polarize positions. Some approaches are based on placing the entire problem within the patient; some have gone to the other extreme, attributing individual disturbances to the contemporary social condition. In past educational settings, the pupil always was at fault when dissonance occurred; supposedly objective teachers and clinicians screened and diagnosed the *child's* problem. Now some would say that it is always the problem of the teacher or the school—the child himself is innocent. If one takes an *interactive* position about behavior,[3] however, such diverting polemics would not cloud the real difficulty, which is to find valid and reliable assessment devices attending to both aspects.

The stance adopted here is that behavior is a consequence of a unique combination of *both* the self and the environment. Thus, identification must eventually include systematic coverage of both the individual and the environment in the distressed system.[4] To illustrate this concept in the school environment, Kelleher[5] has diagrammed the "teacher-pupil interactive chain"; there are also pupil-peer and pupil-task interactions, as well as reactions to the physical environment. It should be recognized that the psychological potential of any environmental stimuli still depends on how the element is perceived by the pupil: the same teacher's behavior may agitate one pupil and soothe another. We should remind ourselves that, psychologically, *all* of the child's behavior is "reasonable" and "normal" given the internal and external conditions operating at that given moment; only when these responses are judged against some standard of desired or acceptable behavior are the given responses considered "impaired."

This concept introduces another complication in assessing children's behavior. The role of an infant, a child, or even an adolescent is a subservient and difficult one. The child's dependency, combined with adult arbitrary judgments about behavior, may produce highly subjective standards of deviance. The standard may be merely adult irritation or expectation of undue perfection: Disturbing behavior to one teacher may be evidence of highly valued independence or creativity to another. Because teachers are group workers, they are particularly sensitive to behavior that upsets the group process. Differences in tolerance, settings, and concept all enter into individual judgments of the behavior labeled "impaired." Therefore, various identification processes have been developed to reduce variance in individual judgments, to provide common base lines, and to safeguard the pupil against idiosyncratic decisions. An explanation of these processes is the concern of this section.[6]

Before examining the specific details of these processes, however, three other problems must be noted which confound interpretation of conditions surrounding deviance. The first is philosophical in nature: How much latitude should be allowed for freedom and how much for conformity? Deviance is always from some norm of behavior. Schools, with their classic emphasis on conformity, are often overrigid and demanding. And yet the democratic ethos requires adherence to certain minimum standards of behavior.

The second problem is whether the implied blame falling on the child for this deviance is justified. Historically, the implication has been that deviant behavior is "bad," "willful," and "volitional." Thus, a disturbed child became ipso facto a bad child by his own choice. Yet the child has "learned" his current behavior through life experiences. So the converse—that no child is accountable for his behavior—is equally perplexing, and psychologists have considerable difficulty with this problem. Like the nondeviant child, the deviant youngster has acquired behavior patterns through learning experiences and individual potential. Given the behavior patterns that deviant children internalize and the external conditions with which they are confronted, their responses are normal for them. If we wish to change the responses, we must teach them something new or change their external conditions.

The third problem is that child screening and diagnosis are often a prelude to a label (e.g., "delinquent," "childhood schizophrenic"), which in turn is prelude to a self-fulfilling prophecy that encapsulates them and sometimes even condemns them. True, diagnosis is the basis of planning a specific program of assistance, but categorizing children discourages attention to individual differences, which is the key to prescriptive planning. Two "disturbed" children are not exactly alike, nor are two delinquents or two autistic children. Each child must be understood in his uniqueness and must be seen as part of his unique milieu. Although the autistic child tends to bring his repertoire with him wherever he goes, variation in setting can mitigate chronic patterns over time. The very anxious, depressed youngster may be slow to respond, even in the most hygenic setting. A relatively limitless milieu might stimulate action from the most quiescent pupil. A punitive setting (e.g., where the staff shames, shocks, applies physical punishments, etc.) accentuates counterhostility. (More subtle punitive settings include sterile routines, perfunctory adult-child relationships, and a lack of concern for the child's rights as a human being.) A child who is relatively mute and withdrawn among peers may warm up in a one-to-one relationship with a kind and gentle reading teacher.

As we shall see, it is possible to organize a set of descriptors to clarify the child's state. His standing on *particular* dimensions is far more important than any general label. Adequate descriptors of the environmental press in which he must react (especially as perceived by the youngster himself) are more difficult to define at present but are just as critical. Moreover, the intervention model must also be sensitive to both inner state and external press. Identification and treatment require recognition of distortions in the inner life space (incorporated attitudes and feelings about the self and others, ego capacities, recognized attitudes and values, and social skills), and outer life space which contains the milieu elements Redl[7] has described so well (the power system, the overt and covert individual and peer codes, staff interactions, grouping patterns, gratifications and punishments, and many others).

These difficulties in screening and diagnosis are very real and demand a sophisticated professional awareness that is always primarily concerned with the welfare of the youngster. Until the culture achieves a more hygenic and effective socializing climate, there will be problem situations to face.

Processes Involved in Screening and Diagnosis

Screening consists of securing a roster of pupils who, at least on the basis of first-level scrutiny, deserve further study. Further study should result in clarification: the youngster has no problem; the problem is transitory; the problem is a response to a situational complex of overdemanding social or academic stresses in school which could and should be altered; or the problem is evident in school, home, and neighborhood and will necessitate careful analysis and specialized assistance.

Teachers have a unique role in screening and its counterpart, evaluation of change. Teachers are the only trained professionals who see all children in many settings, encouraging a broad perspective. In school, a youngster has tasks (work), authority (bosses), and peer relationships (colleagues). In this "Rorschach of Life" the many outpourings of his inner feelings will be evident whether or not special attention is given to them. Teachers' broad experience in the range of normal, age-related behavior can serve as a base for evaluation. Moreover, in many cases, the teacher's contact with the child's home or community life adds additional awareness.

Yet all teachers have biases, set expectations, sensitivities, and the capacity to distort. Of the many approaches to screening, some provide more objectivity than others. In the following articles, we will examine certain devices that teachers can use in screening. The search for devices is endless, and there are several source books devoted to procedures.[8]

It should also be recognized that, in traditional terms, diagnosis and treatment are not entirely separate processes. The adult continually discovers new aspects of the child's world in a diagnosis and the adult's sharing of and reaction to the child's problems are an integral part of the treatment. Diagnosis is progressive, often specific in focus, and existential in appearance, and prescriptive planning must be flexible, open, and always progressing. A thorough discussion of these issues can be found in *State of the Art: Diagnosis and Treatment.*[9]

Quay and his colleagues have conducted a persistent search for individual behavior symptoms that can be observed by teachers and at the same time provide information about recognized patterns of behavior. In a series of studies, his factor analyses have resulted in delineating three scales of deviance: personality, conduct, and immaturity. The following study reports the scales' application to a population of disturbed children.

Personality Patterns of Pupils in Special Classes for the Emotionally Disturbed

Herbert C. Quay
William C. Morse
Richard L. Cutler

Although there has been considerable interest in the kinds of children who might be considered for special class placement and in the ways these children might best be grouped, there has been no systematic investigation of the behavioral characteristics of children in the schools already defined, by whatever process, as emotionally disturbed. This paper reports the analysis of teacher ratings of problem behavior in a large group of children in special classes for the emotionally disturbed in a variety of school systems. The purpose of the research was to investigate the basic dimensions which might underlie the observed interrelationships of a representative number of deviant behavior traits.

Procedure

In the context of a much larger research effort (Morse, Cutler, and Fink, 1964), ratings of problem

Reprinted from *Exceptional Children*, 1966, *32*, 297–301, by permission of The Council for Exceptional Children. Copyright 1966 by The Council for Exceptional Children.

Table 1. Rotated Factor Loadings

Variable	Conduct Problem	Inadequacy Immaturity	Personality Problem	b^2
Defiant, disobedient	69	10	−14	50
Impertinent	68	09	−05	47
Uncooperative in group	65	20	07	47
Irritable	64	07	14	43
Boisterous	63	06	04	41
Show off, attention-seeking	64	00	03	41
Bullies	60	−01	03	36
Temper tantrums	59	−04	15	37
Hyperactive	59	−12	12	39
Restless	58	−12	11	36
Negative	53	24	−08	35
Irresponsible	53	38	−05	44
Swears, profane language	52	04	06	28
Destructive	53	06	07	29
Jealous	52	04	21	31
Inattentive	42	46	00	38
Tense	37	−08	39	31
Hypersensitive	32	03	57	42
Short attention span	32	32	12	22
Dislikes school	32	46	02	32
Shy	−40	27	42	40
Withdrawn	−32	40	36	39
Sluggish	−09	59	15	39
Lack of interest	14	57	06	34
Lazy	19	52	−02	31
Preoccupied	−03	51	18	29
Daydreams	−03	46	20	25
Drowsy	00	45	08	21
Reticent	03	44	31	29
Passive, suggestible	−18	30	22	17
Inferiority	11	02	64	42
Self-conscious	−09	07	60	38
Lacks self-confidence	02	02	57	33
Easily flustered	25	20	52	37
Fearful, anxious	23	09	48	29
Depressed	11	21	34	17
Clumsy	−01	18	27	11
Inability to have fun	−15	22	23	12
Aloof	−13	25	25	14
Plays with younger children	08	10	24	07
Masturbates	12	16	14	06
Headaches	10	15	12	05
Stomachaches	14	24	15	10

Decimal points omitted

behavior traits of 441 children were made by 60 different teachers. The sample of classes varied widely in geographic locus and represented many different philosophies of placement and program operation. The sample was composed of approximately 80 percent boys and 20 percent girls; the mean ages were 9.4 and 9.8 years, respectively.

More complete information about the classes is provided in the earlier publication.

The problem behavior rating scale employed was first developed by Peterson (1961) and represents the most common problem behaviors of children referred to a child guidance clinic. Since its publication, the items of the scale have been

Table 2. Rotated Factor Loadings of Common Variables from Present
Research and Prior Studies

	8th Grade Students (Quay and Quay 1965)			Adolescent Delinquents (Quay, 1964)			Preadolescent Delinquents (Quay, in press)			Present Study		
Variable	P	C	I	P	C	I	P	C	I	P	C	I
Restless	−04	70	15	14	46	37	03	44	04	11	58	−12
Attention seeking	−08	61	19	−07	70	20	01	49	−09	03	64	00
Inability to have fun	31	−15	03	60	23	22	39	−12	10	23	−15	22
Self-conscious	54	00	−11	48	−05	39	59	−08	00	60	−09	07
Disruptive	−12	70	21	−05	77	11	00	67	15			
Feelings of inferiority	57	−07	17	47	05	29	65	06	05	64	11	02
Boisterousness	−03	60	15	−14	71	18	00	69	08	04	63	06
Preoccupation	21	−04	62	60	14	28	18	−21	48	18	−03	51
Shyness	38	−42	00	54	−28	13	59	−27	08	42	−40	27
Withdrawal	15	−18	12	67	−06	04	41	−34	27	36	−32	40
Short attention span	11	44	56	11	59	28	19	37	55	12	32	32
Lack of confidence	63	−17	22	66	12	30	57	03	22	57	02	02
Inattentive	−08	46	58	24	64	18	22	50	52	00	42	46
Easily flustered	34	14	02	55	19	46	60	21	25	52	25	20
Lack of interest	−02	−02	48	49	49	−02	29	−03	47	06	14	57
Reticence	18	−23	08				14	−04	25	31	03	44
Laziness in school	−15	22	59	20	55	00	09	24	66	−02	19	52
Irresponsibility	00	29	51	34	75	00				−05	53	38
Daydreaming	20	13	57	70	08	26	−07	41	50	20	03	46
Disobedience	00	62	22	11	74	00	−03	64	06	−14	69	10
Uncooperativeness	−07	36	25	15	74	01	−04	59	13	07	65	20
Aloofness	22	−32	20	29	−01	02	20	−30	27	25	−13	25
Passive, suggestible	14	13	38	21	47	30	28	12	27	22	−18	30
Hyperactivity	08	54	−01	03	37	53	−05	60	09	12	59	−12
Distractibility	−11	59	36	30	34	62	03	46	53			
Impertinence	07	33	11	21	62	29	−16	57	02	−05	68	09
Lethargy	02	−17	27	62	22	−05	29	−16	58	08	00	45
Nervous, jittery	35	28	−14	42	22	43	40	39	17	39	37	−08

Decimal points omitted.

subjected to a series of factor analyses on a variety of populations (Quay, 1964a; Quay and Quay, 1965; Quay, in press). These studies have almost uniformly shown that three factorially independent dimensions account for about two-thirds of the variance of the interrelationships among the problem behaviors.

The first dimension is composed of aggressive, hostile, and contentious behavior which has been labeled, at various times, conduct disorder, unsocialized aggression, or psychopathy. The second dimension represents anxious, withdrawn, introvertive behavior and has been labeled personality problem or neuroticism. The third dimension involves preoccupation, lack of interest, sluggishness, laziness, daydreaming, and passivity. This

factor generally has accounted for much less of a variance than the first two dimensions, and its meaning is less easily decided upon. The labels of inadequacy-immaturity and autism have been suggested.

While the design of this study did not permit the assessment of two rater reliability, the results of prior research have suggested that the scale can be used reliably by parents and teachers alike.

For statistical analysis, those traits rated present in at least ten percent of the cases were intercorrelated and subjected to a principal axis factor analysis using the squared multiple correlation as the communality estimate. Factors having at least one variable with a loading of .40 or greater were then rotated to Kaiser's (1958) Varimax criterion.

Table 3. Coefficients of Factor Similarity for Studies of Ratings of Problem Behavior

		Present Study			Eighth Grade Students			Adolescent Delinquents		
		P	C	I	P	C	I	P	C	I
Eighth Grade	Personality	.94	−.42	−.28						
	Conduct	−.58	.93	−.39						
	Immaturity	−.51	.04	.70						
Adolescent Delinquent	Personality	.59	−.72	.41	.75	.02	.60			
	Conduct	−.83	.85	−.04	.00	.84	.72			
	Immaturity	.48	.09	−.59	.58	.55	.44			
Pre-Adolescent Delinquent	Personality	.85	−.66	.00	.72	−.09	.27	.86	.23	.63
	Conduct	−.54	.92	−.44	−.06	.93	.45	.27	.87	.48
	Immaturity	−.22	−.29	.81	.26	.29	.89	.62	.62	.49

Results

Rotated factor loadings are presented in Table 1. The three factors rotated accounted for 76 percent of the variance.

The first factor is clearly that of the conduct problem or unsocialized aggressive dimension, with the largest loadings appearing on such behaviors as defiant, impertinent, uncooperative, irritable, boisterous, etc. As noted above, the rating scale has been used in other studies; it is thus possible to compare the factors found in this research with those previously identified. Table 2 presents the variables common to both the present research and a number of the earlier studies, along with their respective factor loadings. Inspection of the pattern of loadings suggests a high degree of comparability across all of the analyses for the conduct problem factor. This apparent comparability was assessed by the calculation of Tucker's coefficients of factor similarity (Quay and Quay, 1965) which are presented in Table 3. As can be seen, the values are uniformly high among those factors labeled as "conduct problem."

Factor two, loading such variables as sluggishness, laziness, lack of interest, preoccupation, dislike for school, and inattentiveness, seems a representation of the factor identified in earlier studies as inadequacy-immaturity. It has also been suggested (Himmelweit, 1953; Peterson, Becker, Shoemaker, Luria, and Hellmer, 1961) that this factor is perhaps associated with autism or a prepsychotic condition. Unfortunately, none of the samples studied to date have contained adequate numbers of clearly autistic or frankly psychotic children to test this hypothesis. At present it seems best to consider this dimension as representing behavioral immaturity. Whether the basis is developmental or regressive remains a question for further research. The pattern of coefficients in Table 3 indicates that, despite difficulties of interpretation, this factor is comparable to those identified earlier in terms of salient variables.

Factor three, composed primarily of such behaviors as inferiority feelings, self-consciousness, lack of self-confidence, fearfulness, and depression, is clearly the dimension of personality problem or neuroticism identified in the earlier research. In this study, however, this dimension accounts for less of the variance than does inadequacy-immaturity—a reversal of the usual state of affairs. Comparability with previous studies is again indicated by Table 3.

Discussion

The results of this study indicate clearly that the behavior problems of children in a wide sampling of special public school classes for the emotionally disturbed can be understood within the three dimensional framework identified in earlier studies of ratings of problem behavior in other kinds of children. Prior research has also demonstrated that these three dimensions can be found in the analysis of both life history data (Quay, 1964b; Quay, in press) and responses to personality questionnaires (Peterson, Quay, and Tiffany, 1961). Certainly these behavior dimensions, objectively observable and reliably rated, provide a potentially more useful way of looking at problem behavior children than does the application of psychiatric nosological labels which are of doubtful reliability even when applied to adults (Schmidt and Fonda, 1956).

The fact that, in the present group of children, the inadequacy-immaturity dimension accounted for a relatively greater proportion of the variance than has usually been the case suggests that children displaying these behavioral characteristics are perhaps more likely to find their way into special classes than are children whose behavior is more anxious and withdrawn. Whether this is due to the Wickman effect (Wickman, 1928) or whether children with immaturity characteristics are perceived as "more disturbed" or even frankly autistic by school personnel is not clear. What does seem clear is that despite a lack of overt aggression, such children are less able to function in the regular classroom than are the more neurotic children. In a later publication it is planned to report on the relationship of the scores of the children on the three factors to many of the other variables reported in the earlier monograph (Morse et al., 1964).

In other research, in addition to the dimensions reported here, there has frequently appeared a constellation of behavior traits which has been labeled subcultural or socialized delinquency. The failure of this syndrome to emerge in this study is likely due both to the fact that few items in the rating scale tap this factor, and to the fact that children representative of this syndrome are not quite so likely to be found in classes for the emotionally disturbed. As one of us has indicated elsewhere (Quay, 1963), these children are not truly emotionally disturbed and represent a quite different educational problem.

Even at this juncture it seems clear that differential programs are likely to be required to remediate both the behavioral and academic difficulties of "emotionally disturbed" children. While we can expect to find few children who are so clearly representative of a given syndrome as to be clearly one "type" or another, we nevertheless can experiment with classifying children with the three dimensional framework for the study of the effects of differential treatment methods. One of us has commented at greater length elsewhere (Quay, 1965) to the effect that present theory, however rudimentary, does suggest different ways to approach different children.

Article References

Himmelweit, Hilde T. A factorial study of "children's behavior problems." Cited in H.J. Eysenck. *The structure of human personality*. London: Metheun, 1953. P. 88.

Kaiser, H.F. The Varimax criterion for analytic rotation of factor analysis. *Psychometrika*, 1958, **23**, 187–200.

Morse, W.C., Cutler, R.L., and Fink, A.H. *Public school classes for the emotionally handicapped: a research analysis*. Washington: The Council for Exceptional Children, 1964.

Peterson, D.R. Behavior problems of middle childhood. *Journal of Consulting Psychology*, 1961, **25**, 205–209.

Peterson, D.R., Becker, W.C., Shoemaker, D.J., Luria, Zella, and Hellmer, L.A. Child behavior problems and parental attitudes. *Child Development*, 1961, **32**, 151–162.

Peterson, D.R., Quay, H.C., and Tiffany, T.L. Personality factors related to juvenile delinquency. *Child Development*, 1961, **32**, 355–372.

Quay, H.C. Some basic considerations in the education of emotionally disturbed children. *Exceptional Children*, 1963, **30**, 27–31.

Quay, H.C. Personality dimensions in delinquent males as inferred from the factor analysis of behavior ratings. *Journal of Research in Crime and Delinquency*, 1964, **1**, 33–37. (a)

Quay, H.C. Dimensions of personality in delinquent boys as inferred from the factor analysis of case history data. *Child Development*, 1964, **35**, 479–484. (b)

Quay, H.C. Dimensions of problem behavior in children and their interactions with approaches to behavior modification. Paper read at a symposium, University of Kansas, Kansas City, March, 1965.

Quay, H.C. Personality patterns in preadolescent delinquent boys. *Educational and Psychological Measurement*, in press.

Quay, H.C. and Quay, Lorene C. Behavior problems in early adolescence. *Child Development*, 1965, **36**, 215–220.

Schmidt, H.O. and Fonda, C.P. The reliability of psychiatric diagnosis: a new look. *Journal of Abnormal and Social Psychology*, 1956, **52**, 262–267.

Wickman, E.K. *Children's behavior and teachers' attitudes*. New York: Commonwealth Fund, 1928.

Behavior Problem Checklist

Col. No.	Please complete each question carefully.
(1-8)	1. Name (or number) of child _____
(9-10)	2. Age (in years) _____
(11)	3. Sex_____ (M 1, F 2)
(12)	4. Father's Occupation _____
(13)	5. Name of person completing this checklist
(14)	6. What is your relationship to this child? (circle one) a. Mother b. Father c. Teacher d. Other_____ (Specify)

Please indicate which of the following constitute problems, as far as this child is concerned. If an item does *not* constitute a problem, encircle the zero; if an item constitutes a *mild* problem, encircle the one; if an item constitutes a *severe* problem, encircle the two. Please complete every item.

---

(15)	0	1	2	1.	Oddness, bizarre behavior
(16)	0	1	2	2.	Restlessness, inability to sit still
(17)	0	1	2	3.	Attention-seeking, "show-off" behavior
(18)	0	1	2	4.	Stays out late at night
(19)	0	1	2	5.	Doesn't know how to have fun; behaves like a little adult
(20)	0	1	2	6.	Self-consciousness; easily embarrassed
(21)	0	1	2	7.	Fixed expression, lack of emotional reactivity
(22)	0	1	2	8.	Disruptiveness; tendency to annoy & bother others
(23)	0	1	2	9.	Feelings of inferiority
(24)	0	1	2	10.	Steals in company with others
(25)	0	1	2	11.	Boisterousness, rowdiness
(26)	0	1	2	12.	Crying over minor annoyances and hurts
(27)	0	1	2	13.	Preoccupation; "in a world of his own"
(28)	0	1	2	14.	Shyness, bashfulness
(29)	0	1	2	15.	Social withdrawal, preference for solitary activities
(30)	0	1	2	16.	Dislike for school
(31)	0	1	2	17.	Jealousy over attention paid other children
(32)	0	1	2	18.	Belongs to a gang
(33)	0	1	2	19.	Repetitive speech
(34)	0	1	2	20.	Short attention span
(35)	0	1	2	21.	Lack of self-confidence
(36)	0	1	2	22.	Inattentiveness to what others say
(37)	0	1	2	23.	Easily flustered and confused
(38)	0	1	2	24.	Incoherent speech
(39)	0	1	2	25.	Fighting
(40)	0	1	2	26.	Loyal to delinquent friends
(41)	0	1	2	27.	Temper tantrums
(42)	0	1	2	28.	Reticence, secretiveness
(43)	0	1	2	29.	Truancy from school
(44)	0	1	2	30.	Hypersensitivity; feelings easily hurt
(45)	0	1	2	31.	Laziness in school and in performance of other tasks
(46)	0	1	2	32.	Anxiety, chronic general fearfulness
(47)	0	1	2	33.	Irresponsibility, undependability
(48)	0	1	2	34.	Excessive daydreaming
(49)	0	1	2	35.	Masturbation
(50)	0	1	2	36.	Has bad companions
(51)	0	1	2	37.	Tension, inability to relax
(52)	0	1	2	38.	Disobedience, difficulty in disciplinary control
(53)	0	1	2	39.	Depression, chronic sadness
(54)	0	1	2	40.	Uncooperativeness in group situations
(55)	0	1	2	41.	Aloofness, social reserve
(56)	0	1	2	42.	Passivity, suggestibility; easily led by others
(57)	0	1	2	43.	Clumsiness, awkwardness, poor muscular coordination
(58)	0	1	2	44.	Hyperactivity; "always on the go"
(59)	0	1	2	45.	Distractibility
(60)	0	1	2	46.	Destructiveness in regard to his own &/or other's property

(61)	0	1	2	47.	Negativism, tendency to do the opposite of what is requested
(62)	0	1	2	48.	Impertinence, sauciness
(63)	0	1	2	49.	Sluggishness, lethargy
(64)	0	1	2	50.	Drowsiness
(65)	0	1	2	51.	Profane language, swearing, cursing
(66)	0	1	2	52.	Nervousness, jitteriness, jumpiness; easily startled
(67)	0	1	2	53.	Irritability; hot-tempered, easily aroused to anger
(68)	0	1	2	54.	Enuresis, bed-wetting
(69)	0	1	2	55.	Often has physical complaints, e.g. headaches, stomach ache

Quay has worked out specific educational designs for each of the three dimensions.[10]

Another screening procedure relies on observations of specific behavior in the classroom. Such processes are in keeping with behavioristic approaches because they are neither clinical nor inferential. Werry and Quay[11] have contributed in this area. Walker[12] presents both a conceptual rationale and a device for obtaining information on three levels: (1) a fifty-five-item behavior checklist; (2) a seventy-five-item rating scale, which includes frequency, teacher reaction, and pupil response, and (3) a ten-minute observation form for task orientation. Walker suggests uses for the information that make it a teaching as well as a screening device. The "teacher-reaction, pupil-response" is also the start of an ecological analysis. Because many behavior observation schemes deal with "on-task" or "in-seat" behavior, the meaning of the deviance still must be inferred. Withdrawn pupils might score well and yet still have problems in such instances.

Long, Fagen, and Stevens[13] have developed a schema which is educationally oriented, useful to the teacher, requires only twenty minutes per pupil, and has an interesting four-part format. The "Pupil Assessment of Self in School" assesses the pupil's perception of (a) his functions in school, (b) performance of his work, and (c) his relationship to peers and the teacher. The eight-item "Self Control Behavior Inventory" is rated by the teacher on a four-point scale. Sample items include "remembers directions," "anticipates consequences of behavior," and "can delay actions even when excited," each with behavioral examples. The third part concerns "Patterns of Achievement." Seven styles are suggested, such as "slow start but sudden increase," "slow constant increase" and "erratic achievement." The fourth part, "Significant Life Events Inventory," presumes that ecological aspects such as injury, illness, economic stress, and separation from parents are significant. Although these external conditions can only be assessed in terms of how the pupil responds to them, this aspect of screening is certainly an important contribution.

Interest in preschool and early screening has encouraged the development of rating devices for this age group. Bell, Waldrop, and Weller[14] have provided an explicit eleven-point rating scale for each of nine dimensions ranging from "frenetic play" and "emotional aggression" to "vacant staring" and "chronic fearfulness." To utilize the teacher's knowledge, Kohn and Rosman[15] have done considerable analysis of their dual social competence scale and symptom checklist. Walker[16] has discussed in detail 143 socioemotional measures and discussed theoretical problems involved in assessing young children.

The *Pupil Behavior Inventory*[17] has both an elementary and junior high school form. Teachers have responded well to it for several reasons: it is fast, the thirty-four items and rating scale are comfortable to use, and the final dimensions (classroom conduct, academic motivation, socioemotional state, teacher dependence, and personal behavior) represent areas of high interest to the educational setting.

Hammer[18] has provided a rating scale of fifty-seven items for the following disturbances: classroom behavior; attitudes toward the self; behavior with the teacher; relationship with peers; inappropriate infantile behavior; physical functioning or appearance; speech; sexual; and difficulties in learning. The individual items provide significant screening and appraisal cues for teachers.

Perhaps the broadest, gauged screening procedure specifically for emotionally disturbed pupils was developed in 1961 (and revised in 1974) by Bower and Lambert. The procedure, marketed through the Educational Testing Service, functions from kindergarten through high school. Some information on the high school follow-up was published in 1972.[19] It was found that scales used in elementary school were good predictors of unsuccessful status in high school. Teacher ratings were especially potent predictors. Perhaps the most significant factor in Bower and Lambert's approach is the threefold study. Rather than depending solely on teachers, personality tests, or peer perceptions, they used a combination of all three. Teachers rate eight dimensions of pupil behavior on a normal distribution grid; pupils provide peer perception on age appropriate devices; self-perceptions provide self-concept data. The information is collated and weighted to provide one total evaluation. The problems in screening are to get behind the pupil's denials and defenses and the teacher's possible biases, and to somehow take advantage of the knowledge gained from the peer culture. These are all access points within the confines of the school milieu.

In-School Screening of Children with Emotional Handicaps

Eli M. Bower
Nadine M. Lambert

What Is Meant by "Emotionally Handicapped"?

An understanding of what is meant by "emotionally handicapped" is a prerequisite for effective use of the screening process. Mental or emotional health is inferred from the degree of freedom an individual has in choosing from among alternative kinds of behavior. Conversely, mental or emotional disturbance can be inferred from individual behavior which is limited, inflexible, and restricted. Such limitations or restrictions serve to reduce the individual's relative freedom of choice in social and educational endeavors. The reduction of personal maneuverability and flexibility in a changing environment increases the individual's difficulties in adapting to the pressures and changes of life. As a result, the emotionally handicapped person shows increasing susceptibility to behavioral difficulties and interpersonal friction. . . .

Specifically, the emotionally handicapped child is defined as having moderate to marked reduction in behavioral freedom, which in turn reduces his ability to function effectively in learning or working with others. In the classroom, this loss of freedom affects the child's educative and social experiences and results in a noticeable susceptibility to one or more of these five patterns of behavior:

1. *An inability to learn which cannot be adequately explained by intellectual, sensory, neurophysiological, or general health factors.* An inability to learn is, perhaps, the single most significant characteristic of emotionally handicapped children in school. Non-learning of this kind may be manifested as an inability to profit from *any* school learning experiences as well as an inability to master skill subjects. The non-learner may fall behind almost imperceptibly in the first few grades but finds himself in deep water by the time he reaches 4th grade. There are some students, too, who seem to be keeping pace until they reach junior high school, when they begin to flounder badly.

By whatever symptoms the inability manifests itself, we will, as educators, seek the cause or causes. And once we have ruled out intellectual, sensory, neurophysiological, and general health factors, there remain emotional conflicts and resistances to be investigated as major causes of learning disabilities.

2. *An inability to build or maintain satisfactory interpersonal relationships with peers and teachers.* It is not just "getting along" with others that is significant here. The term "satisfactory interpersonal relations" refers to the ability to demonstrate sympathy and warmth toward others, the ability to stand alone when necessary, the ability to have close friends, the ability to be aggressively constructive, and the ability to enjoy working and playing with others as well as to enjoy working and playing by oneself. In most instances, children who are unable to build or maintain satisfactory interpersonal relationships are noticed by their peers, or are most clearly *visible* to their peers. Teachers, however, are also able to identify many such children after a period of observation.

3. *Inappropriate or immature types of behavior or feelings under normal conditions.* Inappropriateness of behavior or feeling can often be sensed by the teacher and peer groups. "He acts like a baby almost all the time," or "He acts funny lots of times," are judgments often heard that describe such behavior. The teacher may find some children reacting to a simple command, like "Please take your seat," in wildly disparate or incongruous ways.

What is appropriate or inappropriate, mature or immature, is best judged by the teacher using his professional training, his daily and long-term observation of the child, and his experience working and interacting with the behavior of large numbers of children.

4. *A general pervasive mood of unhappiness or depression.* Children who are unhappy most of the time may demonstrate such feelings in expressive play, art work, written composition, or in discussion periods. They seldom smile and usually lack a "joy of living" in their school work or social relationships. In the middle or upper grades a self-inventory is usually helpful in confirming suspicions about such feelings.

5. *A tendency to develop physical symptoms, such as speech problems, pains, or fears, associated with personal or school problems.* Often, this tendency is first noted by the child himself. Illness may be linked regularly to school pressures or develop when a child's confidence in himself is under stress. Speech difficulties resulting from emotional distress are usually painfully audible to the teacher and parent.

To sum up, then: the significant patterns of behavior in children indicating a need for closer scrutiny by a teacher are: inability to learn, unsatisfactory interpersonal relationships, inappropriate behavior, unhappiness, repetitive symptoms of illness after stress. . . .

What Is Meant by "Screening"?

A major caution in the use of the instruments and process described in this *Technical Report* is to be aware of the fact that this is a *screening* process, and is *not* intended for diagnosis or classification.

A second caution: the screening process has little to say about the causes of emotional difficulties. It has been designed to answer the question: Which children are not functioning well in a particular behavioral dimension? It cannot answer these questions: What caused the difficulty? Is the difficulty serious or minor and transitory? What can be done about it?

The purpose of screening in the area of emotional handicaps is similar to the purposes of other screening activities carried on by the school: for example, the screening programs for vision and hearing problems. To illustrate: the vision screening program in California public schools has four

objectives which would be equally applicable in screening for emotional handicaps:

1.   To insure early in their school careers a more adequate identification of pupils with defects;

2.   To help pupils with defects to receive more intensive individual study and, if necessary, remedial services;

3.   To help teachers become aware of such disabilities and to help teachers to cope with disabilities educationally;

4.   To provide necessary educational adjustments for groups of pupils in the school who can profit from such programs.

Effective screening for emotional handicaps is dependent on procedures or instruments which can be administered, scored, and interpreted with the same ease and effectiveness as those for screening visual handicaps. The efficacy and economy of screening for emotional handicaps are based on the assumption that some defects or handicaps can be detected early and remedied with greater ease and less effort than handicaps allowed to develop fully.

The same thoughtful professional care and discretion need to be exercised in this type of screening as in any other. Parents need to be informed about the objectives of the process and to be assured that the school will follow up the screening by advising and consulting with those parents whose children may need additional help. The administrator and the teaching staff need to understand the purposes of the program and to carry out the procedures of the process in an informed and motivated manner. The entire procedure, including the administration and scoring of each instrument, has been developed to ease the burden of work for the teacher. Effective screening, however, does not occur through effortless magic. Teachers and administrators will need to put the same effort and attention into the details of this screening process as they would into testing vision, hearing, or achievement. . . .

Certain broad criteria emerged as likely to be important in any process for the screening of children subject to or susceptible to emotional disturbance, especially in a process to be used on a large scale in many schools:

1.   It should be possible to complete the screening procedure with only such information as the teach-

er could obtain without outside technical or professional assistance;

2.   The procedure should be sufficiently simple and straightforward for the average teacher to undertake without long training or daily supervision;

3.   The results of the procedure should be *tentative identification* of children with emotional problems—leading the teacher to *refer* to competent specialists those children who could benefit most from thorough diagnosis;

4.   As a corollary to 3 above, the procedure should *not* encourage the teacher to diagnose emotional problems, nor to draw conclusions about their causes, nor to label or categorize children; in fact, the procedure should actively discourage the teacher from undertaking any of these highly technical interpretations;

5.   The procedure should be one which neither invades the privacy of individuals nor violates good taste;

6.   The procedure should be one which does not offer a threat to any child;

7.   The procedure should be inexpensive to use.

With these criteria, and others that emerged as the work progressed, development was begun of screening procedures for identification of emotionally disturbed children at several different levels of schooling.

Behavior Rating of Pupils (All Grades)

One of the most important and useful kinds of information obtained by the school is the teacher's professional judgment of children's behavior. Teachers see children over a period of time in a variety of circumstances: in stress situations, at work and at play. Their judgment and observation have been sharpened by professional training and by day-to-day experience with the normal behavior of children. Often the teacher's rating can be the single most effective index of a pupil's growth and development.

Few professional persons, no matter how well-trained, can make ratings of others with absolute certainty and complete comfort. Don't spend too much time worrying about whether your rating for a particular child is "right" or "wrong." Make your best judgment of each student, then go on to the next. Remember that it is not your judgment alone that will be used to determine whether or not a pupil is developing emotional difficulties. Your perception of a child's behavior will be combined with the perceptions of the child himself and those of his peers—to make the final judgment about screening a child.

The Class Pictures (Peer Rating— Kindergarten to Grade 3)

After you have completed the *Behavior Rating of Pupils*, your next step in screening is to plan for administration of the peer ratings. The peer rating instrument for kindergarten and primary grades, *The Class Pictures*, must be given to each child in your class individually. This may take fifteen to twenty minutes of time for each child. Administration of *The Class Pictures* to the entire class, however, may be spread over a period of time—up to, but not exceeding, one month.

Administer the instrument to children one at a time when the rest of the class is engaged in seat work of some kind or occupied in other activities which do not require constant supervision. Such a schedule will require a minimum of interruption in your regular teaching program.

The Class Pictures are composed of twelve picture cards with a total of twenty scoring items (one or two items on a card). Five of the items are pictures of boys in situations related to emotionally maladjusted behavior; five are pictures of girls in situations related to emotionally maladjusted behavior; five are pictures of boys in situations related to positive or neutral types of behavior; and five are pictures of girls in situations related to positive or neutral types of behavior.

The Class Pictures have been developed as a means of analyzing, in a systematic and measurable way, how children are perceived or "seen" by their peers. The responses of most pupils to the pictures will not surprise you. Some responses, however, may seem unrealistic and inappropriate. *Accept each child's responses without comment unless the child obviously misunderstands directions.* Your role during the administration of *The Class Pictures* is one of test proctor and recorder of responses.

The Class Pictures are used with children who have not yet learned to read or write well. Therefore, the responses of each child will need to be recorded individually by you. You will, of course, have to make special provision for the rest of the class while you are administering *Class Pictures* to individual children. If an additional school person is available, he may work with the class while you administer *Class Pictures*. The actual administration should always be done by you. If you are able to organize the class into working groups, *Class Pictures* may be administered to a few individuals daily during such work periods—but you will decide for yourself how best to accomplish this task.

On the test each child is asked to consider which of his classmates is most like the child in every one of the twenty situations. Some children will pick twenty different names. Others may name one or two peers for several or many different items. Still others may make no response for one or more items. *Do not expect any fixed pattern of responses.*

When the responses for every child in the class are collected, the teacher can tally the number of times a particular child is chosen for each of the twenty pictures. The total number of times a child is chosen for *all* of the pictures indicates how clearly or how vividly he is "seen," or perceived, by his peers.

The number of times a pupil is picked for the ten *negative* pictures indicates the degree to which he or she is *negatively* perceived by his peers. By dividing the number of times a child is picked for the ten negative pictures by the total number of times he is picked for all twenty of the pictures, a per cent, indicating the ratio of negative perception by peers, is obtained and used in screening.

The mean or average number of negative selections of emotionally handicapped boys and girls has been found to be significantly different from the mean number of negative selections in the general school population of that grade and sex. Consequently, the per cent of negative perception has been found to be a reliable indicator of those children whose behavior, as observed by peers, indicates some degree of emotional difficulty. The higher the per cent, the greater the possibility that the child has emotional problems. The per cent of negative selections on *The Class Pictures*, when combined with teacher ratings and self-ratings, has been found effective in primary grades for screening children with emotional handicaps.

A Class Play (Peer Rating— Grades 3–7)

A Class Play is a peer rating instrument with greatest applicability in grades 4, 5, and 6, though it has been used with success in grades 3 and 7. It should be administered reasonably soon after you have completed the *Behavior Rating of Pupils*. It should take no more than 35 to 45 minutes.

Section I of the instrument contains descriptions of twenty hypothetical roles in a play, with instructions directing each pupil to choose a classmate who would be most suitable and natural in each of the roles. A second section of the *Play* (Section II) elicits from each pupil an indication of the roles he would prefer, or which he thinks other people would select for him. This section has thirty different quartets of the twenty roles, with a question aimed at finding out how the child sees himself in relation to each role.

The scoring of *A Class Play* is very much like the scoring of *The Class Pictures*. Each pupil names a classmate for each of the roles in the play. By counting the number of times a pupil is picked for each of the roles in the play, and then counting the number of times each pupil is picked for the *even numbered* (negative) roles, a percentage is obtained indicative of the positive or negative perception of each pupil by his classmates. This score is used in the screening. . . .

Student Survey (Peer Rating— Grades 7–12)

The *Student Survey* is the peer rating instrument for use in the junior and senior high schools. In order for this test to have validity, it is necessary to administer it to a class in which the students have had an opportunity for some social and intellectual interaction, as well as for observation of one another in a variety of classroom situations. Previous work with this test has shown that social studies or English classes are usually best for this purpose.

Some students in the junior and senior high school may be sensitive to the kinds of questions asked on the *Student Survey*. It is important, therefore, that you anticipate the possibility of such sensitivity and take steps to allay any suspicion or resentment. For example, some teachers have found it helpful to have ready an envelope into which all the tests can be placed when the students are finished. This helps to reassure the class that the test results are confidential and reinforces statements made in the instructions that the results will not be discussed with others.

Section I of the *Student Survey* consists of twenty items. Ten are illustrative of maladjusted or emotionally disturbed behavior and ten are illustrative of neutral or positive behavior. For each statement of behavior, the students are asked to list the name of a classmate who is most like the student described in the item.

Section II of the *Student Survey* contains the same twenty behavior statements randomly arranged in thirty groups of four statements each. The student is asked to select one of the four statements in each group as the one which he thinks others in the class might apply to himself. The responses to Section II can be used to compare the peer ratings of a student with his self-rating. The value of providing two sections in the *Student Survey*, a peer rating and a self-rating on the same items, is, that after scoring both sections, the teacher is able to measure and analyze how a student sees himself in relation to how he is seen by others. . . .

A Picture Game (Self Rating— Kindergarten to Grade 3)

A Picture Game is designed to give a measure of young children's perception of *self*. It is used along with the *Behavior Rating of Pupils* (teacher rating) and *The Class Pictures* (peer rating) to identify pupils who are vulnerable to, or handicapped by, emotional problems.

A Picture Game consists of 66 pictures, including two sample pictures. Each picture is illustrative of normal home and school relationships and events. With the exception of the two sample cards and the first ten pictures, each picture is emotionally neutral in the portrayal of the relationship or event. The child is asked to sort each picture into one of two categories: "This is a happy picture" or "This is a sad picture." The sorting is

done by placing each picture in the "happy" or "sad" side of a two-compartment box which has a happy face shown on one compartment and a sad face on the other. The child categorizes each picture in accordance with his perception of it.

The first ten pictures the child sorts are stereotypes: obviously happy or obviously sad situations. The purpose of including them in the test items is to check on each pupil's understanding of the task. If a child sorts the first ten pictures correctly, you can be fairly sure that he has understood the process well enough for you to use his score in screening. If, on the other hand, he does not sort the first ten pictures correctly, you will need to meet with him individually and ask him to sort the pictures again for you, making certain that he understands the process. Some children *choose* to place pictures differently from others. If you find that such children understand the process but continue, on readministration, to sort the pictures in an independent fashion, make a note of it on the "Class Record Sheet," and use the child's score in screening. . . .

Thinking about Yourself (Self Rating—Grades 3–7)

The purpose of *Thinking about Yourself* is to elicit from the pupil himself an *intra-self* measure of the relationship between a pupil's perception of his environment and his conception of what it ought to be. What is looked for is the degree of discrepancy between a pupil's self perception and an ideal self, between his perception of himself as he *is* and as he would like to be.

Many pupils with serious emotional problems cannot bring themselves to disclose their difficulties in writing, or are uncomfortable about disclosing them. Their responses will therefore very much resemble those of other children in the class. These youngsters are most likely to be screened by teachers and peers.

There are other pupils, however, who do not manifest their difficulties to teachers or peers, but who rise to the opportunity to express inner discomfort and *can* communicate their disturbance on a self rating instrument. Since the average discrepancy between self and *ideal* self has been found to discriminate between pupils with emotional problems and those with normal behavior adjustment, *Thinking about Yourself* provides a meaningful and useful screening dimension not available from teacher or peer ratings. . . .

A Self Test (Self Rating—Grades 7–12)

A Self Test is intended to obtain a measure of the difference between the way a pupil sees himself and the way he would like to be—in other words, a measure of the difference between self and ideal self. To the extent that a student is able to disclose the differences or similarities between these two aspects of self, the instrument is useful in screening. However, some pupils with moderate or serious emotional problems cannot bring themselves to disclose the discomfort or dissatisfaction which this instrument invites them to disclose. Their responses, therefore, will very much resemble those of other students in the class. These youngsters are more likely to be identified by teachers and peers in the screening process.

There are other pupils, however, who do not manifest their difficulties to teachers or peers, but who rise to the opportunity to express inner discomfort and *can* communicate their disturbance on a self rating. For these students, the *Self Test* provides the opportunity. Since the average discrepancy between self and *ideal* self has been found to discriminate between pupils with emotional problems and those with normal behavior adjustment, *A Self Test* provides a meaningful screening dimension not available from teacher or peer ratings.

A Self Test contains forty statements describing people behaving in a number of different ways. In Section I, the student is asked to indicate how strongly he *would like* to be or *would not like* to be the person described. In Section II, the items are repeated and the student is asked to indicate how strongly he feels he *is* like or *is not* like the person described. The two responses by the student (i.e., whether or not he *wants* to be like and whether or not he *is* like) are then compared in the scoring process, after which the amount of discrepancy between the two "selves" is compared. . . .

These procedures cover three domains—teacher, pupil, and peers. Other domains—parents, specialists, and institutional stress—complete the inner and outer ecological model. What is needed is a total institutional mental health index of the stress-support provided a particular pupil by a given school environment. Sarason's School Anxiety Scale and other devices that sense the pupil's perception of his relationship to teachers and subject matter contain the makings of such an index. Many existing rating scales, each with a specific purpose, help the teacher objectify judgments about pupils. For example, Kvaraceus has developed the *KD Proneness Scale and Check List* for early identification of delinquents.[20] His insightful work contains observations for all types of screening.

Lesiak[21] has addressed himself to the problem of teacher screening in a broad context and proposes a total battery for all educational handicaps: intellectual, visual, motor, auditory, and sensory, as well as behavioral. In the area of adjustment, the three devices are the Devereux Elementary School Behavior Rating Scale of 10 items (such as "resists or refuses doing what is asked," "provokes peers"); a Teacher Nomination of Classroom Adjustment; and Rating of Classroom Behavior. While our emphasis is on the affective aspects, it should be recognized that these are always in the context of the total child, who usually has other problems as well.

Screening Primary-Grade Children for Educational Handicaps: A Teacher-Administered Battery[1]

Walter J. Lesiak, Jr.

The purpose of the present study was to conceptualize, implement and evaluate a screening procedure and battery of instruments for the evaluation of primary-grade children that would use classroom teachers as the major task force. The intent of the project was to explore the possibility that with the use of modified existing instruments (group and individual) administered within their classrooms, teachers rather than school psychologists could identify children with potential handicaps in the areas of intellectual functioning, behavior disorders, visual-motor functioning, auditory perception and sensory impairments. . . .

During the conceptualization phase two guidelines were established as a rationale for instrument selection. First, all instruments were to be administered by classroom teachers and aides with a minimum of preservice training. Second, each instrument was to provide maximum data on a particular handicap rather than sampling across handicaps. In this connection, instruments were preferred that not only identified and categorized children with handicaps but had instructional program planning implications. Operationally, the two guidelines resulted in the selection of appropriate group instruments, modification of existing individual instruments for group presentation, and the development of new experimental measures. With this approach the role of the school psychologist shifts from that of an evaluator of teacher-referred children to that of a program consultant with such responsibilities as instrument selection, inservice preparation of teachers, data analysis, test interpretation, and recommendations to the system based on the available data.

Method

Subjects

Twenty-two female classroom teachers who represented six school districts participated. From a potential pool of 106 primary teachers (grades K-3), a representative random sample was drawn with grade level, rural *vs.* urban school, and the size of the school district as criteria. These included four kindergarten, six first-grade, six second-grade, and six third-grade teachers who were employed in 13 different elementary schools. Teachers ranged in age from 22 to 64 years and in teaching experience from three to 27 years. The 22 classrooms provided 545 children who were evaluated on the selected battery. From kindergarten to third grade the numbers of participating children were 94, 143, 140, and 168, respectively. The average class size for the selected grades ranged from 23 to 28.

Procedure

Three inservice sessions were needed to implement the study. The first session involved the six school superintendents who agreed to: (a) field test the group identification procedure, (b) permit the selected teachers to attend a one-day workshop, and (c) permit teachers to spend one week to evaluate children within their classrooms. The second session included the 13 building principals of the participating schools. Interestingly, the principals were most concerned about the random selection of teachers from their buildings and attempted to substitute teachers whom they felt had better classroom control, were more experienced, reliable, etc. The third session, inservice training of the teachers, involved one school day in which the purpose of the study and each teacher's role as evaluator were presented. Because of large geographical distances between school districts, teachers were divided into groups of 10 and 12 for the third inservice session. This grouping permitted each teacher to drive less than 30 miles for the inservice meeting. Each teacher received a packet of materials that indicated the

---

From *Psychology in the Schools*, vol. 10, no. 1 (1973), pp. 88–101. Reprinted with permission.

[1]This study was funded under Title VI ESEA grant 1969–70, Madison County, Ohio. The project was conceptualized and implemented with the assistance of graduate students in School Psychology at the Ohio State University under the direction of Donald C. Smith. Linda Adamsen, Phillip Scott and Mary Ellen Davy were of invaluable assistance in completing this project.

specific schedule and sequence of testing activities for each day, directions for administration, and test materials.

For kindergarten and first-grade children, testing required five half-day sessions. Second- and third-grade children required three half-day sessions. All materials were returned by teachers within a two-week period. Although the majority of materials were administered by teachers, four aides were utilized in the study. Three aides were trained in the administration and scoring of the Slosson Intelligence Test and Wepman Auditory Discrimination Test, while one aide scored and tabulated all materials for analyses. Three of the aides were parents with high-school educations, and one was a single female in her junior year of college. The aides were recruited by asking each superintendent to suggest individuals who he felt were reliable and available for a concentrated period of time. The final selection of aides was made on the basis of availability and ease of driving to various schools. Each aide contracted to work 50 hours at $4.00 per hour. The total cost of the testing materials and aides was approximately $1500.00.

Measures

To accomplish the purpose of using classroom teachers as the major task force in the identification of educational handicaps in primary-grade children the screening battery included a combination of standardized group measures, individual tests modified for group presentation, and new experimental measures. The specific measures to evaluate intellectual functioning, classroom behavior, visual-motor functioning, auditory discrimination, and sensory functioning are presented in Table 1. Each measure is discussed in the following section.

Table 1. Areas of Potential Handicap and Measuring Instruments

Intellectual Functioning

    Cognitive Abilities Test (K-3) (CAT)
    Group Draw-A-Man Test (K-3) (GDAMT)
    Teacher Nomination Scale of "Slow Learning" Children (K-3) (TNS)
    Slosson Intelligence Test (selected cases, N = 111) (SIT)

Classroom Behavior

    Devereux Elementary School Behavior Rating Scale (K-3) (DESB)
    Teacher Nominations of Classroom Adjustment (K-3) (TNCA)
    Teacher Ratings of Classroom Behavior (K-3) (TRCB)

Visual-motor Functioning

    Group Rutgers Drawing Test (K-1) (GRDT)
    Group Bender Visual Motor Gestalt Test (2-3) (GBGT)
    Individual Bender Visual Motor Gestalt Tests (selected cases, N = 82)
    Gross Motor Screening Inventory (K) (GMST)

Auditory Discrimination

    Group Auditory Discrimination Test (K-3) (GADT)
    Individual Auditory Discrimination Tests (selected cases, N = 188)

Sensory Functioning

    Teacher Vision Checklist (K-3) (TVC)
    Teacher Hearing Checklist (K-3) (THC)

Intellectual Functioning

1. Cognitive Abilities Test (CAT) (1968). This revision of the Lorge-Thorndike series measures oral vocabulary, relational concepts, quantitative concepts, and multi-mental concepts (ability to see relationships and to classify). Primary I was used for grades K and 1, Primary II for second and third grades. One section of the CAT was completed per day for kindergarten and first-grade children. Second- and third-graders completed two sections per day. A cut score of 90 or less was used on the CAT to identify tentatively a potential intellectual deficit. Children who scored 90 or below were given the SIT (see below) for confirmation of below-average intellectual functioning.

2. Group Draw-A-Man Test (GDAMT). In this task the children were asked to draw a picture of a man on plain unlined paper. Directions were modified from the original test (Goodenough, 1926) to read, "Draw a picture of a man. Draw the best man you know how. Make a whole man, from the top of his head to the bottom of his feet. Don't leave anything out." Drawings were scored for quality and quantity of production by the Goodenough standards and yielded a developmental age score. The degree to which the chronological age exceeded the developmental drawing age was considered suggestive of the degree of below-average intellectual functioning.

3. Teacher Nomination Scale (TNS). To explore the feasibility of teacher nomination to identify children of limited intellectual ability a paragraph was developed that presented characteristics frequently descriptive of "slow learning" children. In this study "slow learning" referred to children with intelligence scores below the low-average range. The paragraph read as follows:

Their social and motor development are somewhat immature when compared to the range in the classroom. They are generally the children who are least successful with school work and tend to find school unrewarding. They have particular difficulty generalizing and expressing themselves due to a less precise and limited vocabulary. Since they learn at a slower rate, they are continually falling behind and are less ready for new work when it is presented.

During the inservice meeting each teacher was asked to nominate children from her classroom who fit the above description. The nominations were compared with CAT scores below 90 to provide data on the accuracy of teacher judgments as to "slow learning" children.

4. Slosson Intelligence Test (SIT) (1964). The SIT is an abbreviated intelligence test designed for use with children and adults. Individual items were modified after those of the Stanford-Binet and Gesell Developmental Schedules. The SIT was administered by aides to all children who scored 90 or

below on the CAT. The SIT was used to evaluate the degree to which the CAT correctly identified children who fell below the low-average range of intelligence.

Classroom Behavior

1. Devereux Elementary School Behavior Rating Scale (DESB) (1967). The DESB is a teacher rating scale of overt problem behavior related to classroom achievement (Spivack, 1967). The teacher is directed to rate the behavior of each student on a 5- or 7-point scale compared to the behavior of the average youngster in the normal classroom situation. The 47 items are grouped into the following behavior factors: classroom disturbance, impatience, disrespect-defiance, external blame, achievement anxiety, external reliance, comprehension, inattentive-withdrawn, irrelevant responsiveness, creative initiative, and need for closeness to teacher. Raw scores for each behavioral factor are converted to standard scores in the manual and interpreted as within the average or deviant range. From this instrument it was possible to develop individual and composite classroom profiles of deviant behaviors related to classroom achievement.

2. Teacher Nomination and Rating of Student Adjustment. To measure teachers' perceptions of classroom behavioral adjustment in relation to the DESB scale two nomination procedures were used. In the first procedure, teachers were asked to nominate the three most maladjusted and the three best adjusted children in their classrooms (TNCA). These nominations were obtained during the inservice meeting prior to their knowledge of the DESB scale. No specific behavioral description was provided. In the second procedure, after she had completed the DESB scale each teacher was asked to rate each child, compared to her present group, as among the best adjusted, average adjusted or least adjusted (TRCB). No specific guidelines were presented for the rating decisions. Each of the teacher nominations and ratings was correlated with the 11 behavioral factors on the DESB. This procedure identified the factors most related to teachers' perceptions of classroom adjustment.

Visual-motor Functioning

1. Group Rutgers Drawing Test (GRDT). A modified version of the Rutgers Test (1952) was developed to evaluate the functioning of kindergarten and first-grade children. The major modifications included reproducing the designs on two sheets of 9 x 11 paper. As with the original directions, the child copied the design in a space below each standard. Specific guidelines and directions for group presentation were developed. Each teacher administered the GRDT to one half of the class in a session. Scoring followed the original manual and resulted in age-equivalent scores. A discrepancy between the Rutgers age score and the child's chronological and/or mental age was suggestive of inadequate visual-motor functioning.

2. Group Bender Visual Motor Gestalt Test (GBGT). A method for group presentation of the Bender test was developed for second- and third-grade children (Amorose, 1970). Each standard design was reproduced on a 9 x 11 sheet of paper. There was one design per page with the axis of the card and paper in the horizontal orientation. Directions indicated that the child could erase and make a second attempt, but the child was to keep the packet (nine sheets stapled together) with his name toward the top of the desk. When children were noticed turning or rotating the packet they were reminded of the proper orientation. Designs were scored by the Koppitz (1964) standards. With this procedure it was possible to compare each child's total number of errors to those of the standardized sample. Children who made more errors than expected for their age sample were identified tentatively as experiencing some difficulty in the visual-motor area. The adequacy of the group procedure was evaluated by comparing obtained group error scores with those obtained by the traditional individual method of administration.

3. Gross Motor Screening Inventory (GMST). Twelve motor tasks were presented to kindergarten children. These included balancing, jumping, hopping, skipping, arm and leg coordination. Scoring was based on a yes-no criterion. Kindergarten teachers received training in the administration and scoring of the inventory during the inservice program. Standardized norms are not available for this instrument, but norms can be established for each school district. Children who scored below the established norms were identified as experiencing difficulty in the gross motor area of development.

Auditory Discrimination

1. Group Auditory Discrimination Test (GADT). A group auditory discrimination test was devel-oped and evaluated during this study. From the various forms of the Wepman scales (1958), 20 item pairs were selected randomly as the auditory stimuli. Fourteen item pairs contained different words, while six pairs had the same words. The record blank was one sheet of paper with 20 boxes identified by a number and a familiar object (ball, wagon, tree, house, etc.). For kindergarten and first-grade children each scoring box was identified by the object. Numbers were used with second- and third-grade children. Aides presented the auditory stimuli to approximately 10 to 15 children at a time. Children responded by placing an O (same) or X (different) in the appropriate box for each pair presented. Scoring was based on the number of x and y errors in relation to each child's chronological age. This procedure utilizes the Wepman Manual Scores and permits identification of children with inadequate auditory discrimination skills. The adequacy of the group procedure was established by testing eight classrooms of children within three weeks after the group testing program according to the traditional individual method of administration.

Sensory Functions

Two teacher-oriented checklists were developed to identify children with possible vision and hearing difficulties. On the vision checklist (TVC) teachers evaluated each child for such observed behaviors and conditions as head tilt, rubs eyes frequently, watery eyes, redness, etc. Children who received five or more check marks on the items were referred to the county health facility for evaluation. The hearing checklist (THC) involved the same format and procedure for referral.

Results

The results of each measure are presented within the context of the particular handicap evaluated. In addition to the basic demographic data as to how the sample scored on each measure, relationships are presented between measures and between the group and individual method of presentation.

Intellectual Functioning

Table 2 presents a comparison of the means and standard deviations between the CAT and SIT for the total group and across grade levels for all

Table 2. Comparison of the Means and Standard Deviations Associated with the CAT and SIT Tests for Children Who Scored 90 or Below on the CAT

Test	N	r	X	SD	t	p
Total Group						
CAT	111	.57*	79.0	8.9	7.95	.001
SIT	111		89.7	11.1		
Kindergarten						
CAT	14	.70*	71.5	7.8	4.36	.001
SIT	14		89.0	11.7		
First Grade						
CAT	36	.64*	79.9	7.8	5.20	.001
SIT	36		92.8	12.2		
Second Grade						
CAT	27	.31	80.7	7.2	3.23	.01
SIT	27		88.3	9.8		
Third Grade						
CAT	34	.65*	78.4	9.8	3.56	.001
SIT	34		87.2	10.2		

*$p < .01$

children who scored 90 or below on the CAT. The CAT scores consistently were significantly lower than those attained on the SIT and ranged from an 18-point difference at the kindergarten level to a 9-point difference at the third-grade level. Differences between the means were statistically significant at either the .01 or .001 level. Pearson correlations computed between the CAT and SIT scores indicated substantial positive relationships at three grade levels and for the total group. At the second-grade level the relationship was slight and not significant. When a CAT score of 80 or below was used as the basis of comparison to SIT scores, the findings were consistent with the above results. The mean CAT was 71.5 (SD = 7.2) compared to a SIT mean of 84.6 (SD = 10.9) (N = 52, t = 7.18, $p <$ 001). The results thus consistently indicate that when compared to the SIT the CAT tended to underestimate significantly children's levels of ability.

To validate the accuracy of the aides' SIT administration and scoring, 27 children were selected randomly for reevaluation on the SIT by intern school psychologists. A comparison of the means and standard deviations of aide scores to intern scores indicated no significant difference between the groups (t = .03, $p <$ .01). The .80 correlation between IQ scores is indicative of a high to very high relationship of administration and scoring between aides and interns.

The coefficients of correlation between the CAT and GDAM measure were .40, .45, .39, .37 respectively for the four grade levels. The correlations were significant ($p <$ .01), but of low strength. Teachers' accuracy in the nomination of "slow learning" children (TNS) was 68 percent correct compared to CAT scores. The behavioral description was written to elicit children who generally scored below 90 on an intelligence scale. On this basis, 76 of the 112 children nominated scored 90 or less on the CAT. By sex, 62 percent of the boys were nominated accurately (36 of 73), while 80 percent of the girls were identified correctly (31 of 39). By grade level, teacher accuracy was 58 percent, 67 percent, 70 percent, 75 percent across the grades. When grade and sex were combined the percentages of accuracy were respectively, KM 56 percent, KF 67 percent, 1M 65 percent, 1F 69 percent, 2M 53 percent, 2F 92 percent, 3M 67 percent, 3F 81 percent. However, 38 percent of the children who scored 90 or less on the CAT were not nominated. Of the 47 children (19 males, 28 females) not nominated, 33 fell within the 80 to 90 IQ range and 14 fell below 80 IQ. Of the children not nominated, 70 percent were in kindergarten and first grade. The results suggest that teachers identified older children more accurately and found it most difficult to identify younger children within the 80 to 90 IQ range. Although teachers were more accurate in the nomination of girls than boys as "slow learners," there was a tendency for teachers to overlook younger girls who were in fact of below average intelligence.

Classroom Behavior

A comparison of teachers' inservice judgments (TNCA) of the three best adjusted and three most maladjusted children correlated .90 (N = 132, $p < .01$) with their later ratings of classroom adjustment (TRCB) (least, average, best) based on completion of the DESB scale. Thus, teachers' initial global judgments were quite consistent with later behavior ratings that utilized systematic behavioral data. The CAT correlated .49, .51, .58, .51 with behavior adjustment ratings across grade levels. Behavioral factors on the DESB that indicated a substantial or marked relationship to the classroom adjustment rating were:

Kindergarten: impatience (−.51), external reliance (−.59), comprehension (.60), inattentive-withdrawn (−.48), creative initiative (.48), likely to quit (−.47).

First grade: impatience (−.61), external reliance (−.59), comprehension (.69), inattentive-withdrawn (−.63), creative initiative (.53), can't change task (−.59), likely to quit (−.54).

Second grade: external reliance (−.54), comprehension (.60), inattentive-withdrawn (−.63), can't change task (−.59), likely to quit (−.51), slow to complete work (−.54).

Third grade: impatience (−.60), external reliance (−.71), comprehension (.66), inattentive-withdrawn (−.72), can't change task (−.59), likely to quit (−.63), slow to complete work (−.59).

Table 3. Comparison of Ranked Teacher Attitudes to Ranked Frequencies of Behavior and Relationship to Classroom Adjustment Rating

Behavior Factor	Attitude Rank	Frequency Rank	Importance in Classroom Adjust. Rating
Classroom disturbance	1	2	low
Impatience	6	4	high
Disrespect-defiance	2	6	low
External blame	8	8	low
Achievement anxiety	7	6	low
External reliance	5	1	high
Inattentive-withdrawn	3	3	high
Irrelevant responses	4	5	low

Note: Correlation between attitude and frequency rank was rho = .54, $p < .01$.

A summary profile suggests that the behavioral factors most related to the teachers' ratings of a favorable classroom adjustment are low impatience, low external reliance, high comprehension, and low inattentive-withdrawn behavior. The older the child the greater the importance of factors such as likely to quit, slow to complete work, and can't change tasks. Behavioral factors of little influence in teacher ratings were classroom disturbance, disrespect-defiance, external blame, achievement anxiety, and closeness to the teacher.

A subsidiary study was utilized to determine whether teachers' attitudes toward the seriousness of a particular behavior would affect their observance of the behavior (Adamsen, 1970). Teacher attitudes were ranked for indicativeness of maladjustment according to the eight negative factors on the DESB scale. These attitudes were related to the rank frequency of the observance of that behavior (see Table 3). It was found that while group rankings between attitude and observed frequency were correlated positively (rho = .54, $p < .01$), comparison for individual teachers yielded results that ranged from high negative to high positive correlations. Thus, while attitudes were reflected in frequencies of rating behaviors on the DESB, this relationship was not applicable to individual teachers. In some cases, high frequencies of behavior noted in children related to the teachers' failure to perceive the behavior as important. The data suggest that teachers' attitudes toward the severity of the behavior are not related consistently to the frequency of observing a particular behavior or related to the behavioral factors most associated with a positive classroom adjustment rating.

Visual Motor Functioning

Within kindergarten and first grade the GRDT mean age equivalents approximated closely the chronological age means (kindergarten, CA = 70.4, GRDT = 70.5; first grade, CA = 83.2, GRDT = 81.5). Significant positive correlations were established between the GRDT and CAT and GDAM at both grade levels (kindergarten .56, .52; first grade .54, .52; $p < .01$).

For the second and third grade visual-motor measures a subsidiary study evaluated the reliability, practicality, and viability of the group method of administering the Bender Gestalt test (Amorose, 1970). The sample consisted of 82 second- and third-grade children who were administered the Bender individually 3 weeks after the group measure. The mean CA of the 21 boys and 17 girls in the second grade group was 7-4 years with a mean IQ of 98. The mean CA of the 23 boys and 21 girls in the third grade was 9-1 years with a mean IQ of 96. Major findings of the study were: (a) an analysis of variance indicated that the difference between

the individual *vs.* group method did not attain statistical significance at either grade level (F = .012, .044 $df = 36, 44$ $p = > .05$); (b) although a counterbalanced design was not used, results of score differences were not significant or substantial, which suggests that the order of presentation with a 3-week lapse between group and individual administration had little or no effect; (c) data from a teacher questionnaire indicated that the group method of presentation was satisfactory in terms of adequacy of directions, administrative procedure and testing time (30 minutes); (d) booklets can be produced at a reasonable cost by use of a high-grade stencil.

Results on the gross motor screening inventory were incomplete. Follow-up indicated inconsistent presentation procedures and scoring standards. Inservice training apparently was insufficient to result in a consistent scoring approach.

Auditory Discrimination

With group measures as the data base, less than 5 percent of all the children were judged to have inadequate auditory discrimination on the basis of y errors (words are the same). The percentages of inadequate discrimination for each grade level based on x errors (different words) were 47 percent, 57 percent, 31 percent, 25 percent respectively. Wide variability in the percentage of inadequate discrimination was noted between classrooms at each grade level. (Kindergarten: 55 percent, 53 percent, 26 percent, 23 percent; first: 90 percent, 83 percent, 62 percent, 54 percent, 37 percent, 22 percent; second: 68 percent, 61 percent, 27 percent, 16 percent, 1 percent, 0 percent; third: 90 percent, 28 percent, 17 percent, 15 percent, 13 percent, 0 percent).

Table 4. Comparison of the Means and Standard Deviations for Group and Individual Auditory Discrimination Errors

Test	N	X	SD	t	p
Group x error*	188	2.3	3.4	5.33	.001
Ind. x error	188	4.5	4.5		
Group y error**	188	.26	.56	3.05	.01
Ind. y error	188	.53	.93		

*correlation between x errors = .67, $p < .01$.
**correlation between y errors = .21, $p < .05$.

Table 4 indicates a significant difference for the mean x and y errors between the group and individual method of presentation. Consistently, children made fewer errors on the group presentation. The correlational relationship between individual x and group x errors was substantial, while the y error relationship, although significant, was negligible.

Sensory Functions

Thirty-six children or 7 percent of the sample were identified by teachers as manifesting visual problems, while 4 percent were identified for hearing problems. All were referred to the county health facilities for evaluation. Four were found to need further visual evaluation and 5 needed additional audiometric evaluation. Thus, less than 10 percent of the sample was nominated and generally less than 25 percent of those were judged valid referrals by the health facility.

Discussion

A number of findings and implications emerged from the present study. Although the CAT and SIT were correlated significantly, the CAT was found to underestimate consistently the intelligence of a substantial number of children when compared to the SIT. While IQ differences between the measures decreased with age, the CAT averaged approximately 10 IQ points lower than the SIT. This would be considered a serious limitation if the CAT were used as a major criterion for placement in an educable mentally retarded program and if the SIT were to be considered an acceptable measure of intelligence for children of below-average functioning. In the present project, however, the CAT was not considered primarily a placement criterion, but rather an alternative group measure of ability. On this criterion the procedures for administration and scoring were judged efficient and effective by the school personnel, and results indicated a normal distribution of scores. With regard to the second issue of the adequacy of the SIT as an accurate measure of intelligence for below-average children, recent findings are less encouraging than earlier studies. With a representative sample of elementary school children, correlations between the SIT and Stanford-Binet of .90 or greater were reported (DeLapa, 1967; Mooney, 1971). However, when a sample of

special education children was used the correlations dropped to .59 between the SIT and Binet (DeLapa, 1967). Subsequent studies that correlated the SIT and WISC full scales on populations of educable mentally retarded and learning disabled children reported correlations of .44, .50, .57, .65 (Lessler, 1971; Swanson, 1971). Thus, some question has been raised as to the ability of the SIT to identify children as candidates for special education when compared with standard intelligence tests such as the WISC and Binet.

The CAT findings suggest that additional research is needed to compare directly the results of the CAT and WISC or Binet for below-average children to determine whether in fact the CAT does underestimate intelligence. From a screening point of view, however, it appears that since the CAT provides lower scores than the SIT, children who score below a certain IQ score (90) on the CAT can be evaluated on the SIT by an aide. Children who subsequently fell below an established SIT score (80) then would be seen by a school psychologist for evaluation. The relevant use of paraprofessionals for screening was demonstrated by the finding that aides were able accurately to administer and score the SIT with no prior psychological testing experience. However, it must be remembered that the aides were not selected randomly, but had been recommended by school administrators as reliable individuals.

Evaluation of the behavior descriptions to nominate "slow learning" children was encouraging. Interviews with teachers indicated that in the majority of cases nominations were based on the behavioral paragraph rather than on available test data. Combined with the finding that teachers found it most difficult to identify younger children, this suggests that school psychologists may want to develop specific behavioral descriptions by grade level and arrange inservice meetings to discuss these characteristics. Perhaps teacher accuracy in referring younger, below-average children could be increased by providing behavioral descriptions rather than permitting each teacher to refer children based on her own perceptions of retardation.

Results obtained on the DESB and teacher scales provide data on a number of issues. First, while not applicable in every case, there was a significant relationship between teachers' perceptions of the severity of a behavior and the frequency with which it was rated. The interpretation of a rating or behavior checklist therefore should consider the possibility that teachers' attitudes toward a particular behavior may affect their observance of that behavior. A second finding of interest was that four behavior factors correlated consistently across all grade levels with teachers' perceptions of classroom adjustment. These factors were low ratings on impatience, external reliance, inattentive-withdrawn behavior and a high rating on comprehension. This finding may suggest the need to arrange inservice meetings with teachers to assist them to develop more acceptable, desirable behaviors and also to decrease less desirable behaviors associated with classroom adjustment. The findings from the DESB also could be used as the basis for individual teachers to understand areas of behavior difficulty within their classrooms and to design methods to deal with them. Some of the behaviors and combination of behaviors that could be used for teacher consultation and classroom planning include: underachieving behaviors, acting out or poorly controlled behavior, feelings of powerlessness.

Attempts to measure visual-motor functioning by group procedures suggest further consideration of this approach. While individual Rutgers scores were not used as the criterion, GRDT scores were developmentally comparable to chronological ages of the groups. The mode of presentation for the GRDT was judged by teachers and participants as appropriate and efficient for classroom administration. When compared with the individually administered test results, the group Bender test indicated no significant differences in the number of errors. However, since a counterbalanced design was not used the above results should be considered tentative. The lack of a consistent administration and scoring procedure on the gross motor inventory suggests that additional training is necessary for kindergarten teachers to utilize these materials effectively.

The group auditory discrimination test was found to produce significantly fewer errors than the individual test. It was anticipated that the group measure would result in greater errors and thus would serve as an initial screening measure. Such a use would not be feasible with the present measure, since the group method underestimated rather than overestimated errors. A possible explanation for this finding is that sufficient control was not exercised to prevent children from copying responses. However, the group results do provide relevant educational data in that the percentage of inadequate performance varied from less than 5 percent to over 75 percent between classrooms. Such variability would provide the basis for within- and between-school programming in the area of auditory discrimination.

The use of teacher checklists to encourage referrals to medical personnel for initial and reevaluations of visual and hearing deficits, although positively received by teachers and the medical community, was relatively unproductive. Discussion with teachers after they had completed the checklists indicated a general concensus that the behaviors presented often lacked specific reference points. As a consequence, many teachers tended not to check an uncertain area but were overly cautious in their judgments. Although not confirmed in this study, it is felt that behavioral checklists may be a worthwhile adjunct to routine visual and hearing screening tests in the schools.

To summarize, if one accepts the point of view that the identification and educational classification of children is important but is secondary to, and for the purposes of, facilitating educational modifications within a particular environment, a number of identification and programming uses appear feasible with the proposed battery.

1. A combination of CAT, GDAM, and teacher nomination could serve as an initial identification procedure for children with below-average ability before the children manifest obvious academic failure patterns. Children identified on the above measures then could be evaluated individually by aides on the SIT and other selected measures. If ability scores were again low the services of a school psychologist might be requested. The above procedure might reduce significantly the number of children referred as retarded who do not eventually qualify for special class placement.

2. With the addition of achievement measures at the second- and third-grade level the battery may identify children with potential learning disabilities. Through the use of the educational definition of learning disability as (a) a discrepancy between ability and achievement, (b) differences in learning processes (visual-motor versus auditory), (c) not the result of retardation, sensory deficits, emotional and/or behavioral factors, children could be screened initially with this battery. Aides and the school psychologist would further evaluate identified children.

3. Programming implications for the school system and individual schools can be drawn from this battery. For example, curriculum adjustments may be considered for schools with large percentages of children falling within the 75 to 90 IQ range. Similarly, educational modifications and/or inservice programs may be suggested for schools typified

by children with inadequate auditory or visual-motor skills and disruptive behavior patterns.

4. Programming for individual teachers also is feasible by utilizing the data derived from the cognitive, behavioral, visual motor and auditory measures. From the point of view of the teachers, feedback after the project indicated that they felt more inclined to utilize test results to modify classroom instruction when they were involved directly in the data gathering process. Thus, teacher involvement in the battery administration may result in a more positive reception of recommendations from a school psychologist.

The results of the present study and the implications for data usage suggest that a screening battery administered by classroom teachers and augmented by aides may constitute a procedure whereby a school psychologist could initially identify and gather relevant data about primary-grade children who manifest handicaps that may interfere with present and future educational functioning.

Article References

Adamsen, L. Effect of teacher attitudes in rating pupils on the Devereux Behavior Rating Scale. Unpublished intern project, Ohio State University, 1970.

Amorose, R. A group method for administering the Bender-Gestalt test. Unpublished intern project, Ohio State University, 1970.

Armstrong, R.J., & Mooney, R.F. The Slosson Intelligence Test: implications for reading specialists. *The Reading Teacher,* 1971, *24,* 336–340.

DeHirsch, K., Jansky, J., & Langford, W. *Predicting reading failure.* New York: Harper & Row, 1966.

DeLapa, G. Correlates of Slosson Intelligence Test, Stanford-Binet, form L-M, and Achievement Indices. Unpublished doctoral dissertation, West Virginia University, 1967.

Furr, K., & Wilson, R. The California Short-form Test of Mental Maturity 1963 edition as a screening device for educable mentally retarded programs. *Journal of School Psychology,* 1968, *7,* 47–49.

Garrett, H. *Elementary statistics.* New York: Longmans, Green, 1956.

Goodenough, F. *Draw-A-Man Test.* New York: World Book, 1926.

Koppitz, E. *The Bender-Gestalt test for young children.* New York: Grune & Stratton, 1964.

Lessler, K., & Galinsky, D. Relationship between Slosson Intelligence Test and WISC scores in special education candidates. *Psychology in the Schools,* 1971, *8,* 341–344.

McLeod, P. *Readings for learning: a program for visual and auditory perceptual motor training.* New York: Lippincott, 1965.

Minimal brain dysfunction national project on learning disabilities in children, phase two, educational, medical and health-related services. Washington, D.C.: Public Health Service Publication No. 2015, 1969.

Rogolsky, M. Screening kindergarten children: a review and recommendations. *Journal of School Psychology,* 1968, *7,* 18–25.

Slosson, R.L. *Slosson Intelligence Test (SIT) for children and adults.* East Aurora, N.Y.: Slosson Educational Publications, 1964.

Smith, S., & Solanto, J. An approach to preschool evaluations. *Psychology in the Schools,* 1971, *8,* 142–147.

Spivack, G., & Swift, M. *Devereux Elementary School Behavior (DESB) Scale Manual.* Devon, Pa.: Devereux Foundation, 1967.

Starr, A. The Rutgers Drawing Test. *Training School Bulletin,* 1952, *49,* 45–64.

Swanson, M., & Jacobson, A. Evaluation of the SIT for screening children with learning disabilities. *Journal of Learning Disabilities,* 1970, *3,* 22–24.

Thorndike, R., Hagen, E., & Lorge, I. *Cognitive Abilities Test.* New York: Houghton Mifflin, 1968.

Wepman, J. *Auditory Discrimination Test.* Chicago: University of Chicago Press, 1958.

More complex screening batteries have been proposed by many authors. One example is Bruce T. Saunders, who has proposed a screening-identification-diagnosis-prescriptive sequence, which depends upon the teacher with subsequent support from more specialized personnel for intensive diagnostic efforts.

A Procedure for the Screening, Identification, and Diagnosis of Emotionally Disturbed Children in the Rural Elementary School

Bruce T. Saunders

Several problems have been delineated that seriously interfere with the development of educational programs for the emotionally disturbed child in rural areas (Saunders, 1971). Noted among these problems are specific demographic-geographic considerations, low per-capita income, lack of trained personnel, and the lack of any real impetus and direction from any authoritative sources within the rural states. For example, at the time of the preparation of this manuscript there are two classes for the emotionally disturbed in the state of Maine on the public school level, one in Waterville and one in Bangor. In addition to these two classes, the Division of Special Education, Area of the Emotionally Disturbed, University of Maine at Orono will operate three or four Special Resource Classes for emotionally disturbed children as internship experiences for graduate students. Essentially, there will be six classes for emotionally disturbed children in the public schools of Maine. The current level of services for the education of disturbed children is quite minimal in Maine, and it is very unlikely we can expect any serious commitments to programs within the near future.

If one considers the current school enrollment in the state of Maine as of June 1970 (241,198 Total, 175,525 K-8, 65,673 High School[1]) in relation to the generally accepted estimate of incidence of serious emotional disturbance in children, which ranges from 4 percent to 12 percent (Lambert & Bower,

1961), we are concerned with a minimum of 7,000 children. Further, Glidewell and Swallow (1968) have reported that if one considers mild as well as moderate and severe emotional handicapping conditions the estimate of incidence is as high as 30 percent, and we then are concerned with 52,658 children in K-8 alone. Glidewell and Swallow (1968) have indicated clearly that estimates of incidence vary considerably with individual screenings of emotionally disturbed children and, obviously, once an initial screening has been completed there exists some responsibility on the part of the schools to provide programs for those children for whom such programming is indicated.

The SID Program

The author, in conjunction with several graduate students, has developed a relatively efficient and inexpensive procedure for the screening, identification, and diagnosis of emotionally disturbed children in the rural elementary school. The procedure is referred to as SID (Screening, Identification, and Diagnosis) and has been developed to be directed by an SID Coordinator and administered by the classroom teacher. The goal of this program was twofold: (a) to provide a badly needed service to children in rural school communities; and (b) to continue to develop the level of sophistication and competence of the graduate student to deal with emotionally disturbed children (Saunders, 1971).

From *Psychology in the Schools*, vol. 9, no. 2 (1972), pp. 159–164. Reprinted with permission.

[1]Telephone conversation between Commissioner of Education, State of Maine, and David Johnson, graduate student at the University of Maine.

Screening

Screening refers to a gross estimate of the total number of children in a school system who are in need of specific identification in order to determine the actual incidence of emotional disturbance. Screening is based upon the use of a modified form of the Lambert and Bower Behavior Rating of Pupils. Screening indicates which children, by name, should be considered for the identification phase of the SID program.

The screening phase of the SID program is organized by an SID Coordinator and is administered by the teacher. SID Coordinators are trained at the University of Maine, and the SID program is considered a tool in the special educators' areas of specialization. The procedure requires approximately one minute per child of the teacher's time. It requires 30 minutes for a teacher to complete a BRS for each of 30 children in her class, which then are returned to the SID Coordinator for analysis.

The SID Coordinator scores each BRS by adding the ratings for each of the eight categories, but omits the rating 3. The total score is referred to as the BRS raw score. After the BRS raw scores from high to low are calculated, the child with the highest raw score on the BRS in the class is given rank number 1. Tied ranks are handled in the traditional manner; namely, the mean rank for the tied-rank position is utilized for the tied scores.

After the SID Coordinator has rank ordered the BRS, the highest 40 percent of the rank-ordered BRS then are considered in the identification phase of the SID procedure. Our initial research in the SID procedure indicated that the top 30 percent of the rank ordered BRS will have areas of significant emotional disturbance or behavior disorder in the identification phase of the program. With many classes, the correlation was still significant when we included the top 35 percent of the BRS. Therefore, the top 40 percent of the BRS must be utilized in the identification phase. If a teacher has a class of 30 pupils, at least the top 12 rank-ordered BRS scores should be considered in the identification phase of the SID program. In each of 11 classes studied in developing the SID program, correlations significant at the .05 level consistently were observed between the BRS X Burke Behavior Rating Scales for the top 35 percent of the ranked BRSs (Ayer, 1971).

The screening phase of the SID program is utilized because it provides a considerable saving in time and money. The screening of a class of 30 pupils takes approximately one hour, including the work of the Coordinator. The identification phase requires approximately 20 minutes per child of teacher's time. The screening phase saves a great deal of time, since only 40 percent of the original class needs to be considered in the identification phase. If the identification phase were utilized without the initial screening, the teacher would be required to spend 11 hours of her time for a class of 30 pupils and the Coordinator would spend an additional seven and one-half hours. Further, the screening costs the school $.25 per child and the identification costs $1.00 per child. A considerable financial savings is realized through initial screening prior to the identification phase.

Identification

Identification refers to a considerably more sophisticated procedure that generally indicates which children will require specific diagnostic evaluation and indicates the nature of the diagnostic evaluation, *i.e.*, personality assessment, intelligence testing, testing for specific learning disability, neurological assessment, etc.

The identification phase of the SID program employs the Burke Behavior Rating Scales, which also are organized by the SID Coordinator and administered by the classroom teacher. The Burke Scales are best employed subsequent to a brief training session with the teachers conducted by the SID Coordinator. Approximately half an hour should be allotted for this purpose. The SID Coordinator should instruct the teacher to complete the Burke Scales on the top 40 percent of the rank-ordered BRS and supply the teacher with the names of the children whose BRS scores placed them in the referred group. The SID Coordinator should not indicate specifically why these children have been selected for further evaluation. After the teacher completes the Burke Scales, they are returned to the Coordinator for analysis.

After he has scored the Burke Behavior Rating Scales as indicated in the manual, the Coordinator interprets the profile to determine whether the pupil will require further diagnostic evaluation (Burke, 1969).

The Burke Scales contain 116 items that cluster into the following 20 factors:

1.   Excessive Self-blame

2.   Excessive Anxiety

3.   Excessive Withdrawal

4.   Excessive Dependency

5. Poor Ego Strength

6. Poor Physical Strength

7. Poor Coordination

8. Poor Intellectuality

9. Poor Academics

10. Poor Attention

11. Poor Impulse Control

12. Poor Reality Contact

13. Poor Sense of Identity

14. Excessive Suffering

15. Poor Anger Control

16. Excessive Sense of Persecution

17. Excessive Sexuality

18. Excessive Aggressiveness

19. Excessive Resistance

20. Poor Social Conformity

When he analyzes the profiles, the SID Coordinator will observe that each of the 20 factors will have three columns into which the raw scores obtained on the factor (sum of the items included in the factor) will fall. The raw score will fall into one of the three columns: Not Significant, Significant, or Very Significant. Any child who attains a score in the Significant or Very Significant range should be considered for further diagnostic evaluation. The determination for specific referral for diagnostic evaluation follows careful consideration of the meaning of the factor and the extent of the deviation. Further, pattern analysis as well as spike analysis should be considered in referral for diagnostic evaluation (Burke, 1969).

The Burke Beahvior Rating Scales provide diagnostic information by identifying:

1. Patterns of disturbed behavior that distinguish among several groups of children.

2. Changes in behavior patterns over a period of time.

3. Areas in a child's personality where further evaluation might take place advantageously.

4. Information useful to school personnel to be utilized in parent conferences.

5. Which children will do well in special classes.

Diagnosis

When further diagnosis is not indicated, the Burke Manual suggests specific programming for mild and moderate levels of difficulty. When diagnosis is indicated, the SID Coordinator will determine whether the referral should be a request for a complete evaluation or whether specific diagnostic information is indicated. The SID Coordinator may determine whether neurological, educational, psychological, psychiatric or pediatric consultation is indicated. In some cases, social welfare agencies should be consulted.

Diagnosis refers to the integrated evaluation of specific areas of psychological-educational functioning and includes intellectual, achievement, projective, educational, developmental and sociometric assessment. In addition, specific medical and neurological evaluation may be indicated. The diagnosis phase of the SID program may follow from a recommendation based upon the results of the screening and identification phase or, in the case of clinically observable false negative, from direct behavioral observation and teacher referral.

Generally, the SID Coordinator is not prepared to complete a full diagnostic evaluation. When a child requires specific diagnostic evaluation beyond the training of the Coordinator, three resources for evaluation are available in the state of Maine: Community Mental Health Centers, licensed psychological examiners, and licensed psychologists. Some of the SID Coordinators are prepared and qualified to perform specific diagnostic evaluations.

The diagnostic evaluation should be reported in a manner that is meaningful to school personnel. It is the responsibility of the SID Coordinator to provide appropriate feedback of the diagnostic evaluation and to prescribe specific educational programming for each child based upon the results of the evaluation.

Some of the more frequently employed diagnostic instrumentation includes:

1. Detailed developmental history

2. Detailed educational history

3. Wechsler Intelligence Scale for Children (WISC)

4. Stanford-Binet (Form L-M)

5. Illinois Test of Psycholinguistic Ability (ITPA)

6. Peabody Picture Vocabulary Test (PPVT)

7. Children's Apperception Test (CAT)

8. Thematic Apperception Test (TAT)

9. Bender-Gestalt

10. Wide Range Achievement Test (WRAT)

11. Vineland Social Maturity Scale

12. Rorschach Psychodiagnostic Techniques

13. Rating Scales (Devereux Elementary School Behavior Rating Scale, Burke Behavior Rating Scale, etc.)

14. Standardized achievement testing

15. Detroit Tests of Learning Aptitude

The SID Coordinator should be responsible for items 1, 2, 13, and 14, which should accompany a referral for diagnostic evaluation.

It is crucial that the reader understand and be committed to the principle stated by Caplan (1964):

It is insufficient merely to identify the vulnerable child. One serious limitation even of highly sensitive early identification is the lack of available resources for remediation and follow-through.

The SID Coordinator is thoroughly trained in appropriate prescriptive techniques and further is able to utilize community resources to the child's best advantage. School personnel should be committed to programming for individual children before they request the SID program in their districts. In addition, the Division of Special Education is preparing an authoritative manuscript that will detail a number of models for the deliverance of Special Education Programming in rural areas. This manuscript will be available to interested educators and will be subject to constant revision as new models are developed.

The author is involved in a continuing research and demonstration project, the objective of which is to refine the SID program. Further research will be reported in the literature as projects are completed.

Article References

Ayer, J. The paired use of the Teacher Rating Scale of the Lambert and Bower Behavior Rating Scale and the Burke's Behavior Rating Scale to screen public school population for deviant behavior. Unpublished manuscript, University of Maine.

Burke, H.H. Manual for the Burke's Behavior Rating Scale. El Monte, Calif.: Arden Press, 1968.

Caplan, G. Principles of preventive psychiatry. New York: Basic Books, 1964.

Glidewell, J.C., & Swallow, C.S. The prevalence of maladjustment in elementary schools. Joint Commission on Mental Health of Children. Chicago: University of Chicago Press, 1968.

Lambert, N.M., & Bower, E.M. A process for in-school screening of children with emotional handicaps. Technical Report, California State Department of Education, Sacramento, California. Princeton, N.J.: Educational Testing Service, 1961.

Saunders, B.T. Emotional disturbance and social position within the non-graded classroom. Psychology in the Schools, 1970, 7, 269–271.

Saunders, B.T. Meeting special educational needs in rural Maine. Paper presented at Council for Exceptional Children, Topical Conference, Memphis, Tennessee, December 1971.

Because of the overlapping problems of emotional and learning problem children, two particular articles are included. The first, a general discussion of learning disabilities, theories, and explanations, is one of the few that clarify the interrelationships between the physical and psychological aspects. The overall common sense and integration of Ross's approach is impressive. Whether his category "dysfunction" is basically perceptual or conceptual is discussed in the next article.

Learning Difficulties of Children:
Dysfunctions, Disorders, Disabilities
Alan O. Ross

Psychotherapists' interest in learning problems of children antedates by a good many years (Liss, 1940) society's recent salutary concern over such questions as school dropout, cultural deprivation, and compensatory education. A review of the literature on learning problems, however, leads to the inescapable conclusion that despite their sustained interest clinicians have made little progress in coming to a better understanding of this problem. We cannot permit ourselves to be complacent about this state of ignorance, for whenever a child's scholastic achievement is below his potential the cost to him and to society is great indeed.

It would appear that one of the major reasons for this lack of progress is the conceptual confusion which plagues this particular area of inquiry. Whether one wants to engage in research on learning difficulties or desires to treat children with this handicap one must first come to grips with the basic question of definition and criteria. This paper will address itself to these points.

Learning difficulties is a broad and undifferentiated term that is often used as a diagnostic label for children brought to the clinician's attention. It is obvious that such a label merely describes an observation and thus explains nothing. It is a tautology to say that a child has a low score on an achievement test or that he failed to be promoted because he has a learning difficulty. In order to achieve finer discriminations among children of this type it seems useful to distinguish between different categories of learning difficulties.

Before discussing these categories, however, it is necessary to examine what is meant by learning difficulties. Learning is inferred from observed changes in performance which are presumed to be related to certain antecedent events called training or teaching. Because learning can only be manifested by performance, a learning difficulty must be defined in terms of difficulty in performance, thus calling not only for a measure of performance but also by a means of determining whether a difficulty in performance is present. A comparison of actual performance with expected performance would seem a simple way of ascertaining a discrepancy reflecting learning difficulty but it will be immediately apparent that expected performance is often a highly unreliable estimate and that inadequate actual performance may be reflecting disruption of performance and not lack of learning. The complex question of criteria for the evaluation of performance and the estimation of potential will receive further discussion but for the present a child with learning difficulties will be defined as one whose academic achievement falls below his intellectual potential.

The evaluation of academic achievement is usually in the hands of the teacher, who is thus not only the individual charged with helping the child learn but also the judge of what the child has learned. This dual role may confound the evaluation, for the teacher is thus asked to judge not only the child but also himself. Yet many children are classified as having a learning difficulty solely on the basis of their teacher's evaluations as these are recorded in the form of grades on report cards. Regardless of whether the teacher can be an objective judge of a child's achievement, grades invariably reflect not only achievement but also a variety of other judgments, such as those relating to effort, classroom behavior, and personality. The problem is confounded by the differences in educational philosophy which underlie the assignment of course grades in different schools and school systems so that a child who receives failing grades in one school might, for identical performance, be given passing grades in another.

From Alan O. Ross, "Learning Difficulties of Children: Disorders, Disabilities," *Journal of School Psychology*, Vol. V, Winter 1967, pp. 82–92. Reprinted by permission of *Journal of School Psychology*. Based on a discussion of papers on learning problems in adolescence, presented at the annual meeting of the American Orthopsychiatric Association, New York, March, 1965. Preparation was supported in part by Grant MH588 from the National Institute of Mental Health, United States Public Health Service.

The difficulty is not reduced but rather increased when the criterion for the presence or absence of a learning difficulty is based on whether or not a child was promoted from one grade to the next. While failure to be promoted is usually an indication that the child has not met the minimum requirement of his grade level, the converse is not necessarily true since promotion is very often an administrative decision, based only in part on the absolute academic performance of a student. Sometimes such questions as class size, physical appearance of the student, or a judgment of whether the child is likely to benefit from repeating a grade enter into the question of promotion.

One method of increasing the objectivity of the evaluation of a child's school achievement is to use quantitative measures based on standardized tests. Sperry and her associates (Grunebaum *et al.*, 1962) use the Metropolitan Achievement Tests for this purpose and classify a child as having a learning difficulty if his scores on this test place him at least two years behind his chronological age in one such major skill as reading, spelling, or arithmetic, and at least one year behind his age group in a second such skill. It will be recognized that chronological age can only be used as a base if the child is of at least average intelligence, as was the case in the studies just mentioned.

In order to arrive at a more generalizable formula one would have to compare achievement test scores with intelligence test scores so as to obtain a quantitative statement of the degree of learning difficulty. Unfortunately, intelligence tests, when used in such instances, do not necessarily give a valid base from which to judge whether a child's school performance is meeting his potential. We know that the same psychological factors which can disrupt learning and achievement test performance also frequently interfere with intelligence test performance. In fact, intelligence tests are in most respects no more than tests of school achievement. It is thus possible that a child shows no discrepancy between his achievement test scores and his intelligence test scores simply because both scores are equally depressed. Estimating a child's potential from his performance on an intelligence test requires considerable skill and experience and is, in the final analysis, no more than a clinical judgment but, unlike the teacher's judgment, it is based on an independent evaluation.

It must also be recognized that achievement tests are not entirely valid, for there are some children who, for reasons only vaguely understood, do very well on such tests but exceedingly poorly in class, while others who do very well in class perform poorly on the formal achievement test. Yet granting these limitations, it would still seem that a definition of learning difficulty in terms of discrepancies between intelligence and achievement test scores provides a more satisfactory basis for the detection of learning difficulties than the often subjective grades and arbitrary promotion record furnished by the school.

A Diagnostic Framework

Children whose measured academic achievement falls below their intellectual potential and who can thus be said to have learning difficulties seem to fall into three major categories: Learning Dysfunctions; Learning Disorders; and Learning Disabilities. Each of these categories can be viewed as having two subdivisions so that the diagnostic framework to be suggested identifies six distinct types of learning difficulties (see Table 1).

Learning Dysfunctions

The first major category, Learning Dysfunctions, includes those children who manifest perceptual disorders which interfere with their school performance without significantly disrupting their overall intellectual abilities. The category thus covers children who are at times said to have "perceptual motor problems", "cerebral dysfunctions", or "minimal brain damage". The subdivisions under this category take cognizance of the fact that children with perceptual disorders of this kind are frequently exposed to peer competition or pressures from puzzled and anxious parents or teachers to which they, in turn, respond with psychological reactions that further complicate their difficulties.

The first subdivision includes children without such secondary psychological problems. Help for children in this group would call for modifications in the educational approach designed to overcome or bypass the handicap. This may involve perceptual training in one or more modalities or help with establishing perceptual-motor integration. The special educational techniques described by Kephart (1960) can serve as a prototype of the kind of help required by such a child. For some of these children perceptual channels other than the visual or auditory may have to be used to help them benefit from teaching, and the special educational methods employed will often have to be highly individualized and based on a careful assessment of each child's capacities. In such an assessment the focus should be on the child's present condition and future potential, with the emphasis on how he can be helped to reach this potential. Questions of the etiology, though important from the standpoint of prevention, are not of the essence when an individual child is to be helped. Techniques based on operant conditioning are now available through which reading behavior can be experimentally studied (Staats, 1965) and reading as well as other forms of abstraction can be taught, even to severely impaired children, through the systematic application of basic learning principles in such a manner that each child can progress at his own individual pace (Bijou & Baer, 1963; Barrett, 1965).

The second subdivision under the category Learning Dysfunctions includes those children who do manifest secondary psychological reactions to the stress occasioned by the learning difficulty. These reactions may take the form of aggression with or without hyperactive and disruptive classroom behavior, social withdrawl with verbalization reflecting feelings of inadequacy and inferiority, possibly accompanied by somatic complaints or regressive phenomena with immature and passive manifestations. These reactions, in other words, may run the gamut of the complaints usually seen by child therapists and the specific form they take

for an individual child probably depends not only on his general reaction pattern but also on the manner in which the demands for academic achievement are expressed by his immediate environment.

Following the suggestion of Schaefer (1961) one might speculate that the child of the mother who tries to handle his learning dysfunction in a hostile-rejecting fashion will develop an aggressive reaction, while the child whose mother is the hostile-controlling type will be more likely to react by withdrawal. The regressed, passive-immature child might well be the product of the affectionately-controlling mother who expresses her anxieties around his learning dysfunction by overprotective behavior.

The relationship between learning difficulties and the interaction between mother and child has received a good deal of attention but there has been little progress in reaching a better understanding of the phenomenon. A search of the literature discloses repeated statements suggesting that it is the mother's covert hostility toward males and her infantilizing and overprotecting of the boy which is at the root of the learning difficulty. This causal statement is based on the observation that many boys with learning difficulties have mothers who are either covertly hostile or overprotecting. One might, however, interpret this correlation to mean that these behaviors on the part of the mother are her reactions to the child's learning difficulties. At any rate, before the causal question can be resolved it would be important to determine whether these particular maternal characteristics are absent in mothers of boys without learning difficulties.

Table 1. Learning Difficulties

Learning Dysfunctions		Learning Disorders		Learning Disabilities	
Without secondary reactions	With secondary reactions	Primary	Secondary	Chronic	Reactive
Special education	Special education *plus* therapy	Therapy *plus* remedial education	Problem-focused intervention	Therapeutic education	Therapy (plus tutoring)

The secondary psychological reactions to learning dysfunctions can thus complicate the diagnostic picture when the reaction is seen as the cause of the learning difficulty. A child may be anxious and therefore not able to learn or he may not be able to learn and therefore become anxious, yet in both cases, not learning may increase anxiety, thus further interfering with the capacity to learn. An ability to distinguish between antecedent and consequence, while not necessarily essential in helping an individual child, may serve to advance our understanding of learning difficulties and possibly aid in developing preventive measures.

Clinical contributions to the literature on learning difficulties frequently link these to problems in the handling of aggression, and the usual inference is that aggression is the antecedent, the learning difficulty the consequence. The formulation often assumes that the child, having learned that the expression of aggression is dangerous, has come to inhibit competitive, self-assertive and striving behavior to the point where this generalizes to school achievement. This formulation is based on the clinical observation that boys with learning difficulties are frequently passive and inhibited but attributing causal implications to this observation is again not justified. Before this causal relationship can be accepted one must rule out the equally plausible hypothesis that passivity and inhibition are the consequences of the frustrations encountered by a child who is unable to learn. It may well be that conflict around aggression and inhibition might be an important factor in many learning difficulties. One should recall, however, that conflict around the expression of aggression is one of the most frequently encountered problems in the boys of today's society so that it is not particularly surprising to find this conflict also among children with learning difficulties.

We all too often look for the cause of learning difficulties in the child's personality. Not having found conclusive answers there, our search has carried us in ever-widening circles into the environment. We have studied the child's interaction with his mother, then with his father, later with both parents, and most recently we are looking at family interaction as the source of the difficulty. The next round of this outward search involving the community and society has already begun, but it may be appropriate to question whether we are going in the right direction in this search. Instead of moving ever outward from the child it might be necessary to turn back and look inside the child who is, after all, the

learning organism. It may well be that atypical cognitive capabilities are the basis of many of the learning problems which most confound us. The things we are trying to teach and the manner in which we teach them would thus be far more crucial to investigate than some of the child's interpersonal interactions. It is, for example, entirely feasible that a child who has difficulties with his schoolwork has a disrupting influence on the family and not vice versa. Since not all children learn at the same rate or in the same manner, a careful analysis of the individual child's specific learning difficulty should lead to highly individualized remedial efforts.

Help for children with secondary psychological reactions to learning dysfunctions would have to entail not only special education but also attempts at alleviating the confounding psychological disorder. These two therapeutic approaches, the one habilitative, the other rehabilitative, would have to be closely coordinated and ideally carried out under the auspices of the same institution, be it the school or the clinic. The reason for this close coordination becomes obvious when one examines, as an example, the child who has developed a fear of failure as a result of repeated failure experiences in his academic endeavors. Such a child is unlikely to benefit from even the most sophisticated special education until he can face a task with even a modicum of confidence, but he is not likely to gain confidence until he has had some success experiences. Helping such a child to break out of this self-defeating cycle calls for great skill and close collaboration between therapist and educator. Ideally, in fact, these two roles had best be combined in the same person.

Learning Disorders

The second major category in the classificatory scheme here proposed, Learning Disorders, covers cases usually referred to as "neurotic learning inhibitions" but within this group it seems again useful to differentiate between cases where the disability is primary and those where it is secondary. In either case, the disorder might be conceptualized by viewing academic performance as behavior which is disrupted or prevented by incompatible responses. Children with primary learning disorders are those for whom learning itself is aversive and whose avoidance or escape behavior to learning occurs both in and out of school. Where this difficulty has been present from the very beginning of school it is synonymous with the primary neurotic learning inhibitions described by Sperry and her co-workers at the Judge Baker Guidance Center (Sperry *et al.*, 1958). The reason a different terminology is here suggested is that the term "primary neurotic learning inhibitions" carries connotations derived from a theory which states that the cause of the problem is that "the major displacement of the internal conflict has been made directly upon the school material" (Grunebaum *et al.*, 1962). In trying to focus on the helping process, such etiologic speculations are here purposely avoided.

One important aspect of the primary learning disorder is that it represents a cumulatively worsening process due to the pyramidal nature of education. A child who has been unable to learn the basic tool subjects in the primary grades experiences an ever-increasing disability, since later teaching is always based on competencies presumed to have been established earlier. It is an unfortunate paradox that the brighter a child, the more severely handicapped he will become because his very brightness may mask the degree of his disability. In the first few years of school such a child can usually achieve a passing grade on examinations and achievement tests, thus hiding how little he has learned. Only a careful comparison of his estimated intellectual potential with his actual achievement will reveal the discrepancy, but since individual intelligence tests, the only basis on which intellectual potential can be even roughly estimated, are rarely given routinely, cases of this nature may go undiscovered for many years.

Because of the cumulative nature of this difficulty, help for such a child requires not only intensive psychological treatment aimed at strengthening the learning-appropriate responses and weakening the incompatible behavior, but he would also need massive remedial education designed to help him catch up with all the basic skills he failed to learn during the years of his disorder. Here again close coordination between the two rehabilitative agents is essential. A child of say, 12 years of age who has to start learning grade two reading and arithmetic will need considerable psychological and social support in order to aid him to accept remedial work. Even after effective learning is made possible, a great deal of continued remedial work and tutoring may be necessary, for unless such a child can be brought up to his age-appropriate grade level, his school experience will continue to be unrewarding and his achievement will consequently continue to suffer.

Secondary Learning Disorders are those where not learning itself but behavior prerequisite for learning is disrupted. It is here that the *true* school phobia should be classified for these are not children who avoid learning but who avoid school, that is the physical setting and not the acquisition of knowledge. Unless the intense and disabling fear reaction has generalized from school to books and subject matter, such children are often able to learn in any setting other than school. The writer (Ross, 1964) has previously proposed that where such generalization has taken place and fear or anxiety interfere with the ability to engage in learning it might be possible to institute a program of desensitization therapy based on a learning set paradigm.

Kennedy (1965) reports remarkable therapeutic success with carefully defined cases of school phobia when they are quickly identified and rapidly treated immediately after onset. Viewing school phobia as a learned reaction, Kennedy's group treated it in a systematic six-step approach extending over a period of three days. All 50 cases treated in this manner over a period of eight years responded with complete remission and a follow-up study showed no evidence of substitute symptoms or recurrence of the phobia.

In school phobia, fear of school keeps the child from learning in school. A somewhat related problem which should be classified as a Secondary Learning Disorder is that of the child whose marked hostility toward school or teacher disrupts his ability to learn. Again the reaction is not to learning *per se* and a different teacher or a different school may well succeed in working with such a child.

In most of these secondary learning disorders the onset is fairly sudden and occurs after a substantial period of consistent academic success. As Kennedy (1965) has shown, it is important to intervene early because once too much essential subject matter has gone unlearned, failure is likely to beget failure as anxiety over school achievement mounts and self-reliance declines. Left unattended for too long, cases of this nature can become confounded by further psychological reactions not unlike those discussed under the category of learning dysfunctions. In intervention does take place early, neither extended treatment nor remedial education is necessarily required. It is undoubtedly among this group that we find the greatest number of spontaneous remissions and remarkable academic success after an interlude of alarming failure. The greater the child's intellectual capacity, the easier it is for him to bridge a brief hiatus in learning and to catch up with his scholastic peers.

Learning Disabilities

The third major category in the classificatory scheme here proposed is Learning Disabilities. It is composed of children whose ability to perform in school is disrupted or made impossible by psychological disorders which do not have their primary focus on learning or on the school situation. Unlike the cases in the previous category, these children have disabling problems unrelated to learning, school or teachers.

In this group too it seems useful to differentiate two subdivisions. The first would be composed of cases with long-standing and pervasive disorders, such as infantile autism or childhood schizophrenia. This group will be referred to as Chronic Learning Disabilities. Little is known about how to help children with disorders of this type but among the most promising approaches are those of therapeutic education, where treatment and teaching coincide and where teacher and therapist are one and the same person. Inasmuch as a severe disorder of this kind disrupts most, if not all, of the child's behavior, it is necessary to build or rebuild his entire response repertoire in both object, personal and interpersonal relations; and whatever approach might be used, it must basically be one of painstaking teaching. Recent work in this area suggests that the systematic application of principles of learning to the treatment of autistic children carries great promise. Davison (1965), for example, reports the case of a nine-year-old autistic boy who is undergoing social-learning treatment and who, after only six months of such treatment, was no longer engaging in tantrum behavior, responded positively to the world about him, followed verbal instructions, and was beginning to read and write. A case of a nonverbal 4½-year-old autistic boy reported by Hewett (1965) shows that is is possible to establish a basic speaking vocabulary in such a child by the use of operant conditioning speech training. It is of interest to note that these techniques can be successfully applied even though there remains considerable diversity of opinion regarding the basic etiology of infantile autism (Ferster, 1961; Rimland, 1964). All that is necessary in order to help a child is to establish that he is *now* unable to engage in appropriate behavior and to find a way through which such behavior can now be taught. What brought the child to his present state is of secondary, largely theoretical interest.

The second subdivision includes children who, after a period of sustained success, fail to perform adequately in school because psychological problems essentially unrelated to school or to learning interfere with their ability to acquire academic subject matter or to reproduce such subject matter, thus showing that they have acquired it. This group will be referred to as Reactive Learning Disabilities. Children in this group are usually reacting to a crisis or trauma in their environment and this reaction interferes with their cognitive processes so that their capacity to absorb new learning or to recall old learning is impaired. Anxiety about separating from the mother with the resulting refusal to go to school which is sometimes erroneously classified as school phobia is one example of a disability of this type. Another might be the child who has experienced the traumatic loss of a close relative and is in acute depression. In each instance it is not learning or school or teachers who elicit avoidance reactions and this differentiates this group from the Secondary Learning Disorders previously described.

Among the children with Reactive Learning Disabilities are also those who are reacting to their parents with negativism and hostility and who find that these can be expressed in a potent fashion by not going to school, not learning or not showing that they are learning. Less directly, pervasive hostility toward a parent may be preoccupying the child in the same manner as the crisis or trauma previously mentioned.

In cases of this nature treatment must address itself to the problem which disrupts learning and if effective therapeutic intervention can take place soon after onset so that adequate functioning can be restored quickly, the child should be able to continue his academic endeavors without requiring special tutoring. However, here too the possibility exists that if weeks and months go by without grade-appropriate learning so that the child falls further and further behind his classmates, secondary psychological reactions in terms of fear of failure and feelings of inadequacy can develop to complicate the diagnostic picture and make treatment more difficult.

Before concluding this outline for a framework within which to classify children whose academic achievement falls below intellectual potential, it should be pointed out that all of these categories are based on the premise that the child's basic intellectual potential is adequate for the tasks demanded of him in school. This suggestion for a nosologic system does not cover the mental defective or the severely brain damaged child whose achievement is at par with his limited intellectual capacity. Nor does this system cover the disadvantaged children whose lack of appropriate achievement is due to poor teaching, inadequate educational facilities, or cultural handicap, situations where the source of the difficulty clearly lies outside the child, calling for remedial action on the part of society.

In hopes of contributing to the better understanding and alleviation of children's learning difficulties, we have proposed a diagnostic framework which differentiates between Learning Dysfunctions, Learning Disorders, and Learning Disabilities. In each case the category and subdivision used points to the specific kind of help required by children so classified, for unless diagnostic efforts lead to constructive intervention they are no more than an academic exercise.

Article References

Barrett, Beatrice H. Acquisition of operant differentiation and discrimination in institutionalized retarded children. *Amer. J. Orthopsychiat.*, 1965, *35*, 862–885.

Bijou, S.W., and D.M. Baer. Some methodological contributions from a functional analysis of child development. In L.P. Lipsitt and C.C. Spiker (eds.) *Advances in Child Development and Behavior*, Vol. 1, New York: Academic Press, 1963.

Davison, G.C. An intensive long-term social-learning treatment program with an accurately diagnosed autistic child. In American Psychological Association, *Proceedings of the 73rd Annual Convention*, 1965.

Ferster, C.B. Positive reinforcement and behavioral deficits of autistic children. *Child Developm.*, 1961, *32*, 437–456.

Grunebaum, Margaret, G., I. Hurwitz, N. Prentice, and Bessie M. Sperry. Fathers of sons with primary neurotic learning inhibitions. *Amer. J. Orthopsychiat.*, 1962, *32*, 462–472.

Hewett, F.M. Teaching speech to an autistic child through operant conditioning. *Amer. J. Orthopsychiat.*, 1965, *35*, 927–936.

Kennedy, W.A. School phobia: rapid treatment of fifty cases. *J. Abnorm. Psychol.*, 1965, *70*, 285–289.

Kephart, N.C. *The slow learner in the classroom.* Columbus, Ohio: Merrill, 1960.

Liss, E. Learning: its sadistic and masochistic manifestations: *Amer. J. Orthopsychiat.*, 1940, *10*, 123–128.

Rimland, B. *Infantile autism: the syndrome and its implications for a neural theory of behavior.* New York: Appleton-Century-Crofts, 1964.

Ross, A.O. Learning theory and therapy with children. *Psychotherapy: Theor., Res. and Pract.*, 1964, *1*, 102–108.

Schaefer, E.S. Converging conceptual models for maternal behavior and for child behavior. In J.C. Glidewell, (ed.) *Parental attitudes and child behavior.* Springfield, Ill.: Charles C. Thomas, 1961.

Sperry, Bessie, N. Staver, B. Reiner, and D. Ulrich. Renunciation and denial in learning difficulties. *Amer. J. Orthopsychiat.*, 1958, *28*, 98–111.

Staats, A.W. A case in and a strategy for the extension of learning principles to problems of human behavior. In L. Krasner and L.P. Ullmann (eds.) *Research in behavior modification.* New York: Holt, Rinehart & Winston, 1965.

The selection reprinted here, by Rabinovitch and Ingram, is notable for the insight of its observations of a series of cases seen in a psychiatric setting. The article is part of a series of studies leading to the development of a new scale through the examination of test data and the "sensing" of interview and case-history material. Three major diagnostic groupings are formulated. We do not know in what percentages these types are found but we do see clearly what they are. Then the syndrome of "primary retardation" is developed in detail with concrete examples. The generalizations drawn from the cases and the etiology are woven into the practical implications for treatment.

Neuropsychiatric
Considerations
in Reading Retardation

Ralph D. Rabinovitch
Winifred Ingram

A close, interdependent relationship between our schools and our psychiatric clinics and hospitals is generally recognized as essential for effective work with school age children. Two relatively new developments have further highlighted the need for this integration of effort. On the one hand there is the rapid growth of special education classes for the emotionally disturbed in the public schools, and on the other hand expansion of specialized classroom programs in psychiatric day-care and in-patient centers.[6]

In our work in both public school and psychiatric settings we have been impressed with the high incidence of reading and language problems among the total referrals. We have been particularly interested to note that in those schools that have developed special psychiatric or social adjustment rooms, the regular classroom teachers have tended to recommend children with both personality and gross reading problems. Even severe disturbance tends to be found tolerable in the classroom if the child is making adequate academic progress. This was not anticipated when some of these programs were established and we now find teachers trained to work with the emotionally disturbed faced with virtually illiterate children whose special remedial needs they do not feel competent to meet. Similarly, through bitter experience, we have learned that for a significant percentage of the *boys* admitted to Hawthorn Center's day-care or in-patient units, psychotherapy and milieu therapy alone are insufficient for rehabilitation; intensive specific remedial reading therapy must be added. Of necessity, then, our multidiscipline group has been forced to give major research and clinical attention to reading problems.

A severe burden imposed on child, family and clinic worker alike is the tendency of many school people and pediatricians to refer the child with the assumption that the psychiatric clinic will find the learning problem to be due to an "emotional block" and that through the magic of psychotherapy, perhaps limited to a few interviews, the child will be "released" to learn adequately. Unfortunately some of us in child psychiatry and clinical psychology have fostered this attitude in the past, overgeneralizing dynamic formulations. The problem is much more complex and there is a need for careful differential diagnosis in each case studied.

Two broad factors in the child's reading functioning must be assessed: (1) The mastery of specific techniques and skills necessary for reading; (2) The application of skills in the learning situation.

In recent years there has been a valid emphasis by educators on content in learning, on the social meaningfulness of what is taught, and this has led to many positive changes in curriculum. Repetitive drill work has been reduced in both language and arithmetic, much to the benefit of the victims of schooling. In the large majority of children, reading skills tend to evolve spontaneously, stimulated and directed by good teachers. With these children con-

From Ralph D. Rabinovitch and Winifred Ingram, "Neuropsychiatric Considerations in Reading Retardation," *Reading Teacher*, XV (May 1962), 433−439. Reprinted with permission of Ralph D. Rabinovitch and Winifred Ingram and the International Reading Association.

tent becomes the major concern. But, unfortunately, there are some for whom written material remains meaningless and for whom there can be no content because the *technique* of reading itself is lacking. Despite the highest level of motivation and effort, they have difficulty learning to translate letter symbols into concepts. The *process of symbolization* is impaired and learning through "normal" teaching methods cannot be expected.

In some of these cases history indicates brain injury (encephalopathy) as the probable cause of disability. In other cases no history is found and the disability is felt to be due to a developmental neurological deficit.

Using the broad term "reading retardation" to describe all cases in which there is a significant discrepancy between mental age on performance tests and level of reading achievement, we can, then, define three major diagnostic groupings:[7][8]

1.   Capacity to learn to read is impaired without definite brain damage suggested in history or on neurologic examination. The defect is in the ability to deal with letters and words as symbols, with resultant diminished ability to integrate the meaningfulness of written material. The problem appears to reflect a basic disturbed pattern of neurologic organization. Because the cause is biologic or endogenous, these cases are diagnosed as *primary reading retardation.*

2.   Capacity to learn to read is impaired by frank brain damage manifested by clear-cut neurologic deficits. The picture is similar to the early-described adult dyslexic syndromes. Other definite aphasic difficulties are generally present. History usually reveals the cause of the brain injury, common agents being prenatal toxicity, birth trauma or anoxia, encephalitis, and head injury. These cases are diagnosed as *brain injury with resultant reading retardation.*

3.   Capacity to learn to read is intact but is utilized insufficiently for the child to achieve a reading level appropriate to his mental age. The causative factor is exogenous, the child having a normal reading potential that has been impaired by negativism, anxiety, depression, emotional blocking, psychosis, limited schooling opportunity or other external influence. We diagnose these as *secondary reading retardation.*

Unfortunately the criteria for definite differential diagnosis are still uncertain and the problem is complicated by much overlap in etiology in individual cases. It is difficult to be certain in the cases of suspected secondary reading retardation, the problem being to rule out a basic developmental deficiency mild in degree. Through the years our research group has come to view the incidence of secondary retardation as lower than we had at first anticipated. While the meaningfulness to the child of what he reads will be strongly conditioned by his life experience and personality, and while the rapidity of his progress in learning will be much influenced by his social opportunities, his basic mastery of symbolization is probably much more neurologically determined than we had once thought. Detailed studies of the reading skills of severely disturbed inpatients, presenting a wide range of psychopathology and attending school in residence, should prove helpful in assessing the effects of specific relationship and life experience distortions on the reading process and its application. Such studies are now in progress at Hawthorn Center.

Of all the children with reading problems those with primary retardation present the greatest challenge. In our research we have devoted major attention to this group. Beginning with the surface symptom we can define the syndrome in terms of the following levels of process disturbance:

1. Reading Retardation: The level of disability is usually severe and apart from a small sight vocabulary, learned by rote, and sporadic simple phonic skills there may be almost no functional reading ability. Arithmetic competence is usually also low although it may be somewhat higher than the reading level. Greatest impairment may be in spelling, reflected in the child's attempts at writing to dictation.

2. Reading Process Disturbance: Analysis of the child's reading performance indicates difficulties in both visual and auditory areas and directionality also tends to be impaired. Visual recognition and discrimination on a perceptual level are intact but letter forms and combinations cannot be translated into meaningful concepts. In a similar way, in the auditory sphere, differences in vowel sounds are appreciated when presented orally, but the sounds cannot be translated into their letter symbols. For example, when a series of short vowel sounds "i, i, e, i" are presented orally, the "e" is readily recognized as different from the "i's" but the crucial step required for reading and spelling, the translation of the sound into its appropriate letter symbol, is impaired. The difficulty then is in symbolization in both visual and auditory fields. Complicating the problem may be left-right directional confusion with or without mixed laterality. Some typical illustrative examples of writing to dictation by children with a severe primary syndrome follow:[5]

Paul is aged twelve, referred for psychiatric study because of severe depression. He is in the fifth grade, having repeated both the third and fourth grades. On the Wechsler Test performance I.Q. is 114, verbal I.Q. 82. Tested reading level is preprimer despite a performance mental age of fourteen years. Diagnosis is severe primary retardation. Paul produces the following when asked to write to dictation "The boy came home":

[handwritten:] ICⁱᵇ ƧIL LΙⅽⁱ GⱾLe

Paul's production reveals total confabulation with no capacity to deal with letters as symbols. Both visual and auditory skills are grossly deficient.

Bill, aged nine, was referred because of school truancy and acting-out behavior in the classroom. Originally considered mentally retarded because of inability to learn at school, psychometric testing indicates that Bill is of normal intellectual potential, performance I.Q. being 94; verbal I.Q. is 72. Reading level is low first grade. Bill writes "The boy came home" as follows:

[handwritten:] The doy nor house

This child depends totally on his visual memory and has virtually no phonic skills. He recalls "nor" as a word and just hopes that by chance it will turn out to be "came." He struggles with "boy," but cannot differentiate from "dog" and the contamination "doy" emerges.

Tom is diagnosed as having primary reading retardation at age seven, midway through the first grade, which he had repeated. At that time he wrote "The boy came home" as follows:

[handwritten:] ⵟ2Ƨ T LΟⅠⵌ

An intensive remedial program was instituted and at age nine he has progressed to this point:

[handwritten:] the doy came home

Tom still reverses "b's" and "d's" but he is well on the road to reading competence.

3. Broader Language Deficits: While in everyday conversation the child may appear to manage relatively well, careful attention to the language pattern reveals frequent difficulties in specific name finding, imprecise articulation and primitive syntax. Typical examples drawn from the responses by severe primary cases to test questioning follow:

Why is it better to build a house of brick than of wood? "Well just in case a hurricane the house can break down, but you put the brick on, it can just hit it but not break nothing down." (Age nine years)

What must you do to make water boil? "You should put it under a fire." (Age ten years)

How did he get hurt? "He sprang a thing, a arm when he felled out of that tree." (Age eleven years)

Is it night-time or day-time now? "Day-time. It's, well, clouds are out and stuff. It's white the clouds, it's lightsen up, the clouds and stuff." (Age nine years)

Is it morning or afternoon? "It's in the noon-time. Noon. In the noon." (Age nine years)

These tend to represent extreme examples, but we look for similar disturbances in expressive language in all cases of the primary syndrome.

4. Specific Concept-Symbolization Deficiency in Orientation: The symbolization defect is not limited to the reading processes alone, but is found to be more basic. There is difficulty in translating orientational concepts into symbols. Thus while the child has no trouble appreciating which of two people is taller, he cannot define their height in feet. Similarly, while he knows clearly that he wakes up in the morning, he may be unable to express this knowledge in terms of a specific hour. To explore further this orientational factor we have devised the Hawthorn Center Concept-Symbolization Test with questions relating to personal information, time, quantity and dimension, number, directionality and laterality. Drs. Ingram, Katz, Kauffman, Langman and Lynn of our group are now completing standardization of the test which we hope may prove helpful as a diagnostic and prognostic instrument, especially with young children, and as a partial key to therapy need.[4]

5. Body Image Problems: Even more basic, there may be disturbances in personal-orientation or body image but these have been much less clearly demonstrated. Now we are using Benton's Laterality and Finger Localization Test and other approaches to study further this aspect of the pathology (1).

All of us working with children with severe reading problems recognize the need for more precise differential diagnostic criteria. We are approaching this problem in two ways. First, a longitudinal study of reading progress of classes of children in public schools is under way. A large battery of tests has been given, starting with first grade, and two groups have been isolated for detailed comparative investigation, those at the highest and at the lowest end of the scale of reading competence; from this study, now in its fourth year, we hope to isolate prognostic indices. Second, our psychologists are attempting to refine differential diagnostic criteria through detailed analysis of psychologic test data, obtained from children presenting a wide range of psychopathology, including language and reading disabilities. Tests used are the Wechsler, the Stanford-Binet LM, Bender-Gestalt, Draw-A-Family, Hawthorn Center Concept-Symbolization Scale and Benton Laterality and Finger Localization Battery. Thus far all data point at least in one direction: the problem is not one in perception per se, but rather in the translation of perceptions and concepts into meaningful symbols that can be used in reading and related language functions.

The total symptom complex of the primary reading retardation syndrome gives, we feel, a clue to the etiology: a neurological deficit, often familial in origin, and expressing parietal cerebral dysfunction (2, 3).

No discussion of neuropsychiatric considerations in reading problems can avoid mention of the inordinate suffering experienced by otherwise normal children, cut off from communication channels, increasingly vital for survival today. With limited resources to meet their specific needs we are obliged all too often to limit our involvement with them to documenting their successive psychological reactions from initial anger to guilt feelings, depression and ultimate resignation and compromise with their aspirations. Work in clinics throughout the country has encouraged us to hope that early intervention by well trained language therapists may permit many children with primary reading retardation to develop at least functional reading competence. Major needs are for early diagnosis and the provision of intensive remedial programs in the public schools. In addition, an adjusted curriculum throughout the school years, relying minimally on literacy, must be devised for some students. It is interesting, if disconcerting, to note how much further advanced our speech correction programs are, in comparison with those for reading therapy. It may be that the speech correction workers have been more aggressive in presenting their reasonable demands and have in the past had more clearcut programs to offer. But now, as reading diagnostic issues are becoming clarified and as specific remedial techniques are evolving, the time is ripe for implementation of large-scale special education reading services in our public schools. Such programs, financed by special reimbursements available in many States, must take their place alongside those already established for children with speech, visual, hearing, orthopedic and other handicaps. In view of the fact that no responsibility of the public school is greater than to teach all children to read, the inclusion of remedial reading as a recognized branch of special education would seem as logical as it is essential.

Article References

1. **Benton, A.L.** *Right-Left Discrimination and Finger Localization: Development and Pathology.* New York: Hoeber, 1959.

2. **Critchley, M.** *The Parietal Lobes.* Baltimore: Williams and Wilkins, 1953.

3. **Drew, A.L.** "A Neurological Appraisal of Familial Congenital Word-Blindness." *Brain*, 79:440, 1956.

4. **Langman, M.P.** "The Reading Process: a Descriptive Interdisciplinary Approach." *Genetic Psychol. Monographs*, 62:3, 1960.

5. **Missildine, H., and L. Eisenberg.** "Physician's Role in Management of Retarded Reader." *Feelings*, 3, No. 9, October 1961.

6. **Morse, W.C.** "Education of the Socially Maladjusted and Emotionally Disturbed Children." W.M. Cruickshank and G.O. Johnson, eds., *Education and Exceptional Children and Youth.* New York: Prentice-Hall, 1958.

7. **Rabinovitch, R.D.** Learning and Reading Dis-

abilities, in S. Arieti, ed., *Handbook of Psychiatry.* New York: Basic Books, 1959.

8. **Rabinovitch, R.D., A.L. Drew, R.N. DeJong, W. Ingram,** and **L. Withey** "A Research Approach to Reading Retardation," in R. McIntosh, ed., *Neurology and Psychiatry in Childhood.* Baltimore: Williams and Wilkins, 1956.

A rare follow-up study of serious learning disability cases gives a pessimistic view of the future.[22] [23]

Procedures combining elements of screening with diagnosis have also been developed. The purpose is to identify a problem and to seek out general patterns or syndromes of behavior —to diagnose the specific nature of the problem. As we review the procedures for assembling this information we will find many facets and styles. Melvin Zax and Emory Cowen and their associates have done some of the most extensive work on identification and prevention over the years.[24] They have found it possible to identify pupils in the first grade who will be problems by the third grade. Their detection procedures include a group intelligence test, the Goodenough Draw-A-Man test, and behavioral observation by the psychologist. Teachers rate ability and adjustment and social workers interview the mother concerning her child's developmental history, adjustment, and other family conditions. This investigation produces a general evaluative criterion rather than specific familial situations that predict particular pathologies.

One of the most frequently used methods for analysis of deviant behavior is the case study. Its basic purpose is to integrate the total life experience. When done well, it serves as a compendium of information and understanding by combining identifying information, psychological test data, gleanings from observation and interviews, and in-depth interpretation. A conceptual system is necessary for organizing a case study. Without it, the study may lack appreciation of the sociological press under which the child lives in the home, school, and community.

Rothney[25] has a well-rounded discussion of the content needed in a case study. He differentiates between census and personal data.

By census data we mean items such as name, age, height, weight, place of residence, and place of birth which may be essential in the identification of the person and his setting. Personal data are derived from the observation of any subject, regardless of his census classifications. The difference between these kinds of data is that the census materials are verifiable items which can *be obtained from records but which do not permit interpretations that apply solely to an individual. The personal data permit interpretations by an investigator from his observations of how a particular individual performs and behaves. (page 6)*

Rothney does not believe that any outline should be followed arbitrarily, but he gives the following general guides for data gathering. First, any information that will help in understanding the child should be considered, which means a wider scope of behavior than has traditionally been studied. Second, because of the variations in reliability of information, all data must be evaluated. Third, the child's cultural situation is considered part of the matrix. The reader is encouraged to consult Rothney's book for details.

Many times, additional specific studies are needed to deepen the case study. However, some investigators spend more time collecting detailed information than in developing plans. Additional assessment is needed when one cannot devise a plan because of a lack of understanding, but in many cases, careful thinking with already available knowledge is enough for plans beyond available resources. In short, diagnostic studies should not be substituted for interventions. It is easier to study a problem than to develop plans for change, and to some it is more fascinating to examine than to confront.

But often examination in more depth will be necessary to comprehend a problem. We may need sociological information: What forces in the community—such as gangs in a slum or the "achievement neurosis" in a suburb—operate on the pupil? We may need to know how the family interrelates—the roles and configurations of mother, father, and siblings. (This information is particularly important if the neurotic child is the family scapegoat.)

The psychologist contributes by study of the intellectual and affective nature of the child. Individual intelligence tests reveal both the overall IQ and where functioning may be relatively high or low. For example, is the memory, reasoning, or perception below expected limits? Particularly for children who may have learning capacity deficiencies, the quality of performance is as important as the quantity. (However, to go from test results to a concrete classroom prescription is difficult, and the teacher can make significant additions to the psychological findings.) Projective tests, used to gauge anxiety, fear, and hate, often indicate the particular life area that is the source of difficulty. Drawing, creative writing, stories told about semi-ambiguous pictures, and responses to ink blots are examples of the psychologists' exploration devices. The most difficult result to obtain is a quantified appraisal of moral or values development. Basically, the psychologist tries to reveal underlying emotional states.

Mary Engel[26] has written a classic article on the parameters of the psychologist's testing role with children. The first parameter is control. Because the child is "forced" to the situation, he reacts with uncanny skill to control the situation by using a range of "actions" from silence to hyperactivity. Under pressure he may regress. The conditions she discusses are present in any interview with a child. But giving a test under absolute pre-set conditions adds more stress.

Social workers and psychiatrists contribute to the case study through insights gained in diagnostic interviews with families and children. Although this mode has been seriously criticized for its subjectivity, it is also true that the trained human mind is a most flexible and sensitive instrument. Essentially the interview is an interaction between two human beings. When the interviewer is responding to his own cues, giving hints, or forcing issues, his results will be suspect. However, training and self-regulation minimize these factors to make interviews an important source of insight.

The Problem of Incidence and Differential Diagnosis

Differential diagnosis is critical in designing intervention programs. For example, to set the proper rewards for operant conditioning, one must know what the individual considers a reward. No problem arises when a hungry rat is offered food or a deprived boy is offered new toys, but it is more difficult to predict when a pupil may find a teacher's strong reprimand more rewarding than being ignored. The child's response depends on his motivational system. When a child seeks punishment, is gratified by making an adult angry, or listens but doesn't feel because he lacks empathic concern, differential diagnosis becomes focal for therapeutic planning. Suppose he says "I can't do it" when confronted with a math problem. If the child makes

this statement because he is afraid of failure, the teacher's strategy should be different than if the child sees no value in learning anything about numbers. Differential diagnosis requires that we know the reason behind the behavior so that we can design proper approaches.

Labeling a child neurotic or psychotic is not the level of differential diagnosis that the teacher needs. Although labels should have the same connotation for all who use them, the categories are usually too general. Chapter 1 of this book illustrated the individuality of youngsters, even those with the same general diagnoses. The purpose of differential diagnosis is to plan differential treatment. Although no two children are alike, particular types show recognizable contrasts. To a degree symptoms are arrayed in patterns that indicate certain handling. A psychopath does not benefit from the same adult response as does an anxious neurotic.

Although many psychiatric interviews with disturbed younger children and adolescents are brief "verifying" snapshots, a skilled child psychiatrist has the potential of offering first-hand diagnostic information on how the child sees his life and where the basic problems lie. With young children, play therapy may be utilized, and with older children semiprojective interactions in completing stories or making up a TV play.[27] Drawings may be encouraged. Talking with adolescents, especially defensive ones, requires great skill, for the interview is also a relationship experience for the youngster. The importance of the interview is to help the youngster give his ideas and fantasies. Werkman[28] considers the most important interview question to be: "Why are you here?" And asking the child about three wishes he would make, his family, school, and peer life, give direction to further probes in important areas. Before the interview is over, however, there should be closure to help the child regain his defenses and know that help will be given. Goodman has an excellent series of suggestions on the interview.[29]

The purpose of screening is to locate potential problems. The purposes of further study are (1) to be certain the behavior is not a normal response to a situation that must be changed; and if not, (2) to reach a diagnosis of the nature of the problem. The conclusions from these studies lead to planning. Thus, it is necessary to collect material from the various sources to understand what interventions are appropriate. Rabinovitch[30] calls this procedure "clinical ledger and functional diagnosis." From the presented symptoms, one goes to the dynamic situation. Although some dimensions are easier to scale than others, the goal is to gather the information into a profile summary:

Functional Diagnostic Dimensions

Level of Intellectual Performance: Abstraction, Problem Solving, etc.
Verbal IQ
Performance IQ
Rote learning   each with a function and capacity rating
Social concepts

Neurological Integration
Large-muscle coordination
Small-muscle coordination
Visual-motor coordination

Language Skills
Oral comprehension
Oral expression
Reading: oral
                  sight vocabulary
                  phonetic skills
                  comprehension
Spelling
Arithmetic

Clarity of Ego Boundaries

Level of Depth Relationships: Empathy

Self-Concept—Self-Esteem

Relationships and Identifications

Freedom from Disabling Anxiety

Acculturalization: Opportunities and Exposure to Learning Experience

---

Where one goes from here is described in following sections and in a summary outline by Cheney and Morse.[31]

As we bring this chapter to a close, we turn to an examination of the overall incidence and nature of childhood mental illness, which is presented in some detail. Various recent studies by the Joint Commission on the Mental Health of Children have found that estimates of the amount of school maladjustment range from a low of three and four percent to highs of 12 and 22 percent of the pupils. But no consistency in definition or process of identification exists and one expects considerable variation from one community to another.

Perhaps the most recent comprehensive compendium of information on elementary school disturbance is found in a study done by Glidewell and Swallow for the Joint Commission. Glidewell and Swallow[32] have summarized studies and theory concerning maladjustment in the elementary school. Their figures suggest 30 percent of the children studied had some difficulties. Five to 25 percent had intrapersonal tensions; and 10 to 30 percent had interpersonal difficulties, ranging from withdrawal to aggression. Obviously a child may have more than one kind of difficulty.

A comprehensive examination of the whole problem is presented in the *Report of the Joint Commission on Mental Health of Children.*[33] A few summary statements should motivate the reader to study the entire volume.

The Commission considered in its study nearly one-half of the American population—that is, the approximately 95,000,000 persons under 25 years of age. Of this number, it is estimated:

Two percent are severely disturbed and need immediate psychiatric care.

Another eight to 10 percent are in need of some type of help from mental health workers.

Of the approximately 10 million under 25 who

need treatment and/or care the Commission estimates:

Eighty percent suffer from emotional disorders due to faulty training, faulty life experiences, and externalized situational conflicts, such as difficulties with school, sex, siblings, parent-child relations, and social problems. These groups can usually be treated by general practitioners or pediatricians trained in mental health; school counselors; child development specialists; social workers; paraprofessionals who have been sufficiently oriented; and other persons working in settings not primarily established for treatment of mental illness.

Ten percent show deeper conflicts, which have become internalized within the self and create emotional conflicts (the so-called neuroses). The services needed by this group range from outpatient services to Re-Ed and/or residential care; however, all these services need to be interrelated in harmonious working referral and treatment arrangements, so the child can easily move from one to another of these services as each is required for his needs.

Five percent show physical handicaps and require specialized facilities and intensive care. Of the estimated 7.6 million physically handicapped children who need services, 5.6 million receive some services. The present services, however, require many improvements. Mental health services and educational services particularly need to be increased and improved.

The remaining five percent suffer severe mental disorders (for example, schizophrenia, severe mental retardation, etc.) and require more intensive care and often institutionalization.

According to our best estimates, only about 500,000 children are currently being served by psychiatric facilities (clinics, hospitals, private therapists). (page 38)

They further indicate the need for early identification and reveal that

The admission of teenagers to state hospitals has risen something like 150 percent in the last decade . . . Instead of being helped, the vast majority are the worse for the experience. The usual picture is one of untrained people working with outmoded facilities within the framework of long abandoned theory (where there is any consistent theory), attempting to deal with a wide variety of complex and seriously sick youngsters and pro-

ducing results that are more easily measured by a recidivism rate that is often 30 to 50 percent, and occasionally higher. (page 6)

It is clear that special education has a major role to play for all disturbed children, but the Commission has a sorry status report.

We have many reasons to point with pride to our educational system. Yet, few would deny that there are glaring deficiencies. There are old goals which have yet to be realized. There is the unfulfilled dream of an equal education for all—one fitted to the unique nature, needs, and aspirations of each child, one which develops the competence and skill necessary for an individual sense of mastery and accomplishment. For many children, we have made little or no advance toward these goals. For example:

Only 13 percent of the 800,000 emotionally disturbed children identified as needing special education currently receive such assistance.

Of the estimated 5,500,000 handicapped children who need special education because of their disabilities, only one-third receive any educational assistance.

An estimated 50,000 migrant children must travel each year when they should be in school; many of these children are excluded from attending local schools on the basis of their transient status.

Millions of poor children and those oppressed ethnic minorities are still herded into old, inferior and segregated schools where they lag further behind their more affluent counterparts as they advance into higher grades. (pp. 72–73)

Two important questions remain to be answered. First, for what reasons are children referred for clinical help? Second, what syndromes are found when the children are studied?

The table below shows the types of problems found in children *referred* to community and school clinics. Roughly three percent of the child population is referred when resources are available. Most of them can be classified as problems for teachers. However the problems of children placed in special classes for the emotionally disturbed are perceived by the teachers as somewhat different. Aggression and management problems occur most often, academic problems are second with hyperactivity, withdrawn behavior, and perceptual problems much less frequent.[34]

Referral Problems of 2500 Outpatient Children*

Referral Problems	Under 6		6-10		10-14		14-18		All Ages			Percent of All Cases		
												Total as % of N	in 2 Community Clinics	in 2 School Clinics
	M	F	M	F	M	F	M	F	M	F	Total			
Academic difficulties	3	0	358	126	322	117	146	54	829	297	1126	45	27	56
Mental retardation	16	9	166	94	180	123	50	35	412	261	673	27	6	40
Aggressive, antisocial behavior	45	12	242	65	192	39	115	45	594	161	755	30	45	20
Passive, withdrawn, asocial behavior	38	15	174	74	110	50	60	25	382	164	546	22	32	14
Emotional irritability and anxiety symptoms	45	16	205	86	108	46	49	25	407	173	580	23	34	16
Hyperactivity and motor symptoms	24	12	139	59	69	24	20	5	252	100	352	14	22	8
Sexual behavior problems	6	1	12	10	13	6	6	6	37	23	60	2.5	4	1
Toilet training	27	7	50	25	36	14	0	2	113	48	161	6.5	12	1
Speech defects	25	9	62	19	26	9	10	1	123	38	161	6.5	6	7
Miscellaneous	14	17	90	38	71	51	34	29	209	135	344	14	20	9
Totals	243	98	1498	596	1127	479	490	227	3358	1400	4758	190.5	208	172

*Average complaint: 1.9 per child

From G.M. Gilbert, "A Survey of 'Referral Problems' in Metropolitan Child Guidance Centers," Journal of Clinical Psychology, 13 (1957), 37-42.

The examination table that closes this section adds recent figures to some of the material presented. It is quoted from *The 1966 Survey of* *the American Association of Psychiatric Clinics for Children,* part of a longer report to the Joint Commission on Mental Health for Children.

Comparison of Distribution of Diagnostic Categories for National Institute of Mental Health and American Association of Psychiatric Clinics for Children Facilities

	79 AAPCC Facilities		1,301 NIMH Facilities	
	Diagnosis	Treatment	Not Treated*	Treated
Brain syndrome	7%	5%	10%	6%
Mental deficiency	6	3	14	3
Psychotic disorder	8	12	5	6
Psychophysiological disorder		4	3	1
Psychoneurotic disorder	21	26	8	14
Personality disorder	27	25	23	22
Transient situational personality disorder	26	25	39	48
Total	100	100	100	100

Omits "undiagnosed" and "without mental disorder."

Note: AAPCC clinics tend to see more psychotic and psychoneurotic children, and clinics reporting to NIMH see more transient situational disorders. This difference is probably based more on differences in diagnostic terminology than on differences in symptoms.

Comparing these percentages with the diagnoses in Morse's study *Classes for the Emotionally Handicapped,* referred to above, we find that 60 percent of the children in Morse's special classes, including those who internalized or acted out, are neurotic, corresponding to "psychoneurotic" problems in the table. Eighteen percent in the classes have disorders similar to the "personality disorders" in the NIMH table. Brain syndromes account for seven percent of the children in Morse's classes and academic failure (an added category) for seven percent.

Although the final article by Bower is built around the concept of prevention, it speaks lucidly to the issue of identification and screening, with particular focus on the educator's role. If the conclusions of this paper are correct, mental health experts may well be taking their cues from teachers. Bower, an outstanding researcher and theoretician in the school mental health field, has shown many ramifications of current mental health mystiques.

Slicing the Mystique of
Prevention with Occam's Razor
Eli M. Bower

Prevention is a word with many shades and ranges of meaning. I have read somewhere that in colonial days Philadelphia health officials sought to prevent an epidemic of yellow fever by repeatedly firing a cannon from the steps of City Hall. This was certainly an unique preventive approach; however, it lacked any evaluation, since no one really knows how many mosquitoes were killed by this procedure.

Occam's Razor turns out to be a more formidable preventive weapon than Philadelphia cannon. Occam's Razor was tempered by a few cutting remarks about human functioning which, loosely translated and brought up to date, could be stated thus: "Don't complicate simple things." For those who prefer a more literal translation, Occam's words were: "Assumptions introduced to explain something should not be multiplied beyond necessity."

The focus in this paper is not so much on the hard-nosed data about early identification of children with potential problems, but the mythologies and encrustations about mental health and education which have kept this kind of an attempt feeble and ineffective. We will need to change blades in Occam's Razor more than once, before we get any program of real significance and impact operating in this area. Now what is the mystique which needs slicing and why?

The state of a child's mental health or ill health is best known and judged by a mental health professional (psychiatrist, clinical psychologist or psychiatric social worker) rather than by less "sophisticated" professional persons who live with the child on a day-to-day basis.

About ten years ago, the State of California decided to invest a sizable amount of money and some of my time to find out whether emotionally disturbed children could be identified early in their school life and, if so, could something be done to immobilize, interrupt, or intercept this kind of development. We found we could identify children with beginning learning and behavior problems, if we effectively and economically used perceptual ratings of students by teachers, peers, and the students themselves. Not surprisingly, we found our measures of the state of emotional development of students to be highly reliable and, on the basis of what good sense and little research we had, to be valid. At this point, however, some of our mental health colleagues began to shake their heads. Remember, they said, the old Wickman study in which considerable doubt was raised about the ability of teachers and schools to recognize the symptoms of serious emotional problems. How do we know that the children you have identified are *really and truly* the mental health problems of our society? Are children identified by teachers (and peers and themselves) really emotionally disturbed? And what is more important, how do you know that these are the children who will eventually become mentally ill? The last question was always posed with the all-knowing scowl of the pipe-smoking scholar searching for the first star in the night sky.

Let me resurrect Wickman's study for those too young to have been exposed or too old to remember. Wickman asked a group of 511 teachers and a group of 30 mental hygienists to rate the seriousness of 50 behavior traits of children. What set the fulminating cap sizzling was the finding that ratings made by the mental hygienists and those made by the teachers had zero correlation. Wickman him-

Reprinted from *American Journal of Public Health.* Vol. 59, No. 3, March, 1969. Copyright by the American Public Health Association, Inc., New York. Reprinted by permission.

self was not at all dismayed by this result, and was most emphatic in pointing out that the directions to each group had been significantly different. The teachers had been asked to rate the behavior as problems in the present reality of the classroom, while the mental hygienists were directed to rate the behavior on the basis of its effect on the future life of the child. Teachers were also told to define the seriousness of a problem by the amount of difficulty it produced in the classroom. The mental health group was asked to rate problem behavior in relation to its importance to a child's mental health. When the smoke cleared and the ratings of the two groups were compared, it became obvious that teachers were concerned with behavior that related to classroom disruption; mental health people, on the other hand, focused attention on behavior that was disturbing the child's inner psyche. Each group was looking at the problem in terms of their own professional biases and from their job-related firing lines.

Although Wickman was careful to point out the limitations of his study, this did not prevent many alexic professionals from jumping to unwarranted conclusions. Two educators examined 12 texts in psychology and educational psychology which mentioned Wickman's study, and found only two which gave a clear and concise statement of the study and its findings. Most discussed the study as indicating that, as judges of the mental health status of children, teachers were way off base. The basic assumption, of course, was that the mental health experts were right and that teachers were wrong.

The myth still exists that someone, somewhere, somehow, knows how to assess behavior and/or mental health as positive or negative, good or bad, healthy or nonhealthy, and independent of the social context wherein the individual is living and functioning. It is possible that the teacher who focuses on the child's observable behavior in school is closer to an operational reality of mental health than can be determined in an office examination. What a teacher is judging is how a specific behavior affects him as a key professional person in a primary social system and how well a child can play the role of student in a school. Similarly, when a child in a play group can not play the play role (adhere to the rules of the game), the nursery school supervisor will find his behavior a problem in that setting. In both instances, the lack of these role skills isolates the child from his peers. A child with an absence of emotional responsiveness to a parent will be a problem in a family setting where such responsiveness is

one of the expected behaviors of children and of satisfaction to parents. But each behavior can only be judged as positive or negative in relation to the social system in which feelings or behavior are expected and prescribed.

Each of the social contexts in which children function have specific goals, rules, and competencies that act as guides for assessing prescribed and expected behavior. A school is a system which demands learning competence; a play group requires rule-abiding behavior; a family should provide an opportunity for some interchange of healthy hostility and affection. Life is lived by children within primary humanizing institutions, each of which require specific functioning skills and behavior appropriate to its goals. I have no idea what mental health is in the abstract, but I would like to define it as comprising the kinds of competence and reality-testing which allow a child to function effectively in the humanizing institutions where he is asked to live. Specifically, these are the home, the peer or play group, and the school.

The fact is that teachers gather enough information about children in their routine operations to make highly accurate professional predictions about the course of a child's school life. However, there is little or no magic in such predictive data unless, in the process of gathering such data, the key professional person in the system is moved to act. For example, there is very good evidence that it is possible to detect potential delinquents at an early age if the Social Prediction Scale, developed by the Gluecks, is used. Why is it not used as a preventive tool? By and large, I would guess because the process of prediction requires operations not consistent with the goals and processes of the institution. In addition, the prediction itself has little curriculum implication or program consequences for the key professional worker in the school—the teacher. Prediction processes must lead to positive action by someone in the system, and this is especially critical in the case of problems which have not as yet become major crises to the teacher. How often one hears a kindergarten or first-grade teacher in a teachers' room react to a fifth- or sixth-grade teacher's description of the gory adventures of a problem child. "Oh, him—he was somewhat of a problem in the first grade," is the likely comment. "I thought he might get over it." The upper-grade teacher sadly shakes her head, indicating a less optimistic state of affairs.

But can teachers and schools be effective screeners of children with beginning mental health problems? In a 1963 study, teachers were asked to rate children on five steps, ranging from the first which was: the child has no problems and is obviously extremely well adjusted; there is absolutely no need for referral, to the last: the child has problems of sufficient severity to require referral. Following this, a sample of children were seen by psychiatrists in privately conducted interviews of, predictively enough, about 50 minutes each. There was a marked lack of agreement between professional groups in classifying children who had severe adjustment problems and needed referral. The investigator thereupon concluded that teachers cannot adequately serve as case finders in mental health screening.

In discussing this research with the investigator, two questions were posed: (1) to what extent do you feel that a 50-minute appraisal by psychiatrists to be a more valid assessment of a child's functioning capabilities and liabilities in a school setting than a teacher's day-in-day-out experience; (2) how, exactly, do teachers react to the concept and meaning of the term "adjustment" and "referral?" One teacher explained her meaning of adjustment: "I guess it means how well a student gets along in school and with others. Now I have this one student who gets along pretty well and I guess is well adjusted, but can't seem to learn anything." While the concept of adjustment is understood by teachers, its operational implementation is somewhat out of the frame of reference and functioning of teachers. Most feel that in rating "adjustment," they are attempting to fill the role of a psychiatrist; somehow, they rate the degrees of intrapsychic conflict and chaos in the minds of their students. Whatever rating adjustment means, teachers should stick to school-related behaviors and roles which can be operationally defined and observed. Does the child get into fights? Can he pay attention when necessary? Does he learn to read? Is he always in a blue funk? Does he get sick? Does he get hurt? Can he express an idea?

To put the shoe on the other foot, another study compared the predictive skill of a teacher, psychologist, and child psychiatrist in judging which kindergarten children would learn up to their IQ potential in first grade. A total of 56 kindergarten children were included in the study. Each professional person related to the children as he would normally. The teacher taught and observed, the psychologist tested, and the child psychiatrist used a standard play situation. All three did a good job of predicting the achievement, but the teacher's was best. The psychiatrist had a tendency to predict underachievement more frequently than it occurred. He suggested that the reason may be that some of the clinical anxiety which the psychiatrist picked up in the children—and which he expected to lead to underachievement—actually produced overachievement. This is, of course, the nub of the problem. Only when the teacher observes how a child may use different aspects of his personality and self can he assess the nuances of how the child mediates what he has, be it anxiety, IQ, shyness, or aggressivity. The investigation confirms Robins' study (discussed later) that (1) raters in general are better at spotting potential positive achievers than the negative ones; (2) teacher judgments provide the most economical and efficient guides to predictions of school success.

The Nonmagic of Teacher Referrals

Another wicked slice with Occam's Razor needs to be taken at the notion and concept of "the referral." In the past, teachers have been so convinced of their lack of mental health expertise and so impressed with the competence of their mental health colleagues that the only significant help for problems which they could verbalize was: "If we only had adequate referral resources." We have invested this process, at least for teachers, with a penicillin-like magic which, unfortunately, is dissipated in the realities of limited knowledge and manpower. The referral concept for the majority of teachers is one where the child is taken elsewhere, where something magical is done to straighten him out, and then returned to school a healthy, well-motivated student. This rarely turns out to be the case. Occasionally, referrals are consummated to the satisfaction of the teacher. When this happens, it is evident that some mental health expert has learned to translate what he knows clinically and psychodynamically into the frame of reference of the teacher and into educational processes and objectives. Unfortunately, there are only a few referral agencies that have the competence to do this or know how to begin to do this. Most teachers have high regard for mental health persons and their professional competence. When the secrets of a problem are revealed to a teacher, she often stands aghast at the marvels of modern psychiatry, psychology, or casework. Indeed, she is thrilled to be a partner to such mighty revelations. She may reenter the class with a better understanding of the "why" and "what" of the student's difficulty, but with her major problem still unanswered: "How do I teach this child?"

There is another assumption about teachers

and referrals which needs slicing. If, in a hypothetical community, there were available immediate, convenient, and useful referral services (each of these will affect the process significantly) and teachers were encouraged to refer children who needed help, one would not get the most serious or the most difficult problems. A referral is the result of a dyadic realtionship between a teacher and a child in the context of a class and a school. One psychologist who attempted to help teachers in an inner city school wanted to know why he got so few referrals. The teachers laughed at the question, and pointed out that if he were serious they would be happy to send him three-fourths of their class. There is also the phenomenon that when a teacher refers a child, she does so because *she* is puzzled or anxious about his behavior. Many teachers will not refer students with serious problems if they feel they understand some of the background and causes of the problems, but will refer less serious problems when the behavior or learning difficulty is puzzling or anxiety-provoking to them.

It is no longer possible in this day and age to think of referral services as desirable or necessary, if one is concerned with the basic preventive question: how do you increase the ecological competence of a humanizing institution to serve more children more effectively? One way would be to develop mental health professionals (clinical behavioral workers) who would not be walled off from the primary institutions by having to deal with its casualties, but could become an active partner with the teacher, principal, and parents in monitoring and enhancing the behavior of all children in the school.

The Object of Early Identification Is to Identify Cases Early

It took me quite a while to realize that the notion of early identification meant different things to different professional groups. One of my psychiatric colleagues used to puzzle me by his lack of enthusiasm for research in this field. Once, when I confronted him with this, he replied: "I don't see why you get worked up about this early identification of emotionally disturbed children. We've got more cases than we can handle right now without finding some more."

His notion of early discovery had to do with what is known in the profession as "cases." My notion of early discovery has to do with the discovery of a child in a primary institution, such as a school, who is having beginning trouble in coping with the demands and processes of that institution. The essential assumption is that, left alone, a beginning problem either finds a wise and highly competent teacher or it continues to grow. In our California studies, children identified as emotionally handicapped fell further and further behind in reading and arithmetic achievement, and were increasingly deemed by their peers to be negative or inadequate students. After five years, they were seen in child guidance clinics and appeared in the Juvenile Index for vehicle code and penal code violations in stark contrast to a randomly selected group of their classmates. This was replicated and amplified by the Minnesota Study which confirmed the fact that children identified by the California materials as emotionally handicapped fall further and further behind their classmates in achievement, and get stuck on a track which leads to severe educational embarrassment and incompetence.

The humanizing institutions to which children are mandated are unfortunately social systems that tend to reward those who succeed in them and punish those who fail. Programs of early identification in schools must therefore not only find failing and problem children early; but, in the process of finding them, must provide for the institutional changes which will make the discovery worth while. This means that processes of early identification must be carried out by key persons in specific humanizing institutions in the context of the goals and processes of that institution, and in such a way that alternative possibilities for action are natural outcomes of the process. Program of early identification which require teachers to do non-teacher-like jobs will not last and cannot be effective. Moreover, such programs cannot enlist mental health workers to visit homes to make clinical appraisals of how a child is disciplined at home, the degree of affection shown to him by his parents, and so on, critical as this kind of information may be. Early identification processes which solely aim at identifying children with "mental health" problems are no more than exercises. They must lead to and be conceptualized in a program framework, and must be translatable into valid interventions within the humanizing institution where the child is living and is attempting to function.

Nobody believes it is possible for all children to experience our humanly constructed humanizing institutions in a positive and ego-enhancing way.

If one can remove one's home-grown complexities and professional blinkers about this sordid world and its people, it is possible to conceptualize humanizing institutions which can carry out their goals and processes for greater ranges of children and eventually for all children. Either we do this or pay the cost in lives and money for remedial or rehabilitative institutions such as prisons, mental hospitals, welfare programs, alcoholic and drug wards. It is also well to remember that when children cannot function in institutions devised for their benefit, they hurt and they bleed. One does not have to ask whether they have broken a leg or cut an artery before administering first aid. It is questionable whether the children identified as emotionally disturbed in school are really and truly disturbed or if they represent the group who will later become mentally ill. I suspect more of them later become antisocial, inadequate, dependent, alcoholic, drug-addicted, and physically ill than a random group of adults. This conclusion is supported by an interesting study of 524 adults who were seen as children in a child guidance clinic and 100 controls of the same age, sex, neighborhood, race and IQ. The purpose of the study was to describe, through a longitudinal natural history, the kinds of childhood behavior problems that present serious danger signals and those that do not. Robins' study is interesting in that there was an unexpected dividend in the data on the control group.

Let us first look at what happened to the 524 adults who had been seen as children in the child guidance clinic. Robins divided them into two categories, antisocial and nonantisocial, on the basis of behavior which led to referral. She found that antisocial children by and large became antisocial adults. Not only were these adults more often arrested and imprisoned than expected, but they were more mobile, had more marital difficulties, poorer occupational and armed service histories, used alcohol and drugs excessively, and had poorer physical health. "But," Robins adds, "from one point of view . . . what we have found is not so much a pathological patient group as an extraordinary well-adjusted control group."

Such a control group was selected from the files of the St. Louis public schools by setting quotas for year of birth, sex, census tract, no clinic visit, IQ above 80, no grade repeats, and no record of expulsion or transfer. Microfilm reels were spun and selection made in the Las Vegas tradition. This, however, turned out to be a winner. Using these four not high standard criteria (IQ over 80, not seen at the municipal psychiatric clinic, no grade repeated, and no expulsion from school), Robins had selected a group of 100 adults of whom only two ever appeared in juvenile court and who, as adults, had good psychiatric adjustment and social competence. She concludes that while having repeated grades in elementary school certainly does not efficiently predict serious adult problems, having not had serious school difficulties may be a rather efficient predictor of the absence of gross maladjustment as adults. Perhaps we have been so concerned with the prediction of deviant behavior that we were not aware how well we could do in predicting effective behavior.

In light of our earlier comment about predicting eventual mental illness, Robbins found no clear connection between type of deviance in childhood and type of problem in adulthood. For example, those adults with antisocial behavior in childhood not only showed antisocial adult behavior, but also showed a greater degree of social alienation and more psychiatric and physical disabilities. As a result, Robins found that children referred for antisocial behavior have a less promising prediction than children referred for other reasons. This is a group that vitally needs mental health services, as teachers have repeatedly pointed out to their principals and mental health consultants.

Conclusion

Don't complicate simple things. Prevention is getting children through our health, family, and school institutions "smelling like a rose." A little soap, a little affection, and a little learning are the holy trinity of prevention. If we can send rockets to the moon, we certainly can do these three little things for the human condition on earth.

Summary

The combination of culture and individual biological limitations produces a significant amount of deviation. The major underlying syndromes in these deviations are in values—deficit or atypicality, neurotic patterns, and psychotic patterns with various combinations; seldom is there a pure example of any one. Theories on the causes of deviation have recently undergone thorough scrutiny, and a concept of interaction is gradually replacing the "either/or"—person-caused or society-caused—behavior malfunction theories.

Acting-out children and adolescents, an increasing proportion of the total maladjusted child population, are receiving inadequate help. Besides the typical psychoses and neuroses, we must deal with new patterns of alienation, delinquency, violence, drugs, sex, and fear. To an increasing extent, the schools will have a key role in this effort. Confronted with mandatory legislation and legal action, the schools can no longer ignore these children.[33] Nor can school programs be primarily custodial, for the "right to treatment" will be the quality control for future school provisions.

Teachers are often the first to encounter children who need help; they can screen out cases that require careful diagnosis and plan hygienic measures within the educational system.

The teacher has a verified and central role to play in the screening process. Childrearing institutions must become more humanized; the school must incorporate necessary identification, supporting and correcting resources within its structure. Teachers and education are keystones in mental health screening and interventions. As educational accountability increases and the line between special and regular education is lost, a three-fold program will develop following identification: (1) primary prevention through affective educational programs; (2) secondary prevention, with provisions such as the crises teacher (described in Chapter 3); and (3) tertiary prevention, the specialized programs (presented in detail in Chapters

Chapter 2 Footnotes

1. **C. Hersch,** "The Discontent Explosion in Mental Health," *American Psychologist* 23 (1968): 497–506.

2. **William C. Rhodes and Michael L. Tracy,** *A Study of Child Variance,* ISMRRD (Ann Arbor, Mich.: The University of Michigan Press, 1972).

3. **Carol Cheney and William C. Morse,** "Psychodynamic Interventions in Emotional Disturbance," in *A Study of Child Variance: vol. 2: Interventions,* ISRRD, eds. William C. Rhodes and Michael L. Tracy (Ann Arbor: The University of Michigan Press, 1972).

4. The leader in this aspect is **Rudolf Moos.** See *Evaluating Treatment Environments:* A Social Ecological Approach (New York: John Wiley & Sons, 1974).

5. **Daniel Kelleher,** "A Model for Integrating Special Educational and Community Mental Health Services," *Journal of Special Education* 2–3 (Spring 1968): 263–272.

6. A complete discussion of this and other related matters can be found in **W.C. Morse,** "Concepts Related to Diagnosis of Emotional Impairment" in *State of the Arts: Diagnosis and Treatment,* eds. K.F. Kramer and R. Rosonke (Washington, D.C.: Bureau of Education of Handicapped, 1974), contract no. [OEC-0-9-252901-4539(608)].

7. **Fritz Redl,** *When We Deal with Children* (New York: The Free Press, 1966).

8. **Buros, Oscar K. (ed.),** *The Sixth Mental Measurements Yearbook* (Highland Park, N.J.: Gryphon Press, 1965); D.G. Johnson and J.W. Bommarito, *Tests and Measurements in Child Development: A Handbook* (San Francisco, Jossey-Bass, Inc., 1971); J.P. Robinson and P.R. Shaver, *Measures of Social Psychological Attitudes* (Ann Arbor: Institute for Social Research, 1972); A.L. Comrey, T.E. Backer, and E.W. Glaser, *A Source Book for Mental Health Measures* (Los Angeles: Human Interaction Research Institute, 1973); M.J. Kaufman, M. Semmel, and J.A. Agard, *Supplementary Materials to Year 1,* Interim report, Part II (Bloomington: University of Indiana, no date); Project Prime has instruments not only for children but for all aspects of special education programs.

9. **William C. Morse,** "Concepts Related to Diagnosis of Emotional Impairment" in *State of the Art: Diagnosis and Treatment,* Kay F. Kramer and Richard Rosonke, eds. (Des Moines, Iowa: Midwest Area Learning Center, 1975), pp. 113–117.

10. **H.C. Quay,** "Facets of Educational Exceptionality: A Conceptual Framework for Assess-

ment, Grouping, and Instruction," *Exceptional Children,* vol. 35, no. 1 (1968): 25−32.

11.   **J.S. Werry and H.C. Quay,** "Observing the Classroom Behavior of Elementary School Children," *Exceptional Children,* vol. 35, no. 6 (1969): 461−470.

12.   **H.K. Walker,** "Empirical Assessment of Deviant Behavior in Children," *Psychology in the Schools* VI (1969): 93−97.

13.   **N.J. Long, S.A. Fagen, and D.J. Stevens,** *Psychoeducational Screening System for Identifying Resourceful, Marginal, and Vulnerable Pupils in Primary Grades* (3565 Brandywine St., NW, Washington, D.C.: Psychoeducational Resources, Inc., 1971).

14.   **R.Q. Bell, M.F. Waldrop, and G.M. Weller,** "A Rating System for the Assessment of Hyperactive and Withdrawn Children in Preschool Samples," *American Journal of Orthopsychiatry,* vol. 42, no. 1 (1972): 23−34.

15.   **M. Kohn and B.L. Rosman,** "A Social Competence Scale and Symptom Checklist for the Preschool Child," *Developmental Psychology,* vol. 6, no. 3 (1972): 430−444.

16.   **D.K. Walker,** *Socioemotional Measures for Preschool and Kindergarten Children* (San Francisco: Jossey-Bass, 1973).

17.   **R.D. Vinter, et al.,** *Pupil Behavior Inventory* (Ann Arbor: Campus Publishers, 1966).

18.   **M. Hammer,** "A Teacher's Guide to the Detection of Emotional Disturbance in the Elementary School Child," *Journal of Learning Disabilities,* vol. 3, no. 10 (1970): 35−37.

19.   **N.M. Lambert,** "Intellectual and Nonintellectual Predictors of High School Status," *Journal of Special Education,* vol. 6, no. 3 (1972): 247−259.

20.   **William C. Kvaraceus,** "Early Identification and Prediction," in *Anxious Youth: Dynamics of Delinquency* (Columbus, Ohio: Charles E. Merrill, 1966).

21.   **W.J. Lesiak, Jr.,** "Screening Primary-Grade Children for Educational Handicaps: A Teacher-Administered Battery," *Psychology in the Schools,* vol. 10, no. 1 (1973): 88−101.

22.   **John G. Frauenheim,** "A Follow-up Study of Adult Males Who Were Clinically Diagnosed as Dyslexic in Childhood," Ph.D. dissertation (Detroit: Wayne State University, 1975).

23.   **William Cruickshank and Daniel P. Hollahan,** *Perceptual and Learning Disabilities in Children,* vol. 1, *Psychoeducational Practices.* (Syracuse, N.Y.: Syracuse University Press, 1975).

24.   **Melvin Zax and Emory L. Cowen,** "Early Identification and Prevention of Emotional Disturbance in a Public School," in Emory Cowen, Elmer Gardner, and Melvin Zax eds., *Emergent Approaches to Mental Health Problems* (New York: Appleton-Century-Crofts, 1967), pp. 331−351; and David R. Beach, Emory L. Cowen, Melvin Zax, James D. Laird, Mary Ann Trost, and Louis D. Izzo, "Objectification of Screening for Early Detection of Emotional Disorder," *Child Development,* 39:4 (December 1968), 1177−1188.

25.   **John W.M. Rothney,** *Methods of Studying the Individual Child* (Waltham, Mass.: Blaisdell Publishing Company, 1968). See especially Chapter Two.

26.   **Mary Engel,** "Some Parameters of the Psychological Evaluation of Children," *Archives of General Psychiatry,* 2 (June 1960), 593−605.

27.   **R.A. Gardner,** *Therapeutic Communication with Children: The Mutual Storytelling Technique* (New York: Science House, 1971).

28.   **S.L. Werkman,** The Psychiatric Diagnostic Interview with Children," *American Journal of Orthopsychiatry,* vol. 35, no. 4 (1965): 764−771.

29.   **Jerome D. Goodman,** "The Psychiatric Interview," in *Manual of Child Psychopathology,* ed. Benjamin B. Wolman (New York: McGraw-Hill, 1972), pp. 743−766.

30.   **W.C. Morse and Ralph Rabinovitch,** *The Nature and Education of Disturbed Children and Adolescents* (New York: McGraw-Hill, forthcoming).

31.   **C. Cheney and W.C. Morse,** "Psychodynamic Interventions in Emotional Disturbance," in *A Study of Child Variance: Interventions,* vol. 2, eds. W.C. Rhodes and M.L. Tracy, Institute for the Study of Mental Retardation and Related Disabilities (Ann Arbor: University of Michigan Publications Distribution Services, 1972).

32.   **John C. Glidewell and Carolyn S. Swallow,** *The Prevalence of Maladjustment in Elementary Schools.* A report for the Joint Commission on the Mental Health of Children (Chicago: University of Chicago, 1968). 116 pp. mimeo.

33.   *Crisis in Child Mental Health: Challenge for the 1970s* (New York: Harper and Row, Publishers, 1970).

34.   **William C. Morse, Richard L. Cutler, and**

Albert H. Fink, *Public School Classes for the Emotionally Handicapped: A Research Analysis* (Washington, D.C.: Council for Exceptional Children, 1964).

35.   **J. Regal et al.,** *The Exclusion of Children from School: The Unknown, Unidentified, and Untreated* (Council for Children with Behavioral Disorder; Council for Exceptional Children, 1972).

3

What Kinds of Help Are Available Besides School?

The children described in the previous sections can be helped. If circumstances go well, they may simply grow up and out of some problems, especially if they have encouragement from teachers, a good school system, and supportive peers. Their chances are improved if they have families who can face difficulties with honesty and accept them without becoming immobilized by self-blame. This asks a lot—often too much—from people who are intimately involved with the hurdles and holocausts of children in distress. If experiences are not sufficiently regenerative, however, or if a disturbance is too firmly established to be outgrown naturally, troubles are likely to increase and to cripple the child's life and the lives of others.

Fortunately, many kinds of help are available. The most pervasive kind is given by carefully planned school programs staffed by talented, trained teachers. Besides school programs there are many other sources of treatment or therapy for children with emotional problems. Types of therapy vary almost as widely as types of disturbances. One method may be more appropriate to a particular child at a given stage of his or her development than others. Sometimes more than one kind of treatment may be necessary, either simultaneously or sequentially. Treatment can take place in the school setting, therapist's office, clinic, or mental health center.

This section will summarize the major forms of psychotherapy now used to treat children. We will approach the subject more or less historically, i.e., we will begin with individual psychotherapy and go from there to group psychotherapy, including one of the newer and more important developments of the past twenty years—family therapy. The discussion on groups will also include: use of media (art, dance, music, psychodrama, bibliotherapy [literature], and writing); group therapy for adolescents; excerpts from a therapeutic classroom session; systems analysis as a treatment device; a discussion on a group of black children; and the necessity of staff training for group leadership.

Many therapies now used are vastly different from one-to-one Freudian psychoanalysis. As a matter of fact, the first analysis of a child did not even directly include the child; it was conducted by Freud and the father of "Little Hans," a severely phobic child. However, Freud's first method implied that success in treating the child was contingent on the parent's active cooperation.

There are also exciting, new, dynamic approaches which help agencies and schools deal with families without making the family or child assume the role of patients. These are based on the premise that most adults and children are motivated to do better and can do better if the specifics needed for change are made evident. These briefer, ego level programs are described by Leventhal and Love.[1][2]

Individual Psychotherapy and Psychoanalysis

Freud predicted that he would be remembered for formulating a theory that really wasn't new—about the forces underlying human behavior. Particularly, he said, philosophers, writers, and artists knew and described the inner human drives. He felt his contribution was to take their observations and insights and to systematize them into a way of thinking. His theory came from experience with hundreds of sick people who could not be helped by other medical disciplines. His prescription for treatment came from philosophy rather than pharmacology: "Know the truth and it shall set you free." The method rested on leading or helping the patient to become aware of the truths about himself.

Freud's theory might be called an education theory. The therapist is a teacher. His subject matter is the patient himself; his curriculum is the patient's past experience, present world, and unconscious feelings. The methods used to help the patient gain awareness, insight, and consequent change, while set down by Freud in specific terms for treating adult neurotics, have been modified according to the knowledge and convictions gained from treating not only neurotic adults, but also psychotics and criminals, as well as children suffering from emotional illnesses.

Freud's basic premises resulted in an intense study of children and their development. His theory of the libido, which might be defined as affectional energy, starts at the breast. This energy can develop naturally in a child who is able to put up with the pressures of society; or it can be blocked, deterred, or turned in ill-fated directions. Freud's emphasis on early childhood experiences focuses psychoanalytic, psychiatric, and educational thought on parent-child and teacher-child relationships. His theory of the unconscious makes sense out of seemingly senseless behavior. Failure to achieve where potential exists, somatic complaints without perceptible causes, crime or misdeed without apparent reason become understandable in the light of unsuspected human needs and conflicts that, if blocked too long, find alternative means of making their presence felt.

Since the psychoanalytic treatment of adults focused largely on childhood, it was natural that children themselves be scrutinized. If illness began in the early years, could it be prevented or caught before it developed further? Could society or education help from the outside? Could the therapist help from the inside? Could parents and teachers alter the course of a child's development to free his energy for constructive living in place of pathological living?

The first case of child therapy was undertaken by Freud himself. Little Hans was treated indirectly by Freud for a phobia of horses. That is to say, Freud supervised the treatment through Hans's father. Hans's father would come to Freud frequently, reporting in detail his son's actions, angers, pouts, tears, and joys. When he could, he would report little Hans's dreams as they had been told to him; the interrelations of mother, father, governess, and Hans were also reported. Freud would interpret what he heard, explaining to Hans's father what the information implied for the management of little Hans in the context of the social mores and goals that were expected of that child in Austria at that time. By this means, little Hans's phobia of horses, which like most phobias spread to other things and consequently decreased his ability to play and learn, was ultimately cured. This was the first child analysis.

In the early years of psychoanalysis, Anna Freud, Sigmund Freud's daughter, and Melanie Klein both worked with children. Although both based their work on Freud's formulations, they disagreed with each other on many basic questions of treatment, such as the relationship between therapist and child, the use of dreams and symbols, the length and conditions of treatment, and the handling of parents. Melanie Klein took the major part of Freud's adult theory and applied it to children. Anna Freud, however, modified her father's theory in a way which was consistent with the child's basic dependence on parents. She was more concerned with the child's total environment—his friends, his neighborhood, his teacher. Space limitations unfortunately prevent our including any selections from the work of Anna Freud or Melanie Klein. They were, with G. Stanley Hall in the United States, the founders of child psychiatry, and the reader is urged to examine some of their work. An important book by each is listed in our bibliography.

During World War II, Anna Freud lived in England, where she cared for and treated hundreds of children who had been bombed out of their London homes or whose parents had sent them to her to escape the bombing. Her studies of these children's reactions to trauma, disaster, death, and separation are fascinating. The work of Melanie Klein, who also lived in England, where she had her loyal followers, has had less appeal to American therapists. But her dramatic theories have proven particularly successful with borderline psychotic children and in application of the principles of groups and group structure and behavior to adults as well as children. They have found expression in the Tavistock theory of group relations and in the work of Wilfred Bion, both of which are described below in the section on groups.

The mental health movement in the United States has a rather different history from that of the corresponding movement in Europe, where interest was first centered on the adult incapacitated by emotional illness. In America, on the other hand (true to our reputation for being all wrapped up in our children), the mental health movement began through child guidance clinics which were started by the psychologist G. Stanley Hall in the 1890s. It is interesting to note that it was via psychology rather than psychiatry that we began our major efforts.

The following article is an excerpt from the work of an American child psychoanalyst, Dorothy Baruch. She works along the lines described by Anna Freud. The case excerpted here should be of particular interest to school people, since it is the story of a boy (Kenneth) who acted out his unconscious conflict through severe physical symptoms and through school failure. This child was operating at a 101 IQ at the beginning of treatment, at 140 at the close of treatment.

In this selection the parents' involvement in the child's pathology is emphasized. Dr. Baruch saw the mother (Cathy) individually on a regular basis and the father (Vic) from time to time. Both parents also participated in group therapy for parents with children in treatment. Both of these techniques are used increasingly when treatment of children is undertaken. It is rare that children under the age of 15 are seen, save in hospital or residential treatment settings, without insistence that some form of regular therapy be administered to parents. Frequently, depending on the theory of the therapist, teachers too are interviewed by the therapist for the purpose of getting, and sometimes giving, information relevant to the child's growth. Sometimes parents are seen by the child's therapist, as in Dr. Baruch's case. Sometimes separate therapists are used; multitherapeutic measures are used with parents, as in the example given here.

The following selection was chosen for four major reasons: (1) It is the case of a child who was treated for a learning problem—in reading and spelling. (2) It is an example of the most typical kind of therapy done in this country: work with a child and a parent in a child-guidance clinic. The child's therapist was a psychologist; the mother's therapist was a psychiatric social worker. (3) It is the record of one complete case. (4) It indicates the use of one type of group therapy with parents—the psychoanalytic-oriented group.

One Little Boy
Dorothy Baruch

At home Kenneth wheezed steadily for the four days and nights between that session and the next. He was quiet. He was good. But he coughed and struggled for air during the night and breathed with painful tightness during the day. The doctor did what he could.

But Kenneth kept on wheezing.

The doctor questioned me: Were we moving too fast? I said I'd watch it; perhaps we were. Kenneth had been such a good boy for so long that it was frightening him to open up to his own view this other part of himself—a part that lies deep in every one of us—hidden but ready to splash out in the bitter word, in the twisted temper, or in the flood-burst of mass riot, lynchings and war. In small or large measure we manage, each in our own way, to keep it underground, according to the smallness or largeness of the hurts we have suffered, accord-

ing to the onus we have leveled at ourselves for unwelcome feelings and according to the quantity and depth of the bitter gall we have stored.

Kenneth had been hurt. I knew only part of it all at the moment. Anger had, as result, accumulated inside him, and had given rise to fantasies mixed with tremendous fear and guilt. He could not show this anger or he might do too much. He might lose the last remnants of his mother's love. Therefore, unconsciously he did let the anger turn back on its course till he himself was both donor and recipient in the pain of illness, in the tragedy of failure, and in the fantasied hurts more dreaded than that of the wounded soldier and more dreadful to bear.

He would have to bring anger to the surface where he could look at it and with my help gradu-

Reprinted from *One Little Boy* by Dorothy Baruch (New York: The Julian Press, 1952; Delta Paperback, 1964) by permission of the publisher.

ally understand and integrate it into the protrait that he painted of himself in his mind.

Release had to come as a primary step if he was to survive in wholeness. I knew this. But I knew also that if it came too fast, it would threaten to inundate him so that he might close up the floodgates anew with reinforced blockades.

In his next session, Kenneth again chose the soldiers. At the start, he dared not follow his impulse to strike down the enemy. Hesitance encased him like lead-gray fog. But at last his desire broke through—throwing a spotlight on terrain that had been veiled from view. And with it, his face was illuminated.

His bombs struck not only mountains but men. His bullets, born in swift flight by his hand from enemy to enemy, crackled mercilessly. Faster and faster. The open voice replaced the closed whisper. Free breath in and out of lungs replaced the stoppered sibilance of his wheeze.

"The bomb got em!" jubilantly. "One man. Two. Three . . ." He went down on one knee, crouching in triumph over the strewn men, his yellow head bent to inspect the havoc he had finally managed to deal after such struggle. His words spilled out. And with them, in the risen excitement, a small trickle of saliva dribbled from his mouth to the floor.

He looked at the dark spot of spittle on the linoleum in stunned silence.

"I—I'll clean it up," he whispered.

Stiffly he rose from his bombs and his soldiers. He walked to the closet hook where a cloth hung and to the sink where he wet it. He wrung out the cloth like a well-taught robot, and brought it back to the spot on the floor.

"I—I didn't mean to get the floor messy."

"I know it, Ken. But really, in here it doesn't matter. You can do lots of things in here that you think aren't proper outside."

But he could not hear me or dared not show that he'd heard.

Slowly and with painstaking thoroughness he mopped the wet space, went back to the sink, washed the cloth out, wrung it, mechanically hung it back on the hook. And with another word but with the rasp of his wheezes breaking the silence, he came straight into my lap.

I thought: To him messing means being bad. So also do injuring and killing, even in play, mean being bad. They're different sides of the same coin, different facets of resentment, or anger, or hostility—call it what one will. Inside of Ken, the reservoir was full to spilling over. In his play, when it was draining out through the drama of killing, it did not need for the moment to drain out in asthma. In such play, though, it showed more of its true form. Ken could not escape its meaning as completely as he could when it came out in sickness or failure. Sickness and failure were great camouflagers. With them he could say in the space beyond words where unrecognized thoughts exist more as feelings: I'm being good, not naughty. I can't help it, after all, if I fail or am sick.

Since messing was less bad than injuring or killing and since injury and killing had frightened him so much, it was obviously not the messy spittle in itself that had sent Ken back in fear to being a baby seeking arms' shelter. The spittle was merely the proverbial last straw.

I would try to help Kenneth get firmly acquainted with the milder forms in which his "badness" showed itself before tackling what to him seemed more dangerous. I would arrange materials and set up the playroom so that it would automatically limit what Kenneth brought out. Instead of waiting for him to get the soldiers from the cupboard, I would have clay or paints out on the floor in readiness, as an invitation to mess rather than injure or kill.

Then bit by bit as he tackled what was less frightening to him and saw that he could live through it without being overpowered by his feelings or deserted by me, he might perhaps gain courage to explore more deeply. I would try as we went along to help him feel less guilty and less afraid and to understand his feelings better, not through mere words of explanation but through the experiences which we would share. Perhaps then —very gradually—the more dreaded feelings might lessen until he could say, in effect, I can handle what's left of them. I'm not really so bad! I don't need to be afraid any longer that my feelings will push me into such terrible actions that I'll either be deserted or destroyed. I needn't turn them back on myself and punish myself with illness and failure. I needn't keep them walled off and hidden as if I were telling myself, "These feelings, they're *not* part of *me*." Instead, I'll be able to let them slip into place as part of what I am. If he could reach this point, he would no longer need to stand over himself, cruelly denying himself and trying to relish denial in place of pleasure. He would no longer have to drain energy from his school work, for instance, in order to keep reinforcing the walls. The energy that had been used for hiding would be freed for work and play, for enjoyment and laughter, for friendship and love.

All this I hoped might eventually happen. I would try to help Kenneth achieve it. But essentially it was Kenneth himself who had to do it. Would he be able to? Was there sufficient courage and vigorous urge left in him, not only for living but for aliveness? How far would Kenneth be able to go?

I had finger paints waiting ready for him next time, right in the middle of the floor.

"What are they? . . . Where are the brushes? . . . Where are pictures to color? . . . I don't do well in free art in school. I like paint-books better. I almost never go outside of the line."

Poor, tight little Kenneth, afraid of what his brush's unsteadiness might mean, feeling that he must not go beyond the line—seeking the shelter of its neat constraint.

I told him you did this kind of painting with your hands, that was why it was called "finger painting."

He wanted gray. And when we got a blob of it onto the paper, he touched it very gingerly with one finger. "Look how dirty my finger got."

He stared unhappily at it.

"Will my finger get clean again? Will the mess come off?"

"Let's try with the soap and water at the sink."

We did. And he saw.

He took a big breath. "It does come off."

He started afresh. With the tips of all the fingers on one hand. With whole fingers down. With palm in, slithering, until the sticky paint was covering the inside of his hand. "See how dirty?"

Again doubt. "Will *this much* come off?"

Back to the sink. "I'd better see."

He scrubbed until I wondered if he'd left any skin.

To the paints with both hands sliding in. Back to the sink. Again to the paints. Again to the sink. Paint and scrub. Prove that he wouldn't have to keep tell-tale signs of dirt on him, then he could get dirty. But the proof was hard to believe. And so it had to be sought again and again until he could finally say with more certainty, "I *can* get them clean."

Both hands went in, then, and the paint slid up past the wrists. "I'll make them real, real dirty." He was smearing the paint now, over the backs of his hands and between his fingers. "I'll get them all dirty. Ahrrr, ahhrrrr, I'm messy! Ahhrrrr!" He growled and stuck up his hands toward my face in a menacing gesture as if he were going to smear me. A pouncing gesture, his fingers spread like claws. His head was back, his eyes guardedly on me, and a sound came from his lips. It was laughter but it was not the full-throated sound that rises from the gay heart. Rather the ghost-sound of an echoed, hollow denial of fear.

I wondered if he saw me swallow.

Even though it was thin and shallow, coming from no farther back it seemed than his palate, still this was the first time in the short long month he'd been with me that I'd heard Kenneth laugh. . . .

Blaine did not call Cathy. But he called Vic into his private office, and from behind Mr. Taylor's great mahogany desk, he told Vic that he was reorganizing the business and for the time being would not need Vic's services.

Vic said, "That's all right." Nothing more. Next day, however, he went back and doggedly questioned, "What's wrong, Blaine? Why are you letting me out? It's important for me to know."

Blaine had said there was nothing against Vic. Only right now he needed men of a different type, more aggressive. "You're the research type, Vic; the inventor, the investigator. Right now that's not what this place needs. We need people who can promote. Push. Why don't you open a consulting service? When we come up with a tough problem we'll use you. It's a deal. But at present we don't need your kind of a man here full time."

That night there was a group psychotherapy session. Cathy came in, the air of a crusader about her, her dark head high. Vic followed, dragging his feet.

Glancing around the already gathered circle, Cathy chose the straight-backed chair from the two that were still empty and Vic, looking helpless, sank into the low armchair and huddled over himself.

The hum of greetings between the group members stopped as the doctor glanced at his watch. "Well," he said, swiftly surveying each face in the circle, "it's time for us to get to work."

There was silence and a few moments of waiting for some group member to spontaneously start to talk about whatever lay on his mind. For into this warm, big room with the quiet of shadows on the wall and the circle of waiting faces, these people once a week brought their troubles and feelings and fantasies just as Kenneth brought his into the room where he played. Here, the doctor and I, as joint psychotherapists, had come to stand as a new father and mother. Under our guidance, these men and women with their diverse problems had grown to speak as freely as they would alone.

Tonight it was Cathy, not Vic, who began.

"It isn't fair," she protested. "It shouldn't have happened to Vic!"

She went on to recount what Vic had told her.

She was angry, she said, at Mr. Taylor for not having protected Vic. "After all the years that Vic's been there. Why, he's been Mr. Taylor's right hand man. I think it's a darn rotten deal. Especially being told he's not the aggressive type!"

Cathy's voice was patiently sweet with martyred indignation. "That's like a slap in the face! What if Vic isn't the aggressive type? Vic's got a lot of other qualities . . ."

With quick perspicacity, several group members picked up Cathy's feelings. They now came out with thoughts that people ordinarily keep unsaid.

This is part of group psychotherapy. For when a person sees in the group how others react to him with the covers of pretense shorn off, he can at one and the same time see how he affects people outside the group. How he reacts in turn with hurt or anger, with impotence or with gesures of appeasement, stands out in clean silhouette. He can see more clearly what he is and how he is and what there is in him that upsets others and brings trouble onto himself. In the circle of the group he experiences safely and without harm in microcosm the under-cover reactions which in the macrocosmic circle of his life outside the group bring him trouble.

With perceptiveness reaching with honesty toward honesty, one group member now hit on the falseness in Cathy's exaggerated sympathy.

"Come on off your pedestal, Cathy."

And another, "You're damned mad at Vic for not being more aggressive and you know it."

"I'm not." Cathy sat straighter and stared around the circle of faces, her hands trembling. "I'm not mad at Vic. Why should I be? I feel sorry for him. I'm mad at that damned Taylor."

"How do you feel, Vic?" another group member asked.

"I *don't* feel, I guess. That's still the trouble. I don't think it matters too much, if you know what I mean. I think Blaine's suggestion about my opening a consulting office is a good one and that's what I'm planning to do, and some of the clients I've worked with will come to me, I'm sure, as soon as they know I'm on my own. I think Blaine himself will use me, and I'll do all right. I'm not really worried."

This time the group reacted to his feelings. Some were friendly, some were challenging, some were frankly angry at him for the absence of vigor in his response. He persisted passively, "It doesn't bother me!" He showed no anger at their anger. No backfiring to their challenges. No appreciation, either, for the friendly concern.

Finally the doctor pointed out, "You have the same problem here, don't you, Vic, that you had on the job? You take all the criticism here without protest. You don't work up any aggressiveness. Let's see, now, how does it really make you feel when the rest of the group jumps all over you?"

Vic looked at the floor and swallowed. He uncrossed his long legs and recrossed them. "It doesn't matter, if you know what I mean."

"What do you mean, Vic?"

He swallowed again and turned toward Cathy, his great hands hanging limply over the arms of his chair. "It doesn't matter," he said and added without change in pace or pitch, "It doesn't matter as long as Cathy thinks I'm all right."

The response rose quickly from various people.

"You sound like a little boy feeling fine as long as his mama says he's O.K. Just like me."

"As long as mother thinks you're wonderful, you don't have to struggle. The world can go by."

Vic's eyes were narrowed like blue slits of water almost lost in their hollows a great distance off. "My mother did think I was wonderful. My mother and Cathy."

His voice did not as usual plod on in monotone to indecisive end without ending. It paused in distinct waiting as if for something to rise from inside him rather than to come from the group.

"My father was away a lot, travelling for a firm he worked for. When he was at home, he was cold and aloof and disapproving of everything I did. I never felt close to him. I'd try to do things to please him when he was around, like getting his slippers for him or kissing him goodnight because he expected it of me, but I'd kiss him gingerly and notice how sharp his whiskers were, like barbed wires telling me to stay on my own side of the fence and not to get in his way or his territory or something, if you know what I mean. I tried to do things to please him, but it never did any good. He'd pack up and leave. I never really had a father. We never were close. I took Mr. Taylor as a father, I guess. I looked up to him and admired him and felt close to him and showed him I was there to do whatever he said. I guess that's got something to do with it, my always doing what he said. If I'd shown more initiative I might be managing the firm now. But I always looked to Mr. Taylor as the one who held the reins. He was so much older . . ."

"The man with the whiskers!"

"Well, I took him that way. As a father."

"And now the only father you ever had walks out and leaves you. But it doesn't really matter, you say, because you have Cathy. I used to say my father could walk out and go to hell and I wouldn't care. But I've seen recently that it mattered a hell of a lot. I was just covering up that I cared, so that the caring wouldn't hurt quite so much."

The doctor came in again. "You thought it didn't matter then, Vic, because you had Mother. You tell yourself it doesn't matter now because you have Cathy."

Vic nodded slowly. "Mother and I were close. But somehow I guess it did matter. I had to be man of the house, if you know what I mean . . ."

"What, Vic?" I asked.

"Well, I did things for Mother. Took care of the furnace and chopped wood and shovelled snow and other things, too, that were more just for her. Just between the two of us, if you know what I mean." He looked for all the world like a frightened overgrown boy who wanted to slink out and hide in some dark retreat with his guilty but cherished secret.

"What, Vic? What sort of things?" I hoped he could share with me now the secret things he'd shared with his mother earlier, only now show them openly in front of these other people, discovering as he did so that in reality he had nothing to fear.

"Well," he swallowed and cleared his throat, "things like brushing her hair. She had blond hair, long and like silk. When she had it unbraided it came to below her waist. She'd let me unbraid it. And I'd run my fingers through its length, straightening it all the way . . ." Vic's eyes were now very blue, focused as if off into distance. "She had a white ivory hair brush with a woman's figure carved on the back. Only a hole had been burned into the girl someway by a branding iron. That's silly, by a cigar or cigarette, I don't remember. And I forget where the hole was in her, what part of her was missing, just that there was a hole somewhere. I'd like to brush her hair; it felt soft and good and there were other things, too, like that, if you know what I mean."

"That felt good?"

He nodded.

"Well," he looked down at the floor. "Well, she'd like me to sleep in bed with her when *he* was away, and I'd wash her back for her when she bathed. She liked me to do it, take care of her, sort of . . ."

"She thought you were wonderful, Vic," the doctor said gently. "How did you feel, Vic? Protected and safe?"

Vic's eyes almost closed till the blue scarcely showed. He looked down at the floor away from everybody, as if he were afraid to meet anyone

squarely. Then, in a voice that was duller and flatter and yet tighter and less flaccid, he answered, "No. Not safe really. No. I didn't really feel safe with my mother. I don't understand it. There was something about it. Well, it seems to me somehow . . . It came to me just at this moment . . . I never thought so before, but . . . Well, as if she had in some way expected too much."

"Like Cathy now?"

He scuffed his great feet on the floor in a helpless gesture, and very slowly shook his head. . . .

"I can't club her!" Kenneth had said. "But I can do other things."

"If I were Hamburger," he elaborated one day, "I'd show her I was angry. I'd jump on her bed and get paw marks all over it. I'd get real mad and growl and bark. I'd chew up her purse and get mud on it. I'd be a real mad and happy Hamburger. Really happy to be mad."

He looked at me soberly. "I'd like to be like that. I'd like to do things, too, to show her how I feel. I'd like to be a real-happy-to-be-mad-Kenneth. But if I got too outspoken it would just get me into a mess of trouble. I can't do it with her. I know that. But I can get the mad out in here with you."

He became freer and easier in reporting what had gone on at home and in the neighborhood. "My boy friend Gene took me to a movie. He treated me. I feel more like a friend!". . . "And me and a couple of other boys got some flower seeds and planted them in the empty lot.". . . "And we're working on a model airplane."

He was freer, too, in expressing his feelings. He was angry at his mother when she was late to meet him at the dentist's one afternoon. He was angry when she forgot to pick him up at school as she'd promised to do. He was angry at her and at his father when they proposed taking back his room for their study and moving him in again with Brad.

"It makes me furious," he announced, glowering. "It'll put me right down again at Brad's level, three years younger than I am. I'll have to turn the lights off earlier and turn the radio off earlier. Just the idea of the whole business makes me mad . . . They don't care how much Brad disturbs me. I don't know what I'll do if I have to move in with that brat . . ."

He stopped and a crafty look came into his face. "Oh, yes, I do know. I'll cough and I'll sneeze and I'll wheeze. I'll get the asthma again. I'll annoy them with it every night. Every night about every half-hour I'll call them in and I'll be such a nuisance keeping Brad awake that he'll be all peevish and shrieky and they won't be able to stand either of us together, and then they'll *have* to give me back my own room . . .''

Even though he thought he could not manage to talk about it to his parents, he had.

At dinner that evening when Brad was especially silly, Ken saw an opening. He threw a glance in Brad's direction, and then turning to his mother, he announced with utter disdain, ''That there's my brother. I love him. I could murder him. And if you put me into that room with him, I will.''

He reported to me a few days later, ''I was surprised. She took it O.K.''

He grew more expansive. ''It's really remarkable. She really can take it from me better than she used to. I guess because she's learning to bring her own crossness out in little fire-cracker explosions. She doesn't hold it all in the way she did. You should see her at home sometimes. She looks like a witch.

''But it's still hard for me to say things to her. It's still easier to say them to you.''

He looked pensive. And then very slowly, as if he were pushing to see his direction through fog, he struggled to bring into words what had long been one of his greatest fears. ''Sometimes I want to let go. Over some little nothing, almost. Some little thing happens; only it isn't little when it gets to me. It seems big. I guess because it sets off something *big* inside me. The biggest wish to SOCK that you ever knew. It's so big that if I socked anybody with that much steam I—I—think I'd explode.''

In great simplicity, Kenneth had elucidated what many people never come to understand. He had been so afraid that he might act on his inner anger and carry out to the full what it dictated that he had kept himself tightly in check. Immobilized almost. So afraid had he been of the push and the force of hostility in him that he had closed up and denied that any was there. In his unconscious mind, however, it had continued to propel him until again and again he had turned it back onto himself, punishing himself for the bad wishes and thoughts, getting sick, feeling guilty, cringing and failing.

If a child's emotional hungers are satisfied by his mother in the helpless beginnings of life when he cannot fend for himself, then he can take in better stride the necessary denials which must be imposed on him as he grows. If he were to put the matter into words, he might say, ''I get angry, yes, at big people for their forbidding me things I want. But still I know they are fundamentally with me and for me. They care about me. They proved that to me when I was small.''

On the other hand, when forbiddings follow early deprivations and a child has not come to the place where he feels he can trust his parents to love and understand him, he is apt to feel they deny him because they don't care about him. Then hurt and anger and rage and fury mount far more stormily. They must be barricaded all the more tightly. It's as if he said to himself, ''I must not even look to see that these feelings exist. If I acknowledge them, they may burst and destroy me and my world.''

Kenneth, however, had looked. With me to support him, he had come through pain and fear to a place of seeing. The pain and fear had grown small enough to endure, and Kenneth had built inner courage enough to tolerate the remnants that still were there and always would be. The trust in me that he had come to feel so profoundly had helped him to make up for his earlier lack of trust in his mother and father. It had helped him move forward toward trust in himself.

Now, since he trusted himself more securely, he could trust himself to manage feelings that he had not felt capable of managing earlier.

Before coming into therapy, he had built up a way of managing himself that was in truth self-demolishment. His way of checking himself had not lain in control but in paralysis. He had virtually immobilized effective functioning in his fear lest unwanted feelings come through. As a result he had not been able to bring out normal aggressiveness. The drive and the push had been so checked that he could not even tackle school subjects with the verve that comes when feelings flow freely into any act. It was as if he had posted a demon of punishment at the streets' intersection, always keeping the ''Go'' sign off and the ''Stop'' sign on.

But now he felt it less necessary to call on the demon. Kenneth felt himself more able to judge and choose and guide what he should do. He could use his eyes and look over the terrain and take into account what the traffic could bear. He could say to himself, ''I'll not go up that street; it's better not to. I'll move along this other street instead. The first street's not safe; the second one is.'' He could say to himself, ''It's not possible to let my feelings run along this action pathway. But along this other one, it's all right.

''I can't let my feelings run out in the act of clubbing my mother. That way is no good.

''But I can talk to my mother sometimes about my feelings. Though only very occasionally.

''I can talk my feelings out to you and to myself . . .

''I've been mad at my mother lots. I was mad at her the other day because she promised me I could go to the store with her and then she went off and completely forgot that I was waiting. I'd like to have called her an idiot. But I knew if I did, she'd get too sore. So I drew little idiot pictures and knew in my mind who they were."

Or again, "I'd like to sock her really. But she's a woman and so I can't. I went and socked my ball, though, all around the block."

He could manage these feelings now more consciously without shoving them all into his unconscious mind. He had acquired the basis for true *self-control*—for managing the outflow of feelings, neither denying nor letting them run wild. He saw what he could do and what he could not do in more realistic terms.

Kenneth had seen too that he could not gain good, warm sensations in his body through possessing his mother. But the deep and human universal wish to experience body-feelings of pleasure was in him. He needed to know, just as all of us need to know, that these can exist without a person's having to feel dirty and bad. He needed to know, just as all of us need to know, that he would have to steer and control the outlets in accordance with our culture's demands, again not by blocking or denying or paralyzing them, but by finding legitimate action-pathways for them to travel along.

We talked about this just as we talked about finding outlets for his feelings of anger. I reiterated what he already knew: that he wouldn't be able to make love to a woman until he was big. But that of course he would think of it and wish that he were already big all the time of his growing.

He made a finger painting in gorgeous colors, warm and glowing magenta-red against a background of aquamarine. A great shaft ran up the center with hands curved around it.

He stood off and surveyed it, and nodded in quiet satisfaction. "A penis with hands touching it. It feels good."

Then, dreaming forward into the future and back into the past, he bridged the time span between with the first marriage dream of every small boy. He worded it now without confusion, knowing it could not be. "Sometimes it wants to go into the mother's baby hole. But naturally it can't."

And then, musingly, he recalled other ways toward solution that he had essayed. "Remember, when I used to poke into the big job hole? I would pretend then that I was poking in the mother's baby hole, exploring, sort of. Trying to find out what was in there.

"And then when I thought how bad it was to want to go into the baby hole the hands would grab

and hurt the penis to hold it back and punish it. That's the red . . ."

I wondered if I saw him flinch, ever so slightly? Were there still in the red of blood's tinge, some things that frightened?

He could see now, however, that hurting himself was not the answer. "That's no use!" he declared. "It's better to make it feel good with the touching. In bed at night. Instead of counting sheep!"

Here again was a legitimate action-pathway, owning up to the feelings and controlling their outflow; not needing to let sex any more than aggression remain a dark demon, unmanageable and bad.

"I can't poke her. But I can do other things."

He had brought out the wish and we'd worked together. The baby wish of dependency on one hand, to push all of himself into his mother, to crawl back into her sheltering body. The man-dream of aggressive independence on the other hand. The wish to conquer and possess. He had faced his fear of letting either side of the impulse flow out into action. The fear of being engulfed and eaten as the baby guppies had been eaten by their mother. The fear of injury to a part of his body, his leg being amputated, hurt by an enemy whose identity even now he had not grasped.

He had explored his feelings and the fantasies enough to glimpse the comforting fact that he could keep them imagined. He had met the stirring in him enough to know that *he could impose restrictions on himself without imposing punishment.*

Kenneth had seen that he could not bring out his wish to "poke" into his mother. Not directly. But there were some more "reasonable" ways of solving the wish, some action-pathways along which it might legitimately go.

"Noises are more reasonable than noses going into ears," he announced one day.

"How do you mean, Ken?"

"Well, when Hamburger barks, his noises go into your ears. That's more reasonable than his little wet nose poking in."

I nodded and waited.

"My noises go into my mother's ears," he elaborated, "just like Hamburger's bark. I used to poke coughing and wheezing noises into her ears. Now I poke different kinds of noises in. The kind she likes better. Good noises, like when I told her yesterday that I'd gotten a spelling prize in school and good grades."

I commented that he was poking his nose into books apparently. He laughed and said he was getting quite nosy. At school, too, he'd wanted to find out what a couple of boys were whispering about and he'd gotten into a fist fight. "Not a bad one. Just enough to show them I could get in on the show. Then, you know? The one I fought with deserted the other and whispered to *me!*"

I checked with the principal. "Yes. He actually did fight. I'd seen it coming; he's been ever so much more aggressive. Fortunately, I'd prompted his teacher that if he should fight, she should just stand by and not let it get too hot. But if possible not to stop him. He's needed so badly to get to where he *could* fight. He held his own, too, the other day when a boy tried to take his place in the line. He said 'No' and actually pushed the other youngster away. And he's getting along better now on the playground; takes more part in games and has made some good friends."

"How about taking a test?" I asked him one day.

"One of those I.Q. things?"

"Yes."

"To see how my mind works?"

"To see how well it's been poking its nose into all kinds of business, finding out about this and that."

He took it in stride as a challenge, eager to see what the test was about.

I was not surprised when the results came to me.

This boy, who two years earlier had been labeled too low to pass with the rest of the children, this boy who had been told to repeat his grade because his score was "only one hundred and eight"—*this boy's intelligence quotient now showed above one hundred and forty.*

I felt as if a gift had been laid in my lap.

Kenneth was now able to use the intelligence that had always been his. It was no longer blocked and tied down along with feelings that had to be held in. It wasn't the test result of itself that pleased me, but rather what it indicated of the general freeing in Kenneth. The test result was a sign that things were going well. So was the absence of asthma. Kenneth had had no attack for over two months, ever since the session after he had painted the great elephant club that had killed his "bad" mother.

Kenneth put into his own words a few weeks later what was happening. "I think I'm getting healthy," he announced. "If this keeps up, I'll soon be able to get a Life Insurance policy."

But Cathy and Vic were having a hard time and in my mind lay the question: was Kenneth healthy

enough to take in his stride the things that might come? . . .

Three days later Vic called me again. His voice, half-raised, had stumbled back into the tense monotone. He had to see me today.

He came in.

Things were in a terrible mess, he said. He groaned and put his head down into his hands, burying the tears. He didn't know what to do. He hadn't phoned Loretta the next day but she had phoned him. The same urgency was in her as on the previous night. She had made up her mind to have him. She knew he loved her. This old-time business of honor was stupid. If he didn't do something decisive about it, she would. He had pleaded for her to wait in order for him to have time to work things out.

But she hadn't waited. She'd gone to see Cathy and she'd spilled things. And Cathy was furious. Cold and aloof in her now justifiable sense of having been offended.

He couldn't forgive Loretta for having done this. And Cathy wouldn't forgive him. She was keeping him out.

Cathy was bitter. "I can just see Vic giving Loretta what he never gives me. Spending time with her when he has no time for me. Talking to her when he won't talk to me. Loving her. Probably sleeping with her, though he says he hasn't . . ."

With me, Cathy was alternately cold and stormy. To Vic she was vindictively cold and hostile.

She became more depressed, feeling life had ended. "Except that I've got Ken. He's wonderful. He's been sweeter to me than he ever has been. As though he's sensed what's been going on."

And from Ken, who called and came in to see me: "I've been really afraid the last few days that Daddy might leave me with Mother. There's something all wrong.

"I keep wondering what it's all about. They still fight too much inside and not enough outwardly. Sometimes I think maybe they have financial worries and that's it. I know they have. But I think it's more the inside feelings that count.

"In the bedroom. That's where it's always the worst.

"They seem to be saying they wish it was all over with. They sit on the bed talking to each other. Maybe trying to love and having trouble. They've had too much trouble trying to love each other.

"I don't know what it is, but something happened. And I've been worried and scared that now they *will* break up the family and get a divorce. I'm mad at them for it. Why don't they grow up and get along? I'm mad at my father mostly for still not really trying to get at his feelings. He still pulls too much into himself, and that way he'll never get things straight.

"I don't like to think of their divorcing. It's frightening. Then I'd be my mother's only man."

For weeks Vic moved in a fog. And then something happened that, with its impact, brought long delayed decisiveness into his life.

It was a Saturday with the children home from school and Ken asked if he could go with his father to visit a job on which Vic was consulting.

Vic looked abstracted. "Why yes, Ken. Come on."

They went across the street together to where Vic had parked the car along the curb. Ken climbed in front in the seat next to Vic. Vic started the motor. And then it happened. With a racing engine Vic went crashing into the car parked ahead.

Ken was thrown forward against the windshield.

"I didn't know what had happened," Ken told me. "I only felt scared. I didn't know till afterward that I had a big lump on my forehead and cuts on my head and chin and fingers. I grabbed for the door and tried to open it. It was stuck someway, and that bothered me more than anything. I just had to get out and I finally did.

"I walked out and stood there and saw Mother coming across the street. And then I blacked out. When I came to, I was lying on the sidewalk. Daddy was walking away and Mother was still coming toward me. She came right to *me*. She didn't talk to Dad."

"I don't know how it happened," Vic said. "I don't see how it could have. The car parked in front of us was at least five feet away. Even a poor driver could have maneuvered out easily. But I crashed into it. As if it were a premeditated act."

But this was not all. A few weeks later it happened again.

Two accidents in such rapid succession!

"That coincidence," Ken muttered, "certainly had an awfully long arm."

He had stood the first accident with amazing fortitude, but this second one was too much for him. He came in wheezing. He felt that somehow the accidents had been his fault.

Why, I wondered, was he retreating to self-condemnation? For what was he punishing himself?

Soon I found out.

A few days before, Cathy had done an unusu-al thing. She had gone into the bathroom with Kenneth supposedly to help him into his pajamas. Quite incidentally, however, she had looked at his body in its eleven-year-old development.

"She looked at my hair there and told me I was growing big there. She told me I was growing into her man."

"So," I said, "you thought maybe that Daddy was trying to hurt you for that reason when he bumped the car. That he was jealous of your being Mother's man? And you're blaming yourself because in a way you'd like to be."

He assented and then retracted. "I did, I guess. But really it was all in *my* mind, not in Daddy's. I know my Daddy didn't mean to do it . . ."

For a moment I wondered whether to press truths that I knew he could grasp. But the horror and the terror of having to live with a father who wanted to harm him was too frightening as a certainty. Especially when he felt, as he'd said, that his father was not really working on his problems. Better to let it rest in the shadow of an imagined possibility from which Ken could choose to escape as he wished. Better to let him handle it by covering it over. For the present, at least. Of most importance for him now were his own feelings toward his father, rather than understanding his father's feelings toward him.

"How does the whole thing make you feel toward Daddy?" I asked.

He nodded knowingly and all at once the wheezing was cleared. "I guess that's one thing I've been hiding. I've been holding it in. He's so big. I've been kind of scared of saying it to myself. But I'm sore at him really. I'd like to do something violent to him. Maybe he didn't mean to do it. But I'm mad at him anyway. He should have been more careful. It *was* his fault. He had absolutely no excuse . . ."

As Ken went on angrily, he grew easier. He had not gotten at the ultimate reason for his anger. But he was at least placing his anger where he knew it belonged rather than turning it back onto himself.

To Vic, the impact of the whole episode kept growing. At first he tried to deny that unconscious motivations had played any role. Then something came out that helped him. One part of the first accident had bothered him more than any other. This stuck in his mind until one night, in the group therapy session, he confronted Cathy with it.

"*I* was in that accident, too, Cathy. I, too, was in the smash. It wasn't only Ken who was in the car. I was there when it hit. But you . . . how did you act? As if there were no one there but Kenneth. You came across the street, Cathy, and you didn't say one word to me. You passed me by and went straight to Ken . . .''

Cathy and Ken! Ken and Cathy! The combination made a pattern in his mind which met with another pattern. His own pattern long ago.

For days and nights the tremendous import of this filled him until from out of the crucible of the deep suffering in him there rose a conviction stronger than words.

At last Vic knew that he couldn't let this happen to his son, the thing that had happened to him. His father had left home. His father had left him with his mother. He himself had been virtually leaving home, seldom being there and when he was there not really being present. Being abstracted and away, his feelings apart. He was leaving Ken with Cathy as his father had left him with his mother.

He couldn't let this thing happen. He had to dig in and stop escaping.

Vic knew finally that he had to become a man.

Many months later Vic brought into another group therapy session something that had happened to him the previous night.

It seemed that the white moon had been shining in the window onto Cathy as she lay asleep beside him in bed. He had raised himself on his elbow and had looked down on her to see if she was all right, since she had just recovered from a rather heavy cold. A sense of eeriness crept into him as he watched the covers rise and fall with her breathing. Her face was relaxed, her lips slightly parted. From between them came the slightest of snores.

He caught his breath, his chest tightening, the dryness coming into his mouth. Panic filled him. He wanted to run. To get up and get out.

This had happened before. With Loretta. But earlier also. With his mother when he was a boy. The rise and fall of her body as she breathed. Her closeness in bed. The small snore creeping out with its rhythmic hum.

How many had been the times when he had been filled with ineffable yearning to reach out and run his hand through her long, soft hair. Being with his mother was good and close and warm. Until his father came home.

Vic had told himself that his mother preferred him to his father. That when his father returned home and he, Vic, was shoved off into the small room across the hall, his mother's mood would slip from its ordinary unsmiling and serious quiet into sadness that held in it the quality of resignation.

And then Vic recalled an incident he'd lost long ago.

His father had come home on the previous night and Vic once more had been put to bed in his own room. The next day he got up before the pale morning moon was out of the sky. He'd dressed himself quietly, somehow vaguely planning to go outside in search of something. Something perhaps to fill the lonely void inside him.

He opened and closed his bedroom door and stood in the hall, the door to his mother's room darkly closed. And then it was that the sounds came to him which for all the years since he had been struggling to keep lost. Little chirruping unwonted sounds creeping out through his mother's closed door. And the sound of her laughter, secretively gay.

This quiet woman who, he'd always believed, was sexless. This serious woman who never laughed! His father was doing something to her to make her lips part in this gurgling enjoyment.

After his father had gone again and Vic was back once more in his mother's bed, night after night he would rise on his elbow and gaze at his mother sleeping.

Then the wish would creep into him along with the shadowed fear that made him slice off the wish before it pushed over the threshold into awareness—the wish to know what secret things he, too, might do to her to make her laugh.

Long after the episode lay buried, the wishes still prompted him to run away. He left home as soon as he was old enough to get a job. He travelled across many states to remove himself physically from that which he carried with him, ironically, in his innermost thoughts.

"I see it now," Vic said, a new composure showing in the increased easiness and strength in his voice. "Some of you people in this group take refuge in confusion. My way has been to take refuge in composure. My calm, cool quietness was a way of escaping the thoughts and feelings I felt I had to escape , . .''

He glanced at the doctor, smiling in sudden hesitance and letting his eyes drop, still somewhat fearful that this man whom he now took as a kind of father might punish him as his real father might have if he'd seen into his thoughts. The doctor might perhaps reach out and burn a hole into him with his cigarette, as his real father might have burned a far graver, deeper wound with a branding iron. Like the hole in the figurine on his mother's ivory brush. Like a hole his father might have slashed with his keen-edged razor.

"I can see now," Vic continued, "that any reaction I have had to any woman is essentially a reaction to my mother. I took refuge in the composed assurance that I'd solved my problem by leaving it when I left home. But I hadn't. I hadn't left my mother. She was still with me, inside me. I carried her across the country with me. And I carried along with her all my reactions of fear about getting close to a woman. Cathy! Loretta! It wouldn't have mattered who.

"But now that that's out in the open, I don't need to run after some Loretta-shaped promise to happiness. I can see that it's up to me to clear out the underbrush, and then the road to happiness with Cathy won't be too hard. She's really the woman I want."

Gradually as the months passed Cathy, too, saw things. One night in the group something was said that made her slip back into what she had used as *her* refuge, the sweet, martyred, long-suffering air behind which she hid the feelings that made her afraid.

This touched off something in another group member, a man who was full of the fury he had carried from his past. He sprang up now and took it out on Cathy. "You're just like my mother," he shouted, "with your holier-than-thou attitude."

He rose and started across the room toward her, towering in his violence, his fists whitely clenched.

For a split second, Cathy's teeth flashed in white and gleaming exultation and the flush of excitement flooded into her cheeks. Then she flinched and paled and started trembling. She wanted to run, but she stayed.

She was frightened by violence and excited by violence, both. She veered from violence and steered toward violence, both. The happiest days of her life had been when her father had turned to her. And this he had done in violence more than in peace. Her only sure way of getting her father had been to provoke him to the point of violence. Then in the mad bursting of temper he became all hers.

"His spankings were the only way through which I could consistently get him."

His spankings actually had been his most dependable gift.

But violence could become too violent and hurt could become too grave. The fear had grown to overshadow the excitement, and Cathy had sought safety in marrying a man unlike her father, mild and retiring, with whom she could control her own feelings along with the control she exerted over him.

That she had needed also to control Blaine she came to see far more clearly, and why. She had wanted a man, yes. But only a man whom she could dominate. Otherwise, in her own excitement, she might provoke hurt beyond endurance, such as her father might have given her a long, long time since.

Gradually Cathy saw these things in their many-sided aspects with the shadows and the colors reaching from them. As she was able to show these to her doctor-father and her therapist-mother without being destroyed as she had feared in her childhood that her own father and mother might destroy her, she grew less fearful. She no longer needed to take refuge in tenseness and apologetic sweetness. Moreover, she could let her most impelling wish come to flower—her deep and basic wish to have a man.

Time moved on. Changes came into being slowly—almost imperceptibly. Like the shift of the seasons. Barely noticeable, the changing, till the change was there.

Vic was Cathy's man now. And she was his woman. There were fights between them as there always would be and always are in a marriage that has any vigor. But there were moments of ecstasy also, and moments of peace.

The reader may want to delve deeper into the literature of individual psychotherapy. There are many volumes in the annual series "The Psycho-Analytic Study of the Child."[3] Helen Leland Witmer edited the excellent *Psychiatric Interviews with Children*,[4] a potpourri of theoretically different, individual child therapies.

Erik Erikson's work is based in psychoanalysis, but his background of teaching and anthropology led him to a theory of child therapy that gave the impact of society's far greater role. He spearheaded the trend toward ego-psychology, which postulates that the child's ego is composed of (1) what he innately brings into the world, (2) what his experiences have led him to be, (3) the interaction of child and society, and (4) how he uses both unconscious and conscious forces to deal with life and the meaningful people in it. Erikson's books, *Childhood and Society* and *Martin Luther, A Study in Identity*[5] describe the child's struggle to develop his own identity. It is critical to recognize that dynamic approaches are broader than Freudian or neo-Freudian. The concern with a child's inner life, fantasy, affective feelings, motivations, and impulses are a concern for many psychologists and educators.

Regardless of the theoretical framework, play is an essential ingredient for treating young children. Virginia Axline's book, *Play Therapy*,[6] is a classic in this area. Subsequently, much has been written about different forms of play therapy—game files have been compiled, film strips, records, video tapes—the materials put out by Marlo Thomas in 1974 are notable. In France, therapists are particularly fond of using puppets and marionettes for psychodrama with children; French literature in the field abounds with helpful material and case histories. These materials and many others we will discuss are every bit as valuable for group therapy or the therapeutic classroom as with individual treatment.

When working with children who do not conform to the neurotic mode for which psychoanalysis and intensive psychotherapy was intended (and these days most of our severely troubled children do not fit this mode), different therapeutic methods and theory are required. For references on working with hyperaggressive youth, Fritz Redl's and David Wineman's *The Aggressive Child*[7] and Fritz Redl's, *How We Deal With Children*[8] stand out. Bruno Bettelheim's *Love is Not Enough*[9] as well as his later books on the subject are classic material for treatment of the autistic or schizophrenic child.

Educators are very familiar with another type of treatment—behavior modification, or operant conditioning. Behavior modification techniques are often applied on an individual basis, a particular program worked out for each child, but they are used even more often within a group setting. To some people, it is a panacea; as a result the temptation is not to examine the dynamics behind the behavior as long as the bothersome behavior is eliminated. Current literature has placed much emphasis on behavior modification; it would be redundant to do so here. For these reasons, and because we would prefer to concentrate on those areas that are so much a part of the school's own armamentorium, only a brief discussion of the subject will be found in this book (see "Treatment Groups" by Ruth G. Newman, p. 158).

Groups

The preceding articles have indicated some of the major pathways that psychotherapy has been traveling in order to help individuals lead more fulfilled and productive lives. Because of the increasing pressures and complexities of modern, particularly urban, society, there are increasingly greater needs for treating the severely emotionally disabled, the somewhat incapacitated, and the victim of society-bred illness. Treatment for emotional disturbance is needed for couples, families, and larger groups as well as individuals; the needs for treatment are apparent among the people in such places as private offices, clinics, hospitals, schools, and churches, as well as on street corners and playgrounds. There are many forms of treatment. The articles in this part of the book treat a major aspect of therapy and education. Both the mental health worker and the educator need to understand the forces at work in groups and how they can be effectively used to teach or treat.[13]

The structure, leadership, and methods of groups vary according to their purposes. As you read about those described below, you should keep in mind your own varied experience of groups. There are bound to be a number of enlightening parallels, if you are looking for them.

Groups:
How They Grew And What They Do
Ruth G. Newman

These days the Group is the Thing. There are haphazard groups; groups emphasizing verbal communication; nonverbal groups; long-term therapy groups; short-term groups; groups to study group behavior; groups to train for leadership in groups; discussion groups; meditative groups; marathon groups; role-playing groups; psychodrama groups; sensitivity groups; and encounter groups. There are groups for delinquents, for debutantes, for miners, for ministers, for alcoholics, for drug addicts, for adolescents, for kindergartners, for couples, for the divorced, for the old people, for teachers, for students, for principals, and for politicians. Groups abound to study interracial relations and international relations. There are even groups broken up into subgroups which study the interaction of their constituent groups. Consequently, it is no wonder that many people, responding to a phenomenon that has much of the appearance of a fad, look askance at groups or are frightened or repelled by them. At the other extreme, there are those who are so imbued with the experience that they become group-addicted, getting their "kicks" from group experience and, like any other addict, are unable to do without that experience, sometimes even permitting the group experience to replace any efforts at sustaining relations in ordinary unscheduled life situations. It is understandable that, with such varieties of response, there is a wide variety in the methods of groups and in the quality and kind of group leadership.

With all this groupiness, what is seldom understood by loyal advocates of one or another particular kind of group is that the underlying aims and primary tasks of groups vary as much as does the quality or method of leadership, and that the only fair way to judge the effectiveness of a group is to ask whether or not it accomplishes or approaches its aims or primary tasks. Its task may be to learn how to solve a specific problem, or to alter behavior, or to arrive at some insight, or to treat the emotional disturbances of group members, or to discuss something of mutual interest. It may achieve other things as well, but the important question is whether or not it does what it sets out to do. If a group is fundamentally for teaching or learning, the group cannot be held responsible for the fact that someone who joined it for therapeutic experiences failed to get what he wished or had, as sometimes happens, an overwhelming emotional experience. He was not in the right group.

It is the responsibility of the group leadership and of the person joining a group to be clear about just what the group's primary goal is. An ideal group leader understands what is happening in a group on many levels at every moment. Without a general awareness among its members of the direction the group is to go, the group will at best probably fail in its purpose and may at worst be destructive. This is true for a teaching group, a staff meeting, a therapy group, a seminar, or a political policy-making group. A group needs a knowledgeable leader who is clear about the group's task and aware of potential pitfalls.

All groups need far better tools for screening group members in order to avoid some of the worst hurdles and hazards. But the screening methods presently in use are either overly pedantic or too loose to be effective. There are few experiences more immobilizing, for instance, than that of the child who is placed in a group which repeatedly excludes him. Eventually he develops a pattern of self-exclusion, so that he holds himself apart whenever he meets new groups of people. There is a need for some good research into the requirements of group-

ing as well as into the training of leaders appropriate to the tremendous variety of groups required by modern society. Some understanding of groups as such is essential to an understanding of families; of schools; of the types of teaching appropriate to different children; of local, national, and international politics; and of the interrelations among various groups within single institutions (such as the schools, which encompass to one or another extent boards of education, administrations, teaching and non-teaching staffs, parents, students, in some respects the entire community). The present high interest in groups is a graphic indicator of their importance in modern society.

Far from being a new concept, groups are of course one of the oldest means of human survival. Like other animal species, early man grouped himself into herds, and the herds subdivided themselves into leaders and followers according to the task at hand. From the herds there evolved the more differentiated tribes, and from the tribes the clans—the groups at each level more specialized and finely differentiated than those above. Warring, working, and negotiating with each other, the smaller groups defined for themselves territorial boundaries, and nations developed. Various forms of cultural ethics emerged as different groups developed differently. Some of the sources of differentiation were psychodynamic, some were economic, and some were ecological and climatic. The various hostile forces of nature solidified the group-proneness of humans all over the earth. Within larger groups there developed subgroups for the purpose of achieving one or another of the particular goals of the society. Tribal custom, personal abilities, and hereditary roles helped determine grouping (much as they do in contemporary schools and classes). Religious groups, food-acquiring groups (hunting groups, herding groups, planting groups), women's groups, children's groups, and even out-groups (the excommunicated or the especially venerated) all found a place, their power varying according to the particular needs of the large group at the moment. Human society would not have survived if there were not in the human species an instinct for grouping. (The word *instinct* is to be taken literally, on the basis of anthropological and historical data.) There is in men a need for simultaneous difference and sameness in relation to one another.

Perhaps because of its instinctual sources, man's group-proneness has never, as such, received much attention. Perhaps the most self-conscious use of groups has been among statesmen and churchmen. From Ikhnaton to Lenin, from Moses to Martin Luther King, the democratic Jefferson, the manipulative Machiavelli, the power-driven Napoleon or Hitler, the socially conscious Roosevelt—none would have achieved what they did without knowing how to relate to and manipulate the groups they dealt with directly and those they dealt with indirectly through representatives. They knew how to use man's instincts for group life to serve the purposes in which they believed, for good or for ill.

Even in the little arena of the classroom, no teacher would survive a school day without knowing how to deal with a group. All of the teacher's actions have some effect—productive, destructive, or something in between—on the members of the group, the class. "Johnnie, move your chair to the back of the room," "Susie, come sit by me," "Laurie, you help Ken," "Nancy, it's your turn to choose your spelling team." How did the students accept these instructions? Why? What was the price? What was the value? Did the teacher have any unconscious motivations? Did the students perceive them? What task did the teacher want to achieve? Was that the best way to do it or just the way everybody had done it—or the way the syllabus or the supervisors had said to do it?

The teacher faces similar questions in his association with other groups, such as the other teachers he works with and the parents of his students. What *did* happen at the teachers' meeting yesterday? Why didn't he speak up? Why didn't he say what he wanted to say and had planned to say? Why did what he said come out too weak, too strong, too wheedling, too belligerent? What about the parents' meeting he had to lead? What went wrong? What went right and why? Did he or did he not accomplish the task? Did he spend too much time with the N's to the rejection of the B's? Why did he shut himself off when the racial issue came up? Was he scared by it or was it right to do so at that time and place?

A person in a group finds himself in a variety of roles—roles which are continually changing. He is violent. He is withdrawn. He is convincing. He is misunderstood. He reaches one or more people. He is isolated. He is the leader one minute and the dependent follower the next. He considers himself guided by rational methods, yet he finds himself acting on utterly irrational, overwhelming motives. He is hated for leading although he has been made to lead. He is scorned for following although no one

would follow *him*. He is singled out by one member and ignored by the others. He is the doctor, and therefore isolated or the patient, and therefore the center of everyone's attention. He incorporates in himself everyone in the group, and yet he remains, if he is at all healthy, his own unique self.

The knowledge that a person acquires about himself in groups helps him to understand his colleagues and his pupils. Experience with the emotionally disturbed is especially good at teaching a person his own defenses and vulnerabilities. More intensely perhaps than any other groups, the emotionally disturbed represent all the phases of oneself and of everyone else; that is one reason these groups often make a person so anxious: they strike chords of intense anger, of hopelessness, of withdrawal, of isolation, of loneliness, of the struggle to succeed, of competition, of winning, of losing, of hatred, of need, of love, of hunger, of the whole gamut of human conditions. But though some of these conditions may be uncomfortable and unattractive, a teacher needs to know what it's like to experience all of them in order to deal with them intelligently in his students.

When working with groups of children, a teacher must beware of thinking he can improve the group by ridding it of the child who is causing a disturbance. If he removes such a child, he can be certain that another child will assume the role of disturber, and he can be fairly sure that both are being egged on by that seemingly quiet fellow in the third row. To try to eliminate the uncomfortable parts of that whole which is a group is to restrict experience and to imply that life is something it is not. To accept the inconvenient elements of group experience and to channel them constructively is to enrich that experience for both teacher and students.

Classroom groups are best organized around the task at hand. What does the teacher want the children to achieve? An academic skill? Personal insight? An exchange of ideas or feelings? A cooperative project such as a mural or a play? A different kind of group is appropriate for each of these purposes, and a teacher should choose each group with leaders who will be able to inspire confidence in the group's ability to achieve the particular task at hand, leaders who can lead without demanding that other group members abdicate all responsibility. From his experience with groups as participant and observer, a teacher finds in time reasonably workable rules for grouping according to the task at hand, be it short- or long-range.

Groups that Study Groups

With the recent upsurge of interest in groups and group theory, a number of organizations have arisen with the purpose of studying groups and group behavior. The National Training Laboratory is one of the sources of such study. It is in this center that the concepts of the "sensitivity group" and "sensitivity training" evolved, the idea being to develop a program through which a participant might become more sensitive to himself in relation to the other members of a group under a variety of experiences. The task is *not*, as many people interpret it, to make one a more sensitive person (it may or not do that); the task is to make each individual member more effective in terms of the total group. The major center of the National Training Laboratory is in Washington, D.C. It also has a summer center in Bethel, Maine, and other centers in California and elsewhere. Although many kinds of group experience are offered, it is best known for its small groups consisting of about eight to twelve people and a group trainer. They are called T-groups, for training groups. As with any group, the T-group's quality and the direction it takes depend largely on the leader, though these are of course modified by all of the group's members. Such groups emphasize informality (first names, any kind of dress, familiarity with the leader), openness, intimacy, and emotionality, since one premise of these groups is the belief that the inhibition of these qualities creates barriers among people that affect them in all of their dealings. The emphasis given to these qualities varies tremendously from group to group.

The National Training Laboratory has attracted many industries, departments of government, social agencies, and schools, for the training of groups among their staff members. Some varieties of these groups, such as encounter groups and those of the Esalen Institute, have been criticized for being anti-intellectual and undisciplined as well as for arousing more feelings, letting loose more hostility, and breaking down more defenses than some group members are able to handle; it has been said that organizations need to be run by rational rather than emotional means. But in spite of the criticism, many people continue to find group experiences of these kinds useful. Many varieties have developed: bio-energetics; massage groups; all kinds of encounter groups, which are an intensely emotional undertaking; the contact group, which is often non-verbal; the transactional or game-theory group, which uses group games as models of pressure situations (deriving from the theory presented by Dr. Eric Berne in a bestselling book, *Games People Play*); and the gestalt group developed by Dr. Fritz Perls, in which a group member dramatizes some partially conscious tendency in himself with the help of the other group members. *Please Touch* by Jane Howard is a readable book that describes NTL groups and their offshoots.

The center for a different approach to the study of group behavior is the Institute of Group Relations at the Tavistock Institute in England. In America, similar studies are being done at the A.K. Rice Institute for Human Relations. These groups have their theoretical sources in the ideas of Dr. Wilfred Bion, whose work began with the rehabilitation of Royal Air Force fliers during World War II. These groups were subsequently developed among various people in England and later in the United States: doctors and hospital staffs, trade unionists, churchmen, government workers, educators, and people generally who were interested in social change. Many, including this author, feel that the Tavistock model contributes more to an understanding of the subtleties and covert processes within groups in relation to leadership—particularly important to the complexities of today's society—than any other theory.

The emphasis in the Tavistock groups is on learning through experiencing groups and simultaneously being able to reflect about the experience. One of the goals of Tavistock groups is to determine which factors encourage and which discourage a work group in achieving its task. These groups examine the relationship between a group and its leadership; they are interested in the sources of authority within a group and in the question of the responsibility of individual group members for the direction a group takes and the decisions it makes. They come to recognize the power of the group in determining the roles, active or passive, of individual members, and they learn what it is to accept or reject those roles. The meaning of leadership and the significance of the various barriers that exist between people, such as the leader and the led, are important considerations of these groups.

In addition to the small group, similar in size to the T-group of the National Training Laboratories, the A.K. Rice–Tavistock model makes use of larger groups, a format which has many applications to modern, particularly urban, society, where such groups as the school assembly and the student protest meeting are increasingly familiar. The large group experience on the Tavistock model is often disconcerting and confusing, though it is also enlightening in that it demonstrates the difficulty of communicating in a group too large for face-to-face confrontation.

The A.K. Rice groups hold periodic conferences, lasting from a few days to two weeks, at which their exercises in the study of small group, large group, and intergroup behavior take place. The intergroup exercise offers dramatically instructive experience in the difficulties of relationship, communication, and negotiation among various groups. It has obvious analogies in the United Nations, in national politics, in labor-management relations, in school board-administration relations, in staff-administration relations of schools and hospitals, and in relations among different racial and ethnic groups. The formation of conservative, liberal, and radical attitudes often takes place in groups, and various individual roles emerge, such as the stranger, the belonger, the excommunicated, the defector, the informer, the rebel, and the go-between. One of the most revealing aspects of these exercises is the difficulty groups have simply in agreeing on a method for the study of group behavior, the difficulty of agreeing on the means for carrying out the group's task once the task itself is agreed on, the difficulty of negotiations among groups, and the chaos and sense of futility that often ensue from these efforts. A most dramatic presentation of the complicated concepts demonstrated by the Tavistock groups can be found in Kenneth Rice's book, *The Conference in Group Relations*. A particularly moving account of the interpersonal dynamics among a small group of men faced with actual life and death decisions regarding the future of a whole nation and perhaps even the world is provided in Robert Kennedy's *Thirteen Days*, a firsthand account of the Cuban missile crisis as it was handled by the top advisors to President John Kennedy.

The National Training Laboratory directs its attention to the individual within a group: how he comes across, how his behavior affects others in the group, and how he reacts to others. The A.K. Rice-Tavistock groups concentrate on the *gestalt* of the group: what forces are released by the group; what pressures and what unconscious group attitudes, covert and overt, are aroused. Because leadership, the authority to work, and responsibility are the foci of this model, the staff behave in a much more formal manner, carefully keeping time and space boundaries between themselves and individual members while work is in progress, so as to be able to keep their full attention on the group and its conscious and unconscious behavior as they study problems of roles within the group, forces that emerge, leadership, competence, and the consequences of taking on or abdicating responsibility.

In addition to Wilfred Bion's *Experience in Groups*,[1] see the excellent articles by Margaret J. Rioch, "The Work of Wilfred Bion on Groups" and "We, Like Sheep."[2, 3]

Article Footnotes

1. Wilfred Bion, *Experience in Groups* (New York: Basic Books, 1962).

2. Margaret J. Rioch, "The Work of Wilfred Bion on Groups," *Psychiatry*, 33 (1970):

3. Margaret J. Rioch, "We, Like Sheep," *Psychiatry*, 38 (1972):

The following article is an excerpt from a book about all aspects of the school groups: the school as a miniature social system; classroom groups, staff groups, parent and community-action groups, administration and teachers-union groups; the nature of group forces and group roles in the school; and the treatment of children in and out of the school setting. The excerpt deals with treatment in groups of children and youths who can stay within the school setting in regular or special classes, but who, on a problem-continuum from ordinary to severe disturbances, can use group treatment when properly administered.

Treatment Groups
Ruth G. Newman

Living sometimes brings to children, as it also sometimes does to adults, problems of such a nature that they may become immobilized. Anxiety or panic besets them to such an extent that they cannot concentrate, and even when they appear to be doing their work, they can neither comprehend or retain it. Like as not, they are unable to sit still long enough to hear the task assigned, let alone to pursue it. When these problems come only from the outside and are temporary—let's say, when a child's parents have separated, or his father has lost his job; or when his mother is ill or the gang has ostracized him or when a beloved pet has died—tension abounds in the family, and the child may become morose or cross. He may feel ignored, belittled, picked on, rejected or unworthy. Or he may be recovering from a bad flu or suffering from undernourishment, both of which conditions make for low tolerance of anxiety, easy loss of temper and clouds of depression. These things he will get over, but if they go on too long beyond their causes, in order to keep the situation from becoming worse, to keep what began as superficial from turning into a deepset response, the child often needs help, usually of a temporary nature.

Help for problems of this kind may be given as therapy within the school building, or it may be given in a clinic or private office outside the school. In most cases recognition that a child needs help comes first from the school. In these instances, therapy is usually preceded by parent conferences and a diagnostic work-up by a school psychologist, a referral clinic or a private facility. In the latter cases, the school needs to have some way of determining whether the child is actually getting help outside and if so of what kind; it needs to know whether the therapist wants to keep in touch with the school or not. The therapy decided on may be individual and may or may not include the family or it may be in a group of peers. There are sometimes special and good reasons for treatment to be individual, but if these are not apparent, this kind of child will probably be very well able to use a group, for in a group he can discover that, as well as his peers, the adults involved can help him gain insight.

If the problems are in fact largely born of circumstance, this type of child tends to be that boon to group therapists, the child who himself takes to therapy as a thirsty man to water, and who is able also to be helpful to others in the group. When he leaves the group, he has learned something more about himself, about his interpersonal style. He has become more aware of the habitual ways in which he has defended himself in situations that make him anxious, and of how he comes across to others; he gains, as well, many more insights that can be of use to him throughout his life. If he is too young for such self-recognition and ability to do something about it, his parents, through parallel or collaborative group work, will have gained the ability to hear his cues and act upon them, and to seek counseling themselves. At the time of crisis, the problems of this group of children *feel* to them no less bad or intense than those of far more distressed children, and sometimes their actions in class are as disturbing or even more so, but the distress lasts less long, and the situation, if caught and recognized, does far less damage to the child or the class, and can be handled more readily. This type of child is well served both by short-term group psychotherapy where some unconscious material can be dealt with, some basic needs served, and coping mechanisms explored, and by inter-active groups such as sensitivity training offers. These groups can meet either in or out of school. There are many kinds of therapy groups. I will describe the basic ones briefly.

From *Groups in Schools* by Ruth G. Newman, Copyright © 1974 by Ruth G. Newman. Reprinted by permission of Simon and Schuster.

Non-Treatment Groups

What do we mean by the term "non-treatment group"? Most commonly, the kind of circumstances that beset a youth above the age of twelve may be alleviated by responsibly led encounter or sensitivity groups in which the group concentrates on its collective behavior and feelings in the here and now, groups in which the individual members get and give feedback on what is happening to them, from and with each other, as well as from and to the adult leader(s).

The leaders of such groups usually behave and dress in a very open and familiar manner. They not only use their own feelings, as every good therapist does, but relay these feelings and the behavior they generate to the individuals in the group in order to indicate how what a person is doing may make others feel. The leaders and the group attempt to explore alternative modes of behavior which might be more successful, or at least more satisfying and so presumably more easing to one's own soul and relationships. Groups serve as a laboratory: they offer a safe place to try on different roles to see which ones fit one's own temperament and needs most usefully. Different leaders use different styles and techniques, but in general the sensitivity or "encounter" type of group attempts to deal with problems in the here and now, largely using past material only where it seems relevant to present behavior or feelings. It emphasizes relationships, closeness, caring, as therapeutic tools to help the individual. Though it often arouses unconscious or reminiscent material and sets up anxiety-provoking happenings, it is not a sine qua non of the sensitivity group dogma that the unconscious be looked at as it is in most psychodynamic therapy or in the Tavistock Model groups. The aim is to enable an individual to see himself and others in a group, and to get help from the group and the leader toward personal growth and development. This is often all that is needed to alleviate the pain and paralysis that derive from these circumstances and to allow them to come close enough to the surface, in time and place, to be looked at and appraised.

Adolescents as well as adults who are shy of "psychotherapy" are often very willing to try this kind of experience. It is particularly apt for adolescents, with their loneliness, their struggle to find themselves, their dependence on group approval and their need to test out adult authority. The search for the self fits in well with the identity struggle adolescents face. When led by skillful leaders, such a group does well in helping the person without deepset problems who needs to grapple with developmental changes, which by themselves at crisis periods of growth (such as adolescence or aging) can cause great anguish.

Sensitivity or encounter groups are often held in the school, though sometimes they are held outside. It is essential that if the school is the sponsoring agency the leaders have some contact with the counselor and teacher—not to breach confidentiality, but so that school people can be made aware that the child is working on his problems, and that while he is doing so, his behavior in class may, for a while, seem more tense or dreamy, and even, at times, bizarre. It is equally important, or more so, that the parents be fully aware of the groups their children are in. It needs to be made absolutely sure that the parents have given their permission. Again, with younger children especially, the group's value is enhanced appreciably if the parents too are involved in a group, or in individual counseling experience.

Sensitivity and encounter groups are also used widely for staff training, and will be discussed in that context in Chapter XII. Although "sensitivity" and "encounter" groups may differ in technique, the goal of *individual* growth through interaction is paramount in both kinds of group. The difference between the two depends on the particular school of thought or techniques used by the leaders.*

Leaders of the two types of group differ not only because of differing professional interests but also because of different theoretical biases. Right now, the largest number form a cluster around what is called "Gestalt" and "transactional therapy." "Gestalt" is represented in the practices of the late Fritz Perls and Laura Perls. "Transactional therapy" is exemplified by Eric Berne in his *Games People Play*. A similar kind of eliciting interaction and insight is that of Virginia Satir who emphasizes a role-playing dramatic approach. Her interests have been largely in family therapy, where the family is seen as a group, but her methods have since been extended to other groups as well.

"Marathon" groups—groups based on the principle that when people are tired their usual sets

---

*The National Training Labs launched the sensitivity groups. National Training Labs is an organization associated with the National Education Association. Its program is based on the work of Kurt Lewin; its founders are Leland Bradford, Ronald Lippitt and Kenneth Benne. Sensitivity training has gone through many phases since its inception, and now has centers throughout the country. Its staff and trainees are active in many groups, some in business, many in education and training, some in therapy, and some as an expression of social concern.

or behavior patterns can be broken down more easily, and that insight and change can thus occur—are used by most sensitivity and encounter leaders. Sessions may run anywhere from eight to forty-eight hours at a stretch. Some more conventional groups who meet regularly once a week for one and a half hours include a few modified marathons in which the participants can go home to sleep for brief periods. For many reasons such exercises are clearly inappropriate for young children.

There can be dangers for adolescents (in fact for everyone) in the extremist types of groups. Some adolescents can't take the kind of closeness forced on them, because they are not yet sufficiently clear about their own identity and unity as persons to have whatever patterns they have developed for themselves battered down without time to assimilate the why and the how and the what it all means. Many, who in their daily lives are overexposed to badgering, cannot take the force of group-badgering which insists that a person feel what the group thinks he should-ought to-must feel. He may not feel what the group wants him to feel and may either fake it—which is not useful—or get group-pressured into feelings, phoney or real, he can't deal with. Another danger, when these groups are adapted to children, lies in precisely that quality which appeals to adolescents and to many adults. Since one of the goals is to develop closeness, intimacy, sharing, the procedures involve the breaking down of existing boundaries. But such boundaries are needed, especially by young children, to give some steering power, some individual sense of how the skin separates one person from another, of where the limits of do and don't, can and can't really fall.

Where boundaries are not a problem, such groups are appealing and useful, and when they are led by people who know adolescents, they are particularly useful with that age group. They can be invaluable to facilitate open communication, to help one realize feelings, to make one aware that the supposedly unacceptable parts of oneself are often liberating and energy-producing. A responsible leader of a sensitivity type of group for adolescents in the school or outside would give careful attention to the problem of who should join and who should be eliminated. He would be careful not to mix adults who are emotionally adolescent with chronological adolescents.

A leader may use many Gestalt and transactional techniques, but he must not allow the activity

to reach a point where the adolescents are forced into a closeness they cannot tolerate, or led into sexual fantasies or acting-out which would make them too frightened or too guilty. Fooling around with people's defenses while setting loose group forces is at best a precarious business. The safeguards lie in the leadership. Still, keeping this in mind, groups which concern themselves with the three areas of particular moment to adolescents—peer relations, self, and authority—can be valuable aids.

Before we leave the subject of sensitivity groups for school-age children, it should be said that in modified form a sensitivity group may be useful in the earlier years as far down as the second or third grade. It may include all or only some members of a class; and it can be a useful device when included as a means to teach sex education or social values and to stimulate intellectual growth as well.

Psychotherapy Groups

There are certain children whose problems have deeper roots than those we have so far discussed. In their lives too, circumstances may arise which cause traumas, and these may bring to light or exacerbate pre-existent difficulties. It requires careful diagnostic procedures to distinguish the problems with deep roots from the more superficial ones. Children with deep-rooted problems fit well into psychotherapy groups.

To pass over the perennial debate about whether the problems that beset humans are rooted in physical constitution, chemical imbalance, genetic fault, environmental happenstance or cultural pressures, let us agree that all these factors do exist and do create stresses. It is rare to be able to say with any validity that a particular individual's misery or mis-adaptation is caused by one aspect and not by the others. Whatever the causes, the difficulties in living exist, and all we can do is take the best information we have available and try to find the best way we now know to work with a particular child, given his assets as well as his liabilities. We do know *some things* beyond trial-and-error methods. If the chosen mode of approach does not work, we try another and another, or we combine two or more, or we eliminate the ones that don't work. Since people are the instruments of these methods, we have to consider not only the receiver of treatment, but the giver as well—and most of all, in nearly all therapies, no matter how mechanical or "controlled," we have to look at the relationship that exists between the giver and the receiver of treatment. Moreover, at the same time that we become more sophisticated in what we know, we have learned that with all humans, but particularly with children, we have to look at the homes they live in, the culture and values they absorb, and the school and the people who teach and treat them. With this assortment of factors in mind, we can proceed to review—we can only skim over them—the various types of therapy where groups become a central aspect of treatment.

Many times it has become clear that certain children do far better in working out their problems—no matter how deep-seated—in a group with children roughly about their own age level than in individual therapy. Their fear of adults is mitigated and their fear of exposure is lessened by the knowledge that others have problems too. Groups confront difficulties in relationships with peers, a prime cause of problems. From these confrontations, understanding, whether vocalized or acted upon, can be gained. For children, a group is a more everyday setting than what Fritz Redl calls the "pressurized cabin" atmosphere of the therapist alone with one child, in a situation outside the context of daily life. Sometimes groups are made up of children with the same kinds of problems. Most often it has been found that a mixture of many kinds of children, exhibiting many different kinds of behavior and exemplifying within themselves a variety of inner dynamics, do better together than children all of one kind or type. Depending on the need, family and group treatment are offered either simultaneously or in sequence. If the therapists of each—the family and the group—collaborate closely, this can be very successful.

Sometimes a child is so emotionally deprived, or so beset by his inner dynamics, that he requires individual one-to-one treatment. He may need only this form of treatment, or he may need it as a prelude to group therapy. The group therapy then becomes a safe testing ground for what he has learned, a kind of graduation exercise from individual treatment, where the child makes transition from the complete attention of one adult to the more difficult and more usual situation where one must share adult attention, and find a way to have one's own needs met while leaving room for the needs of others. Sometimes a child is so fearful of adults, so tight and clammed-up, that he can better manage to get help from a group of peers than from one adult. If this is all he needs, well and good. If he needs more, the group may serve as a prelude or a support to his using individual therapy either after the group, or along with it.

Family Therapy

Since the family constitutes the central group in anyone's life, but especially in the life of the young, and since the younger one is, the more closely one tends to replicate relationships known, heard, hated or yearned for, in the original family, we find family-group sessions useful in diagnosing the major cause of a child's trouble and in getting at the characteristic modes of family interaction. Since family therapy is a relatively new form of treatment, there are many theories about it, some conflicting and some overlapping.

The least group-centered of the lot is the Systems Approach represented by Dr. Murray Bowen. In this approach, the family is understood to be a group, but is not treated as one. Instead, the therapist sees the mother and father and treats them as a couple, first talking and listening to one, then to the other—allowing some dialogue between them, but not using group process. Like all the theories of family therapy, the Systems Approach sees the child who is in trouble, the child because of whom the family comes for help, as "The Index Member" of the family, the one in whom the family trouble is stored. The child is seen as acting out the unconscious—or at least unspoken—difficulties of the family. To Bowen and his group the clue to the difficulty is to be found in a detailed and thorough study of the genealogy and present network of the family—their physical story, their economic status, their job choices and educational histories, their divorces and deaths and illnesses. The further back one can go and the more widely one can study the offshoots of the family, the better for the purposes of this kind of approach. Therefore, even though the Bowenites say with passion that they eschew the treatment of the central family as a group, they are, curiously enough, ready to engage in the study of unusually large groups, not to offer them therapy, but rather to use them as information sources. The literature of this type of therapy abounds in fascinating studies of family happenings: reunions, births, funerals, weddings, anniversaries and birthday parties. The patients are asked to study these rites and occasions to determine patterns; some therapists try, when possible, to get themselves invited so that they may explore and see at first-hand what goes on. In this way the large live family is used as a group tool.

Network Theory

There is only one other branch of psychological treatment I know of that uses the large group, and it uses the group for therapy. That branch is Network Theory, a new outgrowth of family therapy that is used in families where the crises derive from sticky chronic conditions that have not yielded to other forms of treatment, no matter how lengthy or how drastic. Such treatments may have ranged from long years of individual treatment to hospitalizations; they may have moved from group to family therapy and back, with all stages in between. The formulator of Network Theory is Dr. Ross Speck.

In this form of treatment, the organizing therapist and a team of therapists act as consultants to the family in trouble for a definite and short-term series of "network" meetings, anywhere from two to about six in number. For example, a mother and daughter in a family have such severe trouble that neither can leave the other alone. Neither can let the other live separately; yet neither can live with the other without terrible battles. Thus serious destruction ominously hovers about them as well as over the rest of the family and their friends. Suicide and murder attempts are not unusual in such severe situations, whether between husband and wife, or between parent and child. The two central figures, together with the whole family, are asked to invite to a group meeting everyone they know—relatives, ex-wives, lovers, teachers, friends, doctors, counselors, service people who have become involved, bosses—any and everyone. The bigger the group, the theory goes, the better: it dilutes the problem. The idea is to get all these people involved and so to generate a mild form of anxiety that has been so severely aroused in the focal pair of miserable people. After group anxiety has been aroused—and that's not hard to get going in a large group—and the feelings expressed, the group breaks up—in the same room—into committees (small groups) each to tackle one aspect of how they can help with the problem. The notion is that in this way the spiraling trials and failures of the focal couple can be broken into, diluted, and monitored by a concerned multitude; the family-trap is thus hopefully broken by sheer weight of concerted pressure from all sides. A further concept here is that the extreme differences between the pair in trouble, by being taken on by a network of people, can be worked out by compro-

mise, and through compromise alternate ways of acting and reacting be found, if the support of a large enough group is insured. After setting up these "networks," the team of therapists vanishes—as any good business consultant does after he has finished doing all he has contracted to do for the firm. If therapy is needed, either the committees of the network give it, or they see to it that it is arranged for. If housing, a job, school placement, or money is needed, ways of taking care of the problem are worked out. In this context, one of the most fascinating and unusual things Network Theory offers is the use of the chaos engendered by a large group as a therapeutic tool. Gossip too is used, as one offshoot of ways to get opinions whether sound and based on fact, or not. Network Theory suggests an intriguing but as yet unworked-out possibility of using this kind of treatment for school children in deep trouble with their peers or the staff, or for crisis (with a capital C!) in the staff itself.

Some other forms of family therapy, although they differ from one another, can be talked of together, since the therapists who offer them conceive the family as a group and use the interaction between members as a treatment tool. Some are mor group-process oriented than others, but all use the way a family interacts and the roles each is supposed to play for the other and for themselves as a key to the problems of the child in trouble—the Index Member—and the family as a whole. Some family therapists insist on home visits to see the family in its habitat. Some do most of their work in offices. Some invite in-laws and grandparents and close family friends, if this seems important; others stick to the core family. Some use speech alone; others use art and psycho-drama and role-playing and a technique called family-sculpturing. In family-sculpturing one derives a whole family situation or character from the interaction of therapist and one family member, creating the script with body movement and words.

Family therapy as a systematized way of dealing with people in trouble grew out of work with families in which there was a very damaged schizophrenic son or daughter, often one who was hospitalized. Time and again it became clear that on those occasions when the family was seen in combination with the sick child, the family guilt about that child seemed not to give way even when the child got better. It came to light that the group guilt had a genuine reason for existing beyond the constant useless jumping back and forth between periods of mea-culpa and woe-saying, and periods of anger and withdrawal of all interest. The proof-of-the-pud-ding was seen time and time again as lying in the fact that when the sick one (the Index Member) got well, the family as a whole would fall apart, or would appear to be in danger of doing so, until ei-ther the sick one got sick again, or the family dealt with its problem otherwise. Without outside help it would seem each member felt he could not afford to take on his own problems and allow the elected one a measure of health without responsibility for keep-ing the whole rickety structure from collapsing. A second proof was seen in the great number of fami-lies (any school, like any mental health agency, knows the number is legion) in which as soon as one child who has come as "The Patient" has been treated, and has become well, another family mem-ber, usually a sibling, at once gets into trouble just as bad as the first child's, or even worse. The thera-pists developing this form of therapy began with hospitalized schizophrenic patients whose families illustrated this group phenomenon to the extreme; it was taken up soon thereafter by agencies where the repetitive pattern of breakdown in the family, a re-catching of the disease after "the cure" of one mem-ber, was part of a vast intake picture. Names often associated with exploration in this field are: Acker-man, Wynn, Shapiro, Bloch, Jackson, Whittaker, Minuchen, Rycoff and Paul; many of these (along with Bowen) are still working in the field, as are many others.

The reason why I have given this detailed sum-mary here is that the record indicates how a com-mon and damaging group phenomenon can affect the core group structure, the family, as well as peo-ple outside the family group. One member of a group is made the scapegoat—that is, he is sacri-ficed to keep the group together, to take away the pain and unacceptable feelings from others in the group, thus dumping the pain on the chosen group member. We have seen this phenomenon in the classroom of the teacher who is shaky about her own leadership, or the teacher whose personality does not allow expression of hostility, affection, rage, or fear. The cure for such scapegoating in any group, just as in family therapy, is to try to get each member, along with the leadership, to own his "unacceptable" feelings by exploring them, and to help each member not to allow himself to play the lethal game of being the scapegoat or sacrificial lamb.

Three Special Forms of Group Psychotherapy

There have been two broad lines of thinking out of which group therapy as it is practiced today has de-veloped. The first has come from the medical model or the psychoanalytic school; in this each patient comes with his individual problems as he would for individual treatment, but is seen within a group. The group happily profits from listening to one of its members work on his problems with the trained leader. The group members may have more or less opportunity to react to the material presented, de-pending on the convictions of the group leader. With some group leaders—those whose interest is more in group interaction—the group that is listen-ing may be led to relate to the problems with their own experience and insights, and thus play more of a role in being therapeutic agents; with others, the procedure is largely a dialogue, with the leader engaged with one member after another.

This "classical" approach, as it is called, is typically represented by Slavson, the man who is the father of activity groups for youngsters. Its lead-ers are all professionals, usually trained in individ-ual one-to-one treatment, who have come to group therapy later in their experience.

The second broad line of thinking may be rep-resented by such groups as Alcoholics Anonymous and Synanon. Here people with a common prob-lem get together to keep guard over each other, with the conviction that the force of a group whose com-mon experience binds them together can help each member in times of stress or temptation. The group mitigates loneliness, satisfies dependency and serves as a cathartic agency. It tries to mobilize itself, often by faith either in an overseeing agent, such as God, or, if not God, the group itself and its leadership. The leaders here are often people from the ranks of the group, though sometimes professional leaders will be brought in to work alone or in unison with the indigenous leaders. The power of the group has been seen to be extraordinarily helpful for motivat-ed individuals, especially for those given to an ad-diction of some sort: alcohol, drugs, obesity, gambling, smoking and the like. (About the only type of group that has not so far been constructed on these principles is a group to deal with people who have become addicted to groups as a substitute for direct life experience.) Here the group is paramount, and group process is the therapeutic tool. Dependency is the prime mover and the attempt is to transfer the dependency from a drug or a consuming obsessive pattern to the group. At this stage this therapy may be likened to methadone treatment as a means to get someone off the habit. Later, at least in some cases, the goal may be to free the person from gripping dependency needs, but for some it is clear that, once formed, the group must always be behind one to rescue one and to use one as rescuer in turn. Thus, along with caring for dependency needs, this type of group makes for a lifestyle, a social life, a release from isolation and loneliness; it is a route for helping and being helped that makes an individual feel needed and necessary.

The Bion-type group is quite different from the first two (see Chapter III) yet in some ways combines elements of both: for here the psychoanalytic unconscious material is basic and so is the treatment of the *group* as an entity. Treatment is of the group as a group; it is not focused on individuals. Thus, group process here too is paramount. The leader is trained in group behavior, covert and overt, and the recognition of covert processes is a sine qua non of insight. Dependency may be one phase of the process, but others are considered equally important as life-factors: Fight, Flight and Pairing must be continually dealt with as well for the group to do its work and become a work-group. In Bion group therapy, in contrast to group education, the task is allowing individuals within a group structure to deal with conscious and unconscious ways of coping with life, and thereby to free them from crippling aspects of their lives by offering alternatives.

These three broad categories of group psychotherapy cover most of the types of groups that are now used in therapy, including behavior modification groups, hypnosis groups, and drug-induced groups, as well as activity groups, art and music and body therapy groups, psychodrama and scream therapy groups. Some theories and some techniques are applicable to classroom teaching; however, since the task is a quite different one, the application needs to be effected with discrimination and care to avoid confusion of goals. Having said so much, I believe it is clear that the sensitivity and encounter groups talked of above fit better into the second and third categories than the first. The Gestalt (despite the fact that the word itself means "the whole") fits better into the first category, since in Gestalt groups people are treated in a coupling between leader and subject with the rest of the

members of the group looking on, relatively inactive until their turns arrive. The network group, whether its developers are conscious of that fact or not, is in some ways more Bionesque; in others, more like communes and self-help groups.

In view of the existence of all this potpourri of group structures, it is difficult to know which child in trouble will fit into what group and why. That decision is best left to the diagnostic process once the child is referred. The trouble is that conventional diagnosis seems to be getting rustier all the time. Since the school is nowadays laden with looking after a child's behavior as well as his intellectual development, and since that behavior is linked to the use of his intelligence, and both to his inner dynamics and the stress of developmental changes, it would seem mandatory that the school, or one of its delegates—teacher or counselor—be automatically included in the diagnostic process. Though this is indeed sometimes done, especially if the treatment planned is to come from within the school, it is not done often enough. True, teachers and counselors could use more skill in sharpening their observations and translating them, but if their summaries were included automatically along with records of testing and interviewing, we could cut down considerably on mistaken placement in both classroom and treatment modality, and the damaging consequences of doing the wrong thing or nothing would be much mitigated.

As a rule adolescents who need treatment do better in a group than in individual treatment, but there are many exceptions. Many younger children do better in a group or in family sessions than in individual therapy, since individual therapy often divides their loyalties and their ability to work out ways of relating to peers and parents. Here too there are many exceptions. In both cases the exceptions depend on the amount of pressure internal forces are placing on the child. If those forces tend to be so all-consuming that the child cannot deal with a group, or so idiosyncratic that no group seems appropriate, or if they are such as to lead him to destroy any group he is part of, then individual treatment is mandatory. Most workers still think first of individual therapy and then of group in diagnostic placement. It is useful to have diagnosis include a group experience of two or more sessions; that would make it possible to judge whether a child would do better with individual or group treatment, and if group treatment is indicated, might tell what kind of group the child would do best in.

In making a decision about the kind of treatment group to send a child to, if indeed he is to be sent to any group, the school could add essential information concerning the extent to which the child fears classmates, how he handles himself in those toughest of all periods in the school day—the transition periods—and how he acts in the lunchroom, playground, study hall or rest rooms. What is his concentration span? Can he get started? and once started, can he stop? Does he talk excessively? How does he show how he feels—or does he? How does he play? How does he win and how does he lose? What is his attendance record like? his health record? Does the nurse have data? The gym teacher? Is he one who waits in the principal's office, and if so for what kinds of offense? What role does he play in the classroom—bully, scapegoat, clown, or sad sack? Do his parents come to meetings? What are their superficial attitudes toward him? How does he make the teacher feel—pitying, furious, indulgent, amused, bewildered? Is he over-intellectual? Is everything always the other guy's fault? If so, would an art therapy group or a psychodrama group help? Is he a loner or a mixer or a leader? If any of these, a low-keyed talk group might be a good choice. What developmental phase has he reached? Does he need work in behavior control, or does he need the chance to explore his body and mind in an activity group or encounter group? Are parental pressures such that he needs a place to help him relax and meet only minimal demands, or does he require higher expectations of himself? Is he ashamed of being tall, small, fat, dumb, bright, different? Is his or her sexual development a terror to him, and the thought of sex a nightmare? Does he try to act older or younger than his years? Does he attach himself to one person? Does he bribe or steal or brag to get friends? All of these are questions to which an alert teacher can contribute answers for the use of the diagnostician, along with the picture his parents give of how he behaves at home. Both accounts, compared with what the psychologist or psychiatrist finds, tell us how the child sees himself, how others see him, what his emotional and mental capacities are. The composite picture may indicate what group he will fit into and be able to use, and whether individual treatment should be considered simultaneously or uniquely.

All of the above assumes that a teacher or counselor, the school social worker and the psychologist all agree that a child would benefit by help. A conference of school people that decides that Tessa has really been crying too many days in class, or that Louis has been running into the locker room to hide under people's coats too many times, will strengthen the recommendations given at a parent conference, and will give the person responsible for diagnosis and placement a clearer prescription as to how to proceed and what kind of treatment to seek.

Behavior Modification

We have not gone into the various kinds of therapy—those which may be offered in or out of school—which are based on principles of Behavior Modification. This particular form of therapy has become more and more popular among psychologists and in schools in these last years. There are a complex set of reasons why Behavior Modification therapeutic techniques are particularly popular in the schools. Schools have good pragmatic reasons for being concerned with behavior. "Deportment," as it used to be called, has always been the teacher's concern, and the teacher is often rated on how well her children behave. Misbehavior is usually defined as anything that "doesn't go" in Mr. N's or Miss M's classroom or in Mrs. P's or Mr. Q's school. Behavior is rarely seen as the psychologists see it—as any action or reaction, verbal or otherwise, that responds to stimuli from the environment. Behavior is even more rarely seen from the psychodynamic point of view—as not only reactive to outside stimuli, but as symptomatic of what is going on in the inside world of the child to make him perceive outside stimuli as he does and make him react to them as he does. Behavior Modification gives school people a tool they can apply to many situations in the realms of both cognitive learning and "deportment." Since Behavior Modification therapy derives from learning theory, the psychologist's domain, it is a natural alliance between education and psychology. It can deal with the behavior that bothers the teacher at the moment; it need not concern itself with bringing in past happenings in the family or personal history.

Behavior Modification is an outgrowth of Pavlovian conditioning psychology in which animals were taught to produce a number of responses by means of punishment or reward. By the same means they were taught to avoid other behavior, to "unlearn" it. The process of "unlearning" was called "extinction" (of a habit or response). Pavlovian theory was later applied to people—both reward and punishment have been used to teach new modes of behavior or new cognitive material. In the Soviet Union, Pavlovian theory is the basis for most psychological therapy. It is often used both here and abroad to make extinct various patterns considered undesirable, such as stuttering and smoking and drug-taking.

In its more sophisticated form, now in use in some parts of this country, Behavior Modification involves a thorough inquiry into a child's total pattern of behavior, and an even more detailed exploration of the problem that is of particular concern—for example, school-phobia (which lends itself well to this form of treatment) or poor study habits, or not being able to control actions, anger, or body movement. The detailed inquiry tells the therapist all he can learn from everyone involved—child, parent, teacher, friends—about the patterns of behavior and what kind of thing sets the problem in motion. It also tells him what is seen as a *reward* in the case of a particular child. The famous M & M candy may work for some small children, but it may not work at all for others—it certainly does not work for older children. Money may work for some, records for others; chits to be used toward the purchase of a guitar or a motorcylce, or a TV or a sleeping bag or a trip to the seashore, may work for a good many. Once a program is worked out, detailed as any program designed for a computer, and once a reward system is evolved, the plan can be put into effect. From then on, any avoidable stimulus that would work to upset the new learning is avoided; any stimulus that would work toward the goal is encouraged. This means, for instance, that if a given piece of behavior is considered undesirable and therefore to be made extinct, it must be ignored; in behavioral terms, not the slightest word is said about it, for ignoring is "punishment." If such an act is performed, a scolding, or even a mention, may act as a reward in the form of attention-getting, and the aim is literally to get the child to forget it. After each success, rewards appropriate to the particular child, or tokens that will mount up to realize the reward, are given because desired behavior requires attention to impress it on the child. After the behavior is "conditioned," harder and harder assignments are made until the desired goal is reached. Though rewards continue to be given, it takes more and more work to get them. The goal is finally to have the wanted behavior so ingrained, and the satisfaction from it so clear, that rewards are no longer needed to "reinforce" the learning. The success of the process is measured by what happens when rewards and programming stop. Is the new learning really learned or do old patterns re-emerge in an orgy of backsliding? How much reinforcement is needed, and at what intervals? Results vary.

Many behavior modification people began as purists, insisting that all that was needed was the program and the reward. Though punishment in the form of shock, electric or verbal, has been used in some instances—electric shock with, for example, autistic children; psychological shock, visual or oral, in a remedial reading institute for children with learning disabilities—punishment is not really commonly used. This is partly because there are some data that tend to prove people respond more lastingly to reward than to shock; there is too the fact that public opinion reacts more favorably to the use of rewards than to the use of punishment.

Behavior Modification has been found to be most successful when carried out in groups, since the presence of the group and competition among members seem to act as reinforcements in themselves.

More recently Behavior Modification people have found it most helpful when working with children and youth, rather than with rats, cats and dogs, to "reinforce" the learning by means of adding talks with the group leader—a kind of combined psychodynamic and Behavior Modification practice. Clearly, since the leader or the people who are directing the program dictate what must be done with the children, this kind of group falls within the dependency AA-type model. But of course, the leaders must be professionals, well-trained in Behavior Modification techniques.

There has been considerable success with this method, especially when the relationship between the group leader and the children is seen as being as basic to the treatment as are the program and the reward-systems themselves. But the method does not work for all children. For some it does not work at all; for others, results may be temporary. It does seem to work particularly well for many children with severe learning disabilities, especially those whose psychological problems appear to be more the result than the cause of school failure—children whose inability to conquer a basic skill has led to severe feelings of incompetence and apathy.

For the successful use of Behavior Modification in groups, no matter where they are, within the classroom or as an addition to the class offices outside the school, it is essential that parents be involved. The younger the child, the more important is this axiom. The reason is obvious. The purpose is to get rid of certain behaviors or learnings and to instill new or different ones, and this is to be achieved by completely ignoring the old pattern and continuously reinforcing the new. If then the child goes home and is scolded or punished for the very behavior that is to be assiduously ignored and is ignored in the behavior that is to get immediate notice and reward, the outcome will at best be highly questionable. Parents are usually seen either singly or, more economically and more usually, in groups. They are given explanations of what is going on in the treatment of their children, and told why and how they must help, and what will hinder progress. These parent groups are basically educational in function, but they may and often do turn into discussions of dynamic issues, such as feelings, causes, traps parents fall into, and traps they themselves set, with or without awareness.

The danger lies in the fact that since Behavior Modification *seems* easy to do, it is often looked at as a panacea for all troubles, instead of as simply a tool—one tool among many—to approach some problems, but not all. It also causes many people to be concerned about the obvious possibilities for misuse, for Behavior Modification carries about with it an Orwellian, brainwashing character, generating fear that someone up there or out there will decide what people ought to think, how they ought to act, what they ought to like; the fear that someone's thinking—the psychologist's, the teacher's, the dictator's—will "condition" all of us to be robot-automatons, all uniform assembly-line products. Particularly frightening is the political misuse the technique can be put to—e.g., in the service of the status quo or of a dictatorship or a religious fanaticism.

Nevertheless, with proper monitoring and caution, and in the hands of people who are aware that they are using potential dynamite, Behavior Modification can be a helpful group tool in the classroom and in the clinic. As a group, delinquents or children caught in the immobilizing trap of unusual learning disabilities are often particularly appropriate choices for a program of Behavior Modification when it is combined with an understanding of what is going on and why, so that they may have some awareness about what is happening to them. But this is true of any theory.

Before we leave the subject of Behavior Modification, it should be said that in diluted form, and not in its pure culture, this technique is frequently used in all of the groups we are to be concerned with in the rest of this chapter, especially at the early stages of group formation and definition of the task and the methods. This is true particularly with those groups of children who have a hard time with impulse control and sitting still. For instance, at the outset of a program, even though the methods chosen for the group are psychodynamic, an activity

group leader may distribute Cokes to the children to reward a few minutes of sitting silent so that he can suggest to the children what activity is available today and where the materials for it are. The handing out of Cokes is a diluted form of reward, but it serves its purpose. The collaboration of a group psychotherapist with someone who knows Behavior Modification techniques has proved successful with persons who are hyperactive, or those who suffer from apathy and withdrawal.

Once it is decided that a child (or a youth) needs a group, the problem becomes what kind of group to choose and what kind of group leadership will best meet the needs of this child at this particular stage of his physical, mental and emotional development.

Many children have a hard time talking, especially about their feelings. So of course do many adults, especially men who have been trained not to talk about their feelings. To make it possible for such children (or adults) to benefit by psychotherapy, an education or re-education job must be undertaken to open them to treatment—much as a surgeon will not operate until the patient is in good enough health to tolerate an anesthetic and the strain of the surgery. In psychotherapy, ability to receive therapy is even more important, for the treatment depends entirely upon the give-and-take process between patient and therapist. Unlike other treatments, it cannot be done *to* a patient; it must be done with him. The unhappy myth that the psychiatrist knows all, that the psychologist comes equipped with a crystal ball, is often encouraged by the practitioners themselves with their mystique-laden jargon and props. Given a therapist who is able and willing to give up this voice-from-on-high role, group process can break the myths down. Even in adult or pure talking-groups, it becomes impossible to keep up the myth of unseen voices making wise, oracular comments. Children's therapy has always been a nail in the cross of this mystique, since from its inception child-therapy forms of play have substituted for or have supplemented talk. Messages about feelings and circumstances of life are given through toys, puppets, games, pictures, charades and other materials as clearly as through words, or even more clearly. The therapist, depending on whether he came from the Anna Freud, Melanie Klein, or Virginia Axline schools of training, may talk a little or a lot, may interpret or only reflect what the messages given out by the child's use of material mean, but it is still the child who expresses the messages by his play or by his use of materials.

Play and materials, as much as or more than talk, are the language of children. This is especially true of slum or ghetto children whose parents are beset with work and weariness, and who themselves have not been trained to use words as either tool or weapon, and therefore find the demand that they say how they feel overwhelming.*

Even if language were available as a tool, even if in itself learning abstraction and symbolization were more familiar, the question of using these techniques with people whom you have no reason to trust becomes a gigantic hurdle. Why should any child trust a strange adult with his feelings when clearly his family, whom he is expected to trust, have not understood them or been able to use them—when his teachers, with whom he is at least acquainted, seem not to be able to understand them, and when these very feelings appear to be the reason he is in enough trouble to need special help? Besides, he probably isn't sufficiently at home with his own feelings to know what they are, let alone to name them. Even God took a few days before he named things in the world, so the troubled child, especially the nonverbally educated child, has legitimate precedent! It becomes the therapist's job to ease the pathways of communication and hack out new paths where none existed before.

A group therapist may, for a time, have a hectic and bewildering experience, but his task is made easier by the fact that he is dealing with a group, who by their manner and interests and separate means, suggest materials, games, images, which he can follow up and use as channels for getting feelings expressed and dealt with. Interestingly enough, a by-product of successful therapy is usually the ability of a child to use speech more ably than ever before, not only in the realm of feelings, but as a tool for thinking—that is, for solving cognitive problems as well as emotional ones. The therapy, itself, if successful, is educative, and the therapist (along with the group) has been the teacher. This is amusing, because many therapists vigorously deny their teaching role just as they too often object to the teacher's playing a therapeutic role. Yet many of the children without any intervention other than psychotherapy in their lives, do far better in the conceptual school subjects after therapy. One may say that this is true because their emotional problems

have been sufficiently solved to allow them to use their energy in school study; it is hard to disentangle emotional from intellectual effort, but there is much evidence to indicate that the mere ability to translate feelings and thought into words is indeed a successful by-product of the group venture.

Keeping all this in mind, we turn now to those forms of group therapy that use materials as the focal point of group organization, and where words only supplement or come out of the materials being used. The group leader, depending on his point of view and personal style, may interpret much or little. His interpretations will, to be sure, affect the course of the ideas and the problems produced, but the primary point here is that the group itself use the materials to state and to work on the problems of its members.

Activity Groups

Slavson, as I mentioned earlier, was the grandfather of activity group theory. F. Redl, W. Morse and many others could also be mentioned as utilizing a natural child-group structure in the service of treatment. Such a group, often called a club, may meet together at regular intervals, anywhere from once a week for a few hours, to several afternoons or evenings a week after school, or in school or at a designated camp. The group is together because all the members exhibit some kind of behavior which troubles either them or, more often, their schools, homes, or community. They may meet indoors or out; there is usually a room or "clubhouse" set apart for their use. They may, with the leader's help, or at first on the leader's initiative, find projects that they are interested in—building a playing field, fixing over the clubhouse, etc. They may play checkers, monopoly, pool, card games, baseball, basketball, etc. They may box, trampoline-jump, learn acrobatics or dance. They may work in crafts and make things in wood, plastic, clay, basketry. They may cook or sew or sing. The activities, though directed and sometimes suggested by the group leader(s), derive from the age-level interests and needs of the members. At first, it is unlikely that they will, no matter what their ages, all be able to do the same thing at the same time. That may come in time, if it comes. How they win, how they lose at games, the effect on them of competition, how they cheat and how they get found out, how they steal or lie within the group—all these things are significant and make great group material to work on. How do they

*See John Dewey and Alfred North Whitehead, as well as Joseph Barrett's "Cognitive Thought and Affect in Organizational Experience" in *Science and Psychoanalysis*, Vol. 12, N.Y., Gruner Stratton, 1965; and James McWhinner, "Forms of Language Usage in Adolescence and Their Relationships to Disturbed Behavior and Its Treatment" in G. Caplan and S. Lebovic (eds.), *Adolescence: Psychosocial Perspective.* N.Y.: Basic Books, Inc. 1969.

handle a fight? Do they look for a fight, start one, run from one—always get licked, always bully, or get bullied? How do they handle the use of tools, a tool that won't work, an object that will not work? How does a member act if the object was broken by himself, by another group member, by the group leader? Observations based on these questions offer a direct route to basic problems. How do the members handle the problems of attendance—their own or other people's? How do they handle lateness or no-shows, trips that are postponed, defections of particular pals, switches in loyalties, their own inclusion or exclusion and that of others, new members, the loss of old members, change of adult leadership? How are crises handled—crises that arise out of the group itself or in their lives? How do they relate to the leader, to the others in times of stress or need, to their own needs or to the needs of others? These are all basic problems to everyone; with skillful handling and appropriate interpretation or restraint of interpretation, depending on the state and readiness of that particular child at that particular time, working them out is the therapy.

Activity groups can be geared for children as young as three and four, and as old as eighteen and nineteen. The materials used, the games played, the projects engaged in, will differ of course according to age, sexual development and sex interest, but, if well led, groups of this kind are excellent for children and young people of all ages. The age range needs to be fairly homogeneous, though in day-camp settings or residential-camp settings where there is a sufficient number of group workers or leaders so that subgroups can be formed and so that the older members can, as part of their advanced treatment, help younger or newer ones, the age range can profitably be quite wide.

Leading activity groups is a demanding job. It requires certain skill and a certain kind of temperament. In many cases, the kind of ability to handle children exhibited by talented recreation teachers, nursery-school teachers and camp counselors is more valuable than the more intellectualized talent of the garden-variety psychotherapist. In other words, the prime essential here is a feel for children at a given age level, ease with them and enjoyment of them, and the kind of sense of humor that children understand and can share and respond to. In addition to such a temperament in its various phases, what is most important is empathy with what it feels like to be a child and in trouble—in trouble beyond the power of a child to mend or alter. Actual skill at games, crafts, arts, can be learned. But imagination, the ability to use ideas, the

flexibility to let something you have planned drop and to take on something that seems more youth- or child-motivated—these are rarer traits, harder to use and equally necessary to success in this field. Many sophisticated psychiatrists who are good at other forms of therapy are not comfortable in this kind of group and need training to relax into para-verbal modes. Many times it has been found helpful to use group leaders who are themselves relatively untrained in psychiatric know-how or in psychologic know-what-for as the major leaders, under the supervision of a psychiatrist or psychologist or with the professional taking the role of assistant. In such groups co-workers or teams of leaders are especially useful. Collaboration and supervision time is of the essence, since with the best will in the world, and even with the help of tape recorders and videotape, one person cannot help but miss much significant material. Lest I be misunderstood, let me add that I am not saying that trained therapists should never lead activity groups, but simply that they need more training and some re-educating to do so, for their professional training itself has in many cases trained them out of or beyond the flexibility and ease with the nonverbal messages and language of childhood that are required. This kind of retraining is essential to any good group leadership, especially with children and young people.

Art Therapy Groups

Over the past years, art therapy has grown up to be an entity in itself. It has left the area of occupational therapy and now has its own theory and practices, and of course its own group differences in point of view. It could be said that art therapy began through acceptance of Hermann Rorschach's projective tests, tests in which diagnosis is based in significant part on how the client perceived the world. Perceptions, anxieties, distortions, conflicts, and quality of mind were revealed by what one read into the white cards on which there were only ink blots in black and mixed colors. As the projective tests grew and multiplied, material from them yielded much useful data about the functioning and non-functioning of adults and children alike. The study was further advanced by the use of many additional kinds of materials: story pictures, self-created pictures of persons, houses, trees, etc. Models were provided with which people, especially children, would create mini worlds according to their own perceptions; mosaic blocks were introduced too, and games and mazes and comments on films, scenes and anything imaginable.

What a person creates is clearly a projection of himself. Any artist knows this. Conceal himself as he may school himself to do through techniques and skill, somewhere the personality shines through—if one can read the message, even the message the person does not intend to give. That message may come through to anyone, but the skilled psychologist is especially trained to read it. The less skilled a person is in using a medium to express himself, the more clearly he reveals himself. For that reason, especially in pure diagnosis, it is better, when using drawing, painting, or clay productions, to have one of those many people who say "I can't draw anything" or "I never touch a paint brush" than an aspiring Picasso. What one is after is not a product, but a communication from the inside of a person.

This seeming paradox is relevant to the selection of an art-therapy group, especially for children and youth. The group leader may want children who like to use art materials. Those that do like to tend to be better at it than those who turn away from these media. Yet one doesn't necessarily want skilled artists; indeed, it is more difficult to read the messages of those who are so naturally skillful that they can glibly cover over and conceal their inner selves. The dilemma is a far more conscious one among art therapists than among therapists who deal with verbal wares. It is true one hears of too great ease or glibness with words, of intellectualizing as a form of resistance, of talking too much in order not to say anything important, but people are not excluded from talk groups because of their verbal skills. Still, it might be wise to get verbally gifted people into art, dance, or pantomime activity therapy. The point I am making here is twofold: (1) simply being willing to use art materials is enough to admit one into an art group; and, (2) the quality of the products, though sometimes surprisingly good, is not the important thing. The important thing in an art-therapy group is the same as in other groups: the decision about what to do; the time it takes to get started; the throwaways, the erasures and crossings out, the slips and errors, the mess; the disgust and frustration; the rage with the leader, with others, with oneself; the envy expressed; the comments before, during, and after a picture or other art form is made; as well as the fun, joy, recognition and even ecstasy over finding new ways to express one's feelings and thoughts. The heaviness of the lines, the overlap of colors, the personal symbolism of the colors selected, and the personal forms, abstract and/or concrete, that emerge to ex-

press oneself and one's own image; the mood of the pictures and the changes in that mood; the joint interpretations and comments of the group; the kind of contribution each member makes to a joint production such as a group mural or group clay structure: all of these are the essentials out of which the therapy grows. The group therapists—at least one of whom should be cognizant of and comfortable with the use of art materials, and one, or preferably both, of whom should be aware of the processes of personality development and its pathology—may, depending on their point of view, interpret much or little. They may use group processes and group awareness; they may be direct or indirect in their approach. They may wish to limber people up with body or at least arm exercises; they may or may not use music; they may meet many times a week or once a week. They may themselves see individuals in the group aside from the art-therapy sessions for talk sessions, or they may prefer not to do so, but rather to send individuals elsewhere if, through the art groups, material comes up that the child needs extra work on, as indeed often happens. When this occurs, the leaders, if they are group-wise, will let the group know what is happening, so that the issues arising out of being special, or the worries over having problems, can emerge. Having more come up than can be handled in one session a week, let's say, can be a common group concern.

Many art therapists leave the choice of subject completely free. Others, especially those working with school age and adolescent children, find it useful to assign topics to serve as a basis for drawing, painting, modeling, or sculpting. The following suggestions have been found to be useful to groups, both because they get children unstuck from the "I don't know what to draw" defeat before it defeats them, and because the topics are such excellent starters for group discussions:

Make pictures of all the people you live with, or of your family; label the people. Draw something happy, something sad, something frightening, exciting, or funny. Make an angry picture; make a happy one. Make a picture of the group. Make a picture of someone in the group you think could help you. Let's make a joint picture about fun, about dating, about girls and boys, about parents or teachers. These pictures can be either realistic or abstract. When I was first involved in this sort of work, I thought it would be hard to get children to use art media abstractly. I was dead wrong. Children catch on right away, and the comments that are made about their own and other people's abstract pictures or products are tremendously revealing and helpful in the group. So impressive are the results of well-led art-therapy groups for ghetto children, for torn-apart adolescents, for tied-up, constricted children, for children who find talking—especially to adults—next to impossible, that I would like to see all adults who want to become therapists go through an art-therapy experience. They would not only find out much about themselves and about the children they think uncommunicative, but would find themselves more in touch with a children's world.

Music and Dance Therapy Groups

The same principles that operate in art therapy operate also in the use of dance or music as therapy. Just as in the case of art, music and dance were first used with hospitalized patients. It was found that many patients who could not and would not communicate in words would do so when they were allowed to use one of these other expressive forms. We have found that catatonic schizophrenics—patients whose body postures are so rigidly held that they seem (but often only seem) not to take in stimuli, and who do in fact emit no reactions or next to none—react especially well to the use of music, rhythm and body movement. In doing so, they often assume postures and positions or go into patterns of movement that relay to the insightful therapist what they are experiencing in their inner world; they may even give some clues as to how they got that way.

When dance and music therapy was taken out of the hospital and into psychiatric offices and some schools, we established the truth of something that had been guessed before, and even applied by a few experimentally minded, gifted teachers: that brain-damaged children and hyperactive children, especially those with minimal brain damage, respond extraordinarily well to music and dance treatment. Aside from the gains that can be achieved, first toward communication and through that toward relationship with the therapists and other group members, it is a useful cue to teachers that music and body movement can be used well in the classroom for this kind of child. There is something so basic in telling what is going on in oneself by physical stance, kinesthetic sensation and rhythmic movement, that children like the very ill respond to it (once their embarrassment or awkwardness is overcome) with ease. Likewise, there is a part of all of us that helps us reach out of ourselves and respond to the sounds and rhythms, tunes and harmonies, related to nature. A good leader, with the help of music and dance, can set this element in ourselves in motion more easily in a group. Helping patients to do the choreography is as therapeutic as it is revealing.

It is important in using these forms, whether interpretive as in dance or listening, or active as in choreography and instrument playing, that boundaries be set to fit the personality of the group members. That is to say, hyperactive children and brain-damaged children with few controls need more formalized, less free, dance and music forms, while rigid, inhibited, tense youngsters require greater freedom. For this reason, the group leaders (or at least one of them) must be aware, beyond their use of music and dance, of the significance of the disturbance the children are burdened with, so as not to exacerbate the difficulty while they are trying to alleviate it.

Writing and Reading Therapy

It seems paradoxical that many of the people who most love words and what they can do, and who depend on writing words or reading them as their major solace, often have so much trouble communicating orally, face to face with other people. Yet that is true for many. Among this group are many adolescents. Experience has shown that often those who fear any face-to-face encounter, especially in a group, respond well, *even in a group*, when they are allowed to write at home or alone in privacy, and then share what they have written with the group. They may be asked, too, to write comments on what they have read, and to share these as well. Sometimes, at the beginning of such a group, anonymity is used to ensure privacy for the shy person. The progress of the group can in part be measured by the willingness of the members to own their productions and ideas. At the end of such a group, we may hope to find that the members are able to say what they feel to one another and in front of one another, without needing a piece of paper with words on it to protect them or to hide behind. Sometimes in such groups, journals are kept and shared—the teens are diary-keeping years. Sometimes the device is used of having letters written either from one member to another, or by a group member to the group leaders or to the group as a whole. This brings to mind a story told about Abe Burrows: In talking to a class of aspiring writers at the University of Pennsylvania, he answered their questions about how to write by advising practice. "Write," he said. "Write all the time. Write letters. Try writing home!" People in writing-therapy groups write. Some write poetry, some stories or essays or scenes from plays. They experiment with forms old and new. They write to one another and collaborate with one another. They try group writing and group reading. It is often an exciting experience which develops skills in thinking as well as writing. It gives a community of interest and a pathway out of isolation, loneliness, shyness and self-consciousness. Stutterers, whose trouble often · lies in self-consciousness and hostility, do particularly well in such groups. Writing becomes an avenue for the expression of difficult feelings such as anger, hurt, competitiveness and affection. The difference between such a group and a good writing seminar is that the task of the group is therapeutic, and therefore the quality of the product, which is sometimes first class and sometimes pretty awful, is secondary to the fact of communication itself. The important thing is getting to be at home with one's own feelings and being able to own them in public, changing one's attitudes so as to be able to live a more satisfying life within oneself and among others.

Psychodrama

Of all the therapies which use nonverbal (as well as verbal) ways of expressing feelings, conflicts and dilemmas, probably the best-known and most widely used is psychodrama. Since this form requires group participation, whether playing a role in a play or being part of the actively engaged audience, it is essentially a group form. Many people have developed psychodrama in many ways and have adapted the technique, or parts of it, to their own uses. Curiously, the term is not generally associated with the name of its founder, Moreno, though he has written extensively on the theory, practice, and application of psychodrama. Moreno heads an institute where he trains people to use the technique, and he has trained many psychodrama leaders in hospitals and institutions and agencies all over the country, and in fact, in foreign countries as well. There are too many skilled followers of Moreno's ideas to mention here, and too many innovators whose work is based on his. Suffice it to say the field is still being

explored, and uses for the method broadened and deepened. Gestalt theory and transactional theory use snatches of psychodrama in their exercises and in their dream work. Transactional therapy also uses the technique to demonstrate the games that take place among people and to indicate less dangerous alternatives than those employed in these games. Virginia Satir and her school use psychodrama in family therapy in the technique known as family sculpturing. Other groups use it too in moments or full sessions of role-playing. (See Viola Spolin's *Theatre Games*.)

Essentially psychodrama is an opportunity for people to "act out" in a useful way their fantasies, dreams, fears and preoccupations, on the one hand, and the situations which do already, or which later on may, give them trouble, on the other. For example, a member of a group might report a dream and have various members of the group act out parts of his dream. Perhaps they switch roles in the middle, perhaps not. The dreamer may act as director and actor or as either one, or he may serve as audience. Fritz Perl and others exploited the technique of using objects: the chairs and cars and attic windows in the dream are mimed by the dreamer and personified by him. Another example: a child may report an obsessive fear of dogs. He is asked to choose others to help him, and all with him act out his fear, which may be general or may have arisen out of a frightening experience. Or a youth may be going to an interview that means a great deal to him—a job, college-admission, a first date with a girl he likes. He tells the group his concerns and with him they act out the interview or date.

The uses of psychodrama for children or youth of all ages are many. Children like to play-act and like making their own plays as they go along, so it is a popular activity. Children like to create their own experiences and feel them out in a safe place away from outside criticism and belittling. One adaptation has been used by a theatrical group in which the players are actors and respond to requests from an audience of children: Act out this or that. The actors do so, and the children respond. One can deal with material once it has emerged, and the audience helps get the problem posed and sees solutions being added before their eyes. There is no age above three that cannot use psychodrama as therapy.

It is amazing to note the different feelings one gets by becoming for a moment another person or object in one's own life-drama. Attitudes and patterns of thought alter and are often helpful.

The following selections are examples of different uses of child groups, specifically illustrating some of the aspects discussed in the previous selection.

The first piece describes a therapy group using puppets—a form of psychodrama particularly well-suited to children.

The Use of Puppetry in Therapy
Adolf G. Woltmann

"Hit him!" "Kill him!" "Watch out, he is still alive. He is going to kill you!" "Turn around quick. He is coming after you. He is going to bite you!" "Hit him again and kill him!" "You better run home to your mother. This place ain't safe!" "Kill him!"

Excited voices of children fill the room. Some children stand up with their fists in the air, ready to come to the rescue of the little character on the stage. Others sit quietly, but their flushed cheeks and heavy breathing betray their tense emotional state. A few hide their heads in their hands, as if afraid of watching the struggle between the little puppet and the crocodile. The fight on the puppet stage continues. With a stick twice his size, the little puppet boy subdues and apparently kills the fierce puppet crocodile.

The animal sprawls lifelessly on the stage, but as soon as the puppet boy turns his back, it reopens its threatening mouth, lifts its head, and chases the little boy all over the stage. Another battle ensues. The crocodile is hit and killed again, only to come back to life and to harass the little boy until finally, the puppet boy is victorious over the fierce animal. This time the killing is final. The crocodile is pushed off the stage. The puppet boy bows and acknowledges the rousing applause from his responsive audience. The tense excitement is gone, the atmosphere relaxed. The children are happy that their beloved puppet actor has escaped unharmed from this life-and-death struggle.

An examination of scenes like the one just described raises a number of questions. Why do some children clamor wildly for killing, while others hide their heads? Why do some children move their hands as if they had to fight the animal aggressor on the stage, while others shrink away from such aggression and advise the puppet character to run away and to find safety and refuge in the sanctum of the home and the presence of the mother? Why do the children relax when their puppet hero is victorious? Why do some children urge the crocodile to eat up the puppet? Obviously, these puppets have specific meanings for each child. What determines these meanings, and what do they convey in terms of the child's thinking, reaction, and participation?

It is assumed that each child identifies himself, in a manner specific to him, with the puppet characters and with the actions portrayed by them. It is further assumed that this identification leads to projections in the sense that each child projects his own feelings, desires, wishes, and anticipations into the puppet show. . . .

The hero of all the puppet shows that were used in the therapeutic puppet shows at Bellevue Hospital is a boy by the name of Casper. His pointed cap and multicolored costume render him ageless, so that he can easily portray youngsters between the ages of six and 12. The origins of this type go back to about 5000 B.C., when it appeared on the East Indian shadow stage as a servant to a rich master. Bascially, he is a comedian who causes his master to become involved in all sorts of compromising situations. The same type is also noted on the Greek and Roman stage, either as a living actor or as a puppet. He has become world-famous as the English Punch, having been introduced into Great Britain by Italian showmen during the time of Queen Elizabeth. In France, he has thrived under the name of "Guignol," in Russia, as "Petrushka," and he entertained German children first as "Hanswurst" and later on as "Kasper." The Turkish shadow puppet, "Karagöz," belongs to the same family. Basically, this type represents the man on the street with all his ambitions, strivings, and desires. He stresses primarily the earthy and material things in life. Like all of us, he oscillates between courage and cowardice. He seldom is at a loss for words, but more often than not, he uses physical force to defend himself and to settle an argument. He is both

Adolf G. Woltmann "The Use of Puppetry as a Projective Method in Therapy" in Harold H. Anderson and Gladys L. Anderson, *An Introduction to Projective Techniques: And Other Devices for Understanding the Dynamics of Human Behavior*, © 1951, by permission of Prentice-Hall, Inc., Englewood Cliffs, New Jersey.

clever and naive, full of hope and in deep despair, trusting and rejecting. Since he is only a puppet, he can act out his audience's innermost wishes and desires.

This type was used in the Bellevue puppet shows as the main character. The nature of the therapeutic aims and the age distribution of the audiences made it necessary to change him from a man into a boy. Right from the start, we noted the great popularity that he enjoyed among the children of the ward. An investigation into the children's responses and reactions over a period of several years gave us pertinent clues to his popularity. We learned that most children identified themselves very slowly with him. He seemed to express their wishes and desires, and his combination of words with actions was a real demonstration for them of how problems could be handled and settled.

Casper and his fellow puppets cannot simply be defined in psychoanalytical terms, but there is no question that the various sides of the total psychic structure are reflected differently in the various puppets. Casper is the expression of strong infantile desires which demand satisfaction. He knows that he must adapt his drives to the demands of reality. This satisfies the demands of the superego. We must therefore see in Casper something of the Freudian "idealized ego" which reaches for reality without being in conflict with the "id" or pleasure principle. The monkey, which plays an important part in some of the shows, gets his gratifications easily and corresponds in many ways to the "id" which has not been restricted. . . . Casper's parents take over the role of the superego. We believe that the child sees his parents as dual personalities. The Good father and the Good mother love and protect the child, feed him and show him affection. The Bad father and the Bad mother inhibit the pleasurable impulses of the child and train him in a manner not always agreeable to him.

In order to underline the superego function of the father, we made him appear as a plainclothes detective, connected with the police department. He thus not only represents authority in the family setting, but also personifies the controlling force through which law and order are maintained in the community. The Bad mother in the puppet shows is portrayed by the witch. She is the product of folklore and fairy tales. As such, she does not need any specific introduction because the children immediately sense what Casper or any other puppet might expect from her. In one of our shows, she denies food and rest to Casper, makes him work hard, and belittles all of his attempts to please her by

being orally aggressive to him. In another show, she helps Casper to get rid of his baby sister. The part of the Bad father is portrayed by the giant, the magician, and also partly by the cannibals. The giant, through his enormous body, is a physical threat to Casper. The magician, through his magic and clever scheming, is intellectually superior to Casper. The cannibals show hostility to Casper and threaten him with oral aggression. They would like to cook and eat him. Cannibals appeared on the European puppet stage about 200 years ago, probably as a result of mercantilism and colonization, which brought Europe in contact with primitive cultures.

The crocodile or alligator plays a very important part in a good puppet show. This animal represents oral aggression in a two-fold way. Those children who like the crocodile identify their own oral aggression with the big mouth and the sharp teeth. The child's oral aggression against the world is frequently met by counter-aggression, directed by the environment against the child. Therefore, those children who are greatly afraid of the crocodile usually express their own fears of counter-aggression. This probably appears to them as punishment and as fear of the harsh, forbidding forces in the world about them. Occasionally, children become overwhelmed by their own aggression. Fear of the crocodile might then be expressed in the words of an eight-year-old boy who said during a group discussion about a puppet show: "I am afraid of the crocodile. It might eat me up myself." The crocodile or alligator made its appearance on the European puppet stage with the cannibals.

The figure of the devil is another puppet character of long standing. Like the witch, he is a product of folklore and fairy tales, to which have been added theological identifications. He needs no special introduction, because every child immediately knows what he stands for. How intense the projection of youngsters into a puppet show can become is best illustrated by the example of a six-year-old boy. When the devil suddenly and without any prior warning popped up on the stage, this boy bolted from the room, shouting, "Casper, pray for Jesus Christ. The devil is here."

Added to these major actors are minor characters that serve to round out any specific plot. In one of our shows, Billy, the bad boy, and his mother appear. Billy is the negative Casper in the sense that he completely rejects authority, sasses and hates his mother, beats up Casper, and is very demanding and overbearing. The contrast between the good Casper and the bad Billy has served for many illuminating discussions about various family constellations, attitudes toward parents, and the consequences that might ensue if the balance of power were shifted toward the child. Another character type, General "Hitt-'em-and-kick-'em from bang-'em-and-'slang-'em," serves as Casper's Prime Minister and Chief Executor when Casper tries to build up a government for children and finds it expedient to eliminate adult control and authority.

This enumeration of puppet types may suffice to stress that puppets are capable of representing specific personalities either directly or indirectly, or specific sides or aspects of personalities. With such an array of types, there is hardly any limit to the portrayal of problems.

Over and above the flexibility that is provided through the grouping of these various puppet types, there are other psychological factors that make hand puppetry an ideal medium for tackling and solving problems.

Puppetry is a make-believe affair. A puppet consists only of a head and a costume. The hand and the voice of the puppeteer give it a pseudo-life. A puppet might be beaten, but it does not feel real pain. It might be killed, but since it consists of inanimate material to begin with, killing is never real but only simulated. Situations may be very threatening, but puppetry carries with it the reassurance that everything on the stage is only a make-believe affair. This by no means detracts from the realness with which the children follow the actions, identify themselves with this or that character, and project their own wishes into the show. The make-believe nature of puppetry allows it to go beyond the limits of biological life. It is perfectly normal that a bad character like the crocodile is killed, comes back to life, is again killed, and so on. Children are not concerned about the killing, but clamor for the reassurance that takes place each time the bad and threatening character is killed. Solutions to problems have to be experienced again and again before complete mastery is achieved. However, should severely neurotic or psychotic children feel threatened by the show, one can easily reassure them by taking them backstage, where they can see for themselves that the puppets are not really alive, but are only doll-like characters guided by the puppeteer.

This make-believe nature of puppetry is further expressed by the combination of puppets used. A puppet show in which only realistic characters appear is too logical and does not allow for fantasy digressions. A puppet show in which only fantasy characters act is too unreal and fantastic and does not allow for identifications on a reality level. A good puppet show, like a good fairy tale, should therefore combine both realistic and fantasy factors. This mixture of reality and fantasy makes it easier for the child to enter into the spirit of the problem presented, and aids in the identification. Since parts of the show or some of the puppets (witch, devil, giant, and so on) are symbolic expressions of attitudes, the child himself feels free to project his own attitudes into the show.

Children, by and large, enter quickly into the make-believe nature of the puppet show. Yet it will happen that very disturbed and psychotic children object to a puppet show because their own main problem consists of a severe struggle between maintaining a reality appreciation and giving in to their own delusions. One psychotic youngster felt compelled to wash not only the puppets, but also the stage. He claimed that the puppets and everything connected with them were dirty and had to be cleaned. Dirt, to this child, represented the threat of insanity, whereas clean and white stood for reality. Another one of our young patients objected to the puppet show as being too mechanical, and called me the "mechanical man." This little girl went through a rapid phase of deterioration toward the end of her stay in the ward and always went into hiding when a puppet show was given. These and similar experiences taught us that severely psychotic children might conceive the puppet show as a threat to their endeavor to hang on to reality. These children were much more aware of the make-believe nature of the puppet shows, and therefore reacted in a very marked fashion. They felt threatened and had a strong desire of defending themselves against such make-believe.

Another important prerequisite for a good hand puppet show is the *close interaction between the audience and the puppets*. Several centuries ago, it was quite common for the actors on the legitimate stage to address some of their lines, and also offhand improvisations, directly to the audience, which, in turn, talked back. This form of audience participation is no longer practiced on the legitimate stage, but it has been kept alive on the puppet stage. Before the show starts, the children are told that they are expected to enter into the show by telling the various puppets what to do, suggesting modes of action, warning of threatening dangers, and aiding the actors verbally in whatever way they can. The puppets, in turn, speak directly to the children. Casper, for instance, might ask his audience whether or not he should play hookey from school. He acts dumb, tells the children that he never did such a thing, and asks them to instruct him on how to go about it. It is self-evident that the answers Casper receives contain valuable clues to the children's thinking and experiences. In this way, material is produced that would be extremely difficult to extract in an individual interview. The children are not aware of the fact that they themselves give away clues to their own behavior. On the contrary, they feel highly flattered that Casper takes them into his confidence. They really have the feeling that they themselves are running the show. This makes it clearer why it was said that a good hand puppet show should consist of a skeleton-like, flexible script, because without this, such improvisations and audience interaction could not take place. It is not uncommon for the puppets to deviate temporarily from their script to follow some suggestions from the audience, and to return to the regular plot at the proper time and continue with the play until a new interruption causes another deviation. . . .

Groups in the School

The everyday groups in which children naturally gather in and around schools provide the ideal setting, because it is "natural" (not imposed by some form of clinical intervention), both for studying children in groups and for putting our knowledge of groups to work. It is very important that teachers understand the structure, purposes, and form of the groups they work with every day.

The reader is referred to George Dennison's excellent book, *The Lives of Children,* an account of one year at the experimental First Street School in a New York City slum. The book illustrates the intelligent and sensitive handling of children in their own groups, children of various races who had been cast out or considered unteachable by the city school system, although none was intellectually incapable and some were gifted. Mr. Dennison is a writer and teacher. His point of view and that of the school derive somewhat from A.S. Neill's Summerhill, somewhat from Leo Tolstoy's rural experiment, but most of all from John Dewey's philosophy as he originally intended it, not as it has been distorted by some of his earlier apostles and later critics.

The following excerpts are included because they represent different kinds of in-school therapeutic groups. The first comes from *P.S. Your Not Listening,* by special education teacher Eleanor Craig. The second is from a book by one of the authors, and describes how groups were run as part of the consultation process. The third is a systems analysis study on the school to see if it functioned for the benefit of the population.

P.S. Your Not Listening
Eleanor Craig

(An early session of a therapeutic school-group.)

"Mmm . . . sick."

"Where don't you feel well, Kevin?"

"Sick, mmm." His words were barely audible. "I'm homesick, that's what. She doesn't believe me."

I patted his back. "It's hard to come to school when you've been absent."

Suddenly he leaped up, darted into the closet, and closed the door on himself.

Douglas became alarmed. "Listen Kevin, we were having a good morning till you started messing up."

Kevin stuck his head out, then began to pull the door shut on his neck.

"Don't, don't!" Douglas yelled. "You're going to hurt yourself!"

"So what," Kevin answered flatly. "I want to."

"Make him stop, Mrs. Craig." Douglas pleaded. "He's wiping his sweat on us!"

Jonathan bounced in his chair. "Whooeee, he's blowin' his top! He's gonna blast off!"

Kevin's face was scarlet from the pressure on his neck. I rushed to the closet and yanked the door from his grasp. He crumpled to the floor gasping. Douglas began to whimper.

Eddie, scornful of Douglas' concern, mocked, "You worried about that tomato face? That crazy tomato face is your friend!"

"See what you've done?" Douglas sobbed.

"You bum!" He bolted across the room. "You've embarrassed me! Eddie thinks I've got nutty friends. He thinks I taught you to be nuts!" He kicked Kevin in the stomach.

Kevin doubled up in pain, while Douglas went on his all-time rampage. Picking up a chair, he hurled it across the room. Two legs flew off as it cracked a section of blackboard. Coats and jackets were hurled out the window, followed by the wastebasket, papers, and workbooks. I tried to reach him, both physically and with words. He was grunting and snarling, upsetting desks and chairs, scattering papers everywhere.

He grabbed a new tin of chalk from the closet and dumped it, sawdust and all, on Kevin, yelling. "I don't care if you get hurt! I don't care if you die!"

The chalk bounced off Kevin's motionless body. Sawdust filtered into his hair, his eyes and mouth. He gagged and spat.

I caught Douglas' wrist, but he kicked my ankle and ran, calling back. "Shut up, shut up, shut up . . . ." I pursued him to the door and watched him zigzag down the hall, ripping everything off the bulletin boards on both sides as he ran.

Luckily an intercom had just been installed. Miss Silverstein's secretary answered sweetly.

"Doris quick! Tell Miss Silverstein [school principal] that Douglas is somewhere in the building, and we need the nurse immediately for Kevin."

"Hmm? Really? My gosh. Oh, okay."

Seconds later, Miss Silverstein and Mrs. Rogers, the nurse, rushed in, visibly distressed by the havoc in the hall. Our room looked like the aftermath of a tornado.

Kevin had recovered enough to howl. Eddie was prancing around, holding the broken chair aloft. "That boog did it! He broke school property! Now who's a punk?"

Jonathan, having taken cover under his desk, was grunting suspiciously. He zapped the nurse and principal with his invisible atomic gun. "Pow—bam—got ya—you're dead!"

Mrs. Rogers went to Kevin. Eyeing me accusingly, she demanded, "What happened to him?"

"Douglas kicked him in the stomach."

"My God! He could have a rupture!" The nurse, in her late forties, was a tall, heavy-set woman, capable but formidable. Effortlessly, she scooped up the limp child. Chalk and sawdust rained from both of them. "This whole setup just babies kids, lets them get away with murder. In a bigger class they wouldn't dare behave this way. Four kids in a room, a waste of time and money! Just spoiling them, that's what I say."

Her words came with such vehemence that I realized she had felt this way from the beginning. I thought of the innocent classmates these children had victimized previously, but it was no time to justify the program.

She stormed out, Kevin draped limply in her arms. . . .

(A later session in the same therapeutic school group.)

"I had a disturbing conversation yesterday," Ceil [school psychiatric social worker] was saying before school on Friday. "Just as I was leaving the office, Eddie's mother called.

"She'd locked him in his room for the day and gone to modeling school. A policeman was waiting inside when she got home. One of the neighbors had seen Eddie climb out his bedroom window onto the roof. Afraid he'd fall, she called the police. But he just stood there exposing himself. The officer said he wouldn't file a juvenile report, but threatened Mrs. Conte with child-abuse charges if she locked him up again. Can you believe, she doesn't see anything wrong with that? She's just furious at the boy for getting her in trouble."

"Oh, God, that's so discouraging, Ceil," I said. I was facing the window. The bus had turned into the driveway.

"I thought about him for hours." Ceil picked up her briefcase. "At least we know, now, more of what's going on. Maybe we'll have to face an unpleasant decision. As long as he's in that home, Eddie may never be better."

"They're here." I heard the door open. "What's your schedule?"

"Send him in at nine. I'd like to see him first."

"Okay. I'm anxious to talk to you after school," I said.

"Right, but we'll have to cut it short. Don't forget the reception for our new boss at four in the Administration Building. Have a good day."

Seeing Eddie come down the hall, I knew his two-day absence had served no purpose. Rather than helping him understand that disruptive behavior was unacceptable, it had increased his need to act out. We had to find an alternative to exclusion for children whose problems were aggravated at home.

Eddie was already provoking Douglas, crisscrossing in front of him, impeding his progress. "I'll bite you anytime I want! My teeth are good weapons. I bite my sister, too."

"Use them again and you'll be swallowing them." Douglas held up his lunchbox menacingly. They stopped, ready to fight, a few feet from our room.

"Good morning, Doug," I called. "Take a look at the new puzzle on your desk." Hand on his back, I guided him in. "And Eddie, I'm glad you're back." I directed him straight ahead with the other hand. "Mrs. Black wants to see you first today."

While Eddie was with Ceil, the rest of the class did creative writing. More and more, our mornings were passing peacefully and productively. Even rewards, stars, prizes, and privileges were less urgently sought. The feeling of success, the satisfaction when work was well done was becoming a goal in itself.

But Eddie's return an hour later interrupted the day's progress. "You're not telling me what to do! I'm not sitting down!" he yelled as he jogged in.

"You're standing up?" I said.

"That's right! So would you if you got whipped like me. I hate getting whipped. It doesn't do any good. I'll just do it all over. Next time I get locked in I'm gonna make a bomb. I'll blow up the stinkin' house. Then I'll get out."

"Whoo-ee! You'll get out in a hundred pieces!" Jonathan now was much more aware of the other children. Though he had not yet learned to converse, he made occasional comments.

"Here's your folder." I handed it to Eddie. "Where are you going to stand?"

With a red crayon he scrawled "fuck you" across the cover.

"Psst!" Kevin stage-whispered to Douglas. "What'd your grandmother say about that mad dog bitin' you?"

Eddie turned pale. He clutched the folder to his chest and watched Douglas anxiously.

"I wouldn't tell who did it." Douglas rubbed his bandaged wound. "I may be mean, but I'm not that mean."

Eddie sagged with relief. He looked around, headed for the windowsill, placed his folder there and opened it. He stood as he wrote. After a brief silence, he turned toward the group. "Hey Doug, wanna have a race? See who's done first?"

"I would've, but you've been takin' too much sweat out on me. It's just 'cause you hate dark skin, right?"

"Naw! It's 'cause I didn't used t' like ya. But now I do."

"Okay," said Doug cautiously. "Ready, get set, go!"

Kevin was irked at being excluded from the competition.

"Let's hide the punk's lunch" he said to Douglas.

"No thanks." Douglas kept working.

Within an hour he was raising his fist in a victorious gesture. "I'm winning! I'm winning!"

From Eddie's vantage at the window he could see that Douglas' last assignment, tracing the human body from his science book, was almost completed.

Eddie threw his pencil down. His voice was high-pitched, whiny. "You big bragger! Just because I don't feel like bragging!"

Too pleased with himself to be offended, Douglas said, "I'm sorry, I was conscientious of braggin'."

Julie handed Eddie his pencil, which had rolled under her chair. As if pleading his case, he said to her, "He's makin' me nervous! It's not nice to brag, ya know."

"You're doin' good, Eddie." Julie glanced at his work and returned to her own, cutting sandpaper versions of those troublesome letters b, p, and d.

Then Douglas, with a side glance at Eddie, shouted with enthusiasm, "I'm losing! I'm losing!"

"Liar! You liar!" Eddie threw his papers and books across the room. "You know you were winning!"

"Think, Eddie." I stayed beside Jonathan, hoping the incident would go no further. "Why would Douglas say he was losing?"

"Because I've got manners," Douglas interposed. With both hands in the pockets of his ragged jeans, he walked confidently toward the window. "Just take five minutes off, Mrs. Craig. I can handle this."

"Thanks, anyway," I said. "Only one teacher to a room."

Forgetting his sore bottom, Eddie boosted himself onto the windowsill, away from Douglas, who was addressing him. "You better start respecting your elders, kid. I say I'm losing, I'm losing. Don't forget who's already nine."

Feeling threatened, Eddie knew only one response. He crouched, readying himself to jump down on Douglas.

"If you say you lost, Doug," I spoke loudly, "that means Eddie gets first choice for the afternoon.

"I take woodworking." Eddie abandoned the attack.

"Uh-uh," Kevin muttered under his breath. "That's what I choose."

"S-S-S. Pow-pow." Jonathan rocked back and forth in his seat.

"We use words, Jonathan. Remember?" I said. "What's the trouble?"

"I don't know any word beginning with S. Pow-pow." He held up the anagram.

"Easy." Douglas turned away from Eddie. "Psychological. Like disturbed children. And it's psychological how black people and white people treat each other. Don't ya hear the S?"

Jonathan rummaged through a mound of letters and produced S-I-K-O-L-O.

"Still," Douglas looked out the window, "white people might get black themselves if they stayed in the sun too long."

Julie was listening thoughtfully. "Or a beautiful brown like you," she said.

"Gee, thanks. I never heard such a complimentary thing about my skin." He lifted his desktop and poked through the contents. "How about havin' my eraser?"

Julie didn't reach for it. "Maybe my mother would like it." Her eyes were downcast. "She's mad at me, but I'm not sure why."

"Why don't you think about yourself?" He tossed it on her desk.

"I don't like to." She toyed with the eraser. "It makes me feel sad."

Kevin nodded. "Me too," he said softly.

She smiled at him. "You're like me."

The blush began at his neck and spread to the roots of his hair. . . .

(A much later session of the same therapeutic school group.)

The night before, Ellie had been in the kitchen until after ten decorating brownies with blue and white peace symbols for a class sale. Now, with silent acknowledgment to her I proposed a bake sale for our class.

"Cool. Me and my grandmother'll make raisin cookies."

From that day on, my wish for group activities was realized. Even Jonathan worked on the posters that were proudly distributed to every class. Excitement mounted. Central School had never had a bake sale. Other children came to our room to ask about it.

Arithmetic time was devoted to making price signs. Debates were held on which class should come in first. Douglas, of course, opted for the

oldest. Julie argued. "The little kids won't buy as much. Let them choose before everything's gone." Surprisingly, she won unanimously. Even Douglas was swayed.

I sent notes home, explaining the purpose of our sale and thanking parents in advance for their cooperation.

When the great day came, Julie dragged in a carton containing a hundred cellophane bags of popcorn. Kevin's mother drove him and delivered a chocolate sheet cake, cut into fifty servings. Mr. Brenner took Eddie to the store en route to school. He purchased twenty double packages of cream-filled cupcakes, each of which he sliced in quarters. Douglas ceremoniously removed the covers from the two shoe boxes he'd carried. Both were filled to the brim with plump golden raisin cookies.

Jonathan came empty-handed.

"You're the only one who forgot," Julie scolded.

"You bum!" Eddie said.

Jonathan sought solace with his paper friend, but both were relegated to a corner in preparation for the customers. The merchants stood behind double desks, on which they spread the goods. There was a hectic scramble to sort out price tags, and a frantic search for the magic marker when Douglas insisted that none of the prepared cards indicated the true worth of his cookies.

"Ten cents each," he insisted.

"For one cookie?" said Eddie. "You're flaky."

"I'm chargin' five cents for my cake," said Kevin.

"Five cents is fair for everything," Julie decreed.

"Now listen," Douglas thrust a cookie in her face, "these have eggs and margarine and genuine raisins. Do you know how long it takes one single grape to become a raisin?"

"They're beautiful," I said, "but if you charge too much, kids won't be able to afford them."

"Okay, okay, five cents." He held up his hands in resignation. "But for five cents they're not getting raisins."

At nine-fifteen the first graders filed into our room. At the same time, Jonathan's mother appeared and left a tray of candied apples. Julie quickly arranged a desk for Jonathan, who with his paper ghost was recalled from the corner. He and his silent partner sold every apple.

Douglas did not participate. He'd moved his wares to the "office," where he stood with his back to the class.

By the time the second graders arrived, he, too,

was in business—a mound of crumbling de-raisined cookies on one desk, tiny piles of raisins on the other, both products labeled "5¢ Each."

The last group of sixth graders left at eleven-thirty. By now the room was a shambles, desks and floor littered with waxed paper, crumbs, candy-apple sticks, and mashed popcorn. But from the beginning the event was a social success. Children who were reluctant to enter our room, having heard who-knows-what about its occupants, found it not only safe but perhaps even enviable.

"Hey, you got only five kids and all this audiovisual jazz?" one sixth grader said admiringly.

"You're lucky, getting to have a cake sale," a little girl told Julie.

I was delighted with the effect of such recognition, particularly on Kevin and Jonathan. As the morning progressed they changed from mumbling self-effacing boys to confident salesmen, enjoying positions of authority.

Miss Silverstein was our last customer. She bought everyone's leftovers and lingered to hear Douglas announce the final tally. Eleven dollars and thirty cents, all but one dollar in small change.

"Boss!" Douglas said. "That's a lotta bread!"

"Will you bring it to the hospital today," Julie asked me, "and tell 'em it's from us?"

"Better yet," Miss Silverstein paused in the doorway, "I'll call now and let their office know how hard you worked.". . .

(The final session of the same therapeutic school group: Tuesday, June 18; the last day of school.)

At first, Douglas and Julie had asked about Kevin often, but this past week they had been spending the entire day with their new classes. I was receiving glowing reports from Mrs. Tefft and Miss Flynn. Both children would return to their neighborhood schools in September.

All morning Eddie and Jonathan helped me carry books to the storeroom, collect paints and crayons, and take down papers and charts. Until today, Eddie had seemed almost relieved about going to Green Valley, but now, knowing that he'd soon be on his way, he was edgy and apprehensive.

"It's your fault, isn't it?" he asked, continuing to sweep the floor. "You're the one who kicked me out."

"You know that's not true, Eddie. You understand why that school's a better place for you."

"Sure!" He threw down the broom. "Because you're so selfish and critical. Admit it, goddamnit!

You don't think I'm good enough, but you're keeping that crazy fatso."

Jonathan had improved to the point of caring when he'd been insulted. He stopped polishing his desk and sat back pensively. "I never call you names."

"I'll call you anything I want. Freak. Bastard. Bum." Eddie began circling Jonathan's desk.

"Come on, Eddie." I shook my head. I wanted this one day to be pleasant for all. "Anyone can say those words, but what does it prove? Think about the things you've said you liked at Green Valley, and stop feeling angry at Jonathan and me."

"Don't worry!" he shrieked. "I'm glad—glad to get outta this stinkin' place."

School was closing early, and the bus was due at noon. At eleven, Douglas and Julie returned to clean out their desks. When they were done, I served cookies and punch at the reading table. We ate together for the last time, conscious that this whole year together would soon be a memory. I looked at each child.

Douglas gulped the drink and held his cup for more. "I miss my ole buddy Kevin today."

"I'm gonna miss everybody." Julie nibbled her cookie. She edged her chair until it was touching mine.

"I'll miss you all too. But I'll be seeing your new teachers next year, so I'll get to hear about you."

Eddie ate cookie after cookie but said nothing.

Douglas slammed his fist against the table. "Don't make bad predictions, Mrs. Craig. I'll always be loyal to Central. You sound like we'll never even visit here again."

"Visiting's not the same Douglas." Julie looked out the window. "We won't even know the kids."

Douglas stopped eating. "I guess I'll never get to play under the new lights in the gym." He sounded gloomy.

Jonathan smiled at me for the very first time. "I'm glad I don't have to worry about missing that."

Julie put both hands on her hips. "Just because you're getting retarded doesn't mean it's good to stay back."

"Now, Julie," I said. "You know that Jonathan is not really staying back. He's—"

"The bus is here! The bus is here!" Eddie leaped up, knocking over his cup of punch. "Quick! I gotta do something." He grabbed a paper, ran into the closet, and closed the door. He was out in a minute and dropped the paper in his desk. "There, I left ya a note."

Pleased, I went to speak to him, but he dashed by me and out of the room.

Julie threw away her cup and napkin, then flung herself at me, her arms clutching my waist.

"Happy vacation, Julie." I hugged her. She was quivering. "You go ahead to the bus. I'll be out to say good-bye."

That left Jonathan and Douglas, still at the table. "C'mon," Douglas was leaning toward Jonathan. "Make one last goofy sound like you always used ta."

"Heck no!" Jonathan stood up and pushed in his chair. "Are you crazy? Do you think I wanna be in this class forever?"

While they were getting ready, I couldn't resist a peek at Eddie's message. Raising his desktop, I picked up the crumpled note and unfolded it slowly.

He had blown his nose all over the paper.

Sickened and discouraged, I walked to the door behind Jonathan and Douglas. Ceil must have driven over to say good-bye, I thought, seeing her standing beside Julie. Eddie was already in a rear seat by a raised window. Not wanting his upsetting note to be our last communication, I went to the bus and spoke through the opening.

"I got your note, Eddie. Someday you won't feel so angry. Come back and see me." I barely re-

moved my hand before he slammed the window.

Julie kissed Ceil and me. Jonathan allowed us each a brief hug and hurried onto the bus.

Squinting in the sun's glare, Douglas extended his hand. "Well, it's been nice knowin' ya."

I clasped his hand in both of mine and looked into his expressionless face. It was hardest to say good-bye to Douglas, perhaps because he'd been the first and always so unpredictable. "Have a wonderful summer, Doug."

"Summa? Oh, God! Oh, God! Not summa! It's summeRRR. Can't ya hear the R?" He shook his head, hopped on the bus, and shouted out toward Ceil. "Help her, Mrs. Black. She still can't speak our language!"

The driver closed the door.

Ceil and I stood waving. I struggled to maintain a smile and call out a last good-bye, but my throat was hopelessly jammed.

Eddie was crouching. Only the tip of his head visible. Julie blew an abundance of kisses. Douglas, leaning out perilously, waved both arms in a slow crisscross pattern. Jonathan didn't wave. But through the window I could see him mouthing "good-bye, good-bye" until the bus turned the corner.

The Summit Group
Ruth G. Newman

As I entered the outer office I heard fire alarms ringing and saw some students walking out. Inside sat Fred, head down on the table, dejected. I went over, genuinely glad to see him for the first time since June, shook his hand, and asked him how things were. He answered that he was in the process of being kicked out of school. "What for?" I asked. "For this," he said, handing me a four-page mimeographed paper. I sat down and read it. It was a lurid but not completely inaccurate account written by Fred of some of the bad conditions at Urban High. Though smacking of yellow journalism, much of it had a basis in fact. It was calculated to make the most of the racial discrimination that

existed, and to angrily point out the better conditions for learning at high schools in wealthier and whiter neighborhoods. The fire bells and the walkout were a demonstration by some of the students against Fred's impending dismissal. Fred had not, in fact, been expelled, although an irate assistant principal was threatening him with it. It seemed that he had fallen, like so many politicians before and after him, not on the issue of paper and its contents—although it was reasonably clear that that was what was behind the excitement—but on a technicality. In a rage, he had refused to give his home address since he no longer lived with his aunt, and the school had a right to expel him if they had no proof that he lived in the district. By that time he had calmed down sufficiently so that I could say, "Oh, for heaven's sake, Fred, give them your

From *Psychological Consultation in the Schools* by Ruth G. Newman, Basic Books, Inc., Publishers, New York, 1967. Reprinted by permission of the publisher.

address; then let's deal with issues here at school where maybe something can be done about some of the things you brought up, and let's see how to do it. If you get kicked out nothing will be gained." He blurted out his address, which was in the Urban district. The assistant principal, though still angry, decided to let the matter go. I started to talk to Fred about the good things in the paper and also about his use of exaggeration, distortion, and forgery in making his case.

I used the word "forgery" because, while the articles in the paper were signed by several other students besides Fred, these others were objecting to the use of their names, since the articles they had submitted bore little relation to those printed. I asked if I could see all the students involved, some of whom were members of the student government, and said I wanted to see if we could tackle some of the problems mentioned in the paper. Thus what I called "The Rebel Group" got started. There were four boys and six girls, and all of the tracks, from Honors to Basic, were presented. At first Jenny Jones, who was a counselor at Urban, and I were the only interested, participating adults; later several teachers became actively involved. The group met every week for the rest of the school year and then continued on a monthly basis, with replacements made as members graduated. Within three weeks they were called "The Summit Group." I do not recall who gave it the name—it was not I—but that was the name that stuck. They considered themselves a policy-planning group and did indeed affect the school and its policies.

We began by sorting out the problems Fred had brought up—separating those which we, as a group within the school, could do anything about from those which required more community social action. In time, members of the Summit Group became quite active in writing letters to the newspapers and making appearances on radio and television on subjects relevant to the city's problems or youth viewpoints.

I shall summarize, briefly, some of the concerns and activities of this group. The most immediate problem at Urban was the student body's fear of "outsiders" who broke into the building—often with knives, sometimes with guns—and made serious trouble. Groups of these outsiders, many of whom were dropouts from this and other nearby schools or unemployed graduates, hung around outside the building intimidating, blackmailing, and beating up Urban students on their way to and from school. The Summit Group made suggestions about what the students themselves could do and asked

for faculty help in guarding doors. They also asked Dr. Tilden and me to approach the police for better, more understanding police coverage of the block at certain times, and this was the beginning of some work with the police on their relations with teenagers.

Within the school, the first issue that emerged was the fact that the school newspaper served no function of communication. The journalism teacher insisted on an expensive, high-standard product which could enter into competition with papers of other schools for prestige and awards. The students found this frustrating because measuring up to her standards meant printing only one or two papers a year. I suggested a weekly newsletter which could be cheaply mimeographed and distributed and would be quite distinct from the "ideal" school newspaper. Many of the teachers became interested and cooperative. English teachers, typing teachers, and the faculty sponsor of student government all helped, and some worked hard on the actual physical production—proofreading, typing, mimeographing, collating, stapling. The newsletter came out for two cents a copy and became a regular feature of the school life. It provided editorial comment on problems, news of school and personal events, reports on programs, and discussion of issues. When Dr. Tilden, the principal, took a leave of absence she used the newsletter to address the students, telling them where and why she was going. The Summit Group was rightfully excited and proud.

Another in-school problem that was tackled was the almost unbearable noise and confusion of the cafeteria. The Summit Group, with the help of cooperative teachers, planned movies, social activities, and record and combo playing at certain times during the lunch break to tempt masses of students away from the overcrowded lunchrooms and neighboring halls.

Of course there were issues that did not lend themselves to direct practical solutions, but these were at least aired and discussed. Child labor laws (originally made for their protection) prevented many youngsters from getting needed jobs after school. According to the law, no one under eighteen could work after ten o'clock at night. Restaurants and all-night garages don't want to hire anyone who has to quit at ten, since this necessitates a second shift. The Summit Group reported that many kids who wanted to continue in school dropped out because they had to work full time and could do so only in the daytime hours. Some stuck to night school, but some soon gave up.

It was through the Summit Group that I learned of the difficulty some bright students had, not in achieving college loans or scholarships, but simply in raising enough money to apply. Lacking the ten- or twenty-dollar fees, many gave up the idea of going to college or chose inferior colleges simply because of the lower application cost. Apprised by the Summit Group of this problem, the volunteers from the Council of Jewish Women generously started a fund to assist in paying application fees, but it is clearly not a problem unique to Urban High.

As the year progressed the students trusted me with their fears and resentments, knowing I was not there to judge them and was genuinely interested in their feelings and ideas. Many faculty members cooperated in helping them with Summit Group projects. Beginning with the newsletter, and continuing on through the next year, the faculty sponsor of student government attended all their meetings. He liked them and they him, and it was not long before he helped them to articulate their problems even more clearly than they had before.*

In December of that year I was asked by an educational organization to get a tape of student opinions on the difficulties in the high school which contribute to discouragement and to the decision to drop out. I asked the Summit Group if they would like to help me. Seven of them agreed enthusiastically when it was established that neither their names nor the name of the school would be given. This would leave them free to be honest without getting themselves or their faculty in trouble. I warned them that my name was often associated with Urban. I pointed out that if the tape were picked up by the press (as it subsequently was), the connection with Urban might be made. They still agreed to come to my office to make a recording. On the appointed day five of them appeared after school; the other two were sick. Here is a summary of their criticisms, their positive statements, and their constructive suggestions.

Students' Thoughts about Why Fellow Students Drop Out

---

1. There is not enough selection of elective courses, and students are bored with those available.

---

*This man was later shot and killed by an intruder trying to rob the school bank.

2. The necessity to work often causes a drop in grades and discouragement.

3. The inability to cross tracks prevents academic students from taking business courses, which in turn means that they lack money-making skills at graduation. (It seems that academic students must take five academic majors, leaving them no time for courses such as typing. In addition, typing classes are already overcrowded, so there is no room for the few who might manage to carry the extra-heavy schedule.)

4. There are not enough counselors. This means that the counselors have no time for the kind of individual relationships and mental health counseling that the kids feel they need. Most teachers are too busy or too harried to offer individual encouragement to students.

5. Teachers put pressure on bright students to prepare for college regardless of the students' own inclinations.

6. The classes are large and overcrowded. There is a need for more business classes. Some subjects, such as language and math, should be taught in much smaller classes.

7. Students over eighteen are not eligible for school tickets on buses. For some, the extra cost of fifty cents a day is prohibitive. This is most likely to affect Basic or Regular students.

8. There is pressure on good students to excel in all subjects, as well as in extracurricular activities. This pressure, on top of outside jobs and home chores, does not allow for proper rest.

9. There are not enough textbooks; in some courses there are too few; in others there are none. Those that are available are often outdated and are often issued weeks or even months late.

10. Students are asked to buy supplementary books that they cannot afford.

11. There is inadequate equipment and a lack of facilities, especially for science courses.

12. Reading problems are usually a big factor in dropping out. The subject matter of readers used in remediation is insulting to high school students. There should be heavier emphasis on reading in the low grades, and individual remediation should be offered in the upper schools. Mobile libraries at all school levels should be expanded.

13. To stay in school it is necessary to have pride

in oneself and in one's work. Teachers don't help a student build up such pride. Instead they often give false praise which the student knows is not deserved, or they withhold praise from the student who needs and deserves it.

Suggestions Made by Students

1.   The work-study program is very good. It should be available to more students in the school and extended to other schools.

2.   Remedial reading help from the volunteers is very good, and the program should be enlarged.

3.   There should be more counselors; they should be better trained; their work load should be reduced.

4.   There should be two kinds of counselors: (1) mental health counselors and (2) grade placement, section placement, and vocational counselors.

5.   There should be better testing to determine aptitude before track placement is made. There should be consistent review of students' records and achievements for more flexible placement and checkup on requirements for graduation.

6.   More high schools should be built and staffed.

7.   There should be special counseling services for possible dropouts who are in precarious positions. They need to talk; they also need special attention.

8.   There should be better-trained teachers interested specifically in Basic students, so that there would be less busy-work and more learning.

9.   There should be adjustment in scheduling and school hours to make it possible for students to have jobs and continue their schooling at the same time.

10.   Volunteers should be used to lighten the counseling and clerical load at rush periods, such as the beginning of the school year, mid-semester, and report-card times.

11.   All students should participate in some extracurricular activities. Then they would have more pride in their school and more sense of belonging to it. Expansion and re-examination of areas of particular interest to students should be made to revamp the extracurricular program.

12.   There should be more personal contact between teacher and student wherein the teacher will listen to the student and find out what help is needed.

13.   There should be recognition of the outside interests and problems of high school students.

14.   There should be more recognition of true economic need and more imaginative ways to meet this need within the school program.

The following selection shows how group analysis, conducted with full awareness of the system within which the group exists, is a particularly effective means of therapeutic and educational intervention. It is a way to bring about desired changes in behavior and achievement, as well as to affect emotional attitudes, because it goes directly to the heart of those problems in the system that have aroused or exacerbated the child's destructive or futile behavior. Omitted from the article as reprinted here is an excellent discussion of systems analysis theory as a useful, consultative means of approaching mental health problems within a school; the entire article is strongly recommended.

An Alternative to Traditional Mental Health Services and Consultation in Schools: A Social Systems and Group Process Approach

David L. Singer
Mary Beth Whiton
Matthew L. Fried

Psychologists can aid the school with its task of education in two major areas. The first is by applying their knowledge to strengthen the *technical aspects* of education. For example, principles of learning and child development can be used to make curriculum and teaching skills more effective; research techniques can be applied to issues within the school.

More important, we believe, is the assistance psychologists can provide through their understanding of the dynamic aspects of education, the psychosocial phenomena which affect learning. The interests, goals, needs, and anxieties of individuals and groups within a school are constantly in dynamic interplay and are constraints on the success of education, all technical factors notwithstanding. These, rather than individual psychopathology, are the most significant hindrances to the work of education. Consider, for example, the students who are withdrawn and antagonistic because they feel, either with or without justification, that their teacher is "out to put them down." Consider also their teacher, who feels frustrated and unappreciated. Until this barrier to effective work is somehow overcome—either by compromise or resolution of the conflict—even the best curriculum, presented with sound principles of learning and using the best equipment, will have minimal effect.

Constraints on education occur at many levels: school, classroom, faculty, individual, etc. The school, for example, may be assigned covert tasks by the society at large or by its own school district. One such covert task is the perpetuation of cultural values, myths, and mores. The current furor over sex education in many communities has made clear the fact that, for many, the task of educating children is secondary to the task of value perpetuation. Or consider the "model" inner city school on whose fate a program and funds for the whole district hinge. Increased moral support, attention, and concern may enhance educational effectiveness; pressure and anxiety generated by the district office and constant politicking may make the teaching staff so uncomfortable that they lose some of their patience and effectiveness.

As an institution, the school has an organization, and this too is a source of constraints on work. *Authority relations*—the dynamics between persons in authority and those under them—pose problems on all levels: for the school as a social system, within grades or departments, and particularly within classrooms. Whether that authority is seen as legitimate is often an issue. *Peer relations*—the dynamics between "equals" in a group or social system—are similarly active at all levels. Membership in various groups, both formal and informal, generates loyalties, differences, rivalries, and anxiety, which at times can cloud judgment and lead to social misperceptions. Other constraints on the school's performance of its primary task come from the aspirations, fears, and fantasies of its members concerning competence, adequacy, achievement, and success.[1]

---

[1]These phenomena were described by Bennis & Shepard (1956) and Slater (1961). A more theoretical presentation can be found in Rioch (1970). Although these principles and theories were largely developed through observation of self-study groups, in our experience the same processes are operant in classrooms, committee meetings, and other group settings, though perhaps in a more subtle form. For a somewhat more sociometric discussion of classroom social structure, see Glidewell, Kantor, Smith, & Stringer (1966).

From *Journal of School Psychology*, vol. 8, no. 3, copyright 1970 by Behavioral Publications, Inc. Reprinted by permission.

Conflict and anxiety are inevitable, existential givens which occur within each individual, group, and social system, though in differing ways and degrees. How they are handled is crucial in determining either a constructive or maladaptive outcome for the individual or the educational process. Conflict and anxiety can be accepted, dealt with openly, and resolved if possible. If resolution is not possible, they can be lived with and integrated into the system. An opportunity to observe and participate in this process is an essential part of the educational process. The avoidance of anxiety can only limit, and therefore impair, the educational process.

How might these various dynamics manifest themselves in real life, and how might a psychologist use his understanding of them to facilitate education? Let us consider several situations. In each case, the problem solving approach is the same: (a) identifying a source of interference with the educational process, (b) understanding its dynamics, and (c) recommending and/or providing some sort of intervention.

Example 1: Situation: Defense against anxiety by flight.   A drastic and unexpected rise in absenteeism is occuring among the entering seventh grade class in a large urban junior high school. The psychologist learns that a new program has been instituted in which each child has an individually tailored program, based on his level of competence in each subject, which results in his having a unique class schedule. He knows that facing a new school and making the transition to a departmental system are both anxiety arousing. The new program, he believes, is depriving the children of a stable peer group which is a necessary source of emotional support; they are playing hookey to avoid this anxiety. He recommends that children be assigned programs in groups of five rather than on an individual basis.

Example 2: Authority relations in first grade.   A first grade teacher reports that her class has become increasingly disruptive, and suspects that several of the children are too disturbed to be in a regular class. The psychologist notes that the teacher is seven months pregnant and upon inquiry finds that she has not discussed this fact with her class. He suspects that the class is dealing with fears of abandonment by her and/or replacement in her affections by the new baby. Observation of the class confirms this guess and leads him to believe that the disruptive children are those for whom sibling

rivalry is a particulary anxiety arousing issue. He recommends that the teacher discuss her pregnancy and her future plans with the children and help them to express their feelings and fantasies about the event. He offers to sit in and help the discussion along.

A work sample: "Children who could not learn."[2]   One of the elementary schools in a suburban community requested psychological testing from the psychology service for an entire class: 13 fourth and fifth graders, 12 black and one white. All of the children had a history of conflict in previous classes and all were behind in academic work. The white child had been diagnosed previously as schizophrenic.

The purpose of the class was to provide intensive remedial education for the children so that they could be reintegrated into regular classes. However, the teacher, a reading specialist, felt frustrated in her attempts to get the children moving. She wanted psychological testing to tell her whether these children had the ability to benefit from her special class.

That the whole class had been referred for testing suggested that psychological testing was not going to be very useful. Most of the children had been tested before, and it seemed likely that the problem lay in the relationship between the class as a whole and the teacher. Nonetheless, it appeared that to gain any confidence from this teacher and therefore any authorization to work with her on redefining the problem, the children would first have to be tested. (We saw this as an essential compromise, and learned from it the value of explicit contractual agreements. Had the contract between the psychologists and the school been more explicit, and a consultative role for psychologists been authorized, such testing probably would not have been necessary.) As we interpreted the tests, most of the children were functioning at the "low average" level of intelligence with no indications of brain damage. These findings were of little help to the teacher, but they eliminated the possibility that the children were not able to learn.

Observation of the dynamics within the classroom led to a different view of the problem. The children appeared to be actively engaged in a struggle to sabotage any attempts at learning and teaching. There was an unspoken agreement among them to present themselves as dumb and uncon-

---

[2]Similar work in a different type of institution and with older students is described in Klein & Gould (1970).

trollable. Any individual attempt at or interest in learning was quickly sabotaged by the rest of the class. This problem was unwittingly compounded by the teacher, who heaped lavish praise on a child when he learned something, further alienating him from his peers.

We tentatively concluded that, as self defeating as this behavior appeared, it probably served to protect the class from a more central source of anxiety and threat. We therefore decided to work with the class as a group and to provide consultation for the teacher. We assumed that the class would re-enact with us the conflicts and expectations underlying its relationship with the school system which were interfering with learning. Within this context, we hoped to clarify with the class what we saw. Our focus was to be in terms of the group as a whole, rather than on individuals. We also hoped to provide for the children a model of forthright communication and a choice between continued sabotage of learning, or more effective problem solving around the underlying issues which could free them to learn.

Our goals with the teacher were to help her to understand what was going on between herself and this class, to understand particular dilemmas facing these children as a group, and to encourage her to try more straightforward ways of dealing with them. We shared our view of the situation with the teacher and presented our recommendations. She agreed, but with some understandable skepticism. Meetings with the class were set up for the last hour of the school day twice a week. The teacher was not present at these meetings; we met with her immediately afterwards. During the first meeting we introduced ourselves to the children as psychologists who were working with them because they "weren't making it in school." We further explained that they could choose the activities, and that we would try to help them to understand more clearly what went on in the classroom.

At the outset the class appeared chaotic, as if they were demonstrating the same pattern with us as with the teacher. They appeared to be implicitly asking us if we were going to play a punitive, authoritarian role, and testing to see if we could be induced into believing that they could not control themselves. We told them this was how we saw it, and refused to assume responsibility for control of the classroom. When, for example, fights among different children broke out in the first few sessions, the class pointed the fighting out to us and demanded that we intervene. We commented that the

fights continued only because the other children sat by, and we wondered aloud why the rest of the class didn't stop them. At first the response of the class was to protest innocence and blame the fighters. Then they started to stop fights by themselves, and after the third week, fights were seldom seen.

In the following weeks the focus shifted from the unruliness of the class to the one white child who was constantly brought to our attention by the rest of the class for his "crazy" behavior. While this boy's behavior was bizarre at times, the class teased him unmercifully and took great glee in getting him to perform his routines. The message to us seemed to be that *he* was the locus of all the craziness in this class. This emphasis on the white boy's "craziness" led us to believe that these children had come to regard themselves as crazy and bad, and we discussed this with them, too.

The next issue which evolved was race. When the children liked us, they told us we were really black; when they were angry they called us racists. On one occasion they accused us of having murdered Martin Luther King.

The pieces of the puzzle were now beginning to fit together. It was clear to everyone that the school regarded these children as bad, unteachable, and a general nuisance. While five years ago these children would have been thrown out or punished, because of changing times they were now being provided with "compensatory education." Perhaps the placement of one psychotic white child with these black children, who were far from crazy, says something about the latent attitudes of the school and community. As we worked with the children, there was abundant evidence that they interpreted it as a statement that the white school and community regarded them as crazy. The children in this classroom appeared to mirror the feelings of their parents, the black minority in the community, many of whom worked as domestics for the white, middle class majority.

Although being regarded as crazy was frightening to the children, it also had its comforting aspects. They all had low self esteem and a tremendous fear of failure and humiliation. As "crazy children" they could feel absolved of their responsibility to control their behavior and, more importantly, to take advantage of the available learning opportunity.

For the rest of the semester we continued working these issues and acknowledging the children's feelings. We pointed out continually that they were not making it better for themselves, but that they were, in fact, playing into their own worst fears. We confronted them with the choices they were constantly making. As time went on it became increasingly difficult for them to pose as irresponsible and incompetent to control themselves.

At the same time we were working with the teacher, discussing issues that were coming up in the group. We also discussed problems she had encountered and attempted to suggest possible ways of handling situations. When the black-white issue emerged, for example, we suggested that the posters in the room be replaced by real-life pictures including prominent Blacks. At times our comments seemed to fall on deaf ears. Yet, after a while they would quietly be accepted. Thus, despite protests that "pictures don't mean a thing to these children," posters with black faces were on the walls several weeks later.

Our work was not without difficulty. For one thing, there was ambivalence on the part of the principal and the teacher. The principal became very uncomfortable when the class seemed out of control and at times threatened to throw us out of the school. In retrospect it is clear that we did not adequately inform him about our ideas and technique. The teacher also became uncomfortable when too little or too much was happening. She and the school had taken a risk in allowing us to work in this experimental way. What if we succeeded and she didn't? How would it look if we failed? What would it mean to other teachers if she succeeded in teaching these children? What is the school's responsibility if children like these really *can* learn? What are the implications for the community?

Clearly, we were not working in a vacuum. We also frequently felt confused and helpless, and outside consultation was needed to provide perspective.

By the end of the year, the class appeared to change their attitudes toward school and behavior in school. Absenteeism was down and achievement scores rose at least three grades for a majority of the children. For the most part they were no longer unruly and disruptive. These changes were not solely the result of our working with the class. They also reflected our successful collaboration with the teacher, who had changed many of her attitudes and ways of dealing with the children. She was much more open and straightforward. Near the end of the year, after a frank discussion of sex in our class meeting, the children wanted to test the teacher and revealed to her what we had been talking about. She came through with flying colors as she replied, "I'm older than the psychologists and probably know more about sex. Now, what is it you want to know?" And at the end of the school year she reversed an earlier decision and arranged to work once again with this type of class and requested a psychologist to do group work with them.

Our work with this class and teacher appears to have been a success. Yet, we must wonder how long-lasting these effects will be, and, in keeping with our social system perspective, about our impact upon the school as a whole. Any change within a sub-system will inevitably have repercussions for the entire system, either producing resistance and backlash or providing impetus for further positive change.

Article References

Bennis, W.G., and Shepard, H.A. A theory of group development. *Human Relations*, 1956, *9*, 415-457, in W.G. Bennis, K.D. Benne, and R. Chin (eds.) *The planning of change.* New York: Holt, Rinehart, and Winston, 1961.

Biber, B. Integration of mental health principles in the school setting. In G. Caplan (ed.) *Prevention of mental disorders in children: Initial explorations.* New York: Basic Books, 1961.

Glidewell, J.C., Kantor, M.B., Smith L.M., and Stringer, L.A. Socialization and social structure in the classroom. In L.W. Hoffman and M.L. Hoffman (eds.) *Review of child development research.* New York: Russell Sage Foundation, 1966, 2.

Klein, E.B., and Gould, L.J. Fuck you with flowers: Metaphor & organizational dynamics. *Journal of Applied Behavioral Science*, 1970.

Losen, S.M. The school psychologist—psychotherapist or consultant? *Psychology in the schools*, 1964, *1*(1), 13–17.

Miller, E.J., and Rice, A.K. *Systems of organization.* London: Tavistock Publications, 1967.

Newman, R. *Psychological consultation in the schools.* New York: Basic Books, 1967.

Rioch, M. The work of Wilfred Bion on groups. *Psychiatry*, 1970, *33*, 56-66.

Sarason, S.B., Levine, M., Goldenberg, I.I., Cherlin, D.L., and Bennett, E.M. *Psychology in community settings.* New York: Wiley and Sons, 1966.

Slater, P.E., Displacement in groups. In W.G. Bennis, K.D. Benne, and R. Chin (eds.) *The planning of change.* New. York: Holt, Rinehart, and Winston, 1961.

Drugs in Therapy

Although drug therapy may be used with the school program or any other special therapeutic interventions (individual, group, or family), it may be eschewed as an interference in the child's growth, learning, or ultimate cure. It should never be used without thorough diagnosis, constant monitoring and evaluation, and direct supervision and recommendation of a medical doctor. It cannot work, even under the best circumstances, without the parent's or surrogate parent's collaboration.

The use of medicinal drugs in the treatment of children's emotional disturbance is a controversial subject. Some believe they are tremendously helpful; others are fearful of their use. Both sides have their points. The answers depend, obviously, not only on the child and the drug, but on the doctor and what he intends to accomplish. It is important to work with the child, his family, and his school in making the use of the drug not too alarming or special a matter for the child to handle. The meaning of the drug to the child, the way in which he understands it, is also important. Leon Eisenberg is one of the most authoritative physicians in the field. He combines the mental health point of view with a vast pharmacological knowledge.

The Role of Drugs in Treating Disturbed Children
Leon Eisenberg

Few topics of discussion generate more heat and less light than the proper role of drugs in treating disturbed children. At one extreme are those physicians who argue that meaningful treatment is possible only by using the insights provided by psychotherapy—that drugs, if they function as more than placebos, do so only as chemical straight jackets for troublesome children—and that their use serves to delay recognition of the real psychopathology in the family. At the other extreme are those physicians who consider drugs the agents of choice because drugs attack disturbed function at the physiologic level, the place at which they believe the ultimate pathology lies. Partisans of this viewpoint usually also deride psychotherapy as an insubstantial metaphysical occupation, hardly worthy of the honorable calling of a physician. The controversy engages the passions of psychologists, social workers, and teachers, as well as parents. The first law of psychopharmacology might be formulated to state:

the certainty with which convictions are held tends to vary inversely with the depth of the knowledge on which they are based.

There is as yet no universal and completely validated theory of human behavior that would permit a confident prediction of the utility of drugs. Even if we had such a theory the final decision would remain an empirical one. If an agent works well, then a physician, whatever his theoretical persuasion, will be a fool not to use it. For an empiricist, the relevant question becomes: What are the facts?

Experimental Principles

First, it is necessary to consider how the "facts" are obtained. If we wish to know whether aspirin lowers fever we need first of all accurate thermometers to measure fever. Then, we need a group of febrile patients to study. Next, since we know that fever is usually a transitory rather than a perma-

From Leon Eisenberg, "The Role of Drugs in Treating Disturbed Children," *Children*, Vol. 2, No. 4, 1964, pp. 167–173, U.S. Department of Health, Education, and Welfare.

nent condition, we need an experimental design that permits us to discriminate between a drug effect and a "natural" return of the patient's temperature to normal levels. This might be accomplished by having matched groups of patients, one treated by aspirin and one untreated, or perhaps one treated by aspirin and one treated by a second drug. But hold! What does the word "matched" mean in this context?

We know before we start the experiment that the fevers of a cold, of pneumonia, or malignancy, and of brain injury differ from one another in their mechanisms, duration, and susceptibility to modification. Furthermore, the course of the same disease differs in young and older patients; also, if other treatments are administered, these may influence the course of the fever.

Thus, a proper experimental design will require that the control and experimental patient groups be equivalent on those variables known to influence the phenomenon under study: in this case, the variables include diagnosis, age, other treatments, and other factors such as severity of condition and duration of illness. Moreover, we have to assume that other variables not known at the time of the study may be important. Since we cannot match patients on unknown factors, we attempt to take this into account by the random assignment of patients to one or the other group.

With these elementary conditions fulfilled, we must now include a sufficiently large and representative sample of patients to permit the meaning of any obtained differences between groups to be subjected to statistical analyses. These are simply mathematical procedures that enable us to determine how often the observed difference might be likely to arise by chance alone.

Again, the word "representative" requires attention. If we are to have any confidence that our treatment is useful for certain diseases, then we need to be reasonably sure that our sample is representative of patients with the diseases under study. For example, if they were all adults, we would not know whether the findings would hold true for children—indeed, for aspirin we would get quite different results.

Perhaps this simple model will illustrate the ingredients of a well-planned drug study: specification of the phenomenon to be studied; accurate instruments to measure the phenomenon; control for subject variables likely to influence outcome; random assignment to treatment groups; numbers sufficient to permit statistical analysis of findings; and a representative study population.

Effects of Expectation

But we have thus far not considered a major element in drug studies particularly relevant in psychopharmacology—the psychological effect of administering medication upon both the patient and the physician. We have all had the experience, when ill, of beginning to feel better once the doctor arrived, even before treatment began. Countless studies have demonstrated, both with objective signs (blood pressure, heart rate, skin lesions, and so forth) as well as with subjective symptoms (depression, anxiety, pain), that the expectation of a beneficial effect is often in itself sufficient to cause striking improvement.

When the medication is given to a child, it may influence him psychologically in one of two ways or both: (1) directly through his own expectations; (2) indirectly through altered parental behavior generated by anticipation of change in the child. Also, the physician or technician who judges the response may read into it results in keeping with the expected outcome. This is not "cheating"; the bias is usually outside the observer's awareness. Consequently, special precautions are necessary to keep from the patient and the doctor knowledge of the medication the patient is taking. This is done by giving a placebo, an inert substance made to resemble closely the active drug. The record of which patient is getting the drug and which the placebo is kept coded and is not revealed until all results have been scored. Such an experiment is termed "double blind.". . .

Principles of Drug Treatment

Our observations have led us to the following principles:

1. *Drugs can be useful agents in managing pediatric psychiatric disorders when chosen appropriately and applied with discrimination.* They can control symptoms not readily managed by other means and can facilitate psychotherapy by allaying symptoms that disrupt learning. If they are not the panaceas portrayed in advertisements, neither are they the poisons claimed by their foes.

2. *Skill in using drugs requires knowledge of their pharmacologic properties and sensitivity to their*

psychologic significance.[1] Every drug study reveals the potency of placebo effects—benefits occurring from relationship with physician and from positive expectations of patients. These effects can be used to potentiate pharmacologic results by recognizing that the prescription of medication is an important communication to the patient and his family; contrariwise, they can have a negative impact if the physician regards drugs solely as weapons to impose control or as measures of desperation.

3. *No drug should be employed without firm indications for its use, without careful control of the patient, and without due precautions against toxicity.* With any potent drug toxicity is inevitable; to justify its use the severity of the condition and the likelihood of benefit must outweigh the possible toxicity. Toxicity studies on adults cannot be safely extrapolated to children because of differences in the immature and developing organism; clinical decisions must be based on data from pediatric studies.

4. *An old drug is to be preferred to a new drug unless evidence of superiority for the latter is clear.* This principle of pharmacologic conservatism is based upon the fact that unexpected toxicity from a new agent may be apparent only after prolonged experience with it. This is not pharmacologic nihilism. Drugs can make a decisive difference in treatment, but their very potency commends us not to use them lightly.

5. *Drugs should be used no longer than necessary.* Dosage should be reduced periodically, with the goal of ending treatment if symptoms do not return on lower dosage.

6. *Dosage must be individualized.* Each person is metabolically unique. Undertreatment as well as overtreatment can result in erroneous conclusions about unsuitability of a particular medication for a particular patient.

7. *The use of drugs does not relieve physician of responsibility for seeking to identify and eliminate the factors causing or aggravating the psychiatric disorder.* All currently available psychopharmacologic agents treat symptoms not diseases. Symptomatic relief is not to be disparaged. But to prescribe drugs for a child whose symptoms stem from correctable social, familial, biological, or psychological disturbance without attempting to alter the factors causing the symptoms is a disservice to the child.

There is no assumption here that psychotherapy is necessarily any more of a specific than drug therapy. It, too, has symptomatic and nonspecific effects; exacting proof of its efficiency remains to be provided. It, too, can act as an anodyne if not accompanied by searching efforts to correct the untoward life stresses acting upon the youngster. The justification for psychotherapy appears to lie in its possibilities for modifying learned unhealthy behavior patterns. However, the patient may become accessible to psychotherapy only after the acuteness of his symptoms has been diminished by pharmacologic methods. It should be emphasized that control of symptoms by drugs is not an end in itself; symptom control provides a climate in which the patient can learn new and more effective patterns for coping with his environment.

Drugs have a definite but limited role in the treatment of disturbed behavior. Medical evaluation of new drugs seems to follow a time sequence characterized by: early enthusiasm, growing criticism and awareness of toxicity, premature calls for discard, and final sobriety with moderate agreement on indications and dangers. Drugs are neither the passport to a brave new world nor the gateway to hell. With thoughtful selection, careful regulation of dosage, and close scrutiny for toxicity, they add a significant element to a total plan of patient care.

Article Footnote

---

1.   B. Fish, Drug Theory in Child Psychiatry: Psychological Aspects. *Comprehensive Psychiatry* (February 1960 and August 1960).

Chapter 3 Footnotes

1. **Theodore Leventhal and Gerald Weinberger,** "Evaluation of a Large-Scale Brief Therapy Program for Children," *American Journal of Orthopsychiatry,* vol. 45, no. 1 (January 1975): 119–133.

2. **Lenore Love et al.,** *Troubled Children: Their Families, Schools and Treatment* (New York: John Wiley & Sons, 1974).

3. "The Psycho-Analytic Study of the Child" (International Universities Press).

4. **Helen Leland Witmer, ed.,** *Psychiatric Interviews with Children* (Cambridge: Harvard University Press, 1946).

5. **Erik Erikson,** *Childhood and Society* (New York: W.W. Norton, 1950); *Martin Luther, A Study in Identity* (New York: W.W. Norton, 1961).

6. **Virginia Axline,** *Play Therapy* (Boston: Houghton-Mifflin, 1947).

7. **Fritz Redl and David Wineman,** *The Aggressive Child* (Glencoe, Ill: Free Press, 1953).

8. **Fritz Redl,** *How We Deal With Children* (New York: Glencoe, 1968).

9. **Bruno Bettelheim,** *Love Is Not Enough* (Glencoe, Ill.: Free Press, 1950).

10. Two new interesting approaches are worth examining: For elementary age, a school approach is presented by Rose:

Sheldon D. Rose, *Treating Children in Groups.*

For the secondary level, Brendtro:

Larry K. Brendtro and Harry J. Vorrath, *Positive Peer Culture: Use of Direct Interaction Approaches with Adolescent Delinquents* (Chicago: Aldine Publishing Co., 1974).

4

What Kinds of Schools and Programs Are Provided?

Once a child is identified as having learning and behavior problems, educational recommendations usually include a modified educational program. The biggest problem confronting the schools is not formulating such a recommendation, but carrying it out. Finding the right educational and therapeutic setting for a child with severe educational and emotional problems is a search even Sherlock Holmes would find difficult. Securing an appropriate placement is a result of luck and the social influence of race, money, and parental status. Attempts to rectify these biases by legal action against public school systems and mental health agencies continue to have a marked influence on the kind and quantity of special education services for troubled children.

The next article, by Weintraub and Abeson, is an excellent overview of several basic special education issues that are being determined, not by professionals or research data, but by court action. This article describes the first steps in a national movement to obtain legal rights for handicapped children by forcing public schools and local governments to assume the responsibility of providing suitable education for all children.

Appropriate Education for All Handicapped Children: A Growing Issue

Frederick J. Weintraub
Alan R. Abeson

In these days, it is doubtful that any child may reasonably be expected to succeed in life if he is denied the opportunity of an education. Such an opportunity, where the state has undertaken to pro-

From the *Syracuse Law Review.* Copyright 1972 by Syracuse University College of Law. Reprinted by permission.

vide it, is a right which must be made available to all on equal terms.[1]

With these words the Supreme Court of the United States ruled illegal the provision of educational services to any child on a basis unequal to that provided any other child. That historic 1954 decision focused on the elimination of racial segregation in the nation's public education programs. The same words have relevance today, but are being seen in recent judicial decisions to affirm the rights of another segregated group of children, the handicapped, to an equal education. . . .

In *Mills v. Board of Education*, the parents and guardians of seven District of Columbia children brought a class action suit against the Board of Education of the District, the Department of Human Resources, and the mayor for failure to provide all children with a publicly supported education.

The plaintiff children ranged in age from seven to sixteen and were alleged by the public schools to present the following types of problems that led to the denial of their opportunity for an education: slightly brain damaged, hyperactive behavior, epileptic and mentally retarded, and mentally retarded with an orthopedic handicap. Three children resided in public, residential institutions with no education program. The others lived with their families and when denied entrance to programs were placed on a waiting list for tuition grants to obtain a private educational program. However, in none of these cases were tuition grants provided.

Also at issue was the manner in which the children were denied entrance to or were excluded from public education programs. Specifically, the complaint said that

plaintiffs were so excluded without a formal determination of the basis for their exclusion and without provision for periodic review of their status. Plaintiff children merely have been labeled as behavior problems, emotionally disturbed, or hyperactive.

Further, it was pointed out that

the procedures by which plaintiffs were excluded or suspended from public school are arbitrary and do not conform to the due process requirements of the fifth amendment. Plaintiffs are excluded and suspended without: (a) notification as to a hearing, the nature of offense or status, any alternative or interim publicly supported education; (b) opportunity for representation, a hearing by an impartial arbiter, the presentation of witnesses; and (c) opportunity for periodic review of the necessity for continued exclusion or suspension.

The history of events that transpired between the city and the attorneys for the plaintiffs immediately prior to the filing of the suit demonstrated the Board of Education's legal and moral responsibility to educate all excluded children, and although they were provided with numerous opportunities to provide services to plaintiff children, the Board failed to do so.

On December 20, 1971, the court issued a stipulated agreement and order that provided for the following:

1. The named plaintiffs must be provided with a publicly supported education by January 3, 1972.

2. The defendants by January 3, 1972, had to provide a list showing (for every child of school age not receiving a publicly supported education because of suspension, expulsion, exclusion or any other denial of placement): the name of the child's parents or guardian; the child's name, age, address, and telephone number; the date that services were officially denied; a breakdown of the list on the basis of the "alleged causal characteristics for such nonattendance"; and finally, the total number of such children.

3. By January 3, the defendants were also to initiate efforts to identify all other members of the class not previously known. The defendants were to provide the plaintiffs' attorneys with the names, addresses, and telephone numbers of the additionally identified children by February 1, 1972.

4. The plaintiffs and defendants were to consider the selection of a master to deal with special questions arising out of this order.

The defendants failed to comply with the order resulting in plaintiffs filing, on January 21, 1972, a motion for summary judgment and a proposed order and decree for implementation of the proposed judgment.

On August 1, 1972, U.S. District Judge Joseph Waddy issued such an order and decree providing:

1. A declaration of the constitutional right of all children regardless of any exceptional condition or handicap to a publicly supported education.

2. A declaration that the defendant's rules, policies, and practices which excluded children without a provision for adequate and immediate

alternative educational services and the absence of prior hearing and review of placement procedures denied the plaintiffs and the class rights of due process and equal protection of the law.

In commenting on compulsory school education provisions the court pointed out that

failure of a parent to comply with Section 31-201 constitutes a criminal offense. D.C. Code 31-207. The Court need not belabor the fact that requiring parents to see that their children attend school under pain of criminal penalties presupposes that an educational opportunity will be made available to the children. The Board of Education is required to make such opportunity available.

The defendants claimed in response to the complaint that it would be impossible for them to afford plaintiffs the relief sought unless the Congress appropriated needed funds or funds were diverted from other educational services for which they had been appropriated. The court responded:

The defendants are required by the Constitution of the United States, the District of Columbia Code, and their own regulations to provide a publicly-supported education for these 'exceptional' children. Their failure to fulfill this clear duty to include and retain these children in the public school system, or otherwise provide them with publicly-supported education, and their failure to afford them due process hearing and periodical review, cannot be excused by the claim that there are insufficient funds. In Goldberg v. Kelly, 397 U.S. 254 (1969) the Supreme Court, in a case that involved the right of a welfare recipient to a hearing before termination of his benefits, held that Constitutional rights must be afforded citizens despite the greater expense involved. . . . Similarly the District of Columbia's interest in educating the excluded children clearly must outweigh its interest in preserving its financial resources. If sufficient funds are not available to finance all of the services and programs that are needed and desirable in the system, then the available funds must be expended equitably in such a manner that no child is entirely excluded from a publicly supported education consistent with his needs and ability to benefit therefrom. The inadequacies of the District of

Columbia Public School System, whether occasioned by insufficient funding or administrative inefficiency, certainly cannot be permitted to bear more heavily on the 'exceptional' or handicapped child than on the normal child.

Regarding the issue of appointment of a master the court commented,

Despite the defendants' failure to abide by the provisions of the Court's previous orders in this case and despite the defendants' continuing failure to provide an education for these children, the Court is reluctant to arrogate to itself the responsibility of administering this or any other aspect of the Public School System of the District of Columbia through the vehicle of a special master. Nevertheless, inaction or delay on the part of the defendants, or failure by the defendants to implement the judgment and decree herein within the time specified therein will result in the immediate appointment of a special master to oversee and direct such implementation under the direction of this Court.

At the time of writing there are many cases before the courts on right to an education for handicapped children. Several of these cases are bringing interesting new dimensions to the issue. In *Association for Mentally Ill Children v. Greenblatt*,[2] plaintiffs have attacked the placement system as "arbitrary" and "irrational" since some children are placed while others remain on waiting lists. In *Kivell v. Nemointin*,[3] in Fairfield County, Connecticut, the Superior Court ordered the Stamford Board of Education to pay $13,000 in back tuition costs to the parents of a handicapped child who obtained private education for their child after the public school was unable to provide an appropriate program.

In the ruling, the court said it would

frown upon any unilateral action by parents in sending their children to other facilities, if a program is filed by a local board of education and is accepted and approved by the state board of education. Then it is the duty of the parents to accept the program . . . a refusal by parents in such a situation will not entitle their child to any benefits from this court.

Other avenues of legal change in assuring the

right to an education are occurring. Increasingly, attorney generals are being confronted by the issue and ruling favorably. On December 22, 1971, the Attorney General of the State of New Mexico issued an opinion upholding handicapped childrens' rights to an education.[4] He noted:

 ·   *In providing equal learning opportunities for all children, the state, in our opinion, is required to offer equal educational opportunities to all children in the state. Thus, children who qualify for special education are entitled to a free public school education. . . .*

 Obviously, if these children are entitled to the same free education as all other children, they are also entitled to free textbooks and transportation, as long as free textbooks and transportation are offered to all other children. The state's obligation is to provide equal educational opportunities to all children in the state, regardless of their physical or mental capabilities. . . .

 Section 77-11-3.2, supra (Chapter 109, Laws of 1971) refers to the availability of state financial support as a condition of offering special education programs. Because the state has the obligation of offering equal opportunities to all children regardless of learning ability this condition cannot be presumed valid. In the past this phrase has been interpreted as meaning only state financial support directly earmarked for special education, but under the reasoning of this Opinion, the condition can be tied only to the total availability of state funds for free public school education.

Another active avenue for legal change has been state legislatures. During 1971, 899 bills promoting education of the handicapped were introduced in state legislatures; of these 237 were enacted into law.[5] Approximately seventy percent of the states have enacted laws mandating educational programs for the handicapped,[6] a substantial increase from the less than fifty percent of several years ago. In 1971, the Council for Exceptional Children published a set of model state laws for the elimination of exclusion provisions in compulsory attendance laws and the establishment of comprehensive educational services for the handicapped.[7] On April 25, 1972, the major provisions of the model were signed into law in Tennessee.

Former U.S. Commissioner of Education Sidney P. Marland set in 1971 the goal of full educational opportunity for all handicapped children by 1980.[8] While this commitment is laudable, and as the movements noted above imply, attainable, it assumes that these children have no present rights.

The right to an education is not something that educators, politicians or the public grant when it is convenient. Certainly, it will take some time to develop the needed programs and personnel, but the right to an education can not be postponed and must be guarded with judicial overview.[9] For law is the only means that minorities have to assure appropriate behavior from the majority, when such behavior can not be expected.[10]

The case of Harris described earlier represents misclassification. As a result Harris was incorrectly and unnecessarily placed in a special education program.

There has been, since 1970, an increasing amount of litigation questioning the placement of children in special education on the basis of evaluation instruments which are prejudical to the children on the basis of spoken language, cultural background and normative standardization. Much of the logic utilized in these cases is derived from *Hobson v. Hansen*.[11] In ruling that the "tracking" educational placement system utilized by the Washington, D.C. Public Schools was illegal, Judge Skelly Wright considered the evaluation procedures the district utilized.

[E]vidence shows that the method by which track assignments are made depends essentially on standardized aptitude tests which, although given on a system-wide basis, are completely inappropriate for use with a large segment of the student body. Because these tests are standardized primarily on and are relevant to a white middle class group of students, they produce inaccurate and misleading test scores when given to lower class and Negro students. As a result, rather than being classified according to ability to learn, these students are in reality being classified according to their socio-economic or racial status, or—more precisely—according to environmental and psychological factors which have nothing to do with innate ability.[12]

In January, 1970 a suit was filed in the District Court of Northern California on behalf of nine Mexican-American students, ages eight to thirteen.[13] The children came from homes in which Spanish was the major language spoken. All were in classes for the mentally retarded in Monterey County, California. Their IQs ranged from thirty to seventy-two with a mean score of sixty-three and one-half. When they were retested in Spanish seven of the nine scored higher than the IQ cutoff for mental retardation, and the lowest score was three points below the cutoff line. The average gain was fifteen points.

The plaintiffs charged that the testing procedures utilized for placement were prejudicial because the tests placed heavy emphasis on verbal skills requiring facility with the English language, the questions were culturally biased, and the tests were standardized on white, native born Americans. The plaintiffs further pointed out that in "Monterrey County, Spanish surname students constitute about eighteen and one-half percent of the student population, but nearly one-third of the children in educable mentally retarded classes."

Studies by the California State Department of Education corroborated the inequity. In 1966-67, of 85,000 children in classes for the educable mentally retarded in California, children with Spanish surnames comprised twenty-six percent while they accounted for only thirteen percent of the total school population.

The plaintiffs sought a class action on behalf of all bilingual Mexican-American children then in classes for the educable mentally retarded and all such children in danger of inappropriate placement in such classes. On February 5, 1970, a stipulated agreement order was signed by both parties. The order required that:

1. Children are to be tested in their primary language. Interpreters may be used when a bilingual examiner is not available.

2. Mexican-American and Chinese children in classes for the educable mentally retarded are to be retested and evaluated.

3. Special efforts are to be extended to aid misplaced children readjust to regular classrooms.

4. The state will undertake immediate efforts to develop and standardize an appropriate IQ test.

As a result of *Diana* the U.S. Department of Health, Education and Welfare's office for Civil Rights issued a memorandum to school districts with substantial bilingual populations.[14] The memo informed the districts that they would be in violation of Title VI of the Civil Rights Act if students whose predominant language is other than English were assigned to classes for mentally retarded on the basis of criteria which essentially measured or evaluated English language skills.

Since *Diana* several cases have been filed on behalf of other minority groups primarily blacks and Indians. Only one, *Larry P. v. Riles*,[15] has reached some form of judicial decision. This class action suit was filed in late November 1971, on behalf of six black, elementary school aged children attending classes in the San Francisco Unified School District. It was alleged that they had been inappropriately classified as educable mentally retarded and placed and retained in classes for such children. The complaint argued that the children were not mentally retarded, but rather the victims of a testing procedure which fails to recognize their unfamiliarity with the white middle class cultural background and which ignores the learning experiences which they may have had in their homes. The defendants included state and local school officials and board members.

It is alleged that misplacement in classes for the mentally retarded carries a stigma and "a life sentence of illiteracy." Statistical information indicated that in the San Francisco Unified School District, as well as the state, a disproportionate number of black children are enrolled in programs for the retarded. It is further pointed out that even though code and regulatory procedure regarding identification, classification, and placement of the mentally retarded were changed to be more effective, inadequacies in the processes still exist.

The plaintiffs asked the court to order the defendants to do the following:

1. Evaluate or assess plaintiffs and other black children by using group or individual ability or intelligence tests which properly account for the cultural background and experiences of the children to whom such tests are administered;

2. Restrict the placement of the plaintiffs and other black children in classes for the mentally retarded on the basis of results of culturally discriminatory tests and testing procedures;

3. Prevent the retention of plaintiffs and other black children now in classes for the mentally retarded unless the children are immediately re-evaluated and annually retested by means which take into account cultural background;

4. Place plaintiffs into regular classrooms with children of comparable age and provide them with intensive and supplemental individual training thereby enabling plaintiffs and those similarly situated to achieve at the level of their peers as rapidly as possible;

5. Remove from the school records of these children any and all indications that they were/are mentally retarded or in a class for the mentally retarded and ensure that individual children not be identified by the results of individual or group IQ tests;

6. Take any action necessary to bring the distribution of black children in classes for the mentally retarded into close proximity with the distri-

bution of blacks in the total population of the school districts;

7. *Recruit and employ a sufficient number of black and other minority psychologists and psychometrists in local school districts, on the admissions and planning committees of such districts, and as consultants to such districts so the tests will be interpreted by persons adequately prepared to consider the cultural background of the child. Further, the State Department of Education should be required in selecting and authorizing tests to be administered to school children throughout the state, to consider the extent to which the testing development companies utilized personnel with minority ethnic backgrounds and experiences in the development of culturally relevant tests;*

8. *Declare pursuant to the Fourteenth Amendment to the United States Constitution, the Civil Rights Act of 1964, and the Elementary and Secondary Education Act and Regulations, that the current assignment of plaintiffs and other black students to California mentally retarded classes resulting in excessive segregation of such children into these classes is unlawful and unconstitutional and may not be justified by administration of the currently available IQ tests which fail to properly account for the cultural background and experience of black children.*

On June 20, 1972 the court enjoined the San Francisco Unified School District

from placing black students in classes for the educable mentally retarded on the basis of criteria, which places primary relevance on the results of IQ tests as they are currently administered, if the consequence of use of such criteria is racial imbalance in the composition of such classes.

Legal activity may in fact make it possible for handicapped children to receive their constitutional right to an education. "Education for all" is a relatively new concept for the American educational system although it has been emerging for almost a century. The system has long believed in equality, but equality meaning sameness. As Bedau notes "Persons have (received) an equal distribution, equal treatment or equal rights, etc., if and only if they have (received) the same distribution, treatment, rights, etc."[16] Tom Watson, the Georgia populist, epitomized this concept best when he stated, "close no entrance to the poorest, the weakest,

the humblest. Say to ambition everywhere, 'the field is clear, the contest fair; come and win your share if you can!'"[17]

Even today many judicial decisions such as *Hobson v. Hansen*[18] and *Serrano v. Priest*[19] still define equality on a "sameness" doctrine, equal resources to "children whose needs are unequal." Such a philosophy may have been appropriate for a society that was based on family economic production that could absorb those who could not compete equally in the nation's economic system. Today, however, the education of a child is a community concern, for if he is not given skills sufficient for economic participation then he will become dependent upon the community.

If our society reveres economic participation and independence and if education is the major societal process for achieving these goals then a new concept of educational equality is needed for the age in which we live. Coleman defines such a concept as "equality of results given different individual inputs."[20] This would imply that equality exists when students, no matter what their entry behaviors or conditions may be, successfully achieve educational objectives. More simply, equality is achieved when all children learn to read, regardless of the differentiated resources committed to that purpose.

The basic flaw in this concept is that it assumes that all children have innate capabilities for common educational attainments. Thus, using Watson's analogy we need only provide crutches, or other remedial assistance to assure that all children complete the same race. The Coleman definition needs modification to be relevant to the plight of handicapped children. Educational equality should be defined as equality of access to different resources to attain different individual goals.

It is this concept of equality that is now being utilized by the courts in right to education suits. The court in *PARC* ordered the Commonwealth of Pennsylvania to provide every retarded person between the ages of six and twenty-one "*access* to a free public program of education and training *appropriate to his learning* capacities."[21] In *Mills* the court ordered that the District of Columbia "shall provide plaintiffs . . . with a publicly supported education *suited to their plaintiffs' needs. . . .*"[22]

The burden is thus on the educational system to assure that the education program provided to each child is appropriate to the child's needs. The question facing schools is how is appropriateness determined? Certainly the issue has many professional considerations, but the courts and other governmental branches are beginning to exert their influence in the decision making process.

In June 1971, the court in *PARC* stipulated and ordered the Commonwealth of Pennsylvania to place into regulations twenty-three due process steps to be implemented by all school districts. The decree stated specifically that no child thought to be mentally retarded could be denied admission to a public school program or have his educational status changed without first being accorded prior notice and the opportunity of a due process hearing. "Change in educational status" was defined

> *as assignment or re-assignment, based on the fact that the child is mentally retarded or thought to be mentally retarded, to one of the following educational assignments: regular education, special education, or to no assignment, or from one type of special education to another.* [23]

The hearings are to be conducted by persons independent of the school district. Parents are to be informed of their right to be represented by counsel, an independent evaluation of their child to be provided free of charge if necessary, examine all relevant records, cross examine witnesses, obtain a transcript of the hearing and appeal the decision of the hearing. It is interesting to note that the court felt so strongly about the right to due process that the order was issued before the court considered the children's right to an education.

In *Mills*[24] the court reaffirmed the *PARC* due process principles and extended their availability placement procedures for all exceptional children. In addition the court established the right to a full due process hearing before a child may be suspended from school for two or more days.

The movement to due process is seen by some educators as a substantial threat to the stability of the education system. Their main concern is that they believe that it turns total decision making over to the parents. This is not the case. But it does provide to the child and parents the opportunity to have status in the decision making process. All that due process demands of schools is that recommended educational programs be defended in an advocacy setting on the basis of appropriateness to a child's individually determined educational need.

In this age of growing accountability demands on public education, the due process placement concept may prove to be of benefit to the educator. Gallagher[25] has suggested that placement procedures lead to a formal contract between the school and the parent. The contract would specify the obligations of all parties, the educational objectives to be achieved, criteria for assessing their achievement, a timetable for evaluation, and procedures for renegotiating the contract. The purpose of education is to foster learning, not simply to provide programs. Thus appropriateness can only be finally determined if the prescribed learning actually occurs. This type of procedure should enable schools to avoid the situation found in *In Re Held.*[26] In this case a physically handicapped child was enrolled in the public school system for five years, three of which were in special education. During that period the child's reading level never exceeded that of an average first grade pupil. After a year in private school the child's reading skills increased by two grade levels. Thus, the court ordered the state and school district to pay the tuition for the child to attend a private, special school, on the basis that the child's intellectual potential and academic success could only be achieved in that setting.

Educating handicapped children has always been considered by the public educational system to be a "frill" to take care of after every other school need. The reasons used for the denial of educational services to handicapped children are many. They include such statements as the handicapped cannot learn, their presence in school will negatively affect the learning of normal children, these children make non-handicapped children and adults uncomfortable, the cost of their education is too great, and the teachers and facilities are in short supply. Most of these reasons are mere "wives tales." Those relating to the additional resources necessary are reality. Yet the advocacy of law is clear. Appropriate educational opportunity for handicapped children is a present right that must be provided.

Article Footnotes

1. Brown vs. Board of Education, 347 US, 483, 493 (1954).

2. Association for Mentally Ill Children v. Greenblatt, C.A. No. 71–3074-J (D. Mass. 1971).

3. Kivell v. Nemointin, No. 143913 (Fairfield Co., Conn. 1972).

4. New Mexico Attorney General's Opinion (NMAG 71–125) (1971).

5. State-Federal Clearinghouse for Exceptional Children, "Trends in State Legislation for the Education of Handicapped Children" (1972).

6.   Abeson, "Movement and Momentum: Government and the Education of Handicapped Children," 39 *Exceptional Children*, 63–6 (1972).

7.   F.J. Weintraub, State Law and the Education of Handicapped Children: Issues and Recommendations (1971), Council for Exceptional Children.

8.   Martin, "Individualism and Behaviorism as Future Trends in Evaluating Handicapped Children," 38 *Exceptional Children*, 517–25 (1972).

9.   Watson v. Memphis, 373 U.S. 526, 532–33 (1963).

10.   M. Berger, Equality by Statute: The Revolution in Civil Rights 1 (1967).

11.   Hobson v. Hansen, 269 F. Supp. 401 (D.D.C. 1967).

12.   *Id.* at 514.

13.   Diana v. State Board of Educ., C–70 37 RFR (N.D. Cal. 1970).

14.   Memorandum dated May 25, 1970 by Stanley Pottinger, Director of Health, Education and Welfare's Office for Civil Rights.

15.   Larry P. v. Riles, 41 U.S.L.W. 2033 (U.S. June 21, 1972).

16.   Bedan, "Equalitarianism and the Idea of Equality," *Equality* 7 (J. Pennock & J. Chapman eds. 1967).

17.   C. Woodward, *Tom Watson, Agrarian Rebel* (1958).

18.   Hobson v. Hansen, 269 F. Supp. 401 (D.D.C. 1967).

19.   Serrano v. Priest, 10 Cal. App.3d 1110, 487 P. 2d 1241, 89 Cal. Rptr. 345 (1970).

20.   Coleman, "The Concept of Equality of Educational Opportunity," 38 (1) *Harvard Educational Review* 17 (1968).

21.   Pennsylvania Ass'n. for Retarded Children v. Pennsylvania, 334 F. Supp. 1257, 1258-66 (E.D. Pa. 1971).

22.   Mills v. Board of Educ., C.A. No. 1939–71 (D.D.C. 1971) (emphasis added).

23.   Pennsylvania Ass'n. for Retarded Children v. Pennsylvania, 334 F. Supp. 1257 (E.D. Pa. 1971).

24.   Mills v. Board of Educ., C.A. No. 1939–71 (D.D.C. 1971).

25.   Gallagher, "The Special Education Contract for Mildly Handicapped Children," 38 *Exceptional Children*, 527–35 (1972).

26.   *In Re* Held. Nos. H-271 & H-10-71 (N.Y. Fam. Ct. 1971).

In the next article, Evelyn Deno suggests a strategy for increasing the capacity to integrate into the mainstream of education exceptional pupils by redefining the responsibilities of both special education and regular education and by increasing the role and power of the Educational Professions Development Act Program.

Strategies For Improvement of Educational Opportunities For Handicapped Children: Suggestions For Exploitation of EPDA* Potential

Evelyn Deno

One's view of the educational scene is unavoidably colored by personal experiences encountered in trying to deal with educational systems, whether this experience was accrued as a consumer of the system or as a professional trying to improve it. The view from my position is that education is a single continuum on which all children have a place where they should be educated as individuals rather than as parts of systems. The primary educational goal, to me, is to increase the educational mainstream's capacity to accommodate to differences in the individual characteristics that children bring to school learning-tasks. The burden of achieving this goal, consequently, rests with those of us who are concerned with the training of teachers for the classroom.

The second part of this paper contains five suggestions for achieving the goal through possibilities provided by the Special Education program of the Educational Professions Development Act (EPDA). Enacted by Congress in 1967, the Act provides an umbrella for the centralization of many programs concerned with the training of personnel for the schools. A priceless opportunity to integrate regular and special services more effectively is afforded by the requirement that a proportion of EPDA funds be used to enhance educational opportunities for the handicapped.

The Relation of Regular and Special Education

A first-order conviction born out of my experience as a teacher, child psychologist, special education

A monograph published and distributed through the University of Minnesota, Department of Audio-Visual Extension, 1971. Reprinted by permission.

*Educational Professions Development Act.

administrator, and consumer of the literature in the field is that whatever distinctions can be made between regular education and special education are mainly organizational and not substantive, that is, the manner in which learning experiences need to be presented is the main basis of distinction. Whatever learning principles apply to handicapped children apply to all children and end goals are the same in their most essential aspects.

Useless amounts of time and energy are wasted in trying to define for all time and all places what differentiates "regular" and "special" education when the definitional effort addresses to anything other than who is to be responsible for providing what *services*. It is my impression that administrators responsible for implementing whatever is "special" about special education seldom are confused on this point. They are well aware that what is "special" about special education is the delivery system and not the fundamental content of what is to be delivered or the purposes of delivery. Regular educators and academicians seem less certain.

Some special educators find unacceptable the distinction of their responsibility on the basis of the outside capabilities of the regular system. They cringe at the thought of defining their responsibilities as those that regular education rejects or fails to perform. They prefer to rest their identities as special educators on what they perceive to be more positive professional grounds.

This lack of understanding and agreement on boundaries of responsibility is one of the central difficulties standing in the way of better articulation between regular and special education services. In my opinion, *better coordination of regular and special education services is a primary need of our time if we hope to improve education for handicapped children. The EPDA program is in a most favorable position to promote this needed articulation.*

Improved coordination can be achieved only if the factors that make it difficult to mesh the two delivery systems are identified and directly attacked through a fully professional, problem-solving approach. The reasons why the two systems do not mesh to the greatest benefit of all children are understandable. They go back as far as society's original reasons for establishing compulsory public education and they are fed by the natural tendency of any organization to get rid of what makes attainment of its goals difficult and thereby creates discomfort within the structure. These conditions are exacerbated by the unrealistic goals we set for educational pursuits while, at the same time, we use the system to relieve a variety of social problems.

In asking regular education to be more accommodative to handicapped children, special educators are asking regular educators to work harder, at greater pain and cost, and with the prospect of less success per system effort, which is expended in terms of the criteria regular education and its supporting public commonly apply to measure system success. The special educators are making this request at a time when pressures are coming at school systems from every side to perform better and to take on more responsibility for solving social problems. Additional demands to stretch staff time and dollars are not likely to be welcome when demands are as extensive as they now are.

It is particularly hard to defend such a request after a long period in which regular teachers have been indoctrinated with the idea that children with special problems must have treatment by a specialist who is sanctioned by credentials to deal in depth with the kind of atypical behavior presented. A separate financial support system was made available for children defined as "special" under this conception. What we now must do, to some degree, is to unteach what we previously taught. Regular teachers need reason to have confidence in their ability to deal with the majority of the needs of children we previously defined as too "special" to be ministered to by a regular teacher. This confidence can only be accomplished by providing the teachers with the skills and teaching circumstances required to meet the children's needs.

Having found that most children conceived of as handicapped by traditional, medically-based, categorical criteria are probably better off in the regular educational mainstream than sidetracked into segregated special classes, special education needs to share with regular educators whatever expertise it may have acquired over the years or may yet generate through further experience and research. At the same time, it needs to gain better understanding of the potentialities of mainstream provisions. Neither regular nor special education can operate as a monolithic, stand-alone system if it hopes to achieve what is best for children.

The special education field must direct whatever forces it can muster to helping the regular system achieve the necessary understanding and tangible resources to become maximally accommodative to the needs of children who show different learning styles and, at the same time, to insure that specialized education facilities and appropriate treatment options will be available for those residual children who genuinely need special circumstances and methods outside mainstream provisions to maximize their learning. Special education has to organize itself for a double-pronged approach: direct service to children who cannot reasonably be accommodated in the educational mainstream and, working hand in hand with regular education, the development of mainstream technology and implementation mechanisms to improve the total enterprise. Regular educators cannot afford to ignore the richness of technology and curriculum opportunities emergent in mainstream education.

On this assumption, I recommend that we envision educational services on the kind of service continuum illustrated in Figure 1. The tapered design is used to indicate the considerable difference in the numbers of children anticipated at the different levels and to call attention to the fact that the system itself serves as a diagnostic filter. The most specialized facilities are likely to be needed by the fewest children on a long-term basis. Actual work with children provides the best diagnosis if it is thoughtfully conducted.

This organizational model can be applied to the development of special education services for all types of disability. It assumes that there will always be some children who require the help of specialists. It assumes that the characteristics of children who fall out of mainstream provisions will change continuously as mainstream provisions, medical practice, and social conditions change, because learning problems are presumed to be the product of the interaction between the child and the kind of "education" impinging on him at home, on the streets, and in school. Where regular education responsibilities should end and special education's should begin is definable only in terms of the individual case in its particular situation. Under such conditions role conflict is inevitable. What is need-

The Cascade System of Special Education Service

Level I	Children in regular classes, including those "handicapped" able to get along with regular class accommodations with or without medical or counseling supportive therapies	"out-patient" (Assignment of pupils governed by the school system)
Level II	Regular class attendance plus supplementary instructional	services
Level III	Part-time Special Class	
Level IV	Full-time Special Class	
Level V	Special Stations	
Level VI	Homebound	
Level VII	Instruction in hospital or domiciled settings "Noneducational": service (medical and welfare care and supervision)	"in-patient" programs (Assignment of children to facilities governed by health or welfare agencies)

From Evelyn Deno in *Exceptional Children*, vol. 39, no. 495. Reprinted with permission of the Council for Exceptional Children. Copyright 1973 by the Council for Exceptional Children.

ed is will and mechanisms to solve the problem of who should do what, not tighter role-boundary definitions.

The cascade model assumes that children are seldom all able or all handicapped. They more frequently present their teachers with a marble cake of aptitudes and dysfunctions that cannot be adequately described by categorical classification of children on a "he is or he isn't" basis. The organizational model recognizes that children need to be programmed individually, that the only fundamentally meaningful class, for educational purposes, contains an N of one.

This conception provides language and pictures relations in a way that may help to clarify some of the problems to be expected in trying to blend regular and special education services. It places a human bridge in the person of a resource or support teacher at the touch point where the regular and special education systems must mesh if children are not to be caught in the crunch of systems proceeding according to rigidly defined outreach limits. By promoting compatible instructional approaches and more effective case management mechanisms, EPDA can provide critically needed leadership to articulate and synthesize regular and special education resources for the benefit of all children.

Certain central problems are obvious. For one thing, the bureaucratic approach to decision-making is inadequate for the task of making the kinds of decisions that are necessary if an educational system is to honor the fact that a child cannot be classified as either special education's child or regular education's child except in terms of specific teaching objectives cast over a very limited time span. When treatment decisions involve technical judgment and are valid for only limited time periods, the school administrator cannot be expected to have either the omnipotent wisdom or the time to make them in the manner and at the moment they are needed. Just as the field of medicine now finds that it may have advanced too unthinkingly down the specialization path leaving a vacuum of resources at the primary physician level where the discrimination potential ought to be, so has education failed to provide people to be first-level discriminators of need in educational settings. Unlike medicine, which lost the generalist resources it once had to the more prestigious and higher-paying medical specialties, the educational system has kept its general practitioners, that is, its regular classroom teachers. But it disarmed them. They have been drilled into believing that they are only qualified to do as they are told by an administrator or specialist and that they should not try to diagnose or deal with behaviors they are not "certified" to understand and treat. The problem involved here is not peculiar to education, as noted by such writers as Bennis (1969, 1970) and others.

To help us out of the corner into which we have painted ourselves, EPDA might undertake such projects as are discussed in the following section.

Potential EPDA Projects

1. EPDA might sponsor a conference to identify critical factors contributing to the present discontinuity in regular and special education services and to develop recommendations on the directions in which EPDA might invest to promote improvement of understanding and coordinated service delivery.

There are many reasons why regular and special educators find it hard to synchronize their efforts. In spite of the fact that both programs claim similar objectives, the facts are that in practice the two programs have manifested critical differences in emphasis that make it difficult to mesh them.

Both regular and special education programs espouse a humanistic point of view that defines the primary function of the schools as cultivation of the maximum independence of each individual and maximum realization of each child's potential. In fact, neither regular nor special educators have seriously assumed that this ideal could be accomplished. Though regular educators embrace personalized, humanistic, educational goals, the success of the educational system has been evaluated primarily in terms of how useful the system's products are to other institutions of society, that is, how well they fill the roles defined by the social order for its citizens. In practice, schools have given priority in emphasis to this managerial function rather than to the humanistic value verbalized as their primary mission (Green, 1969).

Though special educators will sometimes argue for investment in special education and rehabilitation services on the grounds that taxpayer money will be saved in the long run, humanistic goals are emphasized whether the child is likely to achieve social independence or not. It is possible that the tendency to be sympathetic toward the handicapped and expect little of them has made it more possible for special education to maintain a more fully humanistic orientation. Dedication to this humanistic, best-for-the-individual orientation often creates dissonance in relation to the norm-referenced regular education system.

In keeping with its managerial orientation and the limits of the resources the public provides for the schools, regular education's evaluation criteria and instructional approaches have been aggregate rather than distributive in their focus. The overriding concern has been how well the system is doing "on the average." Regular education's resources have permitted little more than a mass-education approach.

The special education system came into being to serve a distributive function. Its mission was to bring educational opportunity to children denied rightful opportunity under the aggregate approach. To this day its major concerns are distributive—getting the right kinds of opportunity to children who are hard to reach educationally.

Regular education is being challenged as never before on the question of whether it is distributing educational opportunities fairly—not just to those children who learn easily but to those children who do not fit aggregate-approach assumptions. Regular education is increasingly trying to meet the kinds of personalized instruction goals that special education has pursued for some time but it is questionable whether the public is really willing to support individualized, humanistic, and equal educational opportunity for all children. Which children can learn under aggregate mainstream conditions and which must be given a more individually-tailored opportunity if they are to survive socially remains a difficult distributional question.

Differences in how clientele are categorized contribute to discontinuity and conflict. The regular education system has historically organized itself along subject-matter lines geared to norm-derived, age-grade expectancies. Special education has organized itself along medically-based, handicap-category lines in which subject matter objectives are considered subordinate to or at most instrumental in achievement of humanistic goals. This difference in approach creates slippage where responsibilities meet at the regular-special education boundary line. Tests and other assessment devices customarily employed by schools to determine special education's clientele are seldom capable of making the translation from regular education's age-grade and subject-matter frame of reference to special education's personalized objectives and the identified learning styles of individual children. Unless we can achieve a common frame of reference, constructive dialogue will remain difficult to attain and curriculum cripples will continue to be conceived of as constitutional cripples.

2. EPDA might sponsor stipend support and inservice training of regular curriculum consultants and regular classroom teachers in the kinds of content provided for teachers training to work with emotionally-disturbed or learning-disabled children. One would guess that regular classroom teachers, curriculum consultants, and others who received such training—including well-supervised practicum experience with severely disturbed children, learning-disabled children, and other kinds of handicapped children—would emerge as more skillful and accommodating teachers for all children.

During the period required for the mainstream to become more accommodating to the learning needs of individual children, there will continue to be fall-out children who need special help and regular class teachers who need continuous on-the-spot consultative support. We believe teachers talk teacher language and possibly understand teacher's problems more readily than do "outside specialists." The Level II (see Figure I) S.L.P.R. (Special Learning Problems Resource) teacher can render both direct service to fall-out children and continuous, consultative service to regular teachers to help them expand their ability to serve such children. If EPDA funds can be used to help the regular class teacher acquire background that gives her better understanding of what the S.L.P.R. teacher is seeking to accomplish, communication between the regular and special teacher will be facilitated and regular and special education services are likely to be better articulated.

In developing the S.L.P.R. model we may dream that such a teacher might not need to exist some day when more effective regular education systems are attained. The basic purpose of this role is educational improvement, not another self-perpetuating delivery system.

3. EPDA might sponsor with BEH, the National Institutes of Health, the American Psychological Association, and/or other interested agencies a conference or systematic study to determine (a) how behavioral science input is best fed into the decision processes of educational systems to produce desirable change and, relatedly, (b) whether support for the training of school psychologists should be provided below the doctoral level. If so, there should be determination of which federal agency should provide scholarship support for subdoctoral school psychology programs. It seems that no federal program is now willing or able to assume responsibility for support of the subdoctoral training of school psychologists.

4. Support opportunities (scholarships, special study institutes, etc.) should be considered for regular education leadership personnel (administrators, curriculum specialists, etc.) to take work in the special education field, and to provide inservice training for special educators that taps what regular educators can contribute from their expertise to develop better curricula and methods for handicapped children. Special education funding patterns foster excessive ingrowing of special education training and service development. Special education sorely needs to open its doors to the richness in the regular education curriculum domain.

5. EPDA might combine with BEH to support projects directed to developing more feasible strategies for serving handicapped children in the educational mainstream. If more handicapped children are to be served in the mainstream, support funds may need different channeling.

One of the efforts to chart the future services of the field is found in *Exceptional Children in Regular Classrooms*;[1] the whole volume is concerned with the problems of integrating special children in regular classrooms. Two issues that need further discussion are labeling and mainstreaming.

Labeling

The growing argument against labeling exceptional children has reached the hearts of many professional and lay groups in special education. Labeling pupils "emotionally disturbed" or "mentally retarded" sets them apart from others and encourages isolation and rejection by peers and school personnel. It perpetuates a self-fulfilling prophecy in which the pupil learns to behave according to his label, and it leads to fragmented services, so that pupils with multiple handicaps are deprived of special services. Occasionally, students with comparable skills are denied regular class placement because of their labels, which are not predictive of the type of instruction a student needs, necessitating special classes that are extremely expensive to maintain in many communities. A definitive work on labeling is *Issues in the Classification of Children.*[2]

Discarding labels would solve these problems, but it would create several new ones. For example, how will funds be raised for exceptional children if specific needs and services cannot be identified? How will special educators communicate with other medical and psychological professionals who use these categories? Is it possible the issue is not one of labeling, but rather deciding what happens to a child when he is placed in a setting? Frequently, a new field tends to overreact to conflict. Its battle cry might be, "When in doubt, throw it out!" Because labeling is an important issue, the Department of Health, Education, and Welfare awarded Nicholas Hobbs a major grant to study the classification system of exceptional children. This project has resulted in a report covering all aspects of labeling, from theoretical issues to specific recommendations for federal policies.[3]

Mainstreaming or Mayhem

Mainstreaming has become a way of creating social change in public schools. The purpose of mainstreaming is not only to return more exceptional children to the classroom, but also to force the educational system to be more responsive to children's developmental variations.

There has been a great deal of resistance to mainstreaming. Institutional resistance may be active or passive, but its goal is always to crush any innovative program that seeks to change the system's ongoing values and programs. The la-

bels liberal or conservative, humanistic or authoritarian are irrelevant; resistance is simply a matter of maintaining the status quo. Some of the arguments against mainstreaming also come from parents who feel that emotionally disturbed children should not be placed in the same classroom with their normal children. These parents give various reasons: (1) their children will copy the bad habits and inappropriate behaviors of the disturbed children; (2) their children will receive less attention from the classroom teacher; (3) the academic program will be slowed down because of the disturbed children; (4) the class standards and expectations for appropriate behavior will be lowered; and (5) much classroom instructional time will be wasted because of disciplinary problems caused by the disturbed children.

Classroom teachers are also very vocal in their concerns about mainstreaming: (1) classroom teachers are trained mainly to handle normal children, not special, problem children; (2) more class time will be spent handling emotionally disturbed children than the other children; (3) with thirty to thirty-five children in the classroom, it is impossible to handle children with special problems satisfactorily; (4) the school system will not provide the teacher with sufficient materials and support for her to help these pupils; (5) the system will not provide enough planning time for the teachers to set up individualized programs for these children; (6) the academic program will be disrupted continually by the behavior of these children; (7) the typical classroom schedule and school day will be too structured and too long for these children; and (8) special problem children placed in a classroom with a teacher who is neither trained nor has the background to cope with their specific problems will intensify and exacerbate their problems rather than helping them. These concerns must be addressed if mainstreaming is to occur in the public schools.

The roles and functions of the crisis teacher and the diagnostic prescriptive teacher are described in the following two articles and should be extremely valuable sources for helping classroom teachers manage and teach exceptional children in the regular classroom.

A crisis teacher is trained in remedial education and behavioral management to provide direct, immediate help to individual pupils when they are unable to cope with their usual classroom demands. Many children who are referred to a special class could be taught and managed in a regular class if a crisis or resource teacher were available to provide them with temporary support and control. The crisis teacher must work closely with classroom teachers and supportive services and make referrals for diagnostic and intensive help; the prescriptive teacher is a highly skilled, educational diagnostician who works with referred children, individually or in groups, until she can prescribe a curriculum that will give the child success and personal gratification. In large schools both services are needed.

The Crisis or Helping Teacher
William C. Morse

Development of the Concept

There is both a theoretical and practical background to the role of the crisis or helping teacher. First, as to the theoretical matter. At a time of problematic behavior it has been the general practice in schools to wait until a youngster "cools down" or until the migrating specialist comes to deal with a problem. This has serious limitations when one considers the nature of children. While there are times when a child stores up and retains incidents over a long period of time, much of the time they exist in a brief time module, responding to conditions of the moment. Time serves as a sponge, absorbing especially the reality which does not fit with the needs of the pupil. A burst of anger may be replaced by quite a different tone by the time someone gets to the incident. Adults spend a great deal of effort reconstituting the situation, but it seldom goes far beyond a simulation—except for the adult.

Now some schools are crisis prone: in fact there are those which seem to move from one crisis to the next with hardly a pause. But the traditional response to the crisis is usually a dictatorial confrontation, often with a strong emotional reaction on the part of the adult. To expect the behavior changes which are implied is akin to belief in magic. Those who have had the most extensive training in child behavior and management are usually the most remote from the action. Crises are often a condition where schools are least effective.

But crises can be considered a resource for helping youngsters. Caplan has proposed that intervention is most effective at the time of crisis. The theory of crisis intervention is not a surface substitute for dynamic understanding. Characteristically, the efforts of the on-the-line workers have been relegated to a second level importance. Such personnel have been given the responsibility for stemming the immediate tide as a sort of stopgap process, while those with deep involvement have assumed the responsibility for the real corrective influence. Crisis intervention concepts permit no split between what has to be done on a managerial basis and the most significant interaction with children.

The importance of all of this for contemporary mental health ideology is as follows. Studies of life histories show that those making successful adjustments differ from those who make unsuccessful adjustments less in the degree of stress they have faced than in how adequately they learned to cope with that stress. Thus, two case histories can be identical as far as the potential genesis of pathology is concerned, but one turns out reasonably well-adjusted while the other does not. Corrective influence and good mental health are the result of satisfactory solutions to the life crises. The proper intervention provided at the time of a crisis is significant teaching.

This is not to say that people are always particularly "teachable" at a time of a crisis, in the sense that they stand there awaiting help to learn how to cope with a particular situation. It merely means that at that time of crisis a person is in turmoil and seeks some resolution. The object of crisis intervention is to assist with coping action which will have long term value. The Harvard group which has dealt with this problem has studied overwhelming crisis situations such as accidents, bereavement, and other catastrophic life events. Caplan states that during such a period a person is more susceptible to being influenced by others than in times of relative psychological equilibrium.[1]

With the spread of the concept of crisis intervention, particularly using life space interviewing, adults must take care not to consider every incident as a profound life experience for extensive intervention. Particularly with youngsters, that which seems a crisis to adults may not be that at all. It should be clear that the less the individual himself feels the sense of crisis or press, the less likely will the event fit this system.

This brings us to a psychological definition of crisis. An event with a great deal of explosiveness is not necessarily a significant crisis if it is unrelated to the child's abiding problem. The selection of a particular event for potential crisis intervention requires just as much sophistication as does any interpretation in traditional therapy. Bloom has provided help on the problem of definition.[2] Is the crisis in the eye of the "crisee" or just in the eye of the beholder? Is it sensed by the child or only the teacher? Many so-called crisis situations may have no meaning as far as the primary individual is concerned. It is a crisis to the external consumer of the behavior. Many interventions fail because they are poised with an inadequate awareness of this fact. Events which are crises to adults are often satisfying, ego-building and gratifying to pupils. Stated in simple terms, a crisis occurs when the child's coping capacity is overloaded. This may be generated by external conditions such as confronting of difficult academic or behavioral tasks. Or a crisis may be a consequence of internal perceptions, distorted or accurate. The coping failure is of such severity that the child cannot be helped by the typical, mild supporting tactics which teachers use day in and day out. Thus, a crisis is a psychological duress which may or may not be accompanied by overt signs.

Caplan states that a crisis is a relatively sudden onset of disequilibrium in a child.[3] The disequilibrium is acute enough to be differentiated from previous functioning. These become turning points for personality consolidation and there is a relative saturation of negative feelings such as anxiety, depression, anger, shame, and guilt not contingent with what one expects. These are states of turmoil. Caplan points out that many children who are facing an identity crisis will have a period of this type but are not necessarily emotionally disturbed unless this develops into a chronic negative pattern. He also differentiates between developmental and accidental crises. The developmental crises are transitional periods which one anticipates for both normal and disturbed children. For example, the third grade and beginning of school are significant periods. The onset of adolescence constitutes a developmental crisis period. These conditions are precipitated by loss of basic support or some threat or a challenge which puts heightened demands on an individual. Caplan sees these as pathways leading to increased or decreased capacity to cope with one's environment.

We should be wary of the idea that children are always more *easily* influenced at a time of crisis, at least by the adult who is attempting an intervention. In a state of heightened emotion, an individual is more prone to search for cues from some aspect of his inner or outer environment to solve his dilemma. He may take his directive from another child who provides a pattern of what to do about a stress situation. The point is that during this extreme crisis period he is in a labile state.

It is obvious that crisis teaching requires the person who provides the help to be available at the time of the crisis. As a matter of fact, it has been found that the inability of a teacher of disturbed children to resolve chronic crises by providing reasonable coping assistance results in growth stalemate. The important point, from Caplan's view, is that a small force acting for a short time during the period of acute crisis can produce more pronounced impact for change than would otherwise be possible. This is the most central concept of the whole procedure. Of course, interventions are not only verbal but also include manipulation of all aspects of the environment. One uses the emotional potency of the situation to help the child understand what he is feeling and what can be done. When you let a child "cool-down," the impetus for change often cools too. In fact, many helpers spend a good deal of time in regenerating the problem so that it can be discussed. It is even sometimes necessary to actually create a crisis in order to have effective material to deal with, even though the child was a continual problem in a classroom, but at a lower level of intensity.

We have examined the theory of crisis intervention. Now for a look at the practical considerations. Teachers have observed the following. A disturbed child is not in difficulty 100 percent of the time. In fact many of them handle the classroom, most of the time, in an adequate fashion. Also, when a youngster is in the process of falling apart, he needs more adult investment, a fact well known to the classroom teacher. Most often the assistance he needs is too extensive to provide. When there is time it is often too late. In the school setting, the child with problems does not come in neat behavior or academic packages. It is frequently necessary to move back and forth in both arenas to help. A personality specialist is one thing; a remedial tutor another, but both are needed. Further, influence attempts not directed toward helping the pupil with the school reality may be fine, but not what a return to the classroom requires. Most of all, teachers want a teacher type person always available as a back up resource. Itinerant workers are not enough. Furthermore, with the increased pressures being put on schools, with an effort to do something more with the failing pupil, with the resistance to separation of problems in special classes and with stress involved in integration, teachers want help, not advice, and direct assistance rather than consultation. This led to the design called the crisis teacher.

Style and Service

While schools use such space as is available for the helping teacher, the preferred situation is a small classroom divided so that two individual children or two small groups can be worked with at the same time. To the usual remedial art and game resources are added the "hardware"—typewriter, language master, and tape recorders are typical. Some teachers have found teaching machines a real asset.

The helping teacher works both in the emotional and academic life of the pupil. As a special teacher for disturbed pupils, the training includes an intermeshing of both aspects. At one time, the child may be too upset to work on an academic task and a variety of means will be used to begin business. Life space interviewing may work; sometimes a child has to wait himself out for a while. He may draw, type on a note what he can't speak. Usually conversation can be started. It is a complex matter to decide when and what issues are reasonable to approach. Where the trail goes depends upon the nature of the problem. It may be that the presenting issue is a clear academic problem—"how to divide big numbers." Not at once, but over a period of time, every effort is made to get at such underlying factors as are needed to help the child adjust. But the child is seen as a unified total with academic and emotional spheres all as one. This does not imply that probing needs to be done when academic failure is a major source and can be approached directly. The teacher is not wed to any theoretical approach except the total problem-solving approach involved in situational analysis. One examines the nature of the child, the life space press and access points. The self-concept and self-esteem of the child may give leads to the proper interventions. What are the gratification channels available? While there may be elaborate conclusions of what should be done, there is the reality problem of deciding what *can* be done. Interventions in any part of the internal system by life space interviews, remedial help, planning, and so forth will be developed. It may mean writing a contract to support an

inadequate ego or teaching study skills. It may mean an attempt to change the regular teacher's handling, a peer discussion or a design with parents—not always done exclusively by the crisis teacher of course. One goes as far as finding a big brother for identification. Plans may include groups of children, as in the case of sixth grade children assisting first grade ones—none of them being good readers. There is a search for any natural resources which can be utilized.

The term "crisis teacher" was soon replaced with "helping teacher" for several reasons. Schools do not favor being stigmatized as crisis institutions and indeed should not be. Also, helping is the more favored activity. Further, handling crises smacked too much of after the fact, while prevention was the intent. The actual stress-producing conditions cannot be ignored. In addition, there was the issue of what does a crisis teacher do between crises? This implies that a crisis must always be a visible upset in the system. This is not the truth: a youngster may slip into a depressed state when he feels no hope, and he is certainly a case needing help. Further, there are many children who are achieving far below any reasonable expectation. Often reading assistance has not been effective because the problem is motivational and not tutorial. In short, there is enough individualization work to do in any school to employ the full effort of a teacher when there is no uproar.

This helping teacher must really know curriculum at the school level served, must be steeped in remedial teaching techniques and must be skilled in life space interviewing, a style of interviewing in contrast to non-directive interview of therapeutic work for the teacher who must handle diverse types of behavior problems. Since each school is unique, the modus operandi will fit the specific needs of a given school. However, there are several generalizations which may serve as guidelines.

The helping teacher has the most direct relationship with the child and his regular teacher. Referral procedures are the responsibility of the total staff. When a teacher feels that a pupil cannot be helped through the regular classroom alone, it may be because his behavior is disturbing to others or because he is failing in his own efforts to cope with tasks. One does not await a complicated diagnosis or parental permission because the pupil is not, in the usual sense, a special case. His behavior "in situ" provokes the referral. When possible, plans are worked out in advance with the regular teacher. When not, the regular teacher may take the pupil directly to the crisis teacher and present the reality situation in a nonrejecting, non-moralistic but frank manner. This special service is not a dumping ground or a discard heap. Rather, the two teachers discuss sympathetically the educational complexity at hand. Cues relative to the pupil's attitude about the referral are faced directly and the crisis teacher goes over possible goals. The pupil returns to the classroom, after an episode, only when he is deemed intact and ready: it may be soon, or it may take days. The referral back procedure involves the same teacher team work, and the fact of an integrated effort is made clear to the pupil.

Pupils come and go, sometimes on a regular basis as seems advisable but often on an episodic basis when specific pressure accumulates. Of course, at times the special teacher may be working with more than one pupil. As crisis demands decrease, there are always those less demonstrative problem children to be given individual help.

As indicated, the work which goes on during the special session is determined by the pupil's problem. Children seldom compartmentalize their relationships or their quandaries. Home, school, and play are intermixed. General attitudes and school work motivation come in confused combinations. Consequently, the teacher has to take a broad humanistic approach in crisis teaching. The interaction may take on characteristics of a "man to man," a parental surrogate, or a counselor, as well as the general teacher role. Free of large group responsibilities, immediate achievement goals, and time restrictions, this teacher can operate with a new flexibility. Perhaps it will be individualized tutoring, an informal talk, a diversionary activity, or an intensive life space interview session around the feelings and tension evidenced in the pupil. In short, what is done is what any teacher would wish to do were it possible to determine action by the needs of the child rather than respond to a large group process in the classroom.

The difficulty may turn out to be a learning frustration, an interpersonal conflict, or an internal feeling. As the crisis teacher sizes up the situation, plans are made for immediate and long-term steps. This teacher may get the outpouring of the child's inner conflict and must be prepared to handle whatever the child brings as well as refer special problems to other services. At times several children may be involved, and group work is called into play.

It is particularly important that the child learns he will be listened to and that his problem will be considered, even to the point of initiating joint sessions with his regular teacher to discuss conditions. There are few of the "secrets" and confidentialities which some professional workers make much of at the expense of the exchange of necessary information among parties involved with the pupil's school problem. While it is obvious that this takes utmost skill and sensitivity, it should also be clear that co-equal members of a staff can be open with the child, and no professional worker is "handling" another. All too soon we are faced with the fact that the total staff, with all the insight it can muster, will still not be able to influence the lives of some of these children at any more than a surface level. Problems may stem from the family or outside influences beyond school reach. On the other hand, if we can help a pupil meet what are for him reasonable social and academic school expectations, this is itself a worthwhile goal, although other problems remain.

The teacher's role with teacher peers has come to be an aspect with great significance. Most school consultation depends for its momentum on the expert (often from the outside) relating to a person asking for help. The consultant is seldom in the setting all the time and has limited knowledge of all that goes on there. This enables the teacher to take or leave advice, and to protect himself by various means if the implied dependency role with the consultant is not acceptable.

There is another style of consultation, mutual problem-solving, which Ruth Newman (among others) has clarified. Production of viable solutions is the test, rather than implied expertise. This is the stance the crisis teacher takes with colleagues. When the focus is on mutual collaboration to help the child, many of the role conflicts disappear. But this is a most difficult part of the work. Seldom can an effective remedial effort be staged unless the two teachers work in concert. Skill in problem-solving style consultation is thus one requirement for the helping teacher.

A word should be added about the type of effort planned for the child. Most workers develop facility with one technique over another, but the approach must be kept flexible. Interventions should be relevant to the problem, whether they involve changing certain conditions (or stimuli, rewards, etc.) in the life space or are directed to insight or relationship. Whatever is done should be done on the basis of prescription to fit the nature of the child's problem and the access to change, from operant to classical therapy.

Relationship to Other Specialists

Some of the helping teacher's clientele will already have been studied intensively by specialists. Other pupils will be new and present baffling questions to the crisis teacher and staff. Here, specific data on classroom behavior, psychological study, visiting teacher investigation, or material from a psychiatric examination may be in order. Perhaps it will become evident that the pupil's needs are for individual case work or family contact which can be best done by the visiting teacher or counselor. Since these specialists participate in the planning, trial decisions are the product of mutual discussion. The sharing of cases becomes the sharing of a problem-solving venture. In this way, the school principal, specialist, crisis teacher, and classroom teacher work as a team: possessiveness and contention are a luxury schools cannot afford.

The phrase "diagnosis on the hoof" has been used to differentiate this type of diagnosis from the studies done to categorize children. The set is, what can we do to help the pupil? What more do we need to know to help? This is in reverse of using diagnosis as a substitute for planning and remedial effort. Often we already know more of what is needed than we can seem to do. When the reverse is true and we need information to determine practice, this must be provided. While the crisis teacher is the functional entrée to the educational system in a given school, this does not imply that all the requisite information or skills could possibly reside in this individual. Many others will be needed, but they should not be brought in on a hit-and-miss, sporadic basis. When the crisis teacher monitors and integrates the effort, the experts are required to produce more than theory. Now there is a resident worker to follow up on ideas and to test the contribution. Actually, this changes the whole role of external consultation.

Relationship to the Milieu at Large

Two things are frequently missing in a problem saturated educational milieu. Little overall effort is being put in for preventative mental health. Defensive, protective police and authoritative repression become the stance because "school must keep." Here the crisis teacher serves as a mental health influence on the school at large through turning attention to causes and restorative possibilities, even including changes in the school system itself. There is dedication to reducing the abrasion of daily contacts in the school through the use of any viable procedure. While a particular child is in focus, the whole system is really under analysis. This scrutiny, while indirect, is an important change possibility. Change built on solving problems is more penetrating than preachment.

The second general milieu function is that of ombudsman or advocate. In many distressed schools the perception of depersonalization is acute. Youth feel they are handled without concern for their individuality. While no crisis teacher can be cast in a role of solving all the difficulties, the able ones have developed skills in bringing the estranged parties to discuss matters without fear of loss of face. Again, the overall life space interviewing approach has been useful. This is the psychological alternative to the legalistic approach which is accelerating at a rapid pace. Exclusions spawn lawsuits, particularly as the deprived learn of their rights. As racial incidents become more explosive, some non-authoritative bringing together of the contending factions is necessary. In a small way, the crisis teacher sometimes serves this function.

Thus the crisis teacher can be effective only to the degree that his effort is part of a total school milieu dedicated to the maximum understanding and help of the deviant child. Case conference and strategy planning meetings are held with the total school staff. Some planning for particular children can be done on a sub-group basis. The orienting principle is this: all of the adults who deal with the pupil share in constructing the plan and evolving the strategy. Many times school management failure is a consequence of inadequate communication and time to work this out is required. Just another specialist alone will not make the necessary impact on the school environment. Also, regardless of what is accomplished in the special work, the real purpose is to assist the child to function as adequately as possible back in the regular classroom setting. The classroom teacher continues to spend most of the many hours with the pupil and any plan will have to encompass these times as well as that time the child spends with the crisis teacher. Therefore all adults must be aware of the dynamics and think through the most appropriate management procedures. Frequently, after an encouraging start, an improvement plateau is reached and new plans must be evolved based upon a more complete understanding of the pupil and how he reacts.

It is particularly important to have someone looking at the totality of the problem and alert to introducing new techniques which are appropriate to the matter at hand.

Evaluation

Efforts are currently underway to study the nature of the crisis or helping teacher program. Like everything else which is introduced to the educational complex, it soon is made to serve diverse purposes and is distorted to the will of the administrator or inclination of the practitioner. There should be some knowledge concerning the variety of patterns and the perimeters of utility of such a service.[4] The various roles and time spent in particular functions are under study.

Some general information on the program in Ann Arbor gives an indication.

Most children who participated in this program in one school between 1961 and 1964 received aid for seven to nine months, although some were involved for much shorter periods while others required help for ten to twenty months. During the three-year period, twenty-four children in the first through sixth grades were seen on a regular basis.

Of these, 12 students participated for more than one year. The fraction of the 24 derived from each grade was: first grade, 8.3 percent; second grade, 16.7 percent; third grade, 4.2 percent; fourth grade, 8.3 percent; fifth grade, 16.7 percent; sixth grade, 45.8 percent. These data show that the major effort was directed toward children in the upper grades. This policy was established to help children who would soon have to meet the demands of secondary school, and to determine the effectiveness of the program in intensive short term application with children who required the most help.

Since its inception, the greatest pressure has been to service the more seriously disturbed, older children, despite the belief that the most effective and efficient use of this service would involve younger children, where the cycle resulting in underachievement is not yet firmly established. Although sex was not a factor in the selection process, only 2 of the 24 were female.

Assistance was offered in all phases of the academic curriculum. However, the record shows that the greatest need was in reading and arithmetic. Help was also offered in the following subjects,

listed in approximate order of decreasing priority: spelling, language and writing, penmanship, book reports, social studies, oral reports, and science.

While the program is basically oriented toward improving attitudes and motivation, objective appraisals of such changes are unavailable. Nevertheless, subjective evaluation by independent observers, including classroom teachers, guidance counselors, etc., leads to the conclusion that the program has achieved these goals in many cases.

The average rate of gain in achievement for the twenty-four students was +2.3 in reading and +1.6 in arithmetic, with a range of −.9 to 5.0 in reading and +.5 to 5.0 in arithmetic (an expected gain is +1.0). Many of the pupils were two years or more retarded at the start, which conditions the meaning of this.

The report concludes with a review of the problems. In a population of 500 children in this instance, only about half of the underachievers were usually the more seriously disturbed. Time was too short for productive relationships in some cases. So much was dependent on the nature of the regular classroom teacher, and not all were receptive. Were changes temporary or permanent? The prognosis for junior high of those with deep-rooted problems was limited. In a more recent review of children going on to junior high, only 3 of 10 were considered ready, but such predictions are notoriously poor.

On the other hand, based upon the current scene, many pupils in the Ann Arbor group appeared to be on the road to success.

The following positive results were achieved: (a) A healthy, and generally fruitful relationship was established with almost all of the children. Even where it appeared that no measurable gains were made, this was the first time that many of these children experienced society's concern for their welfare. (b) Most of the group became more highly motivated, exhibited less anti-social behavior, and advanced significantly in their academic work. (c) Some of them learned to adjust to highly unfavorable home environments. (d) Negative experiences, such as crisis, were used to strengthen the child's resources so that he learned to meet future crises in a positive manner. (e) Many more children were involved than could be accommodated in a segregated class room. For example, all crisis children in the school were included. (f) The mental health problems of the school were defined as a result of the process of evaluating the students in each class for the program. Other plans were made for students who needed assistance, but who could not be accommodated in this program. (g) An ancillary, but important, benefit was the immediate, on-the-spot assistance that the program offered to the classroom teacher. Furthermore, the total staff, and particularly the classroom teacher, accepted and promoted the concept that each child be treated as an individual within the framework of his present and potential abilities.

In another system, intensive interviews were conducted with a random sample of the pupils involved in a system-wide elementary program. It included 13 boys and 8 girls. Each child was rated by the teacher, evaluated by the helping teacher and the interviewer, and given a self-concept and card sort scale on his attitudes.

The interviews included discussion of the problems the pupil felt he had, what the helping teacher did, what (if any) changes took place, and parent attitude. The youngsters were most open. Boys saw their problme as mostly behavior—fighting and the like; while girls saw mostly academic difficulties. Many feared they would fail. Their views coincided with the perceptions of the conditions by the helping teachers. Most of the pupils had serious difficulties, several having failed at least once and others being diagnosed as almost hopeless by the psychiatrist. They spoke of their sibling hostilities, parental problems, school discouragement, and lack of hope. They felt they were getting aid in academics and could give specifics relative to behavior control. All but 2 said the help was useful. Only a few instances was any direct work done with parents.

On the Coopersmith self-concept scale, the averages for self, social, and school were all at the thirtieth percentile or lower. Some individuals were at the very bottom of the scale.

On the level of moral development or value internalization (after Peck and Havighurst, *The Psychology of Character Development*) this group of pupils is rated lower than most other disturbed populations. These pupils were more anxious about school, had lower morale about school, saw themselves more as troublemakers, and felt their adult relationships were negative more so than other groups of disturbed children in school or hospital programs. They did perceive themselves as more adequate in peer relationships than those in other groups, however. The lower the anxiety, the higher the self-esteem.

The teachers rated pupil progress greater in social adjustment than in school achievement. Self-esteem was rated improved. Of course, they started so low that even with improvement there was still a long way to go.

Several pupils were seen as making no changes at all. Improvement is indicated in pupil feelings of being able to cope with school and interpersonal relationships.

The problem of evaluation is most complex, and these efforts are hardly a start. The hope is to first study what the child needs and then to indicate the prescription. Evaluation has to include relevance of what is done. Further, improvements may be washed out by subsequent in or out of school difficulties. Children seldom get the continued support they are supposed to need.

Further, whatever we do as planned, known intervention may be infinitesimal compared to what happens elsewhere. It is easy to credit or debit a program with impact when in actuality we do not know really what was significant to the child in his life. This difficulty is common in all types of evaluative effort. But it is still essential that external indices of success or failure and the pupil's internal perceptions be codified and data assembled on new and traditional programs of intervention.

Article Footnotes

1. G. Caplan, *Prevention of Mental Disorders in Children* (New York: Basic Books, 1961).

2. R. Bloom, "Definitional Aspects of a Crisis Concept," *Journal of Consulting Psychology*, 27: 6 (1963), 498–502.

3. G. Caplan, "Opportunities for School Psychologists in the Primary Prevention," *Mental Hygiene*, 47: 4 (October 1963), 525–539.

4. Some descriptive material on practice with particular cases has been made available. ("The 'Crisis' or 'Helping Teacher' in the Public School: Theory and Practice," Special Education Committee, School of Education, University of Michigan, 1966.)

The Diagnostic-Prescriptive Teaching Process
Judy Tarr

The diagnostic-prescriptive teacher (DPT), along with her colleague the crisis-resource teacher, represents a rapidly growing trend in public education. The traditional arrangement has been a line-staff organization with the supplementary staff holding advanced degrees or titles, thus placing them above the classroom teacher in the organizational tables.

In contrast to the traditional organization, the diagnostic-prescriptive teacher is a new staff position. Although the position requires specific training and expertise, it is substantially an extra teacher working alongside the classroom teacher in the dual role of assisting colleague and change agent.

The diagnostic-prescriptive teacher is usually assigned to a classroom of her own, but has no regularly assigned student body; thus, she is free to work with classroom teachers and their students in a variety of ways. It is essential that the DPT have strong convictions about her role. The unprepared DPT can find her classroom miraculously filled every period of the school day with other teachers' problem children. The DPT room can easily become the most notorious classroom in the building—notorious as a dumping ground for unruly and uncooperative students.

To enable the DPT to fulfill both roles—assisting colleague and change agent—strict adherence to a procedure which includes a referral process, mutual planning with the referring teacher, and working whenever possible in that teacher's classroom, is strongly advised for new DPT programs.

Step 1. The referral process may begin formally, via a written form by the referring teacher, or informally, via a verbal exchange in the hall, teachers' lounge, or over lunch. In well-established programs, students sometimes refer themselves. Each of these avenues constitutes a legitimate request which the DPT should act on within a day or two. Even when her overload does not permit the DPT to take on a new referral, it is vital that she take time to meet with the referrer, to clarify the nature of the referral and explain why the request cannot be im-

mediately fulfilled. A mutually agreeable time to follow through at some later date should be worked out, or, if the referring teacher is using the service for the first time, an arrangement to assure her of priority in the near future. Delays in response to requests become a source of discouragement to classroom teachers and may provide opportunities to criticize the program.

Step 2. An initial conference with the referring teacher is the critical step in establishing a working relationship. Her reception may range from appreciation for your work to barely concealed hostility and a perception of the DPT as a "know-it-all" hired by the administration to report back on inept teachers. Although most receptions will be more moderate, the DPT should allow ample time during this first conference to explore the teacher's feelings and perceptions about the referred student, the teacher's relationship to the student and the student's class, and the idea of working together on the student's problems.

Increasingly, DPT's (and others placed in helping change agent positions) are required to have training in consultation, human relations, and active listening (reflection, empathy) skills. These skills are crucial in establishing, clarifying, and maintaining any kind of productive relationship with colleagues. Another downfall of a new resource program is likely to be a "let me tell you how it ought to be done" approach by the DPT.

There should be three outcomes of this initial conference, and the first should receive the greatest amount of time: (1) exploration of the referring teacher's feelings and perceptions of the student's problems; (2) identification and clarification of the teacher's primary concern, which may not necessarily be her originally stated concern; and (3) agreement on the next action to be taken.

Step 3. If the DPT does not know the student, the next step is usually to invite the DPT to the student's class and observe his functioning. Because problems classified as "learning" problems frequently turn out to be classroom behavior problems, and vice versa, the DPT is urged to develop a brief profile of the student based on her observational data, the referring teacher, and other staff who know the student. Specific testing is not precluded, but much of the data needed to make useful program adjustments can be more efficiently obtained through skilled observation and interviews. Overeagerness to employ formal testing materials can result in consuming time better spent implementing strategies formulated from observational data and thoughtful hypothesis.

A balanced student profile would include data on the receptive, expressive, and integrative functions. Reception includes visual reception functions, such as visual discrimination, visual memory, figure/ground discrimination, figure constancy, visual closure, and acuity. The auditory reception functions parallel the visual. If formal testing seems warranted and the specific dysfunction unclear, the Slingerland Test for Specific Language Disability or the Illinois Test of Psycholinguistic Abilities provide comprehensive profiles.

An often overlooked reception function is the student's cognitive level of development. Piaget's definition of cognitive functioning as preoperations, concrete operations, and formal operations are especially useful for describing how a student best learns new material or under what conditions he can apply learned material to new situations. The Attribute Games[1] provide interesting cognitive activities useful for both diagnostic and developmental functions.

Expressive functions comprise a second major area of a student profile. Both written and verbal expression are currently receiving the attention previously given to reading as specific language disabilities. Because schools place a high premium on written expression, a student with a specific language dysfunction in written expression might be labeled a bright student who is lazy and earns barely passing grades.

Visual-to-motor and auditory-to-motor (written) functions need evaluation. Too often, classroom instruction relies on a student receiving verbal stimuli accurately and swiftly and just as rapidly and accurately translating it into written form (notes) while at the same time attending to the next auditory stimulus. The auditorially handicapped student with a specific language dysfunction in auditory-to-motor output will understandably be enormously frustrated with such an instructional mode.

A simple, informal test of written expression is the "Copy, Compose, Dictate" test, advocated by followers of the Orton, Slingerland, and Gillingham techniques for teaching children with specific language dysfunctions. The student is given consecutive paragraphs typical of his grade level. He copies the first paragraph, the next he writes from dictation, and the third he composes from some subject matter of his choosing. Analysis and comparison of errors and strengths provides data for hypotheses about auditory and visual functioning, as well as samples of written language expression from the three different stimuli.

Integrative functioning, a complex process sometimes mistakenly interpreted as a measure of intelligence, is specifically correlated with the "pay off" in school. It is, briefly and colloquially, the process of "getting it all together" and giving it back to the teacher as a report, critique, essay test, original story, science experiment, debate, etc. Bloom's hierarchy of mental processes, beyond the memory level, offers a framework in which to assess a student's integrative functioning and within which to promote development toward higher levels of integrative functioning.[2] Bloom defines mental tasks from memory, at the lowest level, through translation, interpretation, application, analysis, and synthesis, to evaluation at the highest level.

Bloom's hierarchy is also useful in helping a classroom teacher analyze the nature of task demands. An overemphasis on lower-order tasks requiring only memory, translation, or interpretation can result as easily in disinterested, disruptive students as lecture note-taking demands on the auditorially handicapped student.

Lastly, a well-rounded student profile includes information obtained by interview and observation: interests, his unique skills, knowledge, and hobbies; attitudes about school, peers, and teachers; self concept; and learning style. To define a student's learning style, the DPT might raise such questions as: Does he respond best in one-to-one or group instructions? Does he do better in student-oriented or authoritarian settings? Does he do better on small, well-defined assignments, or self-defined, loosely controlled creative projects? Does he respond better to immediate feedback or to report card grades?[3] Student learning style and appropriate, supportive classroom organization is developed by Marshall Rosenberg.[4]

Diagnostic Teaching

Testing has been the subject of much current controversy. I hold the conviction that skilled observation is sufficiently reliable and considerably more efficient when dealing with large numbers of students and classroom teachers who are not in a position to act on elaborately detailed data. Classroom teachers will make legitimate requests for specific diagnostic or achievement tests to employ as a basis for classroom grouping or leveling of instruction, and the DPT's service of such one-shot requests in an efficient and helpful manner can build bridges of good will with skeptical teachers. Taking the time to personally deliver the graded tests and providing a summary of the results afford a natural opportunity to initiate conversation about programs and pupils.

Step 4.   The pupil profile and the DPT's observations of the student in the classroom become data for a second conference with the referring teacher. Although the DPT's active listening and clarification of issues will again constitute a large portion of the conference, a specific plan of action in which the referring teacher participates should result. A word of caution to the eager at this point: Experience proves that most teachers are unwilling or unable to consider drastic revision of their ongoing programs. Their security is vested in their current organization regardless of its effects. The skillful DPT will find that a slow but steady movement toward revision keeps communication open and maintains the classroom teacher's willingness to make changes. A popular approach is to identify the most fruitful, rewarding aspects of the teacher's current style and organization, to work for application (or consistency of application) of these positive aspects, and save suggestions for unfamiliar techniques for some later time in the partnership. As this working partnership develops, the teacher will ask the DPT to recommend and help integrate unfamiliar materials and programs, as well as new behavior management and classroom organizational techniques.

Although the current tendency is to work in the teacher's classroom and thus fill the role of change agent, the DPT is not precluded from taking small, selected student groups to the DPT classroom in important situations. Some reasons for working in the DPT room are: testing out new,

controversial, or unfamiliar programs, materials, or techniques before recommending them for classroom use; using the highly successful VAKT-Orton-Gillingham reading, language techniques, or other remedial programs with easily embarrassed adolescents; and conducting a Glasser problem-solving group or a Dreikurs classroom council with a population drawn from several classrooms or across grade levels.

Step 5.   In a large school, the DPT will need to set time limits on her involvement with any one teacher or student. For a new classroom teacher who is overwhelmed by her first job, the DPT may spend one period a day for an entire semester coteaching and modeling the diagnostic-prescriptive approach: pinpointing the issue, gathering the data, formulating a hypothesis, carrying out the experiment, and evaluating the results. For more experienced staff, the DPT may provide shorter, intense periods of involvement, determined by the time necessary to accomplish some mutually established goal.

Step 6.   Evaluation and feedback are needed regularly from teachers currently using the service, and biannually from the larger staff. Gathering this information is facilitated by the use of a feedback form specifically developed to ask such questions as: How often have you used the service this year? What is your department? Were your goals met? How, or how not? What positive changes in students have you noted as a result of the DPT service? What needs do you have which have not been met?

One final note of recommendation—a DPT service should consist of a team of two DPTs. This arrangement usually allows a fuller utilization of the DPT classroom as an alternative learning center while the other team member is out working as a change agent in a referring teacher's classroom. In addition, the team approach is vital to sustain and revitalize the DPT from the often nerve-racking, uphill, frustrating role of change agent. Without a friendly, supportive teammate, crisis resource teachers rapidly find themselves "burned out," overwhelmed by human resistance to change and vested interest in the security of the tried and familiar. Given a support system, patience, persistence, empathy toward one's colleagues, and creativity in generating alternatives, the DPT offers a much needed service for increasingly troubled children in an era of rapid change and conflict.

Article Footnotes

1. Developed by Elementary Science Study, © 1967 by Educational Development Center, Inc.

2. Benjamin S. Bloom et al., *Taxonomy of Educational Objectives: The Classification of Educational Goals*, Handbook I: *The Cognitive Domain* (New York: David McKay & Co., 1956).

3. Norris M. Sanders, *Classroom Questions— What Kinds* (New York: Harper & Row, 1966).

4. Marshall B. Rosenberg, *Diagnostic Teaching* (Seattle, Wa.: Special Child Publication, 1968).

Milieu Therapy

Another procedure that can be used to mainstream exceptional children is the development of a supportive school milieu. The concept of milieu treatment for children flows naturally from the theory of group work, for the word "milieu" implies the total environment in which a child lives. In other words, it's everything that is done to, with, for, or by a child in the place where he finds himself. A public school in all its facets is a child's daily milieu from nine to three. A boarding school is a child's total milieu, including his substitute home and substitute parent and siblings. The word is used in psychiatry to describe the entire setting of a child in residential treatment (or in all-day treatment). The therapeutic concept varies with the program of the setting. If it is a total therapeutic setting, then milieu treatment will consider: individual therapy, school (which is handled therapeutically as well as educationally), group work and group therapy activities, eating, bedtime and waking, and incidental daily relationships with the staff. The theory behind milieu treatment is that a troubled child needs more than just a few isolated hours of individual or group therapy; he should have every aspect of his life designed to build on his health. Insights can come at meal times as well as at play.

Clearly, a healthy, insightful milieu is good for every child, and all schools strive for it. When a child is troubled, however, it becomes vital that those dealing with him (parents, teachers, activities leaders) are sufficiently knowledgeable to handle him.

Fritz Redl, a provocative and creative blender of therapeutic knowledge and educational programs, details in the following excerpt the many factors, both tangible and intangible, that must be considered in developing the therapeutic milieu for pupils with learning and behavior problems.

The Concept of a Therapeutic Milieu
Fritz Redl

A "Milieu"—What's in It?

Obviously I am not going to use the term in the nearly global meaning which its theft from the French language originally insinuated. For practical reasons, I am going to talk here only of one sort of milieu concept: of a "milieu" artificially created

From Fritz Redl, "The Concept of a Therapeutic Milieu," *American Journal of Orthopsychiatry*, Vol. XXIX, October 1959, pp. 721–734. Copyright © 1959, the American Orthopsychiatric Association, Inc. Reproduced by permission.

for the purpose of the treatment of a group of youngsters. Within this confine you can make it somewhat wider if you want, and think of the "Children's Psychiatric Unit" on the fourth, eighth, or ninth floor of a large hospital, or you may hold before your eyes, while I am speaking, a small residential treatment home for children that is not part of a large unit. Of course, I know that the similarity of what I am talking about to other types of setups may be quite great, but I can't cover them all. Hence, anything else you hold before your eyes while I talk, you do strictly at your own risk.

So, here we are on the doorstep of that treatment home or at the keyhole of that hospital ward. And now you ask me: If you could plan things the way you wanted to, which are the most important "items" in your milieu that will sooner or later become terribly relevant for better or for worse? The choice is hard, and only such a tough proposition gets me over the guilt feeling for oversimplifying and listing items out of context.

1. The social structure.   This is some term, and I have yet to see the psychiatrist that isn't stunned for a moment at its momentum—many would run and hire a sociologist on the spot. Being short on time, I have no choice, but let me hurry and add: this term in itself is as extensible and collapsible as a balloon. It doesn't mean much without specifications. So, let me just list a few of the things I have in mind:

a.   A hospital ward is more like a *harem society than a family,* no matter how motherly or fatherly the particular nurses and doctors may feel toward their youngsters. The place I run at the moment is purposely shaped as much as possible after the model of an American camp, which is the only pattern I could find which children would be familiar with, where a lot of adults walk through children's lives in older brother and parentlike roles without pretending it to be an equivalent to family life.

b.   The *role distribution* of the adult figures can be of terrific importance for the amount of clarity with which children perceive what it is all about. Outspokenly or not, sooner or later they must become clear about just who can or cannot be expected to decide what; otherwise, how would one know when one is getting the run-around?

c.   The *pecking order* of any outfit does not long remain a secret to an open door neighborhood-wise toughie, no matter how dumb he may be otherwise. He also smells the outspoken "pecking order" among the adults who take care of him, no matter how carefully disguised it may be under professional role titles or Civil Service Classification codes.

d.   The *communication network* of any given institution is an integral part of its "social structure." Just who can be approached about listening to what, is quite a task to learn; and to figure out the real communication lines that are open and those which are secretly clogged in the adult communication network is usually an insoluble task except for the suspicious outside researcher. . . .

2. The value system that oozes out of our pores. Some people subsume that under social structure. I think I have reasons to want a separate place for it here, but let's not waste time on the question why. The fact is, the youngsters not only respond to what we say or put in mimeographed writing; they smell our value-feelings even when we don't notice our own body odor any more. I am not sure how, and I can't wait until I find out. But I do need to find out which value items are there to smell. Does the arrangement of my furniture call me a liar while I make a speech about how much at home I want them to feel, or does that gleam in a counselor's eye tell the child: "You are still wanted," even though he means it if he says he won't let you cut up the tablecloth? By the way, in some value studies I have missed one angle many times: the *clinical convictions* of what is professionally correct handling, which sometimes even questionnaire-clumsy workers on a low salary level may develop, and which become a motivating source for their behavior in its own right, besides their own personal moral convictions or their power drives.

3. Routines, rituals, and behavioral regulations. The sequence of events and the conditions under which people undergo certain repetitive maneuvers in their life space can have a strong impact on whether they can keep themselves under control, or whether their impulse-control balance breaks down. Since Bruno Bettelheim's classic description of the events inside a child while he seems engaged in the process of getting up or getting himself to sleep, no more words should have to be said about this. And yet, many "therapeutic milieu" discussions still waste their time on arguments between those who like regularity and those who think the existence of a rule makes life an unimaginative drudge. All groups also have a certain "ritual" by which a member gets back into the graces of the group if he has sinned, and others which the group has to go through when an individual has deviated. Which of those ceremonial rites are going on among my boys, thinly disguised behind squabbles and fights, and which of them do adult staff people indulge in under the even thinner disguise of a discussion on punishment and on the setting of limits? Again—the mere discovery of phenomena fitting into this category is not what I am after. We are still far from having good research data on the *clinical relevance* of whatever specific practice may be in vogue in a specific place.

4. *The impact of the group process.* We had better pause after pronouncing this weighty phrase—it is about as heavy and full of dodges as the phrase "social structure," as previously pointed out. And since this one milieu aspect might well keep us here for a week, let me sink as low as simple word-listing at this point. Items that I think should go somewhere under this name: overall group atmosphere, processes like scapegoating, mascot-cultivation, subclique formation, group psychological role suction, experiences of exposure to group psychological intoxication, dependency on contagion clusters, leadership tensions, etc. Whatever you have learned from social psychology, group psychology and group dynamics had better be written in right here. The point of all this: These phenomena are *not* just interesting things that happen among patients or staff, to be viewed with a clinical grin, a sociological hurrah, or with the curiosity stare of an anthropological slumming party. These processes are forces to which my child patient is exposed, as real as the oedipus complex of his therapist, the food he eats and the toys he plays with. The forces producing such impacts may be hard to see, or even to make visible through x-ray tricks. They are there and as much of his "surroundings" as the unbreakable room in which he screams off his tantrum.

5. *The trait clusters that other people whirl around within a five-yard stretch.* I first wanted to call this item "the other people as persons," but I know this would only call forth a long harangue about feelings, attitudes—Isn't it people anyway, who make up a group?—etc. From bitter discussion experience, I am trying to duck these questions by this somewhat off-the-beat phrase. What I have in mind is this: My youngsters live as part of a group, true enough. But they are also individuals. And Bobby who shares a room with John is within striking distance of whatever personal peculiarities John may happen to throw at others. In short, we expect some children to show "shock" at certain colors on a Rorschach card. We expect children to be lured into excited creativity at the mere vision of some fascinating project outline or plane model seductively placed before their eyes. Well, the boy with whom Bobby shares his room is worse than a Rorschach or a plane model. Not only does his presence and the visualization of his personality do something to Bobby, for John not only *has* character traits and neurotic syndromes; he swings them around his

body like a wet bathing towel, and it is going to hit whoever gets in its path, innocent or not. In short, personality traits remain psychological entities for the psychologist who watches them in the youngsters. They are *real things that hit and scratch* if you get in their way, for the roommate and all the other people on the ward.

We have learned to respect the impact of certain extremes in pathologies upon each other, but we are still far from inspecting our milieus carefully enough for what they contain in "trait clusters" that children swing around their heads within a five-yard range. Let me add: not all traits and syndromes are "swung"; some stay put and can only be seen or smelled, so they become visible or a nuisance only to the one who shares the same room. Also: we are far from knowing what this all amounts to clinically. For the question of just what "milieu ingredients" my ward contains, in terms of existent trait clusters of the people who live in it, is still far removed from the question of just which *should* coexist with each other, and which others should be carefully kept asunder.

6. *The staff, their attitudes and feelings—but please let's not call it all "transference."* This one I can be short about, for clinicians all know about it; sociologists will grant it to you, though they may question how heavily it counts. In fact, the attitudes and feelings of staff have been drummed up for so long now as "the" most important aspect of a milieu, often even as the only important one, that I am not afraid this item will be forgotten. No argument needed, it is self-evident. Only two issues I would like to battle around: One, while attitudes and feelings are very important indeed, they are not always all that counts, and sometimes other milieu items may gang up on them so much they may obliterate their impact. My other battle cry: Attitudes and feelings of staff are manifold, and spring from many different sources. Let's limit the term "transference" to those for which it was originally invented. If Nurse's Aide A gets too hostile to Bob because he bit him too hard, let's not throw all of that into the same terminological pot. By the way, if I grant "attitudes and feelings of staff" a place on my list of "powerful milieu ingredients," I mean the attitudes and feelings that really fill the place, that are lived—not those that are only mentioned in research interviews and on questionnaires.

7. *Behavior received.* I tried many other terms, but it won't work. There just isn't one that fits. In a sentence I would say: what people really *do* to each other counts as much as how they feel. This forces me into a two-hour argument in which I have to justify why it isn't unpsychiatric to say such a thing. For, isn't it the underlying feelings that "really" count? That depends on which side of the fence your "really" is. The very fact that you use such a term already means you know there is another side to it, only you don't want to take it as seriously as yours. In short, there are situations where the "underlying feeling" with which the adult punishes a child counts so much that the rather silly form of punishment that was chosen is negligible. But I could quote you hundreds of other examples where this is not the case. No matter what wonderful motive—if you expose child A to an isolation with more panic in it than he can stand, the effect will be obvious. Your excuse that you "meant well and love the boy" may be as futile as that of the mother who would give the child an overdose of arsenic, not knowing its effect.

This item of *behaviors received in a day's time* by each child should make a really interesting line to assess. We would have to look about at "behaviors received" from other boys as well as from staff, and see what the implications of those behaviors received are, even after deducting from them the mitigating influences of "attitudes that really were aiming at the opposite." The same, by the way, should also be taken into consideration for staff to be hired. I have run into people who really love "crazy youngsters" and are quite willing to sacrifice a lot. Only they simply cannot stand more than half a pound of spittle in their face a day, professional attitude or no.

In order to make such an assessment, the clinician would of course be interested especially in the *forms* that are being used by staff for intervention—limit-setting—expression of acceptance and love, etc. The totality of prevalence of certain forms of "behavior received" is not a negligible characteristic of the milieu in which a child patient has to live.

8. *Activity structure and nature of constituent performances.* Part of the impact a hospital or treatment home has on a child lies in the things he is allowed or requested *to do*. Any given activity that is halfway shapeful enough to be described has a certain amount of structure to it—some games, for instance, have a body of rules; demand the splitting up into two opposing sides or staying in a circle; and have certain assessments of roles for the play-

ers, at least for the duration. At the same time, they make youngsters "do certain things" while the game lasts. Paul Gump introduced the term "constituent performances" into our Detroit Game Study, and referred by this term to the performances required within the course of a game as basic. Thus, running and tagging are constituent performances of a tag game, guessing word meanings is a constituent performance in many a charade, etc. We have plenty of evidence by now that—other things being equal—the very exposure of children to a given game, with its structure and demand for certain constituent performances, may have terrific clinical impact on the events at least of that day. Wherever we miscalculate the overwhelming effect which the seductive aspect of certain games may have (flashlight hide-and-seek in the dark just before bedtime) we may ask for trouble, while many a seemingly risky game can safely be played if enough ego-supportive controls are built right into it (the safety zone to which you can withdraw without having to admit you get tired or scared, etc.). In short, while I would hardly relegate the total treatment job of severely disturbed children in a mental hospital ward to that factor alone, I certainly would want to figure on it as seriously as I would calculate the mental hygiene aspects of other factors more traditionally envisioned as being of clinical concern. What I say here about games goes for many other activities patients engage in—arts and crafts, woodwork, outings, over-night trips, cookouts, discussion groups, musical evenings, etc. Which of these things takes place, where, with which feeling tone, and with what structural and activity ingredients is as characteristic of a given "milieu" as the staff that is hired.

9. *Space, equipment, time and props.* What an assortment of names, but I know as yet of no collective noun that would cover them all equally well. Since I have made such a fuss about this for years, I may try to be shorter about it than seems reasonable. Remember what a bunch of boys do when running through a viaduct with an echo effect? Remember what may happen to a small group who are supposed to discuss plans for their next Scout meeting, who have to hold this discussion unexpectedly, in a huge gym with lots of stuff around, instead of in their usual clubroom? Remember what will happen to a baseball that is put on the table prematurely while they are still supposed to sit quietly and listen, and remember what happens to many a well-intended moral lecture to a group of sloppy campers, if you timed it so badly that the swimming bell started ringing before you

had finished? Do I still have to prove why I think that what an outfit does with arrangements of time expectations and time distribution, what prop-exposure the youngsters are expected to stand or avoid, what space arrangements are like, and what equipment does to the goals you have set for yourself, should be listed along with the important "properties" of a place where clinical work with children takes place? So far I have found that in hospitals this item tends to be left out of milieu discussions by psychiatrists and sociologists alike; only the nurses and attendants have learned by bitter experience that it may pay to lend an ear to it.

10. The seepage from the world outside.   One of the hardest "milieu aspects" to assess in a short visit to any institution is the amount of "impact from the larger universe and the surrounding world" that actually seeps through its walls and finds its way into the lives of the patients. No outfit is airtight, no matter how many keys and taboos are in use. In our own little children's ward-world, for instance, there are the following "seepage ingredients from the world outside" that are as much a part of our "milieu," as it hits the boys, as anything else: Adult visitors and the "past case history" flavor they leave behind. Child visitors and the "sociological body odor" of the old neighborhood, or the new one which they exude. Excursions which we arrange, old haunts from prehospital days, which we happen to drive through unintentionally on our way to our destination. Plenty of purposely pulled-in outside world through movies, television, pictures, and stories we may tell them. And, of course, school is a full-view window hopefully opened wide for many vistas to be seen through it—if we only could get our children to look.

There is the "hospital impact" of the large building that hits them whenever they leave the ward floor in transit, the physically sick patients they meet on the elevator who stir the question up again in their own mind: "Why am I here?" There are the stories other boys tell, the staff tells, the imputed secrets we may be hiding from them whenever we seem eager to divert attention to something else. As soon as the children move into the open cottage, the word "seepage" isn't quite as correct any more. Suffice it to say: the type and amount of "outside world" particles that are allowed in or even eagerly pulled in constitute a most important part of the lives of the captive population of an institutional setting, and want to be given attention to in an appraisal of just what a given "milieu" holds.

11. The system of umpiring services and traffic regulations between environment and child. Those among you who have a sharp nose for methodological speculations may want to object and insist that I am jumping category dimensions in tagging on this item and the next one on my list. I don't want to quarrel about this now. For even though you may be right, it is too late today to start a new chapter, so please let me get away with tagging these two items on here. In some ways they still belong, for whether there are any umpiring services built into an institution, and what they are like, is certainly an important "milieu property" in my estimation. . . .

In short, it runs somewhat like this: Some "milieu impacts" hit the children directly; nobody needs to interpret or translate. Others hit the child all right, but to have their proper impact someone has to do some explaining. It makes a great difference whether a child who is running away unhappy, after a cruel razzing received from a thoughtless group, is left to deal with this all by himself; or whether the institution provides interpretational or first-aid services for the muddled feelings at the time. Some of our children, for instance, might translate such an experience, which was not intended by the institution, into additional resentment against the world. With sympathy in the predicament offered by a friendly adult who tags along and comforts, this same experience may well be decontaminated or even turned into the opposite.

A similar item is the one I had in mind in using the phrase "traffic regulations." Much give-and-take can follow naturally among the inhabitants of a given place. Depending on the amount of their disturbance, though, some social interactions which normal life leaves to the children's own resources require traffic supervision by an adult. I would like to know whether a given milieu has foreseen this and can guarantee the provision of some help in the bartering custom among the youngsters, or whether that new youngster will be mercilessly exposed to the wildest blackmail with no help from anyone, the moment he enters the doors to my ward. In short, it is like asking what medical first-aid facilities are in a town before one moves into it. Whether this belongs to the concept of what makes up a "town," or whether it should be listed under a separate heading I leave for a later chance to thrash out. All I want to point at now is that the nature of and existence or nonexistence of umpiring services and social traffic regulations is as "real" a property of a setup as its walls, kitchen equipment and clinical beliefs.

12. *The thermostat for the regulation of clinical resilience.* If it is cold in an old cabin somewhere in the midst of "primitive nature," the trouble is obvious: either there isn't any fire going, or something is wrong with the stove and the whole heating system, so it doesn't give off enough heat. If I freeze in a building artificially equipped with all the modern conveniences, such a conclusion might be off the beam. The trouble may simply be that the thermostat isn't working right. This, like the previous item, is a property of a given milieu rather than a "milieu ingredient" in the stricter sense of the word. However, it is of such utmost clinical relevance that it has to go in here somewhere. In fact, I have hardly ever participated in a discussion on the milieu concept without having this item come up somehow or other.

The term under which it is more often referred to is actually that of "flexibility," which most milieu therapy enthusiasts praise as "good" while the bad men in the picture are the ones that think "rigidity" is a virtue. I have more reasons to be tired of this either/or issue than I can list in the remaining time. It seems to me that the "resilience" concept fits better what most of us have so long tried to shoot at with the flexibility label. A milieu certainly needs to be sensitive to the changing needs of the patients during different phases of the treatment process. It needs to "tighten up"—lower the behavioral ceiling when impulse-panic looms on the horizon; and it may have to lift it when self-imposed internal pressures mount. Also, it needs to limit spontaneity and autonomy of the individual patient in early phases of intensive disorder and rampant pathology; it needs to throw in a challenge toward autonomy and even the risking of mistakes, when the patient goes through the later phases of recovery. Especially when severely disturbed children are in the process of going through an intensive phase of "improvement," the resilience of a milieu to make way for its implications is as important as its ability to "shrink back" during a regressive phase. . . .

Although boards of education must direct their energies to develop their own reeducational services and programs, they also should admit that some children's behavior is so deviant and bizarre that even special classes in a regular school may be ineffective and inappropriate. They need to shout, without embarrassment, that the schools are not omnipotent and that they cannot keep all disturbed children simply because there is no other place in the community for them to go. Responsibility for the education of emotionally disturbed children is not just a school problem; it is also a community problem. In most cities, it involves the Department of Human Resources, Division of Community Mental Health. Unfortunately, special education and community mental health centers have exchanged only token services and programs. The former provide tutoring and academic programs to children in their inpatient and day-care programs; the latter provide consultation programs and outpatient therapy services. The bureaucratic isolation of these services is dysfunctional to the goal of helping troubled children. The public must demand the integration of these two services to create a force greater than the separate capabilities of each department.

There are a few exceptions. The Mark Twain School in Montgomery County, Maryland, is an outstanding, comprehensive facility for junior high and high school students with learning and behavioral problems. The Liberty School in Milwaukee, Wisconsin, is another example of an alternative program designed to meet the needs of emotionally disturbed adolescents. Finally, the League School, founded by Carl Fenichel, was one of the first comprehensive therapeutic day schools for severely disturbed children. Fenichel's pioneer work with schizophrenic children, who are diagnostically and educationally the most complex and difficult to teach, is a model of what can be accomplished when psychological principles of education are used, evaluated, and modified to meet the unique needs of each child. Fenichel believes that all meaningful learning evolves from and revolves around the teacher and that the teacher is the basis of any behavioral or academic change in the child. In the following article, he describes his criticisms of the psychoanalytic approach to treating schizophrenic children and his belief that these children should not be separated from their parents and placed in residential care.

Psycho-Educational Approaches
for Seriously
Disturbed Children in the Classroom
Carl Fenichel

It is only within the past few years that attention is being paid to the education of mentally ill children diagnosed as schizophrenic, autistic, psychotic or pre-psychotic. Up to recently it was generally believed that education could do little or nothing for these children and that the medical, specifically the psychiatric, profession must assume the major or total treatment responsibility.

Except for a few small, costly, psychiatrically-supervised residential treatment centers that accepted a handful of these children, the majority of severely disturbed children ended up in state institutions or in the private and total isolation of their own homes.

Few of these mentally ill children were getting any kind of help or therapy in the community. The public schools, believing them uneducable or uncontainable, gave them "legal exemptions" or medical discharges. Clinics rejected them as untreatable. Private psychiatric treatment was much too expensive for most families. Even when parents could afford such treatment, it was the opinion of the few psychiatrists and child therapists willing and able to work with the pathology of these children that psychotherapy without the support of a total treatment program met with little or no success.

The critical scarcity of qualified and interested child therapists, the high cost of individual psychotherapy, and the reluctance of most parents to place their child in state hospitals or residential centers made it imperative that new therapeutic facilities and techniques be found.

In 1953 the League School started a new kind of treatment facility—one that attempted to keep severely disturbed children within the community by substituting the day treatment school and the home for the mental hospital.

We began with the hypothesis that behavioral

changes could be achieved by the use of special educational techniques in a therapeutic setting without individual psychotherapy. This hypothesis was based on the assumption that a properly planned and highly individualized educational program with interdisciplinary clinical participation could result in social and emotional growth as well as in educational achievements.

It must be admitted that when we started 13 years ago we were very high in motivation but very short in method, program and direction. We thought we knew the kind of children we were getting when we announced that we would take only those with a psychiatric diagnosis of childhood schizophrenia or with the related syndromes of infantile autism or childhood psychosis. We said that we would not accept children who were primarily retarded or who suffered from neurological impairment.

It gradually became more and more obvious to us that our children didn't fit into the neat clinical packages we had ordered for them in our criteria for admission. Instead we found vast differences in behavior, pathology, prognosis and potential among all these children with a common psychiatric diagnosis. They ranged from the most passive and lethargic to the most impulse-ridden and hyperactive, from those who were completely infantile and helpless to those who were self-managing and independent, from the most regressed and defective to some with relatively intact intellectual functioning.

We found that very many of our children, even after their emotional disturbances were removed or reduced, continued to function on a retarded or pseudo-retarded level. Some showed the paradox of precocity or unique skills in a particular area and serious retardation in others. Many behaved as if they were brain-injured. Often we saw in the same child the co-existence and overlapping of features of childhood schizophrenia, infantile autism, retardation and neurological damage. All too often the specific diagnostic label chosen seemed to depend on

From *Intervention Approaches in Educating Emotionally Disturbed Children*, Peter Knoblock, ed. Copyright 1965 by Division of Special Education and Rehabilitation, Syracuse University, Syracuse, New York. Reprinted by permission of Division of Special Education and Rehabilitation, Syracuse University, Syracuse, New York.

the particular orientation of the agency, clinic, psychiatrist or psychologist making the diagnosis.

Over the years we have rid ourselves of the idea that sticking labels on the wide assortment and complex combination of disturbed behavior and disorders found among all our children tells us what we need to know about them. The fact is that the clinical categories in which these children are placed neither describe a specific illness nor help us prescribe a specific treatment.

The vast majority of children who come to us have all kinds of language handicaps. Many are unable to speak or to understand what is being said. At varying times and places they have been diagnosed as autistic, schizophrenic, aphasic, psychotic, brain-injured, or retarded. None of these terms has much educational effectiveness or program value until—with the help of the psychiatrist, neurologist, speech pathologist, pediatric audiologist—the teacher learns more about the particular language disability or disorder.

We discovered that some of these children were unable to understand language because they were deaf and just didn't hear what was being said. Some were able to hear but were so withdrawn, distractible or self-preoccupied that they had never learned how to listen. Some were able to listen but because of a partial hearing loss could get only part of the message. Others had no hearing loss but because of a suspected central nervous system disorder had difficulty in interpreting, understanding, organizing and using the sounds, symbols and concepts that give meaning to language.

We realized that what each child needs is his own personal prescription of training and education based on a psycho-educational assessment of his unique patterns of behavior and levels of functioning. This means going beyond the medical and clinical work-ups and attempting to identify, analyze and describe each child's specific skills and strengths, disabilities and deficits, lags and limitations in the many basic areas involved in the learning process, including sensory and perceptual intactness, neuro-motor development, spatial relations, body image, visual and auditory discrimination and retention, ability to use symbols, understand language and form concepts. The assessment also includes the many observable secondary symptoms of emotional and behavioral disturbances related to the primary disorders and defects. It then prescribes for the teacher specific remedial, training and educational techniques and activites that attempt to reduce, correct or remove these disabilities, if possible, or to work around them and compensate for them if the disabilities are irremediable.

In a program such as ours where the discipline of special education plays the primary role, the clinical skills and experiences of the psychiatrist, psychologist, pediatric neurologist, speech pathologist, pediatric audiologist and social worker have little value unless and until they can be incorporated into the daily program of the child. The major role of the clinical staff at the League School is not to engage in individual psychotherapy but rather to pool their findings, skills and understanding of each child and then, with the help of the special educational supervisor and curriculum resource specialist, to translate and make all of it available in functional and meaningful form for the daily program of the teacher.

A psycho-educational assessment is never complete. It keeps on evolving as continual observations by the clinical staff and teacher confirm, challenge or raise new questions on the validity of the original findings.

The teacher's role in this ongoing assessment is often the most significant one. Unlike the periodic re-evaluations of the psychiatrist or psychologist that are usually in a one-to-one test situation, the teacher has the advantage of working with and watching the child in a multitude of daily learning and living situations. From this constant teacher-child feedback circuit may arise new insights and understanding of the child's pathology, problems and potentials. Together with the current findings of the clinical staff this should result in a more precise assessment with appropriate program revisions to meet the child's ever-changing needs.

When the League School started the field was relatively unexplored and uncharted with no substantial body of tested and recorded educational experiences to guide us. With rare exceptions, the few who had been working with disturbed children in child guidance clinics, residential treatment centers or in private practice assumed that childhood mental illness was psychogenic in origin. Individual psychotherapy was the treatment favored and prescribed.

Nearly every professional worker accepted the prevailing theory that "disturbed children were made disturbed by the mishandling of disturbed or inadequate parents." In his book "Love Is Not Enough," Dr. Bettelheim interprets the frantic, purposeless activity of children at his Orthogenic School as their defense against parents who prematurely forced them into pseudo-adequacy. A child who is constantly on the run and who talks incessantly is doing so, Dr. Bettelheim believes, to hide his incestuous desire for his mother behind a smokescreen of words and to prevent his father from discovering how much he hates him. Another child's perpetual motion and inadequate coordination is attributed to her need to remain a baby and her mother's need to infantilize her.

While right from the start we had said that the teacher would play the key role in working with our children, we weren't sure what that role should be. The psychoanalytic literature that dominated the field consisted of variations on a theme: "disturbed children had been traumatized by parents who had denied them their rightful pleasures and privileges of infancy." At the beginning we believed that our teachers should play a permissive and relatively unstructured "therapeutic" role that permitted their children the freedom to ventilate hostilities, aggressions and primitive drives until basic intrapsychic conflicts were "worked through" and resolved. We assumed that this was what mentally ill children with weak, fragile egos and strong, overwhelming conflicts needed.

Our children taught us otherwise. We learned that disorganized children need someone to organize their world for them. We began to recognize that disturbed children fear their own loss of control and need protection against their own impulses; that what they needed were teachers who knew how to limit as well as accept them. We learned the need for a highly organized program of education and training that could bring order, stability and direction to minds that are disorganized, unstable and unpredictable.

(This is as good a time as any for me to remind myself and you that no generalization about disturbed children holds true for all of them. Even as I tell you of the urgent need to give these children a highly organized program of limits and controls I immediately began to think of all the children I know and have known for whom this principle would not apply. There are those disturbed children who come to us, fearful, submissive and inhibited with their own built-in defense system of controls, routines and rituals. Such children often need to be stimulated and encouraged by their teacher to loosen up their rigid controls, to ventilate and release feelings that are under tight internal censorship, and to develop enough spontaneity and freedom to venture into new, unfamiliar and unstructured situations.)

There are those who attribute all of our children's problems to weak, inadequate egos and who maintain that "learning deficits could not be eliminated until the child had developed sufficient ego strength."

Now I believe it is generally agreed that by the concept "ego" is meant that part of the self, the "I," or the mind which is conscious, which is most in touch with reality, and which handles the problems of daily living. Unless one wants to invest the ego with a spiritual or mystical quality that must be treated in a metaphysical way one must recognize the absurdity of this kind of circular thinking. How can you develop sufficient ego strength in a child unless you remedy the learning and behavioral deficits which contributed to the ego deficiency in the first place?

Many will insist that sufficient ego strength can come only after inner emotional conflicts have been resolved through psychiatric intervention and individual psychotherapy. They attribute the learning and behavioral disorders of most severely disturbed children to the crippling effects of these conflicts.

We have found far too many immediate reasons for the overwhelming problems and deviant behavior of our children without having to dig and search for them in deeply buried conflicts arising from the repression of the libido, an uncontrolled Oedipal drive or parental deprivation. I strongly believe that the pathology of our children—their disorganization, withdrawal, disorientation and confusion—is more closely related to serious learning disorders and language handicaps than to the repression of traumatic childhood memories or unresolved intrapsychic conflicts.

No one will deny that emotional conflicts can and do interfere with learning and functioning. But far too often, especially with severely disturbed children like ours, we lose sight of the fact that their emotional conflicts and disturbed behavior are usually not the cause but rather the result of specific learning disabilities and deficits which in turn may be caused by some constitutional, neurological or biochemical disorder.

Even if we believed that a child's learning or behavioral difficulties had their origin in early childhood conflict, e.g. maternal rejection, incestuous desires, hostility toward father, etc., the present difficulties and deviant behavior are not only far removed and disassociated from these original causes but are creating new problems which must be met NOW.

No matter what the primary cause of a child's disturbed behavior, we believe the teacher cannot afford to wait until first causes are dug up, "worked through" and resolved. Something must be done NOW to correct the confusion, impulsivity, anxiety and other secondary symptoms that disrupt and overwhelm him today.

Many of our children are inattentive. They cannot focus on what the teacher is saying or trying to get them to do. They seem to be easily distracted by competing stimuli and find it impossible to discard or inhibit responses to the stream of competing, irrelevant stimuli that assail them. The teacher may have to devote much of her time at first toward reducing the distractibility. She may have to protect the child from excessive stimuli by a program that is carefully regulated, simplified and sharply focused. She may be able to reduce the inattentiveness by training or conditioning the child in new ways to respond to certain stimuli or situations. She may have to change the classroom setting by modifying or reducing environmental stimuli. A drug program prescribed by the psychiatrist may improve the child's ability to concentrate on relevant stimuli or tasks.

Many may question the lasting value of alleviating or correcting symptoms since "it isn't getting to the heart of the problem." They assert that all we are doing is to suppress or repress the symptoms, and that unless we uncover and eliminate the primary conflict, other symptoms will arise to replace the repressed ones. All that we would accomplish therefore is to substitute one symptom for another.

We believe that quite the reverse is true: that the removal of one symptom is more likely to facilitate the removal of other symptoms by reducing the child's overall anxiety and confusion and improving his feelings of well-being and self-esteem.

A neurological impairment may be the primary cause of a child's language disorder. However, the many problems and difficulties that the child experiences every time he tries to communicate are likely to result in a wide range of emotional and behavioral disturbances: situational stress, frustrations, temper tantrums, anxiety, withdrawal—any one of which only serves to perpetuate and intensify the language disorder far beyond the original physiological impairment. While the teacher—with the help of the neurologist, pediatric audiologist and speech therapist—works to correct or reduce the language handicap, she simultaneously tries to alleviate or eliminate the many secondary symptoms that accompany it.

Improvement in one area is likely to result in improvement in other areas. Achievement can do for the disturbed child what it does for any other human being: make him feel more self-confident and motivate him toward further achievement. Get an enuretic to stop bedwetting or a child with a reading disability to begin to read and you have achieved something therapeutic that goes far beyond the removal of a symptom or a conflict.

Can a program of special education that operates in a group setting meet the highly individualized and unique needs of severely disturbed children, each of whom comes to our school with his set of symptoms, problems and pathology?

There are children admitted to the School whose behavior and intellectual functioning are so infantile, aimless and disorganized that they need an intensive training program on an exclusively one-to-one basis before they can begin to function meaningfully with a group. They are the very withdrawn and lethargic and the extremely restless and hyperactive children, many of whom need to be trained to sit in a chair, to make eye contact, to look, listen and attend to a simple detail or respond to a simple directive.

Their perception of the world is disoriented, vague and confused. Most of them reveal a totally inadequate comprehension of space, size, shape and sequence and are unable to cope successfully with the symbols and concepts of language and learning.

In this individualized training program the teacher will discover whether the child is ready or has the capacity for learning anything more complex than a conditioned response. Some of these children seem unable to understand or follow anything beyond the most obvious and concrete.

The teacher's communications must be free of all excess verbiage so that the child can grasp essential clues. All directives and questions must be given simply, slowly and clearly. Major emphasis may have to be on simple tasks and activities that will help bring the child's behavior under some control.

Getting a helpless child to work at the daily tasks of self-care: learning to put on and take off his clothes, tie his shoelace, wash his hands, toilet himself, use a spoon, etc.—has many educational and therapeutic implications beyond helping him to take care of basic needs and become self-managing. By involving a child in some of the essential demands and realities of daily living we are taking him out of his own preoccupation with self. We are helping him develop manipulative skills that may facilitate other more advanced skills and activities. The child's mastery of any of these simple tasks will often increase his feelings of adequacy and self-control.

Through well-planned daily programming and procedures with consistency of purpose and direction many of these children begin to have some understanding of what is expected of them. Increased demands and expectations are made upon each child as he progresses. Gradually most of them are able to acquire all the self-managing skills and to perform other tasks and activities that bring their behavior under some stimulus control by the teacher.

Once a child begins to recognize and accept some teacher control, we believe he can benefit more from a group than from an individual setting. With so many of these isolated and withdrawn children a one-to-one relationship serves only to feed their very pathology and need to cling to a dependency figure that each child wants all to himself.

When they first come into a group setting most of our children are isolates who seem to be totally indifferent or oblivious to the presence and activities of other children. Their inability to communicate, as well as their failure to understand social stimuli and to pick up adequate clues for understanding social procedures and group situations make it much too confusing or too threatening for them to participate in group activites—even if they wanted to. The few who try to initiate contact with others don't seem to know how or where to begin.

The individual and group learning experiences of the child and his relationships with his teacher are the basic instruments of our program. To be effective, such programming and relationships require one teacher for every three children. Often a child may need one teacher all to himself for intervals during the day. We are not suggesting that three children to one teacher is the magic or maximum ratio. So much will depend on the severity of the pathology of the children and on the skills, resources and capacities of the teacher.

Much thoughtful planning goes into the process and criteria for grouping. We never forget that it is children and not numbers that we are grouping. A child's impact on the group and the impact of the group on that child must be carefully considered. We must therefore assess each child's specific needs, pathology, management problems and levels of intellectual and social functioning.

Although we have no scientific formula for effective grouping of deeply disturbed children we do try to avoid placing within the same group any two children whose problems and pathology might be intensified or contaminated by their mutual presence and interaction. In order to have effective group activities we try not to have too wide a spread in the intellectual and social functioning of the individual children within a group. At the same time, we try to avoid placement of children with similar management problems within the same group: a group of three non-toilet trained children with one teacher could create obvious management problems for that teacher; a group of *all* hyperactive, *all* withdrawn or *all* nonverbal children would not make for balanced group interaction.

So many of the major problems of severely disturbed children are problems in interpersonal relationships and group living. In teacher-planned and directed group activities and interaction, these children can and often do help each other develop the capacities to work and play and live together—something they must achieve if they are to remain and function within the community. This kind of learning can only take place in a group setting. Social relationships are lived—not taught.

While an educational program for disturbed children within a group setting will inevitably create problems (that can be avoided only by having each of these children living and learning in a vacuum of isolation) the group process and the group setting can be utilized by the teacher to reduce or correct inappropriate and unacceptable behavior. I have seen many omnipotent and domineering children gradually learn to accede to the wishes and needs of formerly submissive children who, in the give and take of living together, and with the support of their teacher, have become more self-assertive.

In the group setting at meal time, rest time, play time and work time, our children learn that certain procedures and regulations are not only fair but essential for group living; they learn to wait their turn, to ask for—and not grab, to share, to postpone, to comply as well as to assert. It is in the process of group living that many of our children begin to recognize and respect the presence, needs and rights of others as well as of themselves.

The classroom curriculum, atmosphere, grouping, scheduling, regulations and routines, and how they are handled by the teacher, all have implications and potentials for positive learning and socializing experiences that can induce change, adjustment and growth.

The educational and therapeutic value of the daily program will depend on how effectively the teacher employs individual tutoring and remediation based on an ongoing assessment of each child's learning and behavioral problems and deficits, and on how well she can integrate each child's individual skills, interests and needs into the programming and group processes of the classroom curriculum.

The curriculum consists of reality oriented, living-playing-learning experiences and activities that offer continuity, stability, security and a sense of achievement. Whenever possible it will utilize many of the educational techniques and materials used with normal children in the pre-school, kindergarten and elementary school classes. Where appropriate, many of the remediation techniques successfully used in classes for the retarded, visual and auditory handicapped, perceptually impaired and the aphasic are incorporated into the program.

Until we know more about the causes and the possible cures of childhood mental illness the most we can hope to do for these children is to correct, reduce or eliminate their learning disabilities, disorganized behavior and emotional disturbances.

While every effort is made to restore or correct the primary disability or disorder we realize that very often this is impossible. We are dealing with many elusive unknowns and with many knowns that we cannot correct. We must therefore select from the wide range of a child's deviant and disruptive behavior those symptoms and disabilities which we can identify, remedy or correct, partially or completely.

Our primary aim is to lessen the anxiety, withdrawal and confusion of the child and to stimulate maturation by helping him cope more effectively with inner needs and tensions and with life situations. This is done by presenting new learning situations and experiences aimed at correcting and gradually replacing inadequate habits and patterns of behavior with more appropriate and effective ones.

The teacher never attempts to uncover or interpret unconscious material in order to "make the unconscious conscious" but tries to build up socially acceptable defenses against those drives and impulses which are so threatening and disorganizing to the child. She tries to fill the gaps and discontinuities in a child's development which if left unfilled will impede future learning and social growth.

It has taken a long time for many child therapists and authorities in the field of early childhood education to discover that a child can derive pleasure not only by satisfying the primitive impulses of the id but by developing an ego that can control these impulses and that can function autonomously and effectively within the realm of reality. It is becoming quite evident that most disturbed children not only can find satisfaction by assuming responsibilities, following directives, completing difficult tasks and mastering new skills—but that they grow and thrive in the process.

Many of our children have never assimilated the pre-academic skills, experiences, and concepts that are essential for reading readiness, arithmetic and other academic work. As the child begins to feel more comfortable with his teacher and his surroundings he is encouraged to approach and explore more of the world. A wide variety of planned experiences, inside and outside the school, may help to enrich, enliven and expand the interests and background of the child preparatory to academic work.

On the other hand there are those withdrawn children with meager and peripheral contact with the world who seem to be more comfortable with the symbols of words or numbers than with people or objects. In such cases, preoccupations with reading or with numbers as a means of escape from the world of people and things can often be used to initiate contact, encourage communication and expand interest in other spheres of activity.

All academic work must be highly personalized and timed to fit the interests, needs, preoccupations and life experiences of each child. The very pathology of a child can often be used very successfully as the basis for beginning an academic program.

The teaching process attempts to modify behavior and growth within an interpersonal relationship. In relating to a teacher, children are reacting not only to the teacher's methods but to her "manner"—her total personality. Much of the success of any teacher will depend on many intangibles such as sensitivity, spontaneity and empathic qualities which cannot be measured.

Each teacher brings into the classroom her own unique style of work as well as her own standards, values and needs. She, in turn, must try to understand the unique style and process by which each child learns. She must develop sufficient self-awareness to recognize if her own values, needs and style of work are furthering or interfering with the program and needs of her children.

A child who can identify with his teacher and gain satisfaction from this relationship is more likely to be motivated to learn, to change and to grow. The relationship however must offer more than the radiance of "love, understanding and acceptance." It must not be used to make the child dependent on his teacher but to help him become a less disorganized and more autonomous human being.

A professional relationship has little meaning unless it has professional purpose. In reacting to the educational and social needs of her children, the teacher's role is an active, directive, comprehensive and diversified one: she *relates* while she instructs, suggests, sustains, informs, corrects, clarifies, protects, modifies, calms, supports, limits, stimulates, reassures, intervenes, encourages and guides.

The teacher will be constantly challenged and, unfortunately, often frustrated by the many serious obstacles and handicapping factors which these children bring to the learning situation: low frustration tolerance, self-preoccupation, short attention span, impulsivity, perseveration, language handicaps, reading disabilities, disorganized thinking and a wide assortment of disruptive, disturbed and disturbing behavior.

The teacher must provide purposed structure and definition for every activity. At the same time, because of the lack of flexibility of most disturbed children, she must often bring increased flexibility to her classroom procedures and program. She must be sensitive and alert enough to stop an activity before it becomes bogged down by inattention, disinterest, frustration or failure. While she must live with the failure and frustration of many of her efforts, as well as her children's, she must, wherever possible, try to build some measure of success—no matter how small—into every individual and group activity.

We have found that working with seriously disturbed children the differentiation often made between education and therapy becomes largely a semantic one. A teacher who fosters self-discipline, emotional growth and more effective functioning is doing something therapeutic. Any educational process that helps to correct or reduce a child's distorted perceptions, disturbed behavior and disordered thinking, and that results in greater mastery of self and one's surroundings is certainly a therapeutic process.

Whether we call it education, re-education, counselling, guidance, remediation, conditioning, rehabilitation—any process that helps a child lose some of his feelings of helplessness and that, to a greater or lesser extent, helps him attain greater mastery of self and life situations is therapy.

A disturbed child's self-image, like that of any other child, is enhanced by experiencing success and diminished by frequent failure. It is imperative therefore, therapeutically and educationally, that we organize a highly individualized program of teaching and a learning procedure and pace for each child to meet his own capacities and needs.

As yet there is very little solid evidence based on statistical studies or controlled research to measure the value of any special educational program.

Nearly everyone who works with children—psychiatrists, psychologists, social workers, teachers—finds it easy to attribute any improvement that takes place to something they did. I am sure that we—who have an intellectual and emotional investment in our children—suffer from some of this same professional vanity.

The truth is that we really aren't sure how much of the improvement any of our children make is the result of the philosophy or program of the League School, the impact of a gifted teacher, the tranquilizing magic of a drug, parental influences and life situations outside the classroom, or a child's own wish and will to be helped.

We do believe however that the discipline of special education can help reshape the chaotic world of a mentally ill child into something more sensible and less threatening. We believe, too, that the teacher who helps promote the highest potential and achievement of a child does strengthen that child's feelings of adequacy, well-being and self-esteem. Can any other procedure or human effort be more therapeutic than this?

In reviewing new programs proposed for emotionally disturbed pupils, three concerns emerge. First, although there appears to be a dramatic increase in the number of new services, most consist of an N of 1; unfortunately, there is little replication of a successful program from one setting to another. Second, programs are given different names, but many are very similar operationally. Third, programs with similar names often prove very dissimilar. These concerns should be kept in mind when describing a particular type of setting and program for children.

Using residential care as an example, let's explore some of these concerns. Residential placement is the last and most severe alternative to helping troubled children. To remove a child from his family and community to a new setting creates innumerable psychological and logistic problems for the family and the child. The justification for such a move is that it will protect the child from destroying himself and others by providing him a supportive, predictable environment designed to meet his personal needs. The goal of residential treatment is to develop a unity of approach, understanding, managing, and reeducating. With this assumption in mind, a representative list of different residential programs is offered to emphasize contrasts.

1. A state hospital, e.g., St. Elizabeth's, Washington, D.C.

2. A state psychiatric treatment center, e.g., Hawthorne Children's Center, Michigan.

3. A private children's psychiatric center, e.g., Menninger Clinic, Topeka, Kansas.

4. A residential treatment school, e.g., Grove School, Connecticut.

5. A therapeutic boarding school, e.g., Green Chimneys, New York.

6. Therapeutic camping, e.g., Wilderness Camp, Hope Center for Youth, Texas.

7. Group homes, e.g., F.L.O.C., Washington, D.C.

8. Halfway houses, Chicago, Illinois.

9. Satellite Family Programs, Dallas, Texas.

10. Town Homes, Dallas, Texas.

11. State correctional institutions, Massachusetts.

12. Detention homes, Detroit, Michigan.

It is reasonable to expect that as children's problems become more severe, residential units would respond by increasing the intensity, duration, and cost of programs. Concurrently, the staff would direct more time and skill for providing supporting services to the child. Unfortunately, this has not been the case. Just as you can't tell a book by its cover, you can't assess the quality of a residential program by its brochure. Burton Blatt is convinced that all state institutions for children must be closed. He feels they are not only dehumanizing and depreciating but an evil that must be eliminated if we accept the responsibility of a democratic society. His book[3] played a major role in the state's decision to close these institutions in Massachusetts.

Man Through a Turned Lens
Burton Blatt

In Paris, on December 10, 1948, the United Nations General Assembly adopted a Universal Declaration of Human Rights. Its preamble spoke of dignity and equality and freedom, once revered concepts that—in recent years—have fallen upon evil days. I am compelled today, more than two decades after adoption of the Universal Declaration, to review some of its Articles.

If "All human beings are born free and equal in dignity and rights," why have I seen, in dormitories for the severely mentally retarded, solitary confinement cells that are continuously filled and with waiting lists for their use?

If "Everyone has the right to life, liberty and security of person," why at the state school for the mentally retarded have I seen a female resident held in a solitary cell for five years, never leaving—not for food or toileting or sleep?

If "No one shall be held in slavery or servitude," why have men been held in state school custody for twenty or thirty years, granted neither a review of their cases nor genuine consideration their discharge and community placement?

If "No one shall be subjected to torture or to cruel, inhuman or degrading treatment or punishment," why have I seen two young state school women in one solitary cell, lying nude in a corner, their feces smeared on the walls, ceiling, and floor—two bodies huddled in the darkness, with no understanding of the wrongs they have committed or those committed against them?

If "Everyone has the right to recognition everywhere as a person before the law," why have I seen another young woman in solitary confinement, day after day and year after year, nude and assaultive, incontinent and nonverbal—except for one day each month when her parents call for her and she is washed, dressed and taken home or for a ride in the country—except for one day each month when she may wear clothes, when she communicates, when she is a human being?

If "No one shall be subjected to arbitrary arrest, detention or exile," why have I seen men and women—state school residents for a half century —never knowing why they were placed there, no longer caring about the outside world, and with no hope that anyone outside is interested in them or knows that they exist?

If "Everyone is entitled in full equality to a fair and public hearing by an independent and impartial

Excerpted from a paper by Burton Blatt and reprinted with his permission.

tribunal, in the determination of his rights and obligations and of any criminal charge against him," why have I seen a state school boy in continuous seclusion twenty-four hours a day, described by the dormitory physician as a "monster"?

If "No one shall be subjected to arbitrary interference with· his privacy, family, home or correspondence, nor to attacks upon his honor and reputation," why have I seen mail to and from state school residents read and censored by institutional supervisors?

If "Everyone has the right to freedom of movement and residence within the borders of each state," and "Everyone has the right to leave any country, including his own, and to return to his country," why have I seen people who have never—in twenty or thirty or seventy years—left the few hundred acres of the state school—they who were delivered there at birth, but will leave only in death?

If "Men and women of full age, without any limitation due to race, nationality or religion, have the right to marry and to found a family," why have I seen the mentally retarded, the epileptic, and others denied such rights by state statutes; why have I seen young women sterilized as a condition for their release from the state school?

If "Everyone has the right to own property alone as well as in association with others," and "No one shall be arbitrarily deprived of his property," why have I seen state school residents deprived of their personal possessions and their entitlements under public assistance?

If "Everyone has the right to freedom of thought, conscience and religion," why have I seen some state school residents required to attend church services and others prohibited from such attendance?

If "Everyone has the right to freedom of opinion and expression," why have I seen a child berated by his state school teacher because of the opinions he expressed; why did I hear the teacher tell him how ungrateful, how wicked he was, in light of the bountiful state that had given this unwanted child everything and expected only loyalty and gratitude in return?

If "Everyone, as a member of society, has the right to social security," why have I seen more securing than security, more solitary than social, more indignity than dignity, more enchainment than freedom?

If "Everyone has the right to work, to free choice of employment, to just and favourable conditions of work and to protection against unemployment," why have I seen state school residents in custody long beyond the time when they merited community placement, in custody because they were performing essential, unpaid work at the institution?

If "Everyone has the right to education," why have I seen children at state schools for the mentally retarded permanently denied any semblance of education, treatment, or training?

If "Nothing in this Declaration may be interpreted as implying for any state, group or person any right to engage in any activity or to perform any act aimed at the destruction of any of the rights and freedoms set forth herein," why have I seen people who have no rights, no freedoms, and who, tomorrow, will have less?

Why have I seen a state school superintendent who did not call for a postmortem, an inquiry, or even a staff conference after the death of a severely retarded child who choked when an attendant fed her a whole hard-boiled egg?

Why have I seen a state school director of nursing leave suddenly for a three-day vacation, without assigning additional staff or someone to replace him in his absence, during the midst of a hepatitis epidemic where, in one building alone, twenty-seven of seventy-one patients were diagnosed as having this dreaded disease?

Why have I seen a severely retarded ambulatory resident, stabbed in the testicles by an unknown assailant while he slept, almost die because no one treated the wound substantially until ten hours later?

Why have I seen children at the state school go to bed each night wearing dungarees instead of pajamas, on mattresses without sheets, without pillows, and not one child "owning" even a single article of clothing?

Why have I seen children nude and bruised, sitting, sleeping, and eating with moist or dried feces covering them and their surroundings?

Why have I seen children lying on filthy beds, uncovered, flies crawling all over them?

Why have I seen children playing in and eating garbage?

Why have I been forced to view my brothers, and the world in which they live, as if I were standing in garbage, as if it were to consume *me*? . . .

Although some institutions are destructive to the well-being of children, other institutions provide children with the humanistic care, support, and skills they could not receive in the community or a mental health center. The next article illustrates how a residential center has developed multiple-treatment programs, from behavior modification to individual therapy, as a way of meeting the individual needs of its students.

Many Methods for Many Needs in a Residential Center
Howard G. Garner

The Junior Campus Program at Starr Commonwealth for Boys is an unusual combination of treatment approaches for behavior-disordered children. Behavior modification, affective education, milieu therapy, group counseling, special education, and the treatment of the home-community-school ecology have been blended into a coordinated treatment program for boys ten to thirteen years of age. Each treatment approach contributes significantly to the attainment of the goal shared by staff and boys alike—the return of each youngster to a healthy family, public school, and community environment.

The initial referral process for a new admission brings the boy, the family, and the referral agency in touch with one of the principal members of our treatment team—a liaison coordinator. The Junior Campus program has two professional staff members who are responsible for maintaining close communication with families, schools, and referral agencies during a boy's stay at Starr, usually a year to a year-and-a-half in length. The liaison coordinator usually interviews the prospective student in his home community so that detailed information can be gathered about the youngster's strengths, interests, and problem areas. Parents, teachers, recreation leaders, counselors, and others are interviewed to provide a clear picture of the problems—both the ones the boy brings to Starr and the ones he is leaving behind. While certain problems are resolved in Albion, Michigan, it is expected that the youngster's family, school, and community will function as a healthy ecological system. The liaison coordinators assist in effecting these changes. We believe the problems are not *in* the child but in his interactions with his total ecology.

The Starr program is designed to achieve change in the boys' relationship skills, self-concept, attitudes, values, self-control, and academic performance. The primary treatment modality for attaining these positive changes is the behavior modification system or "point system" as the boys call it. Points are awarded during every part of the day as positive reinforcement for desired behaviors. The staff has to work hard to teach the youngsters that points are earned by positive behavior because punishment-oriented youth initially see the system as taking away points for misbehavior. The earned points, as in all token economies, are valued partially because of the rewards they bring. Our school store allows youngsters to purchase with their points candy, games, models, and books. Weekly point totals allow the boys to earn additional privileges in a four-level phase system. Boys in Phase IV, the highest level of achievement, can have caged pets, in-town shopping privileges, and other special responsibilities. In addition to individual benefits, the point system rewards cottage groups with pizza parties, movies, ice cream parties, and sports events. The group rewards encourage group support for positive behavior by individual boys. Charts are maintained which show group and individual progress. They are used in counseling sessions to help the boys reflect on past experience and to anticipate the future consequences for their behavior. These charts are also used in providing objective data to the referral agency in each progress report.

The behavior modification system is designed so that the boys avoid long-lasting dependence on the points to control their own behavior. Staff members pair verbal praise and personal concern with the awarding of points. Learning to trust and value interpersonal interactions, the boy develops relationship skills that can transfer to the home community. In addition, before leaving the Junior Campus Program, each boy is allowed to function

This is the first publication of Howard G. Garner's article. All rights reserved. Permission to reprint must be obtained from the publisher and the author.

without the point system to control his behavior. He needs to know and to experience his ability to relate to others, to control his own behavior, and to reach personal goals because of internalized values, reinforcers, and control.

Opponents of behavior modification systems criticize the method as mechanical, dehumanizing, and unfeeling. The Starr Junior Campus Program takes seriously youngsters' needs to be cared for by concerned adults, to examine and express personal feelings, and to gain an understanding of the reasons behind their current problems. Each cottage group has a counselor who conducts four group-counseling sessions each week, during which personal problems are discussed and group support is elicited for problem-solving. Individual counseling is provided when it is appropriate. Moreover, the school program includes affective education where a growing awareness of personal feelings is combined with building an understanding of why others feel and behave the way they do. The boys even found a "Feel Wheel" in an old edition of *Psychology Today* and use it in selecting the feelings to be discussed in class. It is clear that group counseling and affective education are not merely concerned with the control of surface behavior.

The school program focuses on developing skills for return to public school. Individualized instruction is used in reading, math, science, and social studies. Students attend classes in cottage groups and have only two teachers for four subjects in order to minimize the number of social interactions. The special education program combines the behavior modification system, individualized skill development, and a relaxed atmosphere in which, for example, a discussion of feelings can begin in the middle of science class. This educational program serves youngsters with both high school reading achievement and second grade reading skills. One can see the more proficient readers providing tutorial help for the slower students.

Caring for others is seen as a therapeutic experience which the staff has to make available to each youngster.

The cottage program has been greatly improved by the adoption of the team model of organization. Houseparents, childcare workers, teachers and counselors serve as equal members of a cottage team charged with the power and responsibility to develop a treatment plan and program for each boy in the cottage. Thus, afternoon, evening, and week-end program planning and execution are in the hands of those closest to the boys. The quality and therapeutic value of this part of the program are increasing rapidly. Ice hockey, intramural basketball, and fishing are just a few of the activities implemented by the cottage teams. Milieu treatment is most effective when those living in the child's milieu have the responsibility and power to design and refine it. This can occur because childcare workers are involved in the afternoon school program, teachers eat lunch daily in the cottage, and counselors work in the cottage several evenings a week. Therefore, all staff have personal and common experiences to use in modifying the milieu to meet the boys' needs.

The main goal of our treatment program can be demonstrated by our policy regarding home visits. Formerly, a home visit was a reward to be earned by avoiding negative behavior. In our current program boys are assured of one home visit a month. These visits are opportunities for the boy and his family to try out new behaviors and to work on problems. Following these visits our counselors explore the boy's feelings about the visit while the liaison coordinators do the same with families. These visits provide data used in modifying our treatment plans for the boy and for the home ecology. Thus, our home visit program contains and reveals our concern for the interactions between the youngster and all parts of his home environment.

Summary

In order for a community to develop an adequate care program for emotionally disturbed children, it will need the total range of coordinated services that include the school, but also extend well beyond the responsibility of the school. A model program should include a diagnostic and treatment center; assistance to the regular classroom teacher through consultation and program modification; special classes and schools staffed by special educators; mental health facilities for children who have intact homes but are too disturbed for the school programs; therapeutically oriented detention homes for children who are in a crisis; residential schools, hospitals, and camps for children who need intensive treatment in a milieu setting; and finally, a protective institution for children who are unable to respond to intensive treatment. Such coordinated services would make it possible to give the child the treatment he needs, rather than forcing the child to adjust to the service available. It is encouraging to know that a few communities are planning for these varied and necessary services.

Chapter 4 Footnotes

1. **M.C. Reynolds and M.D. Davis,** *Exceptional Children in Regular Classrooms* (Department of Audio Visual Extension, University of Minnesota, 1971).

2. **N. Hobbs, ed.,** *Issues in the Classification of Children,* vols. I and II (San Francisco: Jossey-Bass, 1975).

3. **N. Hobbs,** *The Futures of Children* (San Francisco: Jossey-Bass, 1974).

4. **Burton Blatt,** *Souls in Extremes: An Anthology on Victims and Victimizers* (Boston: Allyn and Bacon, 1973).

5

How Do You Teach These Children?

I try to tell the truth and not lie but my problem is that I can't seem to remember anything or that I'm just not <u>listening</u>. I understand that already but I don't know why I just start listening or just start remembering. Most people think that sounds easy to do, but I wonder why I can't start doing that. Not listening and not remembering has just about got me in trouble everytime I've been in trouble since I've been alive (and take my word for it I've been in a lot of <u>trouble</u>!) I don't mean I've only been in trouble at school but at home too. When I was in first grade I got strait A's and I've gotten worse every year until now <u>unexceptable</u>! I think I would be happier if I could finish my work and relax. I wish I could just dump every paper out of my binder and start out fresh. And see the change. I bet it would be a good one chances are they'd be good changes (<u>90% to 10%</u>). I'd have better holiday's weekends and even in and out of school.

Just as the invisible quality of air can affect our physical well-being, the invisible quality of classroom instruction can affect the emotional well-being of pupils. Silberman,[1] in his book *Crisis in the Classroom,* gives a gloomy view of public education as organized around the theme of mindlessness and hopelessness. The slogan, "clean air smells funny," has resulted because clean air is an unusual occurrence. Creative teaching in the classroom is also an unusual occurrence. This view is supported by the high school dropout rate, which has reached 40 percent in some urban schools. In addition, 20 percent of the school population is not learning at a rate commensurate with intellectual ability. For pupils who lack the linguistic, cognitive, and affective skills necessary for school success, the pain of failure makes it difficult to use the standard instructional methods available in the classroom. In time, these pupils become immune to the curriculum, give up attempts to achieve, and avoid others' help.

When these pupils are referred to special education classes because of learning or behavioral problems, we must be careful not to let our specific goals (such as helping them catch up in basic academic areas, or mainstreaming them in a regular classroom) distract us from our primary goal of "helping pupils learn how to learn." Biber[2] reminds us that the purpose of schooling goes beyond teaching specific skills and facts; it is related to the unseen but essential four goals of education. These goals are: (1) development of sensitivity to the world around one; (2) development of techniques and attitudes for learning by discovery; (3) development of cognitive power and intellectual mastery; (4) development of synthesis in learning through symbolic expression. These educational goals are even more important for children with learning and behavioral problems. These problem pupils need specially trained teachers, teaching strategy, and instructional materials to help them overcome their resistance to learning how to learn.

This section is devoted to the methods of teaching these pupils or the "specialness" of special instruction. Is special instruction the same as regular teaching except that the teacher has fewer pupils and more time, or is it different as, say, a workhorse is different from a racehorse? We think it is different. We feel special instruction takes more than good "horse sense" and a steady mind—these help, but they are not enough.

The act of special learning is independent of the act of special teaching. Special teaching hinges on understanding how the learner processes the material received; in other words, the unique conditions of the learner determine the effectiveness of the teaching. For example, a pupil who considers geography totally irrelevant to his personal life makes a teacher's geography lesson ineffective (at least for himself); a pupil who is fearful of hurting people because of his own aggressive drives learns very little from the experience of dissecting a frog; or a pupil with a visual motor dysfunction may become sullen and hostile when asked to complete a three-dimensional drawing assignment. An understanding of individual differences, interests, and abilities is essential in changing teaching into the desired act—learning. In addition, special teaching means blending cognitive and affective components of living and learning so that troubled pupils may experience school as a vital, exciting, and growth-facilitating environment.

Through flexible, skillful use of the right lessons, materials, and teaching methods, the teacher slowly engages the learner. Curriculum and methodology become the instruments of the teacher who, with a virtuoso performance, can soothe, nurture, and excite a new-found appreciation and love for education. Great pains must be taken to insure the curriculum's relevance to the learner; materials and content are potential sources for enhancing the pupil's self-esteem. Without doubt, the teacher's development of personal competence and the ability to teach in a relevant, challenging way is indispensable to this process.

Conceptual Models of Emotional Disturbance

What to teach, how to teach, and the method of instruction should be related to the teacher's view of emotional disturbance. Rhodes and Tracey[3] have described five conceptual models of emotional disturbance that underlie most strategies of intervention. Table I summarizes the essential elements of the five models in terms of the locus of disturbance, critical factors, and representative intervention. (The five models are presented in their pure form, a condition that, of course, does not exist in reality.)

Distinction between the models is a matter of relative emphasis: the biophysical, psychodynamic, and behavioral models tend to focus on the child, whereas the sociological and ecological models focus on the interaction between the child and his environment. In 1964, Morse, Cutler, and Fink[4] completed a national study on public school classes for emotionally disturbed children. Based on 54 programs throughout the United States, which involve over

Table 1. Summary of Conceptual Models of Emotional Disturbance

	Source of Disturbance	Critical Factors	Representative Interventions
Biophysical Model	Within Child	Genetic, developmental arousal, perceptual, neurological and bio-chemical anomalies.	Psychoactive drugs; genetic counseling; perceptual-motor training.
Psychodynamic Model	Within Child	Early developmental trauma; intrapsychic conflict; dysfunctional ego defense.	Play therapy; expressive therapy; psychoanalysis; insight, catharsis, defense mechanism, ego skills.
Behavioral Model	Child's Behavior	Learned patterns of maladaptive behavior.	Behavior modification; social modeling; desensitization; reciprocal inhibition.
Sociological Model	Environment	Breaking social rules/norms; socialization failure; inappropriate expectations; rapid social change; subcultural norm conflicts.	Social case work; welfare; community development; parent education; family planning; institutional modification.
Ecological Model	Interface between child and environment	Unsuccessful transactions between child and his environment; lack of fit between individual and behavior setting.	Conjoint family therapy; crisis intervention; transactional analysis; any intervention program which simultaneously attempts to work with child and environment, e.g. Project Re-ED.

500 children and 74 teachers, the researchers made use of data from actual visits, structured interviews, questionnaires from pupils and teachers, and group description by teachers and administrators reporting on special classes. One major result of this comprehensive study was their proposed program classification system. They found seven operational styles of teaching: (1) psychiatric-dynamic, (2) psychoeducational, (3) psychological behavioral, (4) educational, (5) naturalistic, (6) primitive, and (7) chaotic. It is clear there is no consistency among educators regarding how to teach these children.

As Erickson conceptualized the eight psychosocial states of man, Hewett[5] proposed a Hierarchy of Educational Tasks, a model consisting of seven levels of functioning. They are: (1) Primary, (2) Acceptance, (3) Order, (4) Explorator, (5) Relationship, (6) Mastery, and (7) Achievement. Each of these educational levels is organized around a critical state of learning. The sequence begins with maintaining pupil attention and evolves into trusting teacher relationships, establishing routines, using multiple sensory aspects of the learning environment, solidifying pupil-teacher relationship, developing cognitive skills, and (on level seven) self-motivation in learning. This system allows a teacher to describe the pupils in terms of their strengths and weaknesses on each level. Referring to this model, Hewett suggests that teaching style and curriculum are determined by assessing the pupil's level of educational readiness and not by preconceived educational methods. Hewett's most successful study was the Santa Monica Madison School District Project in California, in which he elaborated his Learning Competencies and developed his Engineered Classroom Design. Hewett's proposed strategy of teaching has made an important contribution to the field of education, and he was one of the first educators to propose the blend of behavioral and dynamic psychology.

Precision teaching, proposed by Lindsley,[6] is another model of special teaching used in regular classrooms. Based on the experimental findings of B.F. Skinner, his theories view learning problems as products of a faulty environment rather than a faulty pupil. He views the classroom as a living educational laboratory in which the teacher functions more like a scientist studying the performance of his pupils. Decisions to modify a lesson or method are made in terms of classroom data and not personal judgments. Meacham and Allen[7] have developed this strategy of teaching in considerable detail.

In summary, we feel there is no panacea, no single model or theory, to reeducate emotionally disturbed children. The needs of children go beyond present models. This is why we are suggesting the label "psychoeducational approach" as a general term, which can include all psychological and educational strategies of helping emotionally troubled pupils.

The Psychoeducational Approach

The term psychoeducational has been viewed as a theory, methodology, and viewpoint. Fagen's position is that the psychoeducational approach postulates a circular, interacting relationship between thoughts and feelings such that cognitive experience and emotional experience affect each other simultaneously. A pupil who cannot learn to read develops intensely adverse emotional behaviors, just as a pupil with severe anxiety about his performance on tests experiences difficulty in comprehending what he reads.

To give this concept some substance, the following operating principles are considered basic to the psychoeducational approach. We believe:

1. Cognitive and affective processes are in continuous interaction.

2. Accepting the existence of mental illness, our task is to describe the pupil in terms of functioning skills that highlight areas of strength and pinpoint areas of weakness for remediation.

3. The psychoeducational process involves creating a special environment so that initially each pupil can function successfully at his present level.

4. Given this specialized environment, each pupil is taught that he has the capacity and resources to function appropriately and successfully.

5. Understanding how each pupil perceives, feels, thinks, and behaves in this setting facilitates educational conditions for optimal behavioral change.

6. There are no special times during the school day. Everything that happens to, with, for, and against the pupil is important and can have therapeutic value.

7. Emotionally troubled pupils have learned a vulnerability to many normal developmental tasks and relationships such as competition, sharing, testing, closeness, etc. As teachers, we are responsible for awareness of these areas and for modifying our behavior in appropriate fashion.

8. Emotionally disturbed pupils behave in immature ways during periods of stress. They will lie, fight, run away, regress, and deny the most obvious realities. We can anticipate immature behavior from children in conflict; our hope for change is to expect mature behavior from adults.

9. Pupils in conflict can create their feelings and behaviors in others: aggressive pupils can create counter-aggressive behaviors in others; hyperactive children can create hyperactivity in others; withdrawn pupils can get other children and adults to ignore them; passive-aggressive pupils are effective in getting others to carry their angry feelings for days. If a child succeeds in getting the adult to act out his feelings and behavior, he succeeds in perpetuating his self-fulfilling prophecy of life, which in turn reinforces his defenses against change.

10. Emotionally troubled children have learned to associate adult intervention with adult rejection. One staff goal is to reinterpret adult intervention as an act of protection rather than hostility. The pupil must be told over and over again that adults are here to protect him from real dangers, contagion, psychological depreciation, etc.

11. We are here to listen to what the pupil says, to focus on what he is feeling.

12. We are to expect and accept a normal amount of hostility and disappointment from pupils and colleagues.

13. Pupils' home and community life is an important source of health that must be considered by any remedial process. However, if all attempts fail, the school becomes an island of support for the pupil.

14. We must demonstrate that fairness is treating children differently. Although group rules are necessary for organizational purposes, individualized expectations are necessary for growth and change.

15. Crises are excellent times for teachers to teach and for pupils to learn.

16. Behavioral limits can be a form of love, i.e., physical restraint can be a therapeutic act of caring for and protecting pupils.

17. Teaching pupils social and academic skills enhances their capacity to cope with a stressful environment.

18. Pupils learn through a process of unconscious identification with significant adults in their lives. This means the teacher's personal appearance, attitudes, and behavior are important fac-

tors in teaching, which must be evaluated continuously.

Translation of the above principles into a supportive psychoeducational environment pro-vides a means by which the multiple transactions of a pupil's life space can be studied. On the following table, Fagen[8] conceptualizes this learning environment by outlining sources of change, focuses of learner's transaction, and facilitating conditions.

Table 2. Facilitating Conditions in a Psychoeducational Environment

Source of Change	Focus of Learner's Transaction	Facilitating Conditions
Learner-Teacher	Person(s) responsible for interacting with learner to effect positive change	Reality orientation; Flexibility; Respect; Emphatic understanding; Support; Protective limits; Consistency; Appreciation of feelings; Positive modelling & expectations; Involvement
Learner-Curriculum	Tasks, materials, and problems planned for mastery	Reasonable challenge; Relevance; Relatedness; Self-direction; Meaningful choices; Feedback
Learner-Peer Group	Other students interacting with learner on regular basis	Mutual respect & sharing; Openness; Cooperativeness; Appreciation of differences; Balanced groupings; Stability; Support; Feedback
Learner-School System	Rules, attitudes, values, and people organized to support the teacher, curriculum, and students	Cooperativeness; Interdependence; Openness; Mutual respect & sharing; Clarity of responsibilities and policies; Self-renewing; Orderly change mechanisms; Participatory decision-making; Appropriate consequences for deviant behavior; Positive modelling & expectations
Learner-Learner	Self-awareness of personal responsibility for self-control and direction	Identification with positive adult; Life space interviews, and therapy

In the next article, Cheney and Morse give an overview of the therapeutic value of the school and the various curriculum approaches that have been used in helping children deal with their inner and outer worlds.

Psychodynamic Intervention
Carol Cheney
William C. Morse

The school can regulate the degree of comfort vs. stress in many ways: through the careful selection of material, through gradation of steps to assure success, and through ending demands for "perfection." School is a place of work and creativity and of fun and play. The social context of school provides a laboratory for peer and authority corrective role learning for the scapegoat or bully. There are so many reality factors that direct interpretation is a natural expectation. There are peer and adult models available. Competition can be mitigated, cooperation enhanced through educational methodology, if one so chooses. There is bibliotherapy and a vast array of cognitive-curricular approaches. A unique blend of cognitive-affective synthesis can be undertaken systematically. Any environment with such potentials has at once the power to be corrective or destructive. A youngster can find a new target for hate and fear, or new and useful things to do and people to care about. The capacity for utilizing the potential of the school resources for mental health ends requires special education insight as well as flexibility to do what is needed.

The school, from this viewpoint, provides special people who do therapeutic teaching (dealing with the affective-cognitive mix) rather than just remedial teaching. The individualization can include peer and lay parent surrogates, such as proposed in the Teaching Moms concept (Donahue and Nichtern, 1965; Fenichel, 1966). Therapeutic personnel, however, lay or professional, do not become so because assigned a role. One's concern would be with the identification image provided by the person. There should be people available who can help when you are in crisis, or to speak to when you need special help with your "internal curriculum." Crisis intervention as a mental health teaching process has been described by Caplan (1964). Such school resources are especially important for disturbed youngsters (Newman, 1967).

School can even provide help for the child's life in many ways which have long-term implications. We can see in the school normal activities which are similar to established therapies: recreation, work, relationship, group, identification, achievement, music, art, dance, and even Slavson's activity group (Slavson, 1943). If they can become special therapies, the school can use them as therapeutic tools.

The therapeutic consequences of active involvement and participation are facilitated by experiences which are intrinsically appealing to the child's normal interests and curiosity. A study by Kounin *et al.* (1966) has demonstrated that in the classroom a high level of "seatwork variety change" produces an increase in appropriate behavior in both normal and disturbed children. Thus a situation which minimizes boredom and maximizes involvement can improve overall pupil behavior. The open classroom, when it is guided by a perceptive teacher, can embody a high therapeutic potential (Knoblock, 1973; Dennison, 1969). Since the psychodynamic position anticipates interaction, this is not a proposal for laissez faire or for converting the class into a classical clinic type setting (Berkowitz and Rothman, 1960).

One cannot discuss the school situation without touching on the issue of stress, particularly the almost universally experienced test-anxiety (Sarason *et al.*, 1960). One hopes, of course, for the temporary and eventual total elimination of tests, with the substitution of better methods of feedback and evaluation. Many alienated delinquents and deprived children find it impossible to cope with failure induced by present practices. As Kohl (1969) points out, however, nearly all children must deal at some point with batteries of standardized tests, often with baffling coded answer sheets and unfamiliar types of questions. As Glasser (1969) says, schools should be without failure. But until test taking is not a survival skill, special education hopes to gradually, over a period, acclimate the pupil to the harsh reality, starting with possible tasks and no failure. Since mainstreaming is a goal, and since school success is critical to that goal, the matter cannot be ignored. Kohl thus undertook to teach his Harlem youngsters *how* to take the tests that deter-

From William Rhodes and Michael Tracey, eds., *A Study of Child Variance*, vol. 2, Interventions Conceptual Project in Emotional Disturbance, Ann Arbor, Mi.: University of Michigan, 1972.

mined such important things as their class placement, their IQ ratings, etc. As students took practice tests and discussed how tests were structured, "their anxiety decreased to a manageable level, and therefore they were able to apply things they had discovered in their own thinking, reading, and writing to situations that arose in the test (Kohl, 1969, p. 340). After their short introduction to test-taking, students' reading scores jumped one to three years over scores they had achieved a few months earlier.

Curricular Approaches as Interventions

Among the basic considerations for curricular approaches to emotional disturbances which Rhodes (1963) outlines are:

1. The child should have new experiences in relation to his old problems.

2. The child should be surrounded with new opportunities which will call up such positive motives as adventure, achievement, exploration, and discovery.

3. Learning should be active and involve sensory input through as many channels as possible.

4. Activities should center on those goals which the child values most.

5. The child should be encouraged to reflect back on experiences and consider what meaning they hold for him.

In addition to such specific educational interventions as indicated above, there have been suggestions for a restorative curriculum which capitalizes on the latent self-corrective capacities of the disturbed child to enhance emotional growth and mental health. Insight and understanding of emotional problems do not always have to be gained within the highly individualized learning context of counseling or individual psychotherapy. Personal discovery can be made through the curricular context as well. The curricular approaches to mental health vary greatly in their focus, from establishment of basic learning skills to fostering awareness of the child's feelings and needs.

In their experimental study Minuchin *et al.* (1967) used ten sequential lessons to develop basic

skills needed for learning and communication. The subjects of their lessons included:

listening

implications of noise

staying on the topic

taking turns, sharing in communication

telling a simple story

building up a longer story

asking cogent and relevent questions

categorizing and classifying information

role-playing

Several curricular approaches focus more specifically on the child as an emotional being. Such curricula reflect several basic beliefs:

1. It is both unrealistic and undesirable to try to eliminate the child's emotional involvements from the classroom.

2. Children learn best when the subject matter is relevant to their experiences and interests.

3. As Weinstein and Fantini write, "unless knowledge is related to an affective state in the learner, the likelihood that it will influence behavior is limited" (Weinstein and Fantini, 1970, p. 28).

Although these curricula were not specifically designed for use with emotionally disturbed children, these basic concepts (as well as many of the specific techniques within each curriculum) conform closely to Rhodes' criteria for work with the disturbed. The point here is, the psychodynamic approach does not favor an antiseptic, exclusively cognitive or skill-oriented educational experience, for either normal or disturbed children. The fact is that most classrooms for the disturbed already have a surplus of unexploited emotional experiences. The curricular programs which have been developed to exploit experiences are thus very relevant to teaching the disturbed child.

Several curricula and textbooks reflect these concerns explicitly. Jones (1968) discusses "Man, A Course of Study," a curriculum developed from the ideas of Jerome Bruner. The subject matter of this social studies curriculum is man's nature—his universal characteristics and his differences from culture to culture. Much use is made of realistic films and stories depicting important aspects of the lives of men in other cultures. Attention is paid to the cognitive content which they contain. Jones suggests equal time for the affective responses aroused. Materials include allusions to such emotion-laden subjects as the selenecide and infanticide practiced by the Netsilik, the relative values of being male or female, and pictures of the bloody killing of a seal. The subjects presented in the program have been chosen for their relevance to the developmental tasks of childhood, and the relationship between emotions and subject matter is reciprocal. Subject matter should be chosen for its relevance to the child's emotional concerns, and the child's emotional involvement facilitates his work with the subject matter. An example of the interrelation is presented in the discussion of family life in Iraq presented below:

Student: "We don't have the whole family living with us like they do."

Student: "The girls there can't get married until the grandfather dies. That's different from us."

Student: "I agree with Sylvia. My whole family doesn't live together."

Student: "Here it's different about the boys and girls. Here girls learn faster and are smarter, and the mother enjoys having girls around because the boys are just rough."

Student: "I disagree. Boys do just as much around the house as girls."

Student: "Sometimes men can sew better than women. Also the chefs in restaurants are usually men."

Student: "Boys and men are built more rugged."

Teacher: "Therefore?"

Student: "I read a book about the frontier days. When the mother and father died the son worked all his life to help the sisters and brothers grow up and get educated."

Student: "Boys don't change the baby's diapers."

Student: "In Puerto Rico I had to work in the fields and the girls could stay home."

Student: "Mrs. Jackson, I want to defend my statement. Because it is less work to hunt and fish than it is to prepare the food, so the woman works harder."

Student: "Men have stronger constitutions than ladies."

Teacher: "Therefore?"

Student: "If it weren't for ladies, men wouldn't even be born."

Student: "How come they say 'It's a woman's world?' "

Student: "I disagree with the girls who say that girls are better, because if you put a girl in a cage with a bear, she would just cry." (Jones, 1968, pp. 167–168)

In the course of the discussion such important concepts as biological and individual differences, division of labor, and the human life cycle are elicited; identity problems and the loaded issue of sex roles are discussed. Such an encounter reflects the usefulness of incorporating the child's emotional involvements into the process of his education.

The approach of Weinstein and Fantini (1970), whose curriculum of affect was originally developed to address the needs of the underprivileged child, is very similar. They place a strong emphasis on identification of the child's personal concerns, which they group into three broad classes: self image, disconnectedness, and control over one's life. To the psychodynamic psychologist, these are the very things which confound the child with problems, "the intrinsic drives that motivate behavior" (Weinstein and Fantini, 1970, p. 24). Education must speak effectively to these concerns in order to function. Among the techniques which have integrated the affective and the cognitive realms are:

1. Creating situations which arouse the pupil's emotional involvement.

A new unit on revolution, for example, was begun by a new teacher who immediately began to forcefully order all blue-eyed children out of the room. The anger aroused prompted a lively discussion of justice, protest, etc. (Weinstein and Fantini, 1970, p. 60).

2. "One-way glasses."

Pupils practice "seeing specific persons through "glasses" which are colored "curious," "things-aren't-really-that-bad," "suspicious," "gloomy," and so on (Weinstein and Fantini, 1970, pp. 70–90).

3. Procedures to identify pupil concerns.

The Faraway Island.

Students are asked to describe the six people they would choose to accompany them to a secluded island.

Ten Years from Now.

Children are asked to speculate about what they will be doing in ten years. This situation often provides an excellent opportunity for clarification of reality factors.

Time Capsule.

The class selects pictures and songs and makes a tape recording to depict what they think is significant about their lives.

4. Games

Games were devised by the Western Behavioral Science Institute to help students develop their view of self and increase their self-esteem. Examples are presented below:

"Complain, Gripe and Moan."

Each child gets coupons labeled "home," "school," and "block." There are booths of the same names where the children "spend" their coupons to complain about each of these aspects of their lives.

"Spies from Xenon."

Children are designated spies from "Xenon" and directed to report back what makes earth children mad, afraid, strong or happy.

"Amnesia."

An adult appears, dazed. He reports being hit and losing his memory. Through an elaborate earphone arrangement, the children tell him what has been happening and help him reconstruct his memory.

"Mirror."

The child is directed to "stand up in front of that mirror, look right at yourself, and say something nice to yourself" (Weinstein and Fantini, 1970, p. 191).

The goals of the curriculum developed by Raths, Harmin, and Simon (1966) are closely related to those we have discussed. Their approach has grown out of the feeling

that the pace and complexity of modern life has so exacerbated the problem of deciding what is good and what is right and what is worthy and what is desirable that large numbers of children are finding it increasingly bewildering, even overwhelming, to decide what is worth valuing, what is worth one's time and energy (Raths et al., 1966, p. 7).

Their curriculum thus focuses on the problem of *value formulation and clarification.* Their emphasis is on the *child's* own exploration of alternatives, on consideration of goals, and on behavior consistent with his choices; no one tells him what is best.

The mechanisms which Raths *et al.* have developed to achieve these goals include:

1. Value clarification responses.

This technique consists of responding to statements made by the child in such a way that he must clarify his feelings or attitudes to himself and his teacher. Raths et al. (1966, pp. 56–67) enumerate thirty "clarifying responses" such as "How did you feel when that happened?" "Did you have to choose that; was it a free choice?" "What other possibilities are there?" "Do you do anything about that idea?" and "What do you have to assume for things to work out that way?" Appropriate use of such value clarifications requires sensitivity to those situations and statements which suggest unstated values. Raths et al. (1966, pp. 65–72) list five statement topics which lend themselves to value clarification: attitudes, aspirations, purposes, interests, and activities.

2. Value sheets.

These are lists of value-related questions which are prompted by a provocative statement or reading.

3. Role-playing.

4. Contrived incident.

The teacher contrives a situation to "shock [his] students into an awareness of what they are for and against" (Raths et al., 1966, p. 123).

5. Open-ended questions.

6. Public interviews.

The teacher interviews one of the pupils "publicly" on some emotionally-charged question such as "What do you hate about your sister?" (Raths et al., 1966, p. 143).

7. Action projects.

Students participate in projects which actualize the values and goals they have been discussing.

In addition to these proposals, there have also been textbooks developed to strengthen the child's emotional health, self-concept, etc. Limbacher's *Dimensions of Personality* series is designed to help the child learn to "accept himself, others, and their society" (Limbacher, 1969, p. v). The texts contain lessons focusing on self-awareness ("Getting to Know Myself," "Knowing I'm Alive," "My Mirrors"), feelings ("When I Cried for Help," "My Feelings are Real"), and other people ("How Different are We?").

Bruck's "Guidance" series (Bruck, 1968–1970) shares a similar emphasis. The series consists of "workbooks" [sic!]* each of which presents the child with provocative reading material, specific questions raised by its content, and suggestions for discussion topics. The child is presented with suggestions for action related to the lesson, and asked to choose one of those presented or develop his own plan. Later, he returns to the lesson to reflect on how effectively he has fulfilled his plan. The hope is that the teacher will use these as stimulants rather than as workbooks.

Jones' point was that regular curricular experiences have enough emotional stuff, and these can be approached naturally as part of the total cognitive-affective binding together of ideas. With disturbed youngsters there is the life of the class itself, which is laden with emotionally charged "curriculum." These matters should not be handled with

*Author addition

repression, authoritarianism, or rule fixation. Here is where the class converts to a social-emotional laboratory, giving the time needed to penetrate events. It may take additional personnel to help, and the Reality Interview or Life Space Interview is the technique (this is discussed elsewhere). It is mentioned here to point out that curriculum is life, as well as "books."

The implications of this section of intervention techniques are clear. One deals with the affective aspects in the educational context, which of course means that teachers must be as well trained in these procedures as in other mental health techniques. Mental health implies the proper bonding, synthesis and integration of the thinking and the feeling components of the individual. The school, being a microcosm of life, offers a wide variety of opportunities for unwinding tangled lives, and for providing new images to be integrated into troubled personalities.

Article References

Berkowitz, P., and Rothman, E. *The Disturbed Child: Recognition and Psychoeducational Therapy in the Classroom.* New York: New York University Press, 1960.

Bruck, C.M. *Guidance Series for the Elementary School: `Focus—Grade 8 Search—Grade 6.* New York: The Bruce Publishing Company, 1968–1970.

Caplan, G. *Principles of Preventive Psychiatry.* New York: Basic Books, 1964.

Dennison, G. *The Lives of Children: The Story of the First Street School.* New York: Vintage Books, 1969.

Donahue, G.T., and Nichtern, S. *Teaching the Troubled Child.* New York: The Free Press, 1965.

Fenichel, C. "Mama or M. A.? The 'Teacher-Mom' Program Evaluated." *Journal of Special Education* 1 (1966):45–51.

Glasser, W. *Reality Therapy.* New York: Harper and Row, 1965.

Glasser, W. *Schools Without Failure.* New York: Harper and Row, 1969.

Jones, R.M. *Fantasy and Feeling in Education.* New York: New York University Press, 1968.

Knoblock, P. "Open Education for Emotionally Disturbed Children." *Exceptional Children.* 39 (1973):358–366.

Kohl, H. "A Harlem Class Writes." *Radical School Reform,* edited by B. Gross and R. Gross. New York: Simon & Schuster, 1969.

Kounin, J.S.; Friesen, W.V.; and Norton, A.E. "Managing Emotionally Disturbed Children in Regular Classroom." *Journal of Educational Psychology* 57 (1966):1–13.

Limbacher, W.J. *Dimensions of Personality: Here I Am.* Dayton: George A. Pflaum, 1969.

Minuchin, S.; Chamberlain, P.; and Graubard, P. "A Project to Teach Learning Skills to Disturbed Delinquent Children." *American Journal of Orthopsychiatry* 37 (1967):558–567.

Newman, R.G. *Psychological Consultation in the Schools.* New York: Basic Books, 1967.

Raths, L.E.; Harmin, M.; and Simon, S.B. *Values and Teaching.* Columbus, Ohio: Charles E. Merrill, 1966.

Rhodes, W.C. "Curriculum and Disordered Behavior." *Exceptional Children* 30 (1963):61–66.

Sarason, S.B. *The Culture of the School and the Problem of Change.* Boston: Allyn & Bacon, 1971.

Slavson, S.R. *An Introduction to Group Therapy.* New York: International Press, 1943.

Weinstein, G., and Fantini, M.D. *Toward Humanistic Education: A Curriculum of Affect.* New York: Praeger Publishers, 1970.

Teachers report that the initial adjustment from home to school during the first fifteen minutes of class is extremely important and can set the atmosphere for the entire day. For example, some pupils enter the classroom loaded with angry, fearful, or sad feelings that were caused at home, on the bus, or on the playground. Hay and his staff have systematically reviewed the multi-ple problems that occurred during this brief period in their Junior Guidance classes in New York City.

Their report reflects the cooperative efforts of more than 200 teachers of emotionally disturbed children and offers the beginning teacher specific methods that have been proved by practical use.

Good Morning, Boys and Girls

Louis Hay
Gloria Lee

Who Are Our Children?

John enters the room like a bomb. He flings the door open and crosses the room in two or three leaps, vaulting over a desk or two on the way. He proclaims to the group that he has had several fights on the way to school and has beaten one or two boys. He seems wound up like a coiled spring. . . .

Vanessa comes into the room dragging her feet. She pulls her books along the floor behind her. She goes directly to her desk and sits in a forlorn fashion, slumped in her seat. . . .

Henry is late. He slips furtively into the room. He hides his books in the closet, gathers together some art materials, and begins working—yet fully dressed in his outer clothing. . . .

Harold is late every morning. He does not come into the classroom but stands by the side of the door. His shirt is unbuttoned, his shoes unlaced, he wears one sock. His hands are in his pockets holding up his pants because he has no belt. Sporadically, he kicks the wall. . . .

Each morning the emotional bridge from the world of the home to the world of the school must be built anew by each child with the help of the teacher. She helps the child view himself as an ac-cepted individual. For children in Junior Guidance Classes this marks the most significant transition of the day, calling for a rallying and redirecting of psychic energies from the focus of the home to that of the school.

In schools where classes line up in the yard, children of Junior Guidance Classes should proceed directly, singly or with classmates, to their rooms. Each child of this population of troubled children has his own physiological and psychological tolerance for non-mobility. Lining them up invites inevitable disturbances.

Where Have They Been?

At the close of each school day a disturbed child returns home, often reluctantly, to the source of his major conflict. Here the drama that fostered his patterns of maladjustment is re-enacted. This may be a parent-child or a parental conflict or sibling rivalry in which the child becomes a pawn. Peer pressure may also augment dissension. Meal time and bed time are crucial periods with nighttime bringing nightmares instead of tranquility. There may be simple neglect with no breakfast, or little nurturing provisions or over-insistence upon eating. The morning views another occasion for a new round of conflicts at breakfast. For most of our children the home represents an arena of painful experiences in which anxiety and anger mount and aggression or

A paper by Louis Hay and Gloria Lee, with the assistance of Shirley Cohen, Hellie Jones, Lottie Rania, and Judy Schmidt. Reprinted by permission of Louis Hay.

withdrawal is used as a defense. In either case, the price is a loss of self-confidence as well as a loss of trust of the adults. It is left to the teacher each morning to help recreate an atmosphere of security.

The morning period should be a quiet one in both tempo and substance. Problems can emanate from the class structure as well as the materials which lead to a high level of activity or stimulation. Competitiveness should be avoided. This should be a time in which children can be alone if they need to be; can move freely; can obtain needed nourishment; can find constructive release opportunities and can test wholesome social relationships. This kind of atmosphere helps children to move into the day's activities gradually.

How Can the Teacher Help?

The opening period of the day is a time when the teacher is vitally needed by her pupils. She must be available and active. She reveals her *respect* for the children by providing the materials and the opportunities for activities which are fitted to the needs and interests of the children.

The teacher also sets the stage and defines this time by the materials which she makes available and by the activities she allows, encourages and suggests. She is faced with the problems of how and when to help the child who needs adult direction in getting started; how and when to involve the child who flits about interrupting the activities of other children and how and when to introduce new materials.

The teacher is active in the following ways:

1. She observes carefully each child as he enters the room. She uses this morning observation as a comparative basis for noting daily differences in clothing, tempo, mobility, physical well being, etc. She participates most actively during the first period by observing "inner movement" through nonverbal communication.

2. She gives each child some sign of welcome and continued interest.

3. She looks at each child individually to sense which children will need that little bit of extra support this day.

4. She is available to answer questions and mediate controversies.

5. She moves in temporarily to support a faltering group activity.

6. She listens to accounts of experiences from individual children.

7. She interests a child who is at "loose ends" in an activity.

The art of encouraging a child toward initiative without making him dependent on the continued presence of the starter is invaluable in a Junior Guidance classroom. It is therefore extremely important that this period be set within a carefully planned but flexible framework. It must not be a haphazard one.

What Kinds of Activities Can Be Planned?

Early morning projects should be nonthreatening and gratifying. They should not depend upon teacher direction. It may be possible to have an ongoing activity that is carried on only during the first period. The last period of the day can serve as a link with the first period of the next day.

Suggested activities for younger children:

1. Individual scrapbooks (These pupil-made scrapbooks may be no more than three or four pages.)

2. Personal story books, written and illustrated by the children

3. Water painting on blackboard (mop should be available)

4. Surprise box (a large box, decorated, containing enough activities for the whole class)

5. Listening to phonograph or radio (child may be able to assume responsibility for operation of machine)

6. Salt, coarse (for pouring)

7. Writing on blackboard

8. Sorting materials (arithmetic chips for color, kinds of beans, kinds of beads, etc.)

9. Table blocks

10. Small finger puppets

11. Dominoes

12.   Trays of different materials
a. Two or three toy cars and a box for a garage
b. A little bath tub and small plastic doll and water (in limited amount) for bathing doll
c. Pieces of very small furniture
d. Science materials

13.   Easel painting

14.   Sewing and knitting (horse reins, etc.)

15.   Special art materials (felt pens, colored pencils)

16.   Looking at magazines

17.   Puzzles

18.   Housekeeping activities
a. Watering plants
b. Straightening block shelf

19.   Stringing (beads, cut-up straws, macaroni, buttons)

20.   A shelf of special books available only during the first period. This supply of books should be changed periodically.

Older children can be helped to a positive carryover from the previous day through helpful classroom discussion.
Suggested activities for older children:

1.   Special interests (scrapbooks, collections)

2.   Science materials and projects (dry cells, magnets, old clocks or radio to take apart and put together, microscope)

3.   Knitting, weaving and sewing, particularly for girls

4.   Class projects (class newspaper with use of typewriter, writing letters)

5.   Mailbox (for communication among children in class and teacher)

6.   Small scale construction (e.g., models)

7.   Listening to phonograph or radio, with child or children assuming responsibility for operation of machine

8.   Making articles for a younger class (Word Lotto game, Go Fish cards)

9.   Special jobs for the teachers or for the class

10.   Sorting (making picture files, collating rexographed worksheets for the class)

11.   Notes on the bulletin board to the class or to individual children telling them about something special available that day or suggesting a particular activity

12.   Browsing through newspapers and magazines.

Suggested activities for individual children who pose special problems:

1.   Finger painting

2.   Surprise bag for an individual child (two or three small toys)

3.   Care of a doll

4.   Printing set

5.   Miniature slide viewer

6.   Easily assembled construction games such as "Mr. Potato Head"

7.   Follow-the-dot books

Some of the activities mentioned previously, such as stringing, sorting, or using the phonograph for quiet records, prove soothing to distraught children.

Additional Guidelines

1.   Seasonal change should be considered.

2.   This is not a work period with floor blocks, wood working, etc. Activities that require a long period of time and self-investment should be bypassed.

3.   One cannot talk of meeting the needs of children in Junior Guidance Classes at the beginning of the day without planning for the availability of food at this time. Children who are hungry cannot turn their attention to the world around them except in anger. A tray of sandwiches saved from the previous day, a few boxes of dry cereal, some slices of bread and jelly or some cookies are signs of welcome which these children cannot mistake.

4.   The sharing of food is also a natural way for bringing the class together at the close of the morning period. How much easier it is to look ahead to the rest of the day while sipping from a container of

milk, or a cup of hot cocoa, and feeling good about being in this place.

5. This is a time for children to renew their relationships, to talk and play together, to exchange experiences and feelings.

6. At all times opportunities for individual differ-

ences should be respected. One child may enter, sit down and not participate in any activities. Whether he is accessible for some direction from the teacher may vary from child to child and at different times with the same child. Doing "nothing" may be doing much.

The U.S. Office of Education recently proclaimed that reading is not a personal *privilege* that can be given or denied, but a *right* which society must guarantee all children. Whether the problem is immaturity, retardation, poor instruction, deprivation, neurological deficit, emotional disturbance, brain injury, learning disabilities, or all of these, the difficulty of teaching children to read is enormous. Over 10 percent of the school population has reading problems severe enough to require special instruction. Although numerous remedial methods (kinesthetic, phonetic, visual, or auditory) are available to the classroom teacher, there seems to be a consensus among experts regarding the process of teaching. This process includes (1) breaking a lesson down into tiny sequential steps; (2) maintaining clarity and simplicity of structure; (3) using repetition; (4) selecting materials carefully designed to eliminate remedial deficits; and (5) developing highly motivating activities centered on the pupil's level of interest and ability. Fagen, Long, and Stevens[8] have outlined these instructional steps in greater detail.

1. Start at or below functional level.   Always try to proceed from a point that the child can handle. Work up to harder tasks gradually, and avoid presenting tasks that cannot be simplified or modified when necessary.

2. Increase difficulty by small steps.   Try not to force big jumps in skill development unless the child's readiness and self-esteem are sufficient. Usually it will be best to proceed by gradually increasing difficulty, building harder requirements on top of earlier accomplishments.

3. Place teaching tasks in a developmental sequence.   Attempt to organize tasks so that high-order skills follow on development of more elementary skills. Break complex tasks into separate components and order them sequentially (for example, kicking a ball requires left-right discrimination, balancing on one foot, freedom to move).

4. Provide positive feedback.   Be sure to indicate through praise, gesture, pictures, charts,

videotape, or some other method that progress is being made. Do not overdo praise so that it sounds artificial or untrue, but use it freely. Frequently remind the child of gains made since he started—often this offsets discouragement during plateau phases.

5. Strengthen by repetition.   Return to earlier tasks often during the year, and always repeat the last few tasks performed at a prior session.

6. Show appreciation for real effort.   Of critical importance is offering recognition for effort rather than the more usual practice of recognizing results. Work at converting appraisal methods so that success is defined relative to child's baseline level and the progress he has made. Appreciation for goal achievement is also important, but should never be praised at the expense of real effort.

7. Enhance value of skill area.   Unless the particular skill being taught is perceived as valuable by the child, meaningful change is not likely. The enhancement of value is therefore a *sine qua non* for effective teaching.

8. Maintain flexibility and enjoyment.   The planned program is never sacrosanct and should always be subject to modification. Combat boredom, fatigue, and restlessness with appealing educational games that may or may not have teaching value. A change of scenery by interesting trips, walks, or outdoor activities can be beneficial—and these may be used as rewards for hard work.

9. Prepare for real life transfer of training. Keep in mind that learning tasks are not ends in themselves but gateways to satisfactions in everyday life. Transfer can be optimized by extending and generalizing the learning tasks to as many everyday activities as possible.

10. Plan short, frequent, regular training sessions.   Hold teaching sessions at the same time and place, daily if possible, and for periods of no more than one half hour. Sharp, energetic, complete attempts at a few tasks in a short session are better than half-hearted, apathetic tries at many.

Until now we have studied various theoretical models of re-educating pupils, written primarily by university professors. Now we become more adventurous (yet more practical) by presenting four original articles by classroom teachers and practitioners in enough depth and detail to give the reader a generous taste of the creativity, complexity, and beauty of special teaching.

A review of the articles by Rabinovitch and Ross (Chapter 2) will be useful in synthesizing the wealth of ideas and suggested resources presented in Claudia Stiles' article, "A Strategy for Teaching Remedial Reading: I'm Not Going to Read, and You Can't Make Me." Mrs. Stiles' special teaching skills win out in the end, and Roger becomes another example of how children can be helped by a teacher who can integrate the affective and cognitive dimensions of learning.

A Strategy for Teaching Remedial Reading: I'm Not Gonna Read and You Can't Make Me!

Claudia Stiles

This is a story of Roger, an eight-year-old nonreader who slowly emerged from a world of confusion and despair into the promising world of communication and reading. Roger is a boy of average intellectual abilities who was unable to learn through conventional classroom instruction. His history of failure throughout the first and second grades left him with feelings of bewilderment, frustration, and hopelessness. He saw himself as somehow damaged and strangely different, for he was painfully aware that he was unable to learn like other children. He was extremely wary of risking himself to the reading process again and was filled with hostility and fear at the prospect. Unfortunately, his condition is not unlike that of most children who are referred to remedial reading specialists.

Roger was referred to our psychoeducational system by the public schools because of poor academic progress and disruptive classroom behavior. His behavior was characterized by impulsiveness, distraction, anxiety toward change, aggression, and manipulative tactics. His home environment was highly unstable and unpredictable. His mother's immediate concerns centered on his inability to cope with the recent death of his father, his enuresis, nightmares, and his open expressions of hostility toward adults and peers. Through a process of assessment and consultation, we learned that Roger's learning problems were partially due to auditory and visual perceptual problems—both areas are integrally related to the reading process. At this point, because of the complexity of his learning and behavioral problems, it was difficult to isolate the factors which were mutually interfering.

Without delay I began to formulate plans for his remediation. Each of our sessions would be diagnostic, with each day's lesson carefully built on the previous one.

When I explained to Roger that I would be his new reading teacher and that I was there to help him learn, he considered that possibility for a few minutes and responded defiantly, "Whatta ya mean, just the two of us?"

"Yes," I explained. "We will work together for thirty minutes, three days a week."

"When?" he asked cautiously.

I took him into my office and showed him the schedule posted on the wall. He found his name and I explained the hours to him. "Where are we gonna be?" he wanted to know.

We walked down the hall and into one of the reading rooms, which he acknowledged with outrage, "There's nothin' *in* here!"

This was a fairly accurate statement, for the room contained only two small desks and two chairs. "Well, we might add some of our own things later," I explained. Of course, the design was intentional. A learning environment free of auditory and visual distractions is a necessity for children with learning problems. It is also a way of clearly focusing attention on learning and minimizing behavior which interferes with that single goal.

He walked around the room, looked into an empty closet, and announced, "I'm not gonna read and you can't make me!"

"Well, Roger," I replied, "I'll promise you one thing. I'll never ask you to do anything that is hard for you. How's that?"

With an incredulous look on his face he declared, "Well, I might come and I might not!" And with that he vanished to his classroom.

After administering the Gates McKillop Reading Diagnostic Test, I discovered that Roger knew at least six of the initial consonant sounds. I would therefore begin on familiar terrain. For our first lesson I laid out an assortment of enticing little objects on the desk, all of which began with the initial consonant sound of hard *c* with which he was familiar: a cat, a small calendar, a can, and a cup. On entering the room he announced, "I'm not gonna read today!"

"That's right," I quietly assured him, "we aren't going to read today. We are going to do other things." Although this was slightly reassuring, he was not yet ready to sit down and start working. As I began to rearrange the objects, he slipped into his chair asking, "Whatta ya doin' with those toys?"

"Well, I'm thinking of something that begins with *c* (giving the hard *c* sound, not the letter name) and·you can pour hot chocolate into it," I said.

His face lit up, and with a hint of superiority he said, "Oh I know that, it's the cup."

We proceeded in this vein, taking turns guessing objects and focusing attention on the initial consonant sound. I then presented him with a beautiful flocked copy of the letter *c* from the *Alphabet Box*. He traced the letter with his index

and middle finger, and then with a pencil he wrote the letter *c* on the paper I provided for him. Roger's fine motor skills were above average and would serve as excellent reinforcement for acquiring other skills.

I began to add other objects representing the initial consonant sounds that he knew, carefully selecting those that were auditorally and visually dissimilar (*c, m, p, s*) so as to avoid the possibility of confusion and to assure success. We followed this procedure for the three remaining consonant sounds, and he was exuberant over his success in handling this task.

I presented him with a colorful, new, spiral notebook and suggested that we make it his book for all the things he knew. This felt good to him, and he asked if he could write his name on it. It would become his consonant dictionary and would be the first step toward helping him develop independence. If he did not know or forgot something, he would at least know where and how to look it up for himself without teacher intervention. It was also through this method of providing a resource and a record of his growing skills that he would learn to trust me to never ask him to do any task that he was unable to do. I had already cut several pages with tabs for locating four of the consonant sounds he knew, and from a selection of pictures, he chose the appropriate one for each page (see Figure 1).

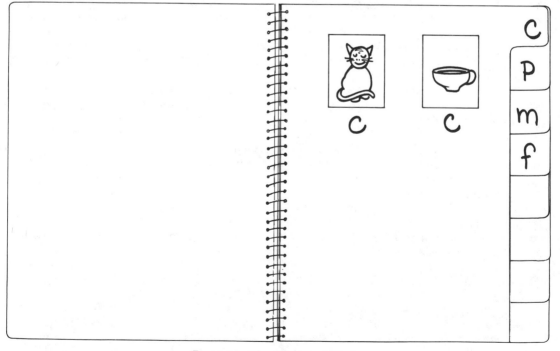

Figure 1.   The Consonant Dictionary

With these tasks completed, we terminated the first of our many reading sessions.

"Is that all we're gonna' do?" he asked.

"That's it!" I replied and off he went.

Roger had not developed any new skills on our first day of remedial reading, but we had both learned a lot about each other and the path that lay ahead of us.

We continued in this way for the next few lessons, sometimes substituting pictures for the objects used earlier and often eliminating pictures altogether as a riddle-game activity. To further strengthen his visual memory, we varied the activity by arranging the pictures, removing one and then taking turns recalling the missing picture and its initial sound.

He was also pleased with the inclusion of the Consonant Race Game. A convenient method of

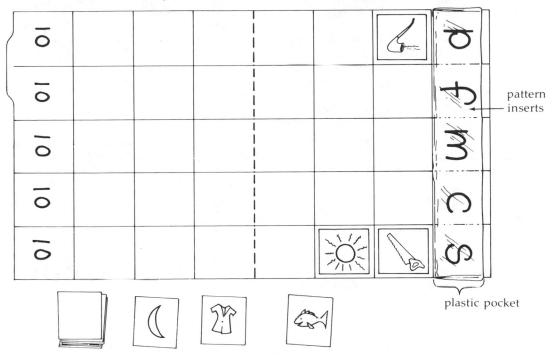

Figure 2.   Consonant Race Game

constructing games for flexibility and storage is to use the back of file folders. The board pattern is marked off for the basic game pattern and a plastic see-through pocket is placed across the top so that different patterns can be utilized for different children's needs (See Figure 2).

We took turns drawing from a stack of picture cards, and then we placed them into the corresponding column depending on their initial consonant sound. The first one who completed a row won ten points and an extra turn. I often included picture cards starred for extra points he could earn by writing the letter which represented the corresponding sound or thinking of another word that began with the same consonant sound. Another valuable and favorite game activity became the Consonant Go Fish Game.

The sequence for learning each consonant sound was first auditory discrimination, then vocal, and then association of the sound with its visual symbol. Helpful guidelines for establishing a learning sequence are:

1. Can he hear it in isolation?

2. Can he hear it in words?

3. Can he pronounce it himself?

4. Can he associate it with the proper symbol?

5. Can he blend it with other sounds to read words?

6. Can he blend it with other sounds to write words?

7. Can he use it rapidly (automatically)?

So far Roger was only able to apply skills through step 4. His ability to use initial consonant sounds would provide him with his first real word-attack skill. I was careful at this time to avoid consonant blends and diagraphs such as *cl, br, st, ch;* these would come later.

Throughout these first few lessons I hesitated to begin work on sight words because of Roger's anxieties and fear about "reading." A very important part of each lesson, however, was spent in my reading the simple Dr. Seuss books to him. I moved my finger along under the words as I read and provided him ample opportunities to furnish the predictable rhyming words and occasionally, to note the familiar, initial, consonant sounds in relationship to recurring words.

It was through this positive introduction to books within a trusting and friendly atmosphere that I hoped to whittle away at Roger's resistance and fear of books and the reading process. Words were becoming friendly things and they were communicating. They were providing us the opportunity for sharing enjoyable moments together as pupil and reading teacher.

We continued to practice correct script forms for each of the sounds he was learning, and he was able to learn the letter names as well.

During our first lesson together, I had noted his confusion in discriminating and writing the letter *p,* inverting and confusing the sound and visual symbol with the letter *b.* The *p, b,* and *d* confusion is typical of many children with visual-perceptual and directional confusions. At the beginning of our second session I presented him with a card on which was printed the letter *p* subtly disguised as a clown, but in such a way as to avoid distorting its essential shape and form (see Figure 3).

Counting on Roger's proclivity toward rhyme and rhythm, we traced over the *p* as we recited together, "*p* is a clown, his leg hangs down." He repeated this rhyme several times, advancing from the card to "invisible" wall-writing, and then to a magic marker on a plastic see-through sheet, which provided an easy flow of movement without restriction. He was delighted with this idea and wanted to take it to his classroom. Of course, I supported this suggestion, knowing that it could serve as a valuable reminder whenever he needed it.

Another simple technique worked well with Roger: the bat-ball idea developed by Mary Mitchell of the Kingsbury Center. Through the use of a miniature bat and ball, tracing, and visual imagery, a child learns to discriminate first the bat (the line) and then the ball (the circle). Both of the words, "bat" and "ball," reinforce the consonant sound and the correct sequence utilized in writing the letter (see Figure 4).

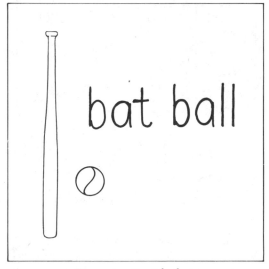

Figure 4.   First the bat
and then the ball.

The effectiveness of any similar technique is the degree to which it is successful in separating out *one* of the mutually interfering elements so that the pupil can develop a sure base for discriminating differences. It is equally important for the teacher to provide many opportunities for drill and easy accessibility to visual reminders.

We continued to work through a process of tiny sequential steps. For at least five or six minutes of each lesson, I concentrated on our consonant ritual. I would give him a sound and he would write the letter, or I would reverse the procedure and give him a letter name. He would write it and then give me the sound. Through similar kinds of drill and the reinforcement of games and varied activities,

Figure 3.   P Is a Clown,
His Leg Hangs Down.

Roger was slowly but surely learning upper and lower script forms, sounds, and letter names. As we began to accumulate many pages, I mounted them into book form, and he was quite proud of the menagerie of brilliant bird, butterfly, and shimmering star stickers that adorned each page as recognition of his good work.

"Now I have two books," he said. "But they aren't real books," he hastily reminded me. In his own way he was letting me know that the prospect of reading books was still highly anxiety-provoking. Learning to read also had other frightening implications for Roger. It represented growing up, becoming independent and accepting responsibility; he was still unwilling to risk himself.

I was amused and highly encouraged one day when, after completing one of these pages, he announced, "I don't think I'll have a bird sticker today. Just write *delicious* on that page up there at the top." (It is important to mention at this point that Roger was a child with insatiable needs for oral gratification, still at the developmental stage of equating food with love, attention, and rewards.) Without hesitation I wrote d e l i c i o u s across the top of the page, and he promptly drew a big juicy hamburger next to it. He then looked carefully at the word, noted its initial sound, and with his finger moved along under the word as we had done with the Dr. Seuss stories, synchronizing without error the *d* and *l* sounds of the word. Perhaps this assimilation of the middle consonant *l* was purely coincidental, but there was no denying his ability to relate the initial sound with the appropriate visual symbol and then the whole word. So this became one of his very first sight words—we were on our way.

With the acquisition of initial consonant sounds Roger possessed a reliable word-attack skill, and he had vividly shown me that he was ready to use it. I made plans for presenting the carefully controlled preprimer level vocabulary in the first of the Bank Street Readers Series, *In the City*. Through the use of many games, work sheets, and related activities, he would learn the twenty-eight words needed to read his first book.

As he entered the room for our next session, he was excited by the huge picture which I had taped to the wall of our room. It was a brightly colored illustration of life in a city: full of streets, buildings, parks, rivers, modes of transportation, and people engaged in a wide variety of activities. We spent a lot of time discussing the picture, locating activities, and identifying buildings by their unique characteristics (a post office flag, a school building, the capitol dome, etc.). We even pretended to devise routes of travel for getting from one place to another. I then presented him with a card on which was clearly printed the word "people."

Instructional note.   I did not choose the word "city" for his first sight word since the soft *c* sound was inconsistent with all that he had learned up to this point. He would learn to deal with exceptions and inconsistencies later.

We then discussed the various kinds of people in the picture and the activities in which they were involved. I provided him smaller copies of the word, and he taped them to the various groups of people pictured throughout the city.

Roger then traced the word, following the VAKT (Visual-Auditory-Kinesthetic-Tactile) procedures.[1] I presented him with a large copy of the

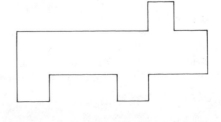

Figure 5.   Configuration

word written in crayon so as to provide a distinct tactile stimulus. He traced over the word three times with his index and middle finger, repeating the whole word as he did so. He did *not* spell the word, but pronounced it as he traced it. In this fashion he could develop a "feel" for the gestalt of the word, not its separate parts as in spelling. I removed the word and he then wrote the word in "invisible" writing on his desk. He was successful at this, so I gave him a pencil with which he could write the word without looking at the original copy. He checked his copy against the master copy and was quite pleased with his efforts. We then compared its

configuration with his other known word, "delicious," cutting around the two words so that they appeared clearly dissimilar in length and shape (see Figure 5).

He was now learning that he could also rely on configuration in discriminating words. Through picture associations, tracing, configuration, and initial consonant sounds, Roger slowly began to accumulate other sight words: *many, go, street, houses, in, city, the.* I began to make little books for him with pictures he could label with appropriate words, phrases, or sentences (see Figure 6).

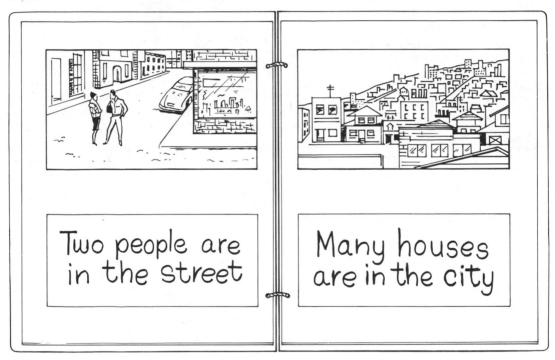

Figure 6.   Teacher-Made Books

He was happily content with his collection of little teacher-made books. They were simple, short, and nonthreatening. They weren't "real books."

During this time we continued our work on the remaining consonant sounds and began the first short vowel sound, *a.* He learned the isolated sound of short *a* by association with the visual clue, an apple. The other vowels would be added as he was ready (see Figure 7). Here again was another simple but valuable resource for helping Roger develop independence.

The phonetic blending process was extremely difficult for Roger, but by using the *Structural Reading Series,* he began to make slow but steady progress. With this method the emphasis is on

avoiding the risk of distorted sounds through the blending process of isolated letters, such as $b - a - t$, by relating the initial consonant with the vowel and then the ending: $ba - t$, $pa - n$, $pa - l$. He used the structural reading dominoes (with words divided in this manner) to build words, followed by writing and spelling tasks, and the reading of short vowel words in context and in games. In this manner Roger was learning to blend words phonetically through a sequence of related sounds and symbols. Because he was able to learn well through multisensory approaches, we also utilized gross motor and kinesthetic skills. I placed enlarged copies of short *a* words on the board. Standing in front of each word, he would blend the words as he moved

Figure 7. Short Vowel Reminder

his hand along under the letters, utilizing his arm, hand, and shoulder muscles to "feel" the visual and auditory left-to-right sequencing process. This procedure also helped him to establish the beginnings and endings of words, auditorally and visually (see Figure 8).

With the acquisition of phonetic words and sight words he was able to read many simple sentences. He was proud of his growing collection of little books made of construction paper and brightly colored pictures. Through short, simple sentence structures he was learning to rely on context as another way of learning words. A regular activity of our reading lesson became the Sentence Cube Game (see Figure 9).

I made three cardboard cubes with words or phrases on each side that could be changed as his vocabulary increased. We would take turns rolling the cubes and then arranging them to form a sentence. This required discerning capital letters at the beginning and punctuation marks at the end of sentences. Points were printed on each side of the cube, and if the words on the sides which were rolled face up formed a sensible and complete sentence, those points were accumulated toward the winning score of 20. He delighted in the absurdities that often occurred (such as "Three cats can work in the store.") his joy undiluted by his gaining no points for arranging these silly sentences.

After months of carefully structured remedial reading sessions, the eventful day arrived. He had

Figure 8. Reinforcement of the Phonetic
Blending Process

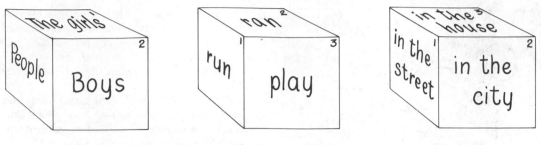

Figure 9.   The Sentence Cube Game

learned all of the sight words needed to read the entire book, *In The City*. I was still a bit unsure of his reaction to such an expectation, but the groundwork had been laid and he had gained not only the necessary skills but increased confidence in himself and his ability to learn.

As he slipped into his chair, he spotted the book lying on his desk. "What's that? Are ya gonna read that to me today?" he asked.

"Oh, I might. Why don'ι we look at the pictures first," I suggested.

That suited him fine and he opened the book. Immediately he spotted "One Two Three."

"Hey, I know that: One Two Three," he shouted. Then he began to race through the book, spotting and reading friendly and familiar words on every page.

"Hey, slow down!" I laughed. "Let's go back to the beginning and see what this is all about."

An excellent procedure in remedial reading sessions is for teacher and pupil to share the reading. The child, as he listens to the teacher read portions of the story, and as he follows along silently, picks up the appropriate use of expressions, inflections, punctuation, and pacing. But that was not to be the case today. Roger was in control of the situation and my offers to read a page or two were refused with a hasty "No, no let me do it. I can do it." And so he did, from the beginning to the end. The other activities which I had foolishly planned for the day were immediately scrapped. Nothing could follow that act.

He was eager to show his new book to his teachers and classmates, so we rushed downstairs to share the exciting news. His classroom teachers had been awaiting this event for weeks, but they were full of "surprised" exclamation over his accomplishment. Upstairs, for future lessons, were three more supplementaries which contained the same controlled vocabulary as *In The City*, but it would be a day or two before Roger was ready to part with his very first reading book.

Roger and I had completed thirty-five remedial reading sessions together. His progress had been slow and often painful, and I was frequently discouraged by the many problems that interfered with his ability to learn. But I made every effort along the way to avoid communicating to Roger that sense of frustration which is so familiar to all remedial reading teachers. Roger would continue to confuse look alike words for many months to come; the assimilation of each short vowel sound would continue to be a difficult process; he would continue to forget without constant review and reinforcement. Many more months of structured remedial reading sessions would be required before he could begin to function independently. Roger had only begun his venture into the world of reading, but he was armed now with a few reliable skills and a growing sense of confidence and achievement.

Reluctant readers are easily discouraged and quickly lose interest if they are not provided access to a multitude of high-interest, low-level reading books. It is important that every remedial reading department be equipped with books which meet these requirements. The children with whom I have worked, from six to twelve years of age, have found great pleasure and satisfaction in the following list of old favorites. Most of these series begin with books at the preprimer level (and gradually progress through third-grade reading levels).

The Moonbeam Series, Benefic Press

The Sailor Jack Series, Benefic Press

The Tom Logan Series, Benefic Press

The American Adventure Series, Harper and Row

Sounds of Language Readers by Bill Martin, Jr., Holt, Rinehart and Winston, Inc. (preprimer through sixth grade)

The Scott Foresman Reading Systems (preprimer through sixth grade)

The Jim Forest Readers, Field Educational Publications

The Wildlife Adventure Series, Field Educational Publications

World Traveler, Open Court Publishing Co. (a popular monthly with selected simplified articles from National Geographic, written at about third grade level)

Article Footnote

1.   Grace M. Fernald, *Remedial Techniques in the Basic School Subjects* (New York and London: McGraw-Hill Book Co., 1943).

Article References

Bank Street Reading Series. New York: The Macmillan Company, 1972.

Consonant Go Fish Game. 2d Series, The Kingsbury Center for Remedial Education, 2138 Bancroft Place, N.W., Washington, D.C., 1971.

Flocked Alphabet Card Set. Keystone Industrial Park, Scranton, Pa.: Harper and Row, 1969.

Gates, Arthur I., and McKillop, Anne S. *Gates-McKillop Reading Diagnostic Tests*, New York: Teachers College Press, 1962.

Stern, Catherine; Gould, Toni S.; Stern, Margaret B.; and Gartler, Marion. *Structural Reading Series*. Westminster, Md.: Random House–Singer Company, 1966.

Except in specific learning dysfunctions in the visual motor area of integration or syntax functioning, writing is a natural expression of thinking and feeling. It should flow with richness and excitement as a pupil moves from concrete to abstract levels of thinking. Instead, there is a general attitude among high school students that a written assignment is equivalent to staying home on a weekend with parents—it's sheer pain!

Many educators are concerned about this attitude and wonder what happens to change the first grader's free and easy experiential story-writing skills into the ninth-grader's dread of weekly English composition. Many critics feel the source of this problem is the teacher's overconcern and emphasis on correct style, proper grammar, and neat handwriting. It is suggested that the fear of writing in imperfect form is so powerful, it discourages pupils from writing anything unless under direct adult pressure. Other critics feel that in our society writing is a "female skill" and consequently not masculine enough for boys to assume. This problem is compounded when it comes to teaching emotionally troubled pupils, who are notoriously resistant to writing. In the next article, Bill d'Alelio demonstrates his ingenuity in motivating a group of severely disturbed pupils to enjoy the pleasure of creative writing. His use of fairy tales, with all their rich fantasy, is an excellent strategy for engaging pupils in writing assignments.

A Strategy for Teaching Remedial Language Arts: Creative Writing

William A. d'Alelio

Many pupils referred to a special class have had negative experiences in writing, and the teacher who attempts to teach creative writing in a typical fashion will encounter a wall of passive resistance or overt refusal. This article illustrates how I overcame my group's initial resistance to creative writing and shares some of the techniques which proved effective in freeing them from enough of their fears to enjoy writing.

One of the basic prerequisites for teaching language arts through creative writing is that your class must enjoy literature. In other language arts areas, a pupil must be able to read a word before he can write it, or recognize a word when he hears it before he can use the word as part of his spoken

This is the first publication of William A. d'Alelio's article. All rights reserved. Permission to reprint must be obtained from the publisher and the author.

vocabulary. In creative writing, the teacher must provide his class with ample opportunity to listen to different forms of literature and to discuss them before he asks the class to write. A selection of fairy tales, poetry, short stories, and tall tales should be enthusiastically read to the group.

I found it useful to begin with fairy tales, because they afford a variety of universal themes and are a good source of high-interest material for class discussion. An example of such discussion follows:

Teacher: *"When the ogre found he had accidentally let the boy and girl escape, what do you think he was feeling?"*

Student: *"He was probably real mad and wanted to get them, and lock them up again, and make sure they would never get away again."*

Teacher: *"What do you think he'll do now?"*

Student: *"He might get out his magic mirror to find out where they went, or he might just go out and look for them."*

A discussion of this sort can center around any of the four elements that contribute to the success or failure of a story: theme, plot, character development, and style. I found it easiest to engage group discussion of the plot before trying to deal with the other elements.

From a pupil's point of view, a good plot involves plenty of action and many obstacles for the hero to overcome. A story with a lively plot also provides the teacher with many opportunities to break for discussion just as the plot is reaching a climax, thus allowing the children to test the rules of sequential story-line development and to explore the many possibilities of action within a story.

Another advantage of using fairy tales for a group's initial exposure to literature is the characteristic clarity of the story lines. A group can learn the basic structure of a well-written story by analyzing the plot development of fairy tales they have heard in class. The clearest method for teaching the progression of a story line is to chart a story's development on the following format:

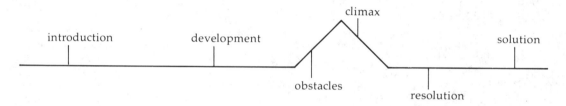

The diagram can be placed on the board, and a story with which the class is familiar can be analyzed by the teacher as an example.

The next step is to have the group analyze another story with less assistance from the teacher. The diagramed stories can be transformed into a mural, with art work by the class and captions by the teacher. An outgrowth of this technique is to provide the class with a partially filled-in diagram and ask the class to make up a story to match the outline.

Once a group is comfortable with discussing plot line, they can be introduced to character development. Character development, in this context, means: Do the children like certain characters in the story and dislike others, and how did the author describe the major characters to make them likable, foolish, scary, etc.? Group discussion is, once again, one of the primary tools for the exploration of character development. The group can be encouraged to discuss the characters of a story through questions such as: "Why do you suppose anyone would want

to go into a valley where they knew a dragon lived?" "Do you think all witches were bad?" "What kinds of things did they do?" Questions of this kind can involve a group in a serious discussion of the characters without the inevitable turn-off of "Who did you like best in this story, children?" Open-ended discussion of characters also lays the groundwork for discussion of how an author lets us get to know his characters as individuals. Group discussions can eventually lead to such questions as: "When the story says 'the prince lived happily ever after,' what do you think he was doing?" "Can you make a guess what a guy like him would be doing from what we know he did in the story?" "What was he like?"

When a group has reached this degree of sophistication in discussing stories, they are ready to move into the areas of style and theme. A good group project is to list descriptive words to fit different characters in a story. An excellent format for this type of listing is a comparison of a good character and an evil one, such as the following:

OGRE	PRINCE	WIZARD	FOOL
ugly	handsome	aged	young
short	tall	clever	sleepy
fat	kind	grey-haired	dressed in
mean	friendly	sly and	funny clothes
dangerous		crafty	stupid and
dangerous		powerful	silly
		good or evil	weak
			harmless

This exercise should be done at the board with the teacher in the role of secretary facilitator rather than active director. (Children will tend to rely on the teacher for "right" answers to this type of exercise unless they are given support to feel their contributions are of merit in and of themselves.) The teacher should try to foster an understanding of classification and descriptive language through comments such as, "An ogre is ugly; we need a word to describe the way a prince looks."

Once children develop an appreciation of literature, they will desire to participate more actively in group projects, such as the listing exercise suggested above. This involvement often starts with a request to draw pictures of characters from the fairy tales, poems, and stories that have been read to the class. The desire to draw pictures of characters can be used as a method to encourage students to start their own written work. A suggestion is for the class to draw pictures of two characters listed for a certain day. The pictures can be drawn on ditto masters and collected. When run off, the pictures can be bound into a folder, with the list of descriptive words as a first page. A page listing the illustrators and their illustrations is an excellent idea as well. Write a sentence to label the picture. Soon, children can be encouraged to make their own "books" by writing lists of descriptive words about characters of their own choice, and illustrating the lists. Another variation of this activity which works well is having pupils label their illustrations with the name of the character, a sentence describing what he is doing, or, at a higher level of development, two or three lines describing what he is like.

Moving into the area of style seems like a difficult task at first glance. This is particularly true when one is working with children who have no great love of language because of their own fear of failure. Again I broke through the initial resistance to stylistic analysis by exposing children to literature before asking them to write lists of characters' attributes. They began to use phrases to describe characters rather than the single adjectives they were using before. A discussion with the group about the advantages of using phrases rather than single words led them to the realization that language is based on chunks of meaning, rather than on single words held together by a capital letter at the beginning of a sentence and a period at the end.

Once a group has reached this realization, there are a number of activities that a teacher can use to reinforce language analysis. One of the first activities we used was an offshoot of the adjective listing. A character was described with adjectives, and the class was then asked to find phrases to replace the adjectives on the board. The format is as follows:

Chauncy the Crocodile

Chauncy is a crocodile who is

green: *the color of grass*

crafty: *always on his guard*

dangerous: *never to be trusted*

lazy: *usually asleep*

scaly: *covered with a coat of armor*

This activity can be adapted for adverbial clauses as well: "Chauncy runs quickly—as fast as the wind." Once the group begins to get the hang of this type of phrasing, they can be introduced to the general use of phrasing in sentences.

Using short selections the teacher has read orally to the class, the group can look for ways sentences can be broken down into meaningful phrases. This can be done by putting the sentences on the board without punctuation and asking the class to decide where the natural breaks occur. The following is an example of the type of sentence which is most useful for this type of exercise:

Harry went out to the garage and got into his car he thought about his basketball game the whole time as he drove to the gym

Another useful exercise for teaching phrasing is to pass out telegram messages typed on yellow paper, without punctuation, and have the group try to decipher the meaning.

dear Steve it was so good to

get your letter last Wednesday
I will be coming to visit your
school this week and hope to see
you then call to let me know where
I can reach you

One advantage of this technique is that it allows the teacher to adjust the reading level of each message while exposing an entire group to the concept of phrasing. Phrasing, for its own sake, will not hold the interest of a class for long—nor should it. It is one of the prerequisite skills for creative writing, not an end in itself. When the teacher anticipates his class has had enough of phrasing, he should be prepared to give them some exciting applied uses of the skill. Three such activities are sentence reduction, sentence transformation, and rearranging sentences.

Sentence reduction is an activity in which each pupil can be made to feel as powerful as a professional editor and as precise as a master detective. A complex sentence with many modifying phrases and clauses is placed on the blackboard and read to the group. The children are asked to figure out the sentence's main idea by crossing out descriptive phrases and language.

One day, Happy, the hippopotamus, who was used to eating and eating and eating, looked in his food trough and saw, to his surprise, that he had no food!

This sentence can be reduced so that it reads as follows:

Happy saw he had no food!

It would be unusual for a class to reduce a sentence to such a bare minimum on the first attempt, but with practice almost any group can become quite proficient and get a great deal of enjoyment out of reducing sentences of this sort. It is truly exciting to see a group of pupils who previously were not interested in the structure of language working with enthusiasm on a task such as this. Don't push them to make more deletions than they can with comfort. With my group, I found that the process of sentence reduction is developmental and that once a class becomes comfortable with it they will really learn how much of our written language is descriptive rather than purely functional.

There is another variation of sentence reduction which bears noting. When a class begins to show a high level of proficiency at reducing sentences, they can begin to work the process in reverse: They can expand sentences rather than reduce them. The teacher would tell the class he has some sentences which he has already reduced, and which he would like to put back in their longer form with the group's help. A sentence such as "Carl was angry" is written on the board with a list of adjectives and descriptive phrases:

Carl _____
        who didn't like to wake up
        the sleepy rhinoceros

was angry _____ !
        who didn't know any better
        when Teddy
        outside his cage
        blew a trumpet

The class then suggests where the phrases fit to make the best sentence. As the class begins to show skill at this type of exercise, more of the phrases can be left up to their imagination. This exercise leads nicely into the next technique, sentence transformation.

Sentence transformation is similar to sentence reduction in that the class is provided with stimulus sentences on the blackboard. In this instance, their output is oral and kids enjoy it. The group's task is to maintain the given structure of several sentences while altering their content. A passage such as:

Who was it that was gliding? It was Wendell, the brown-winged bat!

is placed in the following format:

Who was it that was gliding? It was Wendel the brown winged   bat!
        flying   Franklin   blue   speckled   fish!
        soaring
        hovering
        swimming

Questions are asked, such as: "What if you didn't want to use the word, 'gliding'? What other word could you use?" The children's suggestions are then listed in the column under the word "gliding," and the sentence is read with the substitution of new words. By offering a word which entails a different activity, such as swimming, the teacher can draw attention to the interrelatedness of the two sentences (see diagram above). This activity also provides a good format for introducing such concepts as verb agreement within phrases. "When the first sentence is phrased in the present tense, what happens to the second sentence?" "Who *is* it that *is* gliding?" "It *is* ... etc." A class can become so proficient at this activity that it can produce an entire family of sentences from one stimulus sentence. As with the lists of character descriptions, the different sentence patterns produced by the class can be put into book form. (New sentence families can be added easily if the book is a looseleaf.) Children can be encouraged to illustrate some of their favorite sentences.

One of the techniques frequently used by skilled creative writers is the rearranging of sentence order. An example of this technique is found below:

From the top of the bridge,
the river below is a piece
of sky, until you drop
a stone in it.

Teaching this skill to children is a challenging process, and yet, if they have mastered the other phrasing skills, they can learn it rapidly. Two techniques prove effective in introducing the concept of sentence rearrangement: the first I call scrambling, the second unscrambling. I found it worked best to have pupils unscramble sentences before trying to scramble them. A sentence arranged in an unusual order is placed on the board. The class is asked to underline the phrases which make up the sentence and then rearrange the sentence in a more traditional order. An illustration of this technique, using the sample sentence above:

      (3)   *(1)*
From the top of the bridge,   *the river below is a*
                 (2)
piece of sky   *until you drop a stone in it.*

When the numbered phrases are read in their traditional order, they read:

The river below is a piece of sky, until you drop a stone in it from the top of the bridge.

Scrambling is similar to unscrambling in that the first stage involves breaking down the sentence into its component phases. After a sentence has been broken down, the group can experiment with the various invented combinations from the root sentence. The sentence, "If you think about it carefully, Harry is the kind of person you want as a friend," will yield the sentence, "Harry is the kind of person you want as a friend, if you think about it carefully." When two sentences constructed from the same phrases are read with their natural inflections, it provides a class with a real sense of the significance of sentence order. It is a rare pupil who, hearing the two sentences above read aloud, fails to realize that the second sentence is none too kind to Harry!

The fourth area of literary analysis that can help overcome the fear of writing is theme. Most children will begin to notice basic similarities among the stories and fairy tales which have been read to them over a period of time. Through discussion of theme children come to understand that writing is merely a way of putting concerns and feelings down on paper. Understanding the nature of literary themes can best be developed through group discussion of stories after a class has been exposed to several different themes in two or three different stories. The class should be able to sort out the "scary" stories from the "fun" or "sad" ones. Pupils should be encouraged to discuss their ideas about why writers choose certain subjects, such as the need to overcome obstacles, find love, grow up, etc. They can also be asked their opinions on why sometimes characters who seem to be monsters, frogs, etc., turn out to be good figures, or why many small or weak heroes are the only ones who can kill giants or release people from spells. There are no "right" answers to these issues; they should be seen as an opportunity for pupils to decide what themes they like best and to start exploring what types of actions are appropriate to their favorite themes. At this point many pupils have acquired enough confidence to start their own writing.

There are two general styles of teaching writing: native expression and stimulus-response. The first method has been used by Sylvia Ashton Warner, Kenneth Koch, and Roger Landrum. The basis of this technique is the belief that children, unless inhibited by a fear of failure, are able to produce excellent written work, given an opportunity to do so. Warner and Koch believe in writing assignments that reflect a pupil's interests. Warner asks her class to decide on three words a day they want to learn and then has the class make up a story incorporating the new words. Her concept is that pupils will spontaneously evolve into writers as they begin to sense the security of writing within a group, and that they will soon start to write on their own. She also feels that children will develop into excellent writers without any need for adult intervention in terms of style, once they have begun the process of writing for enjoyment.

Koch's beliefs are similar to Warner's, except that he feels children should be encouraged to explore their natural writing style through individual writing assignments such as "Wish" or "Lie" poems. These consist of personal wishes or lies that each child uses as the basis for each poem:

I wish I had a magic helicopter
I wish I had a long red train
I wish I had a . . . , etc.
                    or
I ate 1,000 pancakes for breakfast
I swam across the ocean before lunch . . . ,etc.

This basic technique is modified by specifying conditions that must be met in each poem, (e.g., each line must be a wish that involves a color). Like Warner's techniques Koch's teaching style is used only to start a pupil writing; the goal is to stop influencing the child's writing as quickly as possible.

Landrum differs from Koch and Warner in method, but not in theory. He tries to engage a pupil in creative writing by getting him to dictate a story into a tape recorder during a one-to-one interview situation. The dictated story is then transcribed and read back to the child. In this way, the child is introduced to his own stories in print and becomes motivated to start writing on his own. Pupils reluctant to tell a story are interviewed about what they are doing in school or at home, and through skillful probing are led to develop their responses into a story.

The stimulus-response style of teaching writing has been with us for many years in one form or another. The class essay about summer vacation is an example of this method through which many of us suffered. Fortunately, many excellent teachers (Ruth Carlson, Mauree Applegate, and Walter Petty) have provided other examples of how to use this method creatively. Their ideas range from hav-

ing pupils react to and write about art masterpieces, such as the paintings of Vincent Van Gogh, to having children collect objects while on a walk, and write a history of the object's life. These teachers believe in the importance of structured style development, and include in their books many suggestions for improving children's writing styles.

Because children in a special education setting have varied learning rates and styles, these teachers' techniques work with some children and fail with others. If a child is having consistent difficulty writing in the native experience style, it may be because he is easily disorganized and so needs the structure of a stimulus-response model. The inverse is also true—a child who is too rigid and too concerned with writing the "right" thing to get anything written at all needs the open-endedness and acceptance of a native-expression teaching style.

The most important thing to realize about teaching creative writing, especially to children who have been rejected and who have an extremely low self-concept, is something which is easy to lose sight of: Behind all of the resistance which you may face initially when you institute creative writing as part of your curriculum, the children *want* to be able to express themselves. The pupils want to be able to write and when they find that they can trust you to help them do it, you and your class will be starting on one of the most exciting and mutually rewarding experiences you can share.

One of my greatest rewards last year was this piece of writing from a twelve-year-old student whose initial response to writing was, "I ain't gonna do none of that shit!"

> *Shout*
> As I sleep
> with my eyes opened
> out of the dark
> I hear a N O I S E
> with my eyes
> but looking around the
> room I only hear
> the silence of
> dark. As I wipe
> the cold sweat
> from my brow.

Article References

Arbuthnot, May Hill. *Children and Books.* Glenview, Ill.: Scott Foresman & Co., 1964.

Carlson, Ruth Kearney. *Sparkling Words.* Geneva, Ill.: Paladin House Publishers, 1973.

Koch, Kenneth. *Wishes, Lies, and Dreams.* New York: Vintage, 1970.

Martin, Bill. *Sounds of Mystery.* New York: Holt, Rinehart, and Winston, 1967.

The knowledge that many emotionally troubled pupils are reading two or more years below their mental age has motivated private educational companies to develop numerous remedial reading programs. Although Huber[9] has reported that low-achieving, emotionally disturbed elementary pupils have even greater deficiencies in arithmetic than reading, there is not the parallel interest in remedial mathematics programs.

Interestingly, emotionally disturbed pupils seem to have more difficulty with subtraction and division than with addition and multiplication. Proponents of psychoanalytic theory suggest that subtraction and division are mathematical processes that "take things away" or "cut them into smaller parts." For deprived and disturbed pupils, the symbolism of these processes creates feelings of sibling rivalry (losing to others) and castration anxiety (losing what little I have left). These interpretations may be true—they at least caution teachers about the symbolic meaning of numbers and mathematical processes—but they have not as yet led to positive solutions. Perhaps some additional interpretations of mathematics learning problems will develop as special educators turn to experimental designs as a way of determining educational remedial programs.

Because so few remedial programs in mathematics are available, a brief summary of some basic programs is listed below:

1.   *The Primary Math Skills Improvement Program* (Special Education Materials, New York) consists of forty prerecorded tapes that involve highly motivating, individualized exercises, reinforcing fundamental skills in sets, subtraction, multiplication, division, and place value.

2.   *Key Math,* by Dr. Austin Connally, *et al.,* (American Guidance Service, Inc., Minnesota) is an individual diagnostic arithmetic test with excellent visual materials. The test covers fourteen skill areas and can be used successfully with pupils who also have difficulties in reading.

3.   *The A B C of Math* (Math Shop, Watertown, Massachusetts) is a complete curriculum series with unusually good manipulative materials such as multi-link cubes, logiblocs, and 3-D numbers.

4.   *The Cuisenaire Rods* (Cuisenaire Company of America, Inc., New York) is the oldest and most frequently used technique of remedial mathematics. The method is concrete, precise, and simple. For most pupils, this is a new way of thinking and feeling about math. All special educators, we feel, should be skilled in this particular technique.

5.   *Math Readiness,* by Dr. May (McGraw-Hill, Early Learning Division, Pennsylvania) is an individualized taped program using an audio and visual approach to instruction. Although it is designed for the primary-age pupil, it can be modified for older pupils who need to begin with basic concepts such as big, bigger, and biggest, right, left, etc.

In the following article, Rose Alpher describes her strategy for remediating pupils with severe mathematical disabilities. Her approach reflects the best of original, exciting, and personal methods of re-motivating reluctant learners. A historical approach to mathematics leaves children with a greater appreciation of the world and knowledge which most pupils in regular classes never receive. It is a special teaching strategy like this one that makes special education special.

A Strategy for Teaching Remedial Mathematics: If I Had $1,000,000 . . .

Rose W. Alpher

Most school curricula manage to strip mathematics of its cultural content, leaving a bare skeleton of technicalities which manage to repel both normal and troubled students. To undo some of this antipathy toward mathematics, my initial remedial approach is to use a historical method that shows the evolution of mathematical concepts. This strat-

egy brings a fresh outlook and a new interest to mathematics.

By allowing pupils to discover through reading graphically illustrated material and trips to the museum, or library, a comparison of Egyptian mathematics with Babylonian or Greek mathematics is first developed. The sole purpose of this historical look is for the pupils to feel an identity, a kinship with early civilizations. The excitement begins when the pupil discovers that the human race, even in its earliest stage of development, was endowed with a "number sense." This number sense permitted early man to realize that something had changed in a small collection of objects when one object was removed or added.

To expand this theme, considerable time is spent with a group of four to six remedial pupils in whimsical speculation. For example, I might ask: "What if we had no number names; how could we report how many pupils are in school? How could we determine how many books we have, or how many chairs we need around the lunch table or in the movie?" Frequently, the pupils answer with primitive methods: "one chair for Larry, one for Tommy, one for Mike, one for Teddy," or by making lines on a piece of paper. Soon they mention counting on fingers, which is my signal to review man's early method of matching persons with sticks or cutting notches in a stick of wood. It is most important at this beginning stage of remediation not to hurry the lessons; they must be relaxed and unthreatening. The pupils must believe they do not

have to learn to add, multiply, or do anything else on a deadline contract. This arrangement relieves the pupil of immediate anxiety because he is still not motivated to learn math.

Another nonthreatening example of numeration is the Roman system. Because pupils are not expected to use it seriously, it can become an enjoyable and familiar system, a nice way of decoding the numbers occasionally found on buildings, in books, and as chapter headings. Of course, I do not expect them to solve math problems using Roman numerals. If, however, the teacher writes the Roman numerals on a chart, leaves it up within view, and from time to time gives them a decoding problem (for example, the Romans wrote 28 as XXVIII, 145 as CXLV, and 1974 as MCMLXXIV), interest is maintained. The pupil's ability to decode and solve a few of his own problems gives him pleasure and immediate gratification. More importantly, a triangular relationship among teacher, pupils, and numbers is built. This relationship is extended further by introducing graphic illustration of the Egyptian system of numeration as shown below:

Number	Symbol	Resembles	Number	Symbol	Resembles
1	/	Stroke	10,000	/	Bent reed
10	∩	Heel bone	100,000	⌒	Fish
100	⌇	Coiled rope	1,000,000	大	Astonished man
1,000	⚘	Lotus flower			

The Egyptians could write 25 as //////∩∩ or ∩∩//////

(Because order made no difference, the ones could come before the tens, hundreds, or thousands.) The pupils are asked to suggest how the Egyptians

might have written, let's say, 2,115. The various correct answers might be:

⚘⚘⌇∩/////   /////∩⌇⚘⚘   ⌇/////⚘⚘

Again, the fun of playing with symbols becomes appealing to the pupils. They remain unthreatened by them, and they are still learning basic arithmetic. This method also can adopt the aura of a fairy tale, or a fantasy of long ago.

At this point, I begin to present our system of

numeration. I help them discover the Hindu-Arabic system, complete with the symbols: 0, 1, 2, 3, 4, 5, 6, 7, 8, 9, and 10. For example, I begin by asking them to write Hindu-Arabic numerals for Egyptian symbols:

1. ∩∩// = 22.   2. ⌇⌇⌇⌇ = 412.   3. ⌇∩∩∩∩∩ = 150.

Then, I reverse the process and ask them to write Egyptian symbols for Arabic numerals.

From this task I begin simple addition:

5	8
6	2
7	6
3	4

The transitional step in acquiring mathematical skills is the mastering of addition; the pupils are told that all they have to learn is how to add. Through examples, they begin to see that multiplication, subtraction, and division are multiple addition. With constant examples I insist on additive subtraction, i.e., 9 and how many is 15, not 15 minus 9. The transfer to standard division and multiplication occurs spontaneously as confidence increases.

Games are introduced which not only include division, fractions, estimating, and rounding out numbers, but also increases the spirit of working together, sharing knowledge, and learning to take some risk. An example of this kind of game is to (1) provide a small bag of M & M's; (2) allow the students to examine the bag, take a small handful, and estimate how many are in their hands, how many are in the bag; (3) give them the cost of the candy; and (4) have them figure out how much per piece. Thus, math sessions become centered around activities; much more interest is generated. One can actually feel the pupils' enthusiasm. They begin to understand concepts and acquire skills. They begin to explore and initiate many of their own ideas (one can see them measuring floors, desks, wallboards, the playground) by which they can demonstrate that they understand the meaning behind the symbol and can use this knowledge in a practical way.

With the functional knowledge of basic mathematical skills, curiosity returns and numbers can be used to expand their life. "What would you do if you had $100, $1,000, or $1,000,000?" becomes an understandable and entertaining question. Whether math is used for dreaming or reality, it's a tool that helps a pupil bring order to a complex world, security at a shopping center, and excitement to his inner life.

Most pupils look forward to physical education and recess periods because, like candy, they are the sweet times of the school day. They are chances to relax, play, have fun, fool around, release tension, and relate to friends instead of books and assigned lessons. Play provides children with vast educational experiences in social learning and physical cognitive skills. An average ten-year-old pupil is a master of numerous individual and group games: checkers, booby trap, Monopoly, fish, old maid, gin, twenty-one, slap, freeze tag, hide-and-seek, steal-the-bacon, drop-the-hankie, baseball, football, basketball, kickball, etc. Games teach children the important lesson that it is impossible to be always first, best, and strongest when playing with peers. The natural feelings of competition, frustration, joy, and disappointment provide meaningful opportunities to learn how to cope with strong feelings that are a part of winning or losing a game.

Unfortunately, emotionally troubled pupils frequently do not know how to play. They never internalize the rules or develop the skills to be successful at games. More important, they usually cannot discriminate between a disappointment and a disaster. For them, play is not a therapeutic activity facilitating growth, but another painful conflict area. It is not uncommon for teachers to exclude these children from the playground because of the problems they create for others. There is little recognition that this decision to remove them from their peer group prevents them from learning the skills they need to play with others. This practice is similar to telling a starving child he will not be fed until his hunger pangs go away. In special education, play is an important basic mean; it should not be taken away or used as an enticement as if it were a dessert.

Research in this area is grossly neglected. One of the original studies in this area was directed by Gump and Sutton-Smith[10] in 1955. They studied how the social interaction among emotionally disturbed children was significantly different between two camp activities, swimming and crafts. They concluded that the activity itself was the important factor in determining the amount of aggression the campers exhibited. This means the type of programming for disturbed children becomes a significant factor. Each game carries its hidden psychodynamics. Significant group forces operate when the teacher selects dodge-ball (in which the group plays against individuals) as opposed to tag (in which an individual is after the group). Some of the specific variables to consider in a game are: the amount of body contact (football); body mobility (statues vs. tag); the complexity of rules and the skill requirements (chess, Monopoly, checkers); the degree of luck (dice and spinner games); the use of space (kickball); the duration of the game (war); the use of props (balls, rackets); role-taking factors (quarterback, pitcher, "it"); and the degree of "horsing around" the game can tolerate (Mother-may-I vs. darts). Unless the teacher knows how a particular game can affect the frustration level of a group or an individual, he may inadvertently contribute to program breakdown and group chaos.

In the following article, Franz Huber translates these concerns for the classroom teacher by describing the four sources of conflict that occur during play. He also offers guidelines for the constructive use of games and sports for troubled children. This article focuses the importance of play for pupils and the skills teachers need to help aggressive pupils control themselves and help the withdrawn become more active, by encouraging cooperative rather than competitive play.

A Strategy for
Teaching Cooperative Games:
Let's Put Back the Fun in
Games for Disturbed Children
Franz Huber

Ms. Smith breathed an audible sigh of relief. Jimmy, the last of the twelve-member, all-boy "academic-social adjustment class" had just passed reluctantly through the door for the twenty-minute recess. Not to play with the others, of course, but to brood and sulk and probably fantasize about what he could do if he had his older brother's ability. Jimmy was so puny and awkward he could barely make foot contact with the spinning, twisting ball so sadistically propelled by Robert, who automatically had taken over the coveted pitcher position. Perhaps Robert was not the most skilled player, but he certainly was the most dominant—overtly so outside of the classroom, and covertly in Ms. Smith's presence. With a look or a threatening gesture he could engender fear and acquiescence in the others. How he was able to buffalo the other boys she didn't quite understand, but didn't he intimidate even her at times?

She could just imagine what was going on out there, for it happened just about the same way every day, whether she went out with them or sent the part-time aide as she did this time. Neither could do much from the sidelines anyway except interact with the stragglers, observe the rest, and be prepared for the anger, resentment, recriminations, hurts, and smoldering hostility after everyone returned to the classroom.

Because her "class" had a separate, later time from any of the other grades, one of them always had to go out. Too many vociferous complaints from teachers, children, and parents about "those kids" had accumulated—their bad language and interfering behavior. From the intense yelling she was now hearing, the customary dispute of someone being either "out" or "safe" was probably occurring outside. Depending on the location, first

base or home plate, these disputes were either settled by individual flare-ups with the toughest boy winning out, or, in a team-against-team conflagration, with Robert's team usually emerging the victor. Then, defenseless Jordie would either drop an easy flyball or let the ball slither through his legs for a home run. How she agonized over Jordie! He was always the recipient of the group's most vehement abuse. Whenever anything went wrong, whether Jordie did it intentionally or unintentionally, or was even involved, he could elicit the group's wrath. He would end up crying and pretending he was oblivious to any peer communication for the next few days. Then he would try again but usually end up in a similar situation.

He wasn't the only scapegoat. Any of the five boys on the lower end of the totem pole could hold that title. Many times she had seen abuse passed on from one child to another, right down the chain. John, a very intelligent but highly manipulative boy, would sometimes be on the receiving end, but generally he was able to turn things around so one of the less sophisticated boys would get it. John had the knack of working things out to suit himself. Yesterday, for instance, contrary to the rules, he convinced everyone that on a force play at third the runner had to be tagged. She knew she should have stepped in as a final arbitrator, but then she wasn't quite sure of the rules herself.

What was probably the worst for her was the reactions of the losers and the winners as they returned from the playground—she could spot them immediately by the way they held their heads. She remembered one authority on play who wrote that children aged ten to twelve weren't that competitive unless made so by adults. That might be true of some kids but not hers. The losers were so dejected, they were unconsolable and spent a good part of the day berating themselves, while the winners, with every taunt and gesture, made sure to remind them of their inadequacies. Or, she would let them stay out ten minutes longer than regulation—there'd be hell to pay, not only from the principal but from her own chaotic group when they came in. As she blew the whistle signalling their return, she wondered which was worse: remaining inside as she did and spending the whole time conjuring up the probable, or being beaten down by experiencing the actual. Did it matter? She still had the same mess to deal with!

It is well-known that disturbed children have major difficulties playing games and sports. It is less well-accepted that normal children and even adults evidence similar problems. What distinguishes the three groups is not so much a qualitative measure of the different kinds of problems that occur, but a quantitative measure of degree, frequency, duration, minimum provocation, and level of incapacitation. In other words, disturbed children react to common frustrations of games and sports (1) with extreme intensity of emotional response, (2) with high frequency, (3) with such long duration that the emotional behaviors pyramid, (4) to such slight provocation that it's barely detectable by the outside observer, and (5) with such a level of incapacitation that it makes it impossible for them to recoup sufficiently for continued participation in the activity. Normal children and adults react with more subdued responses to similar provocation. These exacerbated responses by emotionally disturbed children produce unmanageable trauma for teachers, recreational therapists, or aides, who attempt to have a relaxing time playing games.

Four factors can be identified as sources of conflict: (1) problems that reside primarily in the individual; (2) problems that stem primarily from peer interaction; (3) problems that reside primarily within the structure and organization of the activity; (4) problems that stem primarily from the supervising adult.

The Individual

In most instances, games and sports call for varying degrees of aggression, which should emerge in the form of controlled aggression. This is beyond the usual capability of many disturbed children. They show either too much aggression, resulting in verbal and physical attacks, or too little aggression, producing ineffectuality, defenselessness, and flight. Both responses can be frightening states for the disturbed child.

Closely allied to aggression is the winning and losing syndrome. Winning or losing graciously involves a great deal of understanding and tact. Disturbed children, especially, have not developed the affective skills to accomplish this task. Winning for some signifies complete vanquishment of an opponent; losing involves considerable self-abjection and self-devaluation.

Many disturbed children also do not have the requisite physical skills needed for participation in games and sports with their age mates. Dribbling a basketball, kicking a soccer ball, hitting a softball, all require considerable practice regardless of the inherent physical coordination of the individual. Without sufficient opportunity and sustained practice, these advanced physical skills can rarely be obtained. Consequently, few children enjoy participation in activities which highlight their weaknesses. For many children, it is safer not to play than to try and fail.

Peer Interaction

Peer interaction during latency age is rarely supportive. Peer rivalry is a common phenomenon and eventually produces a status hierarchy within the group. This status hierarchy fluctuates to some extent with the specific activity, but because most games and sports rely on similar skills, the hierarchy remains relatively stable. Lower-status members suffer considerable scapegoating, with displacement of feelings and projection of blame heaped on their least buoyant shoulders. As each child's main goal is to maintain his place within the hierarchy, there is little cognizance of another's plight. Looking through another's eyes and realizing his problems, much less acting to minimize another's pain, is an unattainable task for most children, especially disturbed children. Giving even partial credit to another for a good attempt, or supporting someone in need, is a rare occurrence. This makes it doubly hard for the ineffectual child to win the peer support needed to continue participation or at least bear the moment's inadequacies.

Structure and Organization of the Activity

The structure and organization of specific games and sports should be analyzed to determine their inherent potential for promoting satisfactory or unsatisfactory participant interaction. Most games and sports vary significantly in the general level of frustration. Consider the contrast between softball and soccer. In softball a significant percentage of enforced waiting time is often frustrating: waiting interminably for a flyball in the outfield positions (and when the ball does come chances are it will be out of reach), waiting for three outs to get to bat, waiting for one's turn at bat while other team members bat, waiting for the pitcher to pitch the ball. In soccer, a child has more control over his own destiny. He can go after the ball or not; he can be in the thick of the scuffling or choose to remain on the perimeter. His intensity of participation is governed by his own momentary inclinations, and he is not subjected to forced inactivity. Soccer tends to minimize the frustration induced by inactivity; softball tends to intensify it.

Certain games and activities overemphasize competition, whereas, with slight restructuring, cooperative elements can be accentuated. Take the game "Horse" played on a basketball court with three players. The first player shoots any shot from any position on the court. If the child makes the shot, the next player must duplicate the shot; if he misses he receives an "H." For every miss another letter is added until the word H-o-r-s-e is completely spelled out, and that player is eliminated. (Games in which players are eliminated are doubly hazardous for disturbed children. They must not only suffer through feelings generated by elimination, but early elimination substantially reduces practice time for those with the greatest need. Consider the usual elimination pattern in even a simple game like "Simon Says.")

A slight variation in the Horse game can easily make it a cooperative effort. Choose any word, a longer one preferably, and for every shot made by any of the participants a letter is generated until the total word is spelled out. This transforms the game into a cooperative endeavor with no one eliminated and all receiving equal amounts of practice.

Games and sports can also be analyzed by the degree of focus on the individual participants. High individual-focus games accentuate the crucialness of how a player responds at a particular point in time.

A centerfielder either catches or drops the flyball; all players' eyes focus on that event, and this one play might determine hero or goat status. Tag, with only one child "it," is a also high-focus situation. If more than one child is "it," however, the degree of focus is lessened. Soccer is probably a much lower focus game than softball or kickball because of its complexity and the high probability of chance or fluke occurrences. This reduces the crucial responses for each player. Generally, disturbed children have a higher possibility of surviving low-focus games than those with high focus.

The Supervising Adult

The presence or absence of a supervising adult is of major consequence in predicting the emotional outcomes of games and sports involving disturbed children. Admittedly, presence alone is not sufficiently important to assure any degree of comfort, but, at the minimum, major conflicts can be resolved without the whole activity being jeopardized. Absence of the adult allows for such chaotic conditions that the required mopping-up procedures permeate all subsequent activities. Many teachers feel reluctant to give up precious "free time" or "recuperative time" by providing even minimum supervision for play periods. In the case of disturbed children, this is definitely a short-sighted view. Teachers do not realize how much they can contribute to making games and sports a worthwhile activity.

Guidelines for Constructive Use of Games and Sports for Disturbed Children

The following guidelines apply to any adult with responsibility for supervising normal children or disturbed children engaged in the whole spectrum of games, sports, and activities, both indoors and outdoors. Capability in this role becomes the crucial variable in determining beneficial utilization of these play activities.

1. *Active Participation and "Umpire Services."* Two roles which place the adult in a strategic and highly influential position are active participant and "umpire." (In the active participant role the adult often serves simultaneously as umpire.) As an active participant the adult can control, at least to some extent, the outcome of the game so that extreme imbalance in scores don't occur and can assess

and ameliorate the players' frustration levels by controlling play of the game at crucial times. Although this may come under the heading of manipulation, it is necessary if games are to become a constructive experience for disturbed children. If done skillfully, the adult's control can be practically imperceptible.

Active participation also enables the adult to include children who would otherwise be overlooked by peers before or during the game. In basketball, for instance, few high-proficiency players ever pass the ball to low-proficiency players. Thus, even if willingly on the court, low-proficiency players can be substantially eliminated from play. The adult active participant can assist the low-proficiency player by providing him, for example, with a clear shot or an open pass.

The umpire role is vital for maintaining the game. The umpire must be decisive, judicious, and sensitive to each individual's tolerance level. Decisions that could go either way can be guided by the spirit of the amount, depending on the vulnerability of the children. The umpire's knowledge of the game, his prestige in the eyes of the players, and his judicious decisions based on awareness of the total situation make the role a strong supportive factor in constructive play.

2. Control of Negative Peer Interaction.   The adult maximizes his opportunities to curtail negative peer interaction by being an active participant. Negative peer interaction feeds on itself—one hostile comment frequently leads to another. Scapegoating gains strength in direct proportion to the number of children on the attack. The best control of this destructive form of interaction can be attained by catching it in its incipient stages. At the right time comments such as "Let's play the game," "Good effort," "Tough luck," "He tried," "Aw, come on, we'll get 'em," "Here we go," serve as tolerance builders and diversionary tactics. Quick resumption of play sets up required alternative responses and doesn't allow the disturbed child to work himself into a lather.

The reinforcement of any positive social behavior is also effective. One school went so far as to videotape kids during play and then replay for them individually scenes in which they displayed supportive, helpful, empathetic behaviors to others. The same effect can be more gradually attained through verbal reinforcement of appropriate interactions if the adult is alert to these behaviors. Values, too, need to be reinforced. When kids say "That was a good game," "Who cares who won or lost," "It was a close game," "Everyone had fun," the values inherent in these comments need supporting.

3. Modeling Behavior.   An active way of precipitating prosocial comments, behaviors, and values in disturbed children is to deliberately model these for them. The adult participant's attitude, demeanor, and reactions should serve as an example of behavior worth imitating. When the adult gives credit even for a partial attempt, when he minimizes the player's errors, when he supports all participants and not just certain members, these behaviors are likely to be modeled by the children. The adult, by placing himself in the same position as the players, exerts tremendous influence on the whole tenor of the game through his exemplary behavior and his sensitivity to the individual participant's problems, needs, and pressure points.

4. Building Physical Coordination and Skill. Many disturbed children are deficient in physical strength, coordination, and the physical skills needed for many games and sports, but these attributes can be developed in most youngsters. One pudgy, weak, and uncoordinated fourth-grader, isolated from play because of nonexistent ball-handling skills, became a respectable team member in four months. He was put on an exercise schedule consisting of push-ups, sit-ups, squat thrusts, kneebends, running in place, and isometrics. A high school student coached him in ball-handling skills: catching, throwing, kicking, etc. His physical strength improved considerably. At first he couldn't even begin to accomplish a push-up, but by the end of four months he could do four or five legitimate ones using his arms alone and with his body straight. His game skills improved to such an extent, he was no longer ashamed to play with the others and they began to accept him. His posture, walk, and whole physical manner changed with his newfound control and appreciation of his body. With effort, similar results can be obtained with any group of youngsters. One teacher ingeniously provided six exercise stations throughout the classroom which she used for "activity breaks" whenever the group became restless or needed a diversion. After ten minutes of exercise the boys would return, somewhat more contentedly, to their academic tasks.

5. Planning, Play, Discussion.   The constructive use of games and sports can be facilitated by adequate planning and preparation before actual play and by discussion and wrap-up afterwards. Planning involves a decision about the game to be played, a review and clarification of the rules, a review of good sportsmanship, and a review of how the players can make it more fun for everybody.

This kind of preparation can forestall many problems. After play, a brief wrap-up session combined with quiet rest can provide the transition to other school tasks. The teacher may utilize this time to highlight various aspects of the activity or to commend various members for their play, behavior, or good sportsmanship. Focus should generally be positive rather than a continuation of arguments, conflicts, etc., unless there is an issue that definitely needs resolution.

6. Modification of Games.   Most games and sports can be modified to achieve different purposes. Games are not immutable—they can be changed in whatever way predicates constructive outcomes. Although the majority of games emphasize competition between individuals or teams, most games can be restructured to minimize the competitive elements and highlight the cooperative spirit among the players. Following are some examples of restructuring to make them more serviceable for constructive use.

a. Simon Says.   This game can be played without the noxious elimination of players who miss a direction and thereby receive no further practice in the activity. By not being eliminated, the competitive factor between children is reduced, as well as the competition between teacher and child. If the competitive element needs to be reintroduced, the primary competition can be between the teacher and the total group: seeing how many can or can't be caught at any one time. The teacher will invariably lose, which isn't necessarily bad for the children's morale.

b. Kickball and Softball.   These games are usually organized by teams, with three outs indicating a team change from "at bat" to "field." Often one team is stronger and they remain at bat so long there's little time left for the other team. Futility and frustration galore! If each player has one time at bat in rotation, however, and then automatically the other team comes up to bat, every child has an equal turn at bat and the frustration of three outs is avoided. Runs may still be counted. Another variation allows all players three hits or kicks, running out only the last one. All players rotate through all positions, with the only competition being how far each player hits or kicks.

c. Volleyball.   Volleyball can be a great cooperative game. With one team on either side of the net they can attempt to keep the ball in play as long as possible without it touching the ground; the chal-

lenge is to get higher and higher numerical counts. This form of volleyball is even more fun without a net. Three to ten players stand in relatively close proximity; one player taps the ball in the air with everyone attempting to maintain it there, but no player may tap the ball twice in succession. The higher the counts the more exciting the game gets. It's good for all age levels and gets everyone involved in a cooperative effort.

d. Dodgeball.   This can be a very aggressive game for children—actually striking someone with a ball is overt aggression and repugnant to some children. To some extent, this can be controlled by the balls' softness. Occasionally, the game is prolonged by the group's inability to get a few agile players remaining in the center "out." This complication can be easily remedied, however, by making the circle smaller or giving the participants one or two more balls to throw. This will get them "out" in a hurry. With unskilled players in the center, limit the action to one ball and keep the circle large. This will result in better apparent performance by these children. These two factors—size of circle and number of balls—allow almost complete control of the game by the adult according to whatever intent he has in mind.

e. "It" Games.   "It" games should always start with a strong runner as "It," rather than a slower child who is unable to catch anyone. Also, the cumulative version (all participants caught become "It" until the last child is caught) makes for a more exciting game, brings forth maximum participation, and enables the slower runners to catch the speedier players at times.

"I got it" is a good variation highlighting the fastest runners. Anyone tagging "It" becomes the one who's "got it" and is chased by the group. This game always involves the group against one individual and rarely is the group unsuccessful. Of primary importance in "It" games is the designation of a circumscribed area for play. Otherwise, "It" can run off with the game.

f. Soccer.   Soccer is a good all-around game for the preadolescent age group. It has good running activity, some physical contact, beginnings of teamwork, low-focus and chance occurrences, and quick shifts in offensive and defensive situations that keep the excitement level high. In addition, all children can participate regardless of the level of skill, and all can contribute something to the team. In soccer it is almost impossible for any player to be regarded as a liability. The necessity for umpire services is paramount in this game because of the inherent tendency to use the hands to control the ball. This becomes the one drawback for players forced to get along without these services. It is a pity soccer is not played more in this country because it has so much to offer children.

In conclusion, games and sports can be fun for disturbed children if they are sufficiently supervised, monitored, and controlled by adults, preferably in active participation. Leaving disturbed children alone to work things out for themselves is an overwhelming assignment and usually results in chaos.

The adult must be constantly aware of the psychological aspects of the game and the best ways to ameliorate the negative impact on each child.

Many games and sports need adult restructuring to form the best possible circumstances for play. A perceptive analysis of each game or sport is essential in understanding the effects of these activities on children. It is then possible for any adult to respond with creativity and ingenuity in restructuring these activities to facilitate constructive and worthwhile outcomes for disturbed children.

Although we need to maintain and improve our present remedial services for handicapped children, most future resources should be devoted to primary prevention programs. As special educators, we must change from a crisis "firefighting" educational service to a "fireproofing" service. Unfortunately, fireproofing is less glamorous than firefighting, but it is our only real solution to preventing another ten million children from being overwhelmed by the future demands of society. The first step in establishing primary prevention programs was accomplished in 1973, when the Council of Exceptional Children amended their policy statement to read, "The first level of service and concern of C.E.C. will be the promotion of positive, cognitive, and affective psycho-motor skills in all children that will prevent and/or reduce the frequency of handicapping behaviors." This change in priority will take some time before it influences our training and research activity in special education. At present only a few programs attempt to translate psychological and social skills into an educational curriculum for classroom teachers. Goldstein's[11] social learning curriculum was developed to facilitate social relationships in the classroom. The program involved a ten-phase curriculum to be used primarily with slow-learning pupils in special education. The sections on recognizing and reacting to emotion and getting along with others appeared to be most applicable in teaching young emotionally disturbed children.

Developing Understanding of Self and Others (DUSO) by Dinkmeyer[12] is a comprehensive, multi-instructional curriculum program for pupils K through 4. Based on affective education and developmental guidance principles, the program's primary goal is to develop a positive self-image and value clarifications. Each lower and upper primary program is organized around eight specific themes, such as "understanding feelings" or "responsible choice-making." This program is rapidly gaining the attention and interest of many school districts, because it can be offered to an entire class rather than just special students.

A more cognitive approach to prevention is Schwarroch and Wrenn's The Coping With Series, which consists of twenty-three books for our contemporary society.[13] Using the books as a basis for group discussion, the classroom teacher can drain off and clarify many of the normal developmental problems of adolescence. Books such as Do I Know the Me Others See, and Parents Can Be a Problem stimulate high interest among adolescent pupils.

In 1972 an experimental study was conducted to investigate the impact of the self-control curriculum on observable classroom behavior, school adjustment, and academic achievement. The study sample consisted of 159 second-grade pupils attending three inner-city elementary schools in Washington, D.C.. One experimental control class was selected in each school. Analysis of the data found the self-control curriculum was significantly related to improved school adjustment, with a significant trend toward improvement in observed classroom behavior. Although the data showed no impact on academic achievement, the classroom teachers felt the lessons and approach were useful in increasing their level of teacher satisfaction in the classroom. This program was at best a pilot study. The results, however, were so encouraging that active refinement of the curriculum and additional field-testing of the program is in progress. Although they are still in their infancy, primary prevention programs may become a major focus in special education in the future.

In the following article, Fagen and Long present their self-control curriculum. Based on four years of development and research, their study outlined the following necessary conditions for any primary prevention programs for children. The program should:

1.   be available to all children,

2.   begin as early as possible in the child's development,

3.   focus on the concept of health rather than illness or pathology,

4.   be educationally focused,

5. emphasize normal adult-peer-self interactions,

6. be functional to the teacher,

7. be intrinsically pleasant and satisfying to children,

8. be inexpensive enough to be applied on a mass basis,

9. increase or strengthen skills for effectively coping with the stresses of living.

A Psychoeducational Curriculum for the Prevention of Behavioral and Learning Problems: Teaching Self Control

Stanley A. Fagen
Nicholas J. Long
P.J. Stevens

Children with serious emotional and learning problems frequently exhibit disruptive behavior in school (Morse, 1971). Their behavior often violates the rights of others or interferes with their own basic desires to succeed. Some children are disruptive by explosive, aggressive actions, some display withdrawal or extreme passivity, and others retard their own learning through rigid avoidance of tasks, which arouses strong feelings of inadequacy.

The common denominator for disruptive behavior is a lack of self-control. To effectively cope with the requirements and challenges of the classroom, a child must develop the capacity to control his own behavior, even when faced with frustration. In our terms, self-control is defined as one's *capacity to flexibly and realistically direct and regulate personal action (behavior) in a given situation.*

The Structure of Self-Control

Capacity for self-control depends on the integration of eight skill-clusters, which have been identified on the basis of systematic observation and analysis of disruptive behavior in both a special therapeutic school and a regular school (Fagen and McDonald, 1969). Four of these skill-clusters rely heavily on intellectual or cognitive development; the other four are related more to emotional or affective development. The eight skill-clusters are summarized as follows:

1. *Selection:* ability to perceive incoming information accurately

2. *Storage:* ability to retain the information received

3. *Sequencing and Ordering:* ability to organize actions on the basis of planned order

4. *Anticipating Consequences:* ability to relate actions to expected outcomes

5. *Appreciating Feelings:* ability to identify and constructively use affective experience

6. *Managing Frustration:* ability to cope with external obstacles that produce stress

7. *Inhibition and Delay:* ability to postpone or restrain action tendencies

8. *Relaxation:* ability to reduce internal tension

Each skill-cluster represents a basic parameter of self-control, with each subsuming several interrelated functions. Skills 1-4 are regarded as the more cognitive skills and 5-8 are the more affective skills. Although it appears that parameters load differentially on intellectual or emotional processes, affect and intellect may interact across all areas. For example, "Storage" pertains to memory processes, traditionally regarded as a cognitive ability, but memory may be disrupted by anxiety or emotional stress, even to the point of amnesia. "Appreciating

---

*This article is based on material from *Teaching Self-Control in the Elementary School: A Curriculum for Preventing Learning and Emotional Problems* by S.A. Fagen, N.J. Long and P.J. Stevens. Copyright 1975 by Charles E. Merrill Publishing Company. Reprinted by permission.

Feeling," on the other hand, clearly aims at affective experience but at the same time requires retention of verbal concepts (e.g., sadness, joy, resentment) if affective states are to be correctly identified. Our contention is that cognitive performance is enhanced by the mastery of affective experience, which is likely to be enhanced by intellectual mastery.

Overview of the Self-Control Curriculum

A major conclusion of the 1970 White House Conference on Children stated the strong need for curriculum approaches to the prevention of learning and emotional problems: "We are further finding that curricula which help a child deal with his feelings and emotions, which teach principles of self-control, and which help the child cope with the pressures and frustrations of an industrial society are desperately needed yet almost totally lacking." The following self-control curriculum provides one model for preparing children to cope with these real-life pressures.

The self-control curriculum consists of eight curriculum areas, corresponding to the eight skill-clusters that promote one's capacity to flexibly and realistically direct and regulate personal action. Each curriculum area contains an introduction, including a statement of rationale, a description of units and goals, and suggested learning tasks. The introduction summarizes research that documents the importance of the skill area and states expecta-

tions that a teacher should establish for his pupils. The description of each unit specifies teaching goals for each unit within that curriculum area, and the suggested learning tasks or activities provide the necessary instructions, materials, and procedures for teaching the skills in that unit.

Table 1 presents an overview of the eight curriculum areas and the specific units subsumed within each of these areas.

The curriculum may be flexibly implemented, with the following options available:

Option 1.   The curriculum can be taught in one school year (eight months). Approximately one month should be spent in each curriculum area.

Option 2.   The entire curriculum can be taught in one semester and then repeated (recycled) in the second semester. Approximately two weeks should be spent on each curriculum area.

Option 3.   The entire curriculum can be taught in the first semester of the school year, with the teacher selecting special areas for the second semester. In the first semester, approximately two weeks should be spent on each curriculum area; time spent on any one area in the second semester will depend on the needs of the class and the discretion of the teacher.

Option 4.   Any curriculum area can be taught any time of the year, depending on the needs or weaknesses of the class. The amount of time spent on any curriculum area is left to the teacher's discretion.

Table 1. The Self-Control Curriculum:
Overview of Curriculum Areas and Units

Curriculum area	Curriculum unit	Number of learning tasks
Selection	1. Focusing and Concentration	9
	2. Figure-Ground Discrimination	4
	3. Mastering Distractions	3
	4. Processing Complex Patterns	3
		(19)
Storage	1. Visual Memory	11
	2. Auditory Memory	12
		(23)
Sequencing and Ordering	1. Time Orientation	8
	2. Auditory-Visual Sequencing	7
	3. Sequential Planning	8
		(23)

Curriculum	Curriculum unit	Number of learning tasks
Anticipating Consequences	1. Developing Alternatives 2. Evaluating Consequences	11 7 (18)
Appreciating Feelings	1. Identifying Feelings 2. Developing Positive Feelings 3. Managing Feelings 4. Reinterpreting Feeling Events	4 8 10 4 (26)
Managing Frustration	1. Accepting Feelings of Frustration 2. Building Coping Resources 3. Tolerating Frustration	2 9 22 (33)
Inhibition and Delay	1. Controlling Action 2. Developing Part-Goals	13 5 (18)
Relaxation	1. Body Relaxation 2. Thought Relaxation 3. Movement Relaxation	5 5 3 (13)

Illustrative Tasks for Unit in the "Managing Frustration" Curriculum Area

Frustration is a natural, frequent, and inevitable part of the human condition whenever a wish, desire, or goal is obstructed (Yates, 1962). The term implies both a thwarting stimulus situation and an associated set of negative emotional responses. Although little can be done about the obstacles in the way of immediate goal satisfaction, children can be taught to manage their negative feelings resulting from the stress of frustration.

The "Managing Frustration" curriculum area contains three units: (1) Accepting Feelings of Frustration, (2) Building Coping Resources, and (3) Tolerating Frustration. Taken together the units represent a process for managing frustration: developing supportive perceptions, identifying and maintaining possibilities for success and self-esteem, and increasing capacity for experiencing frustration.

Unit 1. Accepting Feelings of Frustration

Goals. To help children acknowledge and accept feelings of frustration as normal inevitable events; to help children perceive that frustration is not caused by their own badness or inadequacy.

Teaching acceptance of frustration necessitates the arousal of frustration in the presence of unpleasant affect. The following guidelines *must* be kept in mind before inducing frustration: (1) frustration induction should be attempted only after a positive relationship between teacher and pupils has been established in the classroom; (2) degree of frustration should be modulated to assure that initial inductions are mild, followed by moderate inductions. Severe frustration should never be induced but should be dealt with spontaneously as stressful incidents occur within the everyday classroom or school experience; (3) frustration induction must always be followed by clarification and closure procedures, i.e., the teacher should be sure the children understand the meaning and purpose of the frustrating activity before moving on to other things.

Illustrative Tasks: Sharing Group Frustration. Ask for five or six children who want to try a new kind of activity. Bring them together in a small group, with the rest of the class observing. The first objective of the activity is to establish the conditions for frustration, which requires the teacher to introduce a goal that the children are eager to achieve. The goal could be satisfying in itself (e.g., when asked what they might like to do, the children agree that having a race would be fun), or, desired because of a reward to follow (e.g., each team member gets a star, a free period, or some candy if the team reaches the goal). The number of goals that meet this condition are limitless.

The second step in inducing frustration is to interfere with fulfillment of the goal without explanation or reassurance. Thus, after the children begin their efforts to achieve the goal, the teacher makes sure that the task cannot be finished.

Possible Group Tasks.   (a) *A relay race to the blackboard.* Each child takes turns writing his first name, and then going up for a second time to write his last name. Frustration may be induced by removing the chalk or blocking the board (physical obstacles), or announcing that time is up (temporal obstacle). (b) *Passing a message from one person to another by whispering.* The goal is for the last member to accurately announce the message as it was originally presented. Thus, the teacher might show the rest of the class the message to be passed along (e.g., "The tomatoes are growing in the garden," or "The football team plays tonight"), and then whisper it to the first team member. Frustration is induced by talking aloud to the class or the team members while they are trying to remember the exact message (communication obstacle). (c) *Ordering cards.* Ask the members to deal out an equal number of cards from a deck of playing cards, and then see how quickly they can trade cards so that each child gets four-of-a-kind. Team members are told that if they can finish in three minutes they will be rewarded. Frustration is induced by arbitrarily indicating time is up before the deadline (temporal obstacle); by changing the rules so that certain suits cannot be used (general obstacle); or by not including a sufficient number of cards for each child to get four-of-a-kind (physical obstacle).

After inducing frustration in the small group, indicate to the rest of the class that the team did not reach their goal. Then inquire as to how the team member's classmates felt about what happened. For example, "Can someone tell us how he felt when the chalk was missing?" "What did you think when the time was up?" "Was anybody mad about what happened? . . . Anybody sad? . . . Who thought the game was unfair?"

Questioning the observing classmates provides a peer group base of support and identification for feelings aroused in team members. The children directly frustrated can begin to see that they are not alone in their feelings, and that these feelings can be publicly acknowledged without fear of reprisal or humiliation. Following the "group support" period of questioning, the directly frustrated team members should be given an opportunity to express their reactions.

During these periods of questioning for and expression of children's feelings on frustration, several important points can be made: (1) the planned experience was upsetting, uncomfortable, frustrating; (2) different feelings were aroused, e.g., anger, sadness, fear, distrust; (3) upset could not be avoided by anyone; you can't always get what you want; (4) frustration was unrelated to fault or wrongdoing; you can feel badly without being bad; (5) children share similar feelings of upset; (6) it is all right to be upset when we cannot reach a goal; it means we care about things we do.

Follow this activity with subsequent questions and discussion about other situations that frustrate children: "Who can think of other things that seem unfair in school?" "Are there other things you wish you could do or get in school?" "Was anybody disappointed about anything this week?" Focus on expression of feelings relating to frustrations. *Do not explain, criticize, judge, or solve problems mentioned.* The purpose is to develop an awareness that all children experience frustration and have normal and necessary feelings related to such frustrations.

Be prepared to rapidly close the task by summarizing succinctly. For example,

1. "Today we talked about feelings of frustration—the way we feel when we don't get what we want, or hope for, or thought we'd get."

2. "We could see that everybody gets these feelings."

3. "We can talk about these things, and we will do more another time."

4. "These feelings are OK to have; you and all other people (grownups too) will get them a lot. They are part of life and have to be. In school we can learn about them, just like we do other things."

Summary

Much of the present educational and mental health effort has been directed toward managing, understanding or treating maladaptive behavior of children with identifiable problems. It is time to pay at least an equal amount of attention to developing the positive skills that will *prevent* learning and behavioral problems. This article presented a brief overview of a specialized psychoeducational curriculum that can be taught by the regular classroom teacher in the same way reading or any other basic skill is taught.

The Self-Control Curriculum is a positive approach to learning inner controls that are essential to the goals of our democratic society. Current social realities demand that public schools assume a greater responsibility in this area. By 1980, primary prevention programs in elementary schools will be integrated into the regular school curriculum. The Self-Control Curriculum is a prototype of what will be developed in the future for classroom teachers.

Article References

"Confronting Myths of Education—Report of Forum 8." *Report to The President: White House Conference on Children, 1970.* (Washington, D.C.: U.S. Government Printing Office, 1971): pp. 121-142.

S. Fagen and P. McDonald. "Behavior Description in the Classroom: Potential of Observation for Differential Evaluation and Program Planning," *Clinical Proceedings of D.C. Children's Hospital* 25 (1969): 215-226.

W. Morse, *Classroom Disturbance: The Principal's Dilemma.* (Arlington, Va.: The Council for Exceptional Children, 1971).

A. Yates, *Frustration and Conflict.* (New York: John Wiley & Sons, 1962).

Summary

No single theory, discipline, or profession can claim the specialized field of teaching emotionally disturbed children. Although specific research and refinement of theoretical models will continue, the next phase will be a movement to integrate diverse points of view. After all, the common denominator of all these strategies is their commitment to find more effective ways of remediating or correcting learning and behavior problems. In recent years, the relationship between an individual's developmental disabilities and his emotional disturbance has been ascertained. Advances in the analysis of pupils' strengths and weaknesses have prompted remedial education programs rather than institutionalization and psychotherapy for pupils with serious learning difficulties.

Sensitive and skillful understanding and handling of primary emotional problems is needed, of course, but remedial education is also an important tool for altering self-defeating life patterns. Prompt, knowledgeable identification of learning inadequacies, combined with a plan for corrective teaching, can prevent secondary emotional disorders. Furthermore, remedial strategies in the hands of an emotionally attuned teacher can alter the vicious cycles of behavior associated primarily with emotional factors.

There is no magic, no one cure, no short cut in teaching emotionally disturbed children. The task demands an appreciation and diagnosis of the different styles of learning and teaching that are compatible with the ongoing analysis of pupils' strengths and weaknesses.

Following is a list of all special educational materials and regional media centers in the United States. These centers serve as clearinghouses for newly developed methods and materials for exceptional children and are an excellent resource for the interested classroom teacher.

Instructional Materials Centers

Region Served	Director
Indiana, Michigan, Ohio	Mrs. Lou Alonso, Director USOE/MSU Instructional Materials Center for Handicapped Children and Youth 213 Erickson Hall Michigan State University East Lansing, Michigan 48823

New York State and Central New York Region	Mr. Raphael E. Simches, State Director Maurice D. Olsen, Coordinator Special Education Instructional Materials Center New York State Education Department 55 Elk Street, Albany, New York 12224
Western New York Region	Mrs. Elizabeth L. Ayre, Regional Director Regional Special Education Instructional Materials Center State University College at Buffalo 1300 Elmwood Avenue, Buffalo, New York 14222
Southeastern New York Region	Dr. Shirley Cohen Box 101, Hunter College 695 Park Avenue New York, New York 10021
Alaska, Hawaii, Idaho, Oregon, Washington, Guam, Trust Territory of the Pacific Islands American Samoa	Dr. Wayne D. Lance, Director Northwest Regional Special Education Instructional Materials Center University of Oregon Clinical Services Building, Eugene, Oregon 97403
Arkansas, Oklahoma, Texas	Mr. Albert W. Fell, Director The University of Texas Special Education Instructional Materials Center 2613 Wichita Street, Austin, Texas 78712
Delaware, District of Columbia, Maryland, New Jersey, Pennsylvania, Virginia,	Dr. Raymond S. Cottrell, Director Mid-Atlantic Region Special Education Instructional Materials Center George Washington University Washington, D.C. 20006
Minnesota, Wisconsin	Dr. LeRoy Aserlind, Director Special Education Instructional Materials Center University of Wisconsin 415 West Gilman Street, Madison, Wisconsin 53706
Alabama, Florida, Georgia, Louisiana, Mississippi, South Carolina	Dr. Faye M. Brown, Director Southern States Cooperative Learning Resource System Auburn University at Montgomery Montgomery, Alabama 36104

Regional Media Centers

Dr. Robert E. Stepp, Director
Midwest Regional Media Center for the Deaf
University of Nebraska
Lincoln, Nebraska 68508

Dr. William D. Jackson, Director
Southern Regional Media Center for the Deaf
College of Education
University of Tennessee
Knoxville, Tennessee 39716

Dr. Raymond Wyman, Director
Northeast Regional Media Center for the Deaf
University of Massachusetts
Amherst, Massachusetts 01003

Dr. Hubert D. Summers, Director
Southwest Regional Media Center for the Deaf
New Mexico State University
P O Box 3AW
Las Cruces, New Mexico 88001

Chapter 5 Footnotes

1.   **Charles E. Silverman,** *Crisis in the Classroom: The Remaking of American Education* (New York: Vintage Books, 1971).

2.   **Barbara Biber,** "Integration of Mental Health Principles in the School Setting," in *Prevention of Mental Disorders,* ed. Gerald Caplan (New York: Basic Books, 1961).

3.   **William Rhodes and Michael Tracey,** *A Study of Child Variance,* Conceptual Project in Emotional Disturbance, vol. I (University of Michigan, 1972).

4.   **William C. Morse, Richard L. Cutler, and Albert H. Fink,** *Public School Classes for the Emotionally Handicapped,* a research project conducted for The Council for Exceptional Children, National Education Association, 1964.

5.   **F.M. Hewett,** *The Emotionally Disturbed Child in the Classroom* (Boston: Allyn and Bacon, Inc., 1968).

6.   **O.R. Lindsley,** "Direct Measurement and Prosthesis of Retarded Behavior," *Journal of Education* (1964).

7.   **Merle L. Meacham and Allen E. Wiesen,** *Changing Classroom Behavior: A Manual for Precision Teaching* (Scranton: International Textbook Company, 1969).

8.   **Stanley A. Fagen,** "A Psychoeducational Approach to Specifying and Measuring Competencies of Personnel Working with Disturbance in Schools" (Paper presented at The Council for Exceptional Children, April 23, 1971).

9.   **S. Fagen, N. Long, and D. Stevens,** *Teaching Children Self-Control in the Classroom* (Columbus, Ohio: Charles E. Merrill Publishing, 1975).

10.   **Franz Huber,** "Achievers and Non-Achievers Among Severely Disturbed Children" (Ph.D. dissertation, University of Michigan, 1964).

11.   **Paul Gump and Bryant Sutton-Smith,** "Activity Setting and Social Interraction: A Field Study," *American Journal of Orthopsychiatry* XXV:4 (1955).

12.   **Herbert Goldstein,** *Social Learning Curriculum* (Charles E. Merrill Publishing, 1974).

13.   **Don Dinkmeyer,** *DUSO* (Circle Pines, Minn: American Guidance Service, Inc., 1973).

14.   **Shirley Schwarrock and Gilbert C. Wrenn,** *The Coping with Series* (Circle Pines, Minn.: American Guidance Service, 1973).

6

Hygienic Management

The concept "hygienic management" in the education of disturbed children needs clarification. Anyone who has direct responsibility knows that we must "manage"—the goal is at least minimal compliance with reasonable behavior codes based on the generic necessities of social living. However, this responsibility immediately brings into focus the matter of values—whose code?

Many a child and adolescent is justified in opposing how he is treated and the nature of the code to which he is expected to adhere. Often, when the rules are examined, they turn out to be related to adult convenience, conformity for the sake of conformity, and a host of arbitrary issues. It is interesting that the majority of delinquents have their first difficulty not because they steal, hurt someone, or cause trouble, but because they don't go to school, return home when they are supposed to, or break some other code.

Yet the basis of hygienic management in a therapeutic environment must be basic human values: fair play, the right of the individual to self-esteem and hope, nonexploitive interpersonal behavior, respect for members of the community and their possessions. These values we consider the bedrock ethics of our society, although we seldom see them put into full practice. There is no hygienic management possible in a primitive, punitive, suppressive milieu. Most adults punish children when they violate adult propositions. Redl, Glasser and Dreikurs have made it clear that reality should be the basis of intervention rather than adult authoritarianism, whim, or desire for a given state of order. Driekurs[1] holds that

punishment is retaliatory rather than corrective, although folklore has it otherwise.

Adult tolerances to code-breaking differ greatly. One teacher reacts; another ignores. Some believe in allowing youngsters to fight it out among themselves, just short of homicide. Others hold to rigid exterior conformity, with a rule for everything. Sitting in one's seat at the right time is the most significant value for some teachers; "unsitting" at recess when it is "time to go out" is a related value.

One confusion in educational management is over short- and long-term goals. As all group workers, teachers are continually up against group responsibilities which conflict with individual needs. We have yet to learn that helping a youngster improve his self-management and control requires more skill and time than does teaching him arithmetic. We still behave as if we believed in instant character development. When we employ a technique designed to "hold the fort," we should recognize there must also be complementary strategies for the long-term development of reasonable internalized attitudes. There may be times when control is a *sine qua non;* disturbed children by definition are almost always limit-breakers in one way or another. Their limit-breaking may range from occasional violent attacks on a person or physical surroundings, to quiet negation, manipulation, refusal to do work, disinterest, or intense preoccupation with the inner life—shutting out communication with others. Sometimes it is necessary to physically hold a child (with great care and skill), until assistance arrives to remove him to a "quiet room" or time out. Whenever such violations of a child's freedom are used, we must be sure there is no less-constraining procedure available. If such extreme techniques are needed persistently, close examination is necessary to see if we are giving the youngster his "right to treatment."

Although extreme, short-term procedures are inevitable, our real purpose is long-term emotional and social growth. We want to foster healthy identifications and the internalization of reasonable code-values whenever possible. The faster we can initiate significant adult-child relationships and group code support, the faster this will take place.

Hygienic management is the most sophisticated task faced by a teacher of disturbed children. In addition to direct approaches to the child's individual nature through relationship-counseling-interviewing, environmental and situational conditions can be employed to mitigate given behavior. We propose four major channels to management intervention and each may range from processes designed for immediate short-term control to those designed for long-term social and personal development: (1) procedures which focus on the teacher-pupil relationship as generated by teacher behavior; (2) processes which highlight working with pupils in a one-to-one or group format; (3) management components emerging from the design of the learning experience, be it content or method; and (4) procedures designed as a reflection of the group life of the classroom. Obviously, a teacher does not use only one procedure, but rather seeks to mesh the forces of all interventions for short-term control and long-term growth.

Classroom environmental conditions can present many provoking or quieting stimuli for a pupil: other children with "contagious" behavior, a lesson that is dull or too difficult, a teacher who is too lax or too controlling—the list of environmental stimuli is endless. In short, the sources of plans for hygienic management are found in the child's nature (Chapter 1) group interactions (Chapter 3), authority patterns, and tasks. Although dealing simultaneously with all aspects is impossible, basic components of the matrix can be studied to provide considerable assistance to the teacher in handling control problems. Even so-called "external variants" of authority—curriculum and group—are not abstract constants to alter or manipulate in themselves; each condition takes on a specific psychological meaning related to the nature of the individual child's self-concept.

One of the least understood aspects of hygienic management is that it is based on the nature of relationship of teacher and pupils as much as on the specific process employed. One adult can help a child with methods that would never be tolerated from another adult. Exclusion by one teacher is a pupil victory; another exclusion may result in a sense of rejection or a feeling of hopelessness.

What aspects of the child's personal-social matrix can be considered sources of strategy for management? One obvious source is the child's characteristic modes of behavior, his reaction to the environment. With these we use information concerning different pathologies (see Chapters 1 and 2). Psychological planning requires responding to the pupil according to his special nature. The more astute behavioristic methodologies recognize that each youngster has a different hierarchy of pertinent rewards. A dynamic approach acknowledges that the psychopath and the psychotic do not respond in the same way to a particular adult intervention. Thus, effective teachers will move rapidly to individualized responses that are relevant for a youngster at a specific time.

Broad generalizations about management interventions are also possible. (1) The goal is to develop insight into a youngster's behavior. Sometimes it requires reviewing the causes of behavior, but often life space interviewing with appeals to fair play for others, getting work done, or releasing tension. We give "rational" explanations for demands. Thus the behavior problem may become a point of entry for long-term change. (2) The management process attempts to establish clear-cut limits. Sometimes a limit can be delineated verbally, but in a crisis it is often necessary to restrain a child to make a limit explicit. (3) Management recognizes the potent forces of reward and punishment. Because some tasks must be done even if they are not self-gratifying, control may mean an external reward. After all, most of us are motivated at least partly by extrinsic rewards. Many disturbed children find it rewarding to do something 'good' to help others, so the reward need not always be concrete. Role reversal (which makes the child a tutor or helper) has long paid control dividends to teachers. (4) Finally the teacher provides a pattern of behavior for the child through her handling of frustration, failure, anger, and other emotions. The range of control by modeling is from concrete example to imitation and identification. These controls are the interpersonal dimension in intervention methodology.

Generalized methods of control must be used with a sense of appropriate times, places, and children. For example, one does not hold a child who will respond to verbal control. Often, more than one process of control may be incorporated in a situation. Unfortunately, there is no magical solution. The intellectual absorption of psychological knowledge has limited usefulness in an emotionally charged situation. The human animal often reacts first and thinks later. This is true both for adults and for emotionally disturbed children, who live in a fiery world of conflict and possesses a short control fuse.

How will this section help readers who are looking for specific techniques and solutions? By exposure to dimensions of behavioral conflict and management of which the student may not be aware. With intensive experience and adequate supervision, the teacher will find that focusing on specific techniques and pet solutions leads to broad analysis of individual and group interactions on a particular child, rather than yielding a list of rules and regulations.

Most teachers read this section with high expectation because they wonder about their ability to control their feelings when confronted by irritating, explosive behavior over a period of time. These articles should reveal some basis for discipline and management and thus give the professional a way to solve this aspect of teaching.

The first selections deal with the teacher as the source of the teacher-pupil relationship: (1) the teacher relating to different types of emotionally disturbed children, (2) the teacher's own problem, and (3) the teacher's image of his job. The first article by Long and Newman does not attempt to define the teacher's job, nor the teacher's complex role, nor the teaching process per se, but rather attempts to give a picture of the teacher confronting a class of disturbed children. The authors look at the demands made on a teacher, reactions to these demands, and the consequent effect on the children.

The Teacher and His Mental Health

Nicholas J. Long
Ruth G. Newman

Considering the contradictory concepts included under the image of a good teacher, it is little wonder that a teacher is confused about his role. Confusion is often a step on the road to mental health, but it never is, in itself, mentally healthy. At this moment, many teachers seem to be caught in a trap of confusion, not knowing which way is out. It would help them on their journey to define mental health in a most specific sense. For there is no question that a teacher's mental health is of primary importance. His influence over the developing personalities of the children in his charge is a basic determinant of the future he creates, and there are subtle as well as obvious reasons for his influence—more of that later. But let it be emphasized that it is a bad mistake to define mental health as the same for all people. Mental health is a statistical average to which everyone ought to try to conform, not as a norm; it is the quality of mind, body, and attitude that, on the whole, usually leads a person to feel reasonably comfortable—that quality which frees him to use whatever capabilities he has much of the time and which leaves him open and sensitive to what is going on around him instead of needing to defend his own structure.

Mental health does *not* mean, as so many of the statements in education textbooks and lectures imply, that every teacher must mold himself into a pattern of smiling, calm, responsive patience, and have no quirks and no off-beat notions. As a matter of fact, some of the best teachers in the past, as in the present, are, in other realms of life, considered eccentric or painfully shy (see *Goodbye, Mr. Chips*). But in the classroom, "odd ball" or not, many of these people seem to be able to marshal all their resources. Their pupils often love them and/or learn from them. It is not necessary to come off a mental health assembly line to be a good teacher. It is no more necessary (or possible) for teachers to be alike than for individual children to be alike. Uniformity is not the goal for which to strive. It is, rather, to see that teachers like teaching (most of the time), because when one likes doing something one is apt to be fairly good at it; to see that they get pleasure from the children they teach—not all of them, but most of them; that they feel satisfied enough with their work and their lives so that they can view their own successes and failures with some objectivity; and that they feel hopeful enough to keep the capacity to learn and grow, and are comfortable enough to ask for help and to use it.

From Nicholas J. Long and Ruth G. Newman, "The Teacher and His Mental Health," *The Teacher's Handling of Children in Conflict*, Bulletin of School of Education, Indiana University (July 1961), pp. 5–26. Reprinted by permission of School of Education, Indiana University.

Human Beings and Teachers

Focusing then on this specific definition, one may agree with that theme mentioned more than any other in all the literature concerned with the mental health needs of teachers, namely, that teachers are human beings. This would seem a self-evident statement, yet the very fact that it is stated so often implies that in practice it is not so accepted or acceptable a tenet after all. Unquestionably, the insistence of the culture that its teachers, like its ministers and its psychiatrists, be better than everyone else contributes to the contradictory notions concerning a teacher's right to be human.

Common sense, intuitive understanding, and artist's insight, along with present-day contributions from psychology, sociology, anthropology, and psychiatry, have informed us that human beings have a good many feelings they are not proud of and that our culture frowns upon. People feel anger. They feel fear. They feel hate. They feel these things when they are threatened (and indeed they would not have survived as a species had they not experienced these feelings). Being a somewhat more complicated species than other animals, and being more adept at manipulating their environment to fit their needs, they are not so frequently threatened by the enmity of nature as they are by forces inherent in the culture: by approval and disapproval, by need for love and ego enhancement, by need for control, adequacy, and self-regard, for belonging, and for nourishment and warmth of a psychological as well as physiological kind.

This being true of human beings in general, how does the teacher's humanness especially affect his job, and what particular threats does the teacher experience more than, or different from, those of people in other occupations? How can these threats which determine his behavior affect the children he teaches?

Well, take the simple fact that teachers deal with children of all ages and that children, having not been around the earth as long as the teachers, are more primitively organized. They have not yet learned to hide, to control, and to repress their feelings (and considerable mental health time is spent worrying about ways to help them use their feelings and not repress them in unhealthy fashions). Children, directly or indirectly, cry out their needs; perhaps they cannot define them, or place them correctly, or even do anything useful about them, but they make demands one way or another. The teacher must meet those demands, not only of one child, not only of many children, but of groups of children. He must meet these demands or divert them and at the same time teach subject matter. He must do this every day—even when he and his spouse have had a devastating fight the night before; even when he is worried sick about the fact that his own child has been moping about the house and has developed a stutter; even when his mother has become ill and has moved in on him. Even when he has not slept all night worrying over the unpaid bills and comes to school only corporeally, Mary will still need the extra attention she does not get at home before she can start in to work; Bill will still need to be set straight and quieted down before he can launch on algebra problems; Warren will need a hand on the shoulder to bring him back from outer space into earthly contact; and that group of devils in the back row will have to be brought into line.

If these management tasks are not done with some humor, warmth, firm quietness, or cheer, they will not work; and if they do not work, the class will collapse, and it will be one of those days in which everyone would better have stayed home in the first place. To be sure, this is not too different from any business man in any office, except that children are more obviously demanding and they react more readily to the first signs of irritation, disquiet, or panic. Their reactions are less clothed behind social masks, so that their fear, disturbance, or counter-anger is more immediately transferred back to the teacher, who in turn reacts as threatened organisms usually do, with fear or with flight, or, in the exceptional case of someone aware of his feelings, with an ability to see what is occurring and to put a behavioral thumb in the already leaky dike and start afresh.

A Teacher's Self-Awareness

The ability to perceive what is going on outside oneself is no small matter and does not fall naturally like the gentle rain from heaven. It is precisely that ability which is built in by successful psychotherapy and allied techniques. It is what psychotherapy and mental health is about.

This psychological premise is based on the well-documented assumption that the human being is influenced by a multitude of forces from within and from without. A person can afford to be aware of some of these forces, but, because of his culture, his upbringing, his individual personal experiences, and his picture of himself, he cannot afford to be aware of other forces. These latter forces are at least as powerful as those of which he *is* aware, and they may lead him to do all sorts of things which he himself may well not approve of. Moreover, since he cannot accept these things as part of himself, he can have no notion whatsoever of the effect of these actions on people around him, for good or for evil. For example, he probably does not realize that something about Joe in his class reminds him of his brother, Phil, whose very existence made his life utterly miserable all the years of his childhood, and that, without knowing it, he is quite unable to speak to Joe without irritation or to be aware of what *this* boy really is asking for. He may be equally unaware of the fact that the kids in the class are right when they accuse him of playing favorites. He may not know all the times he quite unconsciously smiles benignly at Margaret, how extra patient he is with all her questions and her need for special help. If someone should comment on his treatment of Margaret, he would ask, "Is this not good teaching?" Without special insight, he will never relate the fact that dependent Margaret is most appealing to him because he himself had always longed for someone to answer his dependent needs. He cannot afford to be aware that Margaret has become unpopular with her class because of the favoritism he has shown.

In a different context, Jules Henry[1] has reported a study in which teachers of middleclass children have been observed over long periods of time, their techniques of management noted, and their own self-report of their styles of operation recorded. Two cases out of many were specifically cited in which both teachers thought of themselves as strict disciplinarians. One teacher was quite unaware of the reassuring physical touches she continually gave to a child the minute he began to get out of bounds or the second he needed some extra push, and thus she controlled her class in a manner quite unknown to her. The other teacher was equally unaware of the number of times she pleaded with the children to do what they were asked, because she so needed their assistance. These two teachers would have been just as unaware that they used these techniques out of school with their sweethearts, their mates, their own children, or the clerks at stores with whom they dealt. They had no notion of how they actually went about the business of relating to people. Each had created a picture of himself, as all people do, having little to do with observable reality.

Actually, many of the things that teachers, along with other human beings, do unconsciously are helpful and useful things. Simply because they are done unconsciously does not mean they are bad. It is curious the amount of distrust people have of their unconscious. It is as if they began, as early as possible, to bury there all the things they did not like—their hate, their fear, their anger—and in so doing, they managed to forget that not only these qualities but other feelings have been buried there as well. All those feelings are closeted in their unconscious which, from infancy on up, have made them uncomfortable, have hurt them, or have left them open to attack or criticism. Often these feelings are affection, warmth, tenderness, humor, sympathy, non-conformity, creativity. Frequently, when they have succeeded in locking the skeleton in the closet, they forget that in that very same closet lie their jewels and warmest or loveliest clothes. Teachers who receive more than the usual share of criticism from so many sources tend to be more vulnerable and therefore more fearful of letting their unconscious feelings come to the surface.

The Teacher's Personality Structure

Although there are many teachers who have a natural self-awareness and an inborn talent enabling them to see what really is occurring, there is no one who cannot use additional tools to be able to better see and to better evaluate his own actions. There is no one who does not have shutters in his mind that go down when a particularly threatening experience occurs. What is threatening for one person may be entirely different for another. The way the shutters go down may also be quite different. This is what is meant by the patterns of defense talked of in psychiatry: repression, denial, projection, rationalization, displacement, identification, and the rest. What a person does when his defenses are set into motion may be quite different too. He may greet the threat with flight, with withdrawal, with despair, with increased energy, with extra control, with rigidity, with hostility, with tears, with illness, with laughter, or with sarcasm. These methods of behavior are not lost on the children he teaches, regardless of what the teacher *thinks* he is teaching. Johnny *may* learn arithmetic, but he *surely* learns that Miss J. quickly changes the subject when he says something in a loud voice. In other words, the child learns patterns of behavior more surely than he learns academic subject matter. The younger the child, the deeper the learning.

Of course the child learns his patterns of behavior from home first and foremost. But the school is the child's first venture into a foreign society. It generates in him some new pressures, sets alien standards, and arouses strain in him. Moreover, he spends a large part of his waking life with the teacher—in most cases a larger part than he spends with his parents.

So, if it is an accepted premise that children identify with meaningful adults and that their growth is determined by those people with whom they identify, it is clear that the teacher's ways of reacting are of utmost importance. Furthermore, although it would be nice to think that the child only identifies with the best part of adults, this is not necessarily the case. Since the teacher is in authority and appears to have power, and a child invariably seeks strength or support for his own helplessness, he will identify with, or try to be on the side of, strength; therefore, he may well identify with the more unpleasant parts of a teacher, the very parts, as a matter of fact, that the teacher may have kept out of his own awareness. Or the child, finding a teacher displeasing or too weak to help, may negatively identify. That is to say, if the emotional tone of the teacher has been, in a direct or an indirect way, threatening or non-need-fulfilling, the child may adopt a reverse image and try to become just those things the teacher is not. Thus, what a teacher is, who he is, and how he reacts to the hundred million situations, crises, and interactions that occur in class everyday is the child's armory of knowledge of the outside world. From this he learns how the whole world works and how one copes with anxieties and drives.

Fundamentally, it is not that a teacher is or is not a human being that is at question; it is what kind of humanness he exhibits and how his breed of humanness can be most effectively used in the classroom. The very humanity of teachers makes saintly behavior impossible. No human is always cheerful, patient, and carefree. Moreover, it is not such a good thing to be constantly euphoric. Indeed, if the teacher consistently represses his anger, the children may become increasingly convinced that their own angry and hostile feelings are unique and singularly evil.

Repressed, unaware, unusefully-directed rage and hostility, whether experienced by teacher or child, cannot forever be denied. It comes popping out, at most inappropriate moments, much too much, much too distorted, much too ineffective, much too overwhelming. Or else it appears in physical symptoms such as stomachaches, asthma, headaches, or dizziness. It may appear in nonlearning, in tics, in pretense and indirection, in lying, stealing, or truancy. The more we know about emotional health, the clearer it is that a teacher who gets angry appropriately is apt to be far less harmful to his class than a teacher who is generally irritable. A teacher who can face his own hostility toward a school task, or even toward the behavior of an annoying child, is likely to be one who can warmly take a child's sorrow or dilemma to heart. A teacher who is aware of his own vanity can laugh at himself and is likely to be able to keep the facts of school life in proportion. A teacher who knows he has acted crabby all the morning, because of a squabble at home, can pull himself together and keep the squabble where it belongs. He can proceed to make something more pleasant for the rest of the day. The teacher with awareness knows that, when too many people have been sent to detention hall that week, something may well be wrong not with the class but with himself. . . .

The Straws That Break the Teacher's Back

What first appears in applying informed personal services is the variety of things teachers find particularly frustrating in their classrooms. Ask a teacher to report honestly what most drives him to distraction: sometimes it is the big things like overcrowdedness, or having no time to do a job; sometimes it is the personal idiosyncrasies that make life unbearable. There is no use in placing a hierarchy of importance on the gripes. As anyone knows, a spilled glass of orange juice at breakfast can, at a given moment, be just as upsetting as not receiving a pay raise. It is possible for both kinds of events to be devastating for the time being, or to be met and handled in proportion when awareness and support are available.

Below are some examples of teachers' frustrations as they expressed them. They represent the kinds of frustrations which carefully planned in-service or consultative programs try to meet, in an Androcles and the Lion kind of way, by seeing them as thorns which can, temporarily or permanently, cripple the teacher and keep him from performing, and can consequently hold back the child. A truly good consultative service to teachers could be of help, regardless of which of the following complaints one chooses.

Overcrowding is experienced with a sense of helplessness by some teachers:

In our school district during the past school term there was an overflow of children in our school causing most of the classes to have from 39 to 45 children. There was a constant assignment of new children from other schools in the city as well as from surrounding areas. This impact was felt tremendously in the school program and its operation to accomplish certain goals. As for me, this kind of "bargin'-in" (that was my inner feeling) of from one to two children each week was quite frustrating, as my concern in meeting individual differences was thwarted and my anticipated goals seemed out of reach. I found myself unconsciously resenting the fact that the child was sent to my room, and I became quite peeved if he did not have command of the skills expected of a second grader, for this meant that my job was to take time to help him if I could or at least to provide opportunities to expose him to the skills. I was not even willing to take him where he was and to work from that point, as that would take time, and time was what I didn't have, especially since time had already been sacrificed to register, enroll, and welcome him to the class.

I dread going to school these days—210 children a day, about 40 kids in a class. They tell me a new school is being planned to take up all the kids from the new housing settlement, but until then just try to teach English to 180 kids: the slow ones, the fast ones, the noisy ones. I thought you were supposed to know the kids you teach. I hardly know most of their names, let alone what they need from me. I love English. I have theories about teaching it. All that's been scrapped. Now I'm lucky to simply follow the prescribed dull study plan. I feel I'm not doing a thing for these kids. I'd give my soul for five classes of 20 children each!

I teach kindergarten. Once was, when I had a nice small 16 in a class group. Now I have two sessions: 50 in the morning, 42 in the afternoon, a volunteer parent helper for each class—when they show up. By the end of the day I feel as if I have the D.T.'s, with hundreds of moppets instead of pink elephants passing by. They call this teaching? Not in any child development course I ever had.

Special rules of personal and social behavior, as well as extra and menial chores and low salaries imposed on teachers, are often bitterly resented:

Then there is the "universal" frustration, not so much of salary (although everyone agrees that we are grossly under-paid) as of the benevolences I must cater to. I honestly hold in high esteem the virtues of the YMCA, YWCA, Boy Scouts, Girl Scouts, Red Cross, United Fund, and professional organizations, but somehow they seem to lose their flavor when I am aware that I must join in order to be considered a "good, cooperative" teacher. How nice it would be to join these wonderful organizations simply because I want to join them by choice only!

In the community in which I reside, teachers are somewhat expected to be "saints." This notion, to me, is ridiculous, for teachers, like everyone else, are human. It struck me as funny when I was interviewed for this particular position that the principal mentioned rather pointedly that this area had many people who drank in it, but that pressure was put on to get rid of any teacher who did so. He suggested that if I drank, not to drink in this area.

It would be nice to go into school in the morning and just teach and not have to be collecting money, taking attendance, playing nurse, and trying to discipline those who do not respond to the classroom role. It is difficult to be satisfied with doing just half a job all the time. It is difficult to realize that we cannot be 100 per cent effective but have to settle for much less. It is difficult for me to adjust to this situation as I am more of a perfectionist and like to get the best results all the time.

I hate to quit because I like to teach, but like it or not, I have to resign. My wife is expecting our second child and can no longer work. Since our first child is ill the doctor's bills and living expenses are just too much. I am overtired, tired trying to meet expenses by working at the post office in the Christmas rush and in a factory during summer times. I've been offered a job in an insurance company and, like it or not, I've got to take it. You've got to be rich to afford to teach if you've got a family.

The policy of administration is sometimes felt by teachers to be so outrageous (whether right or wrong) that their total teaching attitudes are affected:

To teach under an administration which focuses its attention upon creating benevolent public relations, even at the expense of school standards, seems to be my outstanding frustration. How is it possible for a high school principal to condone a student's laziness, slowness, and apparent lack of interest in subject matter, in a conference among the child's parents, the child, the teacher involved, and himself, and to state explicitly that possibly the reason for the child's failure was due to the lack of motivation and severity of grading done by the teacher. Mary, the student concerned, was a high school senior. She had failed sophomore and junior English and she was retaking both of these courses during her senior year as she needed both to graduate. Miss T. had Mary for sophomore English. She passed Mary because, as Miss T. said to me, "You can't fight city hall." I did not pass Mary, but when she graduated, she had no record on her permanent record of a failure in junior English. She had instead a "C."

The procedure of giving a contract for eight or nine months seems to have a decidedly negative effect upon the teacher. The implication read into the action is that the employer doesn't trust his judgment and has little faith in the training and prior experience of the applicant—that there is so much possibliity that the teacher will be unsatisfactory that he cannot afford to hire her for a longer period than a year at a time. The result is an undermining of the teacher's performance, self-confidence, and feeling of security.

Most permanently established teachers would not have been asked to take such a teaching load, but many principals feel that they can ask a beginning teacher to accept almost any situation. This is a particularly hard thing to do, because a beginning teacher needs all of the help and encouragement that she can get, and even in the most pleasant situation will have many problems to cope with anyway. I feel that for a teacher, especially a teacher in her first year of teaching, to be so totally out of her teaching field is an injustice not only to the teacher but to the students.

The emotionally disturbed child in the class-

room often generates despair and helplessness in the teacher:

There is a child in the classroom who suffers from an emotional problem. He is withdrawn, sensitive, and nervous—a condition which I know results from his home environment—a broken home, rejection, poverty, etc. I try to work with this child, give him projects that will display his self-worth, encourage him to join in the play activities of other children, give him extra "slaps on the back" for work well done, etc. All of this I do in the limited time the child is in school and under my jurisdiction. After school he goes home, back into the same surroundings that have caused him to be emotionally disturbed in the first place. My work, seemingly, becomes undone; the child enters the classroom the next day in the same condition as he entered the day before. I know the mind, soul, or body cannot be cured in one day, but as this chain of events goes on and on each day, I cannot help but sense a feeling of failure and helplessness.

Suzy was sent to me as an incorrigible seven-year-old who followed no rules, fought with all children, and caused constant room disturbance. She had an I.Q. of 78 on the Kuhlmann-Anderson and 79 on the Stanford-Binet. She was hostile, and yet on the first day of school she threw herself on me, nearly suffocating me with an embrace. Inquiring into her background, I found she lived in a house with seven or eight adults and as many children, seemingly all related, yet no definite relationship could be determined. I could not find out where the father was or even if he were living. Three women claimed to be her mother, but none would talk to me about her. Each said that her grandmother was responsible for her and she went to work at three in the afternoon and worked all night. I was never able to contact the grandmother. The frustration came about because I could find no one who seemed to care enough about Suzy to talk about her or try to help her. During the year I worked on the theory that if I loved her enough, she in turn would feel more secure and want to conform. I felt both I.Q. scores were invalid, because Suzy could think and reason. She was quite capable of finding information and presenting it when she desired.

I can't stop worrying about one little girl in my first grade. She behaves so peculiarly. She doesn't talk most of the time, though she can talk. She answers the other children and me with animal sounds. She hides under chairs like a dog and barks at people. She even bit one little boy. She draws pictures of dogs and insists on eating her lunch on all fours. I've talked to her mother, who is frantic about her behavior, but they have no money to see a psychiatrist. She's been on a clinic waiting list for six months, and I've had the child up for Special Service to test her for three months. In the meantime, the class all laugh at her, and she just gets worse, and I don't know what to do.

Parents are often experienced by teachers as an impossible cross to bear, whether this is because of the teacher's own unresolved feelings about his parents or whether the parents actually *are* obstructionists:

As a teacher, I try to give all the love, energy, consideration, and understanding to each pupil that I possibly can. To have a parent question my attention to another child over his makes me quite frustrated, baffled, and thwarted. If only parents would understand that some pupils require more attention than others and that it is not that the teacher is partial in any respect.

The most frustrating thing I've encountered has been parental attitude. Some, and I must say generally speaking it's the mothers, feel as though their children are bordering on genius. When the mothers classify their dear offsprings as such, the teacher shouldn't expect them to do such trivial things as study a lesson or do a class assignment, but should give the child superior grades in subject matters and satisfactory for attitude.

I have a parent who calls me every night to complain about her child's behavior. At first I tried to be nice and tell her what to do, but nothing is enough. Can't she see I have a right to my evenings, and can't she handle her own child? But I can't seem to cut her off, and I feel helpless to do anything. I've told the principal, and he doesn't seem interested in helping me. "Oh, she'll stop," says he. But when?

Interpersonal relations with staff, where there are differences of opinion or approach or personality conflicts, can be of determining importance to a teacher:

Although students may have difficulty in other subjects, social studies presents quite a problem to several of my students. I believe it is because it involves a great deal of reading and comprehension. Extra time is needed to give those students help who are having difficulty mastering social studies. But what is most frustrating to me is the fact that many of our teachers frown on me for giving special help to students because the teachers feel that the administration will require them to help with special problems also. Then too, some teachers have accused me of trying to impress the administrators because I give some special help.

The school was more of the traditional type, and, although I did try many new ideas and techniques, I found that I began following a somewhat "middle-of-the-road" position. Rather than actually teaching according to the way I had planned, I began to lean more and more to the type of teaching which was customary in the school system. There was not any real pressure from my critic teacher or from the superintendent, who was a personal friend, but I somehow felt that my efforts pleased them more when I followed the line of "traditional" teaching. At the same time, I felt that I was not doing a good job when I did not follow the practices which I had studied in my methods classes. Discipline seemed to be the main objection to the newer methods. Whenever the boys and girls were working on their committees and the room was "noisy," I noticed that I worried about distracting the other rooms nearby. I even began to question the worth of my opinion. I sometimes felt that the older teachers humored me in conversations when I voiced my approval of modern methods and theory. This was not always the case, but I occasionally detected an attitude of "You'll learn. You may think this way now, but wait until you've taught several years." Perhaps this is why I began my graduate work right away rather than beginning teaching as I had previously planned.

I could do my job all right if that sixth-grade teacher would stay out of my way. We have a school where the principal is with us two days a week and with another school three days. When she's not here, that bossy, nosey Mrs. D. just takes over, calls down my kids in the hall when they're not doing anything, criticizes my bulletin board, disciplines my children in front of me, and undermines my authority. The principal is so dependent on Mrs. D.

that there's no use talking to her. Anything Mrs. D. does is fine!

Sometimes deeply experienced personal conflicts can overwhelm a teacher:

I do not like having things on my desk looked at or handled. My desk is verboten. There are always children who want to rifle the papers or just look. They do not want anything, it just seems to be something they do. It doesn't matter to me that I never have anything on my desk that I do not want anyone to see or handle, I just don't want anyone to bother anything that is there. Inside, I have the feeling of "It's mine—hands off!" I know that this is silly, but I feel it strongly. The same feeling carries over to my personal things at home. I want them left alone.

When I may be about to come to a climax in a science experiment, or in the explanation of a transitive passive verb, or have all the attention of every eye and am about to express the punch line, there comes a knock at the door. I may as well answer it, because all hope of competing with that unknown factor of "Who's at the door?" is to no avail. Upon answering, I am handed a clarinet by a mother who says, "Would you please give this to Jeanne? She forgot she had band today." About that time I feel like a plugged-up volcano unable to blow the proverbial top.

If I were to name frustrations, they would come not from teaching but from the fact that I find my family is shorted. I find myself, at the end of the day, weary physically and mentally, often unable to cope with home demands. I will give a short answer to those at home, whereas at school I would weigh my words and answer with a smile. Meeting the needs of two sons, age 15 and 6, and a husband who is far from well could be a full-time job in itself. I feel frustrated in that I have little enthusiasm and patience to give at home after a full day of being enthusiastic and patient with a room full of children.

The other area of frustration is a difficult one to explain and also to admit. When I entered teaching, I had no intention of making it a career. I had hoped eventually to marry and raise my own family. After four years of teaching, I realized I would not meet many eligible men in the classroom. I realized I had to make a choice as to the type of career I wanted for myself. I knew that teaching was the one in which I would feel the happiest and gain the most satisfaction. I am going into guidance and counseling. I like working with people and think I have a reasonable amount of understanding of them. However, at times I feel very unloved and unwanted. I know this is going to hinder my working relationship in some cases. I can remember during my first few years of teaching that I threw myself wholeheartedly into helping students with extracurricular activities. I know I was looking for their appreciation and affection as an outcome of my work. But in most cases the students forgot about my help and enjoyed the activities themselves, letting me sit on the side and watch. How does a single person manage to fill this need for love and affection without becoming the embittered old maid that is often used as a stereotype for teachers? I feel this is an important problem with me. I know the solution cannot come in a short time, nor can anyone else solve it but myself. I would like some suggestions as to possible solutions.

I know one should not dislike a child, but there is one in my class who so offends me that it spoils my whole day. She is sloppy and fat. Her hair is stringy and unkempt. She sits sulky and slumped in her chair, never shows any pleasure in anything, answers in a fresh way, if at all. I know she must have a hard time at home, and I bend over backward trying to be nice. But at the end of the day, I am exhausted from the effort. I even dream about her nights.

As different as these personally recounted examples of frustrations are, there is not one of them that could not be to some degree alleviated by on-the-spot, psychologically sophisticated supervision, consultation, or whatever is called the process of airing one's difficulties, looking at them honestly with an informed and sympathetic person, and being helped not to deny them or let them grow to giant size but to perceive them in a fresh context. Whether by new pathways of communication, or by a reshuffling of the way one sees things, or by simply getting the jumble of enraging feelings into a framework of words, or by a sense of human support, something can grow out of this process for the teacher and the pupils. But this can only be effected when the school and the teachers are openly hospitable to this kind of help, and when the help itself becomes, with increased experience, the kind a teacher asks for. To be of use, it cannot be poured down the throat like medicine; to be nourishing, it must be sipped slowly like the good wine that it can be. . . .

The Disturbed and Disturbing Child in the Classroom

Another of the classroom teacher's common frustrations is the disturbed and disturbing child. Any teacher with the slightest grasp on reality knows full well he will have some difficult children in his class. The course of education, like that of true love, does not run smooth.

But it is true that even *difficulty* is a term that should have *normal* in front of it. There are some children far too sick to be in a regular class. They may be without impulse-control, or their behavior may be bizarre, or they may be withdrawn to the extent of being unreachable. Increasingly, special attention is being given and special provision being made for such children. But where is the severity of their disability first discovered? Rarely in the home. Rarely in the doctor's office. Mostly, severe emotional disturbance is first diagnosed in the classroom.

This means that a teacher—certainly a teacher of the early grades—has to live with, and try to teach, the child who is too ill to be lived with or too ill to be taught. Such a child disrupts the class, demands constant attention, and fills the teacher with a sense of failure and confusion, to say nothing of rage and sometimes of terror or revulsion. All of this causes him to feel guilty as well as inadequate. With the waiting lists of children on special services as long as they are, it is the rule, not the exception, that sees this child in the classroom for months before diagnosis, and longer before replacement. In the meantime, child, class, and teacher are often badly harmed. A growing awareness of this condition indicates the possibility, through teacher training, of earlier diagnosis, a better use of consultation, and increased skills for the teacher to help him recognize and deal with these disturbances on an emergency basis. (The emergency often lasts the whole school year!)

Merely relaying to the teacher the fact that he cannot hope to teach this child and that it is not his fault that the child behaves or feels as he does or learns poorly, is sometimes enough to improve matters. Just knowing this often relieves the teacher, and the child's behavior relaxes in direct proportion to the lessened tension of the teacher. But teaching such children is no easy matter.

Ask any psychiatrist how anxiety-provoking it is to be around very ill people. The teacher is in this spot daily; his anxiety rises sky-high just at a time when he is also forced to deal with his usual load of problems and tasks, and his anxiety makes him less able to do so. Again, to play variations on our theme, the teacher's self-awareness may make all the difference between his survival in school and his collapse, just as it may determine the way a class will survive or the amount of damage the sick child experiences.

Some teachers—often the best motivated—court trouble by becoming over-involved in the child and then feeling rejected and angry when their efforts fail. For some, particular symptoms are too evocative of repressed impulses or hidden childhood experiences of their own. Often, a child placed with a different (not necessarily a better) teacher fares better. Each teacher can take certain kinds of abnormalities and has his own personal aversions, the causes of which may be hidden from his awareness.

To make matters for contemporary teachers even more threatening, the notion of disturbance is even more complex than it used to be. There are, of course, the usual (though difficult on sight to distinguish) characters who are basically healthy but temporarily disturbed over a situation arising at home or at school with which they cannot cope, one which sets them into behavior very like the most disturbed child. The Johnny who throws a book at Peter may be a disturbed child or he may be suffering from an overload of criticism from Papa at the breakfast table. The act is a disturbed and disturbing one, but it can mean anything on the continuum from health to illness.

There are those with disturbances which are indeed very serious and severe but which are not too disturbing to the teacher in the classroom unless he is more than averagely conscientious: these are the too quiet, book-buried, non-social, shy and fearful children, whom teachers are learning increasingly to note, but who do not disrupt class activities as a rule, do not set an entire group into panic or mayhem, and therefore are not so quickly noticed by the teacher.

But in addition, a new phenomenon of disturbance has come to school and makes for a serious fraction of irritation for the class and the teacher. These are children who may not be intrinsically as emotionally flooded as some of the others mentioned, but they are disturbed and most surely are disturbing. They make up the increasing group of lower-class and upper middle-class children who, in a world much more mobile and less rooted than heretofore, have parents who move from place to place on jobs or who are looking for jobs. These children sometimes come from immigrant families (such as constitute a severe educational challenge in large cities like New York), or sometimes from indigent farm or unskilled labor families whose work is seasonal, or from military service people who move from post to post, or from the families of highly skilled young engineers or businessmen whose companies move them back and forth to branch offices in many states. These children have lacked the security of a place and a constant in their lives; they tend to make thin and superficial relationships, to be either desperate followers in order to belong, or desperate leaders in order to shine and to make a mark while the brief candle of their stay burns brightly. Often they make up the gangs and the cliques and the socially worrisome element. Teachers have not yet found ways, other than by trail and error, of dealing with this phenomenon. They have not learned how to relate to these children, how to motivate them for long-term goals or long-term relationships. The very task of doing so, when one thinks about it psychodynamically, borders on the impossible. For these children have learned the hard way not to invest too much in relationships that are bound to change, not to count too much on any way of life when next month or next year the way of life will have to be quite different. Being basically healthy animals, they have learned to adapt superficially to everything in some way or other, and they convey an impenetrable wall when a teacher tries to help them invest themselves emotionally in work, in projects, or in relationships. This problem has just begun to be recognized as a severely frustrating aspect of teaching today.

Reasons behind Choosing Teaching as a Profession

From all that has been said so far, the reader must be beginning to feel as swamped with helplessness as the teachers themselves feel with some of their classes. Why, one begins to ask, would anyone choose teaching for a profession? It is a good question and has been the subject of some study. A teacher's rea-

sons for choosing his profession often underlie the last frustration to be discussed here. What does a teacher hope to derive from teaching? What conscious and unconscious forces may lead to his decision to become a teacher?

There was a time when most teachers were women—when the only respectable job a woman could have was teaching. (This is still in large part true through the elementary grades.) In taking the orders, so to speak, she knew that she virtually sounded a death knell on her hopes for marriage, but she did retain respectability and a sense of usefulness. Unconsciously, a woman might go into teaching to avoid marriage. This may be the case today, as well as in times past, but it is not so easy an escape as it once was, since many teachers are married and the social restrictions on teachers have been modified. However, married or single, respectability is still achieved by the woman teacher. Years ago the rarer man teacher often took to teaching when he found himself to be bookish and unaggressive. This situation still exists, though it is less prevalent than it used to be. Some teachers took to teaching out of a sense of mission or dedication: it was a way to make the world, which did not look so good, better for the future. This is still true, fortunately, and is often found coexisting with many other reasons.

Some teachers fall into teaching. They begin with other fields, find other experiences unsavory, or feel they cannot succeed in them. A job of teaching is open and they attempt it.

Despite the pitiful salaries teachers have always been paid, there are people who feel more secure working on state, county, or city salaries than in business—a teacher's salary, though low, seems reasonably certain. But since low salaries are the rule, the teaching field has become increasingly attractive to many married women. These people often can supplement a limited income by teaching. They can buy the extras at home, or they can contribute to the necessities without the full burden of having to support a family on a teacher's salary. Education schools these days have more and more students who are middle-aged and have children past the toddler stage themselves. For these people, the economic strain tends to be less, but the strain of filling two full-time jobs, teaching and family life, often brings with it its own frustration.

A man or woman may take up teaching because a teacher has been so important in his own development. When he was in school, a particular teacher may have made a great difference in his life, may indeed have become someone to pattern himself on. Some people, contrariwise, take up teaching because of their own school sufferings and because they remember with chagrin and bitterness the poor teaching to which they were exposed, and they resolve to live life over for themselves through others, and this time to do it right. Some people seem to get along beautifully and comfortably with young people of different ages, but they may do very poorly, feel awkward, out of place, and inadequate in adult groups. Such people often make excellent teachers, especially of the very young (though they are frequently the ones who have the most trouble with the parents of the children they teach). These people may be reliving what was a real or a fantasied happier time of their lives. They may be educational Peter Pans and find it necessary to ally themselves with the young folks against the adults. Many of these people, though by no means all, often find it difficult to deal with the authorities in school. They are still carrying on childhood or adolescent rebellions.

Some people are much happier without people. They fall in love with subject matter, with mathematics, or physics, or ancient history. They may have discovered that real, present-day life is simply too much, that relationships demand a closeness that is too frightening; high school or college teaching allows them to legitimately drown themselves in their subject. They are often very skilled in their subject matter, and show a passion and love, when involved in content, that may well be inspiring to some of their like-minded students. These teachers are practically never the ones who find satisfaction in relating to the children in their classes, either as a group or as individuals, unless they find someone who is the budding image of themselves or who seems to be as interested in falling in love with that particular subject matter as they themselves are. These teachers (and some of them are very gifted, if one accepts their limitations) are virtually never interested in the psychology of children or interpersonal relations.

The fact that a teacher may have all sorts of reasons he does not recognize for choosing his profession does not differentiate him from anyone else. It is, again, part of his humanness. The same kinds of reasons, or equally unconscious ones, may impel a person to become a nurse, a doctor, an engineer, a bus driver, an executive, a secretary, a salesman, a plumber, a cattle raiser, a lawyer, or a fireman. The crucial difference for the teacher is that, because he must constantly deal with children and cannot avoid having an important effect on them, he, more than most of his fellow human be-

ings, must be *aware* of the possible reasons for his choice of profession.

Redl and Wattenberg[2] have made a list of 15 of the more commonly stated reasons people tend to go into teaching.

1. Status
2. Family pressure
3. Love for subject field
4. Identification with a former teacher
5. Love of children
6. Fun in teaching
7. Helping to build a better world
8. Self-sacrifice for an ideal
9. Correcting the shortcomings of one's own past
10. Reliving childhood patterns
11. Desire for affection
12. Need for security
13. Halfway house to other ambition
14. Need for power and group leadership
15. Guaranteed superiority

In the discussion above, merely some of these factors have been mentioned. One might not only discuss the rest but add many more. The fact is that people's motives are rarely, if ever, single-purposed, and most people make these decisions on many counts, on a series of personal, rational, irrational, and coincidental factors. Moreover, the reasons a person gives himself for doing something are nearly always the reasons his own self-image can tolerate. People have a great stake in hiding from themselves other reasons, perhaps just as strong or even stronger, which they do not want to face. A teacher afraid of his own aggression may be quite unable to see that he went into teaching not only for love of subject matter but just as much because he had a need for power unfulfilled in other areas. A teacher who takes great pride in his independent, controlled handling of life may not be able to recognize his loneliness and his need for affection as a driving motive. To restate the theme as a coda, the awareness mentioned earlier comes back into the picture again; for the more aware a teacher is of the hidden, as well as the obvious, reasons for teaching, the more fully will be he able to do his job and face its frustrations; for he will be more aware of the areas of satisfaction from which he derives pleasure and will not need to feel so resentful that he is not getting what he intended to get when he took his

teaching certificate. Through awareness, he will have either given up impossible goals and substitute more realistic ones, or he will have found ways to reach the goals unanswered by his job in other areas of his life. . . .

Article Footnotes

1. Jules Henry, "The Problem of Spontaneity, Initiative and Creativity in Suburban Classrooms," *American Journal of Orthopsychiatry*, **29** (April 1963), 266–279.

2. Fritz Redl and William W. Wattenberg, *Mental Hygiene in Teaching* (New York: Harcourt, Brace and Co., 1959), pp. 479–482.

The reader should attend to two aspects of the following selection by Small: (1) the *substantive material* on the preschool, an area of vital and rapidly increasing concern in special education, and (2) the *process* of helping the teacher (in

meeting the problems discussed in the previous selection) through consultation and "back-up" assistance. Without such help, teachers cannot be expected to deal with all the problems of disturbed youngsters.

Consultation with Teachers of "Disadvantaged" Pre-School Children
Edna Small

Introduction

Pre-school experience is recognized as an important part of the educational process, especially for children whose cultural experience does not provide adequate background for first grade tasks. This level of education is being supported by the federal government in such programs as Head Start and has been adopted by some school systems on an experimental basis. Mental health personnel have a real opportunity to provide assistance, both in dealing with emotional problems of particular children and furthering broader preventive goals. We must begin to define the kinds of service most appropriate to meeting increasing demands and to maximizing the experiences of the children involved in these programs.

The following describes one approach to this problem, based on the author's experience for two years as consultant to a program that included five such pre-schools. It departs from other literature on

school consultation by focusing on the most frequent themes that have come up over time rather than on theory or techniques of consultation or consultant-consultee relationships.

Setting

The pre-school system involved consists of five physically separate centers, under shared directorship. Each center has two separate classrooms in operation. During the first year, class size varied between 15 and 18, with a teacher, assistant teacher, and aide assigned to each room. All the children came in the morning, and some stayed all day in a special day-care program. Some staff were part time, but scheduling usually guaranteed two adults in a classroom. Each physical plant had one teacher (with classroom responsibility) designated as head teacher and a school manager to help coordinate supplies, schedules, etc. The second year all schools adopted separate morning and afternoon sessions, with a very small minority of children in day-care programs. Average class size was twenty youngsters, and all teaching staff was full time, meeting separate classes morning and afternoon.

The level of teacher preparation should be noted here. The first year, most of the classroom teachers had prior training and experience in primary education or early childhood development. This was not true of the assistant teachers. In addition, classroom aides, some of whom were young men, were assigned to each room as part of a subprofessional training program for school dropouts. All teachers in this system had direct classroom responsibility, including the teacher in charge of each center. The second year a trained teacher with no classroom responsibility was placed in each center as head teacher, and the school manager position was dropped. The majority of teachers had been assistant teachers the previous fall; former aides became assistants, and new aides joined the program. The Director of the program the second year had been a head teacher the year before and had an excellent grasp of the program and problems involved.

Method of Consultation

After several initial meetings with the Pre-school Director and school administrators, consultative sessions were held with the teaching staff of a given center on the average of once every three weeks. In most centers, these group meetings were attended regularly by the head teacher, classroom teacher, assistants, and, in some schools, the youth aides. The meetings were informal, with no prearranged agenda, and the topics raised ranged from concern about an individual child (the most frequent starting point) to questions of school philosophy and its mental health implications.

The selection of a group meeting as the method of consultation was dictated not by its obvious economic advantage but because of the consultant's conviction that much professional support would be generated by an opportunity to share one's problems with colleagues and to recognize their universality. In addition, it was hoped that the learning that could take place with a given child as the focus, in many instances, could be generalized in a meaningful way, as well as provide teachers an opportunity to exchange useful classroom techniques.

An important aspect of the consultation program was the availability of the "backup" service from the Child Guidance Clinic where the consultant is a member of the staff. Thus, there was a totally cooperating facility receptive to referrals for complete diagnostic work-ups when needed. While consultation was approached with the consultant planning to work primarily with teachers and with the observations rather than seeing children directly, this was never a hard and fast rule.

Themes in Consultation

There were many themes involving teachers' feelings and specific child behavior patterns, both normal and problematic, that came up with most teachers, trained or untrained.

The initial problems presented in all centers concerned children exhibiting some degree of aggressive or hyperactive behavior. As we focused on these children, a frequent pattern of reactions began to appear. Teachers would often report having "tried one thing after another," or "tried to look the other way at times" in order to keep from feeling like a "nag." Thus, there was reduced consistency in expectations and limits for these youngsters. In addition, the teachers frequently had reached a state of extreme annoyance with the child in question by the time his behavior came up for discussion. It became important for the consultant to provide permission for consultant limits by stressing the child's need for such structure in order to reduce the discomfort felt by teachers who found themselves constantly needing to keep an eye on a given child and frequently needing to redirect his activity.

A second part of the problem was the teacher's reluctance to express personal annoyance about a child. This led to the suppression of such feelings until they were of such strength as to markedly interfere with the relationship with the child. The teachers in question seemed relieved by the consultant's comments that recognized how annoying such a child can be, the "normalcy" of their reactions, and more importantly, the usefulness of the feelings the child stirred up as an aid in understanding his needs and problems. They were then much more able to look at the child in terms of developmental level, motility patterns, and very often the relative lack in verbal behavior. We were also able to modify the child's program in terms of his needs without the teacher being "hung-up" on whether she was being punitive, and changes could be interpreted to the child as truly designed for his needs. Thus, one child who at first was terribly overstimulated and disorganized by the unstructured, highly active play on the playground could remain at school with adult supervision and with mutual recognition that the playground was upsetting to him and that he would feel better playing inside. Similarly, the day for several other children was shortened until they could cope with the tasks of the program. Whenever this was done, it was suggested that the child come late rather than leave early so that the child did not feel he was being excluded because of any momentary difficult behavior.

The relationship of relative absence of verbal expression to a pattern of hyperactive and aggressive behavior was often noted with surprise by the teachers, following my inquiry into the verbal area when such other behavior was the presenting problem. Then we could talk about some of the functions of speech, especially as providing an alternative to immediate physical expression of feelings, as enabling delay, and as a way of being able to be in more control of the environment by having a way to conceptualize and express events and desires. Teachers were encouraged not only to limit unacceptable behavior, but also to begin to verbalize how the children were feeling, even when the children could not do this for themselves. Another important general issue was that children had a right to have feelings, even when they were not rational in adult terms.

Discussions about aggressive feelings also led into another general issue: the meaning of "bad language" and how it should be handled. This discussion was facilitated in some schools by teachers having already begun to value the children beginning to verbalize, rather than to act out, feelings. For example, one teacher reported a five-year-old acting out her annoyance by stalking out of the room to the bathroom and yelling "shit" several times. Following this expressive verbal behavior, she returned to the classroom in a much better frame of mind. The teacher was able to see dramatically how this behavior, while not a desirable end-point, was a good step for this child in contrast to her prior physical expression of anger.

The dual purpose of discussing bad language with teachers was to help them neutralize some of the "shock effect" via anecdotes and then to focus on the message rather than the form of the communications involved. For example, at one school the first time the subject of obscenity was raised it was presented in a very abstract form with a lively staff discussion, but with no specific reference to any event. I finally inquired as to what had

triggered this, and learned that in the day's events a three-year-old approached a teacher and said, "I want to suck your titties." We were then able to focus on the clarity of the child's communication and deal with some of the feelings stirred up in the staff by such language, both accepting these feelings as normal, and beginning to move toward being able to respond to what the children were communicating rather than rejecting them on the basis of their language.

A related theme, which again involved the content of the children's verbal communication, came up much later in the year. Teachers began to express their uncertainty as to how to respond when children talked about distressing reality situations. Again, in group discussions, the teachers could express their discomfort with such descriptive communication which made them feel helpless. These were obviously situations over which they had no control, such as observed violence, fires, etc. Again, as in all aspects of consultations, this adult feeling could be accepted and discussed as a very normal reaction. We could then focus on the teacher's assumption that the children were expecting help from them (which was not the case), the value to the children in feeling understood, and the importance of children putting the things happening to them into words as a step in mastery.

Sensitization to children's reaction to change was another clear theme. On several occasions, behavior patterns which had been improving over the course of a year were reported to be recurring. At these times, exploration of the school's situation often indicated a change in teacher or classroom. Via these illustrations, we were able to begin to talk about anticipating such events with children, recognizing the feelings that were involved, and meeting them with reassurance and support whenever possible.

It was interesting to note that initial separation problems were noted less often than was expected by the consultant in a nursery school population. When such were reported, the importance of involving parents or parent substitutes in the transition to nursery school could be discussed. In addition, it raised for the consultant some real questions concerning the degree to which the lack of evidence of separation problems is a healthy developmental sign, or indicates less than normal investment in one object as a trusted image.

For example, many of the children described by teachers appeared to be falsely independent. When hyper-aggressive behavior was reported, I would always inquire into the child's use of adults—requests for assistance or comfort, tendency to cry when upset, etc. When these were lacking, we would assume the youngster did not see adults as a source of comfort and security, and worked toward meeting unexpressed needs. Following one such group discussion, when a youngster's needs had been discussed in the above way, the very sensitive teacher involved went on to wonder why she had not so responded, and discovered that the child's severe ringworm had subconsciously repelled her. Quite skillful handling of this youngster developed, with no need for further consultation.

Another major theme dealt with teachers' unreasonable self-expectations. Thus, the teacher at first seemed to feel a need not only to handle every child who was enrolled in the school, but also to have them make enough progress to enter kindergarten. Throughout, they were encouraged to assess in realistic terms the needs of a given child, and whether these could be met in the reality situation provided by their nursery schools, which was somewhat limited in therapeutic possibilities simply in such terms as the adult-child ratio.

Another type of child discussed was the child functioning at a level far below his chronological age. Often these youngsters were first discussed in terms of their lack of participation and speech. It was important in these cases to inquire fully into their living situations, and to observe them over a period of time in order to work toward the differentiation of environmental versus "real" retardation. For example, two such youngsters were discussed early in the year. One was a boy who only responded "huh" to any approach or question, and later would answer questions by repeating the teacher's instructions; i.e., when asked to say yes or no, he would say "yes or no." The teacher was encouraged to meet with his elderly caretaker, whose speech patterns were much the same. However, her age and illness made it difficult for her to change her style of relating to the child. Over the year, he made marked progress in nursery school and the question of retardation no longer applies.

Another youngster, first discussed at the same time and with similar background factors, has shown no such improvement and is now under further diagnostic study.

In fact, looking at a child over time has been a useful concept to the teachers. If all children presented as problems in the first month were treated as such in terms of focus and referral, most of the important contributions that a nursery school can make, both to diagnosis and to growth, would be ignored. Therefore, while we are always very interested in any child presented for discussion, a given discussion was not seen as an end point, but rather put in a framework of "let's follow the child periodically through the year." This tends to reduce the staff's immediate anxiety, allows for more meaningful differentiation between transient reactions and more serious emotional problems, and keeps the on-going developmental process in central focus.

As indicated above, some problems presented could be best viewed in terms of the environment. For example, meals were not served the first year. One of the youngsters presented early in that year was arousing much concern because of her pattern of coming to school and spending much time in a rocking chair, rocking and sucking her thumb, suggesting a serious emotional problem to the staff. Inquiry into her daily routine, however, suggested a good possibility that she was coming to school hungry. Teachers began to notice this as a pattern with some other children, and ultimately meals were introduced. Similarly, when problem behavior was reported in the bathroom areas where running water was available, the consultant emphasized the "pull" of various things in the environment and the choice the staff had of either programming to avoid such problems by having an adult present, or living with such expected behavior.

At times, the children discussed because of suspected emotional problems were referred for indicated medical clarification. For example, one youngster presented as an overly active boy turned out to have a severe visual problem, and his explanation of fights, "He was in my way," was an accurate view of others in his path as aggressors, as his visual limitations required following a clearly identified track. At other times, children were discussed where the change in their behavior was suggestive of a depressive reaction, and the staff was encouraged to be aware of reality events in the child's life (for example, illness, divorce, births, moving, deaths.)

Working with parents or parent substitutes was another theme that needed continuous discussion. As in many professions working with children, some of the teachers tended to always describe parents as rejecting and at fault in children's problems, with little feeling for the parent involved. At such times, our discussions would focus on trying to help the staff empathize with the parents, recognize the positive motivation involved in getting a youngster to nursery school, and also understand that some of the defensiveness and rejection they felt in parents was the parents' response to years of experience with authoritarian systems that approach them only to complain about the behavior of their offspring. In particular incidents, teachers were helped to find alternate ways to begin to relate to a parent and to work cooperatively rather than feed back further difficulties. At other times, some "problems" of a child's behavior could be easily handled by requesting that parents give explicit permission to their child for some school activity, like using the bathroom here, sitting on the floor, taking off one's shoes, etc.

To a person untrained in nursery school education or early childhood development or to those with extensive experience with older children, the *motility* patterns of normal pre-school aged children can appear pathological. With recognition of the normal needs and preferences of physical activity as well as the availability of activity as a medium for learning, much unnecessary frustration (for both children and staff) from "sitting still" expectations can be avoided. Thus, a child described as "hyperactive" was brought up for discussion. As always, when such words are used, a behavioral description was requested to make clear what behavior was meant. As the teacher described the child in question, the consultant suggested that he sounded like a normal three-and-a-half year old, with perhaps an active constitutional pattern. His need for activity was stressed. On my next visit, the teacher reported with relief that the next time she had felt herself getting annoyed at this youngster's restlessness during group table activity, she had taken him to a more open space and allowed him free movement, and was amazed at the energy and dexterity he displayed, his joy in free body activity like running and somersaults, and his improved disposition. We could then discuss the recognition of motor needs as a first step, needing help next from educators rather than mental health consultants, in learning about teaching techniques that utilize such normal patterns.

Another normal developmental issue highlighted was the importance of recognizing a child's working out a sense of personal identity. Thus, behavior sometimes viewed as "selfishness" could be reinterpreted as a stage in a child's learning to value himself and his property. A beautiful example of this occurred in a youngster being followed in consultation, originally discussed as a shy, nonverbal, non-participating child. Later in the year his teacher described a new "problem"—his annoyance when other kids touched his chair, pushing them away and saying "it's mine." As in many instances,

when the staff could see a specific instance in behavior as part of a larger developmental sequence, they found it less disturbing and could handle it better.

Children's use of fantasy was another area that sometimes presented problems, especially to the untrained. Thus, one four-year-old was described initially as "living in a world of fantasy, cut off from reality." Again, a detailed inquiry into the specifics of actual behavior established that the youngster would often adopt a character such as Batman for the day and not answer questions or follow directions unless addressed properly in his assumed role. The functions of play and fantasy in child-development were discussed, and this child once more was perceived by his teacher as a little boy rather than a potential schizophrenic. Other aspects of this example beautifully illustrated other developmental dynamics. Concerned about his reality-testing, the teacher carefully went through all the child's role characters, indicating that they were real people pretending to be someone else, and if you took off their masks you would see actors. After she had gone through several such examples, our young hero completed the unmasking with typical candor, unmindful of Oedipus: "And if you take off boogey-man's mask, it's really Daddy."

Sexual interest and curiosity, concern about where babies come from, etc., was a frequent problem area to staff, many of whom preferred to pretend that children have no such concerns. The other extreme was to view all boy-girl horseplay as sexual and undesirable. My aim in all such discussion was to put this aspect of child development into perspective, recognizing teacher discomfort, and discussing ways of meeting children's requests for clarification, expressions of curiosity, and worries about mother's pregnancy. As in the related area of "bad language," anecdotes were often useful in getting across how children may interpret things.

Another aspect related to play and fantasy disturbing to untrained staff, especially the young men, was their discomfort when little boys dressed up in women's clothes or took the role of a mother in play. It took much discussion to begin to reassure them that boys as well as girls have to deal with mothering and being mothered, had baby feelings and feelings about siblings, and could usefully work some of these out in play, and that this was *not* a sign of incipient homosexuality.

The final principle is that children move *to* adequate peer relationships *from* a good, trusting relationship with an adult, which builds a sense of self and self-worth. This came up often as questions were raised about kids who did not participate in peer activities, and attempts were often made to force them rather than first build a teacher-child relationship. Other children were mainly involved in "negative" peer contacts, for example, taking things and hitting. Many of the children in the centers, as indicated above, were pseudo-mature and had to first learn that an adult could interpret and meet their needs before they could move to the next step in social development.

Similarly, less experienced staff also seemed at times to make the assumption that the best way to prepare a child for a future requirement was to "practice it." For example, if a child had to be able to sit still, work for longer time periods, etc., in kindergarten or first grade, they should begin doing these things now to truly have a "headstart." Whenever this assumption was implicitly made, we could discuss the alternative, more appropriate hypothesis: that adequate mastery of tasks at a given developmental stage will increase the likelihood of being able to meet future ones, and that it is more important for a three-year-old to do three-year-old things and that this would better enable him to later do six-year-old things than would the expectation of greater maturity, ability to delay, etc., at this time.

The next selection discusses a more specific aspect of pupil-teacher interaction in discipline. Empathic feeling, as advocated by Long, may underlie the ability to move with sequential events (discussed by Kounin) and the ability to accept children (see the Small article). But the explicit goal of empathy is to help the child develop trust. Achieving this goal sometimes requires measures for which teachers are not well prepared, as the three case examples illustrate.

Helping Children Cope with Feelings

Nicholas J. Long
Rose Alpher
Fairfield Butt
Melissa Cully

I couldn't have any bad feelings in my family. I wasn't allowed to be angry, much less say or show it! Sometimes I had hostile thoughts that scared me even though I behaved properly.

I lived in a permissive home, although my parents called it democratic. I could say anything and do anything that came into my head. When I was ten years old, I recall an incident in which I kept teasing my mother and wondering when she would say "Stop it!"

So spoke teachers as they discussed the relationship between their style of managing classroom behavior and their parents' success or failure in understanding and managing their feelings and behavior as children. The discussion became exciting as teachers looked beyond the surface explanation of behavior and focused on how the inner life of a person determines the way he perceives and responds to his interpersonal world. Using this assumption, we will describe the masked ways children express their feelings and how teachers can help them find more acceptable methods of communicating them without exploding, running away or denying that they have feelings.

Teaching: Art of Open Communication

Knowing that you can share your thoughts and experiences with someone and have that person understand and accept them is a wonderful feeling. In this relationship, people move toward each other. They talk and listen to each other. They open up and share their concerns, dreams and aspirations. Whether one calls it love, acceptance, mutual trust or friendship, it has the same personal effect. The

From "Helping Children Cope with Feelings," by Nicholas J. Long, Rose Alpher, Fairfield Butt, and Melissa Cully, *Childhood Education*, March 1969, pp. 367–372. Copyright by Association for Childhood Education International. Reprinted by permission.

person seems complete, has a sense of well-being and an inner warmth that is observable and contagious.

Teaching is the art of beginning and maintaining open communication. It is the capacity of a teacher to empathize with the child, to enter his world in a way that will enable him to manage anxiety, overcome frustration, and become more self-confident and independent. Every teacher is able to achieve this level of successful communication with selected children. Frequently these relationships provide a teacher with the necessary emotional gratification that helps him through the difficult task of teaching large numbers of children who have an increasing range of problems. Consequently, teachers cannot feel the same toward all children.

In our up-tight, turned-off, go-go generation of children, teachers and other adults need assistance in finding ways of maintaining communication with children. It is not an easy task! For example, 10 percent (a modest estimate) of all the children in regular classrooms have emotional problems related to learning, peers, authorities and school rules. At times their behavior is confusing, unpredictable and irritating. While expressing their feelings via fighting, sulking, daydreaming, lying and physical illness, they are unsuccessful in communicating to teachers their deep sense of inner struggle. Instead of eliciting feelings of concern, compassion and cooperation, these children are labeled *troublemakers*—irresponsible and inattentive. For these troubled children, there is little mutual communication and even less emotional acceptance—like living in a foreign country where no one understands your language. Cut off, isolated and rejected by others, these children have little hope that school will be rewarding. As interpersonal frustrations increase, their inappropriate classroom behavior swells until they explode in rage or withdraw from their empty world of interpersonal support. When this happens, they become candidates for Hillcrest Children's Center, a therapeutic elementary school for emotionally disturbed children in Washington, D.C.

Helping Children Cope with Feelings

In helping the Hillcrest teachers understand, relate to, and educate emotionally disturbed children, considerable time and effort are spent discussing and demonstrating the concepts of *decoding, labeling and redirecting behavior.*

Decoding Behavior

All behavior is caused and is the child's best solution for maintaining his state of emotional adjustment. Usually his behavior is his unique way of protecting himself from even greater physiological stress. This leads us to a belief that the problems children cause are not the cause of their problems. The problems children cause are the symptoms of their problems. For example, a child who continues to daydream in class and in turn does not complete his work has a problem. The source of his difficulty lies not in his behavior or symptom (inattention) but in the reasons why he is unable to concentrate. As a result, teachers need to become aware of the child's verbal and nonverbal forms of communication that provide clues to his inner life.

Verbal communication.   When a child is in conflict, language often is used to mislead, protect and mask his real feelings. Consequently, teachers learn to pay more attention to *how* a child is speaking rather than *what* he is saying. By listening to the flow and tones of his words, a teacher can interpret them in terms of feelings, such as anger, seduction, fear, sadness, excitement or nervousness. In addition, one child can say, "Get out of here!" while communicating a feeling of "I love you, please don't go away." Another child can say, "You are the best teacher I have ever had" while sending the message of personal seduction and manipulation.

Since words are learned and reflect the child's socio-economic background, they may have an emotional impact on adults quite different from what was intended. For example, a teacher for six months tutored a withdrawn eight-year-old boy in arithmetic with marginal success. One day he finally understood the place-holder concept. When he completed his assignment, the teacher expressed how proud and happy she was that he had mastered it. In a sudden burst of unmanageable glee, he said, "I know, I'm pretty hot sh—!" Decoding his message, she replied, "It's a good feeling to like yourself!"

Nonverbal communcation.   The more observant we become, the more we listen to what a child says without words. We learn to respond to his body language. We become aware of the many messages he sends with his eyes, muscles, skin temperature, body odor, breathing pattern and body movement. A child learns early in life that if he expresses certain feelings and words his parents react with anger and disappointment. He also learns the spoken word can be held against him as self-incriminating evidence. To avoid this pain, his words can say one thing while his body expresses something different. While all of us react to body language of children unconsciously, the teacher's task is to decode these messages into conscious awareness that leads to the exciting and rewarding statement, "I know now how Mary (or Matthew) feels."

Labeling and Accepting Feelings

As a teacher listens to a child and learns to trust the authenticity of nonverbal communication, the teacher is ready to label the feeling he is experiencing in his own body. Based upon what he sees and feels, a teacher can say to a child, "You look sad. Can I help you?" "It seems to me you are about to explode. Maybe it would help if we could talk about it." "You look very upset. Can I help you?" Or, "I have a feeling that you are concerned about something. Is something scary going to happen to you?"

As you reach out and share the child's inner life with honesty, reflecting his unspoken and spoken language, a new opportunity for a meaningful and successful communication develops. At this time, any impulse to make a moral judgment about the child's behavior needs to be checked.

The next step, accepting the feeling, is far more complex than labeling the child's behavior. For a few teachers, the thought that some children have hostile and even sexual feelings toward them is upsetting. To force teachers to give lip service to something they cannot accept emotionally is more dishonest psychologically than saying nothing. Assuming, however, that most teachers are reasonably comfortable with these feelings, they can express how normal, typical and natural it is for a child to feel the way he is feeling. For example, a teacher could comment, "It's okay to feel sad when you lose something you love. It is the way you should feel." Or, "It is normal for children to be upset or nervous before a test." Or, "I know you are angry at me, but you will feel better when you complete your assignment." The crucial step after labeling and accepting the feeling is to find appropriate ways of expressing the feeling in behavior.

Redirecting Behavior

Just as man has found ways of harnessing the potentially destructive force of fast-flowing river currents into electrical power that has increased his productivity and comfort, teachers can help children learn ways of expressing their feelings through the techniques of ventilation, skill development, and verbal insight.

Ventilation.   A verbal blow-up in which a child says, "I would like to punch him in the nose" or screams or runs away is much healthier than when the child does not talk but instead puts his feelings into action. There are occasions when a child becomes intoxicated by his anger or despair, loses control, and needs to be physically held in order to protect him from hurting himself and others. In most cases, through use of words the teacher can encourage a child to drain off his feelings of frustration, disappointment and fear.

Skill development.   For some children words are not enough. Their bodies are tense and their muscles ache for expression. In other cases the tension freezes up and the child becomes moody and rigid. To release this emotional blockage, the teacher must help the child sublimate or find appropriate activities for his feelings. In school they can be redirected through social studies and language arts (reading about great men and their problems or writing about self and others), art (drawing, pottery, carving), dramatic play (role-playing), physical education (kickball, calisthenics, games), manual arts (sawing, hammering, filing), music (singing, playing or clapping), and homeroom care (cleaning desks, notebooks, chalkboards). All learning must be invested with feeling to give it interest, meaning and purpose.

Verbal insight.   A third alternative is to interview the child. Conflict in the classroom does not always interfere with learning. In fact, conflict can become one of the most unique and useful ways of helping children learn how to cope with and understand relationships between feelings and behavior. This style of intervention, called "life space interviewing," was developed by Fritz Redl.[1] It is a method of talking and listening effectively with children, whether it is for behavioral control, for disciplinary reasons, or for better understanding of how the child sees himself in his selected world. It is the first concrete, practical step beyond suggesting to teachers that they should "accept the child, provide structure, and set limits." It is an essential technique that is taught to the Hillcrest staff under supervision.

Three Case Histories

To demonstrate how our teachers use these concepts, three cases are offered as examples.

The Case of Timmy

Timmy, age 4, came to our therapeutic nursery school as a child of normal intelligence who spoke very few words, who was not completely toilet trained, and who rarely showed the lively interest in toys, activities, and attention from other people. Incidents that might be the cause for expressions of sadness or fright, such as his mother's leaving him on his first visit to school, or slipping while climbing the jungle gym, brought no overt reaction from Timmy. His face often wore a blank stare or a bland smile. Mannerisms included clicking his tongue and holding out his hand while wiggling his fingers. It was not unusual for him suddenly to begin jumping or to break out into hollow laughter.

Tim was growing up in a household where people felt it was safer not to express feelings and handled painful or annoying situations by smiling efficiency. The following incident shows how the seemingly inappropriate behavior of a disturbed child signals his teachers that he is struggling with feelings:

Upon arrival at nursery school one day, Tim's mother stopped to explain that this was the first day of a car pool arrangement and that another mother would be driving him home. Mrs. B. said she knew Timmy was delighted with the new plan, for whenever she had talked with him about it at home he had laughed and smiled. As she stood chatting with the teachers, Timmy stood next to her with his back toward all the women. He didn't look at his mother as she cheerily told him goodbye.

That day Tim seemed helpless in school. He spent a lot of time standing around as if unable to choose a toy to use; he was the last one to be ready for snack; he followed the teachers around the room or came over to touch them gingerly when they were helping another child; and, while he said nothing, he frequently wiggled his fingers. On the few occasions we mentioned the car pool to Timmy, he closed his eyes and put his fingers in his ears. When I announced that it was time to put on coats and go home, Timmy began to jump around. Putting an

arm around him, I said, "I wonder if you're thinking about going home in somebody else's car without Mommy." Timmy laughed. "I bet you don't like that at all" I told him. "You must wish Mommy were coming to take you home today as she always does. It's kind of scary to have things be different, isn't it?" Timmy's laughter stopped as he looked at me. Screwing his face into an exaggerated frown, he took his coat out of his cubby and held it out to me. With help from people who knew how he felt, Timmy could walk forward into a difficult experience.

The Case of Ray

This case describes how a hyperaggressive, impulsive boy is managed by his teacher.

Ray was an eight-year-old inner-city boy of normal intelligence who exhibited severe disciplinary problems in public school. He acted out in primitive aggressive ways, once stabbing a girl in his class with scissors because she made him mad.

During his first week at Hillcrest he bit the teacher, threatened and fought with his peers, and ran through the school. As his teacher set limits on his behavior, Ray was told that there was nothing wrong with having angry feelings, but hitting and running out of class were not acceptable ways of communicating these feelings. Ray was told that setting limits was not punishment but protection.

Over many months the entire staff had occasion to work with Ray. It was a slow but ultimately successful process. When Ray would kick, spit, take objects from the other children, and try to run away, the staff responded by saying that they cared very much for Ray and that caring sometimes meant stopping a child who was out of control. Instead of hitting with his fists, Ray slowly used words to relate his fear and hostility. Ray also had the positive attributes of intelligence, perception, charm, excellent recall, and a sense of humor—all of which were encouraged.

One specific example might help to illustrate this process of expressing his feelings in an acceptable way:

One morning Ray had difficulty learning a new section in his arithmetic book. Feeling inadequate and frustrated, he broke his pencil and started to tear his book. I stepped in, letting him know that I knew he was upset because his work was difficult. For a few minutes he relaxed, but I could still sense his tenseness.

Later, in a team game on the playground, Ray missed catching the ball two or three times because it was thrown too high. He displaced this frustration by kicking a "Frisbie" tossed by a boy playing nearby. The other boy retaliated by calling Ray "short shrimp." Exploding, Ray let loose a barrage of punches. Quickly, I stepped in and carried him to an unoccupied room, holding him securely.

While struggling with me, Ray's intense anger, mixed with feelings of worthlessness, poured out. "I'm garbage!" "Be better if you'd send me back to Junior Village. I should run under the wheels of a truck on Fourteenth Street. I'd be better off dead."

My responsibility at this moment of crisis was to respond to his inner feelings and not to the overt behavior. While I held Ray firmly yet protectively, he said, "My brother and sister messed up our room and blamed me for it!" Here are leftover feelings from home, from the morning academic period in school, from the immediate incident on the playground. I continued to hold Ray until his body relaxed, while letting him know that the people at school care for him, that we feel he's a valuable person, and that a part of him wants to learn other ways of expressing feelings.

Later, when Ray could control himself, I reviewed the incidents of the day, eliciting the different ways of handling them. Ray smiled and said, "I knew I shouldn't have kicked the Frisbie, but I was so mad when Pete called me a shrimp." I commented that when Ray understands his feelings, he will be able to control them. With another smile, Ray said, "I know, and I'm ready to go back to class now."

The Case of Robert

The importance of a consistent teaching relationship to the future improvement of the troubled child is illustrated by his case:

Robert is a highly intelligent, ten-year-old inner-city boy whose life history is filled with personal rejection, school failure, and a general lack of trust. He tested at a low second-grade level but refused to admit that he needed or wanted any help.

His general attitude was one of suspicion, anger and moodiness. During his first year at Hillcrest, the only time he would work in class was with a teacher close by his desk, helping him almost before he asked for it. Slowly he showed a little interest in reading and was assigned to a tutor daily. This relationship became most important to him. Here was an adult he didn't have to share, someone who was able to accept his wide range of problem behavior. As his learning progressed, his ability to trust the school environment improved.

The following incident illustrates Robert's involvement with his tutor:

"I was absent from school for three days. Even though the Principal explained to Robert the nature of my illness, he became depressed and refused to participate in class activities. Understanding his behavior, the Principal listened to Robert ventilate his concerns that I wasn't going to return, that I didn't really like him, and that it didn't really matter to him anyway! When I returned the next day and saw Robert, he broke into a broad smile and said, "How is my beautiful teacher?" I replied, "Wondering how my beautiful student is feeling." During our session that day, we talked about my absence and then read some short stories and poems into a tape recorder together. Showing some interest in the activity, I suggested that he might want to use the tape recorder to write some poems about himself while I went to the library. Upon returning, Robert seemed pleased and asked me to listen to his recording after he left. Much to my amazement and delight, he wrote: "Fear is hate and fire; fear is sadness and loneliness; it is death and heat; fear is something we all have.""

Once more he could trust, he could share his feelings of fear, making them less threatening and more manageable. As feelings are expressed, they are no longer constricting secrets that restrict children from growing.

Article Footnote

---

1. Fritz Redl, *Conflict in the Classroom* (Belmont, Calif.: Wadsworth Publishing Co., 1965).

Before moving to management procedures focused on the pupil, we should emphasize that the teacher's use of relationship requires a great deal of professional sophistication. Relationship is not comprised of gimmicks, but rather the *quality* of interpersonal exchange, which, in turn, leads to influence. The psychological processes which underlie the relationship are modeling and identification. Aspy[2] has proposed specific dimensions such as trust and authenticity and holds that the teacher can assess these qualities in himself. In addition to Aspy's scales, devices for considering trust in human nature and desire to control others can provide insight. Examples are found in the Philosophy of Human Nature Scale[3] and Teaching Styles Questionnaire.[4]

In considering management, "punishment" has been almost synonymous with "discipline." The next two articles show a theoretical and a practical view of this common theme and broaden the significance of the word "punish-ment." Perhaps the key to understanding a dynamic approach to punishment is concentrating on what the experience means to the child, not what it means to the adult (a basic distinction between the operant and dynamic approaches). We cannot take for granted how a child will experience our efforts. Particularly important is the matter of timing, which Redl develops at some length.

The Concept of Punishment
Fritz Redl

Professional Use of the Word "Punishment"

As educators or clinicians, our behavior toward children deserves the name "punishment" only if it is done with a *clearcut goal to help the child.* Thus, it is always a means to an end, and is always employed for the sake of the basic welfare and growth needs of the individuals involved. Whether the actual punishment administered under this policy was correct or helpful; or whether it was stupid, mistaken, wrongly handled; or whether it backfired in its intended effect, is not the point here, as we try to *define* our terms.

It is equally obvious that the use of punishment implies an attempt to produce an experience for the child which is *unpleasant.* It is based on the assumption that sometimes the affliction of an unpleasant experience may mobilize "something" in a child that gets him to think or change his behavior, a change which, without such a "boost" from without, would not have occurred. Tying those two aspects of punishment as viewed in the tool cabinet of the professional educator or clinician together, we might arrive at the following definition, which I think serves our purpose for the time being.

I refer by the term "punishment" to: *a planful attempt by the adult to influence either the behavior or the long-range development of a child or a group of children, for their own benefit, by exposing them to an unpleasant experience.*

The inclusion of the statement that it has to be a "planful attempt, guided by the benefit of the children as a goal," excludes all simple outcropping of adult sadism, bad temper, or personal vengefulness, as well as the use of the child as a prop to assuage one's own anxiety. The statement that all punishment aims at using the production of an "unpleasant" experience in the child marks this intervention technique as different from others. It also raises the crucial question which underlies all speculations about the wisdom of punishment as a tool in a given case: Just what is there to the underlying assumption that producing an unpleasant experience in a child is going to help him rally better to reason and control than he was able to before? For this is obviously the *only assumption* on the basis of which any educational or clinical use of punishment makes any sense at all.

Analysis of the Punishment Experience

"You can lead a horse to water, but you can't make him drink." This age-old saying is rather trite, but many a punishment discussion I have been in would have benefited if this had been written in bold script on the blackboard before it started. For what counts most in punishment is not what we do to *the child,* but *what the child does with the experience to which we have exposed him.* To make a long story short, *this is what must happen within the child if things go well:*

1.   *The child experiences the displeasure* to which we expose him. This "displeasure" can be the loss of a privilege or pleasure he took for granted, or the exposure to something that is unpleasant or even "painful" in some way or other. Or both. For

From Fritz Redl, an original article presented at the American Orthopsychiatric Association meeting, 1959, pp. 9–44.

instance, I can take away his dessert, I can sock him one, or I can insist that he stay in his room while he hears the others playing outside.

2. Whether the displeasure be in the form of frustration or pain on some level, it is bound to produce an *upsurge of anger* in the child. This anger may not be conscious, nor does it have to be strong. But it is normal for the human to react to frustration or pain with an upsurge of fury.

3. The child clearly perceives—at least after the first few moments, the difference between the *source of his predicament* and *the real causes.* The source of his predicament is obviously the adult who inflicted the punishment, or the institution which made him do so. The cause for his predicament, however, is equally obviously *his own previous misbehavior,* for without it the adult would not have imposed the punishment to begin with.

4. The child now directs the anger produced in him by his predicament, not against the source of his trouble but at its cause: *he gets mad at himself* and realizes he would have avoided all this had he only shown more impulse control and wisdom in his actions to begin with.

5. He does however, not only get a little "mad at himself," but he *transforms* this self-directed aggression into *energy that can be used* for his own benefit. By "transforms" we refer to a process by which what was originally personalized fury or self-hatred can be changed into neutralized energy, now available for a multitude of more sublimated ends.

6. He uses this energy, drawn from his fury about his predicament, for two purposes: (a) he forces himself to regret what he did; (b) he forces himself into a sort of "New Year's resolution": "I'll sure not be dumb enough to get myself into a situation like this next time."

7. In a future temptation of somewhat similar kind, he can make use of the image left from the previous incident, and can mobilize self-control power before the act. The previous punishment experience has helped him, not only toward better insight, but also left him with increased energies for temptation resistance.

These, basically, are the steps every child goes through each time a punishment experience to which he was exposed is "handled well" by him—even though these steps are, of course, not really experienced clearly in the process. They are the *condition* for a constructive use of a punishment experience by a child.

How do we know if this can work? It would be easy, with the above outline in hand like a "map,"

to predict exactly just what could go wrong with the way a child handles his punishment experience, and what conditions must be met within a given punishment plan to make a successful ending most likely. It would be easy—but it would take an estimated 80 pages to do it, so let's skip it for the time being. Let's select what seem to me the five most crucial items in this picture—leaving a dozen or so just about as crucial ones unmentioned for now:

1. From what we know about the child, is the specific *form of displeasure* which we selected for a given punishment situation likely to be used by him as an incentive for concern, or is it either going to roll off him without impact, or throw him into a tizzy of irrational response?

Examples. Some children prefer to sit in their room and masturbate anyway, rather than participate in a competitive game with dubious results for them. Sending such a child to his room won't even be experienced as punishment, no matter what *name* we may want to give the procedure. *Or:* A really good moral masochist *loves* to feel sorry for himself and nurse his grudge against the world, which has "done him wrong." Most punishments, for him, do not hold much displeasure, and what little they hold he turns around into self-pitying delight or juicy gratification of a perverted need. *Or:* Being sent back to stay in one's room as punishment for some misdeed or other, might, in itself, be a good "displeasure dose" to rattle a given child into more thoughtful self appraisal. Only—we sent him back while his neighborhood gang was just coming to pick him up for a ball game, and the things we said while we sent him back would be likely to make any self-respecting and emancipation-hungry teenager cringe with unconquerable shame. *Or:* Some children are "allergic" to being alone in a small room. Being sent into one for punishment would produce unbearable panic in them. They are allergic to this type of experience, so you can't use it on them no matter how well they may have "deserved it."

2. From what we know about the child—is he going to be able to *differentiate between "source" and "cause" for his predicament* under the impact of the specific punishment experience which I have provided for him? If the answer to that is no, then you had better save yourself the trouble. Your punishment won't work, and whatever momentary benefit you draw from it will be badly outweighted by the negative side-effects.

Examples. Very little children do not have such discrimination well developed yet. A small child, bumping his head against the table, is likely to turn around and hit the table in revenge for "what it did to him." He is incapable of differentiating the source of his trouble (the contact with the table) from its cause (his own clumsy movement, and not looking where he was going). Some older children regress to that level under the *impact of displeasure or pain.* If that is so, punishment has no chance to help. *Or:* Some people are quite capable of making such distinctions, but they don't want to make them. It is much more gratifying to hate the cop who gave one the ticket than to admit one wasn't driving as one should have. Especially children who are still in the grip of a concerted effort to view the adult as hostile and to deny their own participation in the events of their lives, will construe any experience of displeasure as a "personalized wrong coming from a hateful opponent" rather than consider it a challenge to revise their own style of life. As long as they are in that stage, even the most clearcut form of punishment is going to backfire.

3. From what we know about the child—is he going to be able to *turn his aggression in the right direction,* under the impact of the punishment experience? By the "right direction" we mean, of course, toward that part of himself that made him misbehave, instead of toward the punishing adult, the institution, the world at large, God, or the Universe—or the child in the upper bunk.

Example. Some children are quite capable of knowing and admitting that they were in the wrong and "deserved what they got." Yet, their ego is still totally incapable of coping with any amount of frustration or aggression in a constructive way. Thus, even when correctly mad at themselves, they will have to pour their fury at the people and things around them, or they simply explode into an orgy of diffuse and frantic aggression-discharge. This is especially true for our hyperaggressive child: even at the stage when they begin to feel guilty for what they did, as we hoped they eventually would, they still have not developed enough ego skills to cope with guilt feelings adequately. So, even though they know they are at fault themselves, their aggression still is poured toward the world outside them. As long as that is true, even otherwise well planned "punishments" are of no avail.

4. From what we know about the child—is he capable of sifting and transforming the anger we

produced in him through our punishment, into the type of energy that can be used for increased insight and self control? Among all the puzzles, this is probably the most serious one. For, even if the child gets correctly mad at himself instead of at me the administrator of punishment, or at the institution and its laws, the crucial question still remains: what is he going to do with the fury he now directs against himself? For the fact that aggression is turned against ourselves alone is not enough. It depends very much on just what we do with the aggression we turn against ourselves. Unless the "sifting and transforming gland" for internalized aggression functions well, a child is not going to benefit from punishment received. By "sifting" and "transforming" I am referring to two separate tasks: by "sifting" I mean that the child's ego must be able to decide just how much should be discharged as a waste product. Some children, for instance, discharge all of it as a waste product—none of it sticks and is internalized. Others can't allow themselves any "waste product discharge," so the full brunt of their anger is turned against themselves, which means they are *flooded with much too much repentance, discouragement and self accusation.* The normal child has glands which operate well that way: punished by an adult he can vent some of his anger by mumbling under his breath or slamming that door, some of it by a quickly produced "revenge fantasy against the punishing adult," some of it by diffuse discharge motions, such as, restless pacing of his room, rough manipulating of a ball, etc.—*and only the right amount is then sent to the transformer* to be turned into internalized energy for self-insight and self-control.

Examples. Some children *know* that they are to blame but if the punishment, pain, or frustration, or their already existing proclivity toward guilt feelings is too strong, they simply get *paralyzed* by their repentance and regret, drift into orgies of self-accusation, or they end up feeling no good, incapable of ever amounting to anything, or not worthy of the adult's love or their own self-confidence.

In that case, all the previous steps of punishment worked well, for they *should* have admitted they were wrong, as they did, they should have got "mad" at their own bad behavior, as they did. *Only,* they *did so too much,* and in a totally ineffective way. For simply being mad at oneself is no good, unless one has the energy for doing something about it. *Or:* Some children get angry at themselves, as they should, but they puff out this anger in waste motion rather than in an increase of ener-

gy available for self control. That means they punish themselves by slip actions and "accidents," by
losing their favorite toy, breaking their prize possession, but they cannot use their self-anger for the
purpose of more impulse control. No matter how
"repentant" they seemed to be in their immediate reaction to the punishment, they are as helpless as
they were before at the next onslaught of temptation. Whenever things are wrong with the sifting
and transforming machinery in the child's ego, a
punishment experience cannot be benefited from.

5.   From what we know about the child, is his ego
in good enough shape to cope with the complications of the "time" element in punishment? In
my estimate, the misfiring of punishments which
were otherwise well designed because of this very
factor of timing is the most serious trouble source in
educational as well as clinical practice. I guess I had
better lay this one out a little more in detail. By "time
element" I refer, here, to three entirely different
issues—all of them, however, equally crucial to the
constructive use of punishment by a child.

a. The time relationship between punishment
experience and offense. Public opinion is wildly
confused on this issue. It either assumes that the
two should be in high proximity—or else the child
forgets what he is punished for—or that they should
be far apart—so that the basic issue has time to sink
in, and the adult has enough time to check on guilt,
on issues of justice, and to get his machinery in motion. As is frequently the case, there is a kernel of
truth in both extremes, but neither of them is it. The
reality of the situation is more complex than either
theory would like to have it.

In life with our hyperaggressive children we
have learned that there is great importance to the
issue of timing, but whether proximity or distance is
of the essence depends on many items in each case.
Talking about punishment: some children's awareness that they did something wrong—or even what
they did—evaporates so fast that the act of punishment hits them after it is entirely evaporated. Then,
the displeasure felt during the punishment experience makes little sense, it is likely to be perceived as
rank meanness of an irritable adult rather than as
punishment one has "deserved" for something one
"did." On the other hand, some children's "offenses" were entangled in so many issues, soaked with
so much affect, anger, confusion, delusion, etc., that
no punishment experience can have much chance to
do its trick, unless that confusion is disentangled
first. Knowing this much about the ego of a child
will make it clear that certain forms of punishment

that create complications in the time relationship between punishment experience and offense are by
that very fact counter-indicated.

b. The timing of exposure to the punishment
experience is of crucial concern. Some of our children, for instance, might well "understand" that
they deserved to be sent to their room, and might be
able to "take" that part of it without distortion of
the real facts, at least on occasion. The question to
be asked next, however, is clearly: What will they
do with themselves while exposed to the punishment condition, such as staying in their room, paying back for a damaged item out of their pocket
money, or staying home while others go on a fishing
trip, etc.?

Many children's egos are not in shape enough
to take the time exposure involved in a given punishment. In such cases, this specific form of punishment is counterindicated, no matter how good it
may look from all other angles.

Public opinion, unfortunately, is caught in a
hopeless confusion on this item, too, which causes
no end of trouble even in professional discussions
on the issue. Namely, public opinion has assumed a
fixed relationship between length of exposure and
seriousness of offense. Thus, for a little offense in
the swimming pool, one might assume that a child
should be sent to his room maybe for just 5 minutes. For a bigger offense, maybe it would be "fair"
if he were told to stay out of activities for 2 days.
Well, it may be "fair" all right, but what effect will it
actually produce? As long as Johnny sits there
watching the other youngsters splash around happily while he is sulking about his predicament, but
still under the impression that he "had it coming"
because of the freshness of the memory of what he
did, all may be fine for a while. The moment the
self-perception of what he did is evaporated,
though, the experience assumes an entirely different shape. From then on it is not: "too bad I had to
get myself into this trouble," but, "see, that bastard
waterfront guy lets all these other kids have their
fun, it's only me that doesn't get a break, hell with
him."

In short, the psychological weight of a time
issue has to be weighted with psychological scales,
not with judiciary ones, and the psychology of timing belongs among the trickiest issues I can
think of.

c. By "timing" we sometimes refer to the fact
that the real test of the efficacy of a punishment lies
in the question whether a child can make use of
what he learned from it in the next temptation situation. Thus, its major effect is hoped for from its im-

pact on the future event. This however, means no less than the question of whether a child can, at all, learn from experience, especially from an unpleasant one. And, beyond this, whether he can not only "learn" a lesson from the experience, but whether his ego can supply him with the necessary control energies to make use of what he learned when the next crucial moment comes around. It ought to be clear by now that this is quite a lot to be expected, and I can't help being amazed time and again, that adults are so naively anticipating all the time that few little punishment tricks do not show that long-range effect. The question whether a given child has it in him to "learn" from a given punishment experience is an important one to estimate correctly. For punishment, contrary to popular fantasies, does not teach a thing unless the recipient is in any shape to do the learning. In the case of children with severe ego disturbances, it is clear that this is one of the reasons why one would not expect much help from the punishment department. The ability to tie up a well interpreted experience from one's past with an equally clearly perceived experience from the present, and on top of that mobilize just the right quantity of energy for self control and send it into just the right control-direction—this is obviously a task which a messy ego is likely to flunk. Yet—the use of punishment now makes little sense, unless we have some expectation that its impact can be utilized at some moment in the future tense.

About this issue of the "time element"—we want to assess just how well a child is likely to do in all three aspects of the time issues: Can he take the time relationship between a given offense and a given punishment without getting confused; can his ego sustain him for the *duration* of the punishment experience with all the specifics a given case involves; and is there a chance for some *future usability* of the experience to which we expose him now. If the answer to this is no, punishment isn't worth the effort you put into planning and suffering through it, to say nothing of the complications in the lives of children.

d. Punishment and the problem of in-situational and post-situational support. At this point, I hear you moaning: "Are you trying to tell us that punishment is as complicated as all that? What ever happened to the idea that is was a 'simple' technique, sort of clearcut and very concrete, and much more 'definite' than most of the other intervention techniques we talked so much about?" The answer to that is: Yes. That's exactly what I am trying to convey. The idea that punishment is a simple, clearcut technique belongs in the chapter of optical illusions. What the *adult* does in an act of punishment may be as simple and clearcut as a kick in the pants. What the kid does with this experience and how he reacts to it is anything but simple and clearcut. It involves the most sensitive and vital organs of his psychological organism, as I have just tried to show. In this respect, punishment is much more comparable to a case of surgical intervention than to what you see happen when the guy at the delicatessen slices that salami for you with a sharp knife.

Unfortunately, I have to make it even more complicated, especially when we think of punishment in relation to a disturbed child. The prevalent thinking of the layman still puts most of his effort into finding the "best" form of punishment, having the educator impose it on the child—and from here on in he expects the effect to be sort of automatic.

Fortunately, we already know better than that. We know that even a well planned play experience for a child may need constant support during the time when the child is supposed to be exposed to it, or may need some post-situational followup. This principle, again, is not new. Remember the time spent not only on figuring what game should be selected in the evening, but also on just how we give the children the support they need to live through the game successfully once it gets under way? Remember how important we felt it was not only to physically hold a child when that becomes necessary, but to help him get through this experience without misinterpreting it? Remember how important it was to stick around all through their tantrums, even after we didn't have to hold them anymore, just so we can catch that moment when the child needs or is ready for some activity he can hang onto and pull himself together again?

All this is as true of "punishments" as it is of other experiences in our children's lives. Thus, our responsibility is not ended with the decision to send that child to his room, or to tell him he has to pay part of the damage he has done to the other boy's toy for the next two paydays. The safe-guarding of the right *effect* of a punishment experience is a job that continues as long as that experience lasts, and the real help to make sense out of it all often occurs much later in a post-situational exploitation of the kid's reaction to it. Whenever we figure on any kind of punishment for our children, therefore, it is important to plan just as much for in-situational and post-situational support, as it is to decide what kind of punishment should be tried to begin with. Even a well designed punishment will backfire badly if for some reason we are not able to give the child the support he needs going through it, without distortions, and "learn" from it what we wanted him to learn. With the act of punishment our work with the child on this issue does not end. It only begins. . . . If you ever thought of using punishment in some situations because it "saves trouble" or makes things work more simply, you'd better give that daydream up in a hurry.

Loose Ends for Sale

The "analysis of the punishment experience" which I just presented was not meant to be a photograph; only a map. It makes no pretense of answering your question of just what to do. It only tries to point out a few salient points you will run into if you get into this terrain. . . .

Next, I would like to brush lightly past a few issues that I remember having come up in our staff discussions.

The usage of the term punishment being as loose as it is, we often discuss under the same label situations where we demand that a child "make up" for a hurt he has inflicted, or a damage he has caused. The form this takes may vary. We may insist that he at least "apologize" or show he is sorry; we may want him to clear up the mess he has caused and which inconveniences the other boy in his cabin or room; we may demand partial payment for damage done, etc. I personally do not like to see these arrangements thrown into the same pot as punishments, for they have only a small part of the process in common with them. But I won't quibble about words at the moment. Suffice it to remember that such procedures are actually much more rituals for the restitution of the individual into the grace of the group or of his victim, including an attempt to help him come to peace with himself. The following are the *three major goals* one has in mind when using this technique:

1.   We may want to help the child get the taste of some *consequences* of his behavior, and at the same time offer him a way to *do something about it* that is more or less apt to re-instate the status quo.

2.   By giving the child a chance to "make up for it," we also help him to reduce his guilt feelings and to restitute the previous relationship between him and the person or group against which he has offended.

3.   We also make it easier for the victim of the kid's misbehavior—be it individual or group—to "forgive him," to terminate their own state of wrath against him, and to stop whatever revenge measure they in turn might have in mind. We sort of offer the victimized kid or group a pound of his psychological flesh as a premium for their "forgetting" what he had done to them.

It must be obvious by now, that this technique may have a number of great advantages and may well be used at times to restitute what had been disturbed, which may be a great relief for all concerned. It is also clear, of course, that this only would work where the child has some guilt about what he had done to begin with, where he is clearly aware and admitting that he was in the wrong, is basically ready to wish it hadn't happened, and is himself relieved at the idea of having it all "repaired." The major danger of the technique lies with the case of a child who not only has few guilt feelings, but defends himself against the development of such by a system of "pay as you go" arrangements. Offering this type of child too many opportunities to "pay off for what he did" is inviting his exploitation of this technique to feed his own resistance against real insight and awareness of right and wrong. Great care must be taken in those cases where such "restitutional arrangements" seem feasible, that the youngster gets all the help he needs to interpret his own "making up" correctly, and that we make no mistakes in the nature and duration of the restitutional rituals we may choose. . . .

When a child teases, threatens, pinches, pokes, hits, swears, runs away, or refuses to move, the teacher must be equally concerned with what to do about the *behavior* and what the underlying *causes* of such behavior are. Unfortunately, very little clinical attention is given to the former concern. Teacher intervention is often necessary to protect a child, a group, a program, or property from injury, contagion, disappointment, or destruction. The method of intervention and how it is perceived by both the child and the group raise many fundamental clinical questions that must be examined with the same care as the theoretical discussions of the underlying dynamics of the child. In the next article Long and Newman apply Redl's four-notched scale to the management of surface behavior in a school setting. The techniques presented are not new, but they are particularly well-organized to help professionals conceptualize within a given framework.

Managing Surface
Behavior of Children in School
Nicholas J. Long
Ruth G. Newman

There are four major alternatives to handling behavior. They are: permitting, tolerating, interfering, and preventive planning. Redl emphasizes that no one of these alternatives is better than any of the others. The task is to find the right combination of techniques for each child.

Permitting behavior.   Most rules in a school are made to inhibit and regulate the impulsive behavior of children. During the day, they are told in many ways to stop, slow down, and control their behavior. No one would argue against the importance of these rules in a group setting. If it is important for children to know what they cannot do, it is equally important for children to know what they can do. For example, children should be told that it is permissible to run, shout, and scream on the playground, to be messy when they are fingerpainting, to have some degree of movement within the classroom, to go to the lavatory when necessary, to show some freedom of expression in their creative works, and to express an opposing view without being ridiculed or chastised. Children are reassured when they know in advance that their activities will not meet with adult frowns, shouts, or physical interference. More important, the sanctioning of behavior by adults eliminates much of the children's unnecessary testing of limits. A teacher who permits children to leave their desks and go to the book corner after they have finished the assignment should make this privilege clear. Then a child does not have to sneak a book and feel guilty about it or feel victorious about squeezing more freedom from the teacher than the child thinks he would expect.

Tolerating behavior.   A lot of classroom behavior must be tolerated, but children should have no reason to believe that teachers approve or sanction it. The more common basic assumptions behind tolerating behavior are (1) learner's leeway, (2) behavior that reflects a developmental stage, and (3) behavior that is symptomatic of a disease.

1.   Learner's leeway: Whenever a child is learning a new concept, experimenting with ideas, or trying to win status in the group, the teacher should expect that the child will make mistakes. He should not expect that the child will do it perfectly. For example, many sensitive teachers tell their class that they are not going to be upset when children err in trying to master new academic and social skills. With some groups, the more mistakes they make, i.e., on an arithmetic assignment the easier it is for the teacher to help them clarify their misunderstandings. This was found to be true in the following incident:

I have noticed that Carole (third grader) became very upset if she made a mistake on an assignment. The children were writing to a railroad company for some free material, but they did not know how to address an envelope. I went to the board and showed them the proper form and asked them to

Abridged from Nicholas J. Long and Ruth G. Newman, "A Differential Approach to the Management of Surface Behavior of Children in School," *Teachers' Handling of Children in Conflict*, Bulletin of the School of Education, Indiana University, XXXVII (July 1961), 47-61. Reprinted by permission.

The organization of this selection is taken from Fritz Redl's training notes at the Child Research Branch of the National Institute of Mental Health, Bethesda, Maryland, 1957.

practice. In a little while I noticed that Carole had her head on her desk. When I asked her what was the matter, she said that she couldn't do it and that she already had made three mistakes. I asked her to show me her work. (She had misspelled one word, did not capitalize one of the words, and had the return address crowded up in the upper left-hand corner.) I told Carole that these are the kinds of mistakes that many boys and girls make and that I did not expect her or any of the other children to do it perfectly the first three or four times that they tried. With this encouragement, she started again.

Sometimes it is helpful to talk about "good mistakes" versus "poor mistakes." A good mistake is made when a wrong answer has come out of some sense, so that the logic shines through the error. A poor mistake is one which rests largely on effort or has not even the semblance of logic.

2. Behavior that reflects a developmental stage: Some behavior is age typical and will change as the child becomes more mature. Any attempt on the part of the teacher to alter or inhabit this behavior results in such negligible changes that it usually is not worth the inevitable fight. For example, children in the early grades are impulse-ridden and motor-oriented. Every kindergarten teacher knows this and has accepted the fact that very little can be done about it except tolerate it. This state of tolerance should not be confused with sanctioning it or permitting wild behavior. Another example is that children in the late third or early fourth grade, caught between group pressure and allegiance to the teacher, are notorious for tattling; i.e., "Miss Jones, Johnny hit Mary," or "Johnny pulled a leaf off your flower when you were in the hall." Other illustrations of age-typical behavior are the unscrubbed, unhygienic appearance of the pre-adolescent boy, the primping of sixth-grade girls, the secrets of pre-adolescent girls, and the sex language and behavior of adolescent boys. A classroom example of age-typical behavior is presented below:

At noon, several fifth-grade girls came bursting into the room relating a story about the fifth-grade boys. The boys had discovered several pictures of nude women which were hidden in a bush on the playground. In small groups, they were examining the pictures in detail when a few of the fifth-grade girls "worked their way in" to see what was taking place. The girls screamed and found their way to my room. They related the story; then the bell rang.

The boys entered (without pictures), as though

nothing had happened. Silence prevailed. They knew that I knew. Finally, I asked one of the boys where the pictures were. He explained that they had hidden them in the bushes and planned to secure them after school for more detailed study. I asked another of the boys to bring the pictures into the room. This he did and I, without looking, threw them in the wastebasket.

Then we discussed the situation, emphasizing the value of good literature. The children themselves brought out the idea that such material was available at all newssstands and that anyone could buy it; however, the individual who is attempting to be a good citizen will by-pass such trash. Even the curious boys agreed with the majority viewpoint.

The pictures remained in the wastebasket until after school. Several students sought me out at the teacher's desk, casting glances at the wastebasket all the while. Others, whom I had never seen before, entered the room and quickly left upon finding me there.

Next morning the wastebasket was empty; the pictures were gone. I didn't see them again until I entered the boiler room, where they were on the wall—property of the school janitor.

3. Behavior which is symtomatic of an illness: When a child has a respiratory infection, the chances are that he will cough in class and that the symptom (coughing) will continue until the child is well. This cause and effect relationship is accepted among teachers; however, when a child who is emotionally disturbed shows the symptoms of his illness, such as recurring temper tantrums, fights, and irrational fears, the child is likely to be unpopular with his classmates, his teacher, and even with himself. A psychologically oriented teacher realizes that, when a child suffers from emotional problems, the symptoms are rarely conscious forms of meanness but are simply an explainable outlet for his intra-psychic conflicts. For example:

Some of the things that Martha did were fighting, tearing up other children's property, walking the floor constantly, tearing pages out of her book, name calling, and spitting. Although Martha makes me angry and caused all of us many problems, I feel we have grown a little in understanding that we all have problems and that the class is simply not divided into good and bad, accepted and unaccepted. Martha's behavior has improved during the year and, if I did anything to help it, I was doing it with kindness, firmness, and accepting her as an indi-

vidual, rather than judging her on the basis of her actions.

Interfering with behavior.   While the psychologically trained teacher is aware of long-range goals and is sensitive to the child's core problems, the teacher still has to handle the spontaneous behavior that occurs in the classroom. Some behavior has to be stopped if the classroom learning is to take place. A child cannot continue to act out all of his feelings. The task is to find ways of interfering with the behavior so that it does not disrupt the group greatly but still may be helpful to the particular child. Redl and Wineman in *The Aggressive Child* have listed 21 specific influence techniques that they have been able to identify in their work with aggressive boys. Twelve of these techniques will be developed as they apply to the positive management of children by the classroom teacher.

Before suggesting ways of intervening, the question of when a teacher should intervene needs to be considered. While this question cannot be settled without considering many variables, school psychologists have observed that too many teachers never set limits or intervene until they are choked with counter-aggressive feelings toward a child. When this happens, the teacher is likely to intervene in a way which is unhygienic and too severe. On the other hand, teachers have not been given any guide lines to help them with this difficult problem. They are not really sure whether they should interfere in a particular bit of behavior. Once again Redl gives us the direction and suggests the following criteria for intervention.

1.   Reality dangers: Adults are usually more reality-oriented than children and have had more practice predicting the consequences of certain acts. If children are playing some crazy game, fighting, or playing with matches so that it looks as if they might injure themselves, then the teacher moves in and stops the behavior.

2.   Psychological protection: Just as the adult protects the child from being physically hurt, he also should protect the child from psychological injury. If a group of boys is ganging up on a child, or scapegoating him, or using derogatory racial nicknames, then the teacher should intervene. The teacher does not support or condone this behavior and the values it reflects.

3.   Protection against too much excitement: Sometimes a teacher intervenes in order to avoid the development of too much excitement, anxiety, and

guilt in children. For example, if a game is getting out of hand and continues another 10 minutes, the children may lose control, mess up, and feel very unhappy about their behavior later. Once again, the teacher should intervene to stop this cycle from developing.

4.   Protection of property: This is almost too obvious to mention, but sometimes it is easy to overlook. Children are not allowed to destroy or damage the school property, equipment, or building. When the teacher sees this, he moves in quickly and stops it. But at no time does he give the impression so common in our society that property is more important than people. Protecting property protects people.

5.   Protection of an on-going program: Once a class is motivated in a particular task and the children have an investment in its outcome, it is not fair to have it ruined by one child who is having some difficulty. In this case, the teacher intervenes and asks this child to leave or to move next to him in order to insure that the enjoyment, satisfaction, and learning of the group is unimpaired.

6.   Protection against negative contagion: When a teacher is aware that tension is mounting in the classroom and a child with high social power begins tapping his desk with his pencil, the teacher might ask him to stop in order to prevent this behavior from spreading to the other students and disrupting the entire lesson.

7.   Highlighting a value area or school policy: There are times when a teacher interferes in some behavior not because it is dangerous or disturbing but because he wishes to illustrate a school policy or rule which may lie slightly below the surface of the behavior. For example, he might want to illustrate why it is impossible for everyone to be first in line, or to point out how a misunderstanding develops when there is no intent to lie or to distort a situation. The focus is on poor communication.

8.   Avoiding conflict with the outside world: The outside world in school can mean neighboring classrooms or the public. It is certainly justifiable to expect more control on the part of your children when they are attending an assembly or are on a trip than when they are in their classroom.

9.   Protecting a teacher's inner comfort: Inner comfort is not the first thing to be considered by a teacher. If it is, he is in the wrong profession. For example, if a certain type of behavior makes a teacher feel exceptionally uncomfortable, the behavior may not need to be totally inhibited, but the teacher

may have to learn to be more comfortable with it, whether he likes it or not.

It would be foolish, however, for a teacher, given limits of human endurance, to put himself in a situation in which he is abused constantly or serves as a punching bag for the class. This would not be healthy for anyone. The problem is to distinguish between behavior which is developmental or momentarily cathartic from behavior that is path- ological in origin. Once a teacher recognizes his personal idiosyncrasies and realizes that he is over- reacting to the behavior, in the long run, he might better stop the behavior than do nothing and in- wardly reject the child.

It is obvious that a teacher does not conscious- ly work through all these hygienic steps before de- ciding to stop a behavior. However, the nine points listed above can serve as a guide or reference point against which one can examine his actions. What makes this whole process challenging and compli- cated is that the child behaves in a way which, ac- cording to the proposed list, ought to be stopped but under certain psycho-physical conditions the teach- er does not stop it. After all, life is flexible and usually cannot be condensed into an orderly list of psychological procedures.

What are some of the counter indications against interfering, assuming that the behavior is not dangerous? (1) The fuss that it would create at this time is not worth it! The group confusion that is certain to follow might disguise the real purpose of the interference. In such a case it might be better to wait for another time. There is a written guaranty that it will come. (2) The teacher decides to wait until the behavior deviates to the point where it is obvious not only to the child but also to the entire group. This way the child's typical defenses, such as projection, i.e., "You're always picking on me," or "I never get a fair deal," are clearly inappropriate. (3) The teacher is in too good a mood today. He can- not work up enough genuine concern to impress the child and/or the group with the seriousness of the child's behavior. While this feeling is a common one, it should not be the barometer for inter- vention.

Before returning to the discussion on how to stop inappropriate behavior, there is a need to im- press upon the readers that the following tech- niques are designed to help a teacher maintain the surface behavior of children over some rough spots. They only are stop-gap methods and do not substi- tute for a well-designed program or replace the teacher's knowledge of individual and group psy- chology.

The 12 influence techniques to be discussed are planned ignoring, signal interference, proximity control, interest boosting, tension decontaminator through humor, hurdle help, restricting the class- room program, support from routine, direct appeal, removal of seductive objects, antiseptic bouncing, and physical restraint.

1.   Planned ignoring: Much of children's behavior carries its own limited power and will soon exhaust itself if it is not replenished, especially if the behav- ior is designed to "get the teacher's goat." Assum- ing that the behavior will not spread to others, it might be wise for the teacher to ignore the behavior and not feed into the child's need for secondary gratification. In the following example, the teacher is aware of the underlying meaning of the boy's behavior.

One technique that I find successful is to ignore dis- ruptive behavior. It works most successfully with Frank. When he starts dropping his pencils, or tap- ping his feet, I know that it is a signal that I had bet- ter get over there in a few minutes and help him. I have found, however, that if I confront him with this behavior, he usually argues with me and caus- es additional problems.

In this example, the teacher responds to the motivation of the behavior and not to the manifes- tations of the behavior.

2.   Signal interference: Teachers have developed a variety of signals that communicate to the child a feeling of disapproval and control. These non- verbal techniques include such things as eye contact, hand gestures, tapping or snapping fingers, coughing or clearing one's throat, facial frowns, and body postures. Such non-verbal techniques seem to be most effective at the beginning stages of mis- behavior.

When a student is acting up in a mild way, I have found that a glance in his direction will usually stop the behavior temporarily. Usually I do not have to look at a child for a long time before he is aware that I am looking at him. I have also found that this tech- nique is most helpful with those students who like me. Another signal that I have used is to stand up from my desk when there is a lot of whispering. I hasten to add that there are some children who would have me stand and look at them all day with- out it helping them control their behavior one bit.

3.   Proximity control: Every teacher knows how effective it is to stand near a child who is having

some difficulty. Just as a crying infant will stop crying when he is picked up by his mother, although the actual source of discomfort still exists, the early elementary child usually can control his impulses if he is close to the teacher. The teacher operates as a source of protection, strength, and identification. As one of the teachers explains:

One technique I have found helpful is to walk among the children. As I walk down the rows, I help the children having trouble with their work, or I give the bored ones something else to do. My closeness and help show that I am interested and concerned. It creates a better atmosphere and rapport and diminishes problems. I have found it very helpful and more effective than just standing behind the desk and telling them what to do. When I have a child who needs more than the usual help, I usually put his desk close to mine so that we are both aware of each other.

There are some children who not only need to have an adult close by but who also need the adult to touch them before they are able to control their impulses. This is done by having the teacher put his hand gently on the child's shoulder. This action should not be confused with the teacher who leaves five red marks after he has made physical contact with the child.

The advantages of these three techniques, planned ignoring, signal interference, and proximity control, are that they do not embarrass or even identify the child in the group. The teacher may use all three of these techniques while maintaining his classroom program.

4.   Interest boosting: If a child's interest is waning and he is showing signs of restlessness, it is sometimes helpful for the teacher to show some genuine interest in the child's classroom assignment, asking whether problem 10 was very hard for him or mentioning his personal interest in athletics, cars, etc. Tapping a child's area of interest may help him mobilize his forces and view the teacher as a person whom he wants to please. One teacher described an experience with a child with whom he used this technique as follows:

Craig was crazy about dinosaurs. He read about them; he drew pictures of them; and he even had a plastic collection of them. As you can guess, Craig was a problem. He did not bother the boys or girls or defy me, but he would spend his class time ei-

ther daydreaming or else drawing pictures of dinosaurs. I talked to him many times about this and he promised to stop, but the following day he was back at his drawings. I decided that if I could not fight him, perhaps I could join him in his interest. That night I spent the evening reading the En-cyclopaedia Britannica. The next day I told Craig that I was very interested in dinosaurs, too, and even had a course in college that studied them. Craig was somewhat skeptical of my comment, but after I mentioned some vital statistics about dinosaurs he was impressed that I was an expert in the field. Together we studied dinosaurs but structured the work so that it would only take place after he had completed his regular assignments.

5.   Tension decontamination through humor: There is nothing new about this technique. Everyone is aware of how a humorous comment is able to penetrate a tense and anxiety-producing situation. It clears the air and makes everyone feel more comfortable. The example below shows how one teacher used this technique to advantage.

I walked into my room after lunch period to find several pictures on the chalk board with "teacher" written under each one. I went to the board and picked up a piece of chalk, first looking at the pictures and then at the class. You could have heard a pin drop! Then I walked over to one of the pictures and said that this one looked the most like me but needed some more hair, which I added. Then I went to the next one and said that they had forgotten my glasses so I added them, on the next one I suggested adding a big nose, and on the last one a longer neck. By this time the class was almost in hysterics. Then, seeing that the children were having such a good time and that I could not get them settled easily, I passed out drawing paper and suggested that they draw a picture of the funniest person they could make. It is amazing how original these pictures were.

This example illustrates the phenomenon of group testing. The pictures were put on the board to test the vulnerability of the teacher. Some teachers would have reacted with sarcasm. They might have said that this was infantile behavior and not becoming a fifth-grade class. Other teachers might have given the class extra work or administered a group punishment, such as denial of recess or free time. However, this teacher demonstrated that she was secure, that a drawing could not cause her to regress or to become counter-aggressive, and that she could be counted on during stressful periods. Here is another excellent example of tension decontamination:

As soon as I entered the room two students who had remained in the room during the playground period informed me that Stella and Mary had a fight in the girls' restroom and were at present being seen by the principal. Since both of these girls are good pupils and are well liked by the class, I imagined that they and the class were wondering what I would do when the two girls returned to the room. Fifteen or 20 minutes elapsed before the girls returned. They entered and took their seats and the room became very quiet. I closed my book, looked at one of the girls and said in a rasping voice of a fight announcer, "And in this corner we have Stella, weighing 78 pounds." Everyone laughed. The tension vanished and we proceeded with our work.

Once again humor was used to communicate to the class that everything was all right, that there was no need to worry about it, and that the children could relax and return to their lessons.

6. Hurdle lessons: Disturbing behavior is not always the result of some inner problem. Sometimes the child is frustrated by the immediate classroom assignment. He does not understand the teacher's directions or is blocked by the second or third step in a complicated long-division problem. Instead of asking for help and exposing himself to the teacher's wrath for not paying attention or for exhibiting his educational inadequacies, the child is likely to establish contact with his neighbors, find some interesting trinket in his pocket, or draw on his desk. In other words, he is likely to translate his frustrations into motor behavior. The solution is to provide the child with the help he needs before the situation gets to this stage, as was done in the following example.

Sonya was very stubborn and usually persisted in not doing her work. After making an assignment, I would give the students some time to work on it in class. I would walk around the room and casually stop at Sonya's desk. Noting that she had not started, I would ask her some of her ideas and would suggest that she write those thoughts on paper. She could do the work and would do it if I explained it to her and personally got her interested in it. If I let

her alone, she would usually sit and begin filing her nails or looking at the boy next to her who would become quite flushed. While this technique meant more work for me, it finally paid off because, as soon as she began working, she worked without assistance and began making passing grades.

7. Restructuring the classroom program: How much can a teacher deviate from his scheduled program and still feel he is meeting his "teaching responsibilities"? Another way of asking this question is, "Does the teacher control the program, or does the program control the teacher?" For example, some teachers feel compelled to follow their class schedule with no "ifs," "ands," or "buts." Otherwise, they feel they cannot hope to complete the assigned course of study. Besides, they feel children must learn not be be affected by every passing emotion. They must learn how to concentrate even under undesirable circumstances. Other teachers voice a different position. They feel that the complexity of life and the many extenuating forces make it impossible to follow a standardized course. The task is not so much to teach children as to provide the conditions under which learning can take place. Perhaps these are straw arguments and the question that needs to be raised is, "Does restructuring a program ever facilitate learning?" "If so, under what conditions?" This takes the task out of the realm of "either-or" arguments and places it in the teacher's ability to predict the tension level of the class in terms of feelings of irritability, boredom, or excitement. If the teacher feels that the class is tense but that the tension is decreasing, he may decide not to redesign his program. However, if he decides that the tension needs to be drained off, i.e., verbalized or channelized, before the class can involve itself in the next assignment, he may change his program immediately. Two interesting examples are presented below:

Shortly before a grade school basketball tournament I was forced to cancel basketball practice for the evening. This met with much disapproval from the team members. The lesson for civics that day concerned labor strikes. As I walked into the classroom, I detected the basketball boys were signaling for everyone to remain silent. It looked as though they were going to have fine cooperation from the rest of the class. Seeming to be completely unaware of their intentions, I cancelled our discussion period and proceeded to assign them the written work at the end of the chapter. This work, I explained, was necessary before we could discuss the chapter adequately. The period was spent in constructive work and avoided a head-on clash. Later I talked to the boys and explained why I had to cancel the practice.

The next example of restructuring illustrates how a teacher created an atmosphere of comfort and relaxation.

The children were just returning to the room after the recess period. Most of them were flushed and hot from exercise, and were a little irritable. They were complaining of the heat in the room, and many of them asked permission to get a drink of water as soon as the final recess bell rang. I felt it would be useless to begin our history study as scheduled. So I told all of the children to lay their heads upon their desks. I asked them to be very silent for one minute and to think of the coolest thing they could imagine during that time. Each child then told the class what he had been thinking. The whole procedure lasted roughly 10 minutes, and I felt that it was time well spent. The history period afterward went smoothly, the atmosphere within the room relaxed, and the children were receptive.

8.   Support from routine: We all need structure. Some children need much more than other children before they can feel comfortable and secure. Without these guideposts for behavior, some children become anxious and hyper-active. This is especially true during unstructured time, when children are moved by every wind and breeze of classroom behavior. Most beginning junior high school children find themselves in this state during the first few weeks. One boy summarized his feelings by saying, "It's like one great big surprise. Each hour you go to another teacher and you don't know what's going to happen until it's too late." To help these children, a daily schedule or program should be provided, as this may allay some of their feelings of anxiety. They can predict what is expected of them and prepare themselves for the next activity. As one teacher says:

Each morning I outline the activities for the day with one "leading question." I find that this is helpful to some of the children. When they come into class, they start thinking about the activities we have planned, instead of waiting for me to announce them. This saves time and eliminates the majority of random behavior.

9.   Direct appeal to value areas: One of the most frequent mistakes of an untrained teacher is that he feels he must intervene severely and drastically in order to demonstrate that he has control of the situation. We know that this is not desirable. Another alternative is to appeal to certain values that the students have internalized. The conflict is that some children have not internalized the same values that the teacher has internalized. For example, a teacher cannot appeal to the child's sense of fairness if the child feels he has been "gypped" out of something he has a right to possess. A partial list of some of the values that most teachers can appeal to includes: (a) An appeal to the relationship of the teacher with the child, i.e., "You are treating me as if I did something bad to you! Do you think I have been unfair to you?" (b) An appeal to reality consequences, i.e., "If you continue to talk, we will not have time to plan our party," "If you continue with this behavior, these are the things that will probably happen." In other words, the teacher tries to underline cause and effect behavior. (c) An appeal to the child's group code and awareness of peer reaction, i.e., "What do you think the other boys and girls will think of that idea?" or "If you continue to spoil their fun, you can't expect the other boys and girls to like you." (d) An appeal to the teacher's power of authority. Tell the children that as a teacher you cannot allow this behavior to continue and still want to take care of them. The trick is to learn how to say "no" without becoming angry, or how to say "yes" without feeling guilty.

10.   Removing seductive objects: Teachers have learned that they cannot compete against such seductive items as a baseball in a group of boys or a picture of the latest crooner in a group of pre-adolescent girls. Either the objects have to be removed or teachers have to accept the disorganized state of the group. It is not entirely the children's fault. Certain objects have a magnetic appeal and elicit a particular kind of behavior from children. For example, if a child has a flashlight, it says "Turn me on"; if he has a ball, it says "Throw me"; if he has a magnifying glass, it says "Reflect the sunlight"; if he has a whistle, it says "Toot me"; if he has a pea shooter, it says "Shoot me"; and so on. These objects feed into the child's impulse system, making it harder for children to control their behavior. One of the most exasperating experiences in a teacher's lifetime is to set up a science corner only to have it fingered to death in the first five minutes of bell time.

11.   Antiseptic bouncing: When a child's behavior has reached a point where the teacher questions

whether the child will respond to verbal controls, it is best to ask the child to leave the room for a few minutes—perhaps to get a drink, wash up, or deliver a message. This was done in the following situation.

I had only one occasion to use antiseptic bouncing. One morning during arithmetic study period I became aware of giggling in the back of the room. I looked up to see that Joyce had evidently thought of something hilariously funny. I tried signal interference, and, though she tried to stop, she succeeded only in choking and coughing. By now most of the children around her were aware of the circumstances and were smothering laughter, too. I hurriedly wrote a note to the secretary of the principal's office explaining that Joyce "had the giggles" and asked that she keep her waiting for a reply until she seemed settled down. I asked Joyce if she would mind delivering the message and waiting for an answer. I think she was grateful for the chance to leave the room. When she returned, she appeared to have everything controlled, as had the class, and things proceeded normally.

In antiseptic bouncing there is no intent of punishing the child but simply to protect and help him and/or the group to get over their feelings of anger, disappointment, uncontrollable laughter, hiccups, etc. Unfortunately, many schools do not have a place that would not connote punishment to which the classroom teacher can send a child. To send him to the principal where he sits on the mourner's bench is not very helpful and defeats the purpose of nonpunitive management. However, with staff planning, it is amazing what alternatives can be found.

12.   Physical restraint: Once in a while a child will lose complete control and threaten to injure himself or others. In such emergencies, the child needs to be restrained physically. He should be held firmly but not roughly. Once again there is no indication of punishment, but only a sincere concern to protect the child from hurting anyone. If a feeling of protection is to be communicated, such techniques as shaking, hitting, or spanking him only make it harder for him to believe that the teacher really wants to help him. Some teachers who are ignorant about psychodynamics feel that a child should be punished for such inappropriate and deviant behavior. However, if these same teachers ever had a chance to observe a child who has lost complete control over his impulses, they would soon realize

how frightening and fearful this experience is for the child. These teachers would see the suffering and anguish these children go through. It is no game with them, but strikes at their basic feelings of survival.

The preferred physical hold is for the adult to cross the child's arms around his side while the adult stands behind him holding on to the child's wrists. Occasionally it is necessary to hold a child on the floor in this position. There is no danger that the child can injure himself in this position although he might scream that you are hurting him, or causing him considerable physical pain. Many of the children who need this type of control, go through four different phases. First, the child fights being held and controlled. He becomes enraged and says and does things that are fed by feelings of frustration, hate and desperation. He may swear, bite, and carry on in a primitive way. Most teachers who are not used to being treated this way, find it difficult to absorb this much aggression without becoming frightened and/or counter-aggressive. While we can be sympathetic towards this teacher he must provide the child with non-aggressive handling that he needs during this crisis situation. A professional nurse doesn't take away a patient's antibiotics because he happens to vomit on her. Likewise, a teacher does not reject a child when he needs adult controls the most. The teacher's control system must take over for the child's until his controls are operating again.

During the first stage it is sometimes helpful for the teacher to tell the child softly that he is all right, that in a little while he is going to get over his angry feelings, and that he (the teacher) is going to take care of him and not let him hurt anyone or anything. Once the child realizes that he cannot break away and that he *is* being controlled, the rage usually turns to tears. This is phase two. At this point the child's defenses are down, his coat of toughness has vanished and his inadequacy and immaturity become evident. After this period the child usually becomes silent or asks to be let go, which is phase three. If the teacher thinks the child has control over his feelings and is not going to start the cycle all over again, the teacher should release his hold on the child. It must be emphasized that the teacher, not the child, makes the decision. One evidence that the child is gaining control over his impulses is that his language becomes more coherent and logical. If the child knows who he is, where he is, and what has happened, he is usually on his way up the ladder of integration. As he gains controls, the child usually has to save face, which is often accomplished by pulling away from the teacher or making a sly remark. This is phase four and usually a good sign that the child is ready to move on his own power. Next, the teacher may ask the child to go to the washroom and clean up.

Occasionally, a child may have to be held in the classroom, but this should be avoided whenever possible. If it cannot be avoided, one of the students should get the principal immediately so that the child can be removed from the class. Later, the teacher *needs* to explain to the class and to the child exactly what has happened in order to counter any delusional interpretations of the teacher's behavior.

An important point to remember is that whenever a teacher holds a child and is able to control his own personal feelings of anxiety and aggression, the chances are that his relationship with this child will improve significantly. The message the child receives is: "I care enough about you to protect you from your own frightening impulses. The fact you had to be held is no point against you. I'm not angry, but pleased that you are feeling more comfortable and are in control of your emotions." This kind of support can only foster the child's feeling that the teacher is a person whom he can trust.

Preventive planning.   The fourth of Redl's four alternatives is preventive planning. Sometimes disruptive behavior can be avoided by developing a better school and classroom procedure. If a teacher always has difficulty during transitional periods, if there is undue conflict on the playground or in the corridors, the disturbing behavior cannot be attrib-

uted solely to "problem children"—perhaps the school program is inadequate. For example, if a teacher bores, fatigues, or regiments children into acting out, their behavior cannot be explained in terms of inner conflicts but simply in terms of a poor living design for healthy children. One teacher solved her problem as follows:

In a large elementary school in the heart of Detroit, the staff's major problem during the snowy months was snowballing. Although more teachers were scheduled for playground duty and the severity of the penalty was increased, the problem did not diminish. The children still threw snowballs, but they were much more clever about it. One teacher who was unhappy about additional playground duty suggested that they paint a huge circular target on the back brick wall of the two-story school and actually program more snowballing. After much discussion and apprehension, the idea was presented to the students. They thought it was a wonderful idea, so a student-faculty committee was appointed to draw up some rules and regulations. Once the target was drawn, the problem of snowballing was virtually eliminated. The children threw all their energy into hitting the bull's eye rather than one another. Some children would actually come to school early just so they could have the highest daily score. One teacher commented that many of the "problem children" were very active in this activity and threw themselves out by the time school began. He reported that they were even easier to teach. . . .

In both clinical and classroom applications, behavioristic approaches have gone full cycle to find ways to manage undesired behavior. Teachers have always used contingencies, rewards and punishments, praise, and threats, but their use was so haphazard and unsophisticated that it took a psychological revolution to give these methods understanding and discipline. As with most movements, however, there were (and are) exaggerated claims, esoteric applications, ritualistic and mechanistic approaches, and cults. Children as human beings were ignored; strong aversive stimuli (shocks) and denial were practiced in the name of therapy. M & Ms, checkmarks, and chips become central teaching techniques in some instances.

Yet all of us know that various extrinsic rewards and restrictions are potent forces. We know that a prompt response to behavior is critical if we wish to influence. In short, just as many behaviors are primarily a product of human mo-

tivation, others are "contingency" responsive —most of our behavior combines reaction from both sources.

There are two questions which a teacher asks: How does the behavioral emphasis fit with our short- and long-term goals regarding the kind of human beings we wish to raise? How can we design, whenever possible, implicit contingencies and rewards that are part of the natural setting rather than "tacked on"? This is not to deny that sometimes a specific contingency plan is the best stepping stone to further a youngster's growth or the only access we have.

The emphasis on behavior modification has inundated special education; there is no more popular topic in the literature. Of particular value is Thorp and Wetzel's[5] discussion of the natural environment as the base. Ferster[6] introduced this concept some time earlier.

The following articles are also particularly valuable to the special education teacher: In the first article, Deno approaches contingency management from the viewpoint of an educational

psychologist, searching for help in solving special education problems.

Contingency Management in (Special) Education: Confusions and Clarifications

Stanley L. Deno

. . . Skinner's doctrine that organisms learn from intereaction with their environment is important to us because it places a heavy responsibility on those of us who chose to intervene in the progress of human development. If behavior is in fact functionally related to changes in an individual's environment then responsibility must be accepted by those who deliberately intervene in human environments for the changes in behavior which occur in those environments. This means that when a child becomes more aggressive in an environment which we are managing that we are responsible for that increase in aggression. It also means that when behavior does not change in predicted directions that necessary environmental conditions have not been arranged to bring about the change. A child who is reading no better now than he was when we first began to care for him is a *child we have failed rather than a child who has failed.* Performance contracting and accountability are clearly consistent with interventions based upon Skinnerian philosophy. To adopt such a position leaves us with little opportunity to explain away failure on the basis of inadequacies in a child.

The third doctrine is, perhaps, the most interesting to point out because it is surely the most offensive to us all. The notion that man is by nature an active organism which learns from interaction with its environment and is not by nature anything else must be not only unpleasant for most of us to consider for personal reasons but also unpleasant because it does violence to much of the psychology upon which many psychologists base their professional lives. This last doctrine says in effect that it is foolish to spend time creating grand explanations for behavior and its changes in terms of ficticious nonbehavioral states within an individual—whether those inner states be of mind or emotion. If we ac-

cept that all that man is and does is behavior then we can approach all human problems using the techniques of behavioral science. We treat "mental health" as a behavioral rather than a medical problem. As we shall see later, accepting this assumption does not require us to deny the existence of our "inner lives." It requires only that we treat these private events as behavior when we undertake to change them. The confusions surrounding this point are many, but a reading of Skinner on this point makes it patently clear that our understanding of behavior is incomplete without analysis of inner behavior.

It is well to remind ourselves here that we have very briefly considered three basic assumptions which can fairly be gleaned from the writings of B.F. Skinner, the leading spokesman for behaviorism. While it is interesting to speculate on the validity of these assumptions, what is important here is to recognize that these doctrines are the basis for a philosophy of human nature, and that they need not be embraced when one undertakes to analyze behavior in the manner practiced by Skinner and other behaviorists. One can, I think, practice the functional analysis of behavior without believing any of the doctrines enunciated above.

Functional Analysis

The functional analysis of behavior is an attempt to specify the *environmental variables* of which behavior is a function. The analysis is undertaken for the purposes of predicting and controlling individual behavior. Doing a functional analysis does not require that one believe that behavior and environmental events are all that exist. Nevertheless, it is helpful if one approaches problems of behavior change optimistic that solutions will be derived from changes in environmental variables. If we begin our explanations of behavior change by relying upon inner events that are not

From a paper prepared for distribution at the Institute for College Instructors on Behavior Disorders in Children, August 1971. Used here by permission of the author.

Figure 1. Functional Analysis

Time

Preceding Events	Behavior	Following Events
Relevant (Recurring)		Consequences
1. Instructional Media (Objects, Oral or Printed Communication, Pictures, Automatic Devices)	1. Academic Verbal Nonverbal	1. Things Food, water Physical contact Material acquisition
2. Social Situations (Individual or Group act actions occurring in presence of subject)	2. Social Verbal Nonverbal	2. Behaviors Playing Working
3. Temporal and/or Spatial Relationships among events in 2 and 3		3. Social Contacts Physical Verbal Spatial
Incidental Events	Superstition	
Accidents		

Natural or Contrived (left brace)   Natural or Contrived (right brace)

subject to environmental influence then we must become pessimistic about the possibility that solutions for changes in behavior can be systematically obtained through intervention programs.

The elements of the functional analysis of behavior are simple (see Figure 1): first of course there is behavior itself; second, there are the environmental events which precede behavior; third, there are the environmental events which follow behavior; and finally, there are the contingency relations among those three terms. The term "reinforcement contingency" has risen from the fact that within a functional analysis behavior can be strengthened (reinforced) by changing the events which follow and are contingent upon the occurrence of that behavior.

While heavy emphasis has been given to the final two terms of the analysis (i.e., behavior and its contingent consequences) it would be well to remember that Skinner himself has said that "an adequate formulation of the interaction between an organism and it's environment must always specify three things: (1) the occasion upon which a response occurs, (2) the response itself, and (3) the reinforcing consequences." (Skinner 1969, p. 13) The first term of the contingency (preceding, antecedent or discriminative stimulus events) are as much a part of the analysis as the second and third terms. Rarely are we concerned with strengthening or weakening behavior without regard for the

occasion upon which that behavior occurs (the preceding events). In fact we cannot judge behavior as appropriate or inappropriate in a social system unless we know the situation (the preceding events) in which the behavior has occurred.

H.S. Terrace, in reviewing Skinner's latest book, *The Contingencies of Reinforcement: A Theoretical Analysis*, likens the functional utility of the three term contingency relation in the analysis of behavior to that of the cell in biology:

Indeed, just as the cell or the atom can each assume a variety of forms by changes in the nature of their components, so can the character of a discriminative operant (the relationship between the first two terms of the analysis) be modified by changes in the nature of the discriminative stimulus, the response, and the reinforcing consequences. Most readers are probably familiar with the variations that are possible with the reinforcement term. Reinforcement can be positive or negative, and, depending upon the schedule, reinforcement may follow only a small fraction of the responses that have been emitted. Less familiar are the ways in which the first two members can vary. Discriminative stimuli can derive from either the external or the internal environments. Likewise the response may be overt or covert. It is mainly from contingencies in which a stimulus from the internal environment controls either an overt or covert response that Skinner formulates the examples which encompass activities normally referred to as mental. Internal stimuli and covert responses are assumed to be potentially measurable in the same physical units applied to external stimuli and overt responses. (Terrace, 1970, p. 532)

That the functional analysis is an approach to understanding the controlling relations of all behavior regardless of its character and does not require the denial that covert behavioral events actually occur in the lives of individuals is evident from Terrace's further discussion of Skinner's analysis.

Much of Skinner's analysis of the activities of the mind is directed at showing how awareness of feelings, of thoughts, or of the external world, result from contingencies of reinforcement. In chapters 6 and 8 of Contingencies *Skinner tries to show that private events can and should be conceptualized in much the same way in which we conceptualize conditioned overt behavior. Skinner is quite explicit about the amenability of private events to scientific analysis and about the validity of contingencies as the unit of analysis. "It is particularly important that a science of behavior face the problem of privacy . . . an adequate science of behavior must consider events taking place within the skin of the organism not as physiological mediators of behavior but as part of behavior itself . . . private and public events have the same kinds of physical dimensions. So far as we know, the same process of differential reinforcement is required if a child is to distinguish among the events occurring within his own skin." (Terrace, 1970, p. 532)*

A brief discussion of the functional analysis has been included here to distinguish it from the philosophy of human nature which was summarized previously. Hopefully, it can now be seen that while a philosophy of behaviorism requires belief in certain assumptions, the functional analytic approach which Skinner has used requires only that one be interested in ascertaining the specific preceding and following environmental events which function to strengthen or weaken a behavior. This approach to analysis does not require a belief in the implicit doctrines. It requires only that one be able to apply the three term contingency analysis to events in the behavioral world to determine the contingencies of reinforcement.

Motivation and Management Techniques in the Classroom

While it is true that:
"Naming is not explaining" (The nominal fallacy)
It is also true that:
"Explaining is not changing" (The word game)

First person: You behaviorists are all alike. You care only about what someone is doing, never why he is doing it. What about his real problems?!!

Second person: If I encountered a patient on a ward who spent most of his time smearing feces or walking in little circles I could do something to stop it—you couldn't!

[Quoted without reference.]

Professionals who have embraced the concepts and procedures of behavioral psychology have done so not out of philosophic or theoretic predispositions. They have done so because behavioral scientists have provided models not only for how behavior changes (i.e., explanations) but also for changing behavior. Explanations for a child's ineffective behavior in academic and social settings are of little value to the professional unless they lead directly to alternative procedures for increasing the effectiveness of behavior. Change procedures follow directly from operant conditioning and functional analysis.

Behavioral psychologists have recognized the professional educators' demand for change procedures and have developed what might be called "model systems for changing behavior" which incorporate essential procedures from both operant conditioning and functional analysis. These systems have been disseminated widely in education under the names "Token Economy," "Precision Teaching," and "Contingency Contracting." The salient features of these systems are summarized in Table 1.

Usually, when these systems are presented in teacher workshops, for practical reasons very little time is spent in laying a conceptual base for the system procedures. The systems seem "cookbooky." We will not attempt to provide the basis for each system here, but it should be understood that basis does exist. Unfortunately, learning only procedures without the conceptual basis probably limits the procedure's effectiveness and adaptability for the

Table 1. Three Common Systems for Managing Classroom Contingencies:
A Summary of Salient Features

Token Economies (Allyon)	Precision Teaching (Lindsley)	Contingency Contracting (Homme)
1. Desired changes in behavior are specified.	1. Behavior to be recorded is pinpointed (may be overt or covert).	1. Academic achievement is measured through formal or informal tests.
2. Effective reinforcers are identified and made potentially available.	2. Recorder and Charter are identified (may be behaver).	2. A sequence of daily task assignments is developed.
3. A medium of exchange (token, point, chip, star, etc.) is established.	3. Frequency of behavior is recorded on 6-cycle semilog graph paper (Behavior Research Co.).	3. A Reinforcing Event menu is constructed depicting potential reinforcers (usually high preference activities).
4. Tokens are made contingent on measured increments (frequency, duration, proportion) of behavior specified in objective.	4. Change in frequency described in terms of "multiplier" or "divisor."	4. Performance areas and RE areas are created.
5. Opportunities to exchange tokens for effective reinforcers are made available.	5. An instructional change is made (which may involve change in preceding or following events or both).	5. Contingency Contracts (a statement of how much time in the RE area completing each task will earn) are written for each child.
6. Records of behavior are maintained (usually time series records).	6. Effect of change observed on chart and calculated as change in "multiplier" or "divisor."	6. Contracts are presented to, and accepted by, each child.
	7. Charts are almost always "shared" by Charters.	7. Tasks are completed, checked, and access to RE area is made immediately available.

teacher. It is only when the systems are improperly adapted to the specific instructional setting that remarks such as "I tried behavior modification but it didn't work," or "Behavior modification is fine for some kids, but not all of them" make any sense at all. Failures in these cases are not failures of behavior modification systems; they are failures attributable to the manager's incomplete knowledge of the systems and their bases.

The System: Some Personal Observations

Precision Teaching. Of the three systems summarized in Table 1, precision teaching is the most tightly organized and managed. It is the brainchild of Ogden R. Lindsley of the University of Kansas, perhaps Skinner's best known student. The system is almost a pure application of the experimental methodology developed by Skinner. That methodology places special emphasis on continuous recording of the frequency (previously referred to as "rate") of a specific behavior. Recording procedures in precision teaching are highly developed and continuously modified. The materials and conventions of recording are rigidly adhered to by anyone calling himself a precision teacher. Learning to be a precision teacher involves learning to use the materials and conventions that Lindsley and his followers have developed and that they disseminate through one week institutes on precision teaching offered frequently in Kansas City. The Behavior Research Company of Kansas City publishes and distributes materials to be used by precision teachers. Records of precision teachers are fed back to a computer bank managed by Lindsley. These records are, hopefully, used to develop some scientific facts about behavior.

Although the system appears to be essentially a measurement system, implicit in the measurement procedures is the functional analysis of behavior specified in the first section of this paper. Precision teachers do not use the language of operant conditioning but rather a kind of jargon called "precise basic English" for communication purposes. Perhaps the most interesting recent development in precision teaching is the acceptance of recording what are referred to as "inners" (covert behaviors). It has become proper to count "urges," or "feelings" and to apply change procedures to inner behaviors as well as outer behaviors. This development in particular seems to hold greatest promise for promoting a rapprochement between behavioral and humanistic psychologists. At the same time, however, it tends to fractionate so-called behavior modifiers into different camps.

Contingency Contracting. Contingency contracting is a system developed by Lloyd Homme, another student of Skinner's, who for some time has applied the principles of operant conditioning and the procedures of functional analysis to education. Contingency contracting differs markedly in one respect from precision teaching. Measurements of student performance which are obtained are conventional achievement tests or subject matter tests. Although daily testing is required for contingency contracting, the system does not involve extensive daily recording of frequency of student behavior. The system is based primarily on what has become known as the Premack Principle, which states that if a high-frequency behavior is made contingent on the occurrence of a low-frequency behavior, the low-frequency behavior will increase in strength.

A contingency contract is written on the assumption that behavior on many academic tasks is lower than it is on nonacademic tasks or on academic games. Therefore, an open and explicit bargain is struck between the teacher and the student such that if a student successfully completes a certain unit of work (low-frequency behavior) then he will be able to engage in something else that he might enjoy more (high-frequency behavior). Contracts are carefully written and developed. Homme also encourages teachers to turn over to the student the writing of contracts, which involves both the setting of the task and the reinforcing event. Contingency contracting classrooms are characterized by intense high performance in academic areas and a great deal of movement between performance and reinforcing-event areas.

Token Economies. Token economies are probably the most widely used systems which incorporate the principles of operant conditioning and the procedures of functional analysis. In addition, they are probably the most widely criticized because they seem to involve "bribery," "commercialism," and use of the profit motive. This is unfortunate. For one thing, the "token" has its theoretical origins in the secondary or conditioned reinforcer, i.e., the token is an event which has acquired the power to strengthen behavior only because of its repeated pairings with other reinforcing events. In a token system it is used only as a temporary substitute for the "back-up" reinforcers, which cannot be made immediately available for practical reasons involved in classroom management. Unfortunately many people who have used token systems rely heavily on edible and tangible reinforcers to back up the tokens. It is *this* use of tangible reinforcers which is most susceptible to criticism. The fact that so many token systems have relied on tangible reinforcers suggests that the system managers were either not imaginative enough to use more acceptable back-up reinforcers, or that tangible reinforcers happen to be the most effective reinforcers in most of the systems which were established. Token systems can be effectively used in cooperation with students for mutual benefit, can serve as an excellent device for teaching both academic and social behavior, and, in some ways, are more honest than the subtle manipulation systems we sometimes employ in our relationships with children.

If these short summaries of precision teaching, contingency contracting, and token economies do an injustice to the complexities of these systems, perhaps the brevity has made some of the features of each system more salient. Rather than attempting a more complete presentation (precluded by space limitations), following are general procedures for changing behavior (in that they apply to all behavior), which can serve as a basis for discussions about behavior change.

Procedures for Changing Behavior

Step 1.   *Specify the behavior to be changed.*

All that we do is behavior. In schools behavior is usually termed "academic" (e.g., adding single digit numbers, reading aloud, or writing simple sentences). Some behavior in school is "social" (e.g., talking aloud, leaving the seat, touching another student, or running in the halls). When you pinpoint a behavior begin your description with a gerund ("add*ing*," "read*ing*," "writ*ing*," "talk*ing*," "leav*ing*," and "touch*ing*"). You have adequately described a behavior when two people can independently *count* its occurrence and obtain the same total.

Behavior by itself is never right or wrong; *rules* make behavior (whether academic or social) appropriate or inappropriate.

Step 2.   *Record the frequency of its occurrence.*

Recording is necessary for precision and consistency. If you don't really need to know whether you are successful in changing the behavior you don't need to record. To be sure of success you must record.

To know whether or not behavior changes, it is first necessary to know what it is now. Our subjective judgments are almost always wrong. For that reason you should record a behavior for 4 or 5 days before you try to change it. If the amount of daily observation time changes, record the number of minutes elapsed during each observation period, and divide the number of occurrences of the behavior by the number of minutes observed.

Step 3.   *Change some conditions.*

Two sets of conditions can be changed:

1. preceding events (discriminitive stimuli or antecedent events): The directions or instructions you give to guide performance can be changed. These usually take the form of telling students what to do or how to do it but also include demonstrations by yourself, another person, or pictures, manually or technologically. The *materials* or *situation* connected with the behavior can be changed (e.g., you can change a student's book, the number of problems he must work, the amount of time he has to work, his seat in the classroom, or when he does the assignment). *But be sure to continue recording the same behavior.*

2. following events (consequences): Changing events which immediately *follow* behavior usually produces the biggest change in behavior. You could arrange for any event described below to immediately follow behavior: Doing something different (schoolwork, something social, going to another place—a room, outside, home, a more preferred activity); acquiring or losing something different (adult or peer attention, praise or disapproval, a material item—a toy, tablet, ball, money, food, book). In arranging for a change in an event which follows the behavior, you must assure that the event will occur *immediately* and *consistently*.

Step 4.   *Appraise*

Once you make a change continue it for at least 2 or 3 observation periods and watch your daily record. If the frequency of the behavior doesn't begin to increase (or decrease) make another change. Continue this cycle if necessary.

Article References

McClellan, James. B.F. Skinner's philosophy of human nature. In B.P. Komisar and C.B.J. MacMillan (eds.) *Psychological Concepts in Education.* Chicago: Rand-McNally Co., 1967.

Skinner, B.F. *Contingencies of Reinforcement: A Theoretical Analysis.* New York: Appleton-Century-Crofts, 1969.

Terrace, H.H. Toward a doctrine of radical behaviorism. *Contemporary Psychology,* 1970, *15,* 531–535.

In order to fully appreciate the value of behavior modification, it is important to differentiate the essence of the learning paradigm involved from the "movement." One can recall that the analytic movement, partly as a reaction against earlier mechanistic psychology, was to be a universal solution to all problems: behavior modification has followed the same course as the final solution. But the redress has already emerged, and what we can hope for is a new synthesis rather than a polarization of dynamic vs. behavioristic approaches. Two behaviorists, Levine and Fasnacht[7] have re-examined the results of various studies and point out that token economies may teach children how to earn tokens rather than achieve the real goal in behavior change. Bandura[8] has an extensive examination of the whole issue as it is related to the hidden agenda we all have—the model of man we use which preselects out evidence and emphasis. He points out that the overemphasis on situational determinism is one sided. Fromm[9] and Carpenter[10] have gone into these matters deeply for the serious special education professional.

The next selections deal with various aspects of direct interaction with pupils as individual human beings, emphasizing inner responses to outer conditions. We examine the approach to a pupil's inner perceptions to discover how we can alter the way he sees things and thereby increase his self-management. We will attend to crisis intervention and school-appropriate interviewing, which uses a cognitive or ego level approach to control. Since Caplan's first attention to the psychological resource found in crises, teachers have attempted to apply the concept to work with disturbed children. Teachers of disturbed children encounter crises in abundance; they have to respond somehow. Often their responses are made in desperation. Morse's article translates the crisis intervention theory to the school setting and management problems.

Crisis Intervention in School Mental Health and Special Classes for the Disturbed

William C. Morse

The currently popular concept of crisis intervention has been espoused as an innovation. It has become a central core in the new mental health emphasis. It is part of the basic rationale for the technique of life space interviewing.

At the same time teachers, disturbed children, and other school personnel on the firing line are prone to ask "So what is new?" Responding to crises has moved from a minor to the major enterprise of some educational establishments. Some pupils, too, seem to live in a crisis climate, where quiet is the interlude for recharging the battery. The tactic of confrontation has changed crisis intervention from a technique for the atypical child to dealing with the many vents taking place in schools with activist groups.

Crises are not new, nor is the concept of intervention. Schools pour on interventions. The problem is, these are usually of a reflexive and haphazard type. From our analysis of acts and reactions in the school setting it appears that a good many leave much to be desired. Since they usually lack an awareness of the underlying conditions, they are reactions to symptoms, often with a curbing intention. For example, a boy who skipped a day of school is excluded for several days as a corrective intervention, and the more he skips the longer become the exclusions, the further behind he gets, and the more escape becomes necessary. Frequently a teacher-pupil confrontation is born of a long gestation period of marginal aggravations. Suddenly a minor incident appears catastrophic and there is a reaction. These confrontations are thus compounded of strong emotions and are usually quite one-sided, with no attempt to explore the genesis of the situation or the meaning to the particular pupil. This is true of many special classrooms designed for therapeutic purposes as well as the run-of-the-mill handling of disturbed children in regular educational settings where, in fact, the vast numbers of them are. Why do these interventions tend to be so primitive? There is always time: we are still seeking instant change devices at a cut-rate counter. There is frequently strong emotional investment on the adult's part, which results in undisciplined intervention. Sometimes a passage of time serves as a huge sponge absorbing the true nature of the incident and we have only a charade in the after school appointment. In the past there has been considerable support for cooling-off periods, which is the opposite of crisis intervention or confrontation, and the cooling-off may extend to the point where usable psychological heat has been completely dissipated. Often the person with power to determine the intervention is remote from the circumstances which generated the problem. Rather than reality—which is the essential ingredient of crisis intervention—the once or twice removed person deals with secondhand, frequently distorted perceptions of what really happened. The teacher is so often group bound that leaving the class to participate in the necessary discussion would require a new federal grant. When they do desert the classroom for a quickie, they are anxious over what may be developing back in the classroom. Time again makes the decision. Frequently the incident centers around a teacher who should control immigration and emigration to the classroom and yet a third party, the principal, actually controls it.

The principal is in a very awkward situation. Not knowing exactly what happened, and having past experience or a perception regarding the teacher as well as the pupil involved, he may make certain judgments about the depth of the problem. He is also by role a "fixer" person. This role demands that he *do something* about the incident, and most are hard put to accomplish the impossible. As the superior in the command chain and given the obligation by the teacher for some corrective influence, he is, in fact, often without the resources needed to obtain a change. But this does not allow an escape from the reality problem of doing *something* about the situation. Usually after a dressing down which may be done politely or more vigorously, the pupil is returned to the original setting, often with the realization he will be back soon for more of the same. Of course the teacher who sent him out does not know what has happened with the authority person either. This lack of communication between the parts of the system is a pupil escape hatch. He can forget or ignore a great deal of the interview decision and who will know except in most general terms? It is worth remembering that in a study of special classrooms for the disturbed the actual operating team usually consisted of teacher and principal.

Another important matter is that those who are theoretically the best trained in understanding children and making vital decisions are the most remote from crises. In fact, some of the clinicians are more interested in speculating about the id as seen in projectives than in going where the id is. Working with temporary chaos and violence is for the police segment of education, not for the helping professions.

Schools are slowly coming to recognize that their authority power base has eroded. How, actually can you "make" a pupil behave in a certain way? Is exclusion a threat? In what way can a school enforce its decisions? The whole society has moved away from divine rights of institutions to a base of persuasion without finding new techniques. The old power has vanished; in short, the necessity for reexamining the nature of crisis intervention is that it represents one of our most likely failure areas in educational practice. Even that was no crime until the development of the present theory, which sees the crisis condition as a most significant opportunity for the modification of behavior. Rather than a matter to be avoided, a crisis becomes the situation one seeks in order to have maximum impact.

The theory of crisis intervention does not consist of substituting surface superficiality for dynamic understanding. Characteristically, the efforts of the on-the-line workers have been relegated to a second level importance. They have been given the responsibility for stemming the immediate tide as a sort of stop-gap process with little long-term result expected. The clinical worker with deep involvement has to assume the responsibility for the real corrective influence, slow and eventual though it may be. In crisis intervention the relative importance is reversed. It allows for no split between what has to be done on an immediate managerial basis and the most significant interaction with children in a therapeutic hour. This is not to say that both crisis management and more sedate and typical therapy are not needed. Frequently large administrations of both are required. But one should not contrast these two theories, making one the profound and the other the naive. Practice can certainly be naive or sophisticated in either realm.

The importance of all of this for contemporary mental health ideology is as follows. Studies of life histories of those making successful adjustments differ from those who make unsuccessful adjustments less in the amount of stress they have faced in their lives than in how well they learned to cope with the stress.[1] Thus, we can have two "identical" case histories as far as the supposed genesis of pathology is concerned, but one turns out to be reasonably well-adjusted while the other does not. Corrective influence and good mental health is the result of satisfactory solutions to crises rather than a simple sentence passed upon a person by his life experience. Some turn out well under very poor odds: others had little to sustain them but managed. While the more life adversity the more risk, it is not a simple arithmetic addition. Some learn to cope much more effectively than others.

Thus it follows, we teach how to cope by providing the proper intervention at the time of a crisis, while the child is in the process of learning how to cope. This is not to say that people are always particularly "teachable" at a time of their crises, in the sense that they stand there awaiting help in learning how to cope with a particular situation in a socially acceptable fashion. It merely means that at that point of crisis a person is in turmoil and seeking some resolution. The object of crisis intervention is to provide coping styles which will have long-term utility. In this way it becomes clear that the typical reflective response as now practiced in schools frequently "teaches" coping which is of a nature we do not wish at all. But we cannot avoid teaching something at the time of crisis because the pupil is always learning some means. The Harvard group which dealt with this problem has been interested in studying overwhelming crisis situations such as accidents, bereavement, and other catastrophic life events. Caplan states that during such a period a person is more susceptible to being influenced by others than in times of relative psychological equilibrium.[2] A particular insight we could gain from their studies of major crises is to avoid conceiving every event in a child's life as catastrophic. With the spread of the concept of crisis intervention, particularly life space interviewing, there is a tendency for the adult to saturate the environment with interventions for every real or presumed "incident." Also, with a youngster, that which seems to us a crisis may not be such at all to him. It should be clear that the less the individual himself feels the sense of crisis the less likely it is that we can make profitable use of interventions. Overuse and inappropriate use of crisis intervention will result in a diminution of the potency of the whole process.

One of the first questions which teachers ask is a definition of a crisis. The reason is obvious. So much happens in certain classes of normal or disturbed children that almost everything could be considered a crisis. An event which may have a great deal of explosiveness in it is not necessarily a significant crisis if it is unrelated to the nature of the group's or individual's abiding problem. Of course, in a way, everything is related to everything, but some things are more significantly related or at least the relationship can be exploited. What this means is that the selection of a particular event for utilization under crisis intervention requires just as much sophistication as pacing a given interpretation in a traditional therapeutic effort.

Bloom has made a study of this problem.[3] His research points out a very interesting kind of dilemma: Is the crisis in the eye of the "crisee" or in the eye of others around him, particularly the teacher? Thus many crisis situations may have no meaning as far as the individual primarily involved is concerned. It is a crisis to the teacher who is the consumer of the behavior. Parenthetically, the type of crisis consultation which many of us attempt takes this into consideration: the teacher is most eager to engage in a problem-solving effort at such a time. The issue of "when a crisis" is of great importance and many interventions fail because they are poised with an inadequate awareness of the fact that the one being helped must sense a crisis. Many events which are crises to us are satisfying, ego building, and gratifying to the pupil. Hence, there is no crisis except to ward off any effort to make it one. Stated in simple terms, a crisis is precipitated by overloading the child's capacity to cope. It may be generated by external demands in the environment such as the academic or behavioral tasks he is given. Or it may be in consequence of internal perceptions, distorted or accurate. The coping failure is of such an intensity that the child cannot be supported by the typical supporting tactics which teachers use day in and day out. The crises take many forms. For example a child acts out and becomes a critical management problem. A teacher may recognize a peak of depression sometimes under the guise of clowning. A sharp and noticeable erosion of self-esteem can be the basis of an approach. It may be generated by academic failure or frustration. Frequently, crises are a consequence of contagious social stimulations. Often evaluation experience such as an examination coming up or grades being given precipitates a crisis. Thus, a crisis is a psychological condition of duress which may be accompanied by overt signs but may not.

In another article Gerald Caplan states that a crisis is a relatively sudden onset of disequilibrium in a child where previous functioning was known to be stable.[4] From our point of view we might say that the previous functioning is usually stable but the disequilibrium is acute enough to be differentiated from that previous functioning. These are turning points of personality development and there is a relative saturation of negative feelings such as anxiety, depression, anger, shame, or guilt which are not contingent with what one ought to find. These are states of turmoil. Caplan points out that many children who are facing an identity crisis will have a period of this type but are not necessarily emotionally disturbed unless this develops into a chronic negative pattern.

In a mimeographed paper by Caplan entitled "A Conceptual Model for Primary Prevention," he differentiates between developmental and accidental crises. Developmental crises are the transitional periods one anticipates in both normal and disturbed children. For example, the onset of adolescence constitutes a developmental crisis period. We usually think of the third grade and beginning of school as significant periods. The accidental crises are like accidents in general. You can predict there will be a certain number in a population but not when they are liable to occur. These are conditions precipitated by loss of basic support or some threat or challenge which puts heightened demands on an individual. Caplan sees both of these as pathways leading to increased or decreased capacity to cope with one's environment. In his own experience these people are ready for increased help and are more easily influenced.

When thinking of children, it is important that we be wary of the idea that they are more *easily* influenced. The search for a solution does not always imply that the child is more easily influenced by the adult who is attempting an intervention. In a state of heightened emotionality an individual is more prone to search for cues from some aspect of his inner or outer environment to solve his dilemma. He may take his directive from another child who provides a pattern of what to do about a stress situation. He may regress to more primitive solutions. The point is that during the extreme crisis period the counterbalance of forces in his total personality are labile. Caplan would have us focus our effort on short-term successive acute crises for effective intervention. One gets involved in the ongoing living experience of the youngster. It is obvious that this type of work means that the person who provides the help must be available at the time of the crisis. As a matter of fact, it has been found that the inability of a special teacher for the disturbed to work through such chronic crises results in a progress plateau. The important point, from Caplan's point of view, is that the critically correct small force acting for a short time during the period of acute crisis can produce drastic changes which would otherwise be impossible. This is the most central concept of the whole procedure. From my own point of view it becomes important to recognize that interventions must be thought of not only as verbal but as consideration of possible manipulations of all aspects of the external environment as well. But the idea remains: an effective solving of today's problem is a most promising way of washing out the impact of an unfortunate past. This immediacy with which one attempts to deal with issues is in contrast to the traditional "cool down" theory. Many institutions use a quiet room or have a child quiet down before anyone will talk to him. This is not to say that one would never want some reduction of intensity, but the essential nature of crisis intervention is to use the emotional potency of the contemporary charged situation to help the youngster understand what he is feeling and what can be done. When you let a child "cool down," he has lost the impetus for change. Now it can be seen that this implies a virtual revolution in who does what and why for behavior modification. It is particularly amusing to think of expecting a child to have his problem ready for discussion when he comes in for a therapy hour, 2 p.m., Thursday afternoons. There may have been a blow-up on Monday and nothing significant since then to the time of meeting with the therapist. The child with sustained internal anxiety who is of the talking type best fits the traditional therapeutic approach. As a matter of fact, if one examines counseling with children after the precipitating event has passed it will be pretty clear that a good deal of time is spent in generating the problem to be discussed. One of the reasons so much of the pupil-teacher interaction is nothing more than hollow moralizing is because the child at that point in time has no feeling of an issue about which he has to do something. A teacher working with a child who has a reading difficulty but who denies it may get him to actually read and thus demonstrate his failure in order to be able to begin to do real work with him. Otherwise, the child can avoid recognizing his difficulty and make it impossible to deal with him. It has been my experience in supervising people doing individual therapy that it is sometimes necessary for them to actually create the crisis in order to have effective material to deal with, even though the child was a continual problem in a classroom. The interview process breaks down because it is so remote from reality which the child experiences.

The use of the crisis implies keen understanding of the appropriate interventions. This means knowledge in depth—psychological, sociological and educational—applied at the correct point in time. Actually it requires more rather than less insight in these domains. Inappropriate interventions result in faulty learning rather than real help.

In our own experience there are four places the crisis concept has changed procedures rather radically. One is in consultation, which has changed from supervisory or case analysis of a historical nature to strategic planning. Roles cease to determine function when solutions are sought. No one knows enough to resolve all difficulties. Second is the use of the crisis or helping teacher who is available to operate at the time of severe difficulty and breakdown by handling disturbed children taken from the regular class at the time when they flounder. This teacher works with both emotional and academic aspects in teaching the child to cope. The third major use in working with disturbed children is in the style of interviewing developed by Redl and others entitled life space interviewing. This presumes that working with a child through interviews around the particular difficulty he faces in the contemporary life scene is an effective way to help him learn long-term coping. The last is as a conceptual system to handle the confrontation situations which are more and more frequent in secondary education today. If these are seen as crises resulting from a failure to meet situational demands, there will be less repressive action, which solves little.

We are a long way from really understanding how to make constructive use of severe trouble points, but at least we have a theory to explore. One hopes that it will be taken seriously and not as another verbal gimmick with a catchy sound. We need to school ourselves relative to the theory involved and train ourselves in practice.

Article Footnotes

1. Harold Renaud and Floyd Estess, "Life History Interviews with One Hundred Normal American Males: Pathogenicity of Childhood," *American Journal of Orthopsychiatry*, vol. 31, no. 4 (October 1961), pp. 786–803.

2. Gerald Caplan, *Prevention of Mental Disorders in Children* (New York: Basic Books, 1961).

3. Bernard L. Bloom, "Definitional Aspects of a Crisis Concept," *Journal of Consulting Psychology*, vol. 27, no. 6 (1963), pp. 498–502.

4. Gerald Caplan, "Opportunities for School Psychologists in the Primary Prevention," *Mental Hygiene*, vol. 47, no. 4 (October 1963), pp. 525–539.

How does a teacher mediate a crisis or any condition where teacher-pupil interaction is necessary? Verbal interplay is only one method and changes in the situation or tasks may be required to manage the classroom. But many times external manipulation of conditions is not sufficient. Human beings are verbal, and words can be cues to action. In our experience, all children use a verbal system as part of the way they organize their world. The astonishing verbal expression of deprived children in creative poetry and writing demonstrates how prejudiced adults are when they fail to encourage language-related control. A pupil may be influenced by strong inner feelings or perceptions about his situation, as indicated in Long's article. These need to be explored, clarified, and reassessed.

Most of us have little sophistication in interviewing. We resort to either repressive admonitions or interpretative-depth material, which further inflames the situation we are trying to control. Redl was the pioneer in recognizing that a special interview process was needed to deal sensitively with these life events. We want to help the child gain control of himself and learn to deal actively with his problems. The goal of the interview is to appeal to the intact part of his ego. The following article is the fundamental theoretical paper on life space interviewing.

While Redl does not stress the point in this material, the adult must have an empathic potential—that subtle capacity to see and relate to the deeper feeling rather than the defensiveness of the child—to make the technique effective.

The Concept of the
Life Space Interview
Fritz Redl

It is our contention that life space interviewing plays an important part in the lives of all children. All adults in an educational role in children's lives find themselves in many situations which could correctly be thus labeled.

It is our contention that the life space interview assumes a mediating role between the child and what life holds for him, which becomes just as important as the interviewing that goes on within the pressurized cabin.

It is our contention that in work with seriously disturbed children, even if they are not exposed to the special type of pressurized cabin therapy over and beyond their exposure to milieu therapy, the strategically wise use and technically correct handling of the life space interviews held with the children are of foremost clinical importance.

It is our contention that even where children are exposed to clear-cut pressurized cabin therapy, for special therapy of one phase of their problem, the wisdom of strategy and technique used by their natural home or school life personnel in mediating life experiences for them is of major strategic relevance in its own right.

It is, before all, our contention that what goes on in a life space interview, even though held with the child by somebody not his therapist, in the stricter interpretation of the term, involves as subtle and important issues of strategy and technique as the decisions the psychoanalyst has to make during the course of a therapeutic hour.

It is our contention, last and not least, that any application of total life milieu therapy as supportive to individual therapy, or undertaken in its own right, will stand or fall with the wisdom and skill with which the protectors, teachers, and interpreters in the children's lives carry out their life space interview tasks.

It is for this reason that we shall try to subject some of the occurrences during the process of a life space interview to the same type of scrutiny that psychiatric therapy techniques have for a long time been exposed to in our technical seminars. By the way, one more word about the *term*:

What we have in mind when we say "life space

interview" is the same thing as what my staff, my friends, and my coworkers, while I still lived in Detroit, referred to under the name of *marginal interview*. The reasons for the change in terms are many, and seem to me so strong that they outweigh the equally obvious disadvantages of the switch in name. When I, and many of us in the same type of work, started talking about the marginal interview, it was pretty clear, out of our own context of operation and to us personally, what we felt it was "marginal" to. We meant, at first, the type of therapylike interview that a child may need around an incident of stealing from the "kitty" in his club group, but which would be held right around the event itself by the group worker in charge of that club, rather than by the child's therapist—even though the material around the incident would probably later be getting into therapy, too.

So—it was "marginal" in two ways: marginal in terms of the rest of the life events around which it was arranged; and marginal in terms of the overall job expectation of a group leader, who uses casework or therapy technique even while functioning in his group leader role.

Since I moved into the operation of our residential treatment design[1] within a huge hospital setting, the term "marginal" has lost the clarity of its meaning entirely, besides other disadvantages which the low-status sound of the word "marginal" seems to assume for many people.

In changing to the term "life space interview," we apologize for the possible confusion that might be created because we are using the term here with an entirely different meaning from the one Kurt Lewin had in mind. In spite of this disadvantage, we feel that the term is at least frank in its emphasis on the major characteristics of this type of interview we have in mind: In contrast to the interviewing done in a considerable detachment from direct involvement in the here and now of Johnny's life, such as the psychoanalytic play therapy interview, the life space interview is closely built around the child's di-

Abridged from Fritz Redl, "The Concept of the Life Space Interview," *American Journal of Orthopsychiatry*, XXIX, January 1959, 1–18. Copyright © 1959, the American Orthopsychiatric Association, Inc. Reprinted by permission.

rect life experience in connection with the issues which become the interview focus. Most of the time, it is held by a person who is perceived by the child to be part of his "natural habitat or life space," with some pretty clear role and power-influence in his daily living, as contrasted to the therapist to whom one is sent for "long-range treatment." We are fully aware that none of the similarities or differences implied here are truly characteristic for the two operations; in fact, to find similarities and differences is the goal, not the starting point for our research. For the time being, and until someone with more imagination and linguistic know-how gives us a better clue, we think the term is as good, or bad, as any we could think of to connote what we have in mind. Frankly, we aren't quite used to it ourselves, and you may find us slipping back into calling the whole thing by its old Midwest-flavored name of the "marginal" more often than we may be willing to admit.

Goals and Tasks of the Life Space Interview

First, I want to select for discussion two major categories of goals and tasks for life space interviewing: (a) Clinical Exploitation of Life Events; and (b) Emotional First Aid on the Spot. The difference between these two categories does not lie in the nature of the event around which the need for the life space interview arose—we shall in the future refer to this event as the "issue"—but in our decision as to what we want to do with it; it is also defined, of course, by the question as to just what the situation itself allows.

Let's assume that a group of children are just about ready to go out on that excursion they have anticipated with eagerness for quite a while. Let's assume there is, due to our fault, somewhat more delay at the door because of a last-minute search for lost shoes, footballs, etc., so that irritability mounts in the gang that is already assembled and raring to go. Let's further assume that in the ensuing melee of irritated bickering two of our youngsters get into a flare-up, which ends up with Johnny's getting socked more vehemently than he can take, furiously running back to his room, cursing his tormentor and the world at large, all educators in particular, swearing that he will "never go on no trip no more in his whole life." We find him just about to soak

himself in a pleasurable bath of self-pity, nursing his grudge against people in general and adding up new evidence for his theory that life is no good, people are mean "so-and-so's" anyway, and that autistic daydreaming is the only safe way out.

Well, most of us would feel that somebody ought to move into this situation. The staff member who tries to involve the sulking child in a marginal interview at this time has a choice of doing either of two things:

He may want to be with John in his misery, and to assist the child in disentangling the complicated web of emotions in which he is so hopelessly caught, simply in order to "get him over it" right now and here, to get him back into his previous enjoyment-anticipating mood. This situation seems to be quite comparable to the concept of "first aid"; the organism is capable of taking care of a wound produced by a minor cut, but it might be wise to help it.

On the other hand, depending on how much time there is and how Johnny reacts to the adult's interview strategy, the adult may suddenly find that this opportunity gives him a long-hoped-for chance to help John to come to grips with an issue in his life which we so far have had little possibility to bring to his awareness. Thus, he may forget about his intention of getting John back to his original cheerful excursion-anticipating mood; he may even give in to his sulky insistence that he "wasn't going to go nohow," but he may decide to use this special opportunity to start on an interpretational job. He may begin to tie this event up for John with many similar previous ones, and thus hope to help him see how John really "asks for it" many times, even though he has no idea that he does so, and how his irritably rude provocation or lashing out at other children often gets people infuriated, or whatever the special version of this perennial theme may be. In short, half an hour later our interviewer may be driving after the rest of the group with a somewhat sadder but wiser companion at his side, or he may at least have laid the groundwork for some such insight to sink in at a future opportunity, or to be picked up by his "therapist" at a later opportunity in case John happens also to be "in individual therapy" of the more classical style.

By the way, most of the time we can't be sure before an interview under which of the two goal categories it will eventually have to be listed, for we may in the middle of an interview find good enough reason for a switch from the original intent with which we entered the scene.

This differentiation between "Emotional First Aid on the Spot" on the one hand, and "Clinical Exploitation of Life Events" on the other, however, still leaves us with two rather comprehensive categories before us. I feel that the practitioners among you would like it better if we broke those wider concepts down into smaller units and thus brought them closer to the observational scene.

The Clinical Exploitation of Life Events

Our attempts at pulling out of a life experience, in which a given child is involved, whatever clinical gain might be drawn from it for our long-range treatment goal, may assume some of the following special forms:

Reality rub-in.   The trouble with some of our youngsters, among other things, is that they are *socially nearsighted.* They can't read the meaning of an event in which they get involved, unless we use huge script for them and underline it all in glaring colors besides. Others are caught in such a well-woven *system of near to delusional misinterpretation of life* that even glaring contradictions in actual fact are glided over by their eyes unless their view is arrested and focused on them from time to time. More fascinating even, are the youngsters whose preconscious perception of the full reality is all right, but who have such well-oiled ego skills in alibi-ing to their own conscience, and rationalizing to any outside monitor's arguments, that the picture of a situation that can be discussed with them is already hopelessly repainted by the time we get there. It is perhaps not necessary to add how important it is, strategically speaking, that such children have some of this "reality rub-in" interviewing done right then and there, and preferably by persons who themselves were on the scene or are at least known to be thoroughly familiar with it.

Symptom estrangement.   In contrast to their more clearly neurotic comtemporaries, our children's egos have, in part at least, become subservient to the pathological mechanisms they have developed. They have learned well how to benefit from their symptoms through secondary gain, and are therefore in no way inclined to accept the idea that something is wrong with them or that they need help. A large part of the "preparatory" task at least, with-out successful completion of which the magics of the more classical forms of individual therapy are rather lost on these children, consists in alienating their ego from their symptoms. Hopeful that there must be somewhere a nonpathology-swallowed part of their ego functions waiting for a chance to speak up, we use many of their life situations to try to pile up evidence that their pathology really doesn't pay, or that they pay too heavily for what meager secondary gain they draw from it, or that the glee they are after can be much more regularly and reliably drawn from other forms of problem-solving or pursuit of life and happiness. By the way, the assumption in all this is *not* that one can simply argue such children through well-placed life space strategy into letting go of their symptoms; part of the job needs to be tackled, in addition, by many other means. However, we can *enlist* part of their insight into helping their ego want to liberate itself from the load of their pathology. To make it possible for them, even after they want to, to shuffle off the unconscious coils of their neuroses, is an issue in its own right. We also ought to remember at this point how important it is that symptom estrangement be pursued consistently by all the staff all the way down the line. It would do little good to *talk* in interviews about the inappropriateness of their symptomatic actions, if the social reality in which they live made it too hard for them to let go of those very symptoms. Our action definitely has to be well attuned to our words in this task more than in any other.

Massaging numb value-areas.   No matter how close to psychopathic our children may sometimes look, we haven't found one of them yet who didn't have lots of potential areas of value appeal lying within him. But while the arm is still there, circulation has stopped. Value sensitivity in a child for which his inner self has been liberated still needs to be *used*, and something has to be done to get circulation going again. Admitting value sensitivity, just like admitting hunger for love, is quite face-losing for our youngsters. There are, however, in most youngsters some value areas which are more tax-exempt from peer group shame than others. For instance, even at a time when our youngsters would rather be seen dead than overconforming and sweet, the appeal to certain codes of "fairness" within their fight-provocation ritual is quite acceptable to them. Thus, in order to ready the ground for "value arguments" altogether, the pulling out of issues of fairness or similar values from the debris of their daily life events may pay off handsomely in the end.

New-tool salesmanship. Even the most classicism-conscious therapists confess from time to time that they spend quite some effort helping a youngster see that there are other defenses than the ones he is using, and that doing this may at least partially widen the youngster's adaptational skills. The therapist, however, who operates in the "pressurized cabin" of a long-range classical style individual therapy design cannot afford to waste too much of his effort in this direction, or he would puncture the pressure-safe walls he has spent so much time building up to begin with. So, as soon as the potential to use such mechanisms has been liberated in individual therapy, the adults who "live" with those children can begin to use many of their life experiences to help them draw from them the vision of a much wider range of potential reaction to the same mess. Even the seemingly simple recognition that seeking out an adult to talk it over with is so much more reasonable than to lash out at nothing in wild fury may need to be worked at hard for a long stretch of time with some of the children I have in mind.

The life space interview offers a chance to leave the more general level of propaganda for better adjustment tools, and to become quite specific in the demonstration of the all too obvious inadequacy of the special tool previously chosen by the child. In this respect we feel the same advantage that the salesman may feel who, besides having leaflets to distribute, is given the opportunity to demonstrate.

Manipulation of the boundaries of the self. From time to time one invariably runs into a child who combines with the rest of his explosive acting-out type of borderline aggressive pathology, a peculiar helplessness toward a process we like to refer to as *group psychological suction.* Quite vulnerable to even mild contagion sparks, he is often discovered by an exceptionally brilliant manipulator of group psychological currents, and then easily drifts into the pathetic role of the perennial "sucker" of an exploitation-happy subclique.

The life space interview, of course, offers a strategic opportunity to begin to move in on this. To illustrate what we mean by this concept of "manipulation of the boundaries of the self"—and leaving out all the details as to life space strategy employed in the case—the following example may serve:

Several months ago, we felt that the time was ripe to "move in" on the problems of one of our youngsters around "group psychological suction" de-scribed above, so we decided to exploit incidents of this sort, wherever they might happen, through an increased use of "life space interviews." We felt good when eventually the following incident occurred one day in school: Two boys of the subclique that enjoyed exploiting this youngster were hard at work to get him to "act up" for them. This time their wiles didn't seem to get them anywhere; in fact, in the process of accomplishing their job they got out of hand themselves and got themselves "bounced." They were hardly out of the room when the youngster in question turned to the teacher, with a relieved look on his face, and declared, "Gee, am I glad I didn't get sucked into this one."

Many of our children are more ready than one would assume at first sight to expand their concept of the wider boundaries of their self into including other people, benign adults, their group, or the whole institution to which they feel a sense of belonging, and so on. In an entirely different direction, again, we may want to use life incidents to help youngsters with the problem of acceptance of their self, or of hitherto split-off parts of it. Anything that educators describe under terms such as "encouragement," "inculcating a feeling of worthfulness and pride," and anything that betrays confused attitudes of the children toward their "self" in the form of despondency coupled with megalomanic illusions, etc., might well be grouped under this heading.

In summary, we should underline the implication that these five goals for the use of the life space interview were meant to be illustrative rather than system binding. In all the instances we have raised so far, the real *goal* of what the life space interviewer did was the clinical exploitation of a given life event. It meant making use of a momentary life experience in order to draw out of it something that might be of use for our long-range therapeutic goals.

Emotional First Aid on the Spot

While children are exposed to therapeutic long-range work on their basic pathology, it is important to remember that they are still forced to live with their symptoms until they finally can shed them, and that child development is also still going on. For, while it is true that our children are sick enough to deserve the term "patients," we must never forget that child patients are still *growing youngsters.* This means that the adult, who accompanies them during the various phases of their growth, is also needed as an *aid on the spot* in those adjustment demands of daily life that they cannot well manage on their own. It is our contention that this in itself is an important enough task to deserve special technical attention, and that the opportunity for such "aid in conflict" includes the situations which we term "life space interview." The emphasis here lies in the fact that emotional first aid in itself is a perfectly valid reason for a carefully planned life space interview, even if this special issue around which the interview is built promises no long-range gain in the same way in which we described it in the previous section. As illustration of the goal which a given life space interview may set itself, we should like to enumerate again five randomly assembled subcategories:

Drain-off of frustration acidity. Even normal children experience easily as something quite infuriating the interruption of the pleasurable exploit in which they happened to be engaged. This is especially unfortunate with our type of child who has such low frustration tolerance, for he is over-aggressive and hostility-projective to begin with. It is here that the life space interview has an opportunity to serve as an over-all hygienic device. In sympathetic communication with the child about his anger or justified disgust at the discomfort of having been interrupted, we can drain off the surplus of intervention-produced hostility, and thus avoid its being added to the original reservoir of hate. Such situations offer themselves especially when something has gone wrong with a planned enterprise, or if the mere need to maintain a schedule may force interruption.

Support for the management of panic, fury, and guilt. The trouble with many children is not only that they *have* more feelings of anxiety, panic, shame, guilt, fury than they should or than the normal child would experience, but also that they don't know what to do with such states of mind when they get into them. We have already complained, in *Children Who Hate*, about how difficult it is to help such children to react correctly even if they do feel guilty when they should. It is important, then, that the adult intervene and give first aid as well as therapeutic support whenever heavier quantities of such emotions hit the child or the group. In our own over-all strategy plan, for instance, we consider it important that an adult always stay with the child,

no matter how severe his tantrum attack may become. The knowledge that we are just as interested in protecting him from his own exaggerated wishes, as from the bad intent of other people, has been found quite ego supportive in the long run. By being with the child right after the excitement of a blowup abates, the adult can often help the child "put things back into focus and proportion" again. He can also aid him in the return to the common course of activities or social life of the day without the sour after-taste of unresolved hurt.

Communication maintenance in moments of relationship decay. There is one reaction of our children to experiences of emotional turmoil which we fear more than any other they may happen to produce—and that is, the total breakoff of all communication with us and full-fledged retreat into an autistic world of fantasy into which we are not allowed to penetrate. We get scared, because with children at the borderline of psychotic withdrawal from any and all reality this weapon of defense against help from us is the most efficient one.

It is used especially frequently when events force us to a clear-cut form of intervention in a youngster's behavior, the nature of which seems, at first sight, to offer an especially "clear-cut" point of argument or interpretation to the child. Yet, at this very moment he is liable to drop all relationships with us, and thereby makes us quite helpless in our attempt to offer sympathy, explanation or support. Often, for instance, after a particularly vicious attack upon another child, a youngster will misperceive the motives for the intervention of a protective and battle-interrupting adult to such a degree that he interprets even the most well handled interruption of the fight as rude and hostile "betrayal." To this he reacts with such resentment that the breakdown of all previously established relationships with that adult seems imminent. It is important that this process be stopped right then and there and that we prevent the *next step* in the youngster's defensive maneuver, namely, the withdrawal of all communication and the total flight into autistic daydreams. Often, in such a moment, it is obvious that nothing we could do would make any impact on the hopelessly misconceived image in the youngster's mind. However, our attempt to involve the youngster in some form of communication may prevent the next level of retreat from us right then and there. So we surrender any plan to "talk to the point," but simply try to keep communication flowing between child and adult, no matter on what theme and no matter how trivial or far removed it may be from the issue at hand.

Regulation of behavioral and social traffic.   This specific task of the life space interview doesn't look like much, and we have become painfully aware that people have a tendency to consider it too "superficial" and undignified to be included in items as status-high as the discussion of "interview techniques." Yet, our respect for the clinical importance of our service as *social and behavioral traffic cops* has gone up, if anything, over the last ten years. The issue itself is simple enough and doesn't need much explaining. The performance of the task, however, may get so difficult that it is easily comparable to the most delicate problems that might emerge in individual therapy of either children or adults.

The facts of the situation are these: The children know, of course, what over-all policies, routines, rules of the game of social interaction are in vogue in a given place. Only, no matter how well they "know," to *remember* the relevance of a given issue for a given life situation is a separate task, and to muster enough ego force at the moment to subject impulsivity to the dictates of an internalized concept of rules is still another. Thus, the service they need becomes very similar to the job the traffic cop, when functioning at his best, would perform for adults, and even the most law-abiding ones amongst us may need such help from time to time. He reminds us of the basic rules again or warns us of the special vicissitudes of the next stretch. He may point out to us where we deviate dangerously even though we happen to be lucky this time. Since people do not necessarily learn even from dramatic experience, unless they are aided by a benign and accepted guide, it may be important to go, in a subsequent session, through a stretch of behavioral confusion and to use it for reinforcement of our over-all awareness of the implications of life. Since our children are especially allergic to moralizing or preaching or lecturing of any kind, it would not do to offer them a condensed handbook of behavioral guidelines. It is important to subdivide that phase of their social learning into a number of aids *given on the spot* when needed most.

For example: we have a clear-cut policy on our ward about the child's going to our school sessions, and about the reasons for this, as well as the course of events which will take place if a child gets himself "bounced" for the time being. We have spent great effort to have everybody live this policy consistently so that the unanimous attitude of all adults involved could serve as an additional nonverbal reinforcer of the basic design. Yet, in order for all this to become meaningful and finally incorporated and perceived as part of the overall structure of "life in this place" for our children, it took hundreds of situations of life space interview surrounding school events.

Umpire services—in decision crises as well as in cases of loaded transactions.   The children often need us for another function, which may sound simple though the need for it may be emphatic and desperate: to *umpire*. This umpiring role in which we see ourselves put may be a strictly internal one. It sort of assumes the flavor of our helping them decide between the dictates of their "worser or their better selves." For those instances, our role resembles that of a good friend whom we took along shopping—hoping he would help us maintain more vision and balance in the weighing of passionate desire versus economic reason than we ourselves might be capable of in the moment of decision-making. However, we wouldn't want to restrict this term to its more subtle, internal use. We envision it to go all the way from the actual umpiring of a fight or dispute, of a quarrel about the game rules in case of conflict or confusion, to the management of "loaded transactions" in their social life. Into the last category fall many complicated arrangements about swapping, borrowing, trading, etc., the secondary backwash from which may be too clinically serious to be left to chance at a particular phase. Many such situations, by the way, offer wonderful opportunities to do some "clinical exploitation of life events." But, even if nothing else is obtained in a given incident of this kind, the hygienic regulation and the emotionally clean umpiring of internal or external dispute is a perfectly legitimate and a most delicate clinical job in its own right.

Summarizing all this, we should like to emphasize what we tried to imply all along: All these "goals"—the strategic exploitation type, as well as the moment-geared emotional first-aid ones—may be combined sometimes in one and the same interview, and we shall often see ourselves switch goals in midstream. We probably need not even add that the type of goal we set ourselves at a given time in our project would also be strongly influenced by the phase the children find themselves in in their individual therapy, and of course, just where they are in their movement from sickness to mental health. In fact, the "stepping up" as well as the "laying off" in respect to selecting special issues for life space interview or for purposely leaving such materials untouched is in itself an important part of the over-all coordination of individual therapy and the other aspects of our therapeutic attack on the pathology of a given child.

Speculations about Strategy
and Technique

The importance of a clinically highly sophisticated concept of *strategy and technique* in regard to the life space interview is taken for granted in this discussion by now. That this short symposium cannot hope to do more than open up the issues and point at the need for more organized research seems equally obvious. In view of this, it may seem most advisable to concentrate on one of the core problems of all discussions on strategy and technique, namely, the question of *indications and counterindications;* and to draw attention to some of the most urgent aspects that need further elaboration soon. If we say "indications and counterindications," by the way, we mean to refer to both: indications and counterindications for the *holding* of a life space interview to begin with, as well as indications and counterindications for a specific *technique* or for the establishing or abandoning of a specific strategic move. The question "Should I keep my mouth shut or should I interpret this dream right now?" which is an issue so familiar to us from discussions of individual therapy, has its full analogy in the orbit of life space interview work.

The following criteria seem to turn up most often in our discussions of technique:

Central theme relevance. By this we mean the impact of over-all strategy in a given therapeutic phase on the question of just what situations I would move in on and what issues I would select for life space interview pick-up. It would not do to surround the children with such a barricade of attempts to exploit their life experiences for clinical gains that it would disturb the natural flavor of child life that needs to be maintained; and too much first aid would contain the danger of overdependency or adult intervention oppressedness that we certainly want to avoid. As an example for this: At certain stretches we would purposely keep away from "talking" too much about our previously quoted youngster's proneness to allow himself to be played for a sucker. It is only after certain over-all therapeutic lines have emerged that we decide in unison that such incidents should from now on be exploited more fully. It was felt, at that particular time, that the child's individual therapist would welcome such supportive rub-in from without.

Ego proximity and issue clarity. The first of these two is an old standby, well known from clinical discussions in classical psychoanalytic work. One simply does not sail interpretatively into material that is at the time so "deeply repressed" that bothering it would only unnecessarily increase resistance or lead to marginal problems in other areas. On the other hand, material of high ego-proximity had better be handled directly, else the child might think we are too dumb or too disinterested to notice what he himself has figured out long since on his own. The same issue remains, of course, an important criterion in life space interview work.

The item of *issue clarity* is a more intricate one and becomes especially complex because of the rapidity with which things move on the behavioral scene of children's lives and because of the many factors that may crowd themselves into the picture. Just one brief illustration of what we are trying to point out:

Johnny has just attacked another youngster viciously, really undeservedly. The other child's surprise and the whole situation are so crystal clear that this time we are sure that even our insight-defensive Johnny will have to let us show him how he really asked for it all—So, here we stand, our clinical appetite whetted while we watch the fight. But—wham—a third child interferes. He happened to run by, couldn't resist the temptation of getting into the brawl, and he is a youngster Johnny has a lot of hostile feeling about anyway. Before anybody quite knows what has happened, Johnny receives from that interfering youngster a blow much too heavy and unfair for anybody's fight ritual, and so, of course, Johnny leaves the scene howling with fury, pain, and shame about losing face. Obviously, we had better assist Johnny in his predicament, but the idea of using this life space interview for a push in the direction of Johnny's self-insight into the provocativeness of his behavior seems downright ridiculous at this point.

Role compatibility. Children who live in an institutional setting do not react to individual people as "persons" only. There is also a direct impact brought to bear on them from the very "role" they perceive a particular adult to be in. This issue has long been obscured by the all too generalized assumption that the personal relationship between child and adults is the only thing that counts. To illustrate this point:

When a camp counselor finds her whole cabin up on the roof where they know they shouldn't be, she may have trouble getting them down no matter how much the children may all love her. I, as the camp director walking on that scene, may find it much easier to get them off the roof; in fact they may climb down as soon as they see me coming along. This does not mean that they have a less good relationship to their counselor or a better one to me. It simply means a difference in their role expectation. The counselor for them is seen in the role of the group leader, which heavily contains the flavor of the one who plans happy experiences with them. It is true that on the margin of this role they do know that the adult counselor also has certain "over-group-demanded" regulations to identify herself with and to enforce. However, that part of her role—and for the sake of a happy camp experience we hope so—is less sharply in focus than the program-identified one. In fact, if that counselor got too fussy or too indignant about the youngsters' not responding immediately, or used the argument of the over-all camp regulations against her gang too fast, this would create resentment and a loss of subsequent relationship for a while. The role of the camp director, no matter how cordial individual feelings toward him may be, is much more clearly loaded with the expectation that it is his job to secure over-all coordination of many people's interests. The children would therefore expect the director to make a demand for them to get off that roof, and would not hold it as much against him that he does interfere with the pleasure of the moment or considers the whole camp more important than "Cabin 7" at this time.

The compatibility of the major role of a given adult with the role he is forced into by the life space interview is an important strategic consideration. In our present operation, for example, we felt, during the first year or so, that it was quite important that the role of the *counselor* be rather sharply set off from that of the *ward boss*, the *teacher*, the *therapist*. . . . During that phase it also seemed important for us to protect the counselor from too many unnecessary displaced hostilities, since she has enough to do to handle those that would naturally come her way. In short: During that period of time we felt it important that all requests for going home or for special prolonged week-end visits, etc., were steered to the psychiatrist, who was seen as the ward boss by the children. The transference character of many of these requests and the terrific ambivalence of the children about them, thrown on top of all the aggression manipulation a counselor has to cope with anyway in her daily play life with the child, would have increased the ensuing confusion. The arrangement we created allowed the ward boss to absorb some of the extra frustration acidity unavoidably generated during such interviews, while the counselor was, so to say, "taken off that hook." At the same time, however, we did feel that the counselor is the most natural person to assist the child in *first aid* interviews around his concern about home, mother's not turning up for a visit, etc.

Mood manageability—the child's and our own. With due respect to all the clinical ambition any staff member can have about managing his own mood, there is a limit beyond which he cannot be forced any further. Such limits need to be recognized. Oversimplifying the issue for purposes of abbreviation:

If I work for an hour in order to get the children finally in shape to be quite reasonable and have a good stretch of quite happy and unusually well modulated play with me, I can't possibly act concerned enough if one of them does something that needs a more serious "reality rub-in" for good measure. This is especially the case where we allow a child to play his "cute antics" for the service of everybody's entertainment, and where he suddenly begins to go too far. Even a serious talk with someone who quite visibly found the same antics cute two minutes ago will not have the same strategic chance as a talk with one who was not involved in the original scene.

The item of mood manageability is, of course, an even more difficult one as far as the mood of the children is concerned. The issue may be clear enough, and the event beautifully designed to draw some learning out of it. If the youngster in the meantime gets overexcited, bored, tired, or grouchy, the best laid-out issue would be hopelessly lost and we had better look for another occasion for the same job.

Issues around timing. One of the great strategic advantages of the life space interview is the very flexibility in timing that it offers us. We don't have to hope that the child will remember from Friday noon until his therapy hour next Wednesday what was happening just now. We can talk with him *right now.* Or, having watched the event itself that led to a messy incident, we can quite carefully calculate how long it will take the youngster to cool off enough in order to be accessible to some reasonable communication with him, and move in on him at that very calculated time. Or we may even see to it that he gets enough emotional first-aid from us or from our colleagues so that he can be brought into a state where some insight-focused discussion with him is possible at last. One of the most frequent dilemmas that aggressive and explosive children force us into is the fear of waiting too long to talk about something, because we know how fast they forget, as opposed to the need to let some cooling off take place, lest the interview itself get shot through with the aggression debris left over from the original scene. Sometimes external things happen and the "time" aspect may often work against us. I shall never forget the painful experience several years ago in which I finally had succeeded in working a bunch of quite recalcitrant delinquents into a mood conducive to my talking with them about an issue they didn't want to face. Just then the swimming bell put a rude end to my efforts. To keep them one minute longer while they heard and saw everybody else running down to their beloved free swim would have made shambles out of my carefully built up role as interpreter of the rules of life.

The impact of terrain and of props.   Both the life space interview and the more classical styles of individual therapy believe in the importance of terrain and props. In the long-range therapy, after we have figured out the most goal-supportive arrangements, the problem of terrain and props loses its importance because it can easily be held constant or can at least be kept under predictable control. While the most favorable terrain is always the one in which both partners feel most comfortable, in life space interviewing the terrain may be terrifically varied, and neither it nor the selection of props is often within our power.

In fact, more often than not, terrain as well as props are on the side of the child's resistance, rather than on our side. This is, of course, especially true when we move in on a situation involving extreme behavioral conflict.

For the child, the most comfortable place may be the one behind his most belligerently cathected defenses. From bathtub to toy cabinet, from roof or treetop to "under the couch," his choice of terrain seems endless. In all cases the problem of what emotional charge the surrounding props may suddenly assume remains of high technical relevance. Besides what is going on between the two people, what is going on between *them and space and props* can become of great relevance.

In summary, the choice of a given technique must be (1) dependent on the specific goal we have in mind (2) within a given setting (3) with a specific type of child (4) in a given phase of his therapeutic movement.[2] There is no "odd" or "bad" technique in itself. The very procedure that "made" one situation all by itself may be the source of a mess-up in another, or may have remained irrelevant in a third. However, this reminder, while disappointing, would not be too hard to take, for we have learned that lesson from the development of concepts of strategy and techniques for the psychiatric interview long ago. Rather than relearn it, we simply need to remember the difference between a pseudoscientific technical trick-bag, and a more complex, but infinitely more realistic concept of multiple-item conditioned choice of criteria for the selection of strategy as well as of techniques.

Article Footnotes

1.   Whenever in illustrations the "children on our ward" are mentioned, this refers to the following setting: Closed Ward within the premises of the National Institutes of Health, a large research hospital. The children referred to here: a carefully selected group of six boys ranging in age from eight to ten years at the time of intake, chosen as representative of "borderline" disturbances commonly referred to as "explosive acting-out type of child." They are children of normal IQ, however, and are expected to be free from traceable physical pathology, characterized in their behavior by a rather extreme volume of aggression, extreme forms of reckless destruction, and loaded with an amazing array of learning disturbances and character disorders to boot. The ward on which the children lived was staffed and operated more along the lines of a camping program, with the hospital as a base, but not ultimate limit for the activities. At the time of the presentation of this material, the movement of the children into a newly constructed open residence was imminent. The treatment and research

goals of the operation included the study of the impact of intensive individual psychotherapy (four hours per child per week), of observations in our own school setting (individual tutoring as well as group school), and exposure to "milieu therapy" in their life on the ward.

2. Many of illustrations used in this paper need to be understood as limited by the specific conditions under which the observations were made. For their full evaluation, a detailed description of the over-all program and ward policies for the clinical management of the children and for the guidance of staff behavior would have to be added here. It is, therefore, expected that most of our illustrations will have to be read with this reservation in mind. While literal translation into practice with other children in different settings is not intended, we do imply emphatically that the basic principles we are trying to illustrate here should hold for a wide variety of designs.

Life space interviewing should not be linked with crises alone. Rather it is an appropriate style of teacher-pupil interaction to deal with many issues. Although the process evolved as a control technique, it is now more generally applied. In the following article by Morse, more or less extreme cases are used for illustration, but other less stringent problems can also be worked with in this manner. Redl's article gives the psychological elements of life space interviewing. Morse gives steps and stages that teachers can use to organize interviews. In LSI training programs, discussion and study of actual interview tapes enable the supervisor to help a teacher use the technique effectively. Without supervised practice, it is most difficult to learn any new skill. However, a conceptual system helps teachers practice talking with children in the format of life space interviewing. No one would go through the "steps" in sequence, or even use them all in the same interview. But they provide nodal points in thinking about the process as a model of interaction. This article should be read with Redl's theory article.

Worksheet on Life Space Interviewing for Teachers
William C. Morse

A major problem for teachers is how to talk or counsel effectively with pupils and groups of pupils, whether it be for the purpose of exploring a general attitude, a motivational complex, or a control and management problem with mild or severe implications.

These conditions are apparent: (1) teachers cannot adopt a counselor's role, be it psychoanalytic or non-directive; (2) it is not possible to refer all "working through of problems" to persons outside the classroom; (3) it is not adequate to continue an outmoded moralistic approach or some equally unsophisticated and undynamic method.

Any model worthy of teaching as a profession must embody the deepest understanding of individual and group dynamics. But it must be focused on practice suited to the "firing line" operation of teaching rather than the consultation room. There is considerable disagreement about the role of a teacher, but no one will argue that the profession is sorely in need of new methods for assisting in the socialization processes and for dealing with the increasingly complex and frustrating behavior that pupils bring to the school. Whatever we do should be based on the generic nature of the educative process and the legitimate responsibility of the school. The concept of LSI is geared to these propositions.

Several theoretical developments have produced the present theoretical stance.

1.   The concept of milieu as developed by Lewin and Redl. The application to the school implies an awareness of the total psycho-social system of a school.

2.   The concept of Life Space Interviewing by Redl is designed to work with behavior "in situ."

3.   The concept of crisis intervention by Caplan and others makes it clear that active intervention in times of stress is a most productive teaching opportunity.

4. The concept of differential diagnosis and strategic planning emphasizes going beyond the symptom and applying a variety of stratagems.

5. The concept of coping skills gives a rationale to the newer methodology as a means for teaching the pupil-needed ego skills. There is no belief that this alone will always be sufficient, but it is implied that without such new skills, much traditional therapy pays a low dividend.

6. The empathic relationship which the teacher generates underlies any "technique," and is more imposing in its impact than is method per se.

The following steps are not meant as a formal series, for there will be a great deal of flexibility in the development of any situation. Teachers seldom can conduct an extensive sequence at one interview, but the process can still be seen in its entire scope.

It should be noted that the goals differ significantly. In depth work, the expectation is for long-term gradual emergence of a more healthy personality, with possible regression followed by integration and eventual independence. In LSI, the hope is for a degree of behavioral compliance accompanied by life space relief, fostering adjustment. Marginal behavior then, may be all one expects. Traditionally, teachers act as if they expect to induce an immediate character change by exterior verbal exchange.

I. Instigating Condition

Goal.   In LSI, a specific incident (or series) calling for interference starts off the interview, but not as a moral issue, which is the traditional approach. The choice of proper timing and selection of an incident is critical. Many times it is preferable to allow certain incidents to pass by until one worthy of exploration occurs. There is usually a need for some "on the spot" managerial involvement. In LSI, direct use is made of milieu reality events. Choice of time and place of handling is selected to enforce or mitigate.

Process.   One first works to obtain the individual (or group) perception of the state of affairs. While this is partly a matter of permitting catharsis and ventilation, it is basically the mode of establishing relationship by emphasizing your real interest in the child's perceptions rather than in your opinions. It is

a matter of psychological truth rather than legal truth to which the adult is sensitive. To listen is to accept: it requires empathic feeling. Frequently the interviewer will be faced with resistance that demands tact and skill to penetrate. You end up with his perceptions, and you have already begun to size up the dynamics of the situation.

II. Testing for Depth and Spread

Goal.   Some events are, to the child, isolated incidents. Others stand for something more extensive: "I always get caught," or "I can never do anything." To what is this event attached as the child sees it? One drops many issues that seem to have no significant attachments since to the child these have little meaning. On the other hand, if what happened is a symbol of life for the child, it deserves minute attention.

Process.   What is the basic central issue involved? Is this symptomatic of general life experience? Is it attached to some deep personality aspect? ("Do teachers always pick on you?" "Are all the others leaving you out?" "You always get caught, others don't?") What is the psychological factor underlying the behavioral episode and the reason for the depth of reaction?

III. Content Clarification

Goal.   It should be noted that here the content focus is very different from the traditional approach where there is an emphasis on standardized morality and surface compliance. Nor is the concern with the fantasy, conscious and unconscious content through dreams, early conflicts, and so on as would take place in depth counseling. Nor is the emphasis only on feeling, as in the less directive efforts. It is on what happened in sequence, descriptive at this level and without implied judgment.

Process.   The teacher explores what went on: the reality is reconstructed with attached feelings and impulses recognized. It is accepted in a non-valuative way, although pupils already know we have values in ourselves. We are interested in the world as the pupil perceives it—not in the "reality" world as we would see it at this juncture.

IV. Enhancing a Feeling of Acceptance

Goal.   In truth, the way we conduct the interview is the only way we can cultivate a feeling of acceptance in the relationship with a child. Some have limited capacity to respond, but many find a really concerned, listening adult a new experience. We do not aim for a deep transference as in therapy. We aim to be seen as an understanding, helpful teacher-counselor, a role most pupils already anticipate for us.

In classical therapeutic work, significant transference is anticipated. In traditional teaching, the adult-teacher role is one of authority, paternalistic or autocratic. In LSI it is emphatic, with a deep involvement in understanding. This consists of non-interpretive utilization of basic conscious or unconscious motivations. It requires a non-defensive, assured reasonableness. It is permissive in the sense of recognizing "the right to be heard," not in condoning behavior unsuited to the setting, such as hitting or destroying. The adult accepts that behavior is caused, that change is slow and hard, that motivations must be understood—but on the ego level. Any portion of positive potential is nurtured in contrast to exclusive attention to the pathology.

Process.   Obviously it is not only what is done, but also how the basic tone is established, the acceptance, the ability one has to help the pupil while maintaining the adult role. This is a most complex condition but one many teachers can accomplish. It requires essentially non-interpretive responding to deeper feelings, which sometimes the pupil does not consciously recognize in himself. The significant aspect is to deal with the feeling behind the defense, not counter-attack the defense itself.

V. Avoiding Early Imposition of Value Judgments

Goal.   We aim to put understanding before judgment. Traditionally, teachers appeal to value a system, use threats, admonition, exhortations, and denial of impulses.

In the depth process, transference, resistance, interpretations, insight, identification, and acceptance of impulses (interpretations of unconscious material), high verbal permissiveness, acting out are interpreted. Play therapy and projective devices may be employed in the quest of the "diseased" and deepest level of difficulty. Obviously these methods are suited to the traditional therapeutic settings and not to the classroom.

Process.   In LSI, the perception of the pupil is accepted as a perception, but other perceptions are explored, too. The implications of his view are realistically contemplated in a non-punitive manner. The emphasis is on behavior and methods of coping with his problem in a more satisfactory way. Ego level interpretations may be given only on the basis of the overt data and, ideally, are acknowledged by the pupil in the life setting. Impulse control is studied, support planned, hurdle help provided, and coping skills "taught." Implications of the present behavior are faced in actuality, not as a threat. Arguments over "right" and "wrong" behavior imply the pupil does not know right from wrong, which is usually not the case, and a challenge often sets off a secondary adult-child contention. If no real (rather than abstract) violation of the rights of others has taken place, it may be impossible to find an appeal to the child anyway.

VI. Exploring the Internal Mechanics for "Change" Possibilities

Goal.   The goal here is to find what superego values or fragments are relevant in the pupil's perception of events. It is a matter of presence of guilt and anxiety *vs.* just being caught. The pupil must be free to express antisocial values. Group-related guilt reduction must be explored.

The ending of this phrase moves toward "What should be done about it?" Many issues resolve themselves at this point: on the other hand there may be extensive resistance which has to be handled over a long series of contacts.

Process.   Essentially we ask, what will help the pupil with this problem as he sees it? How can I help, or who can help? Here we get important diagnostic cues regarding his self-concept and goals as well as rationalizations. We see something of his hope or despair, his belief in "instant change." Frequently there is again resistance and denial. The worker can clarify the reality of assumptions which the pupil makes, without judgmental overtones, always looking for evidence to consider.

VII. The Two Resolution Phases

Goal. In the traditional work of teachers, surface compliance is usually demanded for whatever it is worth. In depth work, the anticipation is for eventual transfer to life situations with the expectation that sometimes things get worse in the action arena for a time. In LSI, one cannot expect great changes or even any improvement at times. The whole environment of life milieu is utilized for any relief or alterations it may have to offer. This may mean mitigation of given critical conditions, or planning and building in some support in the milieu. The limited outcome may be evidence that something more intensive in the way of help may eventually be needed—deep therapy, institutional treatment, or whatever the condition reveals. There is no supposition that, in all cases, even a tolerable situation will result. While LSI has the long view, it has to operate in the immediate, so in a sense it requires a bifocal view of events. What can we do to prevent a repetition of this behavior?

Process. (a) *Presenting the "Adult" View.* If the problem has not worked itself out to some reasonable next step, the adult at this stage begins to inject reality factors in an objective way: implications of behavior, standards, expectations. Reality limits are explained in a non-moralistic way. Why some attention must be given to the behavior is covered, but not vindictively. It may be a matter of basic social behavior or the nature of school and its inherent demands or the implications of nonconformity. Considerable skill is needed here to avoid the typical moralistic stance. At the same time adult responsibility must be acknowledged, and the nature of the real world frankly examined.

Process. (b) *Working Through to a Solution —Strategic Planning.* The reality demands are clarified and some reasonable first-step plan is developed. What is going to happen or will happen the next time? Here is where the sanctions, freedom restrictions, need for more intensive help, the special assistance, and behavior contingencies are discussed. It is essential that the plan be one which can be carried out, whether it be removal, a talk with parents, or a discussion with a third party. Thus, we are led again back to the milieu and its potentials. A pupil should be left with a feeling of milieu solidarity and support for him in his dilemma, rather than permissiveness or escapism. Vague and severe threats have no place whatsoever. Discussion of extensive and obviously not-to-happen consequences of continued limit breaking serve only to confuse the issue. On the other hand, there should be no hiding or reluctance to examine what may actually have to take place. We have to help him feel we are non-hostile and that we have hopes of really helping him cope with the difficulty. Since many pupils feel they must test any stated plan, no nonworkable program should be risked. That is, no plan is envisioned which will not be possible to conduct if the pupil needs to test it out. Here needed specialists are worked into the design and all of the school's resources are reviewed for potential help. It well may be that LSI and other methods will work in unison when the problem is a very complex one.

Worksheet on Conceptual Variations in Interview Designs with Children

	Psychodynamic	Life Space or Reality	Traditional
1. Instigating condition	General personality problem, long-term, not responding to supportive and growth correctional effort	Specific incident (or series) of behavior usually calling for "on the spot" managerial interference	Both implied but interpreted as moral issue
2. Goal	Long term expectations of gradual emergence of more healthy personality, possible regression followed by integration and eventual independence	Degree of behavioral compliance accompanied by life space relief fostering adjustment	Induce an immediate character change, exterior change
3. Setting	Office isolation away from immediate life pressures, formal setting, sequence timed	Direct use of milieu reality aspects; choice of time, place to enforce or mitigate as needed	Isolated, integrated, frequent use of group or setting for pressure

4. Relationship	Classical transference resistance inter-personal relationship	Emphatic, child identified role by adult	Adult role of authority; paternalistic, autocratic
5. Content	Conscious and unconscious, fantasy, early conflicts, projection, focus on feeling, impulse exploration	What went on, reality exploration, reconstruction with attached feelings impulses, recognized, accepted	Emphasis on the standard morality interpretation of event
6. Processes	Transference, resistance, interpretations, insight, identification, acceptance of impulses (interpretations of unconscious material), high verbal permissiveness, acting out interpreted	Causal behavior "accepted," clinical exploitation of LS events, ego-level interpretation, impulse-control balance critical, support given, explanations fostered, ego support, hurdle help, "skills" depicted, behavior implications faced	Appeal to value system, threats, admonition, exhortations, denial of impulses
7. Resolution	Eventual transfer to life situations	Support and milieu planning to mitigate critical conditions	Surface compliance or rejection

---

Article References

Bandura, Albert. Social Reinforcement and Behavior Change—Symposium, 1962. *Am. Jo. Ortho.*, 33:4, July 1963.

Caldwell, Bettye M., Leonard Hersher, Earle Lipton, and others. Mother-Infant Interaction in Monomatric and Polymatric Families. *Am. Jo. Ortho.*, 33:4, July 1963.

Caplan, G. Mental Health Consultation in Schools. Milbank Memorial Fund Proceedings, 1955 Annual Conference.

Caplan, G. (ed) *Prevention of Mental Disorders in Children.* New York: Basic Books, 1961.

Dean, S.J. Treatment of the Reluctant Client, *Am. Psych.*, 13:11, November 1959, pp. 627–630.

Dittman, A.T. and H.L. Kitchener. L.S.I. and Individual Play Therapy, *Am. Jo. Ortho.*, 29:1, January 1959, pp. 19–26.

Kitchener, Howard L. The Life Space Interview in the Differentiation of School in Residential Treatment. *Am. Jo. Ortho.*, 33:4, July 1963.

Krasner, Leonard. Reinforcement, Verbal Behavior, and Psychotherapy. *Am. Jo. Ortho.*, 33:4, July 1963.

Lindsley, Ogden R. Experimental Analysis of Social Reinforcement: Terms and Methods. *Am. Jo. Ortho.*, 33:4, July 1963.

Long, Nicholas J. Some Problems in Teaching Life Space Interviewing Techniques to Graduate Students in Education in a Large Class at Indiana University. *Am. Jo. Ortho.*, 33:4, July 1963.

Morse, William C. Working Paper: Training Teachers in Life Space Interviewing. *Am. Jo. Ortho.*, 33:4, July 1963.

Morse, W.C. and E.R. Small. Group Life Space Interviewing in a Therapeutic Camp. *Am. Jo. Ortho.*, 29:1, January 1959, pp. 27–44.

Murphey, Elizabeth B., Earle Silber, George Coehlho, and others. Development of Autonomy and Parent-Child Interaction in Case Adolescence. *Am. Jo. Ortho.*, 33:4, July 1963.

Newman, Ruth G. The School-Centered Life Space Interview as Illustrated by Extreme Threat of School Issues. *Am. Jo. Ortho.*, 33:4, July 1963.

Redl, Fritz. Strategy and Techniques of the Life Space Interview. *Am. Jo. Ortho.*, 29:1, January 1959, pp. 1–18.

Redl, Fritz. The School Centered Life Space Interview. Washington, D.C.: School Research Program, Washington School of Psychiatry, 1963.

Redl, Fritz. The Concept of Therapeutic Milieu. *Am. Jo. Ortho.*, 29:4, October 1959, pp. 721–727.

Redl, Fritz. The Life Space Interview in the School Setting—Workshop, 1961. *Am. Jo. Ortho.*, 33:4, July 1963.

Silver, Albert W. Delinquents in Group Therapy. *Am. Jo. Ortho.*, 33:4, July 1963.

Wineman, D. The Life Space Interview, *Social Work*, January 1959, pp. 3–17.

Zigler, Edward. Social Reinforcement, Environmental Conditions, and the Child. *Am. Jo. Ortho.*, 33:4, July 1963.

In a most realistic review of the psychiatric interview, Goodman[11] lists several basic methods of talking with children: speak slowly and simply; avoid the inquisition; use a "let's pretend" approach; use a natural approach; reserve searching questions until late in the interview; let the child describe the situation; and balance questions with comment and listening. This material is excellent reading for all who talk with youngsters. Glasser has also been an exponent of new and productive ways to work with children. Although he emphasizes the contrast between ego-level and depth approaches, his reality interviewing both on a more traditional basis,[12] and in a group process,[13] are close to the concepts developed here in life space interviewing, which functions on both a one-to-one and group basis.

There is increasing attention to group forces in behavior management and change. In fact, some have said every effective treatment for adolescents depends on group forces. Certainly, when it comes to delinquents, programs like the "Positive Peer Culture" have opened encouraging new possibilities[14] and deserve the attention of all special education teachers.

The next paper in this series shows a most astute use of group goals as a contingency for management (see also Chapter 3). Graubard has a reputation for dealing with difficult inner city teaching conditions and for applying no-nonsense approaches. Again we are shown how a theoretical reward can be the reverse. In this case starting with teacher praise and academic success discouraged what the teacher wanted to encourage because these "rewards" had a negative group valence. In a subculture where school failure is the expected outcome, delinquents reject school as it usually is presented to them. School is a signal for battle.

The author weaves an understanding of what took place by going back and forth between individual and group goals. These youth are basically more defensive about failing than about school learning. When external conditions are arranged to prove to them that they can achieve, they respond with effort and ability that has not been apparent before in their school careers.

The Use of
Indigenous Grouping as the
Reinforcing Agent in Teaching
Disturbed Delinquents to Learn
Paul S. Graubard

It has been demonstrated that the use of teacher praise and attention in its own right can effectively modify the behavior of low achieving and obstreperous children (Hall, *et al.*, 1968). Other studies report that token reinforcement productively changed behavior with the emotionally disturbed (O'Leary and Becker, 1967), the retarded (Bijou, 1966), the culturally deprived (Wolf, Giles, and Hall, 1968) and with a culturally deprived juvenile delinquent (Staats and Butterfield, 1965).

The Staats and Butterfield study was limited in that only a single S was worked with outside of the group, and the teacher did not have to contend with antisocial behavior reinforced by peers. Peers are, of course, a fact of life in school situations. Thus, a study by Zimmerman and Zimmerman (1962) found that teacher praise acted to decrease academic performance in direct contrast to the Hall study. Peer reinforcement might account for the different results of the two studies, for in certain subcultures the peer group can be a more powerful reinforcer than the teacher. Nevertheless, the effect of the peer group is largely unexplored in the educational liter-

Reprinted from an article based on a paper delivered to the 76th Annual Convention of the American Psychological Association, August 30, 1968. Reprinted by permission of the author.

ature, and clinical experience and sociological theory suggest that many learners are caught up in the battle between peer and school values. These students probably comprise a sizeable proportion of the educational casualties in schools. Enough theory has been generated to warrant attacking this problem directly.

The Culture of the Delinquent

For example, Cloward and Ohlin have suggested that the school represents a value system and a way of life that is unacceptable to urban delinquents. Thus a delinquent who is successful in school according to school norms does achieve at the risk of loss of status in his group.

Cloward and Ohlin (1960) have also argued that because of differential opportunities certain rewards of society are denied to many youngsters. These individuals then band together to form a delinquent subculture which is capable of developing its own reward system. Finally, Parsons (1954) maintains that school and academic learning are perceived as unmasculine by delinquents and predelinquents. The group is formed to consolidate a masculine front as imposing as the demands of the schools. Parsons maintains that this is particularly true in urban areas where the female-centered household is more common. In the face of all this, the general pattern is to attempt to win individual students over to the traditional social values of success and reward. This, the "artichoke technique," is not universally successful because of the limited battery of rewards available to the teacher as well as the relatively low power and status of the school when compared with the peer group; and clinical evidence has found (Minuchin, Chamberlain, and Graubard, 1967) that rewards and teaching coming from peers are more effective than rewards and teaching associated with authority figures (for example, teachers) with disturbed delinquents.

The primary purpose of this project then was to ascertain whether the delinquent peer culture could explicitly be enlisted in the acquisition of academic skill and the diminution of anti-school behavior, and to determine if children could learn more effectively and efficiently utilizing the peer group as the reinforcing agent rather than the teacher. Another purpose of the study was to examine the process of how disruptive groups could be managed and taught by a clearly explicated teaching method.[1]

Method

Subjects.   Ss were 8 boys in residential treatment through court order for anti-social behaviors. They formed an indigenous group in that they comprised the residential population of an agency and made up a delinquent subculture within the agency. Ss had lived together for approximately one year. They ranged in age from 10 to 12. They carried psychiatric diagnoses of varying types although the label "undifferentiated" is the most descriptive (Auerswald, 1964). IQ's ranged from 74 to 112. Reading levels ranged from third to sixth grade. Aggressive children were given priority for the classroom.

Classroom.   Sessions were held at a University classroom four days a week for a one-month period during the summer. At the investigator's request counselors did not escort children to and from the classroom. The room, which was similar to public school classrooms in New York City, was set up as a self-contained unit. The room was equipped with a one-way vision mirror and closed-circuit television equipment.

Instructional program.   The teaching day was divided into several segments: a reading period where SRA and Sullivan materials were utilized, an arithmetic period where work sheets were made up, a dramatics period, a social studies discussion period, and a free time if work had been completed with no anti-social conduct displayed during the school day. During this free time Ss were allowed to play games, but the children generally elected to bring their own records and phonograph and dance.

Data recording.   Direct observation of Ss was utilized for the study. Observers, stationed behind a one-way mirror, observed the class for two 24-minute periods each hour. Ss did not know *when* they were being observed although they were fully aware that there was an observer. The observer checked off the action of each S by going down the list of names every 10 seconds for a three minute period. Each S was observed approximately 36 times per hour or 108 times per school morning. Using an observation schema adapted from Becker, *et al.* (1967), Ss were given an "A" for appropriate behavior which was defined as following directions, eyes on work, writing, speaking to the teacher or to peers about school matters, or engaging in following school routines or teacher instruction. Ss could also receive an "I" for Inappropriate Behavior which was defined as disrupting the class, cursing, throwing objects, hitting, being out of seat without permission, and talking without permission. Ss could also receive an "E" for Excused Absence which was defined as going to the bathroom with permission, going for a drink with permission, etc. A more fine breakdown of both appropriate and inappropriate behavior was kept to help us plan programs for individual Ss, but these different behaviors can be subsumed under "A" or "I" for this report. The only school rules which were put into effect were (a) attendance was mandatory (this was an agency requirement), (b) Ss could not destroy property, (c) Ss could not use physical force. (Infraction of these rules meant that Ss had to leave school for the day. This happened a few times during Non-Contingent Teaching Condition A, only one time during Group Contingencies B, and no times during C, Group and Individual Contingencies.)

The observer ratings were checked by two other judges and agreement never fell below 92 percent. This reliability was calculated a minimum of three times each week and never fell below the 92 percent level. Reliability was calculated by Total Numbers of Agreement over Total Numbers of Observation Times 100.

Design

The class was taught under several different conditions. In each case the teacher's performance was continually monitored by two judges to insure that she followed the required (pre-set) teaching conditions. Three conditions were used. The first was Group 1 in which group consensus was evolved for rewards. The Ss selected kites, goldfish, shirts, baseball bats, marbles, and money. Points were assigned to each of these given rewards and the acquisition of these rewards was contingent upon *each* S in the group achieving a minimum number of points. Points could be earned for following school rules and achieving specified outputs of academic work (this was explicitly defined for each subject area). Management of the classroom was given over to the Ss. A bonus bell was rung at variable intervals. At first it was rung frequently (once every four minutes or less) on a random schedule and then at longer intervals. If everyone was behaving appropriately when the bell rung, each S earned 10 bonus points.

The bonus bell was based on the assumption that the more that Ss displayed appropriate behavior the more likely they were to be rewarded. It was used for each condition although it was used less and less as the project progressed.

Group consensus was followed by non-contingent rewards. During this condition the same academic routines and work were followed, but points were awarded regardless of their behavior, and teacher praise, grades, and exhortation were used. In addition, the teacher intervened during periods of obstreperous behavior, wheras under Group consensus obstreperous and inappropriate behavior were ignored.

After the non-contingent teaching, the group consensus was then reinstated. Finally the last condition was initiated. During this condition (Group and Individual) Ss still *each* had to achieve minimum behavior and academic points to win group prizes, but the prizes were changed to snacks such as southern fried chicken, cake, and pizza. Individuals were then allowed to work for their own self-selected prizes, which were again made contingent upon achieving specified numbers of combined academic and behavior points. During the beginning of the project behavior points were worth twice as much as academic points but as the sessions progressed, these procedures were reversed.

Results

The dependent variables in this study were amounts of appropriate and inappropriate classroom behaviors and reading grade levels. Reading gains were measured by progression from lower level SRA material to SRA material of a higher grade level. Each S was able to read and comprehend material at least two color cards above his own baseline during the course of the 20 session project.

Figure 1 shows how Ss performed during each condition. Since conditions were run for different lengths of time and since Ss were absent for varying lengths of time because of dental visits, etc., the most meaningful comparison seems to be percent of behaviors based on total number of observations for each teaching condition.

The probability values of the changes in behavior have been calculated by the Median Test (Siegal 1956) and are shown in Table 1.

Two things must be said about the results.

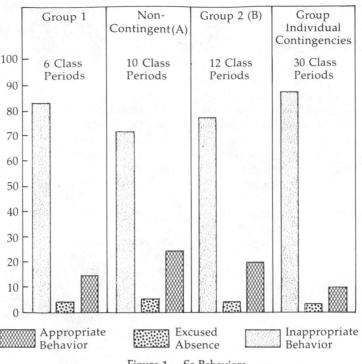

Figure 1.   Ss Behaviors
During Different Teaching Conditions

1.   As the sessions progressed Ss had to complete increasingly longer assignments to achieve the same number of points, while the behavior points decreased in value.

2.   For purposes of this study cursing was considered an Inappropriate Behavior. During the Group conditions the majority of "I's" were received for cursing, an act which appeared to receive tremendous group reinforcement. Given a teacher with a high tolerance level for four letter words the "I" behaviors would have decreased to practically zero.

Discussion

The data shows that the procedures used in this classroom were effective in increasing the academic output of the group, in shaping appropriate classroom behaviors, and in eliminating disruptive behaviors. In fact, during the individual reward condition, for 3 days of the 6 day period there were only two or less disruptive incidents observed in a class that had been especially picked for aggressive behavior, and that had a long history of failure in and expulsion from public schools. While the design of this study does not allow us to gauge the rel-

Table 1. Probability Levels of Change in Behavior during Different Teaching Conditions

Conditions	A	E	I
Non-contingent vs. Gp. 2*	.04	n.s.	.02
Gp. 2 vs. Gp. and Individual	.01	n.s.	.01
Gp. and Individual vs.			
Non-contingent	.005	.02	.005

*Due to the small number of days during Group 1, significance between Group 1 and Non-contingent teaching is not possible to obtain by the Median Test and therefore no statistical analysis was made, but inspection of Figure 1 shows the trend of the direction of the changes.

ative efficiency of this method compared to other approaches such as going directly from non-contingent to individual rewards for example, the fact that this group was able to learn and behave in school is important in and of itself.

The process by which this occurred is worth analyzing, albeit speculatively. The fact that the group gave its consensus for rewards appears to be an important part of the process. Academic prowess and classroom conformity are not values that are highly admired by this population (Brown, 1965; Parsons, 1954). Great pressure is put on children not to conform to rules of authority (Polsky, 1964), and severe punishment is meted out by their peers to those children who do violate peer values. It is felt by this speaker that the group must consciously legitimize learning so that the individuals in the group do not have to concern themselves with loss of status for learning. This is not unlike family therapy where explicit permission must be given by a particular family member before a given topic can be discussed by individuals. In the group reward condition learning is reinforced by the group since the group benefits from the performance of the individual. While there is no direct evidence from this study, it is doubtful if many individuals are strong enough to resist the mores of the delinquent group vis-à-vis school achievement. There is some indirect evidence for this statement since intelligence for delinquents is practically normally distributed (Prentice and Kelly, 1963), but reading levels are consistently low for the majority of delinquent children and achievement is *not* normally distributed.

Once the group had sanctioned learning there was a sudden shift in the performance of individuals and disruptions began to decrease. While group rewards appear to be considerably better than noncontingent payoff, Condition C, group and individual rewards, was introduced because the

eventual goal was to bring these *S*s into the mainstream of education and to have them work with only minimal dependence on the group. In addition, there was a concern about a *least-effort* effect where *S*s would only work to achieve the group minimum. This same effect has also been noted in work with infrahumans.

Individual rewards were then introduced so *S*s could receive rewards in excess of those achieved by the group, and these rewards were contingent on the *S*s own effort. Under this condition, after they had received the group's permission to learn, a dramatic increase in learning was noted with a consequent decrement of disruptive behavior.

The fact that the group took responsibility for itself, gave individual members permission to learn, and could concretely achieve its own goals and rewards appears to have been the paramount factor in the success of this project.

The group managing itself is not unlike aspects of the civil rights struggle where groups and communities will manage themselves, but will not be told what to do. To date, there has been little consonance between the world of disturbed, delinquent children and the school. Instead of being cognizant of, negotiating with, and enlisting the support of the group, educators have traditionally ignored it, and usually this has been done at the expense of the teacher and the children.

Article Footnote

1.   The author gratefully acknowledges the assistance of Sara Unobskey, formerly Director of the Yeshiva University Special Education Demonstration Center, who taught the class.

Article References

Auerswald, E. Developmental effects of poverty in children of hard core urban families: Implications for nosology and treatment. Paper presented to American Orthopsychiatric Association, 1964.

Bijou, S.W. Functional analysis of retarded development, in N.R. Ellis (ed.), *International review of research in mental retardation.* New York: Academic Press, 1966, Vol. 1, 1–19.

Brown, C. *Manchild in the Promised Land.* New York: Macmillan Co., 1965.

Cloward, R., and L. Ohlin. *Delinquency and Opportunity: A Theory of Delinquent Gangs.* Glencoe, Ill.: Free Press, 1960.

Hall, V., D. Lund, and D. Jackson. Effects of teacher attention on study behavior. *Journal of Applied Behavior Analysis,* 1968, *1,* 1–12.

For some children little basic self-control can be achieved without therapeutic assistance. Although individual therapy is not an essential ingredient for control for many children, even when it is, the teacher may find either no assistance available or only episodic, superficial contact, which is even more disconcerting. Therapy is discussed at length in Chapter 3 but should be related also to management problems.

If the teacher takes the ecological model seriously, classroom control may sometimes depend on external changes in the community or the family. Negative build-up from the group or the family can be too much to be dissipated in the classroom. Community mental health has only begun to demonstrate the need to reduce conditions that produce such acting out. But unhygienic influences of poverty, discrimination, and family maladjustment will erode the mental health of youngsters for many years. Traditional approaches are effective against some negative family influences, but the resources are very limited. New approaches to lower-class families and the use of family meetings associated with the school are discussed elsewhere.

Yet the teacher's frustration when problems stem from the "unreachable" family is a source of many control anxieties. One suggestion is to encourage the social agencies to provide "big brothers" and "sisters" so that long-term identifications can be facilitated even though the family cannot be changed. However, the teacher can also try to replace some of the damaging effects of a family by working only with the children.

Involvement with parent associations and individual parents is a necessary management skill for teachers of the disturbed youngster. There are new ways of helping by "teaching" parents rather than "changing" them by traditional therapy. An interesting demonstration has shown that didactic and dynamic elements can be combined in work with parents.[15] When this general process is applied to the school situation, parents are expected to cause change in themselves and in their children through group meetings. The school is an excellent place through which to design such a program. Teachers are encouraged to think of ways to use the school to help parents reduce the pressure on children—pressure that results in management problems in the classroom. Teachers no longer have to give up when the parents are unreachable by traditional techniques. In all probability, special class teachers will soon move from the typical parents' meeting to group-generated parent involvement in organized efforts to help through educational rather than therapeutic roles.

The following article clarifies many of the problems in working with parents. The approach is one of mutual problem-solving.

Conference or Confrontation
Sheila Murphy

All teachers are faced with the uncomfortable prospect of communicating to parents their child's behavioral and academic problems. There are such children in almost every classroom, and each teacher must attempt what at times seems the impossible task of seeking an understanding with the parents, which could lead to a unified effort to discover the causes of the problems and to develop a realistic school and home approach to help the troubled child. This article will isolate and examine some of the elements in a parent-teacher conference that contribute to its success or failure.

A conference is *not* a substitute for a written report; reports or notes are a vital communication link between home and school whether they give or seek information. Writing forces clarity of thought and has the additional advantage of being open for repeated reference and review. A teacher, however, cannot know the effect a letter or report has on the family. Whether parents misread a report or read it accurately and disagree, they do not have the opportunity to respond quickly. Exchanges of written communications can lead to superficial

agreement or disagreement based on no working relationships at all. Therefore, conferences are an essential supplement whenever parents or teacher feel more than an informational exchange is needed.

The conferences requested by the teacher to discuss pupil behavioral and academic problems *must* have two goals: the mutual exchange of information and, more importantly, initiation of a cooperative effort to help the child. This cooperative effort may lead to working on classroom changes, instituting new ways to structure or modify the child's home environment, seeking outside assistance, or simply agreeing to maintain close home-school communication. In pursuit of this second goal, a conference not only allows for two-way communication, but has the potential for attaining a working relationship between parents and teacher.

Five components of a successful conference which can significantly contribute to a more complete understanding of the child and a beginning cooperative relationship are:

1. The Search for a Mutual Perception of the Child

The Search for a Mutual Perception of the Child

Unless a teacher runs her classroom like a household or parents teach reading and arithmetic at home, a child's behavior is not necessarily the same in both settings. A home is usually less structured than school, is infrequently task-oriented, rarely contains 20–30 siblings, and has different relationships. No teacher can look over her classroom and point out the children who are bed-wetters, and parents may have similar difficulties observing academic or social behavior at school. Because the pressures, demands, and relationships are different in the two environments, it is logical that a child's behavior will vary also. The initial difficulty both parents and teacher have in believing the report of the other doesn't necessarily mean either is distorting, denying, or being defensive. A child may not be perceived in the same way because his behavior is not the same.

At the beginning of the conference a teacher must begin with a description of the difficulty, but very soon she must interrupt to inquire whether the description sounds like anything the child does at home. For instance, "Does Kevin seem restless and jumpy?" "In the neighborhood does Kevin get into arguments quickly?" "Do you notice Jan daydreaming or preoccupied when she's with you?" Even more basic first questions might well be, "How does John talk about school?" "Have you heard from him anything about trouble at recess?" "Does he complain about the work?" "Has he seemed angry about me or the class?"

The teacher should also try to imagine situations at home that might elicit the same disruptive or depressed behavior and then inquire about the child's behavior during these times. For example, a hyperactive child may not watch TV because he's too restless to sit through a program even though younger siblings have enough attention span.

If this part of the conference reveals no mutuality of perception, the focus should then become: "I wonder why John sounds so different at home than he is in school?" The parents might feel the difficulty is with the teacher or the school. Again

questions are important. "Is this the first year he's had this trouble?" "What were previous school experiences like?" "How is he in church, nursery school, Hebrew school?" "Is this his first structured group?" There might have been a change in the home: a move, new baby, death, etc.

It is very helpful to have both parents attend the conference if it is at all possible. They might have different perceptions of their child, and these differences can also lend themselves to exploration. If only one parent is present at the conference or in the home, it is beneficial to ask whether the child responds to the absent parent as he does to the observable one. All of these questions help to get a clearer picture of the child, his feelings and reactions.

Because a teacher has two goals for this conference (mutual exchange of information and relationship building), the need for some common understanding on even one aspect of the child is essential. Otherwise, the possibility of a cooperative approach is remote. Agreement might be attained on something as vague as the child's unhappiness with school, or his anger at other children, or it might become more specific—he is overly restless, or slow to learn new tasks, or very lonely, or quick to become frustrated.

This search for some common home-school perception is easier said than done. It is, however, an essential task. Parents and teachers have to agree on at least a partial definition of the difficulty if they are to cooperate in its amelioration.

Communication: What Is Sent and Received

The teacher, in her eagerness to relate the child's problems, may not be communicating what she intends. Independent of the parents' awareness of their child's classroom problems, when they listen to the teacher they hear two things: what the teacher is saying and how she *feels* about it. The child's behavior may be causing disruption and anger in the classroom, but this anger can sound as if it were directed at both the child and his parents. It is helpful to discuss the conference ahead of time with a supervisor or consultant—someone not directly involved with the child—so that the teacher can sort out his own reactions to the child and also his anticipations of the parent. If the teacher expects the parents to be angry, he might begin the conference in a defensive way by attempting to prove a case rather than initiating discussion. This "overkill" of data is likely to make parents defensive and angry or simply overwhelm them. A discussion before the conference may make the teacher more relaxed and objective.

When parents ask questions or respond to the teacher, they too are communicating both content and feeling, and the teacher has the choice of responding to either aspect of communication. The teacher must, of course, respond to the verbal content, but at times the parents' feelings must have priority. If the parent expresses intense feelings, it is impossible for the teacher to continue any useful discussion that could lead to a mutual understanding. A teacher must stop and address these feelings directly: "I guess it feels like everyone's been critical of John"; "It sounds like you've been feeling totally frustrated with the low report cards after you've tried so many different things"; "If you are working two jobs and have four children, all you *need* right now is a new problem." This lets the parents know that the teacher understands them and also helps to separate the feelings from the task of dealing with the child's problem.

Another aspect of communication is the quantity and timing of information given to the parent. Parents cannot absorb in a few minutes what a teacher has been observing for weeks or months. It is necessary to allow parents time to clarify what is being said, or ask questions, or disagree, shortly after the conference is started. The longer the teacher talks before starting a dialogue with the parents, the more intense feelings and generalized questions the parents will have. Communication also means the teacher must know when to stop talking.

Descriptive Behavior vs. Conclusions

After working with a child in a classroom for an extended period of time, every teacher has formed many assumptions and conclusions about that child. When the teacher meets the parents, it is natural for her to want to test the validity of her ideas. At a first meeting, however, the parents won't be at this point. Indeed, they have also formed some assumptions and conclusions about the child, his school, and teacher that may be totally different. For example: John sleeps through reading, the first activity every morning. The teacher, after trying to wake him up for weeks, is convinced he is allowed to stay up too late. At home John might talk about the boring teacher whose reading class is deadly. If the conference is started with the conclusion, "John's bedtime is too late and prevents him from paying attention in class," genuine communication

is already thwarted. The parents will immediately feel an attack and respond with *their* own conclusions.

A description of a child's behavior should be nonjudgmental and allow many possible causes to be mutually explored: physical problems, a learning disability that doesn't allow him to stay at class level (so he avoids anxiety by sleeping), poor sleeping arrangements at home, emotional problems that prevent him from sleeping even when he's sent to bed, etc.

A teacher can't control the parents' unwarranted assumptions, but she *can* attempt to gear the conference to *explore* behavior and problems rather than to merely trade conclusions.

Direct Discussion

Sometimes it is tempting to approach a specific discussion of a tense situation gradually. If a child is failing in class, it can often seem more compassionate only to imply the consequences of a child's current performance. This technique often has the reverse effect on parents; if the problem is vague and not clearly understood, or even if the parents do understand but hesitate to push the conclusion, communication gets more and more tense. If the teacher can matter-of-factly yet directly discuss the difficulty, both parents and teacher are usually relieved.

It is sometimes harder for parents to be direct, particularly if they disagree. A teacher can facilitate a working relationship by helping them clarify their thoughts. If they describe something that seems unfair at school, it is a relief to the parents if the teacher can restate it directly: "John sounds like he feels I am being very hard on him"; "It sounds like the classwork is boring to John"; "He seems to be saying he hates this classroom." In this way, the conference becomes focused rather than vague. The focus may be painful, but it has the potential for a realistic discussion.

The Contract

Hopefully, the end of the conference is the beginning of a home-school alliance. Therefore, the conference should not signal the end of communication. The teacher can make this clear by scheduling another conference in a month, suggesting the mother call her in two weeks to discuss whether the child's behavior has changed, arrange to send home a brief note of the child's daily or weekly progress, or let the parents know when she is available by telephone. Whatever the means, the teacher ends the conference by arranging further communication.

The exact areas discussed and the next steps to be taken should also be very clear at the end of the conference. Sometimes the only agreement may be to wait and see if the situation improves. More often, the conference decides on some specific action by home or school. Whatever the outcome, a clear summary should be stated or given to the parents in writing so that further communication can begin where the meeting ended.

This limited examination of one kind of parent-teacher conference (one called by the teacher when a child needs behavioral or academic help) has discussed its dual goals, and five aspects of communication that maximize the conference's potential for success. Understanding this "skeleton conference" is useful, but of course each conference also has its unique flesh and blood—the people participating.

What Happens When Communication Is Blocked?

There are times when a teacher has no communication with parents. Their anxiety or anger at the school may prevent any meaningful exchange, or they may be too angry with the child to see any possibility of change. Sometimes, other family problems leave no energy for helping their child. Economic, medical, or marital problems may realistically have higher family priority.

There are also times when a teacher reacts to a particular child or parent with strong anxiety or anger—an inevitable and normal occurrence. No one can change shape or personality like an amoeba to suit every other personality.

When available, outside consultants are useful in attempts to evaluate parents' reactions and their possible causes. At times, consultants can chair the conference which may be less anxiety-producing for parents who have a negative relationship with the school. The consultant is seen as an outsider, a noninvolved person who is also nonaligned. Teachers with great self-awareness may wish to invite a consultant to the conference when their own feelings about child, parents, or their own involvement in the situation might lessen their effectiveness.

It is important that a record of the conference and its results (or lack of results) be left in the child's file so the next teacher can build on what was attempted. Thus, in the second or third conference, or from the second or third teacher, parents can see their child's persistent problems. Although an initial conference may produce no immediate understanding, consistent approach may make a later conference successful.

Some conferences will always fail. The more aware the teacher is of some of the pitfalls to be avoided in a conference, the lower the percentage of painful, nonproductive ones. The ideas discussed in this article will hopefully contribute to achieving a maximum use of the parent-teacher conference.

Kounin and his associates have done extensive work on discipline of normal and disturbed children in regular classrooms, using both filmed sequences and immediate observation. The study yields several important findings. It shows the interrelation of discipline and pupil work involvement and the group nature of effective control techniques. He also shows the multiple-level functioning of successful teachers: they react to individual and group behavior and to academic and social responses with a varied sequence of strategies. Many clinical workers find this skill most difficult to achieve. It is interesting that Kounin and Obradovic have found it helpful to use new terms to explain the elements of effective discipline, which they see as teaching —running a classroom—rather than imitating the roles of other professionals.

Managing Emotionally Disturbed
Children in Regular Classrooms:
A Replication and Extension

Jacob S. Kounin
Sylvia Obradovic

In a previous study based on observation of elementary school classrooms containing one or more emotionally disturbed children, Kounin, Friesen, and Norton (1966) concluded that teachers who were successful in managing the behavior of non-disturbed children in a classroom were also successful in managing the behavior of emotionally disturbed children in the classroom. This conclusion was based upon the following findings:

1. A significant positive correlation between the *work involvement* scores of disturbed and non-disturbed children in the classroom.

2. A significant positive correlation between the *deviancy* scores of the disturbed and non-disturbed children.

3. A significant correlation between the *deviancy-contagion* scores of the disturbed children and the *deviancy* and *work involvement* scores of the non-disturbed children.

4. A delineation of specific teacher techniques that correlated significantly in the same direction and approximate magnitude with the behavior of both the disturbed and the non-disturbed children.

These findings were arrived at through analysis of videotapes recorded for a half-day each in 30 elementary school classrooms. Because there were some differences between the first two grades and the upper grades and between seatwork and recitation subsettings (e.g., arithmetic lesson, reading lesson), the breakdowns for grade level and subsetting resulted in some quite small N's.

The present study attempted both to replicate

and extend the earlier study. To obtain a better sample of both seatwork and recitation subsettings for all teachers, the number of classrooms for the first two grades was increased. In addition, the recording time for each time for each class was extended.

Method

The activities in 50 first and second grade classrooms were videotaped for a full day each. (The recording technique was described in the previous study.) Because the recording for one classroom could not be used, the final usable N was 49 classrooms, 24 located in a predominantly middle class suburb of Detroit, Michigan, and 26 located in metropolitan Detroit.

To exclude "extreme" classrooms from the study, only schools whose average achievement scores fell between the 20th and 80th percentiles of the school system's norms were used. The schools selected were large enough to have at least two classrooms for each grade, and one "poor" and one "good" classroom were selected per school—this judgment being based upon whether the children in the classroom showed high or low degrees of work involvement. The designation of children as "emotionally disturbed" was based upon a consensus among the teacher, principal, and, in most cases, a school social worker. Where the child was on a waiting list for the school social worker but had not had a professional diagnostic work-up, the principal investigator accepted a consensus between the principal and teacher, along with some obvious pathological circumstances (such as a child in the first grade being in his fourth foster home).

The sample of children for scoring was selected by the project director from diagrams of the seating arrangements for each academic subsetting in each classroom. Each diagram was divided into four quadrants and a boy and girl from each quadrant

From "Managing Emotionally Disturbed Children in Regular Classrooms: A Replication and Extension," by Jacob S. Kounin and Sylvia Obradovic, *The Journal of Special Education*, Vol. 2, No. 2, 1968, pp. 129-135. Reprinted by permission of *The Journal of Special Education*. The research reported here was supported by Public Health Service research grants from the National Institute of Mental Health.

selected for scoring. The emotionally disturbed children were scored separately.

Each child finally selected for scoring was coded for *work involvement* and *deviancy* every 12 seconds for the duration of a specific academic subsetting, the 12-second interval being used to accommodate the timing device on the videotape machine. For *work involvement*, the children were rated as to the number of times they were considered to be: (a) definitely doing their assigned work; (b) probably doing the work; or (c) definitely not working. The ratio of ratings for "definitely not working" was used as the score for *work involvement*. For *deviancy*, the children were coded as: (a) not misbehaving; (b) engaging in mild misbehavior; (c) engaging in serious misbehavior. The *deviance* score was the percentage of 12-second units in which no misbehaviour occurred. (All scores, for children and teacher, were stated in a hypothesized positive order.) Intercoder reliabilities for different sets of coders ranged from 82% to 100% agreement, with a mean of 95%.

A teacher's managerial success in the classroom was defined by her ability to induce work involvement and prevent deviancy in the children with whom she worked. A detailed description of the categories in which teachers were scored will be given below. To avoid coloring teacher scores with children's behavior scores, different individuals were used to score teachers than to score children. (There was one exception. The coder for *accountability* and *group alerting* for teachers in recitation subsettings also coded children's behavior, but a period of about one year separated the two codings.) Intercoder reliabilities for teacher styles ranged from 79% to 99% agreement, with a mean of 92% agreement.

Findings

There were no significant differences, by *t* test, between the scores of disturbed and non-disturbed children for either *work involvement* or *deviancy*, or in seatwork or recitation subsettings. The correlation between the scores of disturbed and non-disturbed children were .764 for work involvement and .818 for deviancy in recitation subsettings and .567 for work involvement and .649 for deviancy in seatwork settings. These correlations support the conclusion that a teacher's degree of success in managing the classroom as a whole is related to her degree of success in managing the behavior of the emotionally disturbed children in the class. A more precise formulation of this conclusion requires (a) a delineation of what it is that teachers do that makes a difference in how children behave in their classrooms and (b) a determination of whether these techniques have the same effect upon disturbed and non-disturbed children. Table 1 summarizes the correlations between various teacher techniques and the behavior of the emotionally disturbed and non-disturbed children in the classroom. The correlations for the non-disturbed children are shown in parentheses. With few exceptions, the correlations obtained for disturbed children and non-disturbed children are in the same direction and approximate magnitude.

Three conclusions may be drawn from these correlations:

1.   Specific teacher techniques, which can be delineated, do determine how children behave in a classroom.

2.   These techniques are *group* management techniques.

3.   They have about the same effect upon emotionally disturbed children as upon non-disturbed children.

A description of the various teacher techniques rated in the study follows.

Management Categories and Techniques

For the purposes of the study and categorization of teacher behavior, a set of descriptive codewords was used.

The codewords *slowdowns* and *smoothness* relate to a teacher's initiation and maintenance of the class's movement. Slowdowns refers to the manner in which a teacher maintains movement during a particular classroom activity and during the transition from one activity to another; it designates teacher-initiated friction that impedes the group's rate of movement. Slowdowns are created by the forms of teacher behavior classified and coded as follows:

Overdone.   This was used when the teacher engaged in actions or a stream of talk that clearly exceeded what was necessary to get the children to understand or participate in an activity (behavior that would elicit the reaction, "All right, that's

Table 1. Product-Moment Correlations between Teacher Styles and the
Behavior of Children in Academic Settings*

| | Recitation (N = 49) | | Seatwork (N = 48) | |
Teacher Style Dimension	Children's Work Involvement	Children's Deviancy	Children's Work Involvement	Children's Deviancy
Slowdowns	.528	.621	.494	.409
	(.656)	(.641)	(.198)	(.490)
Withitness	.510	.415	.537	.472
	(.615)	(.531)	(.307)	(.509)
Smoothness	.501	.399	.518	.136
	(.601)	(.489)	(.382)	(.421)
Overlappingness	.485	.213	.414	.271
	(.460)	(.362)	(.259)	(.379)
Group alerting	.434	.311	.385	.334
	(.603)	(.442)	(.234)	(.290)
Valence-challenge	.335	.406	.304	.346
	(.372)	(.325)	(.308)	(.371)
Accountability	.269	.206	.086	.124
	(.494)	(.385)	(.002)	(−.035)
Seatwork variety and challenge	.042	.043	.284	.154
	(.061)	(.033)	(.516)	(.276)
Highest multiple correction	(.812)	(.720)	(.685)	(.741)

*A correlation of .279 is significant at the .05 level; a correlation of .361 is significant at the .01 level. Correlations for nondisturbed children are given in parentheses.

enough already!"). It was applied to the following categories of teacher behavior.

Behavior overdone. "Nagging," "preaching," or "moralizing" about the behavior of the class or of a particular child.

Prop and action overdone. Talking too much or dwelling too long on subactions (how to sit, where to put hands) or "props" (pencils, crayons, books) to the point of obscuring the task or its purpose.

Task overdone. Elaborating the task or task directions beyond the point where most children clearly understood and were ready to proceed.

Sheer overtalk. Excessive talking that could not be clearly classified in the above categories.

Target fragmentation. This was used when the teacher directed individual children or small groups of children to do separately what the entire group could do at once—producing a drag in classroom movement and unnecessary delays for the other children. Thus, instead of directing a group of children to go to the "reading circle," the teacher might tell Johnny to go to the circle, then Mary, then Robert, until all were finally seated there.

Prop fragmentation. Equivalent to target fragmentation except that the teacher causes the

slowdown by directing the children to handle "props" separately when they could be managed in an unbroken unit of behavior.

The term smoothness was applied in connection with a teacher's manner of initiating and sustaining movement in the group. *Antismoothness* behaviors were coded as follows:

Dangles. Initiating an activity and then leaving it dangling to attend to something else (e.g., walking away from the group after giving a transition order, watering a plant after raising a question in arithmetic).

Truncations. The same as *dangles* except that in a *dangle* the teacher eventually resumes the activity, whereas in a *truncation* she drops it entirely.

Thrusts. A teacher's sudden bursting in on the children's activities with an order, statement, question, in such a manner as to indicate that the timing was dictated only by her own needs or desires, with no evidence, such as pausing or looking around, of sensitivity to the group's readiness to receive the new message. An everyday example of a thrust would be someone's butting in on a conversation without waiting to be noticed or attempting to ease in by listening to see what was being discussed.

Stimulus-boundedness. Equivalent to a thrust (in the sense of "jerkiness") except that here the teacher's behavior is a response to an event of some kind.

The stimulus-bounded teacher behaves as though she has no will of her own, reacting to an event as a helpless iron filing to a magnet. For example, she might be explaining an assignment or passing out papers, notice a piece of paper on the floor or a child sitting improperly (the event must be one that is not intensive, intrusive, or disruptive of the class), and become "immersed" in the event to the point of paying no attention to the major activity. This kind of behavior may be regarded as the opposite of goal-directed.

Group alerting and *accountability* were used in describing the degree to which the teacher focuses her behavior on the group as a whole, rather than on a single child, when the group is the performing unit. Thus, even though only one child in a reading group might be reading aloud, the group is regarded as the performing unit, since all the children are doing essentially the same work either by listening, reading along, or preparing to recite. The model for teacher behavior in this situation is an individual tutoring session in which the child is either listening to the tutor or performing for him and is held accountable for his alertness, knowledge, and performance. To what extent does the teacher make the classroom a replicate of this tutorial situation?

Group alerting refers to the degree to which the teacher focuses on all the children in a group during transition periods and recitations. Some forms of teacher behavior watched for in coding for group alerting are: (a) creating suspense in the classroom by pausing after a question and looking around before selecting a child to recite; (b) selecting reciters at random rather than in a predictable order; (c) alerting the children that they might be called upon to evaluate a reciter's performance; (d) circulating or deliberately looking around at the group during a child's recitation; (e) presenting a challenging issue to the group during the recitation; (f) acting in other ways indicating that the group is being kept alert and stimulated.

Accountability refers to the degree to which the teacher communicates to the children that she knows what they are doing in relation to the task during a child's recitation—her demonstrated alertness about how the children are performing the designated task. A simple measure of this alertness is the number of children called upon to recite during a given interval.

Another aspect of teacher style that was as-sessed was the teacher's ability to avoid satiation in the children in her group. The average duration of specific activities (a simple notion of "attention span") was found not to correlate with children's behavior. Nor did we feel that we could validly determine the children's feelings about their progress—probably the most important variable in slowing down the rate of satiation. We did attempt to arrive at a measure of variety and challenge in the day's program. In the previous study, the degree of variety in the class's activities, which included non-academic settings, did not correlate with the children's behavior. The latter's correlations with seatwork variety for *learning-related activities* were among the highest obtained. In the present study, variety and challenge were the highest predictors of the *work involvement* scores of non-disturbed children during seatwork, though not during recitation.

At transition points, *valence* and *challenge-arousal* were scored—the degree to which the teacher (without overtalk) attempts to instill in the children a zest for the upcoming task. Valence indicates that the teacher communicates to the children that the activity has intrinsic pleasure—"You'll like this one." Challenge refers to the teacher's communicating that the upcoming task will be intellectually challenging—"This next one is tricky"—and of course delivers on her promise with a task that does require some thought or creativity.

Seatwork variety-challenge was based upon the number of changes in assigned seatwork during a given period of time. Changes were scored in the following categories: (a) academic content (reading, arithmetic); (b) type of intellectual challenge (repetitive, rote copying tasks were scored negative and tasks requiring thought or creativity positive); (c) "props" (routine to unusual); (d) child responsibility (initiates own pace, pace set by other); (e) overt behavior mode (sedentary to active); (f) group configuration; and (g) geographic location.

Another aspect of teacher style that correlates with children's behavior is *withitness*—the degree to which the teacher demonstrates that she is tuned in on what is going on in her classroom—has the legendary "eyes behind her head." This score was based upon the percentage of "desist events"— occasions when the teacher did something to stop a child's misbehavior, selected the correct deviant, and did so on time. The following were regarded as mistakes: (a) admonishing the wrong child; (b) stopping a minor act of misbehavior when there was a more serious one taking place (scolding a child for whispering when two other children were chasing each other around the room); (c) acting too late (after contagion had set in, or the misbehavior had grown worse).

Overlappingness is a measure of the degree to which a teacher attends to two issues when confronted with two issues to handle. (This correlates highly with withitness.) Two types of events were scored: "desist incidents" and "child intrusion incidents" (as when a child from a seatwork group approaches the teacher while she is working with a reading group). Does the teacher give her attention to both demands for her attention or does she go all out to one and drop the other? For example, while working with a reading group and interrupted by a child in seatwork, a teacher high in overlappingness will do something with the reading group (scan, instruct reader to continue) while handling an intruding child, or desisting a deviant child.

Discussion

As noted above, the correlations among these various forms of teacher behavior and children's behavior indicate that it is possible to delineate concrete aspects of teacher behavior that lead to managerial success in a classroom and apply to both disturbed and non-disturbed children. These are techniques that create a classroom ecology which applies to the *group* and not merely to individual children. Advocating this approach is not a simple matter of admonishing teachers to "create rapport" or "make it interesting." Nor does it entail a pre-occupation with personality attributes such as "friendliness," "patience," "love of children," "understanding." Nor is it simply a matter of extrapolating from other adult-child relationships, whether with parents, psychotherapists, or even with tutors. Rather, the business of running a classroom is based upon a complicated technology directed towards developing a non-satiating learning program; programming for progress, challenge, and variety in learning activities; initiating and maintaining group and individual movement in classroom tasks; observing and eliciting feedback for many different events; coping with more than one event simultaneously; directing actions at appropriate targets; and doubtless others yet to be determined.

We would like to close with an opinion about priorities in the training and selection of classroom teachers, whether for emotionally disturbed children or others. We feel our research shows that techniques of group management and programming should be given more emphasis than they are presently receiving in curricula for prospective teachers. Classroom management techniques (and one might note that none of them necessitates punitiveness or restrictiveness) are neutral, enabling, and facilitate many different educational objectives. The lack of these skills puts a barrier in the way of promoting an effective classroom ecology and achieving educational objectives. Mastery of them frees the teacher to achieve a variety of objectives, including that of helping individual children.

Article Reference

Kounin, J.S., Friesen, W.V., and Norton, A.E. Managing emotionally disturbed children in regular classrooms. *Journal of Educational Psychology*, 1966. 57:1, 1–13.

A final article demonstrates the synthesis of various techniques needed by a teacher faced with a particular classroom problem. Many teachers find the management of profanity most difficult. Opinions on what a teacher should do range from such extremes as "the teacher should swear too, because it shows understanding of the kids behavior," to "swearing is to be stopped at once because it is a signal of defiance and starts contagion." Duffner illustrates how a teacher can conceptualize such a problem as swearing, get behind the symptomatic level, and apply a pragmatic set of interventions.

The Management of
Profanity for Classroom Teachers
Betsy Duffner

On the streets, profanity may trigger annoyance, anxiety, anger or possibly murder. In the classroom, inappropriate language can prove equally destructive to the learning process. The classroom context, however, should differ from the street scene by its stability and structure, which permit development of extinction strategies. Understanding the psychosocial dynamics of profanity in the classroom is a prelude to planning such strategies. This article will describe eleven underlying reasons for students' use of profanity, three possible teacher reactions, and three teaching methods of coping with disruptive language in the classroom.

Students' Use of Profanity

Habitual

In certain subcultures or city environments, profanity is as much a natural part of the language as the amenities "hello" and "good-bye" in other subcultures. A phrase like "go to hell" functions more as a conversational filler than a baiting insult. Students often react spontaneously with such language on the playground, in the cafeteria, or in the school corridor when they relate to their friends. They do not direct habitual profanity toward their teacher. A variation of habitual profanity as reported by a fourth-grade teacher illustrates the use of profanity to express pleasure.

For the first three months of school, Jerry had encouraged, demanded, and pleaded with his friend Paul to play kickball with him during recess. Paul's legs had been deformed since birth, and he had a great deal of difficulty running, let alone playing kickball. He had refused his friend's pleas and remained on the schoolyard periphery.

On the day Jerry's team was to clinch the fourth-grade championship, the line-up was one man short. Jerry begged Paul to be on his team and to save them from a loss by default. Finally, Paul gave in and agreed to play. He asked to be last at bat, but his turn finally arrived, and he moved slowly, in his broken gait, toward home plate. Jerry knew how painful this was for his friend, and he prayed that Paul would make it. The opposing pitcher rolled the ball, and Paul smacked the ball towards third base.

"Look at that son-of-a-bitch kick," shrieked Jerry.

At such moments, the teacher knows that her student's words are not destructive and that he is reacting spontaneously in his own language.

Intentional

Generating Prestige Among Peers. "Man, he's the third baddest kid in the school."

A teacher heard this statement of awe and admiration just after one of her more timid children ventured into audible profanity for the first time. It appeared to the teacher that the timid student was more aware of his impact on the other children than on the math problem he was refusing to do. For some children the necessity to maintain a peer audience is a compelling enough reason to resort to offensive language, despite the painful consequences.

Violating Adult Taboos. Children are aware of society's view of obscenity and of anxious adult reaction to obscene outbursts. Consequently, such language represents a direct attack on the teacher's values and a very effective aggressive technique during a teacher-pupil conflict.

Testing the Authority and Control of a Teacher. The first few weeks of school are a time for testing the teacher's ability to handle provocative behavior, including profanity, and his skill in protecting the educational and social environment of the classroom. At least one student is always prepared to disarm the teacher and to challenge the existent authority in the class. One teacher who was having some difficulty with new procedures for student assembly programs was confronted by a student's remark: "See, I told you guys she didn't know what the shit is going on around here." Although this behavior occurs, most pupils hope their teacher will survive the challenge and continue to function securely.

Avoiding Consequences of Behavior: The Cover-Up Technique.   Scott was pulled off the playground for initiating a fight with a student from another class. Once inside the school building he attempted to control the conversation by remarking on the physique of the female teacher present. Such tactics often obscure the original issue (in this case the fight during recess) and may prevent the teacher from dealing with the precipitating events.

Attracting Teacher's Attention.   Teacher reaction to some pupils' swearing may encourage profanity in others. When more timid students see the attention that profanity attracts, they may attempt the same tactic. "It's better to be yelled at than ignored" was the feeling of one of the more articulate youngsters who tried out this method.

Retaliating.   When a student perceives that he is being backed into a corner, that his choices have been removed, or that he is being threatened or embarrassed, he will often strike back in an attempt to hurt the teacher as much as he feels he has been hurt. The final incident in the short story "Doctor Jack-O-Lantern" (Chapter 1) accurately describes how one student caught in the turmoil of embarrassment, anger, and isolation struck back by fusing aggressive and sexual feelings into one expression.

Exploring Sexuality.   It is important for teachers to recognize that exploring sexuality is a natural part of preadolescents' development. Profane sexual language appears to be the first level of public experimentation. Students are often found giggling in corners over the mention of a sexual term. They will make up new words to stand for the tabooed phrases and whisper them to the student sitting next to them, frequently setting up a contagious chain of laughter.

Displacing Feelings.   Many teachers have been surprised during the first few minutes of class by an unwarranted profane verbal attack by one of their students, such as "Get off my ass!" When explored, the student's frustration or anger is usually connected with someone other than the teacher. The student more than likely was unable to express his feelings in the situation where they originated and subsequently blurted them in a less threatening place. (Some teachers have the same difficulty when they vent their dissatisfaction about working conditions with fellow workers instead of their boss.)

Sexual Fantasizing.   At some point in development most students have fantasies about their teachers' sex life. Pupils will frequently "pair-up" a male and female teacher in the school and imply that the two are sexually involved. Students will imagine themselves to be "courting" an attractive teacher and may make offensive phone calls or send notes proclaiming their feelings.

Eliciting Punishment for Unresolved Guilt.   When students feel they have not been punished sufficiently for a previous wrongdoing, they may break a "rule" to elicit more punishment. They know that using profanity in the classroom is usually a fairly effective way of accomplishing this goal. The following vignette illustrates how one fifth-grader was satisfied.

Larry had just won the last two games of math bingo. As the teacher was passing out the new problem cards, the champ was heard yelling a string of obscenities at the girl sitting next to him. Shocked and confused, the teacher immediately dismissed Larry from class. It was only after a grueling forty-five minute session that the school counselor discovered that Larry had cheated in the two games he had won. After the second game he was overwhelmed with guilt and consequently caused his own removal from class. To Larry, such results seemed just for his offense of cheating.

Of the above uses of profanity, a student may employ more than one at a given time, that is, he may test authority at the same time he evades consequences for behavior. In any case, teachers must respond to profane attacks, and teachers' responses to profanity vary almost as widely as children's motivations for using it. Three common inappropriate teacher reactions will be explained: intimidation, uncontrolled anger, and hurt.

Teacher's Reactions to Profanity

Intimidation

Fear.   Teachers often become frightened when they are confronted with obscene language. They may ignore the student's retort, hoping the student will stop of his own accord. Usually this response not only fails to discourage profanity, but also tacitly encourages others in the class to join in.

Embarrassment.   Most teachers have experienced challenges to their ability to accomplish a task. Failure at these times may cause feelings of embarrassment, anger, and genuine hurt. Teachers are challenged daily to elicit creativity from their students, impart new skills for better growth, and protect the learning environment of their classrooms. Some students focus on the teacher's authority and challenges her to find out if she means what she says. For instance, twelve-year-old Tony seemed determined to discover what his teacher would do if sufficiently provoked.

The class came tumbling in from a recess period still excited about their kickball game. The teacher asked the students to sit at their desks and settle down for the afternoon story time. Tony, who appeared to be in no mood for a calm period, challenged the teacher in sexually provocative terms to carry out her order: "What the fuck are you going to do about it?"

The embarrassed teacher was on the spot to prove to Tony and the rest of the class that she could maintain her authority and not look foolish in the process. She began to react more to her feelings of panic and impotence than to the student who had refused to quiet down. She felt her stomach twist slightly and her mind struggle for the most effective words. Her voice quivered as she issued meaningless threats. The class immediately sensed her shakiness and bedlam prevailed. The angry and embarrassed teacher lived with the chaos for another thirty minutes.

After school, the teacher controlled her fury and damaged pride when she faced Tony in the principal's office, but unfortunately she proceeded to punish him subtly for the next few weeks by calling him last to line up for lunch, trips to the water fountain, and class dismissal.

Anger.   Occasionally, when a student has been justly reprimanded for breaking a class rule, he responds with inappropriate language instead of the expected guilt. This can infuriate the already annoyed teacher who may, in retaliation, level a severe punishment. At this point, the student's rage could get out of control and the conflict escalate into a power struggle.

Hurt.   Most teachers have been temporarily disappointed or hurt by a student with whom they thought they had a respectful and caring relationship. Profane insults from such a student can be upsetting and difficult to understand and may lead to the same kind of retaliatory response by the embarrassed teacher.

The question before all teachers is: How can I solve this problem in a helpful way without being overwhelmed by fear, anger, or hurt? As a special education teacher of emotionally disturbed children, I have found three approaches to be successful and have a personal bias toward the psychoeducational model.

Psychoeducational Model

The psychoeducational model operates under the assumption that teachers can provide students with important tools to change their behaviors by explaining the student's motivations and feelings. Among other places, these tools are provided during the teacher-student discussion that immediately follows an incident of profanity in the classroom. During this meeting, the teacher must communicate her feelings about profanity in the classroom and make it clear that such language will not be permitted. At the same time, the teacher must make every effort to elicit and sanction the feelings of the student which led to the profanity. The teacher's understanding of the student's motivations should supply sufficient trust for the student to attempt new ways of handling frustration, fear, anger, and other strong emotions.

Let us reflect specifically on a few of the possible motives for profanity in the classroom and explore some of the tools provided by the psychoeducational model.

As stated above, the student's reasons for using inappropriate language may be conscious or unconscious. The teacher may find himself attempting to establish whether the student is intentionally, trying to be provocative with such language. The teacher might assume that testing authority, eliciting peer approval, gaining teacher attention, or avoiding accountability for behavior were the student's premeditated goals. Whether or not this assumption is accurate, the teacher's first step is to bring his observations to the conscious level (by labeling the tactic), thereby encouraging the student to look at his own behavior.

Once the student begins to talk (the important second step), the teacher is in a better position to understand the particular student's motivations and the teacher has information that will aid him in the classroom and in further discussions. For example, once Scott's teacher (see above) discovered that Scott often disguises and displaces his feelings, he was then better prepared to "call" Scott on the attempted avoidance maneuver instead of reacting to the profanity tactic itself.

Labeling gives the student words to describe his feelings and behavior—an important third step that encourages the student to think for himself and thus gain strength in coping.

The Token System

An informal reward system administered once or twice daily (for example, at the end of the morning and afternoon sessions), has encouraged students to extinguish profanity from their expression repertoire. Although the student might understand why such language is inappropriate, additional motivation and reinforcement usually increases the student's awareness of his speech and stimulates greater self-control.

Planned Punishment

A penalty of five minutes' silence, partial loss of recess time, or temporary removal of a privilege are not overly severe and act as successful reminders to the student to develop more appropriate methods of expression. The student should know ahead of time the consequences for profanity. Most students will test the teacher to see if he will, in fact, demand that they be accountable for their behavior. It is crucial that the teacher follow through with the consequence if credibility is to be maintained.

In conclusion, the teacher must be aware of why students use profanity as a method of expression. He must realize that unplanned ignoring will not only do little to alleviate the problem, but may possibly engender tacit approval and encourage group contagion. He should not underestimate the amount of guilt most children have after using provocative language in school. Most importantly, the teacher should reflect on what profanity represents to him as an individual and as an educator of children.

Summary

Hygienic management is a very complex topic, taking us from specialized techniques and whole classroom designs to the community and family influences. Teachers who have unusual difficulty in control will need consultation to unravel the causes and trace the ramifications.

It has been clear, too, that part of the problem is manpower, the right person doing the right thing at the right time. The ratio of adults to disturbed youngsters seldom approaches that which is needed. We look in vain for enough therapists, for enough available support personnel, or for smaller classroom sizes. We are going to turn more and more to new staffing patterns in the classroom, where extra hands count most. Aides, assistants, mother helpers, and older youth will contribute even one-to-one help for certain very disturbed children in the early stages of their education. Such help will be required for adequate control.

Hygienic management means helping the pupil find himself and regulate his own behavior more adequately. We seek to teach basic socialization in some cases, a sense of inner belief and security in others. These goals will not be reached without considerable human investment. To keep order is not an adequate goal for management.

Chapter 6 Footnotes

1. **Rudolf Driekurs and Loren Grey,** *A New Approach to Discipline: Logical Consequences* (New York: Hawthorn Books, Inc. 1968).

2. **D. Aspy,** *Toward a Technology for Humanizing Education* (Chicago: Research Press, 1972).

3. Page 517 in Robinson and Shaver Op cit.

4. **L.J. Wehling, and W.W. Charters,** "Dimensions of Teacher Beliefs about the Teaching Process," *American Educational Research Journal* vol. 6, no. 1 (1969): 7–30.

5. **Roland G. Thorp and Ralph J. Wetzel,** *Behavior Modification in the Natural Environment* (New York: Academic Press, 1969).

6. **C.B. Ferster,** "Arbitrary and Natural Reinforcement," *Psychological Records* 17 (July 1967): 341–347.

7. **Fredric M. Levine and Geraldine Fasnacht,** "Token Rewards May Lead to Token Learning," *American Psychologist* vol. 29, no. 11 (1974): 816–820.

8. **Albert Bandura,** "Behavior Theory and the Models of Man," *American Psychologist* vol. 29; no. 12 (1974): 859–869.

9. **Erich Fromm,** *The Anatomy of Human Destructiveness* (New York: Holt, Rinehart and Winston, 1973).

10   **Finley Carpenter,** *The Skinner Primer: Behind Freedom and Dignity* (New York: Free Press, 1974).

11.   **Jerome D. Goodman,** "The Psychiatric Interview," in *Manual of Child Psychopathology,* Benjamin B. Wolman, ed. (New York: McGraw-Hill, 1972), pp. 743–766.

12.   **W. Glasser,** *Reality Therapy* (New York: Harper & Row, 1965).

13.   **W. Glasser,** *Schools Without Failure* (New York: Harper & Row, 1965).

14.   **Harry H. Vorrath and Larry K. Brendtro,** *Positive Peer Culture* (Chicago: Aldine Publishing Co., 1974).

15.   **Michael P. Andronico et al.,** "The Combination of Didactic and Dynamic Elements in Filial Therapy," pp. 129–135, and Michael P. Andronico and Bernard G. Guerney, Jr., "Potential Application of Filial Therapy in the School Situation," pp. 371–377, in *Psychotherapeutic Agents* Bernard G. Guerney, Jr., ed. (New York: Holt, Rinehart and Winston, 1969).

7

The Evolution of Practice:
Evaluation and Innovation

Special education programs in all areas are undergoing rapid shifts, and work with disturbed youngsters is no exception. As Rhodes and Sabin[1] indicate, the development of schools and classes for disruptive and defective children parallels the compulsory education of immigrant children in the 1870s. The trend then was the development of segregated, depersonalized, often cruel custodial care. Major public school involvement in special education began in the period following World War I and was encouraged by the psychological testing movement. The mental health movement of the 1930s brought emphasis on child-guidance and extension of classes.

At present several converging emphases are causing desirable turmoil in our field: mandatory special education laws; legal actions on the right to segregate and the right to treatment; mainstream integration of special children (often following closely the development of special classes in states which only recently organized any programs); anti-institutional (humanistic) approaches; and rejection of classification schemas.[2] It should be noted that concern for educational programs for very seriously disturbed children has also seen a rapid increase with mandatory legislation. A review of studies of "children at risk" is available from the National Institute for Mental Health.[3] Out of this welter may come a new delivery system, but it will probably come only after excesses that fail to distinguish between change and progress.

There are two mainsprings of new direc-

tion: research concerned with evaluation of program impact and creative leadership. Either mode of change is not without risk, and every student who wishes to be a professional in the field will find evaluating data from these two sources a most difficult task.[4] This section cannot cover all the research, nor even sample the views of leadership. Rather, the intent is to raise some of the issues to help clarify this major professional responsibility.

On the subject of evaluative research, seldom has so little basic evidence so greatly influenced direction; the time, however, was ripe for change. At present, evaluative research is required of almost every program. In general, accountability has increased psychologically fraudulent interpretations, and often massive political implications (as with Headstart, where programs were cut because of misleading research).

As MacMillan[5] has pointed out, problems of sample, nature of clientele, diagnosis, and teacher variables (among others) confound the issue. Early exploratory studies in one field of special education are continually offered as proof of intervention ineffectiveness in other areas. Thoughtful analyzers, however, are at last beginning to consider the vast complications in program evaluation. For example, Kendall[6] has given intensive thought to some basic concepts around segregated vs. integrated special education. Because most emotionally disturbed pupils have always been "mainstreamed," we do know certain hazards; among Kendall's eight variables to be considered in efficacy research are attitudes of teachers and children and the "goodness of fit" of the curriculum experience in both the integrated and isolated setting. We know that the administrative format tells little, if anything at all, about the psychological experience of the individual child in either setting. A given psychological intervention cannot be evaluated apart from its prescriptive relationship to the specific problem for which it was intended. Disturbed children are still given the available program, whether or not it is in tune with their needs. Although control groups may be an aid in evaluative research, they often provide further illusions, because no control group ever equals the experimental group in the various significant dimensions. One simple observation should challenge glib acceptance of evaluative results: external interventions (from changing the child's teacher to family therapy) help certain children, and internal interventions (from the "primal scream" to mechanical behavioristic approaches) appear to help other children, but no intervention yet devised "cures" every student.[7]

Even if a youngster has a given problem or set of problems and some type of "treatment" is provided, there are changes in his life other than that aspect which is under our surveillance. The part of his life covered by planned intervention may range from as little as one-half of one percent or even less in many therapeutic efforts, all the way to residential milieus, where almost all his working hours are used for planned interventions. A close examination of the special class day often indicates that what actually takes place there has little if any specific relationship to the child's problem. The same is true of a series of therapy hours or tutoring sessions. Yet we evaluate this "therapeutic" experience as if it had the potency to change a great deal, even when it is not appropriate to the youngster's deep needs.

Based on our own studies of evaluating interventions, we have adopted a research paradigm combining elements of behaviorist and case-study methodology. The behaviorists taught us to look at the individual child and at precisely what is done to change him in specific ways. Case study involves a humanistic-dynamic view. Psychological technology is now available for dealing with single cases, the "N of 1."[8] Cases are combined for group analyses only when they present reasonably "identical" patterns of behavior which then can be related to a given psychological intervention. This is in contrast to the "shotgun" method, i.e., assuming one can unravel the nature of helping disturbed children (though each is a unique individual complex) by applying a common intervention. In group studies two supposedly similar groups are employed,

a control (which gets the treatment) and an experimental (which gets nothing). If there are even small but statistically significant differences found between the groups due to large group size, the "significant" findings almost always cover up a more important result. Some children in each group improve and some in each group do not, regardless of the intervention and the significant group difference. Such assessments of the efficacy of interventions resemble weather reports with the probability of sunshine being just above chance. It may almost as well rain.

The "N of 1" paradigm for evaluating interventions follows this order: (1) gathering in-depth knowledge of the disturbed child to provide a socio-psychological assessment of the situation; (2) developing case-specific interventions directed to the child and/or environment; (3) acquiring evidence of the actual conduct of the intervention in its psychological substance; (4) monitoring of possible unplanned positive and negative life-change events that may be more powerful and extensive than the planned interventions; (5) recognizing that we may benefit from normal growth changes; (6) assessing the short-term outcomes and long-term follow-up. Unfortunately, we usually evaluate what we do, whether it is relevant or not, rather than concentrate on specific relevant interventions. For example, in addition to evaluations of the impact of the special class, it is vitally important to find out and incorporate the impact of changes at home and elsewhere. One cannot assess the efficacy of the given intervention in an ecological vacuum. This is true when a pupil *is* making progress as when he *is not*. A youngster who finds a peer pal, an adolescent who falls in love or gets a job, a family that overcomes poverty, a sibling who quits scapegoating—life is filled with fortuitous events that influence a child's life. Anyone recognizing the complications of children's lives should be hesitant to claim credit for a cure without knowing what has happened in the external and internal reality. Follow-up studies are particularly subject to these limitations, for they often assess the impact of a past program on the basis of an entirely new set of conditions when a pupil returns to the mainstream.

The effects of a special program often extend beyond the focused-on disturbed child, who may improve a little or not at all. Other youngsters who tried to adjust to his presence may now have growing room. His former teacher, unable to meet his needs, may have a resurgence of resources for the others. His parents, at the end of their endurance, may now find relief when not called to school every other day. Perhaps the only value to the child himself will be a reduction in the continual conflict with a hostile environment. Or solving one problem may reveal a more serious deviation. The life space may be evaluated in many ways. Some changes may be for the better and others not.

The lack of generalizable conclusions should not be taken as deprecation of those who have done the studies. Researchers have expended great energy over long periods of time, willing to wait years to find results. Only the consumers who want instant answers and sure conclusions fail to appreciate the equivocal aspects of the research.

In the first article, Redl discusses some subtleties of measuring improvement. As help-giving is a dynamic interaction in Redl's view, any changes affect both the adult and the youngster. One of the particular values of this selection is its application of concepts to day-by-day intervention. We know so many judgments to be partly matters of perception. It is evident that staff expectation does have an impact. Hopes become self-fulfilling prophecy. This can be as true for prognosis-improvement ("he relates so well") as for prognosis-failure ("diagnostic label schizophrenic"). In this far-ranging article, Redl directs our attention to easily overlooked aspects of the improvement process we are to study in detail in this section.

Clinical Speculations on the Concept of Improvement
Fritz Redl

. . . Long ago, Freud made the casual remark that, if an especially brilliant patient uses obviously especially stupid arguments for his defense, then it is a sure sign that there is more to the resistance involved in this than meets the eye. If some people on our level of clinical endurance are thrown into frenzy by a process of "improvement"—the very thing we are actually working and living for day and night—then there must be angles to this that might well stand exploration beyond what we are aware of right now. . . .

Improvement—What Do We Really Mean?

If anything became clear to us . . . when we tried to come to grips with our collective improvement panic, it was the fact of multiple meanings with which this term is bandied about in discussion. This isn't much of a discovery, of course, but since the hesitation—or resistance—against coming to grips with this multiplicity of meaning seems to be very strong, it might help future discussants if we laid bare the major traps in concept formulation right here and now. When people argue about improvements the following four meanings seemed to be involved—and confused:

Meaning A. Improvement—meaning a specific function in mid-air. Thus, one would hear claims that children can read better now than before, that they are able to stick to an assignment, to fulfillment of a task, that they can participate in a competitive game without being thrown by failure or success, or that they can now "allow themselves to learn" how to swim, paint, spell, or what have you. Such claims by the various disciplines involved in the cultivation of such skills would frequently be met by the therapists with an uneasy frown, a polite nod in the direction of the sister-discipline, followed by a hot debate as to whether this "really" constitutes improvement—but that one we shall come back to soon.

Meaning B. Improvement in overall mental health. In this respect, staff would argue whether a given child is getting "better"—usually referring to a rather specific part of his well known pathology. Most frequently though this type of statement ends up in a list of "symptoms dropped," or in more hard to formulate statements about desirable attributes customarily described in our American Culture as signs of well being: less tense, more relaxed, freer to react to reality as it is, less "driven" by irrational impulse, etc. etc. etc.

Meaning C. Improvement from the vantage point of the consumer. By this I mean all the adjustment demands which are made on a child by the

Abridged from Fritz Redl, "Clinical Speculations on the Concept of Improvement," presented at the American Orthopsychiatric Association Meetings, 1959.

surrounding universe, many of which have primarily to do with the comfort and taste buds of those who are on the receiving end of the line of child behavior. Thus one would find statements such as these: He is less rough on trips outside, sticks within rules better, is much quieter, has fewer tantrums and then they aren't quite so hard to live through; when in a sulk it doesn't take quite as long to get him out of it, etc. etc. etc.

Meaning D. Improvement as a "human being." Into this category fall a variety of statements which do not seem to be quite founded in either psychiatric theory or in any special educational creed, and frequently mark themselves quite clearly as different from strictly clinical statements. People get easily embarrassed while making them in the course of a case discussion, and frequently also apologize for them with the type of pride one usually displays when apologizing for something one really deems more important than what happens to be on the official agenda. Thus staff would refer to our children as "more lovable" than before, would insist that Bobby is more of a "Mensch" right now, and he seems to be a more "decent" human being, more responsive to overall expectations or just in terms of plain human charm.

Needless to emphasize—any one of these four different meanings may actually be contained in a given statement in mixture with the other three. . . .

The moral of the story that we want to lead up to today lies in the impact of the above described multiple connotations on staff discussion in an interdisciplinary team. The following chance observations may be of interest:

1.   Individual staff members lose, under the impact of improvement panic, whatever level of *conceptual astuteness* they really possess, at least for the duration of a case conference. Thus you may find a therapist who knows very well that a given teacher who said that Bobby has improved in reading, does *not* for a moment delude herself that this might mean he is cured—you may find a therapist going, in spite of this knowledge, into a long harangue about "improvements" often really being in "the service of resistance" and so forth, which then in turn leads to a somewhat angered insistence by the teacher that skills do count also, after all.

2.   Members of disciplines which have a reputation for being "clinically more sophisticated" than some others (Psychiatry versus Teaching, art therapy versus nursing, etc., as the case may be) have a

tendency to get irritated beyond reason by even modest statements of improvement of part functions or skills, and on the whole pride themselves on a somewhat over-ostentatious pessimism—as though even the mention of improvements would throw them back into a lower status field. The representatives of more part-skill oriented disciplines have a tendency to hide their improvement observations, for fear of being deemed unpsychiatric or clinically too naive for words. The debate thus avoided usually breaks out in displaced areas of clinical or technical issues.

3.   On a good team, members of the same discipline who meet the children in their daily life in different roles or at different times, have a tendency to hide their observations of improvements if their revelation might seem as though they took undue credit for them. Thus, in our case, a lot of quite clearcut improvements remained unmentioned for a while simply because a given counsellor was afraid his teammates might interpret his statements about Bobby's new relationship of trust as though it was meant to tell the others on the team how skillful the speaker was. Such is the price of good battle-morale after return to civilian life.

4.   A frank discussion of these issues and an encouragement to record observed improvements, and never mind what they might *imply* brought about an increase in recording and observations offered, but the effect of such "medication" never lasts very long; it needs to be repeated more often than one might assume.

Improvement—How Do We Know It Is "Real"?

What people are most afraid and ashamed of, on a high-level interdisciplinary clinical team, is to appear overconfident, overoptimistic, too naive in one's expectation about human change, rash in one's claims and "too easily fooled." Working with child patients whose very pathology seems to lay traps for such weaknesses with special wile and skill, this "countersuspiciousness" of the adults in battle with the suspectness of child motivations seems to assume an even higher force.

In discussions, this theme usually comes up under the guise of questions, whether a given claim of improvement is "real" or not. Some of this way of putting it is actually only a concession to the amenities of middle class conduct—for you can't very well tell a teammate that he is a fool who doesn't know what he is talking about and sees improvements where there are none. Rather, one can concede the appearance of improved behavior claimed, as long as one shifts one's incredulity to the question of the substance it might hold.

In actuality, the question "but is it real" seemed, in our struggles at least, to cover six rather discrete issues that should be carefully kept apart:

1.   Is it "real"—or is this only improved behavior, produced as a *defense* against treatment or change?

Example: *The tough kid who becomes quite "goody-goody" after arrival for a few weeks, because he wants to stall for time to "size up the joint."*

The originally obstreperous youngster who suddenly becomes more amenable to adults because he has changed tactics: he takes revenge on them now by manipulating the behavior of his peers into anti-adult escapades behind the scenes.

2.   Is it "real"—meaning, *is it ready for transfer?* In this respect, we do not doubt the appearance of improvement where it is claimed, but question whether it would stand up if situations were even slightly changed.

Example: *Youngster suddenly opening up in a real friendship for one counsellor—does this mean he is reducing his hostile warfare against the adult world, or does he simply reserve this attitude to this one person alone, thus even reinforcing his warfare against the rest of the world.*

Bobby shows more interest in activities on the Ward, gets involved in much more complex art projects there—does this mean now he is ready for prolonged interest spans in his work in school?

3.   Is it "real"—meaning, *is it re-traumatization-proof?* What we really question in that case is not the clarity of improvement, but just how much of the old bad stuff could the youngster take without a relapse. It should be noted, by the way, that I have found many clinicians fall into the trap of General Public Opinion on this score. I find therapists blushing at the thought that somebody might come around a year—or two foster home placements —away from now and say: "See, I told you it wouldn't last"—irrespective of the questions whether the new breakdown wasn't perhaps due to totally unacceptable traumatization of the child. In no

other field of medicine do I find people that trust less in their own domain. A cured pneumonia remains cured as far as the physician goes, and nobody expects retraumatization proofness for the rest of the patient's life.

Example: *Bobby has made tremendous strides in trust, is capable of accepting reprimands or even punishment if handled wisely and with proper care. But what will happen if he runs into a sadist of a teacher, a drunken fool of a foster-home parent, a stupid prediluvian practice of rule enforcement in a next institution?*

4.   Is it "real"—or rather, is the basis on which behavior rests "genuine"? In this frame of reference we do not really doubt the factualness of an improvement claim. What we wonder, however, is how much improved behavior or attitude flows out of real "personality change from within" or how far it is actually maintained only through unusual pressure from without.

Example: *Some children suddenly get scared we might "abandon them" if they are too bad.*

Under the impact of that separation panic, their surface behavior seems to "improve." However, does that mean that the "real problem" has been solved?

Under the impact of a momentary enthusiasm for a special project or a newly found adult friend, we find youngsters acting and promising way above their means. The way they act and feel during that phase is quite visibly an improvement over what we saw before—how solid, though, is the basis on which such improvements are erected?

5.   Is it "real"—meaning: is this improvement worthwhile as measured against the *price we may pay?* This is especially true where our ambition may lead us to squeeze out of youngsters levels of operation which are developmentally premature, thus cramping the style of life they ought to have in order to complete their developmental phase at ease.

Example: *A pre-adolescent who is trapped into displaying a lot of "Emily Post" adaptation to adult taste patterns as to how a little lady or little gentleman should act, thus missing the leeway for rough and tumble play which this age phase ought to have a large dose of.*

An adolescent who is trapped into premature job or vocational ambitions thus becomes a much more "serious" youngster, while he is actually postponing an important shift in adolescent psychosexual growth in a much later phase, or forces himself into a compulsion-neurosis-like state of pseudo maturity.

6.   Is it "real"—or are· we just *having luck for a while?* Often our improvement statements are obviously well rooted, and we are sure we haven't done anything to force the children into a higher level of operation. Only—we soon discover that all that happened was that we had a special piece of luck. Sometimes, it just so happens we hit a day of unusual relaxedness for the program we had in mind, or one of those situations where a "positive mood" simply is in the air from the first waking hour on, or where a lucky surprise, an unusual event, sets the tone so well that even disturbed children, with that much supportive luck, can really *live above their means* for a while. Only, it would be premature to expect their continued function on that level, or to forget what price in regressive interludes we may have to be taxed for after a while.

Example: *A skillfully designed school or play hour would often turn out unexpectedly well. Seduced by such luck, the adults may try to make such planning part of the regular and prolonged diet of the group. If premature, the result is a throwback or regression to, or beyond the original level, and the insight that the experience of such happily "improved reactions" was just a piece of unusual good luck.*

By the way, this element of "living above their means" should not be ignored entirely. The ability to do so for certain stretches seems to be one of the safest signals of imminent ego change.

In summary—all those 6 interpretations of the question whether a given phenomenon of "improvements" is "real" or not, are valid issues in their own right. They need to be viewed separately, though, and confusion between them is among the most dreaded pitfalls in staff debate.

Observations from our own "Improvement Panic phase" as to these issues:

1.   In interdisciplinary team discussions, *disappointments* along the line of meaning No. 6 (is it "real," or did we just have luck for a while) and No. 2 (is it ready for transfer) seem hardest for the staff

to take with grace. They frequently lead to "I told you so" debates rather than time spent on realistic re-appraisal of the scope of improvement exploitability, or they lead staff members to withdraw all their previous improvement statements, rather than to modify their degree of transferability at the time.

2.   *Irrespective of realities* in the picture, *therapy staff* in the stricter sense of the term is inclined to suspect all program and school staff of overexploiting mild improvement cues beyond what the treatment traffic can bear; child care and teaching staff has a tendency to suspect and accuse therapy staff of being "overfussy" and holding the kids back from experiences for which they would be quite ready.

3.   Faced with *predictions* as forerunners of a widening scope of community contact of the child patients—partial, as before changing room, hospital school to community school, or total, as in the case of impending home, foster home, or after care placement—*all staff* tends to become panicky and ends up with predictions much more negative than they really thought the improvements themselves amount to. In short, trust in transfer power of improvement goes down, panic about retraumatization vulnerability goes up. In fact, sometimes it even looks as though we *hoped* or at least *expected* that the subsequent handling of the child will have to be traumatic in nature, for only then could we have an alibi for having thought him ready for discharge to begin with, in case it didn't work out.

Improvement—At What Cost?

In the preceding discussion we mentioned the case where we feel that improvements can be obtained at "too high" a price in terms of other areas of the child's life. Of course, such mistakes will have to be avoided. However—let's face it, all improvements give us a rough time, at least for a while. Of course we somehow know this, and in specific case discussions this problem is invariably raised. Yet, I do not find that literature has given enough emphasis to the very specific problem it constitutes for the child to run around with an improved personality in the same old stable, for the adult to live with a child who has improved program readinesses, and for the institution which has to maintain a disease-protective atmosphere for some of its patients while others need to be put on the path to the way out.

In the following I shall try to list just a few of the thoughts that forced themselves upon us during those months of improvement panic.

Just What Does It Imply for the Child?

The Ego of a child who allowed himself to "improve" while under our treatment and care—and let's forget for a moment just which of the aspects of "improvement" we may be talking about, the problem is there in all of them to some degree—has the following added complications to face, and will need a lot of resilience to bear the burden of improvement with courage:

1. Extra elation and depression load.   Children of the type we are talking about remain, for a long time, quite incapable of dealing with even normal quantities of feelings of elation or depression, excitement or emptiness. Both throw them into frantic gesticulation of their ego instead of eliciting the usual coping mechanisms children have available for such events. Therefore, for a long stretch of time, the therapeutic team needs to avoid any planning that contains too much of a chance for either, and the adult has to substitute for coping mechanisms his controls from without, if either experience should hit the child too hard. Under the grip of improvements occurring within—even of partial ones, such a state of protectedness from elation or depression can no longer be maintained. Widening the scope of their experiences in areas where they are ready for it also implies the exposure to elation and triumph, of sudden insight into the distance between where they think they are as to where they really are, and a sudden onslaught of depression. For all practical purposes then, an ego that is exposed to the right diet of challenging enough experiences to feel elations will also have to take in its stride accompanying accidents of depressions, and will have to be ready for both. Only—often enough the movement in skill or personality area where improved functioning can occur is not necessarily well timed with the development of such coping mechanisms. Result: the children's ego experiences more failures with coping with either than before, which makes life for and with those children more tumultuous than it had been while they were still in the grip of their old pathology.

2. Increased problems in dealing with failure and success, criticism and praise, punishment and re-
wards.   For years we had to learn to avoid exposing our child patients to either of those, since the incapacity of their egos to cope with such experiences or educational techniques is among their primary characteristics. Astounding ingenuity had to be developed by staff to find a way of life in which to spare the children's ego the necessity for such coping, to find forms of child handling and child care which would substitute for the challenge such experiences and techniques involve.

With the emergence of new improvement potentials, this state of affairs, too, can no longer be maintained. Expanded exposure to life of more complexity makes use of such techniques unavoidable. Growing into normal life makes the learning of how to deal with such experiences paramount. Thus, hardly freed from the onslaught of their old pathological impulsivity, these children now have to practice new ego techniques in coping with the consequences of their widened area of potential functioning.

3. Increase in newness panic and additional fear of loss of control.   More newness brings with it also an increase of the anxiety that goes with exposure to new situations—a liability from which we had to protect these children for quite a while. Exposure to trying themselves in situations of increased scope also implies their increased fear of loss of control, of being overridden by an onslaught of impulsivity. In fact, since these children along with the improved functioning also usually develop some level of increased insight into their selves, their own awareness that they *might* be suffering loss of self-control in a new situation also goes up. It seems paradoxical but is an important fact of clinical life that with improved movement toward mental health the self-perception of these children's actual weakness of internal controls becomes more *realistic*, which increase in internal realism, so to say, has in its wake a new wave of anxieties about loss of control. A chain reaction which probably poses one of the most delicate clinical policy problems of all.

4. Fear of commitment, nostalgia for old pathology fun.   This phase of the improvement curve has been better documented in reports on individual therapy with children and adults than the others. It nevertheless introduces new challenges to meet in the children's daily lives. What we are referring to is the well documented fact that the emerging awareness of the healthier ego and what life in health implies, also brings with it the dawning idea of the price one pays for freedom and health, and the demands society—and oneself—is likely to make once one has left the dreary but relatively safe refuge of mental disease. Also—newly tasted gratifications are still wobbly, the secondary gain extorted from old pathology-geared gratification, while spurious is, at least safely predictable and well known. Thus, the "improvement prone" child travels a road more challenging, but also much emptier of the known, and much more unpredictable in terms of the nature of the gratifications to be expected as a reward.

5. *The diversion of improvements as bargaining tools with the world of adults.*   Of all the pitfalls, this is probably the worst one, at least in therapy with the type of children we have in mind today. For, once improvement on several levels has been tasted, these children are not slow in detecting its terrific bargaining power over the adults on the behavioral scene. And once a given piece of improvement becomes a bargaining tool in the battle with the surrounding universe, its *value, clinically speaking, has been nullified.* In fact, the improvement we produced, once it is in the service of such battle against change, is but an additional weapon in the child's hand. We shall talk about the problem of keeping staff from playing into the hands of this vicious and perverse process in a minute. At the moment what we are referring to is the tendency and skill of children on the way to health to bribe and blackmail their surroundings with that very issue of health itself. Only after they have improved enough, can they use regression as an efficient weapon for punishing their therapist or themselves. Only after they have shown considerable gains on several levels, can they successfully trap us into confusing surface improvements with real change, or taking their coins of more pleasing behavior as a sign of advancement rather than of the resistance it really is. The "promise" to be good—by word or deed, the "threat" to regress—by deed or word, are a new piece of agenda on the strategy discussion table during those phases in the children's clinical life.

6. *Estrangement from peer group and peer culture with all that this implies.*   This phenomenon is most visible, of course, when some of the children move "faster" than others in the same subgroup, or if an individual's move out from under pathology happens more rapidly than the behavioral code of the peer group can keep step with. Since this is the more frequent situation anyway, we might list

shortly what the problems of the "improving" child will be under those conditions:

a. Behavior which is rated as "improved" in the world of the therapy-success eager adult may have the opposite rating on the peer code scale, which still has strong natural power in their lives, and needs to retain such for quite a while to come. Thus, for instance, the ability "to ask for help rather than to lash out in wild destructive despair" is a clearcut improvement item on anybody's scale. For the kid who produces such behavior it easily contains the flavor of "sissiness," of "giving in" or "playing up to" the adults, of acting like a "teacher's pet."

b. Improvements in basic health issues invariably also are accompanied by changes in *taste.* Accepting sublimiated gratifications for more primitive ones obviously creates a gap between the child now and the child before, and therefore between him and his less advanced playmates. Thus, we will find two phenomena in the wake of such moves: our improved youngster may become *contemptuous* of, or hostile to, those who still linger in their old rough, obviously crazy and uncomfortable pleasures and behavior, or he may become envious of them, developing nostalgic yearnings for the more simple life of yore. Experiences, by the way, which our youngsters may not yet be able to cope with, even at the time when their improvement in sublimation of their taste-buds already has taken place.

c. *Exposure to additional dare and group-loyalty tests. Ambivalence also toward this new image of self.* Groups don't like to let people go. In the organized adult crime gang, the punishment for estrangement is death. In kid groups it is ostracism or an endless chain of "loyalty tests." Thus, the changing child in the not yet changing group will find himself suspect of being a fifth columnist in the battle against adults, for the very "improvements" he has not yet learned how to savor. He will be exposed to a constant flow of "dares" to show that he is still O.K. in spite of that suddenly discovered eagerness to hold up his hand in class for contributions, to finish products adults are proud of, or his obviously gratifying use of his relationship to a therapist. Thus, our changing individual undergoes a new phase of group conflict at the very time when his first improvements need a chance to emerge.

7. *The turmoil of choice.*   Improved personalities need a wider scope to operate in. The nourishment of improvement potentials invariably implies the in-

crease of free choice. Thus, the very children who, during their sickness, had to be protected by the adult from being exposed to too exciting choice making, because their egos could never bear such a load, will now have to emerge into choice making on a stepped-up scale. Rather than have an adult stand behind them who can hold them when they make the wrong decision, they will have to be kept in a program that gives them a chance to be on their own, to make their own decision whether to behave or to misbehave, so that the consequences of such decisions can then be picked up in therapy or life-space interview work. No matter how closely supervised their overall life frame may remain, this withdrawing of the adult in tactful awe of the importance of an autonomous decision making process is the core of all treatment into health.

The result of this for the internal household of· our children is obvious: wrong decisions have to be made. The ego will then be tempted to use its old alibi and projection techniques to ward off the insight-consequences that might have to be drawn from them. Our "Life Space Interview" records are bursting with colorful illustrations of just this very sort of thing. It is the clinical exploitation of life events—life events which are allowed to occur—that marks this phase of therapy, as against the protection from stress that marked the previous one. While this is the only safe way back into health, it isn't an easy one, and the casualties on this path are not less numerous than those on the previous treatment stretches.

All in all it should be clear by now that we are deeply impressed with the fact that real improvements—on any one of the counts we mentioned above—make additional demands on the child. This is especially true for settings in which the children under treatment live in a group with other child patients, while in part branching out into widened areas of school and community life. While the "group" may, under circumstances, support the way to health, it is also quite likely to try to block it. In either case, the "improving child" will be faced with frustrations and failures which are the result of the widened horizon of his experiential life and to which he would not have been exposed to begin with, had he not improved. Thus, the child's ego assumes, with each "improvement" step, also the challenge of managing more complex life situations, and a new batch of frustrations, anxieties, confusions and fears. Quite a job to perform until, finally, digested experiences of this sort can be

turned, by the child, into a renewed concept of his self.

Improvement—What Is the Cost for the Clinical or Educational Adult?

To lump both of them together isn't really quite fair; for obviously the problems we have to face vis-á-vis the improvement issue will vary considerably in terms of the specific function we are expected to fulfill in the youngster's overall treatment scheme, and the specific role we have to play in his daily life. However—time is costly at this point, so let us oversimplify and abbreviate without too much apology and guilt:

1. Coping with the temptation to over-expect and exploit. Frankly, not all of the resistance of youngsters against our therapeutic wiles to bring about a change is just a function of their pathology. Even without its distorting influence, I can't blame some of them for being leery of being free to improve, for there is one instinct most powerful in all adults in this professional game—a terrific drive to hang onto whatever changes we finally seem to notice; and, while they hardly show us a finger of improvement, to grab the whole hand and try hard to pull them into a level of health they are far from ready for.

We all know that, but we haven't spent as much time learning to recognize our secret wishes in that direction as we have spent learning to know when we are liable to get angry and mad, frustrated or hostile, so we can take professional action against such feelings flooding our clinical gates.

The more skill-oriented professions have a natural tendency in that direction by the very nature of their job. But the therapist, in the stricter meaning of the term, isn't free of it either. It only shows in different ways. In fact, I have seen Bobby's therapist mad at his group worker for expecting the child to enjoy games or experiences still much too frightening to him, just because he had improved some, and yet would find the same therapist disappointed an hour later that a youngster who had been so capable of insight style therapy by now should suddenly return to a phase of non-verbal resistance against any and all interview work, and wondering what mistakes we had made. In short—one of the greatest internal problems of staff is that once they have smelled the flavor of a few moments of success, felt the relief in seeing irrational kids respond with normal reactions, they are liable to forget all they have learned through the years of severe pathology onslaught—or rather, to throw it out of the window as though the millennium had arrived.

2. Bargain basement deals with the pseudo-normal child.   Worse than the temptation to over-expect and exploit improvement potentials is the temptation to fall into the trap of using their promises and "good behavior" or their verbal threats of regression for bargain deals which are clinically as destructive as anything could be. To make this point, which I consider the most important of all, safe against misinterpretation, a slight detour back into our pre-improvement policies seems justified.

The specific type of child patient on whose back, so to say, we discuss the whole improvement issue today, requires, during the first years of therapy, an avoidance of all *punishment* in the usual sense of the term. I cannot re-argue the reasons for this here.

The appearance of marked "improvements" seemed to confront us with the need to plan as carefully about our anxieties about optimism and hope as we had needed to plan about our dangers of hostility and despair. It is my impression that there was no automatic transfer from the principles that had guided us against the wrong reactions to the youngsters' "bad" behavior into the avoidance of the wrong handling of their promises to be "good." In the struggle with all this, the following directives resulted as a side piece to our original batch of training policies:

Whenever we are confronted with it, *we cannot afford* to make them feel our widening of their leeway for autonomy and expressional scope is *"reward"* or *"privilege."*

a. If we did, this would only stir up their "make a-deal" philosophy of life and seduce them into exploitational pseudo-promises and adjustments, and they would *escape the real issue* again.

b. They would not tie up the experience of Reward and Promise with either their own past behavior or with the future predicament anyway, so those rewards and privileges would only be considered a premium for symptom-disguise.

c. However—we must not be considered as being *indifferent* to their improved behavior and attitude. It is important to show them that we are happy about it, but not to the degree that the loss of such recognition would become something to be *constantly afraid of.*

d. Whenever we have to terminate temporarily a new scope in their autonomy and mobility, we must make sure they do not experience this as *punishment.* This must be interpreted quite similarly to our previous intervention policy; we just think you can't make it yet, that's all there is to it. Not whether they were good or bad, but *whether we know they are ready* for an experience is the criterion for them to have it. Thus, we must also protect them from their own *illusionary need to produce phoney or rash promises.* We have to protect them against unrealistic self-expectation just as we used to protect them against unrealistic feelings of defeat.

e. The attitude to be conveyed is: "We love you anyway, we shall do everything to help you 'make it,' whenever you enter a new area of widened autonomous decision making, or experiential tryout of new situations. However, we shall also protect you from trying more than we know you can handle, even if you get mad at us at the time. We are happy about every step forward you can make, but we don't want you to feel you have to produce improved behavior as a prize. We shall help you move at your own rate. On the other hand, the production of improved behavior as a coin for special privileges is out, in this outfit, too. It isn't necessary. What you get, you get because you need it, it is good for you and you are ready for it."

These are the only basic criteria on which the granting of special extensions in autonomy of decision making, and of experiential expansion, depends. To convey such an attitude in the turmoil of daily events is not an easy task, but neither was the handling of negatively experienced interventions mentioned above. Only, staff is usually caught unawares for the latter, and the very fact these kids begin to look and act in many moments of their lives so much like plain ordinary normal kids easily fools us into the same type of bargain deals, or of institutionalized punishments or rewards that, with normal children, are known to work so well. In fact, the healthier these kids get, the harder it is to remain aware of the amount of clinical caution and clinical tact that still has to remain part and parcel of our treatment policy. In all those cases where we made bad mistakes along that line, and tried to rely on promises, threats, rewards, punishments, no matter how mild and wise, we were soon forced to regret it. And even then it was hard for us to realize that the only people we can afford to get mad at for such mistakes are ourselves, rather than the kids who "disappointed" our fond hopes.

3. Improvement muteness because of a repressed

desire to grow. After so many months and years of hard labor without any reliable signs of success that could be trusted, it is hard to avoid a strong wish to brag about a real improvement, or to overtalk it in case conference or in luncheon gossip with the rest of the clinical crowd. Afraid that we might do so, and realizing that this would be misinterpreted by the rest of the gang as a rather prima-donnaish and conceited act, we often defended ourselves against our own narcissistic hopes by not admitting or noting actual improvements to begin with. Thus, one often sees children handled with much too little improvement leeway, thereby slowing up the possible clinical pace. And recordings, just when improvements of all sorts actually set in, become quite unreliable, a not inconsiderable deficit for an operation that is geared toward research.

4. Renewed competitiveness among team members and distorted relationships to "the other field." With the first "improvements" finally becoming undeniable, a new wave of competitiveness is likely to hit an otherwise already quite team-oriented staff. It seemed easier to love each other, and to respect the other guy's discipline, as long as we were all in the same boat of struggling with little visible success against overwhelming odds. Once improvement happens, our narcissistic investments are re-inflamed. This may happen on a personal level —why should Bobby do this (showing reliable behavior when trusted with keys) for counsellor X when I know he would never have done that much for me? It may also happen on the level of displacement into interdisciplinary issues: sure that teacher thinks she got Bobby to read. Little does she know that he would never have allowed himself to want to do so, unless I had opened it all up for him in that therapy hour the other day. To bring this new wave of potential staff conflict under control seems to be a more arduous task for all involved than to become aware of and cope with our feelings of frustration, aggression, and fear.

In summary—there seems to be a considerable implication of all this for the task of pre-service and in-service training of staff, and for the ongoing supervisory process on all levels. Without going into any of these details today, it may suffice to state that the clinical morale and astuteness of a given residential staff well developed for the original onslaught of pathology in the raw, may need considerable re-structuring, in order to be equally foolproof against the terrific onslaught of the first improvement wave.

Improvement—What Is the Cost to the Institution?

When child patients are treated in an institutional setting of any kind—and some of this even holds for the less enduring settings, such as outpatient therapy clubs—the phenomenon of improvement creates new tasks and new problems, which seem to me to deserve much more recognition than they have gained in the past. All too often do we design our institutional framework primarily for the "treatment" of a given disease entity or disturbance of some kind. Somehow we hope that within all this the patient will "get better" and finally be ready for discharge. Not enough do we often realize how the step by step impact of improvements which have already taken place may change the whole treatment need of individual or group, to the point where co-existence with the originally clinically correct pathology service design becomes a problem of first order. To mention but a few of the most obvious observations to the point:

1. Danger to a real "treatment atmosphere" in favor of a system of institutionalized penalties and rewards, or of assessments of part achievements. In a place where most kids have shed their worst primitiveness, it is quite possible to make demands, set standards, which give a smooth image of a well run place, with the kids on the health-proximity end of the line more or less setting the tone and representing the place to the world outside. As soon as this happens, regression becomes a luxury hard to afford, conformity to some standardized expectations becomes a real issue with the group of kids, even if the adults would retain clinical flexibility in their thoughts. Individualization, respect for special anxieties, oddities, and pathological blow-ups become something the institution is increasingly ashamed of. They blush if it happens, instead of taking pride in how wisely they handled it when it occurs. Even a clinically highly sophisticated setting may temporarily suffer such a *relapse into preclinical naivete* just at the very moment when their first successes become clear to all. In our own experience, for instance, I had little trouble convincing even clinically not very sophisticated or highly trained staff of the impossibility of using punishments on kids who have obviously no sense of future or of past. When the children began to improve, I found myself forced to write long essays to reassure even the treatment staff of the difference between intervention and punishment, between normal children at home and child patients on a still closed or just opened ward. . . .

2. The emergency of a system of "caste" and "outcast." The adults may "understand" why Bobby is now ready for more leeway and less tight supervision, more trust with gadgets and less fussiness, and even Bobby may. But how will this affect the other children? For *them*, what I and the child know is simply a concession to his greater self-control looks like rank favoritism of the worst kind. Also, if the group "improves" in too uneven rates, it is unavoidable that some consider themselves quite excluded from "privileges" which the others seem to enjoy, and the concept of the "privileged character" can be as destructive in a treatment setting as in detention homes. Also, once the pressure of such a system of "privileges one enjoys after one has improved" and "absence of rights one is doomed to because one isn't trusted enough" becomes more or less institutionalized, it develops a suction power of its own with disastrous effects all around.

Only the constant vigilance of staff about their own motives, and the careful interpretation—by word or deed—of all events that might give rise to such suspicions to all children involved—including the group of "onlookers"—can safeguard an institution against this trap.

3. Program distortion for the rest of the group. Aside from these interpretational pitfalls, it also easily happens that the program diet which the less improved children get *actually* changes way beyond what is clinically wise. This change may occur in two directions: it may lead to a *pauperization* of the program for those who don't quite seem to be up to it yet. Staff may betray their annoyance with the level of operation of the less improved, and too openly display their understandable gratification with the program for those who are more advanced and therefore more gratifying to work with. Or the change may lead to *stepped up demands* for all, with disastrous results for those who just cannot yet make it. In both cases an institution would lose its clinical value for some of the children, while increasing its fitness for those on top.

4. Differentiation between "regression" and legitimate "improvement mess." One of the hardest issues to interpret to outsiders, and occasionally to oneself, is the fact that improvement, in growing kids, of course does not mean the termination of problems or even of problem behavior. An adolescent, for instance, who spent his pre-adolescent years in a closed ward with a small group of also disturbed peers, and who is really "coming along well," will be *expected* to have to live through all the

usual turmoil of adolescent awakening sexuality, of concern about peer status, of battle with home personnel about his newly discovered status of emancipated young man. Life with teenagers alone, no matter how normal, can be full of problems, and of problem behavior of considerable proportions. Why should "our kids" be an exception to this? And yet, we were very tempted to interpret their first steps into adolescent rebellion as just "regression to their old ways," to react to their normal adolescent overestimation of anything outside and devaluation of what they have at home, as though it simply meant "we never got anywhere, they are as hostile and hard to please as they were when they came." In fact, if your youngsters enter their adolescent phase just at the time when improvements set in and when their scope of activities is branching out into the community more and more, staff is likely to develop some sort of envy toward people outside, who seem to have an easier time with them, than the home base personnel. Yet any parent of any normal child is quite used to just that. The real problem, however, lies in the difficulty to *assess* correctly, even in our own domain, just what we have before us: regression or problem behavior which accompanies their coping with a new part of life. Research in this direction is practically nonexistent; its expansion way beyond its present state devoutly to be wished.

5. Accepting the challenge of the calculated risk—and the public hatred in its wake. It is hard but safe to run a place for the extremely sick. Nobody expects any better from you, as long as you keep them out of their hair. You, yourself, have a constant alibi in your vest pocket—in view of the enormous pathology that stares you in the face, even superhuman effort can't well be blamed for failing.

Once the children "improve," doubt rises, whether we couldn't do "more" for them, and indeed, ever more seems to be needed. To cater to the needs of an "improved" personality on the way back to health, however, is quite a different task from treating a bunch of incurables humanely and with some clinical hope. It involves an increased demand for *calculated risk*. For some institutions, such as mental hospitals for instance, this even constitutes a legal and administrative problem of considerable scope.

To use just one illustration for many: at a certain state in his development, Bobby could be trusted with the ward keys for a short trip down to the coke machine. In fact, he *needed* such trust experiences when half-way ready for them, for how can anybody develop autonomy on a leash? On the other hand, in a mental hospital such practice is strictly against the rule; lower status staff can well be fired for such a breach of rules. Or: Johnny and Max are now in need of partial independence from the group, and of an experience of behaving well, out of decency to the counselor who is "on." Result: this said counselor will of course give in to their requests to "go on up the creek a little for some more crabs while you are packing up, we will be back in five minutes, honest." If the counselor knows his children and their mood, and the clinical phase they are in, such a permission is a clinical *must*. Yet, he better not record the incident, for it is against all laws of the land. And of course, we don't even insist that this judgment was entirely right. We even hope the risk will misfire from time to time, for only such misfiring gives us the chance for the "clinical exploitation of a dramatic life event," which may shorten the child's treatment by months.

In the transition from a closed unit to open life in the community, the cost of the improvement of our children became even more painfully visible. For the public in general has little tolerance for a risk that misfires, no matter how well it was calculated, or how wisely exploited for the therapy of the child. In fact, this may well be one of the reasons why we still have so many closed wards or highly restrictive institutions, and so many fewer places where the "last stretch from sickness to health" could be taken. For, as our societal hatred of those who deal with the dangerous and the mentally sick is what it is known to be—who could take the risk of supporting that last stretch toward mental health, without losing his own?

A careful overall review of the results of various programs will help in the examination of details of research. Lewis's article is far more than a review of past work. His summary of data and theoretical implications serves as a point of reference for future studies. Prediction is the basis of prevention, but one must not try to use a described event as a psychological constant. If school means little to a pupil in contrast to other aspects of life, failing in school will not be a potent event psychologically. Another child may be devastated by such failure. An event that is traumatic to one may be a source of exciting pleasure to another. Coping capacities vary.

After examining what we can learn from earlier behavior about prognosis for future adjustment, Lewis discusses the effect of therapy. In reviewing various methodologies, he illustrates how diverse are the variables used and the conclusions reached. His concluding paragraph is really an explanation of why we are moving so slowly and what the new direction in evaluation research should be.

Continuity and Intervention in Emotional Disturbance: A Review
W.W. Lewis

The treatment procedures used in child guidance clinics are based implicitly on two hypotheses regarding the relationship between emotional disturbance in children and mental illness in adults. The first of these, which we will label the continuity hypothesis, is that emotional disturbance in a child is symptomatic of a continuing psychological process that may lead to adult mental illness. The second, which we will call the intervention hypothesis, is that therapeutic intervention enhances the child's present adjustment and thereby reduces the likelihood that he will experience serious mental problems later in life.

As working hypotheses, these presumed relationships have served us well in allocating our resources in the mental health field and in making operational decisions regarding when and to whom treatment should be offered. As hypotheses, however, they need to be examined from time to time in the light of accumulating evidence that may increase or decrease our confidence in the procedures we employ.

Levitt (1957a) published a review of outcome studies of psychotherapy with children which raised doubts about what we are calling the intervention hypothesis. While his conclusions are relevant to this review, and will be taken up in context, the ev-

From W.W. Lewis, "Continuity and Intervention in Emotional Disturbance: A Review," *Exceptional Children*, vol. 31, no. 9, May 1965, pp. 465–75. Reprinted by permission of The Council for Exceptional Children and the author.

idence that will be considered in this paper is somewhat broader in scope than whether children improve more with psychotherapy or without it.

The continuity hypothesis can be translated into a prediction that children who have been identified as emotionally disturbed will have more problems of adjustment as adolescents and adults than children who have not been so identified. There are two general types of studies that can help evaluate this prediction: retrospective studies of adult mental patients and followup studies of adults who had been seen diagnostically in child guidance clinics as children.

Similarly, the intervention hypothesis can be translated into a prediction that children who have received treatment for emotional disturbance will have fewer adjustment problems than emotionally disturbed children who have not received treatment. Two kinds of studies can help evaluate this prediction: outcomes of clinic treatment in terms of very general criteria, e.g., percent of children who were improved following treatment, and experimental studies designed to investigate more specific changes accompanying treatment.

The Continuity Hypothesis: Retrospective Studies

Retrospective studies generally employ a sample of adult mental patients whose childhood symptoms are reviewed through the case histories, questionnaires, and interviews with informants. Kasanin and Veo (1932), Bowman (1934), Friedlander (1945), and Wittman and Huffman (1945) have all followed this pattern in reporting a correlation between childhood problems and psychosis in adult life. A common conclusion in these studies is that adult psychotics have had visible signs of disordered behavior early in their lives and presumably could have been identified and treated long before they reached a stage of frank psychosis. Two alternative interpretations may be offered. One is that since the person making judgments of the quality and severity of the childhood symptoms knew that the subject was a hospitalized psychotic, a negative halo effect may have been created. The other interpretation is that there is no way of determining how many other children had similar problems but were not studied because they did not become psychotic later in their lives.

Bower, Shellhammer, Daily, and Bower (1960) attempted to eliminate the knowledge of outcome bias by obtaining descriptive ratings from former teachers of hospitalized schizophrenics without the teachers' awareness of their present status. Comparison of these ratings with those for a control group selected from the same high school classes indicated that the teachers had been aware to some extent of the prepsychotic students' deviant tendencies. That there may have been still other students in the same high school classes who had similar symptoms was not raised as a question.

A study by Birren (1944) attempted to eliminate both alternative interpretations by examining psychological reports of children referred to psychologists in a public school system and who later were committed to mental hospitals. Thirty-eight records of this kind were compared with a control sample of nonpsychotics who had been examined at the same time for similar problems. The test records did not reveal significant differences between the two groups of children and ". . . in none of the cases studied was there suspicion on the part of the examiner that the child examined had severe conflicts or would later become psychotic" (p. 93).

The Continuity Hypothesis: Adults Followup

Followup studies of adult adjustment status of an entire population of children who had been referred to child guidance clinics is a defensible way of establishing the correlation between developmental problems and mental illness. Two studies of this type have been reported, both designed to investigate the relationship between particular childhood problems and adult schizophrenia.

The association between withdrawing, internalized tension symptoms in children and adult schizophrenia was the focus of attention in a study of the adjustment of adults seen diagnostically at the Dallas Child Guidance Clinic 16 to 27 years ago. From case history materials, 54 former child patients were classified as internal reactors on the basis of comprehensive social history, one or more psychological examinations and a psychiatric interview. On the basis of followup interviews the authors concluded: ". . . they are on the whole getting along quite well. Approximately two-thirds are classified as satisfactorily adjusted and one-third as marginally adjusted. Only two of the 54 are considered to be sick, and only one of these is in a mental hospital . . . one has the impression that most of the people who we diagnosed as internal reactors turn out to be average, normal people in most respects" (Morris, Soroker, and Burress, 1954, p. 753). Another report on the same clinic population described the classification of case histories of 606 former child patients into three categories of symptoms—introverts, ambiverts, and extroverts. The names of 24 of these former patients were found in the files of mental institutions in Texas, presumably indicating a severe kind of mental illness during adulthood. Of the 164 persons whose records had been classified as introverted, only one was among the group of 24 hospitalized patients. "The results point to the conclusion that there is not adequate justification for the assertion that children who might be classified as introverts are more likely to develop schizophrenia . . . introverted children may be least likely to develop neuropsychiatric disorders . . . which would require hospitalization" (Michael, Morris, and Soroker, 1957, p. 337).

An even more ambitious followup study of former child patients is under way at the St. Louis Municipal Psychiatric Clinic. The subjects are 525 consecutive admissions 30 years prior to the beginning of the followup. In addition, one hundred problem-free control subjects were selected at random from public school records of the same time to match the former child patient group on sex, race, year of birth, and socioeconomic status. Adult social and psychiatric status of both the former patient group and the controls has been determined by a standardized interview with each subject and a search of public records. In summarizing present psychiatric status of the former child patients, 21 percent are in the no disease category. By comparison, 60 percent of the control group are placed in the no disease category (O'Neal and Robins, 1958b). In the former patient group ten percent received schizophrenic diagnoses as adults. In this group too, the withdrawing, internalizing symptoms in childhood problems seemed not to be prodromal of adult schizophrenia. None of the preschizophrenic children had been diagnosed as psychotic, although some suspicion had been expressed in three cases out of 28. Rather, the childhood symptoms of the schizophrenic group seemed best described as antisocial, along with a greater number of areas of disturbed functioning (O'Neal and Robins, 1958a). Comparisons of the former patient group with controls or variables other than present psychiatric status showed a higher rate of mortality in the patient group, a higher proportion who had moved away from the St. Louis area, and a higher proportion of arrests for serious crimes (Robins and O'Neal, 1958).

Continuity Hypothesis: Conclusions

The conclusion that can be drawn from both these child patient populations is similar in one important respect. It is the acting out, disturbing child who is likely to become seriously mentally ill as an adult, rather than the shy, withdrawn child. It is interesting to note in passing that in the much quoted Wickman study, comparing teachers' and clinicians' judgments about problem behavior in children, the teachers may have been better predictors of adult psychiatric status than clinicians. These two studies give us different answers on the larger question—"Do problem children become mentally ill as adults?" The reason, undoubtedly, is the difference in criterion of adult status used in the two studies. When a more rigorous criterion of adult mental illness, admission to a mental hospital, is used in the Dallas Clinic followup, the answer is "no." When the criterion is "no psychiatric disease" determined by examination, as in the followup of the St. Louis patients, the answer is "yes, problem children do have a higher proportion of psychiatric difficulties as adults." The later conclusion is tempered somewhat by referring back to the proportion of control subjects in the St. Louis study who had been classified in the no disease category. They had been selected to provide a comparison with a healthy population, and subjects in whose school records there was any suggestion of problem behavior were not used for control purposes. In this group, who would presumably be somewhat freer of problems than a group selected entirely at random, almost one-half either received a specific psychiatric diagnosis, or their status is not sufficiently clear for them to receive the no disease label. The findings, therefore, seem to offer only mild support for the continuity hypothesis.

The Intervention Hypothesis: General Outcomes of Therapy

The effectiveness of therapeutic intervention on children's adjustment status has received attention in the literature for more than thirty years. In general, the question that has been asked in these studies is "How many of the children who were treated showed improvement in their presenting symptoms?" At the simplest level of investigation there is a statement of the percent of the treated children who were showing improvement at the time the case was closed. These studies can be summarized rather quickly by stating that improvement is usually noted in two-thirds to three-fourths of the treated cases regardless of the treatment setting, the professional discipline of therapist or the age of children treated (Allbright and Gambrell, 1938; Beaumont, 1945; Brown, 1947; Gibbs, 1945; Jacobsen, 1948; Lamore, 1941; Rotenberg, 1947). The most recent and comprehensive figure, based on reports of 994 clinics of cases closed during the year 1959, is 72 percent improvement (Norman, Rosen, and Bohn, 1962).

Conclusions based on the statement of the child's adjustment status at the termination of clinical treatment must be guarded since it may reflect simply the degree of optimism of the therapist at the time the case is closed. Followup studies of treated clinical cases by persons other than the clinic staff provide a somewhat more detached evaluation of the outcome of treatment. The usual format of followup studies is to select a sample of cases from a clinic's file and interview an informant, usually the child's mother, in order to assess the child's adjustment for a period of time after treatment is terminated. The assessment is then summarized as a dichotomous judgment in terms of improvement in presenting problems or adequacy of present adjustment as opposed to no improvement or poor adjustment. In studies ranging from one year to seven or eight years following treatment, the proportion of improvement reported is still mostly within the two-thirds to three-fourths range. Witmer and students (1933) reported 73 percent for a New York clinic, and a range of 60 percent to 84 percent in a study of 16 clinics (Witmer, 1935a, 1935b). Other reports of this kind give improvement figures of 76 percent (Hardcastle, 1934); 73 percent (Hubbard and Adams, 1936); 80 percent (Shirley, Baum, and Polsky, 1940); 63 percent (Cunningham, Westerman, and Fischhoff, 1956); and 71 percent (Rodriquez, Rodriquez, and Eisenberg, 1959).

Most of these studies have made an effort to relate factors other than treatment to successful adjustment at followup. However, none of them report a clear relationship with the length of treatment, whether or not the child finished treatment, the sex of the child, or his age at referral. Some evidence has been found for interaction effects between treatment and intelligence, initial diagnostic classification, and socioeconomic status of parents. One rather puzzling finding in the study by Shirley et al. (1940) was the lack of relationship between ad-

justment at close of treatment and adjustment at followup. Judging success in a dichotomous way, four of every ten children who were judged successful at the end of treatment were unsuccessful at followup, and four of every ten unsuccessful treatment cases were judged successful at followup. Unfortunately, the other studies did not report their data in a way that allowed for a comparison with this finding.

Effects of Intervention

The effects of intervention in treating children's problems can be more rigorously tested if the followup method includes a comparison group of children who have been identified as emotionally disturbed but who have received no treatment. Levitt (1957a) touched off a spirited debate a few years ago by concluding that improvement rates among children who had been treated in child guidance clinics were no higher than improvement rates for children who had been on clinic waiting lists but had never been treated. Following the method used by Eysenck (1952), Levitt established a base line recovery rate of 72.5 percent from two followup studies of children who had been withdrawn from clinic waiting lists (Witmer and Keller, 1942; Lehrman, Sirluck, Black, and Glick, 1949). He then presented data on outcome of clinical treatment with 7,987 children in which the percent improved was 73.3, not significantly different from the control figure. He went on to analyze the difference between reported improvement at the close of treatment and at followup. That the time since identification of a problem in a child might be a more important factor in his present adjustment than whether or not he had received treatment was the Controls were 427 waiting list defectors from the same period of time. Twenty-six outcome variables, including psychological tests, biographical data, self-evaluations and clinical judgments failed to show any significant differences in the psychological adjustment of the two groups. Levi and Ginott (1961) reported a 55 percent remission of symptoms rate in 314 children treated in a clinic, compared to 20 percent remissions in a group of 300 children whose parents had made application for treatment but had failed to complete the intake procedures.

These five studies, comparing more than one thousand treated children with more than one thousand children whose problems were not treated, are almost uniformly discouraging in evaluating the outcome of treatment in a child guidance facility. The Levi and Ginott study alone would encourage optimism, and it is interesting to note that the improvement figures reported in that study, both for the treated and for the untreated groups, depart markedly from figures reported in most other studies. Depending on how seriously one takes the question of the appropriateness of comparison with waiting list defectors, the evidence at least does not increase confidence in the intervention hypothesis. One might wish for an intake arrangement in clinics that would allow children to be randomly assigned to treatment and control groups, to help rule out the alternate explanations based on motivation and severity of symptoms in the waiting list defectors.

Cambridge-Somerville Youth Study

This kind of design was used in the Cambridge-Somerville Youth Study, a program designed to prevent juvenile delinquency. Pre-delinquent boys were matched at the beginning of the study on age, intelligence, social, and emotional ratings and probability of developing delinquent behavior. One of each matched pair was randomly assigned to a treatment group, and received a case work counseling service for a period of six to eight years. By the criterion of preventing juvenile delinquency, measured by police and court records, there were no differences between the treatment and control groups either at the end of the study (Powers and Witmer, 1951), or at followup, ten years after the study was terminated, (McCord, McCord, and Zola, 1959). Included in Witmer's evaluation of the program is a comparison of results using the same for-inference that Levitt drew from his comparison. Followup studies of longer duration tend to report higher rates of improvement than studies at the close of treatment.

Levitt's conclusion has been criticized on several grounds, but primarily on the appropriateness of defectors from clinic waiting lists as controls (Hood-Williams, 1960; Heinicke and Goldman, 1960). It has been suggested, for example, that the initial motivation for treatment is probably not as high, the problems are not as serious, or sudden improvement in symptoms occurred while the child's name was still on the waiting list. Levitt has countered these criticisms by showing that treated

and defector child cases do not differ on 61 factors, including two clinical estimates of severity of disturbance and eight other factors related to symptoms (1957b, 1958a), and that in followup interviews with parents of defector cases only 13 percent attributed defection to improvement of the child's symptoms (1958b). On the other hand, a spontaneous recovery rate of 50 percent has been reported in a study by Morris and Soroker (1953).

Waiting List Defectors as Controls

Whatever the shortcomings in the use of waiting list defectors as controls in studying outcomes of child therapy, it is the only basis of comparison presently reported in the literature. The study by Witmer and Keller (1942) reported a followup study of children eight to 13 years after their clinic contact. In this group there were 85 children who had received treatment and 50 who had been seen only diagnostically. Improvement at followup was reported for 60 percent of the treated group and 78 percent of the untreated group. Lehrman, et al. (1949) also reported a comparison of adjustment of 196 children seen for treatment and 110 children seen only for diagnostic evaluation. A one year followup showed 75 percent of the treatment group with improved adjustment and 70 percent of the untreated group with improved adjustment. A five year followup study of 202 former clients of a child guidance clinic in England was reported in terms of mean ratings rather than percent improved. However, the comparison on ratings between treated cases and cases seen only diagnostically showed no significant differences (Barbour and Beefell, 1955). Levitt, Beiser, and Robertson, (1959) studied the psychological adjustment of a sample of 579 cases, averaging about seven years after the termination of treatment. mat as that generally used for comparison of clinic treatment and control cases. A terminal rating of adjustment was made from case records for each boy in the treatment group. A similar rating for 148 of the boys in the control group was made at the end of the study by an interview with the boys and their parents and by a questionnaire sent to their school. Comparison of the terminal adjustment for the 148 matched pairs of boys showed 71 percent of the treatment group receiving ratings of good or fairly good adjustment, and 74 percent of the control boys receiving similar ratings. The question of degree of disturbance would seem to be clearly answered in this study by the original matching of treatment and control subjects. The question that still may be raised is one of motivation for treatment. In the Cambridge-Somerville experiment none of the boys or their families sought treatment; the service was offered to them.

Studies of the general effectiveness of residential treatment for disturbed children have, to date, been carried out along the same lines as the evaluations of outpatient clinical treatment of children. Controls from a waiting list are not generally available as a comparison group. In most studies a gross report of general adjustment is given either at the termination of treatment or at some specified followup period. In a descriptive survey of 12 residential treatment centers for emotionally disturbed children, Reid and Hagan (1952) reported a general outcome figure for each of the institutions studied. The figures reported by each institution on successful treatment vary from 50 percent to 76 percent, with a cumulative average of about 68 percent for 519 children reported upon. The range is somewhat lower but the average is comparable to the figures reported for out-patient treatment of children. Hamilton, McKinley, Moorhead, and Wall (1961) report a two-thirds success rate at the close of residential treatment of 110 adolescent boys.

Other studies give followup information on children who have been treated in residential settings. Rosenthal and Pinsky (1936) reported a 63 percent success rate, Zick (1943) reported 63 percent, Johnson and Reid (1947) 74 percent, Benjamin and Weatherly (1947) 71 percent and Rubin (1962) 67 percent. The only study of this general type that departs from the approximately two-thirds improved rate for residential treatment is a followup by Morris, Escoll, and Wexler (1956) in which the two-thirds rate was reported at termination of treatment, but by age 18, 21 percent of those who could be located were judged by interviews to be doing well. The rest showed varying degrees of poor adjustment.

The major informational value of the studies of outcome in residential treatment centers is that success is comparable, as far as gross judgments of outcome are concerned, to success with children treated in outpatient clinics. Since there have been no untreated controls employed in any of these studies, it is difficult to draw conclusions relevant to the intervention hypothesis, i.e., that children benefit more by treatment than they would by no treatment.

The Intervention Hypothesis: Predictions Based on Specific Variables

Some experimenters have approached the problem of outcome of clinical treatment by making predictions on variables more specific than whether or not a child improved. These studies have been conducted in nonclinic settings, sometimes with children who have not been referred as problem cases, but have been able to approximate a true experimental design more closely than studies whose intent is to evaluate outcome of clinical treatment. The pattern of reporting on brief play therapy experiences for children is to use questionnaires, ratings, and sociometrics as measures of direct consequences of play therapy, and measure of reading achievement as an indirect index of improvement in emotional adjustment.

Fleming and Snyder (1947) selected seven subjects, who had high scores on tests of maladjustment, for group therapy sessions followed by retest on the initial measures. It is difficult to conclude that the reported changes were a function of the group therapy experience, because of the tendency of extreme scores to show regression toward the mean on retesting. Nevertheless, the study established a pattern of using a nonclinic population of children, a non-waiting list control group, a predetermined length of time for experimental intervention and direct measurement of criterion variables. Mehlman (1953) employed nondirective group play therapy with institutionalized familial defective children. Using personality test scores and behavior ratings as the criterion for change, the study found slightly more changes in the therapy group, compared to controls, on scales of the Haggerty, Olson, Wickman Behavior Ratings. Cox (1953) used an elaborate design to include age roles of children in an orphanage as one of the independent variables in a study of play therapy. His prediction that the older children in the group would show changes in sociometric measures as a function of play therapy was confirmed; personality measurements were in the predicted direction but did not achieve significance. In a study by Seeman, Barry, and Ellenwood (1956), an experimental design controlling for the effects of regression was used, by choosing both the experimental and control group from children with extreme scores on adjustment. Following individual play therapy sessions, the experimental group showed significant changes in reputation test scores, teacher ratings were in the predicted direction but not significant and, for aggressive children, there was a shift away from aggressive ratings. Dorfman (1958) approximated a clinic population in an experimental therapy group by using children referred by classroom teachers for help. The design included a wait control period for the experimental subjects, and matched no-therapy controls, and followup of both groups after one year. Scores from a personality test showed no change during the wait period for either group, improvement in the experimental group during therapy which was maintained, but not enhanced, during the one year followup. An adjustment score from a sentence completion test showed a similar pattern of change for both groups.

A different base line was used in reporting the outcomes of brief psychotherapy with children (Phillips and Johnston, 1954; Phillips, 1960). Disappearance of specific symptoms, present in each child on referral, was used as a criterion for change. Comparisons were made with the remission of symptoms in children treated by conventional child guidance methods, rather than a control group. The comparisons of specific symptom remission favor the brief treatment technique in all of the cases reported.

The use of reading achievement as an indirect indication of change attributable to play therapy is based on the notion that reading is an extremely complex skill, and sensitive to interference from emotional maladjustment in children. Bills used an own-control design to investigate the effects of play therapy on the reading achievement of maladjusted retarded readers (1950a). Standardized intelligence and reading achievement tests were used to establish the degree of reading retardation and to measure change in reading skill. There was significantly more gain in reading scores during the therapy period, compared with the control period, and gains for some of the children continued through the followup. A second study by the same author (Bills, 1950b) tested a corollary hypothesis—that retarded readers who were not emotionally maladjusted would not improve in reading skills with play therapy. Fisher (1953) found improvement in reading ability in a group of boys receiving psychotherapy in addition to a remedial reading program, compared to other children in the same remedial reading program who did not receive psychotherapy.

Seeman and Benner (1954) reported a mixed outcome among two groups of children randomly assigned to an experimental group exposed to a group therapy experience and a control group. Experimental children gained more on reading achievement, showed no difference on sociometric scores, and showed a trend that was not quite significant toward greater maladjustment on a personality test.

Studies in Special Program Settings

Three studies reported specific outcomes in treatment of children in residential settings. Rausch, Dittman, and Taylor (1959) used an observational technique to study the change in social interaction of hyperaggressive boys in a residential treatment center. While the pattern of interaction of these children with their peers did not undergo any change during the time of treatment, there was a significant change in their relationship to adults, a decrease in what the study referred to as hostile-dominant behavior. In their evaluation of New York's Wiltwick School for Boys, McCord and McCord (1956) reported a cross sectional comparison of Wiltwick boys with boys in a public reformatory on personality test scores. Differences included lower anxiety among Wiltwick boys, lower authoritarian tendencies, decrease in prejudices, more satisfaction with the world and with themselves, greater interest in constructive activities and a closer attachment to staff members. The only study approximating a prepost design with experimental and control groups in a residential setting is reported by Weeks (1958), a comparison of boys at Highfields and boys in a public reformatory. No control over assignment could be exercised, since administrative groupings had to be used, so the assumption of initial comparability of the two groups may be questioned. The dependent variables in the study were attitudes in regard to family, law and order, and outlook on life, measured by questionnaire. There was little evidence that either group of boys was able to change basic attitudes measured by the questionnaire in the direction of greater conformity to society's values; in fact some subgroups showed change in the reverse direction.

Only one study reported psychometric outcomes of a day school program for emotionally disturbed children. Haring and Phillips (1962) reported test data for a one year experiment with three groups of emotionally disturbed children in Arlington County, Virginia. Administrative groupings were used to study three methods of instruction. Group I received structured instruction, Group II were children left in ordinary classrooms, and Group III received permissive instruction. Behavior ratings by teachers and academic achievement test results were used in a pre-post design to assess change. Changes during the year on both variables clearly favored the structured method, and the authors concluded that the difference was a function of superiority of the method of instruction. Although gains on both dependent variables did favor the structured group, initial differences, especially between Groups I and III, raise serious doubts about the appropriateness of such a comparison. The administrative grouping resulted in large initial differences on all variables reported, age, achievement, and ratings of behavior. In spite of this weakness in design, it is encouraging that an experimental approach has been introduced into an educational setting and definitive criteria have been used to determine outcome in a program for emotionally disturbed children.

Summary

Two working hypotheses in clinical treatment of disturbed children have been examined in this review. The continuity hypothesis, that emotionally disturbed children will become mentally ill adults, has received only mild support. If one begins with mental patients and reviews their developmental history, he is likely to find a record of childhood problems. If one begins with a population of children identified as emotionally disturbed and follows the whole group to adulthood, the evidence is mixed. Neither of the two large scale followup studies was designed specifically to test the continuity hypothesis, so the conclusion must be guarded. The conclusion of the Dallas study is that it is hazardous to predict particular forms of adult mental illness from childhood symptoms, at least in the language we customarily use to talk about children's problems. In any event, only a small proportion of the total group of children became so disturbed as adults that they had to be admitted to a mental hospital. The St. Louis study, on the other hand, identified psychiatric problems in almost two-thirds of its former child patients, but very few of the problems identified could be called serious or incapacitating, and, as in the Dallas study, no accurate predictions could have been made on the basis of presenting symptoms in childhood. So far as the continuity hypothesis is concerned, we must at least conclude that it is incomplete. The extent to which a childhood predisposition to mental illness influences appearance of problems in adult life is not entirely clear, but it is apparently not a determining factor. In this perspective, Levitt's suggestion that time may be more important than treatment has more meaning. That some disturbed children will grow up to be disturbed adults is undoubtedly true, but many others will grow up to be ordinary adults with no more than their share of problems.

The second hypothesis of clinical treatment, that therapeutic intervention enhances the general adjustment status of disturbed children, has received even less support than the continuity hypothesis. The regularity with which the two-thirds to three-fourths improvement figure occurs in studies of disturbed children, regardless of treatment, suggests a widely shared bias that allows us to see all but the most obstreperous children as "better than they were."

The most convincing evidence for the effectiveness of intervention is in studies using criteria more specific than assessment of general adjustment. While some might argue that sociometric scores, questionnaires, and tests beg the real question of whether the child is better, the fact is that as outcome variables they reflect differential change while global judgments of improvement do not. One way of interpreting this difference, of course, is that as research tools, judgments about general adjustment are simply not as reliable as test scores or ratings on specific items of behavior. However, in the absence of compelling confirmation of the continuity hypothesis, we may need to re-examine what we hope to accomplish by intervention, rather than concluding that the evaluation of intervention is a hopeless undertaking. If we do not postulate a linear relationship between emotional disturbance in childhood and mental illness in adulthood, the treatment of symptoms may be all we can realistically undertake. If we cannot aspire to reconstruction of personality that will have long range beneficial effects, we can modify disturbing behavior in specific ways in present social contexts. This more modest aspiration may not only be more realistic, but it may be all that is required of the child-helping professions in a society that is relatively open and provides a variety of opportunity systems in which a child can reconcile his personal needs with society's expectations of him.

Article References

Allbright, Sue, and Gambrell, Helen. Personality traits as criteria for the psychiatric treatment of adolescents. *Smith College Studies in Social Work*, 1938, 9, 1–26.

Barbour, R.F., and Beefell, C.J. The followup of a child guidance clinic population. *Journal of Mental Science*, 1955, 101, 794–809.

Beaumont, Arlene. Psychotherapy of children by social case workers. *Smith College Studies in Social Work*, 1945, 15, 259–286.

Benjamin, A., and Weatherly, H.E. Hospital treatment of emotionally disturbed children. *American Journal of Orthopsychiatry*, 1947, 17, 665–674.

Bills, R.E. Nondirective play therapy with retarded readers. *Journal of Consulting Psychology*, 1950a, 14, 140–149.

Bills, R.E. Play therapy with well-adjusted retarded readers. *Journal of Consulting Psychology*, 1950b, 14, 246–249.

Birren, J.E. Psychological examinations of children who later become psychotic. *Journal of Abnormal Social Psychology*, 1944, 39, 84–95.

Bower, E.M., Shellhammer, T.A. Daily, J.M., and Bower, M. *High school students who later become schizophrenic.* Sacramento, California: State Department of Education, 1960.

Bowman, K.M. A study of the pre-psychotic personality in certain psychoses. *American Journal of Orthopsychiatry*, 1934, 14, 28–35.

Brown, Marjorie. Adolescents treatable by a family agency. *Smith College Studies in Social Work*, 1947, 18, 37–67.

Cox, J.N. Sociometric status and individual treatment before and after play therapy. *Journal of Abnormal Social Psychology*, 1953, 48, 354–356.

Cunningham, J.M., Westerman, H.H., and Fischhoff, J. A follow-up study of patients seen in a psychiatric clinic for children. *American Journal of Orthopsychiatry*, 1956, 26, 602–612.

Dorfman, Elaine. Personality outcomes of client-centered child therapy. *Psychological Monograph*, 1958, 72 (Whole No. 456).

Eysenck, H.J. The effects of psychotherapy: an evaluation. *Journal of Consulting Psychology*, 1952, 16, 319–324.

Fisher, B. Group therapy with retarded readers. *Journal of Educational Psychology*, 1953, 44, 354–360.

Fleming, L., and Snyder, W.U. Social and personal changes following non-directive group play therapy. *American Journal of Orthopsychiatry*, 1947, 17, 101–116.

Friedlander, Dorothea. Personality development of twenty-seven children who later became psychotic. *Journal of Abnormal Social Psychology*, 1945, 40, 330–335.

Gibbs, J.M. Group play therapy. *British Journal of Medical Psychology*, 1945, 20, 244–254.

Hamilton, D.M., McKinley, R.A., Moorhead, H.H., and Wall, J.H. Results of mental hospital treatment of troubled youth. *American Journal of Psychiatry*, 1961, 117, 811–816.

Hardcastle, D.H. A follow-up study of 100 cases made for the Department of Psychological Medicine, Guy's Hospital. *Journal of Mental Science*, 1934, 80, 536–549.

Haring, N.G., and Phillips, E.L. *Educating emotionally disturbed children.* New York: McGraw-Hill Book Company, 1962.

Heinicke, C.M., and Goldman, A. Research on psychotherapy with children: a review and suggestions for further study. *American Journal of Orthopsychiatry*, 1960, 30, 483–494.

Hood-Williams, J. The results of psychotherapy with children: a re-evaluation. *Journal of Consulting Psychology*, 1960, 24, 84–88.

Hubbard, Ruth M., and Adams, Christine F. Factors affecting the success of child guidance treatment. *American Journal of Orthopsychiatry*, 1936, 6, 81–102.

Jacobsen, Virginia. Influential factors in the outcome of treatment of school phobia. *Smith College Studies in Social Work*, 1948, 18, 181–202.

Johnson, Lillian, and Reid, J.H. Evaluation of ten years' work with emotionally disturbed children. *Ryther Child Center Monograph*, 1947, IV.

Kasanin, J., and Veo, L.A. A study of the school adjustments of children who later in life became psychotic. *American Journal of Orthopsychiatry*, 1932, 2, 212–227.

LaMore, Mary T. An evaluation of a state hospital child guidance clinic. *Smith College Studies in Social Work*, 1941, 12, 137–164.

Lehrman, L.J., Sirluck, H., Black, B., and Glick, S. Success and failure of treatment of children in the child guidance clinics of the Jewish Board of Guardians, New York City. *Jewish Board of Guardians Research Monograph*, 1949, No. 1, 1–1–87.

Levi, Aurelia, and Ginott, H.G. The results of psychotherapy with children: another evaluation. Unpublished manuscript, 1961. Cited by H.G. Ginott, *Group psychotherapy with children*. New York: McGraw-Hill Book Company, 1961, 145–147.

Levitt, E.E. The results of psychotherapy with children: an evaluation. *Journal of Consulting Psychology*, 1957a, 21, 189–196.

Levitt, E.E. A comparison of "remainers" and "defectors" among child clinic patients. *Journal of Consulting Psychology*, 1957b, 21, 316.

Levitt, E.E. A comparative judgment study of "defection" from treatment at a child guidance clinic. *Journal of Clinical Psychology*, 1958a, 14, 429–432.

Levitt, E.E. Parent's reasons for defection from treatment at a child guidance clinic. *Mental Hygiene*, 1958b, 42, 521–524.

Levitt, E.E., Beiser, Helen R., and Robertson, R.E. A follow-up evaluation of cases treated at a community child guidance clinic. *American Journal of Orthopsychiatry*, 1959, 29, 337–349.

McCord, W., and McCord, Joan. *Psychopathy and delinquency*. New York: Grune and Stratton, 1956.

McCord, W., McCord, Joan, and Zola, I.K. *Origins of crime: a new evaluation of the Cambridge-Sommerville Youth Study*. New York: Columbia University Press, 1959.

Mehlman, B. Group therapy with mentally retarded children. *Journal of Abnormal and Social Psychology*, 1953, 48, 53–60.

Michael, C.M., Morris, D.P., and Soroker, E. Follow-up studies of shy, withdrawn children: II. Relative incidence of schizophrenia. *American Journal of Orthopsychiatry*, 1957, 27, 331–337.

Morris, D.P., and Soroker, Eleanor. A follow-up study of a guidance clinic waiting list. *Mental Hygiene*, 1953, 37, 84–88.

Morris, D.P., Soroker, Eleanor, and Burress, Genette. Follow-up studies of shy withdrawn children: I. Evaluation of later adjustment. *American Journal of Orthopsychiatry*, 1954, 24, 743–754.

Morris, H.H., Jr., Escoll, P.J., and Wexler, R. Aggressive behavior disorders of childhood: a follow-up study. *American Journal of Psychiatry*, 1956, 112, 991–997.

Norman, Vivian, Rosen, Beatrice, and Bohn, Anita. Psychiatric clinic out-patients in the United States, 1959. *Mental Hygiene*, 1962, 46, 321–343.

O'Neal, Patricia, and Robins, L.N. Childhood patterns predictive of adult schizophrenia: a 30 year follow-up study. *American Journal of Psychiatry*, 1958a, 115, 385–391.

O'Neal, Patricia, and Robins, L.N. The relation of childhood behavior problems to adult psychiatric status: a thirty year follow-up of 150 subjects. *American Journal of Psychiatry*, 1958b, 114, 961–969.

Phillips, E.L. Parent-child psychotherapy: a follow-up study comparing two techniques. *Journal of Psychology*, 1960, 49, 195–202.

Phillips, E.L., and Johnson, Margaret. Theoretical and clinical aspects of short-term, parent-child psychotherapy. *Psychiatry*, 1954, 17, 267–275.

Powers, E., and Witmer, Helen. *An experiment in the prevention of delinquency*. New York: Columbia University Press, 1951.

Rausch, H.L., Dittman, A.T., and Taylor, T.J. The interpersonal behavior of children in residential treatment. *Journal of Abnormal Social Psychology*, 1959, 58, 9–26.

Reid, J.H., and Hagan, Helen. *Residential treatment of emotionally disturbed children*. New York: Child Welfare League of America, 1952.

Robins, L.N., and O'Neal, Patricia. Mortality, mobility and crime: problem children 30 years later. *American Sociological Review*, 1958, 23, 162–171.

Rodriquez, A., Rodriquez, M., and Eisenberg, L. The outcome of school phobia: a follow-up study based on 41 cases. *American Journal of Psychiatry*, 1959, 116, 540–544.

Rosenthal, F.M., and Pinsky, G.D. Follow-up method in child guidance work. *American Journal of Orthopsychiatry*, 1936, 6, 609–615.

Rotenberg, Gertrude. Can problem adolescents be aided apart from their parents? *Smith College Studies in Social Work*, 1947, 17, 204–222.

Rubin, E.Z. Special education in a psychiatric hospital. *Exceptional Children*, 1962, 29, 184–190.

Seeman, J., Barry, E., and Ellenwood, C. Process and outcomes of play therapy. *American Psychologist*, 1956, 11, 428.

Seeman, J., and Benner, E. A therapeutic approach to reading difficulties. *Journal of Consulting Psychology*, 1954, 18, 541–543.

Shirley, Mary, Baun, Betty, and Polsky, Sylvia. Outgrowing childhood's problems: a follow-up study of child guidance patients. *Smith College Studies in Social Work*, 1940, 11, 31–60.

Weeks, H.A. *Youthful offenders at Highfields: an evaluation of the effects of the short-term treatment of delinquent boys.* Ann Arbor: University of Michigan Press, 1958.

Witmer, Helen. A comparison of treatment results in various types of child guidance clinics. *American Journal of Orthopsychiatry*, 1935a, 5, 351–360.

Witmer, Helen. The later social adjustment of problem children: a report of 13 follow-up investigations. *Smith College Studies in Social Work*, 1935b, 6, 1–98.

Witmer, Helen L., and Keller, Jane. Outgrowing childhood problems: a study in the value of child guidance treatment. *Smith College Studies in Social Work*, 1942, 74–90.

Witmer, Helen, and students. The outcome of treatment in a child guidance clinic: a comparison and an evaluation. *Smith College Studies in Social Work*, 1933, 3, 339–399.

Wittman, M.P., and Huffman, A.V. A comparative study of developmental, adjustment, and personality characteristics of psychotic, psychoneurotic, delinquent and normally adjusted teen-age youths. *Journal of Genetic Psychology*, 1945, 66, 167–182.

Zick, Frances. Outcome of intramural psychotherapy of children. *Smith College Studies in Social Work*, 1943, 14, 127–132.

In a subsequent review, Clarizio[9] concludes that retrospective studies offer only modest evidence that the maladjusted child grows into a maladjusted adult. Both he and Morris's group[10] suggest that neurotic symptoms in childhood do not predict neurosis in adults. However, serious social maladjustment is predictive. In a study more closely related to the school situation, Zax and his associates[11] found that, compared to normal children, first graders with a high potential for being disturbed earned lower grades, scored lower on achievements tests, and were rated by teachers and peers as more poorly adjusted, when they reached the seventh grade. They do not believe that early mental health problems are transient.

Glavin[12] points out that thirty percent of "screened for problem" children who receive no planned intervention have persistent disturbance, but the majority of the emotional disturbances of young school children do not persist over four years. He also makes the point that these figures do not apply to profoundly disturbed children; the figures refer only to those who remained in regular classes.

Kohlberg et al.[13] have written a thorough review of the relationship between childhood behavior and adult mental health. They point out that it is not the *absence of problems* which is predictive of adult status, but the *presence of various competencies* which makes the difference. In general, they find little support for the continuity theory that emotionally disturbed children will become mentally ill adults. Exceptions are found in biological predispositions to schizophrenia and in sociopathic conditions or character disorders that are the result of environmental factors—these two aspects are predictive of future difficulty.

From Kohlberg it is evident that significant physiological limitations and severe environmental conditions must be taken into consideration regarding risk in follow-up studies. The Thomas, Chess, and Birch excerpt presents a reasoned viewpoint concerning the implications of biological aspects.

Temperament and
Behavior Disorders in Children
Alexander Thomas
Stella Chess
Herbert G. Birch

Theoretical Implications of
the Findings

The findings of our longitudinal study of children who developed behavior disorders clearly indicate that features of temperament, together with their organization and patterning, play significant roles in the genesis and evolution of behavior disorders in childhood. Both before and after they developed symptoms, groups of the children with behavioral disturbances differed in temperament from those who did not develop such disturbances. The clinical cases, as a group, were characterized by an excessive frequency of either high or low activity, irregularity, withdrawal responses to novel stimuli, nonadaptability, high intensity, persistence, and distractibility. No single temperamental trait acted alone in influencing the course of the child's development. Rather, combinations of traits forming patterns and clusters tended to result in an increased risk for developing behavioral disorders. Differences in types of behavior disorders and of symptoms, too, were found to be associated with differences in temperament.

A given pattern of temperament did not, as such, result in a behavioral disturbance. Deviant, as well as normal, development was the result of the interaction between the child with given characteristics of temperament and significant features of his intra-familial and extra-familial environment. Temperament, representing one aspect of a child's individuality, also interacted with abilities and motives, the other two facets, as well as with the environment, in determining the specific behavior patterns that evolved in the course of development.

Given our findings on the relevance of temperamental factors to the genesis and evolution

of behavior disorders, we may explore their implications for general theory in psychiatry and child development. As is the case when any significant influencing variable is identified, there is an understandable temptation to make temperament the heart and body of a general theory. To do so would be to repeat a frequent approach in psychiatry which, over the years, has been beset by general theories of behavior based upon fragments rather than the totality of influencing mechanisms. A one-sided emphasis on temperament would merely repeat and perpetuate such a tendency and would be antithetical to our viewpoint, which insists that we recognize temperament as only one attribute of the organism. In our view, temperament must at all times be considered in its internal relations with abilities and motives and in its external relations with environmental opportunities and stresses. Consequently, the relevance of the concept of temperament to general psychiatric theory lies neither in its sole pertinence for behavior disorders, nor in its displacement of other conceptualizations, but in the fact that it must be incorporated into any general theory of normal and aberrant behavioral development if the theory is to be complete. Existing theories emphasize motives and drive states, tactics of adaptation, environmental patterns of influence, and primary organic determinants. The central requirement that a concept of temperament makes of such generalizations is that they come increasingly to focus on the individual and on his uniqueness. In other words, it requires that we recognize that the same motive, the same adaptive tactic, or the same structure of objective environment will have different functional meaning in accordance with the temperamental style of the given child. Moreover, in such an individualization of the study of functional mechanisms in behavior, temperament must be considered as an independent determining variable in itself, and not as an *ad hoc* modifier used to fill in the gaps left unexplained by other mechanisms.

A formulation of the role of the child's own

characteristics that fails to give temperament serious consideration together with other mechanisms is
illustrated in a recent discussion of autistic psychosis. The author, herself a longtime student of
organismic individual differences in children, asserts
an a priori hierarchy assigning prime importance to
"mothering" and secondary importance to the
child's characteristics: "Children who suffer from
this illness have in common the lack or distortion of
a mutual relationship with a mother person . . . in
some instances this deficiency arises because there
was no mother who responded to the baby as normal mothers do—an environmental deficiency. But
the illness also occurs in children who were raised
by normally responsive mothers who provide all
that other children receive. But the child is so
constituted that he cannot participate in the usual
patterns of interaction, probably due to an inborn
deficit yet to be specified. The child deficient in the
capacity to respond is just as motherless as is the
normally equipped child without a mother."

This formulation assumes that autism is a
deficiency disease; and that the essential nutritive element is "mothering." It implies that there is one
pattern of mothering that may be classified as adequate for all children and assumes, on hypothetical
grounds, that such a universal "adequate" for the
mothering process does exist. However, a recognition of temperamental differences and their
significance for development makes it impossible to
accept such universals, whether for the mothering
process or any other environmental influence, and
emphasizes the need to clarify and define "adequacy" in terms of the goodness of fit between the organism cared for and the pattern of care, if such care
is to result in certain socially defined consequences.

A contrasting illustration, in which temperament is seriously treated as a determining variable
rather than as an ad hoc consideration, can be cited
from the recent literature. In a psychiatric study of
children with poor school achievement, Ross defines
a syndrome of behavioral distrubance which he calls
"the unorganized child." He identifies the specific
attributes of the child's individuality and parental
functioning as independent but mutually interacting
influences, and avoids any hierarchal designation of
one as more fundamental than the other. Ross
identifies the pertinent factors involved in the
development of the unorganized child as the combination of the temperamental characteristics of
high distractibility, short attention span, and low
persistence in interaction with the parental attributes of overpermissiveness or disorganization of
functioning. He further points out that specific

manifestations of the syndrome will depend on
whether these temperamental qualities are combined with high or low activity level and intense or
mild responses. Specifically, Ross suggests that the
unorganized child may show restlessness and a tendency to chatter disruptively if he also has a high
activity level, daydreaming if he is less active, and
tantrums when frustrated if he is also intense in his
reactions.

Thus, a truly interactionist approach rejects the
attempt to impose a priori hierachal judgments of
relative importance on child and environment in the
developmental process. Moreover, it rejects the
dichotomy of child versus environment and recognizes that the effective environment is the product
of the selective responsiveness of the child to aspects of the objective situation to which he is exposed. An interactionist approach also cannot be
satisfied with the application of global characteriza-
tions that children have "different constitutional
dispositions" or that some mothers are "good" and
others "bad" to explain all the vicissitudes of normal and disturbed development. What is required,
first of all, is not merely an acceptance of the statement that children differ, but knowledge of how
they differ and how these differences are
continuously expressed as significant determinative
factors in psychological growth. What is also required is not the categorization of parents as better
or worse, more or less hostile, anxious, etc., but the
delineation of those specific attributes of parental attitudes and practices and of other intra- and
extrafamilial environmental factors that are
interacting with the specific temperamental and
other organismic characteristics of the child to produce specific consequences for psychological development.

Motivational and Nonmotivational Factors

Although a long-term study must have a defined
focus if it is to avoid the dangers of diffuseness and
tangential pursuits, it is inevitable that such focused
inquiry will have certain serendipitous outcomes.
Such outcomes derive from the fact that what is
being considered in detail is the developmental
course of normal and aberrant behavioral styles, an
issue which is more broadly encompassing than is
temperament. Consequently, the sequential data on
behavioral development necessary to assess the role
of temperament in development are also entirely

pertinent to a consideration of motivational features of functioning. As a result, the findings on symptom selection and evolution provide a substantial basis for considering the interrelations of motivational and nonmotivational factors, intrapsychic maneuvers, anxiety, and psychodynamic defenses in the development of normal and disturbed behavior. The implications of the findings for these issues can now be considered.

A major aspect of most theoretical formulations on the causes and nature of behavioral disturbances is the extent to which conceptualized intrapsychic purposes and aims are invoked as explanatory principles. Classical psychoanalysis and certain forms of contemporary learning theory present opposite and extreme positions with regard to the importance of such motives in the causation of disturbed behavior. For the orthodox psychoanalyst, motives are all-important. As stated by Freud in one of his final systematic formulations, "The symptoms of neuroses are exclusively, it might be said, either a substitutive satisfaction of some sexual impulse or measures to prevent such a satisfaction, and are as a rule compromises between the two." In other words, the primary force is considered as motivational, i.e., the aim to either satisfy or prevent the satisfaction of a basic drive. The motivational preoccupation of psychoanalytic theory has been ubiquitously evident in its search for the sources of psychopathological phenomena in underlying purposes, motives, and conceptualized goals and aims. A typical contemporary expression can be found in a discussion of child psychiatry in the *American Handbook of Psychiatry*. The general assertion is made that "there is evidence of repression and of the 'return of the repressed' in the symptoms of the neurotic child," and various specific symptoms are considered within this motivational framework. As an example, sleeplessness is stated to reflect "a vigilant attempt at protest against a frightening impression of the environment." At the other extreme, are the learning theorists, such as Eysenck, for whom "neurotic behavior consists of maladaptive conditioned responses of the autonomic system and of skeletal responses made to reduce the conditioned sympathetic reactions." With this formulation goes a denial of the existence of underlying motivational states. Thus, Eysenck states further that "there is no underlying complex or other 'dynamic' cause which is responsible for the maladaptive behavior; all we have to deal with in neurosis is conditioned maladaptive behavior."

Our findings that temperament-environment interactions play an important part in the develop-

ment of behavioral disturbance in the young child suggests that it is frequently unnecessary and unparsimonious to postulate the existence of complex intrapsychic motivational states to account for maladaptation during the period of early development. The concern of such child analysts as Spitz, who have lamented the difficulty of studying intrapsychic states in young children, therefore appears unnecessary, inasmuch as the objective behavioral data obtainable for this age group appear quite sufficient for the study of the course of psychological development. . . .

Concepts of learning theory, based on conditioning, offer a non-motivational explanation for the manner in which specific maladaptive patterns may arise. It does not appear possible, however, to encompass the dynamics of symptom evolution in some of the older children entirely within the framework of a simple conditioned reflex model. Thus, as the growing child's subjective life expands and his psychological organization is increasingly influenced by ideation, abstraction, and symbolic representation, conceptualized motives and aims may, in some cases, begin to play an important part in symptom formation and evolution at older age periods.

To summarize, our findings would suggest that it is merely confusing to attribute elaborate psychological motivational mechanisms to the young child if a simpler explanation accounts for all the facts. In the older child, it may be necessary to invoke such motivational states when efforts to explain the behaviors in terms of simple mechanisms appear inadequate. . . .

Prevention of Behavioral Disturbance

The prevention of behavioral disturbances in childhood covers a vast array of issues, including those genetic, biochemical, temperamental, neurological, perceptual, cognitive, and environmental factors that may influence the course of behavioral development. The child's termperament is only one of the many issues to be considered by professional workers concerned with the prevention of pathology in psychological development, though often an important one. As our findings have demonstrated, the degree to which parents, teachers, pediatricians, and others handle a youngster in a manner appropriate to his temperamental characteristics can significantly influence the course of his psychological development. The oft-repeated motto, "Treat your child as an individual," achieves substance to the extent that the individuality of a child is truly recognized and respected. The other frequently offered prescription of "tender loving care" often has great value in promoting a positive parent-child interaction, but does not obviate the importance of the parent's actual child-care practices being consonant with his child's temperamental qualities.

Finally, the recognition that a child's behavioral disturbance is not necessarily the direct result of maternal pathology should do much to prevent the deep feelings of guilt and inadequacy with which innumerable mothers have been unjustly burdened

as a result of being held entirely responsible for their children's problems. Mothers who are told authoritatively that child raising is a "task not easily achieved by the average mother in our culture" are not likely to approach this responsibility with the relaxation and confidence that would be beneficial to both their own and their child's mental health. It is our conviction, however, that the difficulties of child raising can be significantly lightened by advocating an approach of which the average mother *is* capable—the recognition of her child's specific qualities of individuality, and the adoption of those child-care practices that are most appropriate to them.

A closely related area for examination is the prognosis for true learning disability cases, where parents have been led to expect everything from "cure by growing up"[14] to highly pessimistic anticipations regardless of intervention.[15]

To illustrate Kolberg's thesis about high-risk populations, attention is given to studies dealing with both psychotic children and those with severe social deviance.

There have been several studies of seriously disturbed children. Fairly representative is one by Watt et al.[16] They examined the public school

records of thirty hospitalized schizophrenics and concluded that these persons could have been picked out by screening procedures. However, until a study has been conducted on the subsequent adult status of an unselected sample of children with comparable symptoms, it is impossible to judge their results.

Many studies are retrospective, but the following study by Havelkova has the advantage of more complete initial data. The conclusions can be related to the concepts in the previous report.

Follow-up Study of 71 Children Diagnosed as Psychotic in Preschool Age

Milada Havelkova, M.D.

Though the diagnosis of childhood psychosis has become popular in the past 20 years, the prognosis has remained an unanswered question. A vaguely defined condition, its natural history is obscure. "We are not dealing with a separate and distinct clinical entity; rather we are dealing with a group of clinical syndromes."[13] A follow-up study on a syndrome which may well be a group of diseases would seem to have only minimal value, except as an attempt to separate subgroups with a similar long-term clinical picture.

Psychoses in childhood are rare, and most investigators have observed only limited numbers of children, of different ages, with different types and degrees of illness, treated by different methods —making any real comparison of the findings extremely difficult. Many of the follow-up studies were done at least partly for the purpose of assess-

ing effectiveness of particular treatment methods. In his review of the subject up to 1957, Eisenberg says:

Clinical disorders which are characterized by a prolonged and fluctuating time course provide particularly vexing problems for the evaluation of therapeutic results.

Once again, it seems inescapable that steps in maturation will now and again follow the introduction of new treatment programs. The very eagerness of the investigator, as a physician, to relieve the suffering caused by the illness makes him all too ready to assign the changes observed to the agent he is administering at the time.[8]

From the *American Journal of Orthopsychiatry*, vol. 38, no. 5, pp. 846–857. Copyright ©1968, the American Orthopsychiatric Association, Inc. Reproduced by permission.

Bender, in a study mainly concerned with the existence of the syndrome of childhood schizophrenia itself and with the results of electroconvulsive therapy, was able to trace 120 children out of 143 treated. She reported that two-thirds of the shock-treated group required subsequent hospital care, one-third continuously. Fifty percent were in the community and 25 percent were showing fair to good adjustment. Fifty patients not treated by shock were considered a control group. Of the control, two-thirds were subsequently sent to state hospitals, one-third of them became chronically hospitalized. Only 2 (4 percent) were making a fair to good adjustment.[1]

The well-known Eisenberg and Kanner study[3] has been used by many child psychiatrists as a basis for prediction and comparison. That study was based on 80 autistic children at least 9 years old and known to the authors for at least 4 years. Sixty-three (79 percent) were traced. The median and average age of the children studied was 15 years; the median and average follow-up period was 9 years. The outcome was "good" (patient functioning well, academically and socially) in 3 cases; "fair" (able to attend grade school but of a distinctively deviant personality) in 14 cases; and "poor" (maladapted, with apparent feeblemindedness and/or grossly disturbed psychotic behavior) in 46 cases. Thus, about 27 percent were functioning at a fair to good social level, a figure remarkably consistent with Bender's findings (25 percent). However it became apparent that those children who failed to develop speech, or once having developed it lost it, did much more poorly than the others. Taking as the line of demarcation, speech with communicative value by the age of 5, Eisenberg and Kanner found 50 percent of the "speaking" children achieved fair to good adjustment whereas only 3 percent of the nonspeaking did so. The study failed to reveal any correlation between formal psychiatric treatment and clinical outcome. However, the authors were struck by the considerable efforts extended by schools and parents on behalf of those children who had improved and could not escape feeling that these efforts were important in their recovery.

Brown[6] summarized the current status of 129 of 136 children age 10 or older who had been diagnosed during their preschool years as having "atypical development." The results showed that 59 percent were absorbing enough formal learning to compete in society, 36 percent were receiving schooling through normal education channels, and most of the others were in schools for the retarded rather than for the disturbed. Over one-half seemed

to have made a psychological adjustment that would enable them to function within society.

Using the Eisenberg and Kanner classification of outcome, Bettelheim[4] in his recent book on infantile autism gives follow-up data on 40 patients treated in the Chicago Orthogenic School. For 8 of 40 children (20 percent) the end results of therapy were "poor." For 15 (38 percent) the outcome was "fair", for 17 (42 percent) "good." Bettelheim reluctantly agrees that, as yet, the prognosis is closely related to the child's willingness to speak.

The intensity of feeling expressed in the conclusions drawn from these studies reflects the bias of the authors. It is difficult, and sometimes impossible, to communicate a child's degree of illness even between staff members of the same clinic let alone between members of different clinics. Some of the differences in results in reported series may be due to variations in the method of selection of cases. In Kanner and Eisenberg's group were 32 speaking and 31 nonspeaking children, while in Bettelheim's group were 26 speaking and 14 nonspeaking children. The lack of parallel studies (treated and untreated cases) makes comparison between one clinic and another all the more complex.

Knowing very well that our study suffers from all these imperfections and that our material and methods are not quite comparable to those of others, we have provided our own controls—untreated children. We offer our observations feeling that they can make a useful contribution to the general knowledge about the course of childhood psychosis.

Methods

Our study is a clinical follow-up study of 71 psychotic children (42 treated and 29 untreated). All first assessed during their preschool years, they have been followed for 4 to 12 years and were between 8 and 17 years old at the time of study. Sixty-four children attended the West End Creche (a day care center for disturbed children placed in an established nursery for normal children). Seven comparable cases from The Hospital for Sick Children were added to increase the number of untreated children. The diagnostic criteria used were Kanner's for infantile autism[14] and Bender's description of the autistic and pseudoneurotic form of schizophrenia.[2] Later, the criteria of the British Working Party also were used.[5]

To summarize the criteria for selection: The child must have been diagnosed at preschool age as a case of early infantile autism or childhood schizophrenia, of the autistic or pseudoneurotic form; he must have been followed by us for at least 4 years after the diagnosis was made. Cases of secondary autism were excluded.

Original Assessment

In the West End Creche Treatment Centre the therapeutic and diagnostic team consisted of: a nursery therapist (nursery teacher trained for therapy in the Centre), who works with the child on a one-to-one basis 2 hours a day 4 times a week; a social worker, who works with the parents for an hour once a week or more if required; a supervising psychiatrist. Psychological services were obtained either privately or from The Hospital for Sick Children.

During the diagnostic assessment the child was observed for 4 weeks in different life situations, alone and in a group of normal or of disturbed children. His individual therapist was always present. Semistructured daily reports were made by the therapist and some of the sessions were observed by the psychiatrist, directly or through one-way screens. Additional investigations such as neurological evaluation, EEG, hearing and speech assessment were done during the month if necessary. Family assessment was by interview or home visits.

In the final conference at the end of the fourth week, the diagnosis was made, the degree of illness determined, the child's response to our program evaluated, and a decision made about the best therapeutic plan for him.

The 7 untreated cases added from The Hospital for Sick Children were all assessed in their preschool years. As well known to me as the West End Creche children, they were followed for the same length of time. Direct assessment by me provided a reasonable substitute for the month-long observation at the West End Creche. Most of the cases referred to West End Creche directly or to me in my position as psychiatrist at The Hospital for Sick Children had been already diagnosed by another psychiatrist as cases of infantile autism or childhood schizophrenia. They were sent for consultation and planning of treatment.

Over the years of the study we went through various stages of trying to distinguish the different syndromes as described by other authors. The signs overlap, often making distinction impossible. The problems arise between the autistic forms of psychosis (infantile autism of Kanner and the autistic form of childhood schizophrenia of Bender) and the pseudoneurotic form of schizophrenia of Bender. Slowly we came to call these forms of illness, "phases": autistic, symbiotic (not always present), pseudoneurotic, and pseudopsychopathic. Any one of these developmental phases turns into a permanent form of illness if the child's further development becomes arrested.

We excluded those children in whom the autistic symptoms were considered to be secondary to gross brain damage or to a clear-cut mental defect, since they were unlikely to respond to our therapeutic program. Those children who had delayed milestones other than speech and toilet training, and did not function close to their age level, were considered mentally defective and were also excluded.

Results of Diagnostic Observations

The diagnostic observations during the assessment period contained an element of therapeutic trial. We attempted to determine whether a psychotic disturbance was present, to identify the type and the severity of the disturbance, and to judge the child's ability to respond to therapy.

The Severely Affected: 17 children (24 percent):   The children belonging to this group had typical symptoms of the autistic form of childhood schizophrenia to such a degree that a diagnosis was possible on the first contact. Response of this group to the month of observation was negligible.

The Moderately Affected: 29 children (41 percent):   These children presented patterns of behavior comparable to those in the severely affected group, although they were usually less autistic. Those over 4½ years showed some evidence of pseudoneurotic behavior. During the month of observation favorable signs were noted: the minimal ability to play in a constructive and goal-directed way; the presence of some specific fears and phobias as compared with the purely diffuse anxiety of the more severely disturbed children; the presence of compulsive-obsessive defenses rather than straight withdrawal; some indication of the beginnings of language.

The Mildly Affected: 25 children (35 percent): These children, although presenting typical symptoms, did not show them at all times, so that a period of observation was needed to confirm the diagnosis. Seen when very young they displayed autistic behavior, but at a later age pseudoneurotic behavior. The youngest child whose behavior was noted as pseudoneurotic was 3 years old.

Selection of Cases for Treatment

Children found to be severely affected were not admitted for treatment because they were considered untreatable by our methods. A therapeutic trial given to 3 of these was unsuccessful.

The moderately affected were given preference in selection for therapy since no improvement seemed likely without therapeutic intervention. Only 3 assessed by us as moderately affected could not, for different reasons, be included in our treatment program.

Lack of space prevented treatment of the mildly affected. We felt they could make progress in other settings. Only 6 of this group received treatment in the West End Creche, the majority being referred to ordinary nursery schools in the area. Some of these children, later treated elsewhere as more facilities developed in the community, are included in this study in the "mixed" treatment group.

The Treatment

The treatment for all the children was on a one-to-one basis. Each child had his own playroom as a home base and his individual nursery therapist, who first tried to develop a personal relationship with him and later introduce him into the normal nursery school environment. Although with experience this plan has undergone some modification in detail, we learned much from it. We started with a very understanding and accepting attitude, attempting to build a relationship on the positive side only, with minimal restrictions and directions. During the first 2 years this was changed, because we found by experience that restrictions and normal directions to the child enhanced the relationship with the therapist, making it possible for her to teach the child the skills without which his transfer to normal nursery school environment would be unsuccessful.

Our original idea for a part-time mother substitute was found to be confusing to both child and therapist, creating unnecessary problems between the therapist and the child's mother. Also, some of the children on their arrival already had a relationship to their mothers and took many months to develop a relationship to their therapists. For these, a mother-substitute seemed quite nonsensical. We redefined the role of the therapist as that of a therapist only.

The child's activities in the playroom ranged from pleasurable social and physical contact, learning to dress and undress, eating and toilet training, to learning the use of educational toys, drawing and making letters and numbers. Outings on the streets and into the stores, trips on streetcars and into parks and playgrounds were included according to the child's needs. In retrospect, we feel children tended to follow patterns similar to those of other disturbed children under psychiatric treatment, but their progress was slower.

After the child had overcome his resistance, had accepted the limits placed on him, enrolment in the normal nursery began. At this stage his therapist was able to help him do the tasks he disliked and face and overcome the frightening experience of meeting a group of children. Not all children were able to reach this stage; those who did required one to 2 years of individual therapy first.

Enrolment in the nursery school was slow and gradual. Separation from the therapist was accomplished by replacing the relationship with another more superficial one, a relationship to the teacher in the normal nursery. When the child was able to function in the group without his therapist, we considered him ready to be discharged from the treatment center and admitted to the nursery school. The teachers in the normal nursery were instructed to aim expectations toward "normal" behavior for the child rather than to try to adjust the school to his needs. The period of adjustment to the group took usually about one year. This, added to the early treatment, made a total period of 2 to 3 years.

Casework for the family was provided on a weekly basis to help the parents understand their child, improve their relationship with him, and support the normal aspects of his personality. In the early years of the program, therapy was concerned with the child's environment, and though we made no statements to parents about the origin of the child's illness, their already existing guilt feelings were increased by the therapy. To keep parents motivated to change the environment, we made no attempt to decrease their guilt feelings. This led to later rejection of the child who failed to achieve the improvement they had hoped for from their efforts. This approach was changed.

Realizing that we had failed to recognize our

limitations and had not made them clear to the parents, we started purposely to decrease parental guilt by explaining immediately that the child had a sickness and a very serious one. By decreasing the parents' denial of the child's serious illness, we hoped to be able to handle their hostility and guilt toward the child while he was still under treatment. From our follow-up studies we believe this approach has been helpful in preventing later rejection.

The "Control" Cases

At the beginning of our project there was no other treatment center in our area for psychotic children, so that the most we could offer some children was regular counseling. This proved unsatisfactory. Helping a mother assume attitudes which would make the child less withdrawn and consequently more troublesome without relieving her of the child usually ended by the mother stopping the treatment and placing the child in an institution. In 3 cases the mother actually suffered a serious depression. Consequently we abandoned this form of treatment.

The mildly ill children showed a tendency to spontaneous improvement and were not generally admitted to our treatment program. Borderline cases seemed to improve with maturation, nursery school attendance, and an occasional follow-up interview. Those with whom some regular contact was maintained but who received no formal therapy made up our untreated group. In the "mixed" group were the children followed by us as untreated cases but later enrolled in other treatment programs. Several attended only psychiatric outpatient clinics on a weekly basis. The shortest period of such outpatient treatment was just over 7 months. The longest period of inpatient treatment in this group was 3 years.

Findings of the Study

While observing the children's development throughout the years we found two typical forms of illness: the autistic and the pseudoneurotic. Only 3 children could not be placed in one or other of these categories—they represented a mixture of both forms throughout the follow-up period. A number of children changing from the autistic to the pseudoneurotic form of the illness went through a symbiotic phase in which they related to the mother or the therapist. For a time some children showed such relationships to all people relating to them. Because this reaction has always been temporary in our cases and because, in the beginning, we did not always recognize it, our data on the numbers of "symbiotic" children are inaccurate.

Of the children who remained autistic (29 of 71—41 percent) 17 had originally been assessed as severe and 12 as moderately affected. Fourteen received treatment and 15 remained untreated. Custodial care is necessary for 24 of these children. The remaining 5 are at home. Four children function in an IQ range of 50—70, with the highest being 64. Twenty-five are under 50 IQ. About half are unable to attend school, 40 percent are in classes for the retarded, and the remainder (only 2) are in opportunity classes. None appears to have any chance of becoming self-supporting even to a limited degree.

Among the children who were pseudoneurotic on follow-up, 39 of the 71 (55 percent) presented the picture of the pseudoneurotic form of childhood schizophrenia, some during the assessment but most later on as they approached school age. In 35 of these cases, history or observation had revealed an autistic phase preceding the pseudoneurotic one. We also noted in a number of these children a symbiotic phase occurring between the autistic and the pseudoneurotic one. None of the pseudoneurotic children was without "useful" speech, although there were disagreements among our staff about the degree of this usefulness.

None of those cases in which both phases were identified had come from the severely affected group, though 13 were from the moderately affected group and 22 from the mildly affected. Twenty-one had been treated, 14 untreated. Most, 29, had remained at home. Four were in a residential training center and 2 in custodial care. Sixteen, nearly half, had a normal or higher intellectual function (over 80 IQ); the rest were sub-normal. Fifteen of the 39 were in normal school classes, 17 in opportunity classes, and 3 were unable to attend school.

Age of Change and Prognosis

As some of the children remained autistic while others slowly changed, losing some of their autism and developing pseudoneurotic behavior and speech, the question arose: Do the children who show an earlier change from the autistic to the pseudoneu-

Table 1. The Relationship of the Severity of Illness to the Outcome—71 Children

	SEVERE—17		MODERATE—29		MILD—25	
PLACEMENT						
Home	2	(12%)	16	(55%)	20	(80%)
Institution	15	(88%)	9	(31%)	2	(8%)
Treatment center	none	(0%)	4	(14%)	3	(12%)
SCHOOL						
Normal class	none	(0%)	9	(31%)	8	(32%)
Opportunity class	1	(6%)	7	(24%)	13	(52%)
Class for retarded or none	16	(94%)	13	(45%)	4	(16%)

rotic behavior have a better prognosis, and is the change influenced by treatment?

Since the stages overlap, to determine the time of change, we took the midpoint of the elapsed time period between the last definite diagnosis of the autistic phase and the diagnosis of the pseudoneurotic phase. The age of the child at this point we call "age of change." For example, if the autistic form was last recognized at 4 years of age and the pseudoneurotic form was noted at 6 years, the age of change was considered to be 5 years. In our series this age roughly corresponded with the development of useful speech. Based on the concept of age of change we have obtained the following results:

1. Of the 13 children with "age of change" before 4½ years, 9 (69 percent) have normal intellect;

2. Of the 19 children with "age of change" between 4½ and 5½ years, 7 (37 percent) have normal intellect;

3. From the 3 children with "age of change" between 5½ and 6½, none have normal intellect.

That is, the children who changed earlier had a tendency toward better intellectual function ultimately. In view of the importance of intellect for the child's future adjustment, the early change from the autistic to the pseudoneurotic stage appears to be a favorable prognostic sign.

In order to clarify the role of treatment in the change from autistic to pseudoneurotic phase, an attempt was made to assess the "age of change" in a time relationship to treatment. We found 22 children (63 percent) in whom the "age of change" preceded treatment or who received no treatment, and 13 children (37 percent) for whom the "age of change" fell within the period of treatment.

This provides some sobering thought as it suggests that in the two-thirds of the children who did improve, the development from the autistic to the pseudoneurotic phase occurred without any formal therapy. In view of this it is doubtful whether the decrease of autism in the remaining third of the children was the result of treatment. In fact, it appears quite probable that the decrease of autism may come as part of a maturational process rather than as the result of our therapeutic efforts. It would seem important, then, to know whether treatment can speed up the maturational process by stimulation of the child and by reinforcement of his increasing interest in environment through pleasurable feedback from the therapist.

The Intellectual Function

An attempt was made to assess the current intellectual function of the children and to compare it with our original assessment of intelligence. Unfortunately, these had been (with some exceptions) on the basis of clinical observation only, since the children were not considered to be reliably testable. Although some of the children still cannot be well tested now, the current assessments are much more precise and objective than the original ones. Thirty-eight (84 percent) of the 45 children who live at home or are in treatment centers were assessed on the basis of formal tests. The remaining 7 children were assessed on our clinical observations and on reports from parents and teachers. The intellectual level of the 26 children in institutions was reported to us by the staff in the follow-up reports (see Table 2).

There appears to be a general tendency toward deterioration of intellect on the follow-up, most

Table 2. Relationship of Severity of Illness to Intellectual Function—71 Children

| | SEVERE—17 | | MODERATE—29 | | MILD—25 | |
	Original	Follow-up	Original	Follow-up	Original	Follow-up
INTELLECTUAL LEVEL						
Dull normal, normal, or						
higher (from IQ 80 up)	0 (0%)	0 (0%)	16 (55%)	9 (31%)	21 (84%)	9 (36%)
Borderline (IQ 70—80)	6 (35%)	0 (0%)	9 (32%)	5 (17%)	3 (12%)	5 (20%)
Defective (IQ 50—70)	3 (18%)	1 (6%)	4 (14%)	9 (31%)	1 (4%)	10 (40%)
(IQ under 50)	8 (47%)	16 (94%)	0 (0%)	6 (21%)	0 (0%)	1 (4%)

marked surprisingly enough in the least affected children, those originally considered to have normal intellect. Although real deterioration is no doubt present in many, some over-estimation at the time of diagnosis must have played a role because of our lack of experience in the early years.

Intellectual limitation is serious since it constitutes an additional handicap to the child's emotional and social malfunctioning. From the total of 71 children at the follow-up, 43 (61 percent) were found functioning under 70 IQ. None of these children has much chance of becoming self-supporting. Even the potential of those in the 70–80 IQ range group—10 children (14 percent)—is quite limited.

Treatment Related to Outcome

An attempt was next made to compare the children treated at the West End Creche with the children not treated there. The latter were divided into two groups: (1) those who at some stage obtained treatment in the community (either residential or outpatient) and (2) those who received no formal therapy at any time (see Table 3).

The group treated in West End Creche (mostly moderately affected) now has the highest percentage of children with normal intelligence, where-

Table 3. Treatment Related to Outcome of Mildly and Moderately
Affected—54 Children

TYPE OF TREATMENT	WEC—23	MIXED—16 (untreated controls treated elsewhere later)	NO TREATMENT—15
ORIGINAL ASSESSMENT			
Mildly affected	6 (26%)	8 (50%)	12 (80%)
Moderately affected	17 (74%)	8 (50%)	3 (20%)
Average age when treatment started	3 yrs., 10 mos.	6 yrs., 10 mos.	—
Normal intellect found in	14 (61%)	11 (69%)	12 (80%)
FOLLOW-UP			
Normal intellect	10 (43%)	5 (32%)	3 (20%)
In institution	7 (30%)	3 (19%)	1 (7%)
In school:			
Normal class	11 (48%)	4 (25%)	2 (13%)
Opportunity class[1]	4 (17%)	7 (44%)	9 (60%)
Class for retarded or no school[2]	8 (34%)	5 (31%)	4 (27%)

[1] For children in 50—70 IQ range.
[2] For children under 50 IQ range.

as the untreated group (mostly the mildly affected with the best intellectual function originally) now has the lowest percentage of children with normal intelligence. Approximately half of the children who began the treatment early were able to function in normal classes, while three-quarters of the children who began treatment at a later age were unable to remain in these classes.

Our impression is that, although the treatment did not change the pattern of illness, if begun early it did improve the child's ability to attend school.

Our findings also suggest that treatment may have enabled a better utilization of the original intellectual potential.

Members of the mildly affected group (25) had relatively the same degree of illness. Thirteen were treated and 12 untreated (see Table 4). The results, similar to those shown in Table 3, give further support to our original impression that the treated cases had less loss of intellectual function and better adjustment to school. Early treatment appears to bring better results.

Table 4. Treatment Related to Outcome of Mildly Affected—25 Children

TYPE OF TREATMENT	WEC—6	MIXED—7 (untreated controls treated elsewhere later)	NO TREATMENT—12
Average age when treatment started	4 yrs., 6 mos.	6 yrs., 5 mos.	—
FOLLOW-UP			
Normal intellect	3 (50%)	2 (29%)	3 (25%)
In institution	1 (17%)	—	1 (8%)
In school:			
Normal class	4 (66%)	2 (29%)	2 (17%)
Opportunity class	1 (17%)	4 (57%)	8 (67%)
Class for retarded or no school	1 (17%)	1 (14%)	2 (17%)

Discussion

Some of the findings surprised us. Our orientation had previously been toward treatment of the emotional and social maladjustment of these children without particular focus on development of their intellectual function. In the beginning we ignored, or rather denied, the intellectual defect, believing that it was a "pseudodefect." But after a child's emotional and social adjustment improved, we found that intellectual limitations were present and that these limited the child's independent functioning in the community.

Searching the literature in quest of findings similar to ours, we realized that an emotional block must have prevented us from noticing mental defect in our patients earlier. Despert[7] speaks about deterioration without clearly describing its type. Kanner and Eisenberg[9] describe their "poor" outcome cases as "apparent" feeblemindedness, with grossly psychotic behavior.[8] Grebelskaja-Albatz[11] reported that of 22 schizophrenic children up to age of 8 years, 9 with an acute onset developed mental retardation of varying degrees of severity. Brown[6] states that the majority of those unable to use normal educational channels are attending classes for the retarded rather than for the disturbed, but she does not call the children mentally defective. Bettelheim[4] was impressed that for all 46 children in his study, the "so-difficult-to-establish affective relationship" was achieved far more readily than the "ego-functions"—"including reasoning, reading comprehension, and mastery of the nonaffective aspects of reality." Kraepelin's[15] term "Pfropf-schizophrenia" suggests that the dementia praecox was "in a certain manner grafted upon an already existing disease," and Szurek[18] believes that mental deficiency can be complicated by severe mental disorder. These authors consider intellectual defect as primary, rather than secondary, to psychosis. My own study on the siblings of schizophrenic children[12] indicates the possibility that intellectual defect may result from psychosis at an early age.

The changes with maturation from the autistic to the pseudoneurotic form of emotional disturbance observed in West End Creche lead me to agree with Bender[2] that the presenting form of the illness in a particular age group results from the defensive system typical of the child's maturational level. The very immature, disorganized, and very ill child is capable only of withdrawal when anxious. As he grows older his diffuse anxiety becomes focused, and phobic and compulsive defenses develop. These are the better organized and more intelligent children.

We believed in the past that improvement—the decrease of autism—was a result of our efforts, and we have been surprised to find that it is most likely a maturational phenomenon. Whether we play some role in the development of relationships is still not clear. If we do, it is probably in stimulation and reinforcement of the child's growing interest in his environment through pleasurable feedback provided by the therapist. In some cases where the child's potential to relate was better than his parents were able to use, we may have provided the outside stimulus necessary, but have no proof of this.

Our achievement in the area of learning is most likely connected with the set-up of the treatment center as part of a school and the fact that our therapists were originally teachers. Although we did not attempt to demonstrate any major social and emotional progress in the children, some improvement appears to be a prerequisite to the child's learning, both as an individual and in the group.

The continuing serious problems of even the mildly ill children, and the possibility of a critical time for treatment suggested by our study, led us to change our policy of selection of cases for treat-ment. We now give preference to the mildly ill child, and impress on his parents the importance of early treatment rather than waiting until they are "ready" to accept the child's illness and seek treatment for him.

Summary and Conclusions

Because of the relatively small number of children and the great number of variables involved in our study, no definite conclusions can be drawn. However, our general impression is that childhood psychosis is a serious illness resulting, in most cases, in ultimate intellectual deficit of differing degrees. It appears that this deficit can be only partially prevented by treatment; the children who have the tendency to improve spontaneously can, if treated early and intensively, increase their chances for adjustment in the community, making better use of their intellectual potential and making better adjustment to school. Changes in the clinical form of childhood psychosis, the decrease of autism and the development of pseudoneurotic defenses, appear to occur on a maturational basis in the less severely ill children irrespective of therapeutic procedures. The time of change from the autistic to the pseudoneurotic form of illness appears to have some predictive value. The better outcome of the early-treated children as compared with late-treated very mildly ill children suggests that there is a critical period for treatment.

Article References

1. **Bender, L.** Childhood schizophrenia. *Psychiat. Quart.*, 1953, 27, 663–681.

2. **Bender, L.** Schizophrenia in childhood—its recognition, description and treatment, in childhood schizophrenia. *Amer. J. Orthopsychiat.*, 1956, 26, 499–5506.

3. **Bender, L.** Treatment of juvenile schizophrenia. *Res. Publ. Ass. Res. Nerv. Ment. Dis.*, 1954, 34, 462–465.

4. **Bettelheim, B.** *The empty fortress: Infantile autism and the birth of the self.* New York: Macmillan, 1967.

5. **British Working Party.** Schizophrenic syndrome in childhood. *Brit. Med. J.*, 1961, 2, 889–890.

6. **Brown, J.** Follow-up of children with atypical development (infantile psychosis). *Amer. J. Orthopsychiat.* 1963, 33, 855–861.

7. **Despert, J.** Schizophrenia in children. *Psychiat. Quart.*, 1938, 12, 366–371.

8. **Eisenberg, L.** The course of childhood schizophrenia. *Arch. Neurol. Psychiat.*, 1957, 78, 69.

9. **Eisenberg, L. and Kanner, L.** Early infantile autism, 1943–55. *Amer. J. Orthopsychiat.*, 1956, 26, 556–566.

10. **Eisenberg, L.** The autistic child in adolescence. *Amer. J. Psychiat.*, 1956, 112, 607–612.

11. **Grebelskaja-Albatz, E.** Zur Klinik der Schizophrenie des frühen Kindesalters, Schweiz. *Arch. f.*

Neurol. u. Psychiat., 1934, *34*, 244–253; 1935, *35*, 30–40.

12.   **Havelkova, M.** Abnormalities in siblings of schizophrenic children. *Canad. Psychiat. Assn. J.*, 1967, *12*, 363.

13.   **Hirschberg, J. and Bryant, K.** Problems in the differential diagnosis of childhood schizophrenia. *Res. Publ. Ass. Res. Nerv. Ment. Dis.*, 1954, *34*, 455–461.

14.   **Kanner, L.** Early infantile autism. *J. Pediat.*, 1944, *25*, 211–217.

15.   **Kraepelin, E.** *Psychiatrie: ein Lehrbuch für*

Studierende und Artze, 8th ed. Leipzig: J.A. Batl, 1913.

16.   **Mahler, M.** On child psychosis and schizophrenia. *Psychoanal. Stud. Child.* (New York), 1952, *7*, 286–305.

17.   **Reiser, D. and Brown, J.** Patterns of later development in children with infantile psychosis. *J. Amer. Acad. of Child Psychiat.*, 1964, *3*(4), 650–657.

18.   **Szurek, S.** Psychotic episodes and psychotic maldevelopment in childhood schizophrenia. *Amer. J. Orthopsychiat.*, 1956, *26*, 519–543.

Gossett and his colleagues have reviewed the studies of hospitalized adolescents. They demonstrate a keen awareness of the complications involved in such evaluative efforts and conclude that there is a need for refinement and multiple variables in future work of this type.

Follow-up of Adolescents Treated in a Psychiatric Hospital: I. A Review of Studies

John T. Gossett
Susan Baillies Lewis
Jerry M. Lewis, M.D.
Virginia Austin Phillips

To be ideal, the planning, initiation, and modification of psychiatric treatment programs should be based upon empirical studies of the long-term effectiveness of different treatment techniques. Accordingly, writers in the field of hospital treatment have proposed that those providing psychiatric treatment should conduct long-term follow-up studies.[19, 37] The perplexing problems involved in conducting follow-up studies of psychiatric treatment have received growing attention in recent years.[4, 7, 18, 32] However, in the past 30 years, because of the time, expense, and complex methodological problems involved, few investigators studying adolescents have published such studies. The methodological issues most relevant to the examination of outcome of adolescents treated in psychiatric hospitals will be explored in detail in a subsequent paper.[21]

Methodology varied in the thirteen follow-up studies located in a search of the psychiatric literature.[1, 2, 3, 5, 8, 10, 13, 17, 19, 23, 28, 39, 40] Researchers in the field did not replicate previous studies, and the thirteen are not strictly comparable. For example, the studies emanated from twelve different hospitals whose treatment programs dealt with selected patients with a variety of demographic and diagnostic differences. Also, the criteria for measurement of change varied from study to study. However, in spite of these marked differences, there are some significant similarities. All thirteen studies examined adolescents at least six months after discharge from inpatient facilities. The patients studied were similar in age, and most were diagnosed as severe character disorders or psychotics (primarily schizophrenic). All of the studies included judgments of patient change in terms of improvement (changes in condition from time of admission to time of follow-up), level of function (changes in status relative to "normality"), or both. In each of the studies some attempts were made to correlate patient, family, or treatment variables with treatment success.

From the American Journal of Orthopsychiatry, vol. 43, no. 4, 602–610. Copyright © 1973, the American Orthopsychiatric Association, Inc. Reproduced by permission.

This paper focuses upon the six variables reported to be significantly related to long-term outcome of teenagers who received hospital psychiatric treatment. Three variables concerned the patients themselves (the severity of psychopathology, the process-reactive nature of the psychopathology, and intelligence). Two correlates referred to the nature of the hospital treatment (presence of a specialized adolescent program, and the completion of in-hospital treatment). The final factor pertained to aftercare (continuation of individual psychotherapy following hospital discharge).

The appendix lists other variables that were studied but found to be not statistically significant, contradictory, or of undetermined value.

Pretreatment Variables

Severity of Psychopathology

Clearly the most powerful prognostic sign at the time of a teenager's admission to a psychiatric hospital was an evaluation of severity of his psychopathology. The degree of positive change that took place with treatment was found to relate inversely to this initial severity; that is, the lesser the initial disturbance, the better the function at follow-up.

Severity of Patient Psychopathology. In eight studies, severity was evaluated in terms of diagnosis; that is, neurosis, character disorder, or psychosis.[1, 3, 8, 10, 13, 17, 23, 39] Although these categories overlap, generally the average level of disturbance does not differ among them.

While slight differences in criteria, both of diagnoses and treatment outcome, leave strict comparisons open to question, all investigators made judgments of change in overall functioning following treatment. In a comparison of each patient's functioning at admission and follow-up, between 60 percent and 94 percent of those diagnosed neurotic were judged improved; the median was 83 percent improved.

In the same eight studies, between 33 percent and 83 percent of the patients given a character disorder diagnosis were judged improved; the median was 53 percent. For patients called psychotic (predominately schizophrenic), between 12 percent and 61 percent improved, with a median of 45 percent.

Severity of Family Psychopathology. The three investigators[1, 2, 23] who explored family psychopathology for a family history of psychosis, severe alcoholism, or family separation found no significant relationship between such individual items in the history and long-term outcome. These results correspond to the longitudinal studies comparing disturbed and well-functioning teenagers, which revealed no significant differences in the presence or absence of family psychosis or marked trauma.[6, 27, 29, 30, 33] These comparison studies did reveal significant differences between normal and abnormal teenagers in the degree of coping skills learned in the family setting. This finding suggests that more subtle measures of overall family dysfunction might have predictive value.

In exploring overall severity of family psychopathology, Carter[5] found that a family history with an isolated instance of psychosis, delinquency, epilepsy, alcoholism, neurosis, or behavior disorder did not predict outcome. Yet in cases where there were multiple signs of family disturbance, treatment outcome was almost invariably poor. He noted:

As regards the group of non-recovery cases, 17 out of 47 showed abnormality in the parents. This is 36 percent compared with 17 percent in the fully recovered. There is also a difference in the quality of the abnormality, the parents being either more obviously psychotic or more eccentric and introverted . . .[5]

This finding suggests that the level of family psychopathology (rather than the presence of particular circumscribed individual diagnostic descriptors) might be sensitive in predicting outcome of treatment.

The Process-Reactive Nature of Psychopathology

A number of studies of psychiatrically treated adults have found illness diagnosed "reactive" to have a better prognosis than that diagnosed "process."[9, 14, 15, 16] The pre-adult characteristics that define process and reactive types of disturbance are summarized in Table 1; findings relating these characteristics to outcome with adolescent patients are reviewed below.

Table 1. Criteria For Differentiating Process and Reactive Psychopathology

Process Disorder	Reactive Disorder
Birth to Fifth Year	
1. Severe psychological trauma	1. No severe psychological trauma
2. Frequent or severe physical illness	2. Good physical health
3. Patient considered "odd" child in the family	3. Patient considered "normal" child in the family
Fifth Year to Adolescence	
4. Academic failures	4. Academic success
5. Introversion; isolation from peers	5. Extroversion; involvement with peers
6. Disturbed siblings	6. Normal siblings
Adolescence to Adulthood	
7. Marked verbal and physical passivity	7. Verbally and physical active; normal assertiveness
8. Absence of heterosexual behavior	8. Presence of heterosexual behavior
9. Gradual onset of disabling symptoms	9. Sudden onset of disabling symptoms
10. Lack of clear stress precipitating symptoms	10. Clear stress precipitating symptoms
11. Early onset of severe psychopathology	11. Late onset of severe psychopathology
12. Bland, insidious onset of symptoms	12. Intense, "stormy" onset of symptoms
13. Slow symptomatic response to hospitalization	13. Rapid symptomatic improvement with hospitalization

Adapted from Garmezy[9] and Kantor and Herron.[16]

Early Psychological Trauma.   This variable was not investigated in any of the thirteen adolescent follow-up studies, except in the limited sense already discussed as part of family psychopathology.

Childhood Physical Illness.   The single follow-up study that explored the relationship between early childhood physical illness and later psychiatric outcome produced no significant association.[39]

Evidence of "Oddness" in Early Childhood.   Perhaps the investigation most nearly relevant to this dimension was conducted by Masterson,[23] who found that the presence of "neuropathic traits" in the early life history of schizophrenic patients was not predictive of eventual outcome. Neuropathic traits in this study included behaviors such as tantrums, feeding problems, breath holding, enuresis, night terrors, tics, and nail-biting.

Academic Failures.   Masterson[24] found that schizophrenics and character disorders who had passed all grades up to the time of hospitalization had significantly better outcomes than those who had failed one or more subjects or grades. Pollack,

Levenstein and Klein[28] also found that grade failure or remedial help in the academic backgrounds of adolescent patients were predictive of poor outcome. In the theoretical section of their study they specifically link evidence of early academic failure with the process-reactive dimension.

Isolation from Peers.   Results for four studies tend to support peer isolation in early childhood as a significant predictor of poor outcome. Carter[5] found that psychotic children who had early shown "... defects in amiability, shyness, sensitiveness, loneliness, and moodiness ..." tended to have poor outcome, whereas those with a history of amiability and warmth of personality tended to have good outcome. Masterson[23] found that ability to relate both to individuals and to groups predicted positive outcome for his schizophrenic patients but did not hold for neurotic or character disorder individuals. Pollack, Levenstein and Klein[28] found that friendships, both before and during adolescence, were predictors of positive outcome, while Avery and Kris[2] found similar results for adolescent friendships; in these two studies, psychotic and character disorder patients were combined.

Disturbed Siblings. While we found no studies specifically relating evaluation of adolescent patients at follow-up to the presence of disturbed siblings, Carter's[5] suggestion that overall level of family psychopathology may be predictive of outcome would seem to include the concept that the presence of disturbed siblings is a negative prognostic factor.

Verbal and/or Physical Passivity. Avery and Kris's[2] patients with a history of marked inhibition of aggressive affect had poor outcome. Similarly, Carter,[5] and Pollack, Levenstein and Klein[28] found that patients described as shy, shut-in, passive, or withdrawn had a poorer prognosis than did those showing average or above average levels of activity, aggressiveness, or extroversion.

Heterosexual Behavior. Neither Avery and Kris,[2] nor Pollack, Levenstein and Klein[28] found the presence or absence of heterosexual behavior in the past history of adolescent patients to be helpful in predicting outcome.

Onset of Symptoms. Avery and Kris,[2] Carter,[5] Masterson,[23] and Weiss and Glasser[40] found gradual onset to be predictive of poor outcome, while acute onset was related to a more positive treatment result.

Precipitating Events. Three studies dealt with the influence of precipitating factors. Carter[5] found that, with schizophrenic adolescents, it was rarely possible to identify factors precipitating the psychotic disorder, and that even when they could be identified, they did not have predictive significance. For his non-schizophrenic patients, however, the presence of clearly precipitating factors was predictive of better prognosis. The predictive significance of the presence of a precipitating factor was supported by Avery and Kris's[2] sample but not by Masterson's.[23] Thus, the significance of a precipitating factor as a predictor would seem to be equivocal.

Age of Onset of Severe Psychopathology. The recovery rate in Carter's[5] sample of psychotic adolescents in whom the onset occurred before age seventeen was ten percent. When the onset occurred later, the recovery rate was 55 percent. In Masterson's[24] sample of schizophrenic patients, those admitted after the age of fifteen had a better recovery rate than did those who were hospitalized at younger ages. The opposite was true of Masterson's[23] patients diagnosed character disorders; that

is, the younger the patient at admission, the better the prognosis. Similarly, Warren[39] found that for psychotic patients, early onset had poor prognosis. This was not true, however, in this group of neurotic and character disorder teenagers.

Weiss and Glasser's[40] teenagers who experienced disabling symptoms before age 12½ had poor outcome. Pollack, Levenstein and Klein's[28] group of schizophrenic patients also showed a statistically significant relationship between age of first psychiatric contact and outcome. Those with the best outcome were those who were oldest at first treatment contact.

Clearly, in psychosis, the earlier the age of onset (particularly if prepubertal), the poorer was the prognosis. In neurosis or character disorder, the relationship of age of onset to outcome was equivocal.

Intensity of Onset. In Carter's[5] psychotic group, the more stormy the onset, the better the prognosis. In Masterson's[24] schizophrenic sample, those showing an onset characterized by confusion or fear tended to have a better outcome than did those showing autism or shallow affect.

Rate of Symptomatic Improvement with Hospitalization. A final factor is the rate of symptomatic improvement occurring during early, non-specific treatment in the hospital milieu. In Carter's[5] sample of psychotic adolescents, most of those who recovered had shown marked symptom clearance during the first three months of hospitalization. Masterson's[24] schizophrenics and character disorders had a much higher rate of recovery if they had demonstrated rapid symptomatic improvement soon after hospitalization. This variable did not predict outcome with the neurotic patients in his sample.

In summary, when evaluating psychotic adolescents, a configuration of eight factors suggests a process disorder with poor prognosis: a history of academic failure; isolation from peers; presence of a disturbed sibling; shut-in personality; early, gradual, and bland onset of symptoms; and a slow symptomatic response to non-specific milieu treatment. For those patients diagnosed neurotic or character disorder, the process-reactive dimension is less likely to predict outcome of treatment. However, a pattern of early history of academic failure, peer isolation, presence of a disturbed sibling, gradual onset, and slow response to early, non-specific hospital treatment seemed related, although in lesser degree, to negative outcome.

Intelligence

Carter,[5] Annesley,[1] Levy,[19] Avery and Kris,[2] Pollack et al,[28] and Warren[39] found that below average intelligence signified poor outcome for psychotic patients and was a weaker but, nevertheless, still significant predictor for non-psychotic hospitalized adolescents.

Treatment Variables

While treatment variables have been examined less frequently than patient variables, the few attempts to correlate various aspects of treatment programs with long-term outcome produced three clearly significant factors. These are: a hospital program oriented specifically toward adolescents, rather than incorporating them into adult programs; the degree to which the patients completed the recommended inpatient treatment; and continuation of psychotherapy after discharge.

Special Adolescent Program

Data compiled by Beavers and Blumberg[3] strongly suggested that those hospitals offering a specialized adolescent treatment program had better long-term results, especially for schizophrenic and character disorder adolescent patients. This observation was supported in later studies.[8, 10, 17, 19, 28]

While it was difficult to compare all aspects of the specialized adolescent treatment approaches, one common feature was an academic program.[1, 3, 8, 10, 19, 39, 40]

Completion of Inpatient Treatment

In Levy's[19] study of Menninger's adolescent service, 85 percent of the teenagers who completed the recommended inpatient treatment had a successful long-term outcome. In contrast, for a group of patients whose hospital treatment was "terminated" by the institution, only 33 percent had a successful outcome. That institution terminated treatment if there were highly limiting organic factors, institutional inability to handle the patient, or the patient needed a different type of treatment facility. When a patient's family decided he did not need treatment or was dissatisfied, discouraged, or angry at the hospital and terminated treatment, 58 percent had a successful long-term course.

Failure to complete treatment may be a reflection of the severity of family and patient psychopathology, rather than a separate variable. None of the studies, however, correlated severity of psychopathology and type of termination.

In the Timberlawn sample,[10] 87 percent of the patients completing recommended treatment had successful outcomes, whereas only 42 percent of those for whom treatment was interrupted prematurely (whether by parents or hospital) were rated as long-term successes.

Continuation of Psychotherapy

For most teenagers who receive intensive inpatient treatment, the period of hospitalization is the first phase of a planned, long-range treatment involvement. Accordingly, extended individual, group, or family psychotherapy is frequently recommended at the time of discharge. Some patients and their families accept the recommendations for such follow-up care, but many do not.

Avery and Kris[2] found that continuation of psychotherapy led to better long-term outcome. More specifically, Beavers and Blumberg[3] found that 80 percent of those who continued psychotherapy and 41 percent of those who discontinued were significantly improved at follow-up. Similarly, Gossett and Lewis[10] found significant improvement in 70 percent of those who had continued in psychotherapy and in 31 percent of those who discontinued. Continuation in psychotherapy after discharge may be yet another indirect measure of severity of psychopathology; that is, generally healthier patients may be the ones who continue.

Summary and Discussion

Thirteen long-term follow-up studies of inpatient psychiatric treatment of adolescents in twelve different hospitals have been reported in the last 30 years. Six factors were found to correlate (at statistically significant levels) with long-range outcome: 1) severity of psychopathology, 2) process vs. reactive nature of psychopathology, 3) intelligence, 4) a specialized adolescent treatment program, 5) completion of the recommended hospital treatment, and 6) continuation of psychotherapy after hospitalization.

Demonstration of the predictive capability of these six factors clarifies the need for 1) refinement, to increase predictive accuracy; and 2) examination of combinations of variables, for increased efficiency and understanding of the interaction among them.

Recent data on other variables with theoretical and/or research backing point to additional useful directions for research. For example, research on internal vs. external locus of control suggests that this variable may have predictive significance for inpatient treatment outcome.[20, 22, 31] Also, the reports of young people with histories of heavy psychedelic drug involvement suggest that degree or type of drug usage may have prognostic significance.[11, 25, 26] Patient "likability" has also been mentioned in several studies of adult patients, and might have some predictive significance for adolescents as well.[8, 12, 34, 35, 36, 38, 41]

When primary prognostic variables are identified, the significant components of these variables determined, and the relevance of various combinations of the variables measured, more finely focused studies of those staff and treatment techniques contributing most directly to positive treatment outcome will be possible. Each of these steps is necessary to the planning, initiation and modification of effective, empirically based, inpatient psychiatric treatment programs.

Appendix. Variables Found to Have Statistically Nonsignificant, Contradictory, or Undetermined Relationships to Long-Term Outcome

PRE-HOSPITAL VARIABLES
1. Age at hospital admission [2, 5, 19, 23, 28, 29]
2. Attitudes towards idealism, rebellion, and religion [2]
3. Birth order [1, 2]
4. Diagnostic subtypes or patterns of symptoms [1, 5, 17, 23, 28, 39]
5. EEG results [1, 28, 39]
6. Family moves [2]
7. Family psychosis [1, 2, 5, 23]
8. Grandparents in the home [2]
9. Legal record [2, 39]
10. Physical maturity [39]
11. Previous drug therapy [2]
12. Previous psychiatric hospitalization [2]
13. Religion [2]
14. Sex [5, 23, 39]
15. Socio-economic status [2, 28, 39]
16. Symptoms [1, 2, 5, 23, 39, 40]
17. Type of physique [5]

HOSPITAL VARIABLES

1. Drug therapy [2, 3, 8]

2. Duration of hospitalization [1, 2, 3, 8, 13, 19, 23, 28, 39, 40]
3. Group therapy [2]
4. Hours per week of psychotherapy [2]
5. Improvement at discharge [23, 28]
6. Length of psychotherapy sessions [2]
7. Level of function at discharge [2, 39, 40]
8. Mixed vs. all adolescent living units [3]
9. Mode of treatment of schizophrenia: Insulin vs. psychotherapy [1]
10. Number of family visits [2]
11. Parental therapy [2]
12. Participation in student government [2]
13. Prognosis at discharge [23, 39]
14. Response to psychotherapy [2, 13, 19, 23]
15. School attendance [2]
16. Use of day hospital program [2]

POST-HOSPITAL VARIABLES
1. Ability to relate to family [2]
2. Following recommendations made at time of discharge [39]
3. Length of interval between discharge and follow-up [1, 2, 5, 13, 39]

Article References

1. **Annesley, P.** Psychiatric illness in adolescence: Presentation and prognosis. *J. Ment. Sci.*, 1961, *107*, 268–278.

2. **Avery, N. and Kris, A.** Psychiatric follow-up: One to two years after discharge. In E. Hartmann *et al.* (Eds.) *Adolescents in a mental hospital.* New York: Grune & Stratton, 1968.

3. **Beavers, W. and Blumberg, S.** A follow-up study of adolescents treated in an inpatient setting. *Dis. Nerv. Syst.*, 1968, *29*, 606–612.

4. **Beskind, H.** Psychiatric inpatient treatment of adolescents: A review of clinical experience. *Comprehens. Psychiat.*, 1962, *3*, 354–369.

5. **Carter, A.** The prognostic factors of adolescent psychoses. *J. Ment. Sci.*, 1942, *88*, 31–81.

6. **Clarizo, H.** Stability of deviant behavior through time. *Ment. Hyg.*, 1968, *52*, 288–293.

7. **Fiske, D.** *et al.* Planning of research on effectiveness of psychotherapy. *Amer. Psychol.*, 1970, *25*, 727–737.

8.   Garber, B. *Follow-up study of hospitalized adolescents.* New York: Bruner/Mazel, 1972.

9.   Garmezy, N. Process and reactive schizophrenia: Some conceptions and issues. *Schiz. Bull.,* 1970, *2,* 30–74.

10.   Gossett, J. and Lewis, J. Follow-up study of former inpatients of the Adolescent Service, Timberlawn Psychiatric Center. *Timberlawn Foundation Report No. 37,* 1972.

11.   Gossett, J., Lewis, S. and Phillips, V. Psychological characteristics of adolescent drug users and abstainers: Some implications for preventive education. *Bull. Menninger Clin.,* 1972, *36*(4), 425–435.

12.   Gossett, J., Lewis, S. and Phillips, V. Notes from the ivory tower: Closeness. *Timberlawn Foundation Report No. 62,* 1971.

13.   Herrara, L. Five years later: The adolescent patients as young adults. In E. Hartmann *et al.* (Eds.) *Adolescents in a mental hospital.* New York: Grune & Stratton, 1968.

14.   Higgins, J. Process-reactive schizophrenia: Recent developments. In R. Cancro (Ed.) *The schizophrenic syndrome: An annual review.* New York: Bruner/Mazel, 1971.

15.   Higgins, J. The concept of process-reactive schizophrenia: criteria and related research. *J. Nerv. Ment. Dis.,* 1968, *138,* 9–25.

16.   Kantor, R. and Herron, W. *Reactive and process schizophrenia.* Palo Alto, Ca.: Science and Behavior Books, 1966.

17.   King, L. and Pittman, G. A six-year follow-up study of sixty-five adolescent patients: Predictive value of presenting clinical picture. *Brit. J. Psychiat.,* 1969, *115,* 1437–1441.

18.   Levenstein, S., Pollack, M. and Klein, D. Follow-up study of formerly hospitalized psychiatric patients: Procedural considerations in data collection. *J. Hillside Hosp.,* 1966, *15,* 152–164.

19.   Levy, E. Long-term follow-up of former inpatients at the Children's Hospital of the Menninger Clinic. *Amer. J. Psychiat.,* 1969, *125,* 1633–1639.

20.   Lewis, S. and Gossett, J. Notes from the ivory tower: Internal-external locus of control. *Timberlawn Foundation Report No. 60,* 1971.

21.   Lewis, S. *et al.* Follow-up of adolescents treated in a psychiatric hospital: II. Methodological issues. In process, 1972.

22.   MacDonald, A. Internal-external locus of control: A promising rehabilitation variable. *J. Couns. Psychol.,* 1971, *18,* 111–116.

23.   Masterson, J. Prognosis in adolescent disorders. *Amer. J. Psychiat.,* 1958, *114,* 1097–1103.

24.   Masterson, J. Prognosis in adolescent disorders: Schizophrenia. *J. Nerv. Ment. Dis.,* 1956, *124,* 219–232.

25.   McAree, C., Steffenhage, R. and Zheutlin, L. Personality factors and patterns of drug usage in college students. Paper presented at the American Psychiatric Association, San Francisco, 1970.

26.   Mirin, S. *et al.* Casual versus heavy use of marihuana: A redefinition of the marihuana problem. Mimeographed paper from the Pharmacology Laboratory, Division of Psychiatry, Boston University School of Medicine, 1970.

27.   Offer, D., Marcus, D. and Offer, J. A longitudinal study of normal adolescent boys. *Amer. J. Psychiat.,* 1970, *126,* 917–924.

28.   Pollack, M., Levenstein, S. and Klein, D. A three-year posthospital follow-up of adolescent and adult schizophrenics. *Amer. J. Orthopsychiat.,* 1968, *38,* 94–109.

29.   Renaud, H. and Estess, F. Life history interviews with one hundred normal American males: "Pathogenicity" of childhood. *Amer. J. Orthopsychiat.,* 1961, *31,* 786–802.

30.   Roff, M. Childhood social interactions and young adult bad conduct. *J. Abnorm. Soc. Psychol.,* 1961, *63,* 333–337.

31.   Rotter, J. Generalized expectancies for internal versus external locus of control of reinforcement. *Psychol. Monogr.,* 1966, *80,* 1–28.

32.   Sargent, H. Methodological problems of follow-up studies in psychotherapy research. *Amer. J. Orthopsychiat.,* 1960, *30,* 495–506.

33.   Schofield, W. and Balian, L. A comparative study of the personal histories of schizophrenic and nonpsychiatric patients. *J. Abnorm. Soc. Psychol.,* 1959, *59,* 216–255.

34.   Schofield, W. *et al.* Prognostic factors in schizophrenia. *J. Cons. Psychol.,* 1959, *18,* 155–166.

35.   Sinnett, E. and Hanford, D. The effects of patients' relationships with peers and physicians on

their psychiatric treatment program. *J. Abnorm. Soc. Psychol.*, 1962, *64*, 151–154.

36.   **Sinnett, E., Stimpert, W. and Straight, E.** A five-year follow-up of psychiatric patients. *Amer. J. Orthopsychiat.*, 1965, *35*, 572–580.

37.   **Smith, J. and Wittson, C.** Evaluation of treatment procedures in psychiatry. *Dis. Nerv. Syst.*, 1957, *18*, 387–390.

38.   **Strupp, H.** *et al.* Psychotherapists' assessment of former patients. *J. Nerv. Ment. Dis.*, 1963, *137*, 222–230.

39.   **Warren, W.** A study of adolescent psychiatric in-patients and the outcome six or more years later: II. The follow-up study. *J. Child. Psychol. Psychiat.*, 1965, *6*, 141–160.

40.   **Weiss, T., and Glasser, B.** Social work follow-up: Six months after discharge. In E. Hartmann *et al.* (Eds.) *Adolescents in a mental hospital.* New York: Grune & Stratton, 1968.

41.   **Wood, E.** *et al.* Interpersonal aspects of psychiatric hospitalization. *Arch. Gen. Psychiat.*, 1962, *6*, 46–55.

It will be recalled that Kohlberg also made the point that severe distortion of the environmental conditions has long-term negative predictive implications for later maladjustment.

The next study, also a consequence of long-term research, is of high importance for teachers, especially teachers of disturbed children. A fundamental problem of our culture is our failure to reverse anti-social behavior. Robins concentrates on sociopathic (or in the extreme case—psychopathic) children, who have never internalized an acceptable set of values. They have no empathy for the feelings of others and little regard for the future. They learn little by experience.

This work enables one to compare normal, neurotic, and sociopathic children as adults. Particularly telling is her discussion of the natural history of the sociopathic personality—where the efforts at rehabilitation and the unfortunately negative role of education are clearly evident.

Deviant Children Grown Up:
A Sociological and Psychiatric
Study of Sociopathic Personality
Lee N. Robins

Childhood Behavior Predicting Later Diagnosis

Feasibility of Long-Term Follow-Up Studies

This study describes the adult social and psychiatric status of 524 persons who, because they were seen in a child guidance clinic, were expected to yield a high rate of adults diagnosable as sociopathic personality. Their adult status has been compared with that of 100 normal control subjects. To complete this study, it has been necessary to locate patients 30 years after their clinic referral and control subjects 30 years after their graduation from elementary school and to obtain valid interviews

from them about matters ordinarily treated as privileged and personal. From the interviews, supplemented by materials out of the records of many agencies, an evaluation of the kinds and seriousness of the subjects' adult antisocial behavior has been made, and the subjects have received a psychiatric diagnosis.

The success of the study in locating 90 percent of the subjects, in obtaining interviews for 82 percent of them and adult records for 98 percent means that subjects can be found and interviewed after 30 years, and that abundant record information concerning their adult lives can be located to verify those interviews. Pursuing information ordinarily considered personal and privileged through the structured interview was also surprisingly successful. Eighty-six percent of the sociopaths personally interviewed admitted enough antisocial behavior for psychiatrists to give them that diagnosis on the basis of the interview alone, before seeing record information. Only seven percent of them denied all adult antisocial behavior. While subjects were by no means totally reliable, they tended to minimize their antisocial behavior and push it back in time, rather than to deny it. On the basis of interviews and record information obtained, it was possible for two psychiatrists to reach an agreement as to whether 88 percent of the subjects were psychiatrically ill or well and to make a reasonably specific diagnosis for 71 percent. That it is possible to find subjects, interview them, and make a diagnosis indicates that following populations thought to be disease-prone is a practical method for investigating the development of psychiatric syndromes, although the length and expense of the research indicate it is neither a cheap nor easy method.

The maladjustment of the patients showed itself in their high rate of arrests, low occupational achievement, their mental hospitalizations and numerous subjective symptoms, high divorce rates, alienation from friends, relatives, church, and all kinds of organizations, extensive use of welfare services, frequent moves, excessive use of alcohol, and the transmission of behavior problems to their children.

As a first step in specifying factors which identify those likely to have serious difficulties as adults, it was noted that children referred for antisocial behavior differed much more from the control subjects in their adult adjustment than did children referred for temper tantrums, learning problems, sleep and eating disturbance, speech difficulties, and all problems other than antisocial behavior. The more severe the antisocial behavior, whether measured by numbers of symptoms, by number of episodes, or by arrestablility of the behavior, the more disturbed was the adult adjustment. Children referred to the clinic without numerous symptoms had no worse an outcome than had the control subjects. Clearly then, it was not the stigmatization as a "problem child" which created later problems, but rather the nature and severity of the childhood behavior which had occasioned referral.

The Natural History of the Disease Sociopathic Personality

A comparison of the childhood and adult histories of children diagnosed sociopathic personality with the histories of other patients and control subjects permits describing the sociopath's distinctive family history, symptoms, and course.

The disease occurred almost exclusively in boys referred to the clinic for antisocial behavior, particularly theft. Most of the sociopaths, in addition to a history of juvenile theft, had a history of incorrigibility, running away from home, truancy, associating with bad companions, sexual activities, and staying out late. Most of them were discipline problems in school and, having been held back at least one grade by the time they appeared in the clinic, most of them never even graduated from elementary school. More often than other patients, they were described as aggressive, reckless, impulsive, slovenly, enuretic, lacking guilt, and lying without cause.

Ordinarily referred to the clinic about age 14, the history of behavior problems dated back an average of seven years, beginning early in the school history. Before passing Juvenile Court age, almost four out of five appeared in court and more than half were sent to a correctional institution. Most of them had directed antisocial behavior toward their parents and teachers, and, more often than other antisocial children, they were also involved in offenses against businesses and strangers.

Girls later sociopathic were similar except that they were often referred to the clinic because of sexual activities, and their first difficulties began somewhat later.

Most of the sociopaths had a father who was either sociopathic or alcoholic. As a result, even more of them than of other clinic children came from homes that were impoverished and broken by divorce or separation.

As an adult, almost every sociopath had a poor work history, had been financially dependent on social agencies or relatives, and had marital problems. Three-quarters of them had multiple arrests leading to prison terms. They drank excessively, were impulsive, sexually promiscuous, had been vagrant, were belligerent, delinquent in paying their debts, and socially isolated. Most were disciplinary problems in the Armed Forces if not rejected because of their criminal records. In addition to their antisocial behavior, about half of them described themselves as "nervous," and they had a profusion of various somatic symptoms. The symptoms which best distinguished them from all other diagnostic groups were their poor marital histories, their impulsiveness, vagrancy, and use of aliases. With rare exceptions, they came to psychiatric attention only as a result of conflicts with the law or disturbances created while in prison or Service.

Sociopaths had a higher rate of injuries and deaths by violence than had other subjects. Children resulting from their unions had a high rate of problem behavior and failure to graduate from high school.

At time of follow-up, about age 44, 12 percent of the sociopathic group had given up their antisocial behavior, and an additional 27 percent had reduced it markedly. The remaining 61 percent were still seriously antisocial. The most common age at which improvement occurred was between 30 and 40 years.

The Independent Predictors of Sociopathic Personality

The best single childhood predictor of sociopathic personality was the degree of juvenile antisocial behavior. Sociopathic personality could be about equally well predicted by three measures of antisocial behavior: 1) the variety of antisocial behavior (what we have called number of symptoms); 2) the number of episodes; and 3) the seriousness of the behavior, as measured by whether or not the behavior was of the kind for which children appear in Juvenile Court.

Among children with a wide variety of antisocial behavior, the best predictor of the diagnosis of sociopathic personality was whether or not the child was ever placed in a correctional institution. Fifty-five percent of all severely antisocial children who became sociopaths went to a juvenile correctional institution, compared with only 33 percent of those who did not become sociopaths. The next most powerful predictor was the frequency and seriousness of their antisocial behavior. Almost all (88 percent) of the antisocial children who became sociopaths committed four or more arrestable acts, as compared with 71 percent of antisocial children with other diagnoses as adults. Three approximately equally good predictors were the kind of discipline in the home, the number of siblings, and a history of theft.

In descending order, other predictors of sociopathic personality in highly antisocial children were being male, committing antisocial acts against businesses, and being truant in combination with poor school performance.

Most of these predictors were common not only in the highly antisocial children who became sociopaths but in other highly antisocial children as well. About three-quarters of children with other outcomes also stole and experienced little discipline and more than half committed four or more arrestable acts, were male, and truanted. The largest percent difference between the two groups was with respect to institutionalization—a difference of 22 percent.

Predictors of sociopathy in less severely antisocial children were much more powerful, because while they occurred less uniformly in the sociopaths, many of them were almost absent in children free of antisocial behavior or only moderately antisocial who did not become sociopaths. As was the case for severely antisocial children, going to a correctional institution was the best predictor of sociopathy in less severely antisocial children. Inmates of correctional institutions accounted for 37 percent of the sociopaths in this group, but for only 10 percent of those who had other diagnoses. Next most predictive was having a sociopathic or alcoholic father. More than two-thirds of the presociopaths had such a father, compared with only 21 percent of children who later had other diagnoses. Committing four or more arrestable acts also predicted sociopathy in the less seriously antisocial children, as it did in the severely antisocial. Other predictors, in descending order, were impulsivity, aggression toward child strangers, running away, lying (except to avoid punishment), appearing in Juvenile Court, staying out late, being only children or one of four, and lacking guilt. The largest percentage difference between the two groups was in the proportion with a sociopathic or alcoholic father—a difference of 47 percent.

Many of the variables commonly reported as characterizing the childhoods of patients diagnosed sociopathic personality were not predictors of that disease when the level of antisocial behavior in childhood was taken into account. Although we found, as others have reported, a high rate of parental deprivation and repudiation, school dropouts, slum living, poverty, foster home or orphanage experience, and antisocial behavior on the part of the mother in the childhood histories of the sociopaths, these variables did not predict the disease independently of the child's level of antisocial behavior. The predictors found to be independent of the child's level of antisocial behavior, except for family size, have also commonly been reported as typical of the childhood histories of antisocial adults. Whether these variables do in fact reliably predict adult antisocial behavior can be demonstrated only if they are found to be successful predictors in other follow-up studies of populations of problem children. . . .

Implications of the Findings for Issues in Psychiatry

Child guidance clinic patients studied had a strikingly higher rate than control subjects of sociopathy, and also a somewhat higher rate of schizophrenia, chronic brain syndrome, alcoholism, and hysteria. But they had *no* higher rates of manic-depressive disease or of neurosis other than hysteria. Nor did any particular symptoms or family patterns in the patients predict these latter syndromes. While too few manic-depressives appeared in either patient or control groups to draw conclusions about them, these findings raise a question as to whether adult neurotic symptoms are in fact consequences of problems in parent-child relations or of parental loss in childhood, as is so commonly supposed. In any case, the kinds of juvenile problems and family constellations that led to the referral of these children do not appear to predict neurosis. Indeed, many of the childhood symptoms commonly thought to be early signs of neurosis appeared as often in children well as adults as in those sick. *(sic.)* Shyness, seclusiveness, "nervousness," irritability, tantrums, insomnia, fears, speech defects, hypersensitiveness, and tics were all unrelated to psychiatric outcome. Nor was the *number* of nonantisocial symptoms a good predictor of later psychiatric health. Serious antisocial behavior, on the other hand, was a particularly ominous childhood pattern. These findings suggest that the antisocial child deserves the most serious efforts at treatment if he is not to be a psychiatrically ill adult.

A suggestive finding of the study is the continuity of levels of antisocial behavior between childhood and adulthood, a continuity that cuts across the diagnostic lines we have been able to draw. The level of childhood antisocial behavior not only predicted sociopathy, but also predicted which schizophrenics and alcoholics would be combative and acting out, which relatively quiet and retiring. This tends to confirm two studies of the consistency of personality traits from childhood to adulthood (Tuddenham, 1959; Kagan and Moss, 1962) which also found aggressiveness an especially stable trait, particularly in boys.

The importance of the father's behavior in predicting the child's is also underscored in this study. Antisocial behavior in the father was associated not only with *juvenile* antisocial behavior in the patients, but also with antisocial behavior in adults who had been minimally antisocial as children. Antisocial behavior in the father, in addition, was the only childhood variable which predicted that sociopathic persons would not decrease their antisocial behavior with aging. The findings of this study lead us to recall A. E. Housman's lines:

> When shall I be dead and rid
> Of the wrong my father did?

But the findings do not permit any simple explanation of the mechanisms which relate the fa-

ther's behavior to his offspring's. The fact that separation from the antisocial father by his desertion or divorce or by having the child adopted did not decrease the child's risks may seem to suggest a genetic factor, as Rosanoff *et al.*'s (1941) and Lange's (1931) twin studies argue. There are, however, practical consequences of having an antisocial father that tend to increase the number of independent predictors of sociopathic personality that a child may have: Children of antisocial fathers usually live in lower-class neighborhoods where they are likely to find other children who encourage them to engage in truancy and theft; they receive little discipline because the father is uninterested and hedonistic and because, if he fails to hold a job, the mother must become a breadwinner; they are more likely to be sent to a correctional institution when they come to Juvenile Court because the judge wishes to remove them from an environment he considers noxious. These consequences of having an antisocial father tend to occur whether or not the father remains in the home. In addition, the mother who chose to marry such a man may rear her child in his image even when he is absent or may herself be a "covert" sociopath from whom the child learns attitudes consistent with sociopathy. If the etiological factor *is* genetic, it is still necessary to explain the high prevalence of the disease in men as compared with women, the failure of the few women with the disease to transmit it to their children in the absence of a similar problem in their husbands, and the occurrence of the disease in some children without sociopathic fathers.

Whether or not the important etiological factor is genetic, certain factors frequently cited as etiological in the production of this syndrome did not appear to be so. Parental rejection, as measured by the parent's taking action against the child, treating him in a cold manner, or being excessively strict with him, did not predict sociopathy. Nor was parental deprivation resulting from the death or illness of a parent a factor.

This study provided no evidence that antisocial behavior and neurotic symptoms serve a common purpose, such as a defense against anxiety, so that an increase in one implies a decrease in the other. Antisocial children had as many non-antisocial symptoms as did children with non-antisocial symptoms only; and adult sociopaths who abandoned their antisocial behavior did not develop an excess of somatic symptoms in its place. It was noted, however, that with age, antisocial symptoms tend on the whole to decrease, somatic symptoms to increase. . . .

Some Inferences to Methods for Prevention and Treatment

Since children who will develop serious adult antisocial behavior usually have significant antisocial behavior in their early school years, it is reasonable to plan for their early treatment, not only because behavior patterns may be more amenable to change at that age, but because delay will add a serious educational handicap to the antisocial behavior. Since truancy and poor school performance are nearly universally present in pre-sociopaths, it should be possible to identify children requiring treatment through their school records, refining the group most in need of care by using some of the predictors described above.

This study provides no answers concerning what, if any, methods of prevention and treatment will be effective. Yet the fact that a gross lack of discipline in the home predicted long-term difficulties suggests trying a program in which the schools attempt to substitute for the missing parental discipline in acting to prevent truancy and school failures. The public school might attempt to take over responsibilities that are usually the parents', just as the private boarding school does for upperclass children, perhaps by providing escorts for truant children in the morning and supervised study after school hours to guarantee that tomorrow's assignment is done before the child goes home. By randomly assigning boys who meet the criteria for pre-sociopathic personality to such programs or to control groups and later comparing results, it will be possible to learn whether school discipline in the early grades can interrupt the development of antisocial behavior.

For adults already highly antisocial, suggestions for promising kinds of therapy have been sought in the adult histories of sociopaths in this study who have improved. Findings were meager and could plausibly be interpreted as the results rather than the causes of reform. Nonetheless, since they were the only hints available, the findings might be worth exploring for their possible therapeutic usefulness. The fact that sociopaths maintaining contacts with wives and other relatives tended to improve suggests encouraging wives and relatives to tolerate the irritability and hostility of the antisocial adult in order to maintain some sort of control of his behavior. The fact that brief prison terms may have induced reform also suggests that short incarcerations, preferably followed by pro-longed supervision by parole officers to reinforce the family's control, may be useful. The fact that sociopaths holding jobs in which they had little supervision kept them longer than they did standard factory and office jobs suggest guiding them into occupations in which they have little sustained contact with supervisory personnel, occupations such as construction workers, cab drivers, and bartenders. Finally, one unexpected finding was the attribution of reform by some men to their desire to keep up payments on goods in their possession lest they lose them. While the impulsive and imprudent behavior of the sociopath may make it impossible to induce him to work in anticipation of purchasing objects desired, subsidizing down payments for him on desired goods which cannot be *kept* unless he works may sometimes be effective. Working to keep what one has may require less ability to defer gratification than does working in order to get something one does not have.

Next Steps in Research

Tests of the findings of the present study by replication and endeavors to turn observed associations into tools for therapy and prevention are not the only unfinished business.

The use of a clinic population to study this syndrome had the great advantage of providing a disease-prone population, so that sufficient cases of the syndrome were found at follow-up with a minimum wastage. But it had the disadvantage that one does not know how representative the children followed who turned out to have the syndrome are of all adults developing the syndrome.

Two techniques for overcoming this handicap can be suggested. Wastage can be avoided not only by following a clinic sample, but also by following children whose demographic characteristics suggest that there will be a high adult rate of the syndrome. We are currently doing such a study of a population of Negro men identified from public elementary school records. Negro men were selected because their high level of adult crime, unemployment, and marital instability suggests that they will yield a large enough proportion with adult antisocial behavior to allow the study of the relation of childhood factors to deviance in a population unselected by clinic treatment or court referral. This is not a perfect solution because one must still make the untestable assumption that the childhood factors predicting a syndrome in the sub-populations in which it is common are the same factors predicting it in the sub-populations in which it is rare, but one certainly can come closer to obtaining an unselected sample than by choosing a clinic population.

A second way of solving the problem is to attempt to locate a representative sample of adults with a given syndrome, seek record information about their childhood behavior and their childhood family situation, and compare these results with the same information obtained for control subjects picked from rosters on which the sick adults appeared in childhood but on which their appearance was not dependent on special characteristics of the subjects themselves or of their parents. Such a roster might be birth records or elementary school records, and the control subject might be the next child of the same sex on the roster. The relevant childhood records with respect to which control and patient groups might be compared are, for their own behavior problems, juvenile police records, school records, and clinic attendance and for their social and family history in childhood, neighborhoods lived in and number of moves (as indicated by number and location of addresses on school records), welfare and police records of their parents, psychiatric hospitalizations of parents, and other records of parental problems. The source of a representative sample of adults with a syndrome would vary with the syndrome to be studied. For sociopathic personality, one might choose a sample of persons who simultaneously have police records, welfare records, and multiple divorces. Clinical interviews with persons simultaneously appearing on these three rosters could be used both to make a definite diagnosis and to locate the childhood rosters from which the control subject is to be chosen (e.g., by asking place and date of birth to locate birth registration, or the elementary schools attended, to locate school rosters). This second technique is particularly useful for syndromes which are rare not only in the total population but in any demographically definable group. The only problem in the technique is one of so defining the adult target population that it does produce a representative sample of people with a given syndrome and relatively few people *without* the syndrome (to avoid wasting interviews).

The present study has attempted to solve one part of the equation between childhood patterns and adult outcomes. We have specified childhood patterns which appear to predict sociopathic personality in adults. We have only tentatively answered the question as to whether sociopathic personality can occur in the absence of these childhood patterns, by pointing to the rarity of this syndrome in the control population and in clinic patients free of serious antisocial behavior in childhood. A study of the childhoods of a representative adult sample of persons with the diagnosis of sociopathic personality would complete the equation.

These studies were selected to examine Kohlberg's biogenetic and sociogenetic high-risk groups, and his position has been corroborated. Two other studies are important partly because of their differences. One, *400 Losers* illustrates the problems of reaching the hard core inner city youth with a work program.[17] The problem behavior of the youngsters followed them into the work situation. If they had no work-oriented close identification figures, they were usually doomed to failure. The disasterous outcomes indicate yet again the difficulty of changing the inner and outer ecology systems. In another study of nine child murderers, it was found that their life experience had produced an emotionally empty state (psychopath) and a lack of cognitive coping capacity since they could not use symbols to mitigate their impulses. They could not read. Many had been brutalized as well.[18] The question of continuity of disturbance has also been studied by Shepherd.[19]

We turn now to studies of program-efficacy research. The two major programs for emotionally disturbed children in the schools are the special class and the crisis-helping, or resource, teacher. We turn first to the special class.

The problem we have before us is how to assess the values and limitations of special classes. We must study the psychological impact of segregation on the child who is to be given "this unique opportunity." We must also know what the actual experience in the classroom is—speaking again in psychological terms. Finally, we must know the impact of the "return" process for individual children. Some disturbed children definitely improve in the classes. There is great doubt, however, that all improve. There is even greater doubt that the children retain their improvement in subsequent placement. There is no reason to believe that special classes could be a universal panacea.

The first study is a broad survey of special classes for the emotionally disturbed, conducted with the help of the Council for Exceptional Children. The purpose of the study was to examine the effects of special classes. Definitive findings were elusive, because the methodology had serious limitations, but the sample is fairly large and covers a wide spectrum of classes.

Public School Classes
for the Emotionally
Handicapped: A Research Analysis

William C. Morse
Richard L. Cutler
Albert H. Fink

An ultimate goal of this research was to determine the effects of special public school classrooms for emotionally handicapped children upon the children themselves.

Pre- and posttest data on school achievement were not broadly available, and plans to use these as a major criterion had to be abandoned. Retrospective data from both pupils and teachers were utilized instead, as were evaluative views of administrators and site visitors. In this chapter, both statistical findings and impressionistic views are presented.

Administrators' Evaluations
of Programs

One simple criterion for evaluation of the programs was to pose the question to administrators, "Would you expand your program as it now exists if funds were available?" All but four program administrators indicated that they would. Several were enthusiastic or ambitious, and would add from ten to 20 more classes. Most were more modest, either in their aspiration or their evaluation, and indicated that they would like two, three, or four more classes. A frequent suggestion for expansion set one class per medium size or large size building as a goal. Others defined their needs and wishes in terms of an extrapolation of the present percentage of children served. Estimates of the proportion of children needing special service ran as high as 20 percent of the total population, although the most typical estimate was 10-15 percent. Service by other special personnel was often included in these totals.

Abridged from William C. Morse, Richard L. Cutler, and Albert H. Fink, "Public School Classes for the Emotionally Handicapped," a research project conducted for the Council for Exceptional Children, National Education Association, 1964. This project was supported in part by a grant from the National Institute of Mental Health to the Council for Exceptional Children. Reprinted by permission of the Council for Exceptional Children and the author.

Administrators generally reported heavy demands for additional placements, which is understandable in the light of fairly well-established minimum percentages of known disturbed children. However, on the other hand, in several locations it was difficult to obtain the full complement of pupils for the classes. The reasons for this were nearly as many as the programs reporting the difficulty. Many of the most obvious school problems did not fit the available class in terms of age, pathology, or necessary psychiatric and parental acceptability. Often it was the vexing problem of transportation which prevented enrollment. More than half the programs studied reported waiting lists, and consequent pressures to move more children into existing classes or to develop new ones.

Needed Changes as Seen by
Administrators

While some of the administrators' comments about needed change reflected unique local problems (e.g., "we need to have less clinical contamination" or "we can't seem to lick the transportation problem"), most administrators revealed a desire to serve more children, to enrich and broaden the programs, and to secure more adequate housing. Special equipment, e.g., teaching machines, typewriters, etc., was considered to be a need by many. Mentioned also was the desire to have the administration know the program better, and to be able to offer more or better inservice education. Additional help for the teacher, in the form of more consultation, aides, an itinerant teacher or substitute teacher, was an often expressed wish. While administrative frustration appeared in acute form only rarely, there was an occasional case, and it typically involved a lack of money or authority.

Ratings of Program Success

Table 1 presents ratings of overall program success.

The site visitors tended to see more extremes at both ends of the success continuum. Nearly three-fourths of the programs were judged by them to be either "encouraging" or "outstanding" in their success. Totals for comparable catagories as rated by the school personnel totaled only 50 percent. On the other hand, the site visitors' judgments of clear failure outnumbered those of school personnel nearly three to one.

Table 1. Rating of Program Success

Category	Percent Site Visitors	Percent School Personnel
Clear failure	15	5
Limited success	11	21
Encouraging success	30	29
Outstanding success	40	21
No data	4	25

A good many reasons underlay the judgments of poor success found among school personnel. The level of judged success was most often closely related to the appreciation of the teacher's efforts. Many administrators said that it all depended upon how good or poor the teacher was. If those persons doing the judging agreed with the teacher's methods, they found the program in one way or another successful. If they were not satisfied with what the teacher was doing, they tended to rate success lower. Other specific factors which seemed to be related to judgments of success and/or satisfaction were: (a) not enough structure; (b) too much expense; (c) lack of sufficient opportunity for outside treatment; (d) too few children going back to regular classes; and (e) class size and/or transportation problems.

It is obvious that the true concern about success or failure often goes much deeper and arises out of the total complex of problems previously discussed. This complex involves the establishment of goals, the screening and selection of pupils, the treatment, and finally the reintegration process. Since the goal often is to return the pupil to the regular class remediated and conforming, it is worth asking whether pupils with prognosis for quick recovery are selected. While it is true that few psychotics get into the programs, other criteria, such as family workability, age, etc., also need to be considered in the light of goals set. It is generally most difficult to set up that treatment program within the class which is most consistent with the nature of the pathology. A general approach is almost necessarily imposed on the classroom process, although it is apparent that more specific plans are not made as often as possible. Finally, there is a wide range in the efforts to return the child, as well as in the degree of acceptance he finds when he goes back.

Frequently, case successes stand out in the minds of school personnel. Generalization from the single case is tempting, either to support or to limit the program. Programs that operate for two years or more and return only 10 percent of their children to regular classes may still be regarded as successful because the children seem accepted and more comfortable, and are making some progress. The attitude of grateful parents also seems to play a large part in the feelings of school personnel. . . .

Teacher Prognosis Regarding Individual Pupils

Table 2 presents the views of the special teachers on whether their individual pupils will continue to need the special class.

Table 2. Perception of Pupil's Continuing Need for Special Class

Will Need Special Class for Most of His School Life	Percent Indicating (N = 464)
Uncertain	35
Yes	6
No	42
No data	17

While the teachers' prognoses were not totally optimistic, there were indications of their belief in the recoverability of about half the children. This was in contrast to the relatively small number who were seen as becoming able to return to their regular classes.

Table 3 presents a summary of eventual expected placement. These figures are quite consistent with those seen in the previous tables, with slightly more than 40 percent of the children judged to be eventually capable of returning to a regular public school program. The larger "no data" percentage suggests less willingness to make longer term predictions.

Table 3. Teacher Perception of Pupil's Eventual Placement

Type of Placement	Percent Indicating (N = 481)
Regular public school class	40
Special school placement	13
Vocational training	4
Drop out or expelled	2
Institution	5
Miscellaneous—job, private school	4
Uncertain	9
No data	23

Teachers predicted the degree of each pupil's personal adjustment and academic adjustment, as well as whether or not his general adjustment was expected to meet his parents' expectations. A summary of responses to the first two of these questions is presented in Table 4.

Once again, there was evidence of the teachers' long term faith that a third or more of their children would return to essentially normal circumstances. The outlook for academic adjustment was only slightly better than for personal adjustment, even though it was clear that the teachers' main effort and orientation was toward the educational remediation of the children. The correlation between the two measures is +.59.

The teachers also indicated that a composite 56 percent of their pupils would be able to meet their parents' expectations for adjustment. The product-moment correlation between this estimate and the teachers' own prognosis for the child's personal adjustment is +.40. . . .

Pupil Prognosis for Return to Regular Class

Another aspect of program success concerned the pupil's perception of his own situation and prognosis. Tables 5 through 9 present summaries of findings which reflect on certain major aspects of his self-prognosis.

Table 5. Pupil Expectation Concerning Return to Regular Class

When Pupil Expects to Return	Percent Indicating (N = 519)
Never	8
Not for a long time	10
After a few years	32
Soon, right now	45
No data	6

The pupils' collective outlook was somewhat more favorable than their teachers', and reflected a natural optimism and wish to have things back to normal. This finding was especially interesting in the light of data presented earlier, which indicated that most pupils were quite satisfied with their present classroom arrangement.

The distribution of responses over the categories is strikingly similar to that in the previous table. Since the correlation between the two ratings is only +.38, this is not a simple projection. The ratings in Table 6, however, are related to teacher ratings at only +.15. It appears that teachers and pupils saw

Table 4. Teacher Prognosis Concerning Pupils' Personal and Academic Adjustment

Degree of Adjustment	Personal Percent Indicating (N = 397)	Academic Percent Indicating (N = 406)
Complete	32	39
Limited	54	53
Very inadequate	14	8

matters of individual prognosis quite independently.

Table 6. Pupil Perception of When His Teacher Expects Him to Return to Regular Class

When Teacher Expects Him to Return	Percent Indicating ($N = 519$)
Never	8
Quite a while	31
Soon	55
No data	6

Pupils anticipated the areas in which they would have difficulty when and if they did return to the regular classroom. Table 7 indicates the distribution of the pupils' responses.

Table 7. Pupil Anticipation of Difficulty in Regular Class

Area	Percent Indicating ($N = 519$)
No trouble	14
Academics—(specific subjects—34%)	54
Peers	10
Teacher	7
Miscellaneous	5
No response	10

Academics were the largest potential difficulty area, and expected trouble with specific subjects was a concern of about one-third of the pupils. Troubles with teachers and peers affected less than one-fifth of the respondents. The concern with academic accomplishment in the regular class is particularly interesting in the light of the teachers' earlier reported discouragement in this area, as well as the teachers' emphasis upon interpersonal successes. In spite of the overall academic orientation of most programs and individuals, it appears that this is where the problems continue to exist.

Children also indicated in three specific areas what they felt their prospects were once back in their regular class. To the statement "I will be able to do the work," 87 percent of the 519 children indicated yes; only seven percent indicated no, and the balance gave no response. The respective responses

to the statement "I will be able to keep the rules" were 86 percent, 8 percent, and 6 percent, and to the statement "I will be able to get along with the kids," they were 88 percent, 6 percent, and 6 percent. In terms of specific areas, the pupils' outlook was quite favorable. The high proportion of children who said that they expected academics to be their major problem must have felt, in the main, that they would be able to handle the problem. Once again, the pupils appeared to be able to make distinctions among the three areas, since the intercorrelations among the three ratings ranged from only +.20 to +.32—high enough to be significant with this large N, but not indicating much variance in common.

Pupil Aspirations for the Future

One of the major components in any pupil's motivational system is his notion concerning his prospects for the future. To a degree, this can also serve as an index of how realistic his appraisal of himself is. Students told what they proposed to pursue as a life activity once they were out of school. Table 8 presents a summary of these responses, catalogued according to Reiss' (1961) occupational index scheme.

Table 8. Pupils' Occupational Aspirations

Level	Example	Percent Indicating ($N = 519$)
1	Auto mechanic	25
2	Policeman	14
3	Salesman	15
4	Baseball player	11
5	Draftsman	7
6	Teacher	9
7	Scientist	6
8	Doctor	7
	No data	7

Two-thirds of the children responding aspired to the first four categories, and the mean for all responses was 3.22, with $SD = 2.3$. The pupils aspired generally to occupations which were well within their intellectual capability to manage. In interpreting the data, however, one needs to recognize that many of the children are still young enough that fantasy, rather than reality factors,

Table 9. Children's Perceptions of Present and Previous Classes—Eight
Classroom Conditions Dimensions

Dimension	Previous Mean	Present Mean	t	r	p
Peer relationships	2.23	1.95	8.12	.32	.001
School anxiety	2.41	1.80	18.50	.35	.001
Personal affect	2.52	1.82	17.51	.31	.001
Parental pressure	2.33	1.70	15.86	.37	.001
Teacher relationships	2.46	2.16	9.04	.22	.001
Behavior	2.49	1.81	18.82	.39	.001
Morale	2.36	2.12	8.77	.26	.001
Academic success	2.70	1.95	20.30	.27	.001

$N = 406$

plays the major part in determining responses to such a question.

The children also felt fairly confident of reaching the goals they had set. In responding to a question specifically asking "How good are your chances of reaching the goal you have set?" 6 percent said "poor," 8 percent said "fair," 16 percent said "good," 50 percent said "very good," and 3 percent said "excellent." Eighteen percent of the sample of 519 children gave no response to the question. The mean of 3.4 falling between good and very good, indicates a reasonable degree of confidence.

Self-Perceptions of Change in the Pupils

One very important test of the success of such programs as those studied is the degree to which they induce change for the better in the children with whom they deal. It was not possible to assess these effects by extensive pre- and postprogram data.

It was necessary to rely upon retrospective data as a means of inferring changes which had taken place in the participating children, both from their own point of view, and from that of the teachers who had contact with them in the program.

Schedules A and B, which were completed by the individual children, or by trained recorders from data provided directly by the children when necessary, contained approximately 40 items which were used to assess pre- and postprogram conditions as seen by the children. These 40 items were grouped, a priori, into eight dimensions as indicated in Table 9. Each dimension contained approximately five

items, and the median reliability of the dimension scores was +.60.

Schedule A required that the children respond in terms of conditions as they saw them in their previous school or class. Schedule B sought similar information on the present special class. Differences between previous and present scores on each of the eight dimensions were computed, and a t test for correlated arrays was then applied to each dimension. The items were scored so that a decline in mean dimension score indicated improved conditions from previous to present class. Table 9 presents a summary of this analysis.

In terms of the perceptions of the children themselves, the special classrooms offered significantly better conditions than did the regular classrooms from which they came. The children, as a group, saw improved relationships with teacher and peers, felt less anxiety and parental pressure, and were happier, had higher morale, behaved better, and experienced greater academic success than in their previous settings. There was a considerable halo effect at work among the dimensions. At the same time, there remained little question that a general improvement in reactions to the school situation had occurred.

Changes in the Children as Perceived by Their Teachers

Another means of evaluating changes in the children as a result of their participation in the special class programs was obtained from teacher reports

Table 10. Teacher Perceptions of Changes in Children—Four Classroom
Behavior Dimensions

Dimension	Means		t Tests		r	p
Control	Previous	3.87	Prev.-Init.	7.86	.74	.001
	Initial	4.33	Prev.-Pres.	17.87	.40	.001
	Present	5.47	Init.-Pres.	14.39	.52	.001
Affect	Previous	3.03	Prev.-Init.	6.14	.73	.01
	Initial	3.39	Prev.-Pres.	17.54	.30	.001
	Present	4.97	Init.-Pres.	15.35	.42	.001
Academic	Previous	7.17	Prev.-Init.	2.57	.30	.01
	Initial	7.58	Prev.-Pres.	8.06	.17	.001
	Present	8.55	Init.-Pres.	11.85	.50	.001
Relationships	Previous	2.96	Prev.-Init.	6.62	.73	.01
	Initial	3.35	Prev.-Pres.	20.40	.33	.001
	Present	5.00	Init.-Pres.	16.57	.39	.001

$N = 406$

on perceived differences in pupil ability to control themselves, their affect, their academic achievement, and their personal relationships. Each teacher provided data on his children which indicated their condition on these dimensions as reported to him from their previous class, their condition when initially seen in the special class, and their condition at present. For each of the four dimensions, difference scores were computed between previous and initial, previous and present, and initial and present conditions. Table 10 summarizes the results of this analysis. In each case, t tests for correlated arrays were applied, and the items were scored in such a way that an increase in mean score from previous to initial, from previous to present, or from initial to present, indicated an improvement in the dimension.

Table 10 indicates a significant change in the perceptions of the teachers regarding the condition of their children, not only in the period during which they have had contact with them, but in the period between their previous class experience and their early contact in the special class. Several possibilities may be adduced to explain this peculiar finding. Perhaps the child's condition, as reported to the present teacher by the former teacher, was made to seem worse than it actually was. Perhaps the needs of the present teacher to see improvement were so great that they distorted his judgment or memory. Whatever the source, the changes seen by the teacher were in every case significant, and certainly indicate that things were better from the teacher's point of view.

Variables Related to Change
in Individual Pupils

To go beyond the mere demonstration of these changes and to attempt to account for them in terms of other variables on individual pupils, a total of 78 variables, including the change scores on the eight pupil dimensions and the four teacher dimensions, was assembled. These were subjected to a correlation analysis. The variables included measures of pupil self-confidence and aspiration level, self-prognosis in specific areas, pupil age, family morbidity as judged by the teacher, etc., as well as the pre-, post-, and change scores on the specific pupil and teacher dimensions discussed in the previous section. . . .

This examination was not an encouraging one. A very large number of significant correlations appeared (in part because the size of the sample makes the requirement for significance very low), but the pattern of relationships did little to clarify our knowledge of the factors which were operating to produce change. For the most part, pupil variables related to one another, teacher variables related to one another, but few significant relationships crossed the party lines. For example, considering the eight pupil self-description dimensions (peer relationships, school anxiety, personal affect, parental pressure, teacher relationships, behavior, morale, and academic success) on both the previous and present conditions, significant intercorrelations were found to exist among all pairs except three in the resulting 16 x 16 matrix. The range of significant correlations was from +.10 to +.58, with the median at +.33. These variables also related significantly to most of the change scores which were derived from them, as was to be expected. The several measures of pupil self-confidence and prognosis in specific areas also related significantly one to another, and to the eight dimensional measures and their derivatives, although less strongly.

A similar situation exists when the teacher variables are considered, although the teachers' ratings of such pupil characteristics as control, affect, relationships, etc., are less likely to be highly intercorrelated. It would appear that the teachers did discriminate among the variables, while the pupils were more likely to manifest a general halo effect in their perceptions. Once again, the teacher ratings of previous, initial condition in the special class, and present condition were strongly related within each teacher judgment variable, and also were related to the respective derived change scores. Beyond these expected patterns, meaningful intercorrelationsons were hard to find. A scattering of significant correlations appears throughout the matrix (far more than chance alone would provide), but most of these are so low or so remote in their interpretation as to be of only academic interest.

The level of these relationships is much too low to permit any but the most tenuous conclusions. However, a consistent pattern does seem to emerge, and while it is recognized that they may be the result of rating artifacts, response sets, etc., it is believed that they describe a meaningful syndrome which surrounds the improvements in the child's view of his school life. One would speculate that introduction into the special class, with reduced pressures and more tolerance from the teacher, produces a slight lessening of the child's overt pathology. The teacher in turn responds to this by seeing the child as better than he was described, and a narrow circle of hygienic relationships is developed. It is necessary to remember that every correlation plot has two ends, so that the opposite syndrome also exists for many children who do not see their lot as improved. However, the overall improvements discussed previously are of a significant magnitude, so that the proportion of children who are not benefitted is relatively low. Considering the fallibility of the measures, the difficulties with retrospective data, and the large and varied sample of pathologies, these findings represent an encouraging sign, even though they are obviously not conclusive.

Variables Related to Teacher-Perceived Change in Pupils

It was previously indicated that change scores were computed on four dimensions of pupil behavior as judged by their teachers. These four were: (a) control, (b) academic performance, (c) affect or feeling, and (d) general relationships. Three change scores were actually computed on each dimension, indicating changes from previous class condition to initial condition in the special class, from previous to present condition, and from initial condition to present condition in the special class. For the most part, changes which emerged were of the last two types, i.e., from previous to present condition, and from initial to present condition in the special class. From an examination of the changes, several interesting patterns emerge. The low magnitude of the correlations does not permit sweeping statements about those variables which relate to change as perceived by the teacher. However, there does seem to be a consistent pattern which involves not only teacher judgments, but also pupil perceptions of the improved conditions in their school lives in the special classroom. No causal significance can be attributed to these correlational findings, but it is quite clear that the pupil now feels that he is better off than he was. Whether this is a response to the relief from classroom pressure in the regular school, with consequent amelioration in his general relationships within the special class, or whether the teacher was an active, rather than an observing, agent in the change process is impossible to determine. For whatever reason, students seemed to feel better, and teachers were aware of this in their own view of things. What is cause and what is effect must await rigorous and controlled experimentation.

One other finding is worthy of mention. Running throughout the teacher change variable is the element of academic improvement, or at least less academic retardation. This appears consistently throughout all findings, as does the teacher's perception that the improved children were those with particular academic difficulty before they entered the special class. Once again, cause and effect are difficult to separate, but the importance of the academic process to both the student and the teacher cannot be overstressed. When the child improves academically, he sees his present condition as much more desirable than his former one. Teachers are generally very gratified at the fact that students seem not to be as badly off academically as they thought, and may respond favorably to such children. A most important element underlying the helping process in these classrooms centers around the teacher expectation of academic performance, previous pupil academic failure, and the introduction of academic success experiences into the classrooms.

Following this overall survey, a series of specific follow-up studies have been instituted. Even in an integrated series, it is impossible to get equivalent data from the various settings; these studies will probably raise more questions than they resolve. McKinnon completed a study on special classes.[20] He reports that relatively few of the disturbed children in schools get special help. Some 0.3 of 1 percent of all children are accepted, far short of the number of school pupils regular teachers identify as needing extensive help. In elementary programs, the mean referral age is 8 years, yet the mean acceptance age is 9½ years, a considerable lag. The pupils have all types of adjustment problems and, when referred, are learning at 62 percent of normal rate, although they have average IQ's. During the typical 1½ years' stay in the classes, their learning ratio increases to over 70 percent. Behavior is considered improved, parents are encouraged, and the pupils are positive in their evaluation of the help. Follow-up data are obtained (on the average) over three years after the class. Now 46 percent of the pupils are in regular classes and 21 percent are in special school programs at higher grades. Several have graduated or dropped out, but 11 percent are in in-patient hospitals. The older the pupil, generally the more academically retarded he is. Because of the low learning rate, he tends to fall further behind those making normal progress. Although behavior regressed somewhat after the class, pupils are seen as getting along better in school and in social relationships, except for academics. The best candidate for a special class appears to be the younger child of higher socio-economic status and with a higher IQ. Kotting and Brozovich[21] question how much change has been made in the school environment when the pupils re-enter regular classes. They discuss the ideal candidate for the special class, the one for whom the prognosis would be high. And he is the one unlikely to need the program at all. But as Quay has asked, "Were the classes designed for the specific needs of disturbed children in the first place?"

Asselstine,[22] after reviewing the twelve-year operation of a special class program, feels that two types of children are enrolled. One can be helped by individual tutoring in a regular school program. The other requires medical care, which is usually in short supply. Thus the special class is often a stop-gap measure that does not provide the degree of help needed.

Recently, Hewett and others have evaluated their engineered classroom.[23] The program was able to increase attention to the task, one of the primary goals. Gains in arithmetic were higher in the experimental group; reading gains were not. They feel that the checkmark system is superior to teacher reinforcement, at least at the initial stages, for these pupils. The temporary tangible rewards ceased to be necessary as the children made progress.

We conclude evaluation of special classes with one of the most comprehensive efforts available. This work by Rubin, Simson, and Betwee is an intensive study of the impact of the special class, with every effort to obtain an equivalent control group. Their summary is an astute statement of present school rehabilitation efforts. The reader is advised to read their whole book, where they develop the thesis of three sub-groups—the immature, the learning problems, and the behavior types.

Emotionally Handicapped
Children and the
Elementary School:
Evaluation of the Special Class

Eli Z. Rubin
Clyde B. Simson
Marcus C. Betwee

We now turn to the analysis of the results to determine what changes took place from the time the child entered the special class until the time he was judged ready to leave, and to compare these changes with those shown by the control group which did not experience the special class procedure. For a limited number of our sample, we are able to discuss to what degree the subjects maintained or altered their adjustment pattern one semester after replacement in regular classes.

When we compared the experimental and control groups from point of entry to exit on a variety of measures, we found few differences. The overall results suggest a trend to greater improvement by the experimental group. The more significant changes appear to relate to classroom behavior as seen by the teacher. The changes are least in academic performance and, in fact, there is some suggestion that both groups continue to fall behind academically, with the experimental group doing a little bit better when rated by the teacher, but doing somewhat worse on Achievement Test scores. The results do not indicate any remarkable changes in adjustment as seen either by the parents or the psychiatrist. The changes that are observed, which favor the experimental group significantly, again relate to the child's attitude and perception of school. More significant changes in psychiatric condition are not observable.

It is possible to make some tentative conclusions from *this* data. Although the group that experienced the special class program shows some trends toward greater improvement over the controls, these differences are not strongly convincing that the special class program is a highly significant contribution to improvement in better school adaptation of children. It is apparent from these re-sults that the control children in considerable numbers also showed improvements. Furthermore, the variability within the experimental group on the various measures suggested that the special class procedures may not be helpful, equally, to all members of the group.

Because of the limited sample involved in the follow-up study, few definite conclusions can be drawn. There are some significant trends reflected by the data. There are indications that the experimental group tended to maintain improvement or continue improvement in classroom behavior, both in terms of symptom display and according to the Teacher's Rating Scale, when their behavior was evaluated at the time of follow-up in comparison to that at the time of entry to the special class. On the other hand, the control group showed a better adjustment at follow-up in only a limited number of these same areas. This trend toward improvement in behavioral adjustment was not reflected, however, to any degree outside of the classroom. The parents of the experimental group did report that the children tended to maintain improvements already shown to a greater degree than the control group parents, but none of the differences can be considered reliable statistically. When we turn to progress in academic performance, the experimental group showed some improvement in achievement over that reflected at exit, whereas the control group continued to show academic decline. However, even with this slight improvement, the experimental and control groups continued to show academic retardation. In terms of the teacher's judgment about academic functioning, the teachers who received the experimental children felt that their reading ability was significantly better.

There is no confirmation from our psychiatric or psychological material that improvements in emotional adjustment were significant for either the experimental or control groups. Little change was reflected. With respect to psychological variables, it

Table 1. Comparison of Group Means on Change in Disruptive
Behavior in the Classroom (Behavior Observation)*

Variable	Exp	Control	Difference: Exit to Follow-Up
Disruptive behavior ratio			
In teacher's sphere	3	16	− .8
In independent activity	6	22	−1.6

*A ratio of follow-up/exit was used to indicate change. Scores below 1 indicate improvement at follow-up.

appeared that the control group improved on approximately the same number of variables as did the experimental group.

Thus, this limited follow-up study suggests that the children in the experimental group who had been part of the special class program were able to maintain the improvements gained in the special class with respect to classroom adjustment and to hold these for approximately one or two semesters after replacement in regular classes. A longer term follow-up is certainly indicated to determine if such changes in adjustment leading to more satisfactory performance in school could be maintained in later grades and contribute to a more successful adjustment generally.

Summary

In this chapter, the results of the special class program have been reviewed, comparing the experimental and control groups on a variety of measures from the point of entry to the point of exit, and for a limited sample from the point of entry to the point of follow-up. In general, the findings suggest limited improvement restricted primarily to classroom adjustment and reduction of symptomatic behavior. The results, themselves, are not dramatic nor do they contribute to an overwhelming confirmation of the initial hypothesis—that special class programming is generally beneficial to emotionally handicapped children as a specific method of intervention and correction.

Our experiences in this study have led us to conceptualize the problem somewhat differently. Many of the children in this study made noticeable improvements recognizable by teachers and parents. Although the majority of these children came from the experimental group which had experienced the special class program, there were some from the control group as well. Furthermore, as more experience was gained with the manner of functioning of the children in the special class situation, we became more aware of the heterogeneity of the groups and the fact that certain kinds of behavior were characteristic of some children and not of others. As we learned to identify particular characteristics of malfunctioning in the classroom, we turned our attention to an examination of the behavioral characteristics of our total sample with the hope that we could identify the particular characteristics of those children who benefitted the most, as well as those who showed the least response.

In our statistical analysis we focused on the behavioral characteristics displayed by the children leading to their referral for special class placement. We tried to determine if there were particular behavior symptoms clustered together that were psychologically meaningful and could supply us with more specific information about the characteristics of our sample. At the clinical classroom level, we attempted to identify certain characteristics of academic and behavioral functioning which appeared more closely related to the child's lack of progress in his daily functioning. Utilizing a combination of criteria including level of cognitive-motor adaptive skills and ability for self-control and independence of functioning, instructional groups were composed and more specific content programs were introduced. As it turned out, the statistical approach involving a factor analysis of the behavior symptoms and our regroupings based on clinical impressions were highly correlated. Part 3 will deal in detail with both of these approaches, as well as an alternate method of examining the results of our special class procedures by comparing successful and non-successful groups.

A Michigan study of child mental health has pointed out the inescapable fact: various efforts to help children are bogged down in inefficiency because caseloads are too large. There are not enough places to treat the seriously disturbed youngsters who require a total milieu program with individual therapy. As exemplary institutions for such children do exist, there is no excuse for poor care.

Principles to guide new programs are emerging from the good facilities. Do not remove the child from his environment if he can be helped within it. If he is not a danger to himself or others, or a significant detriment to the rights of his peers, try to help him in his community. When a child is removed, he often gets nothing more helped within it. If he is not a danger to himself community plus the traumatic significance of removal. This feeling of being different and hopeless is openly resisted by many adolescents; younger children, who may well feel resistance, verbalize it less often. On the other hand, separation is a relief to children who see escape from home and school as their only means of survival. A child who lives with very disturbed parents, one who lives in abject poverty, one who suffers from a hostile school—for him even minimal institutional care may be more than he otherwise had. The immediate acceptance of the new "home" by some disturbed children shows the stress of the local environment for them. When the original home cannot be altered, what choice is there?

To undertake the total raising of a child is a profound social responsibility. It is expensive to operate an institution and to attract the needed personnel of all disciplines; the psychological cost of providing deep human bonds and caring in a helping and socializing environment is even greater. Because services so easily become dehumanized, it takes expert direction to maintain morale and tone. The difference in quality between institutions is not in money alone: it is in the character and concern of the staff. The critical help may come from psychiatric therapy, from a teacher and the educational experience, from a child-care worker, or from some change in the parents' feelings brought about by the social workers. When a child needs intensive help, some separation from the community is required.

Even when the level of service in an institution is high, two other conditions must be added. First, establishments (represented by huge state detention and mental hospitals) must be made smaller and closer to the child's community, and made multidisciplinary in substance as well as form. Education must play a major role in this development. In addition, there is the pressing need to search for new designs.[24] These designs will come in many varieties and with new disciplinary arrangements. Some have spoken enthusiastically of the Educateur staffing model, where one person serves a multiple role for sustained total care. Special camps, sheltered workshops, on-the-job training, and the use of sub-professionals are other suggestions.

The amount of responsibility and investment required to restore health in a disturbed youngster is far more taxing than is generally recognized. To continue hour after hour, day after day, month after month, requires special training and a special type of person in a special supportive setting. Otherwise, even the best environmental resources do not provide enough help.

One informative follow-up study on a new design is part of Project Re-Ed's extensive evaluation effort. They did not compare their treatment with others, as essential variables in various studies have not been carefully controlled. Several sources of information were available for this six month follow-up, including home and school ratings and formal test data. But the most interesting material in this report is the discussion of the often neglected conditions that are important in interpreting evaluation findings. Weinstein presents a considered and candid commentary on her results.

Project Re-Ed Schools
for Emotionally Disturbed
Children: Effectiveness as
Viewed by Referring
Agencies, Parents, and Teachers
Laura Weinstein

Two Project Re-Ed schools—Cumberland House Elementary School in Nashville, Tennessee, and Wright School in Durham, North Carolina—were established several years ago under the joint sponsorship of the National Institute of Mental Health, the state of Tennessee, the state of North Carolina, and George Peabody College for Teachers to develop and test a new model for helping emotionally disturbed children. The philosophy, program, and history of the Re-Ed schools have been described in detail elsewhere (Hobbs, 1965; Hobbs, 1966; Lewis, 1966a; Lewis, 1966b; Lewis, 1967). Suffice it to say here that the schools offer a short term residential program for school age, preadolescent children who are too disturbed or disturbing to be maintained at home or in a regular school, but who do not require hospitalization or constant surveillance. (See Table 1 for further description of the first 250 children served by the two Re-Ed schools.) One unique characteristic of the schools is that the primary staff, who plan the program and work directly with the children and others in the children's social world, are specially trained teachers rather than psychiatrists, psychologists, or social workers.

Research on the effectiveness of the Re-Ed schools has been and continues to be an integral part of the Re-Ed program. The data presented here deal with evaluations of improvement in the Re-Ed children by referring agencies, parents, and the children's schools.

Improvement as Seen by the Referring Agencies

Soon after the child leaves Re-Ed, a worker in the referring agency who has had continued contact with him or his parents during his residence at Re-Ed is contacted by mail by the research staff and asked to rate change in the child by responding to this question: Compared to enrollment, is the child's adjustment now *worse, the same, slightly improved, moderately improved,* or *greatly improved?* Interest is in the percentage of children rated in the top categories as opposed to the percentage rated worse, the same, or slightly improved. The referring agency ratings are summarized in Table 2.

Also summarized in that table are responses to the same item made by the child's parents 6 months after he returned home. Despite the relatively brief average length of stay at Re-Ed schools, these percentages compared favorably with the two-thirds to three-fourths rated improved in most other studies of effectiveness of other treatment programs.

Improvement as Seen by the Parents

Parents rate their child's behavior just prior to his Re-Ed enrollment and again 6 and 18 months after he has left Re-Ed. The parents are asked to work independently in making their ratings.

At Cumberland House, followup contacts to collect the post-Re-Ed ratings involve home visits if the family lives in the vicinity of Nashville, with the parents filling out the rating forms under the supervision of the interviewer. For families who live at a distance, initial contacts are made by telephone and then the rating forms are mailed to the parents. At Wright School, all followup contacts are made by mail.

Three scales were developed to measure dimensions of particular interest.

From *Exceptional Children*, vol. 35, no. 9, May 1969, pp. 703–711. Reprinted by permission of The Council for Exceptional Children and the author.

1.   The Symptom Checklist is composed of problem behaviors commonly ascribed to disturbed children (crying, temper tantrums, running away, feeling afraid, etc.). The parents indicate the frequency with which each behavior has occurred in the previous 2 weeks.

2.   The Social Maturity Scale was adapted from the Vineland and its variations (Cain, Levine, Tallman, Elzey, & Kase, 1958; Doll, 1947; Farber, 1959). Thirty-four behaviors are listed; the parents check those the child usually performs.

3.   The Semantic Differential discrepancy score is the sum of the squared differences between the way the parent describes the child and the way he indicates he wants him to be. The polar adjectives represent the factors Becker (1960) derived in his analyses of parent and teacher ratings, plus an activity dimension which seemed especially relevant to Re-Ed children.

At the time of data analysis, 56 Wright School and 111 Cumberland House children had been discharged long enough to be scheduled for the first home followup. Followup interviews were accomplished for 52 of the Wright School and 109 of the Cumberland House children. However, both preenrollment and first followup ratings on the three parent scales were available for only 30 Wright School and 73 Cumberland House children. The primary source of loss was that the scales were not developed until 45 of the children had already been enrolled. Additional losses occurred for children who lacked one or both parents or who had a change in parent figures between enrollment and first followup. Finally, some ratings were not available because parents omitted items or misunderstood instructions; such loss was minor except for the Semantic Differential scale, with which a number of the parents had difficulty.

Results for the preenrollment and first followup (6 months after the child's return home) ratings are shown in Table 3. According to both parents, children from both schools were showing fewer inappropriate behaviors, were more socially competent, and were less discrepant from parental standards and expectations at first followup than before enrollment.

The increased concordance between the child's behavior and his parents' expectations, indicated by the decrease in the Semantic Differential discrepancy score, could have come about in any one of three different ways: the child's behavior could have "im-proved" (i.e., become more like his parents' expectations) while his parents' expectations remained unchanged; the parents' expectations could have become "more realistic" (i.e., more like the child's behavior) while the child's behavior remained unchanged; or both the child's behavior and his parents' expectations could have changed in ways which made them more congruent. Increased concordance between the child's behavior and the expectations for his behavior held by his parents is a basic goal of the Re-Ed intervention, and the Re-Ed strategy focuses, as necessary, both on improving the child's behavior and on making the parents' expectations more realistic. To what extent did the increased concordance indicated by the Semantic Differential discrepancy score data reflect improvement in the child's behavior, and to what extent did it reflect adjustment in the parents' expectations? To explore this, the Semantic Differential scale was scored separately for the parents' descriptions of the children and for their descriptions of how they wanted the children to be.

It can be seen from Table 4 that both parents at both schools described their children's behavior as more socially acceptable at first followup than they had prior to enrollment. The Parent's Ideal for the Child score remained stable over time for mothers at both schools. The expectations of Wright School fathers also remained stable between enrollment and first followup, but Cumberland House fathers appeared to have adjusted their expectations to more closely approximate the behavior of their children. These data suggest that the increased concordance after Re-Ed between the child's behavior and his parents' expectations stemmed primarily from improvement in the child's behavior. Even Cumberland House fathers, who did adjust their expectations, indicated that their children had met them halfway by bringing their behavior closer to their fathers' expectations.

Further analyses of the Semantic Differential scale focused on the child's performance on the individual dimensions. Each dimension was scored separately, with high scores indicating friendly extroversion, lack of tension, lack of aggression, dominance, and activity, respectively. Changes in dimension scores over time are shown in Table 4. At first followup, both parents at both schools described their children as less tense, less aggressive, and more dominant than before enrollment. In addition, mothers described their children as more outgoing. Neither parent indicated any change on the activity dimension.

Table 1. Characteristics at Enrollment of the First 250 Children
at the Two Re-Ed Schools

Demographic Characteristics	Percentage	
	Wright School (N = 94)	Cumberland House (N = 156)
1. Sex: males	78	83
2. Race: white	100	96
a 3. Mean age at enrollment (years)		
Wright School Cumberland House		
10.9 10.2		
4. IQ		
50– 89	29	21
90–109	52	59
110–139	19	21
Mean		
Wright School Cumberland House		
98.1 99.7		
5. Socioeconomic status		
Education of head of household		
8 years or less	15	24
9–11 years	27	18
12 years	18	21
13–15 (including noncollege training beyond high school)	18	23
16 years or more	22	14
Median: Completed high school		
Occupation of head of household		
Median: Skilled labor, white collar		
a 6. Parental situation at enrollment		
Both biological parents	61	54
Both adoptive parents	11	11
One parent, parent and stepparent, or other relative	26	31
Foster parents or child care institution	3	4
Mental Health Status and History		
7. Referring agency		
Mental health clinic or child study center	69	76
Social service agency	11	11
Private physician, psychologist, or psychiatrist	5	3
School and school associated services	13	8
Other (court, priest, etc.)	2	3
8. Referring agency diagnosis (most usual was some variant of "Adjustment Reaction of Childhood")		
Children for whom brain damage ever suspected	21	30
Children for whom schizophrenia ever suspected	12	13
a 9. Type of problem (Re-Ed rating)		
Acting out	41	79
Withdrawn	54	19
Truancy or school phobia, no other behavior problem stressed	2	1
Problems primarily academic	2	1
10. Number of agencies and private practitioners previously working with child for diagnosis or therapy. Includes physician if child saw him because of emotional problems. Referring agency omitted unless it provided therapy prior to Re-Ed.		
0	11	21
1	44	35
2	23	24
3	17	12
4	4	6
5	1	1

Demographic Characteristics	Percentage	
	Wright School (N = 94)	Cumberland House (N = 156)
Mean:		
Wright School Cumberland House		
1.6 1.5		
a 11. Mean age of child when first seen by helping agency (years)		
Wright School Cumberland House		
8.5 8.0		
12. Received medication for emotional or behavioral problems prior to Re-Ed	37	33
13. Arrested or in juvenile court prior to Re-Ed (crimes or truancy)	4	8
School Situation at Enrollment		
14. School enrollment		
Not enrolled in school	10	10
Special class	6	5
Regular class	84	85
15. Had failed one or more grades	66	53
16. School progress not normal (removed from school, failed, special class)	70	60
a 17. Mean grade in school for those in regular class		
Wright School Cumberland House		
4.4 4.0		
Achievement Test Data	(N = 51)	(N = 132)
Retarded in reading	84	86
Retarded in arithmetic	92	92
Mean retardation in reading (years)		
Wright School Cumberland House		
2.0 1.5		
Mean retardation in arithmetic (years)		
Wright School Cumberland House		
1.9 1.6		

Difference between schools is significant.

Improvement as Seen by the Child's School

Before the child leaves his school to enter Re-Ed (if the child is at that time enrolled in school), the Re-Ed staff asks his teacher to fill out a questionnaire describing the child and rating him on a number of dimensions. At school followup, done by the research staff by mail, the child's new teacher is asked to fill out the same questionnaire. Again, interest is in change in scores over time. The timing of school followup is more variable than that of home followup because the fact that children periodically change classes must be taken into consideration. To permit valid ratings from teachers, no school inquiry is made before the child has been with his teacher and classmates at least 3 months; thus, time to first school followup depends upon how close the child's discharge from Re-Ed is to the summer recess. Average time between discharge and first followup has been 6 months, with second school followup done a year after the first.

At the time of data analysis, 62 Wright School and 125 Cumberland House children had been discharged sufficiently long to be due for their first school followup. However, school followup information was not obtained for four Wright and five Cumberland children because their schools had not returned forms or because they could not be traced; neither could followup information be obtained for

Table 2. Improvement Ratings:
Percentage of Children Rated
Moderately or Greatly Improved

Rater	N	Wright School Percentage	N	Cumberland House Percentage
Referring agency	37	73	43	89
Mother	32	87	58	83
Father	22	73	41	78

four Wright and three Cumberland children because they were not enrolled in school at followup.
Thus, a total of 54 Wright School and 117 Cumberland House first school followups were completed. Children who were not enrolled in school
prior to Re-Ed (and had no teacher who could make
initial ratings) were omitted from the pre-post
comparisons, except in those cases where the child
had been expelled shortly enough before Re-Ed so
that his former teacher could provide the ratings.
Additional children omitted from some analyses
were those who were enrolled after particular items
were added to the school questionnaire. Finally,
some items have smaller N's because teachers
omitted them through oversight or inability to make
a judgment.

The Student Role Behavior Scale. This scale consists of items which are fairly specific and closely
tied to the requirements of the student role (e.g.,
Does the child work at desk assignments without
getting distracted or annoying the other children? Is
he willing to share the teacher's attention? Does he
do his homework?). The scale has a maximum of 27
points, with high scores indicating more adequate
role performance. It can be seen from Table 5 that
children from both schools were seen by their teachers at first followup as playing the student role more
adequately than had been reported by their teachers prior to enrollment.

Items 2 through 6 of Table 5 are each based on
3 point scales, with lower scores indicating more socially desirable behavior. At first followup, Re-Ed
children were seen by their teachers as behaving less
disruptively in class, as feeling less personal distress,
as being more able to face new or difficult situations, as working harder and more persistently, and
as relating better to their classmates than had been
reported by their teachers prior to Re-Ed.

Item 7 of Table 5 summarizes results of a 5
point scale requiring judgment of the child's ability
as compared to other children his age. A lower score
indicates greater ability. Of all the teacher rating
items used in the research, this is the only one which
suggested a negative change in the children. After
Re-Ed, the children were seen as having less ability
than before Re-Ed. The meaning of this change will
be discussed after data on academic achievement
have been presented.

Table 3. Parent Rating Scales: Change in Children between Enrollment and
First Followup

Rating Scale	Rater	N	Wright School Rating at Enrollment	Rating at First Followup	t	N	Cumberland House Rating at Enrollment	Rating at First Followup	t
Symptom checklist	Mother	29	34.4	21.7	4.75**	73	41.0	27.9	6.98**
	Father	24	27.6	20.7	2.32*	55	35.6	22.7	7.06**
Social maturity	Mother	30	23.8	28.0	6.47**	71	22.4	27.1	10.05**
	Father	24	23.7	26.7	3.60**	53	22.3	25.9	7.03**
Semantic differential discrepancy	Mother	20	141.9	91.2	3.11**	65	138.6	95.1	4.78**
	Father	18	103.1	70.8	2.43*	42	125.3	71.7	6.45**

*Significant at .05 level, two tailed test.
**Significant at .01 level or beyond, two tailed test.

Table 4. Semantic Differential Scores: Change in Children between
Enrollment and First Followup on Mean Ratings Given by Parents

Score	Rater	N	Wright School Rating at Enrollment	Rating at First Followup	t	N	Cumberland House Rating at Enrollment	Rating at First Followup	t
Description	Mother	20	35.3	41.7	3.21**	65	35.2	41.4	5.18**
of child	Father	18	39.0	45.9	2.85**	42	36.3	42.8	5.56**
Parent's ideal	Mother	20	62.4	63.1	0.41	65	61.6	61.9	0.20
for child	Father	18	61.8	61.8	0.04	42	62.4	59.6	−2.31*
Dimension scores									
Friendly extroversion	Mother	20	19.5	21.2	2.60**	65	19.1	20.6	4.17**
	Father	18	20.3	21.2	1.71	42	19.5	20.3	1.82
Relaxed—nervous	Mother	20	7.1	12.4	4.28**	65	8.1	11.3	4.75**
	Father	18	8.7	12.2	2.73**	42	8.3	11.9	6.78**
Lack of Agression	Mother	20	8.6	12.0	2.62**	65	7.5	11.1	4.08**
	Father	18	10.0	12.6	2.24*	42	8.5	10.6	3.18**
Dominance	Mother	20	15.0	17.4	2.56**	65	17.0	18.3	2.31*
	Father	18	15.7	17.1	2.33*	42	16.3	17.5	2.22*
Activity	Mother	20	13.5	14.6	1.16	65	15.4	15.8	1.32
	Father	18	13.3	14.4	1.84	42	15.2	14.8	−1.02

*Significant at .05 level, two tailed test.
**Significant at .01 level or beyond, two tailed test.

Table 5. Change in Children between Enrollment and First Followup:
Mean Ratings Given by Teachers

Scale items	N	Wright School Rating at Enrollment	Rating at First Followup	t	N	Cumberland House Rating at Enrollment	Rating at First Followup	t
Role behavior	39	12.6	17.4	4.57**	77	13.9	19.1	7.08**
Disruptiveness	39	1.6	1.3	3.02**	77	1.7	1.2	7.35**
Feelings of personal distress	36	2.3	1.8	3.08**	76	2.2	1.6	6.11**
Ability to face new situations	34	2.6	2.0	3.53	71	2.4	1.7	4.51**
Work habits	42	2.7	2.3	3.61**	96	2.5	2.2	4.11**
Relationships with other children	42	1.7	1.4	2.13*	85	1.9	1.4	6.25**
Ability	37	3.1	3.5	−2.46*	77	3.1	3.3	−1.98*

*Significant at .05 level, two tailed test.
**Significant at .01 level or beyond, two tailed test.

Table 6. Rating of Behavioral-Emotional Adjustment in School:
Change in Children between Enrollment and First Followup

	Normal Range	Percentage Mild Problems	Fairly Severe	Very Severe	Mean
Wright School (N = 43)					
Enrollment	2	7	65	26	3.1
Followup	26	35	33	7	2.2
				$t = 6.04**$	
Cumberland House (N = 109)					
Enrollment	9	24	47	20	2.8
Followup	38	40	18	4	1.9
				$t = 8.76**$	

**Significant at .01 level or beyond, two tailed test.
  Three children could not be rated with confidence on this dimension.

Global ratings made by research department. A
rater in the research department makes two global
judgments about the child on the basis of the
questionnaire filled out by the teacher; in making
these judgments the rater uses the descriptions of
the child given by the teacher in answer to
openended questions as well as teacher ratings such
as those discussed above. The research rater is asked
to judge, separately for behavioral-emotional adjustment and academic adequacy, whether the
teacher is saying that the child *is in the normal
range, has mild problems, has fairly severe problems, or has very severe problems.*

These judgments had good interrater reliability. Judgments of behavioral-emotional adjustment
made by two research raters correlated .92 (N = 78)
and judgments of academic adequacy correlated .91
(N = 72). When teachers were asked to make the
same judgments after filling out the questionnaires,
correlations between research raters and teachers
were .89 (N = 150) for behavioral-emotional adjustment and .87 (N = 150) for academic adequacy.
In all cases, means were identical or nearly so.

Results for the behavioral-emotional adjustment dimension are shown in Table 6. Change was
quite striking. About three-fourths of the children
were rated as having fairly severe or very severe
problems prior to Re-Ed; approximately the same
number were rated as in the normal range or as having mild problems at first followup. Overall, there
was a mean change of almost one full scale point.
Results for the academic adequacy dimension,
shown in Table 7, were less striking. Indeed, aca-

demic change reached significance only for Cumberland House children. These results fitted well
with judgments made at discharge by the Re-Ed
teacher counselors. The teacher counselors felt
considerably more satisfied with the changes they
saw in their children's behavior than with improvements in their academic proficiency. Both schools
are currently putting greater emphasis on their
academic programs.

Some sense of what is at issue in the academic
area may be gained from the academic achievement
test information which was collected for Cumberland House children. Where possible, scores
from the last two achievement tests taken by the
child prior to Re-Ed and the first two taken after Re-
Ed are collected; these are standardized tests (usually Metropolitan) taken by the child with his class at
his home school. Primary interest in the scores is in
comparing rate of gain in acquisition of academic
skills prior to and after Re-Ed. Scores from two pre-
Re-Ed tests were available for 84 Cumberland
House children; scores from two post-Re-Ed tests
were available for 53 children; scores on all four
tests were available for 25 children. Prior to Re-Ed,
during the year between the two pretests, the children gained 6 months in reading (rate of gain = .6
months per month of schooling) and 5 months in
arithmetic (rate of gain .5 months per month of
schooling). These means held both for the small
group of children who had all four tests and the
larger group who had scores from both pretests but
not from both posttests. After Re-Ed, the group of
53 children with both posttests showed a month for

Table 7. Global Rating of Academic Adequacy: Change in Children
between Enrollment and First Followup

| | Normal Range | Percentage | | | Mean |
		Mild Problems	Fairly Severe	Very Severe	
Wright School (N = 43)					
Enrollment	16	14	23	47	3.0
Followup	19	14	33	35	2.8
				$t = 0.85$	
Cumberland House (N = 112)					
Enrollment	28	15	31	26	2.6
Followup	43	16	29	12	2.1
				$t = 3.52*$	

*Significant at .01 level or beyond, two tailed test.

month gain in reading and in arithmetic (rate of gain = 1.0 months per month of schooling). The smaller group with all four tests showed the same 1.0 rate of gain in reading and a rate of .8 months per month in arithmetic. These results are quite impressive when contrasted with the frequent finding that disturbed children fall farther and farther behind their peers academically as time passes. The results reported here suggest that growth in academic gap between Re-Ed children and their peers was arrested.

However, learning at the normal, expected rate after Re-Ed is sufficient only if the children have completely closed the gap between themselves and their peers during Re-Ed—if on leaving Re-Ed they are performing at grade level. This did not occur; after Re-Ed the children were about as academically retarded compared to their classmates as they had been at enrollment. The Re-Ed program had succeeded in affecting the children's motivation for learning and ability to learn; it had not been able to make up for their initial retardation. Their continuing retardation is reflected in the ratings of academic adequacy shown in Table 7.

The achievement test data indicated that the children learned better after Re-Ed than before. This conclusion is supported by other evidence from the teacher questionnaires (e.g., significantly fewer children were in danger of retention or social promotion after Re-Ed than prior to Re-Ed). Why, then, did their teachers see the children was having less ability after Re-Ed than before (see Table 5, Item 7)? An interesting *post hoc* hypothesis is that prior to Re-Ed, the teachers saw the children's poor performance as resulting from their emotional disturbance, whereas after Re-Ed, the teachers, being less likely to see the child as disturbed, were more likely to see his performance as accurately reflecting his

ability. If this reasoning is accurate, it lends special credence to the findings concerning the effectiveness of the Re-Ed program. Most of the evidence for effectiveness rests on findings of positive change; one wonders how seriously the individual items can be taken—how much they are all affected by the same halo effect. Support by a finding of negative change would indicate that improvement was great enough to overcome the halo effect.

Ongoing Research

Results from the first home and school followups, which have been reported in this article, indicated improvement in behavioral and academic performance following Re-Ed. Second followup data continue to be collected, and preliminary analyses indicated that the improvements reported 6 months after the child left Re-Ed were generally being maintained a year later.

A major focus of the current research is study (under a grant from the Office of Education) of a group of untreated disturbed children. Study of these children over time will permit evaluation of the extent to which the results reported here reflected rerating effects, improvements related to increased age, or the natural variations in behavior which occur with the passage of time. Until these additional data are available, conclusions must remain tentative, and the results presented here should be considered an interim report. However, the extent of the changes found, and their consistency within and across raters, do lead to optimism that the findings of behavioral and academic improvement following the Re-Ed intervention will hold even after the additional data are in.

Article References

Becker, W.C. The relationship of factors in parental ratings of self and each other to the behavior of kindergarten children as rated by mothers, fathers, and teachers. *Journal of Consulting Psychology,* 1960, 24, 507–527.

Cain, L.F., Levine, S., Tallman, I., Elzey, F., & Kase, D. *Study of the effect of special day training classes for the severely mentally retarded.* Available through ERIC Document Reproduction Service, National Cash Register Co., 4936 Fairmont Ave., Bethesda, Md. ED 00 2979, 1958.

Doll, E.A. *Vineland social maturity scale manual of directions.* Minneapolis: Educational Test Bureau, 1947.

Farber, B. Effects of a severely mentally retarded child on family integration. *Monographs of the Society for Research in Child Development,* 1959, 24 (71, Whole No. 2).

Hobbs, N. How the Re-Ed plan developed. In N.J. Long, W.C. Morse, & Ruth G. Newman (Eds.), *Conflict in the classroom: The education of emotionally disturbed children.* Belmont, Calif.: Wadsworth, 1965. Pp. 286–294.

Hobbs, N. Helping disturbed children: Psychological and ecological strategies. *American Psychologist,* 1966, 21, 1105–1115.

Lewis, W.W. Project Re-Ed: Educational intervention in emotional disturbance. In J. Hellmuth (Ed.), *Educational therapy.* Seattle: Special Child Publications, 1966. Pp. 295–315. (a)

Lewis, W.W. Project Re-Education: A new program for the emotionally disturbed. *The High School Journal,* 1966, 49, 279–286. (b)

Lewis, W.W. Project Re-Ed: Educational intervention in discordant child rearing systems. In E.L. Cowen, E.A. Gardner, & M. Zax (Eds.), *Emergent approaches to mental health problems.* New York: Appleton-Century-Crofts, 1967. Pp. 352–368.

Although it is evident that small "N" comparative group studies have their limitations, we must still learn what we can from such work.

Vacc has tried to include academic and social adjustment in his evaluative studies of mainstreaming vs. the special class.

A Study of Emotionally Disturbed Children in Regular and Special Classes
Nicholas A. Vacc

The emotionally disturbed children in the regular classes achieved less well on the Wide Range Achievement Test and the Behavior Rating Scale than did the emotionally disturbed children in special classes. Further, the emotionally disturbed children in the regular classes were less well accepted than the normal children.

This study was designed to measure changes in achievement and overt behavior of emotionally disturbed children (or children identified as emotionally handicapped by a school psychologist and a psychiatrist) in special and regular classes. In addition, the social position of emotionally disturbed and normal children in regular classes was assessed.

Differences of opinion concerning the relative merits of special class placement and regular class placement for the emotionally disturbed child prevail among educators. Those educators advocating regular class placement feel that the regular school program can be tailored to provide for individual differences. They also feel that the regular class does more than the special class to fit the emotionally disturbed child to his social environment. Educators advocating the special class placement believe that the regular classes cannot make adequate educational provisions for the emotionally disturbed child and that placing this child in a regular class provides no guarantee that the group will accept him socially.

Reprinted from *Exceptional Children,* vol. 35, no. 3, November 1968, pp. 197–203, by permission of the Council for Exceptional Children. Copyright 1966 by the Council for Exceptional Children.

Very little has been written concerning the emotionally disturbed child in a typical school setting. Rhodes (1962) found that studies in this area usually used a small number of subjects, provided little information on the process, and lacked coherence. Morse (1964) made an attempt to gather descriptive data of existing special class programs for emotionally disturbed children. The study indicated confusion on the part of educators about how to proceed in educating the emotionally disturbed child. Morse stated, "There is the obvious need for greater systematization and more rigorous research . . . [p. 131]." The work of Cruickshank, Bentzen, Ratzeburg, and Tannhauser (1961), Haring and Phillips (1962), and Radin (1966) provided indications that programing for emotionally disturbed in a special class setting could be beneficial. Knoblock (1966), in an attempt to improve the education of emotionally disturbed children in regular classes, emphasized consultative services. Balow (1966), after an extensive review of the literature on programs for emotionally disturbed children, reported that the majority of publications have been prescriptions, subjective descriptions, and clinical studies.

The salient points of pertinent literature pertaining to the present study are as follows:

1.   The importance of the need for programs for the emotionally handicapped child has been demonstrated by the identifications of the number of such programs in schools (White & Harris, 1961; Vaughan, 1961; Rogers, 1942b; Bower, 1960).

2.   Ideologies for the rehabilitation of emotionally disturbed children have been primarily clinically oriented; there has been little agreement regarding the best approach (Bettelheim, 1949; Pearson, 1954; Redl & Wattenberg, 1951; Redl, 1962; Newman, 1956; Rogers, 1951; Axline, 1947; Moustakas, 1956; Hymes, 1955; Prescott, 1957; Haring & Phillips, 1962).

3.   Established programs for emotionally disturbed children in schools are limited, and research indicates a lack of uniformity in approach (Morse, 1964; Balow, 1966).

4.   The theoretical research on peer acceptance should be considered in the preparations and evaluation of programs for the emotionally handicapped (White, 1960; Sullivan, 1953; Bossard, 1960; Olmstead, 1959; Phillips & De Vault, 1955).

The specific questions concerning this study of emotionally disturbed children in special and regular classes in Chautauqua County, New York, were:

1.   What is the change in achievement of emotionally disturbed children in a special class as compared to that of emotionally disturbed children in a regular class?

2.   What is the change in overt behavior of emotionally disturbed children in a special class as compared to that of emotionally disturbed children in a regular class?

The specific question concerning the study of the social position of emotionally disturbed children in the regular classes was: What is the degree to which emotionally disturbed children in the regular classes are receiving social choice selections and rejections as compared to normal children in regular classes? In addition, attention was directed to determining the percentage of stars, isolates, and rejectees found within the group of emotionally disturbed children and normal children in regular classes.

In a classroom sociometric situation, a star is a person who is chosen for positive roles so much in excess of chance expectancy as to confirm the existence of social forces of acceptance. An isolate is a person who is chosen for positive poles so seldom in comparison with chance expectancy as to confirm the existence of social forces of neglect or rejection. A rejectee is chosen for negative roles so much in excess of chance expectancy as to confirm the existence of social forces of rejection.

Method

Subjects

The population studied consisted of children attending public schools in the centralized districts of Chautauqua County, New York. Two special classes, each containing eight emotionally disturbed children, were studied. A group of 16 emotionally disturbed children was selected from the regular grades by matching them with children in the special classes on a number of variables: (a) intelligence, (b) chronological age, (c) grade placement, (d) achievement level, (e) comparison of social class position, and (f) the opinion of the supervising psychologist. The comparison of the groups on variables of social class, grade level, intelligence, age in months, and achievement level are presented in Table 1.

Table 1. Comparison of the Groups of
Emotionally Disturbed Children in
Regular and Special Classes

Variable	Special classes Mean	N	Regular classes Mean	N	F	t
Social class	5.12	16	5.43	16	1.36	.86
Grade level	3.56	16	3.62	16	1.16	.12
Intelligence	95	16	93	16	1.02	.65
Age in months	124	16	121	16	1.32	1.22
Achievement level	2.71	16	3.00	16	1.01	.81

The findings indicated no significant differences between the two groups on the variables tested. The computed F ratio suggests homogeneity of variance between all of the sets. On the basis of these statistical tests, it would seem that the emotionally disturbed children in both regular and special classes came from the same population.

The group of emotionally disturbed children in the regular classes was compared with the children in the special classes in academic achievement and overt behavior. In addition, the social position of the emotionally disturbed children in the regular classes was examined in relation to the normal children who were members of the same classes. Sixteen classes were used involving children in grades one through six. The criterion for a class being selected was that it contained one member identified as emotionally handicapped.

Data Collection

The Wide Range Achievement Test and the Behavior Rating Scale (Haring & Phillips, 1962) were administered at the beginning and at the end of the study for the emotionally disturbed children in regular and special classes. A school psychologist administered the Wide Range Achievement Test to each child in October and again in June. The same schedule was followed for the administration of the Behavior Rating Scale. Two Behavior Rating Scales were completed for each child during the two testing sessions—one by a teacher and one by a school psychologist. A minimum of a 35 minute observation period of each child was required for completion of the rating scale.

The Class Play (Bower, 1958), a sociometric questionnaire, was administered in October and again in June by the classroom teacher on a group basis. Every child in the regular classes which had one emotionally disturbed child was involved.

Instruments Used

Wide Range Achievement Test.   The Wide Range Achievement Test was devised by Jastak (1946) for determining achievement level in the basic school subjects of reading, spelling, and arithmetic. In these three skills, the range of the instrument extends from kindergarten to college. Jastak (1946) reported that the test provided a suitable achievement measure for clinical work. The reliability coefficients determined by repeated testing of 280 cases ranged from .88 to .95.

Behavior Rating Scale.   The Behavior Rating Scale was developed by Haring and Phillips (1962) for use in measuring change in overt behavior of emotionally disturbed children. The Behavior Rating Scale is a 7 point Likert type scale consisting of 26 items. The judge rates a child from 1 to 7 on an item of descriptive behavior. The values of the items and raters are averaged to yield a single score. In the current study, the test reliability of 36 means of two raters was .95. Internal consistency of each item to the single score provided data that 23 of the 26 items were consistent at the .01 level.

Analysis of the agreement between the raters is presented in Table 2. The correlation coefficient between raters was .75, a value which is significant at the .05 level. Through the use of the F test, it was established that homogeneity of variance existed between the two groups of raters. The t value between raters yielded results that showed their ratings were not significantly different from each other.

In this study all information reported concerning rater agreement using the Behavior Rating Scale instrument illustrated agreement in scoring.

Table 2. Analysis of the Raters'
Agreement on the Behavior Rating
Scale

Raters	Mean	N	F	t	r
Teachers	4.16	33			
Psychologists	4.10	33			
			1.77	1.20	.75*

*Significant at the .05 level

A Class Play.   A Class Play was devised by Bower (1958) for use as a sociometric device with elementary children. Certain of the parts in A Class Play are representative of negative roles, and others, positive. These roles are based on commonly accepted cultural perceptions. The student is asked to indicate a child in his class who best fits the role as described by his teacher. A child received an acceptance score of one each time his name was given by any classmate in response to a positive question. Since there is no method of determining the extent of acceptance or rejection, there was no adequate basis on which to assign weights to the scores. For data analysis, it was assumed that each child named was accepted or rejected equally on each question.

In its original form, A Class Play contained 12 roles, but for purposes of this study, the 6 roles with the highest discrimination value based on factor analysis (numbers 1, 2, 3, 4, 10, and 11) were employed (Bower, 1958).

Results

This section is presented in three parts: (a) Wide Range Achievement Test results, (b) Behavior Rating Scale results, and (c) sociometric results.

Wide Range Achievement Results

The mean gain scores of the emotionally disturbed children in the regular and special classes are presented in Table 3.

The t value between the two groups was significant at the .05 level. This suggests that the achievement gains made by the emotionally disturbed children in the special classes exceeded those made by the emotionally disturbed children in the regular classes.

Table 3. Comparison of the Emotionally Disturbed Children in the Regular and Special Classes on the Wide Range Achievment Test

Emotionally disturbed children	N	Pretest a		Posttest		Mean gain in grade achievement	F	t
		Mean	SD	Mean	SD			
Special class	16	2.71	1.60	3.26	.98	.56		
Regular class	16	3.00	1.04	3.30	1.09	.30		
							1.37	2.60 b

a Pretest results not significantly different at .05 level

b $p < .05$

Table 4. Comparison of the Emotionally Disturbed Children in the Regular and Special Classes on the Behavior Rating Scale.

Emotionally disturbed children	N	Pretest a		Posttest		Mean gain in grade achievement	F	t
		Mean	SD	Mean	SD			
Special class	16	4.19	.52	3.77	.76	.42		
Regular class	16	4.02	.96	4.26	.85	—.24		
							1.19	4.33 b

a Pretest results not significantly different at .05 level

b $p < .05$

Behavior Rating Scale Results

The data presented in Table 4 contains the F and t values derived from the mean gain scores of the emotionally disturbed children in the regular and special classes. The t value between the two groups was significant at the .05 level. Analysis of the results indicated that gains made by the emotionally disturbed children in the special classes exceeded those made by the emotionally disturbed children in the regular classes.

Sociometric Results

The sociometric questionnaire was administered in the fall and again in the spring in order to determine any change in the social position of emotionally disturbed children with the passage of time.

The results of acceptance and rejection scores on the fall administration of the sociometric questionnaire are presented in Table 5. The data present the comparison of the mean acceptance and rejection scores of the emotionally disturbed and normal groups. This table presents the number of children in each group (N), the mean scores (M), the standard deviations (SD), the difference between the means (D), and the t statistical test.

The results indicated that the emotionally disturbed children were not as accepted within their classes as were the normal children since their mean score was lower than the normal group. The difference between mean acceptance scores of the two groups was statistically significant at the .05 level.

The comparison of stars, isolates, and rejectees in the emotionally disturbed and normal groups for the fall is presented in Figure 1. The method of determining stars, isolates, and rejectees follows that

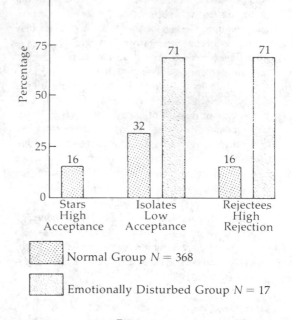

Figure 1.

developed by Bronfenbrenner (1943) to calculate a chance expectance index for each class. With these values it was possible to determine the equivalent t for each cumulative frequency. For example, a significantly low acceptance score indicated an isolate, a significantly high acceptance score indicated a star, and a significantly high rejection score indicated a rejectee. It was possible that a child could be classified into one or more categories providing significance was achieved in each category.

This illustration shows that (a) none of the children in the emotionally disturbed group was classified as a star while 16 percent of the normal group were stars, (b) the percentage of isolates was greater in the emotionally disturbed group than in the normal group, and (c) the largest percentages of

Table 5. Comparison of Acceptance and Rejection Scores of Emotionally
Disturbed and Normal Groups (Fall)

Scores	N		Mean		SD		D	t
	Emotionally disturbed [a]	Normal	Emotionally disturbed	Normal	Emotionally disturbed	Normal		
Acceptance score	17	368	.82	3.01	1.07	14.40	2.19	2.74 [b]
Rejection score	17	368	12.94	2.42	9.77	12.00	10.51	3.51 [b]

[a] The sociometric questionnaire was administered to one additional emotionally disturbed child in the regular class.

[b] $p < .05$

rejectees were found in the emotionally disturbed group.

The results of acceptance and rejection scores on the spring administration of the sociometric questionnaire are presented in Table 6. The members of the emotionally disturbed group were not as accepted within their classes as were the normal children. This difference between the two groups was statistically significant at the .05 level. In comparing the rejection scores, the emotionally disturbed group was more rejected than was the normal group.

The fall and spring acceptance and rejection scores of the emotionally disturbed groups are presented in Table 7, which contain the *t* values derived from the comparisons. The comparisons showed no significant difference. This seems to indicate that the social position of emotionally disturbed children was relatively stable throughout the school year.

In Figure 2 an illustration of stars, isolates, and rejectees of the emotionally disturbed groups is shown graphically for the spring testing. These results were relatively consistent with the results of the fall sociometric questionnaire.

An examiniation of Figure 2 presents the following information.

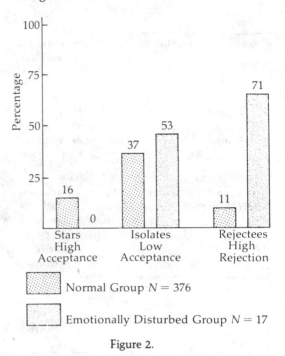

Figure 2.

1. The percentage of stars in the normal and emotionally disturbed groups remained consistent in both the fall and spring testing. The emotionally disturbed children were not chosen positively to any appreciable degree.

2. The percentage of isolates was greatest among the emotionally disturbed group. In comparison with the fall results, the number fluctuated in both groups.

3. The percentage of rejectees in the emotionally disturbed group in the spring remained consistent

Table 7. Comparison of Fall and Spring Acceptance and Rejection Scores of the Emotionally Disturbed Group

Scores	Fall		Spring		D	*t*
	Mean	N	Mean	N		
Acceptance score	.82	17	.71	17	−.11	.31
Rejection score	12.94	17	11.00	17	−1.94	.58

Table 6. Comparison of Acceptance and Rejection Scores of Emotionally Disturbed and Normal Groups (Spring)

Scores	N		Mean		SD		D	*t*
	Emotionally disturbed	Normal	Emotionally disturbed	Normal	Emotionally disturbed	Normal		
Acceptance score	17	376	.71	3.02	.95	13.79	2.19	2.71*
Rejection score	17	376	11.00	2.48	9.55	11.42	8.52	2.82*

*p < .05

with the fall results, whereas the percentage in the normal group decreased slightly.

Conclusions

A comparative description was made on the basis of the analyzed data and the following conclusions appeared justified.

1.   The emotionally disturbed children in regular classes achieved less well on the Wide Range Achievement Test than the emotionally disturbed children in special classes.

2.   While emotionally disturbed children in the special classes made changes in overt behavior in a positive direction, the emotionally disturbed children in regular classes showed changes in overt behavior in a negative direction measured by the Behavior Rating Scale. The mean gain score of the emotionally disturbed children in the regular class-

es was significantly different than the mean gain score of the special class group.

3.   The emotionally disturbed children in the regular classes were less accepted than the normal children. The mean acceptance score of the emotionally disturbed group was significantly less than the mean acceptance score of the normal group.

4.   The emotionally disturbed children in the regular classes were more rejected than the normal children. The mean rejection score of the emotionally disturbed group was significantly greater than the mean rejection score of the normal group.

5.   An analysis of the results of the sociometric questionnaire for stars, isolates, and rejectees indicated that (a) the percentage of stars was greatest in the normal group, (b) the percentage of rejectees was greatest in the emotionally disturbed group, and (c) the percentage of isolates was greatest in the emotionally disturbed group. Although the percentages varied in the fall and spring sociometric results, the data were consistent.

Article References

Axline, V. *Play therapy.* Boston: Houghton Mifflin, 1947.

Balow, B. The emotionally and socially handicapped. *Review of Educational Research,* 1966, *36* (1).

Bettelheim, B. *Love is not enough.* New York: Free Press, 1949.

Bossard, J.H. *Sociology of child development.* New York: Harper, 1960.

Bower, E.M. *A process for early identification of emotionally disturbed children.* Bulletin of California State Department of Education, 1958.

Bower, E.M. *Early identification of emotionally handicapped children in school.* Springfield, Ill.: Charles C. Thomas, 1960.

Bronfenbrenner, U. A constant frame of reference for sociometric research: Part 1. *Sociometry,* 1943, *6,* 363–397.

Cruickshank, W.M., Bentzen, F.A., Ratzeburg, F.H., & Tannhauser, M.T. *Teaching methodology for brain injured and hyperactive children.* Syracuse: Syracuse University Press, 1961.

Haring, N.G., & Phillips, E.L. *Educating emotionally disturbed children.* New York: McGraw-Hill, 1962.

Hymes, J.L., Jr. *Behavior and misbehavior.* New Jersey: Prentice-Hall, 1955.

Jastak, J. *Wide Range Achievement Test.* Wilmington, Del.: C.L. Story, 1946.

Knoblock, P. *Intervention approaches in educating emotionally disturbed children.* Syracuse: Syracuse University Press, 1966.

Morse, W.C., Cutler, R.L., & Fink, A.H. *Public school classes for the emotionally handicapped: A research analysis.* Washington, D.C.: Council for Exceptional Children, NEA, 1964.

Moustakas, C.E. *The teacher and the child.* New York: McGraw-Hill, 1956.

Newman, R.G. The acting-out boy. *Exceptional Children,* 1956, *22,* 186–190, 204–216.

Olmstead, M.S. *The small group.* New York: Random House, 1959.

Pearson, G.H. *Psychoanalysis and the education of the child.* New York: Norton, 1954.

Phillips, B.N., & DeVault, M.V. Relation of positive and negative valuations to social and personal adjustment of schoolchildren. *Journal of Applied Psychology.* 1955, *39,* 409–412.

Prescott, D.A. *The child in the educative process.* New York: McGraw-Hill, 1957.

Radin, S.S., Cary, G.L., Chorost, S.B., Kaplan, S.G., & Garcea, R.A. Orthopsychiatry and special services for emotionally disturbed children in the public school setting: Syracuse Scholastic Rehabilitation program. *Journal of School Health,* 1966, *36,* 245–248.

Redl, F. Crisis in the children's field. *American Journal of Orthopsychiatry,* 1962, *32,* 759–780.

Redl, F., & Wattenberg, W.W. *Mental hygiene in teaching.* New York: Harcourt, Brace, 1951.

Rhodes, W.C. Psychological techniques and theory applied to behavior modification. *Exceptional Children,* 1962, *28,* 333–338.

Rogers, C.R. The criteria used in a study of mental health problems. *Educational Research Bulletin,* 1942, *21* (2), 29–40. (a)

Rogers, C.R. Mental health findings in three elementary schools. *Educational Research Bulletin,* 1942, *21* (3), 69–79. (b)

Rogers, C.R. *Client-centered therapy.* Boston: Houghton Mifflin, 1951.

Sullivan, H.S. *The interpersonal theory of psychiatry,* New York: Norton, 1953.

Vaughan, W.T. Children in crisis. *Mental Hygiene,* 1961, *45,* 354–359.

White, M.A., & Harris, M.W. *The school psychologist.* New York: Harper and Brother, 1961.

White, R.W. Competence and the psychosexual stages of development. In M.R. Jones (Ed.) *Nebraska symposium on motivation,* 1960. Pp. 97–141.

Vacc later followed up special class pupils on a long-term basis and his results are most discouraging, although again they include small "N" groups.[25] He found no advantage to the special class intervention. However, we cannot know how prescriptive the child's actual experience was, nor are fortuitous happenings in the child's life taken into consideration, and finally, there were doubtless some children who improved in either situation and others who did not.

There are even more grave difficulties in assessing the sporadic crisis-resource teacher intervention. Quay and Glavin[26] have studied both classes and resource rooms over a four-year period. Their programs utilized behavior modification procedures and resulted in definite improvements in social and academic behavior. They indicate that the most cost-effective program is the resource room.

The next article hints at issues for the future. It illustrates the forces for change in program design emanating from the professionals who analyze present conditions.

The following article is a concise statement of Rhode's ecological model, an essential direction for new prevention and treatment strategies. It implies a new synthesis, which will include an assessment of the child as part of an interacting system which includes the family, the school, the community, and the social value system. Those who plan to help disturbed children must find ways to function in the social system, as well as directly with the child. They must direct their attention to innovative ways of working with the rest of the child's environment. The professional worker can no longer hide in a classroom or office.

A Community Participation
Analysis of Emotional Disturbance
William C. Rhodes

Introduce a "strange" or "peculiar" child into any microcommunity (a classroom, group cottage, family home) and observe the ripples of discomfort which are triggered off around him. Observe the collective dynamics in his proximal environment; he becomes a disturbing catalyst, sending waves of excitation and of irritation throughout the microcommunity into which he has been inserted.

From William C. Rhodes, "A Community Participation Analysis of Emotional Disturbance," *Exceptional Children,* January 1970, pp. 309–314. Reprinted by permission of the Council for Exceptional Children and the author.

Observe the exchanges which then take place between the child and the collective surrounding him. It is like a reverberating circuit of disturbed mood-behavior exchanges. The child becomes a collective object around which intense collective dynamics ebb and flow. He both absorbs and generates intensive responses to his presence in the microcommunity.

In such a situation, we are observing an ecological exchange, a reciprocity between the child and his living environment which is disquieting and uneasy.

Remove the same child. Place him in a specially constituted setting, one in which the exchange patterns are especially structured to accommodate to him (a therapeutic milieu, for instance) and something happens. The child is no longer so strange. He no longer generates constant currents of mood-behavior excitation. He seems different—more "normal." He is more a part of his microcommunity, more in harmony with his setting.

Having made these ecological observations of a child in a live setting, let us now move to simpler forms of microcommunity life. Let us observe what happens in communities of lower animals when one of the members of the colony provides a deviant or unaccustomed set of species signals.

As reported by Lorenz (1967), when a strange bee, termite, or ant enters an established colony, he sends waves of disturbance throughout the hive, nest, or anthill. The agitated members of the colony attack and destroy him. Lorenz reported that it has long been known that the quality of strangeness which triggers the intense mood-behavior of the colonies is a deviant smell, one that is different from that of the clan. Members of the colony recognize each other by a characteristic hive, nest, or anthill smell and they coalesce in agitation around anyone who enters with a scent that deviates from the accustomed one.

Lorenz reported that it has been known only since 1950 that rodents behave similarly. When a strange rat enters a colony, the information is transmitted like an electric shock throughout the whole colony. The alarm is sounded by the deviation of this intruder rat's odor from the characteristic colony smell. The rest of the colony becomes thoroughly agitated by this deviation.

With their eyes bulging from their sockets, their hair standing on end, the rats set out on the rat hunt. They are so angry that if two of them meet they bite each other. . . . On the day of persecution of the strange rat all the members of the clan are irritable and suspicious [Lorenz, 1967, p. 155].

If a member of the rat colony is removed and put in a sterile environment so that he loses the clan smell, he too will be attacked when returned to the rat community. If he is quickly removed again and placed in the earth and other materials of the colony so that he absorbs the same odor, he can be returned with impunity.

In studies of fish life at the undersea site of a coral atoll, scientists have discovered that by slightly drugging a fish or altering his behavior by placing him in underwater floating fishbowls, they can directly influence the behavior of other fish in the surrounding environment. Members of his own school will flee from his vicinity. Predatory fish will be instantly attracted by his slight deviation from his own kind and will single him out for attack.

A related phenomenon has been reported by Hebb (1949). Hebb was studying the fear reactions of chimpanzees in the Yerkes colony to a deviant or unaccustomed image stimulus of one of its own members. He presented the colony with the disembodied head of a chimpanzee and with an anesthetized chimpanzee. Chimpanzees in the colony fled from these strange, unaccustomed images as though in paroxysms of terror. Later, using detached parts of chimpanzees, he established that such stimulation was a source of profound excitation, usually followed by avoidance but sometimes by aggression.

Here, in the judgement of the author, we are observing the prototype of "disturbance."

Theory

The intrapsychic analysis of illness, the learning analysis of behavioral disorders, and the communication conception of organic deficit (which conceptualizes disorders in the receptor, effector, or integrator organs of the child) all have clinical or experimental support as reasonable explanations of child problems which lead to intervention. The analysis offered here does not challenge these frames of reference as they apply to various conditions in children whom we lump together under the umbrella term of "disturbance." Instead it acknowledges that any one of these hypotheses may be partially applicable to the condition which is labeled "emotional disturbance." However, it attempts to shift the locus of the disturbance from the child to an encounter point between the child and the microcommunity or microcommunities which surround him. It addresses itself to the ecological exchange nature of the disturbance. It searches for an intervention which will address itself to the shared process which is occurring between the child and the microcommunities he is encountering.

The point of departure in this particular analysis of emotional disturbance is not scientific understanding, but ethical intervention into the ecological exchange. The view presented here suggests that intervention into the surroundings of the child should occur simultaneously with any intervention into the condition of the child, because the disturbing events are reciprocal products rather than isolated attributes of the child—live products of the encounter between a child and a participating community (community is used here to refer to the resonating environment surrounding the child). The community participation analysis also suggests that interventions attempted within any of the three frames of reference (intrapsychic, behavioral, or biophysical) cannot adequately deal with the problem of disturbance. In almost every case using these conceptions, the significant variables upon which the interventions concentrate are centered within the child.

This has proven to be an inefficient and ineffective approach for any single child. These conceptions offer no promise of getting to sources and preventing or alleviating the creation and development of such children. Nor can any of the interventions derived from these theories promise to come to grips with the large numbers of children involved. In addition, such interventions do nothing at all about the "normal" children who may be less visibly affected by the same process in the same setting.

In the intrapsychic approach or even in the interpsychic approach, the disturbance is seen as located within the child, and the operations upon the environment or upon other individuals in the child's orbit are tangential or peripheral to the major intervention locus—the child. In the behavior modification approach, in spite of the manipulations of the environment or of environmental contingencies, the focus is upon maladaptive behavior of the child. In the communications or organic approach, the deficit is conceptualized as residing within the child. Any environmental arrangements which are made are attempts to compensate for this deficit.

In the community participation analysis of emotional disturbance, the problem is seen as a community condition. It is a reciprocal condition which exists when intense coping responses are released within a human community by a community member's atypical behavior and responses.

The triggering stimulus, the rejoinder of the microcommunity, and the ensuring transactions are all involved in emotional disturbance. The total process must be considered if one has any intention of intervening in the situation most effectively and most ethically.

One of the signs of disturbance is the increase of energy and the intensity of effort which has to be made by the respondent community in exchanges with the signaling individual. The disturbance might be looked upon as a faulty encounter between the individual and the community in which neither side is able to adapt to the other.

Assumptions in the Community Transaction Analysis

The participating community analysis of child disturbance makes certain assumptions which are critical for intervention. The first assumption is that response release signals are being emitted by a child into the live setting (his microcommunity) surrounding him, and that these signals are activating disturbance in the setting. Instead of saying that the child is maladapted, we might discuss a maladaptive microcommunity or setting (the home, the classroom, the work group, the play group, etc.).

The second assumption is that the released community responses are directly influenced by the culture of the microcommunity in which they occur. This means that the released response is a culturally relative phenomenon. It is colored by the stored culture in the particular community and in the internalized culture of the responders who share the community with the signaler.

In simpler forms of life, the disturbing signal is any noticeable variation of members in the community. Released response seems to be either attack or flight from other members of the collective. Removal of the signaler image halts the triggering, or release, of agitated responses in the collective environment. The environment can then return to its nondisruptive state and the agitation gradually fades away.

In a human microcommunity the transaction which occurs may not be quite so simple. Although the primitive or simple signal-response release transaction may follow the same principles, it is colored by the culture stored in the context surrounding the signaler and internalized in the culture bearer.

Behaviors which are responded to with

agitation in one community context may not provoke the same response in another context, depending upon the incorporated culture of the resonators and the stored culture of the context in which the transaction or encounter is occurring. If, for instance, a child in a slum neighborhood engages in certain kinds of fighting behavior such as gang rumbles, or in acquisition behaviors such as stealing, it may attract no attention from adults in that context because it is not necessarily responded to as a behavioral violation requiring control actions. In another socioeconomic or cultural context and with other responders, it may be responded to as delinquent behavior and delinquent control interventions are called into play.

The important dimensions of human disturbance being stressed here, which are not usually encompassed in theories about emotional disturbance, are those which have to do with the community nature and the cultural relativity of the disturbance. Both of these are considered necessary conditions in the intervention preparations. To say that any child condition labeled pathological is partly defined by the resonance of the microenvironment does not deny that there may be real biological or behavioral differences in the child. It does not deny that the disturbed situation can be, more or less, affected by unilateral interventions into the child. It states, however, that the community resonance is part of the disturbed condition and should be taken into account in the intervention. It says also that the ecological exchange is influenced by its cultural context.

Adaptive Capacity of Communities

The contribution made by the adaptive ability in microcommunities harboring or containing such a signaling individual can be grasped by comparing the self presentations of a schizophrenic child in his "normal" public school community and in a high quality residential treatment community.

Every professional has experienced widely contrasting behaviors in such a child over a very short period of time when he is moved from the ill adapting environment of the classroom to the adaptive or effective coping environment of the treatment setting. The child in the public school is very "sick," whereas, when he is viewed in the adapting residential setting, he is much less "sick."

By comparison of these two microcommunities one can say that the "normal" human community was nonadaptive, and the residential setting provided an adaptive participating community for the child.

Anyone who has read the compelling story of Makarenko (1951) would see the same type of contrast of adaptive and maladaptive participation of communities in the Gorky and Kuryazh colonies. In Makarenko's account, after the Gorky Colony was well established and running smoothly, he was asked to take over a much larger community of children and young people in the Kuryazh Colony. This colony was a "sick" community. There was no order. Classes were not held. Teachers barricaded themselves in their rooms which had been stripped almost bare by the thievery of the colonists. The living quarters were without doors because the children had chopped them up for firewood. The older boys had organized the younger boys to go into town and steal for them. Some of the older boys were highwaymen.

With great reluctance, Makarenko finally took over the Kuryazh Colony. He not only imported the culture of the Gorky Colony, but he brought with him a cadre of Gorky colonists who had incorporated that culture within themselves. As a result of the cultural import, he was able to transform the disturbing Kuryazh Colony into a constructive and flourishing environment.

In a short period of time the Kuryazh colonists appeared quite different from the picture they had presented before the coming of the Gorky cadre. Quite obviously both the individuals and the community were changed.

In either of the two examples presented here we see the very same children in quite different lights, depending upon the community with which they are exchanging. If we examine the schizophrenic child or the disturbing Kuryazh colonists as they behave in the "before" environments, we view serious problem individuals. If we view them in their transactions with the "after" environments, we see quite different individuals. In these examples, the quality of the resonance is certainly different and makes a difference in the observed behavior of the signaler. This analysis suggests another inference that might be made about the signaler within the participating microcommunity. This marked child, who has been singled out as the possessor of the disturbance, can be thought of as a pointer, gauge, or indicator of something which is maladaptive in the responsivity of the microcommunity.

If we follow the reciprocity analysis and the added provision that the reciprocity is being influenced by the culture of the specific community of occurrence, then we can assume that other children in the community may be experiencing similar difficulties. Although the difficulty may be manifesting itself most dramatically in the child who is obviously at odds, the possibility exists that many other children in the same human community are being affected in similar ways.

If the environment and its active coping culture could be adapted to fit this "unusual" child, it is quite possible that it would be making similar changes in adaptations to all of the other children participating in the microcommunity. By using the child as a pointer or register, one is led to the particular part or aspect of community transactions which must be ameliorated. In this way, the child is like an instrument detecting community inadequacies or malfunctions, suggesting the modifications in the reciprocity which must be made.

Displacement and Blame Projection

In the beginning of this article, it was stated that the point of departure of this particular analysis of emotional disturbance was not scientific understanding, but effective and ethical intervention. It was stated that interventions into the interacting cultural environment must occur simultaneously with any intervention into the condition of the child, because the problem of concern was a reciprocal and not a unilateral one.

In our present practices of providing for emotionally disturbed children, we might be accused of displacing the problem upon the least protected part of the microcommunity in which the problem is manifested. We might also be accused of working with that sector of the problem which can least resist our intervention attempts, and which has the least capacity to defend its right against intrusion. We are tackling that part of the community which is least able to point out the complicity of the rest of the community in the problem. It is much easier to practice our intervention upon the child alone because he is helpless to resist our intrusion. The rest of the community resists reciprocal change. The child is more malleable to change. Therefore, the burden of adaptation is usually placed upon the child.

From both an ethical and a practical point of view, this is a very limited solution to the total problem. It fails to alter the ground out of which the problem arises and allows other children to move into the participating community, be affected by it,

and suffer the consequences of such an engagement. The effort made should not only be one of shaping a particular child to fit a static culture in a community, but also one of constant revision in the community's accommodation to wide ranges of differences in individuals. From the point of view of the community, such capacity to accommodate should make for fewer intense, disruptive convulsions in the total community.

Intervention

This analysis can be used as the background and the basis for any number of intervention measures in the ongoing reciprocity. However, it counter indicates any major program which plucks the child from a context of disturbance, attempts to make all of the changes in him, and restores him to the unchanged context out of which he came.

Furthermore, the ideal intervention measures would be those which enter the active disturbed situation, identify the point of convulsive encounter between the child and the surrounding human community, and then trace the problem as far as possible to its cultural source in the surrounding context both within the others in the context and in the cultural practices and artifacts of the microcommunity or ecological unit.

Ethically, interventions into "emotional disturbance" should face the bilateral nature of the convulsive ecological exchange. Such intervention attempts should aim to change the quality and kind of exchange, either by directly structuring more harmonious exchange designs through which the participating parties interact or by modeling and remodeling the context (cultural and environmental) in which the exchange occurs. For this reason, the author favors consultation over psychotherapy as an intervention process. One should enter into the ecological context of the condition and attempt to influence the quality and nature of the exchange between the child and his microcommunity. Such an intervention recognizes the totality of the problem.

The time has come to begin to concentrate attention upon changing the ecological conditions under which children have to live and grow, and thus reduce the number of occasions of disturbance and the number of children who are extruded or alienated from their living units. This is the only way in which our society can hope to come to terms with the magnitude of the problem called emotional disturbance.

Article References

Hebb, D.O. *The organization of behavior.* New York: John Wiley & Sons, 1949.

Makarenko, A.S. *The road to life: An epic of education.* Translated by I. Litvinov & T. Litvinov. Moscow: Moscow Foreign Languages Publishing, 1951.

Lorenz, K. *On aggression.* Translated by M.K. Wilson. New York: Bantam Books, 1967.

We have left so much untouched. For example, there is the need to take a new look at the treatment of delinquents—treatment often avoided by those in special education. The subject is brought to arresting attention in *The Throwaway Children.*[27] Administratively, there is the crucial role of the principal in any educational program for disturbed children.[28]

Some time ago, Hobbs wrote a provocative article concerning the future of mental health work.[29] His pungent observations are as pertinent to the community mental health movement as they were when he wrote it. In fact, his concept, teaching mental health workers a humanistic background and skills in working with people, serves as a model for the special educators' training. The final article by Morse is an application of some of Hobbs' ideas of special education for the disturbed child. In a way, it can be thought of as a summary of new directions, which must be taken if we are to succeed in our work.

Fact and Fancy Regarding the Mental Health Revolution and Its Implications for Educational Programs for the Disturbed Child
William C. Morse

We have heard from many sources that a mental health revolution is here. Fortunately, the revolution includes educational and medical interest that encompasses not only the disturbed child but the mentally retarded as well. The implications are applicable to both.

This revolution comes at a time of great expansion in educational programs for disturbed children. Many states have passed legislation to foster special classes and other school programs for disturbed pupils. New facilities are being built for residential care. County mental health programs are being developed and encouraged by the federal government. Many will have day-school educational adjuncts. Particularly important is the fact that there is more money for these activities and we know programs are more likely to follow money than ideology. There is money at the federal level for training and experimentation as well as demonstration. There is often money at the state level to reimburse public school classes. In fact, some states have provided more money than there are personnel to man the programs. In all of this there are even a few new ideas and new concepts being incorporated. But by far the most vital element of the mental health revolution is the money. Money makes the critical impact. Yet, we know very well that money isn't everything. After all, the Edsel was launched with a big investment and we do not want a mental health Edsel. Money does not guarantee trained personnel. Money does not guarantee innovation. With the manpower shortage money does not even guarantee adequate service. Thus it is that increased monetary resources may actually bring with them lower quality programs.

It is quite clear that schools and educational programs are close to the center of the new impetus in mental health work and already the pain of metamorphosis is evident. It has been my good fortune to be able to study certain mental health operations where the new in mental health approaches was to replace the old. Several aspects soon became apparent. First, it was much easier to verbalize change than to accomplish real change. Second, many of the new and often discussed programs are still in the honeymoon stages. In fact, the plan for one was written up and published before the first child was diagnosed or involved in any ongoing activity. Even though the fact that it was only a plan was clear, people wrote the authors for advice and help even prior to any operation. Many years later the analysis and results of this program were published though the program was no longer operating. A working model finally evolved after the experimental phase, which had been financed, was over. Another matter of note is that programs appearing in the literature often turn out to be idiosyncratic, born and succored by the special talents of a particular person or by conditions in one place. It may be difficult to transfer the program for replication elsewhere.

There is more money but of course it still is hard to get the money we need, when we need it. Still it is easier to find funds than to change an ideology. It is easier to move a brick wall than to alter a mind. One could raise my salary more easily than one could raise the sites of my mode of operation. These conditions raise some serious questions about how profound our participation is going to be in the so-called mental health revolution. Is it a revolution or just a rotation? The actual revolution will not be found in articles in the *Journal of Orthopsychiatry* or in speeches like this one but in the actual work the teachers did today and will do tomorrow in the confrontation of real situations in the classrooms where the children are.

If there is to be progress, new concepts are vital. As educators we must search out the meaning of new concepts which comprise the mental health revolution. Can we manage the implied innovations or will they manage us? I want to take as a basis for our discussion an article by Nicholas Hobbs entitled, *Mental Health's Third Revolution*. This appeared in the *American Journal of Orthopsychiatry* for October 1964. After we are acquainted with Dr. Hobbs' main proposals, we will attempt to apply these to educational programs for the disturbed child. This article is exciting and provocative. It certainly deserves careful attention from those of us who are trying to look ahead to see what our particular professional work may look like in the future. We can only capitalize on a few of his insights here.

Hobbs points out that there are two phases to any revolution. The first phase is that of invention; the second phase is that of engineering. The invention phase is the discovery of new ideas. The engineering phase involves actually creating new training programs and new institutional designs. The author goes back in history to point out that the first mental health revolution started when insane people were, for the first time, treated with dignity. While some of the old conditions and attitudes unfortunately still persist today, basically this first revolution implied that instead of going to look at people in institutions as if they were animals on display, the ill should have our sympathy and receive kindness and care. To Hobbs, the second mental health revolution was a consequence of the work of Sigmund Freud. In Hobb's mind, revolutions generally tend to excess and he thinks Freud's was no exception. At the present time he suggests that this second revolution, by its unfortunate emphasis, requires a counter-revolution to restore balance and common sense. As he puts it, this is needed to prevent the obsession and passionate commitment we have to the world inside a man's skull, to the unconscious, and to the stuff that dreams are made of. He believes Freud not only influenced the physician but the psychologist, the preacher, the teacher, the social worker. All have been captivated by this point of view. While he admits a debt to Freud, he believes that we must break with this heritage to bring on the third mental revolution. While I would agree to the need for new ideas, I think it only fair to point out that to produce the new as a counter-revolution suggests an unfortunate course. Counter-revolutions are also given to excesses.

This proposed counter-revolution can turn out to be essentially negative, throwing out all that is old and embracing anything new, glorifying half truth and spawning messiahs. For example, at the present time, in many circles it is popular to deny any intrapsychic phenomena. We have people who are involved in working with human beings who deny the importance of motivation or causes or anything except a dissociated sample of external behaviors. It is even possible to join a training program for teachers of disturbed children and see a sign on the desk reading, "Stamp Out the Unconscious." The theme seems to be, "if it is new it is good," regardless of what it is. Obviously, no one wants to be old fashioned. To be eccentric and suggest the importance of various kinds of treatment when used at the appropriate point is considered to be the biggest sin of all. One must be a crusader and fight the infidel. This is exciting verbal cabal but ill suited for those of us who try to meet the complexities of actual children. So while as Hobbs says, "the pendulum might need to swing back," can we be alert to the

possibility that a counter-revolution might also produce consequences every bit as unfortunate as those
he feels were involved in the Freudian second mental health revolution itself?

Hobbs goes on to say that we are now in the
third mental health revolution, which he sees as not
identified with the name of a person, but which is
exemplified in the common theme running through
many apparently discrete innovations of the last 15
years. Basically, as he sees it, the concepts of public
health have finally penetrated the field of mental
health. This means we have left the clinical model to
accept the public health model and are seeking ways
to make it work in practice. To quote Hobbs, "Mental illness is not the private organic misery of an individual but a social, ethical, and moral problem, a
responsibility of the total community." When we
think of the implications of this, it becomes clear
that this mental health revolution involves the total
society in which we live. We are every bit as concerned about housing, the size and location of the
schools we build, and the discrimination which is
apparent in our society, as we are in usual mental
health professional concerns if we accept this concept of mental health. One of the immediate difficulties of this concept of mental health is the fact
that the immensity of the problem tends to immobilize many of us who are not used to thinking in
these terms. The fact that the total social fabric must
be altered to achieve the type of a resolution we aim
for is frightening. As a result, many of us would
prefer to stay or beat retreat to the protection of our
own professions and the fractionated relationship
we have with the individuals we are trying to help.
Offices are more circumscribed than neighborhoods.
So are classrooms. This escape is as true for teachers as anyone else. We can close the door and
symbolically reduce our concern. The suggestion
which Hobbs makes, however, is that we must face
the implications in the total community and all of its
life if we are ever to fulfill the goal of the third mental health revolution. It means not only a clinic in
the community but it means a hygienic approach to
the whole social fabric of the community where the
elements of mental health are put into practice in the
many, many aspects of our social existence.

Hobbs moves on as he refers to a study done to
find out what determines the kind of treatment disturbed people receive. The investigators found no
relationship between the diagnosis of an individual
and the type of treatment he got. They studied various diagnostic variables and found these unrelated
to treatment. The one variable related to the type of
treatment received was the socio-economic status of
the patient. It appears that one's socio-economic
groove defines treatment regardless of diagnosis.
Those in the high socio-economic group received
extended, expensive, talking psychotherapy. Those
in the low group tended to get quick therapy,
mechanical, drug or electroshock. Now the basic
issue which Hobbs is pointing out is the need to
individualize and relate programs to the particular
needs as revealed by diagnostic study. Treatment
follows—or should—diagnosis not pocketbooks.
Those of us in special education have a responsibility for suitable programs not based on ability to pay.
We must ask ourselves whether or not the types of
things we do with children are based upon specific
differential diagnosis or whether they are just programs to which the child is supposed to fit. Do the
less affluent in the center city get cheap, quick programs, devoid of what is really needed? How much
relationship is there between our diagnosis and our
differential classroom practice in any class? Do we
imply homogeneity for our class? If we do pretend
we know that it is a fault, since no classroom group,
regardless of how chosen, is really homogeneous.
So, we wonder whether we have met the challenge
of the various varieties of disturbed children which
come to our classes as, for example, those both deprived and disturbed. Have we left these to someone else, or just left them out?

There are other cliches which ignore individual differences in our clientele. One finds such statements as, "all must be in therapy," meaning all
parents, mamas and papas, or the child is refused.
On other occasions one hears, "we wouldn't spoil
our program by allowing therapy." Most of these
statements are made on a global basis without any
reference to a diagnosis or the type or range of children we accept into the classes.

People are talking about their prejudices in program design rather than fitting the program to the
child. We can ask ourselves whether we have included in our special education programs adequate
diagnosis of a sociological, intra-psychic, learning
and neurological factors. We must be specific. Not
only do we have to know a child is anxious, but we
have to find out anxious when, and how much, and
about what. This leads to more specificity about
how to alleviate his tension. One wonders whether
or not the point Hobbs makes concerning treatment needs vs. financial access to mental health
work in general doesn't also apply to much that we
do in educational programs for the disturbed child.

Hobbs' next point is the fact that the available
supply of mental health workers is limited while the
demand for services continues to grow even faster

than the population. As he sees it, in the foreseeable future there will never be personnel to meet the demands for service. He suggests, and I quote, "we must find new ways of deploying the resources of manpower and of knowledge to the end that effective mental health services, for prevention, for diagnosis, for treatment, for rehabilitation, can be made available to all of the people." Now this point has real significance for those of us in our business. What are we doing to deploy our resources for prevention as well as rehabilitation in overall programs for the disturbed child? We know as a fact that many more children are in regular classes than in special classes or special services. Frequently, a school develops a special program or class as a show case and hires us to keep the glass polished. Are we special educators recognizing the responsibility that we have for all handicapped children in the school or do we bask in guilt reduction by helping just our few in our special class? We have to ask ourselves what, eventually, will be the best use of our time. Many of our special class teachers are becoming dissatisfied in being mop-up experts, sloshing around in a mess at least partly perpetrated by the school itself. The question is, do we know how to employ the tactics of prevention? Will the crisis teacher serving the school be better than a class? Is group work for many better than a class for ten? Are the old formats going to be enough?

Hobbs makes a telling point that the mental health specialist (and I quote) "must be a person of broad scientific and humanistic education, a person prepared to help make decisions not only about the welfare of an individual, but also about the kind of society that must be developed to nurture the greatest human fulfillment." Then he shows that the training for the mental health specialists, whatever their sub-speciality, has not been for prevention. He raises the crucial question of who among us knows enough about the social agencies of our community, the effects of social change, of mobility and so on, to really make judgments about the comprehensive mental health program? It requires a sense of responsibility about the total community, and an insight about its workings. I think this raises a question for us in regard to special education. Are we ready to examine our ideology and training to the broad purposes which Hobbs suggests? It has seemed to many of us that we are in an era of increasing specialization rather than more generic training. We appeared to be interested in more and more about less and less. Most of us want or are forced into myopic courses of a highly specialized nature. Our graduate training seldom involves any

breadth of scientific or humanistic education. The fact is, we are in the process of splitting off more and more the deprived, learning disabilities, the perceptually handicapped and so on. As Dr. William Rhodes has suggested, we will run out of children before special categories. It appears that the more generic approach to special education is losing out after a struggle for a hearing. The contest has been joined but the vested interests of your and my special talents are greater than ever and supersede what we know about the actual nature of our children. Namely, we know that it is hard to find pure cases to fit any of our categories. So many children suffer from multiple handicaps while we train ourselves to treat single deficiencies. One argument is that money is easier come by if we split up into all these sub-specialities. Regardless of reasons or rationalizations it is obvious that most of us are being short-changed or are short-changing ourselves in both the broad humanistic and specialized training which Hobbs suggests as necessary to participate in the third revolution.

Hobb's next point is that the new mental health centers may be nothing more than the same thing that we have always had but a reflection of the general urbanization of America as we move from a rural to city social order. He asks, "shall we succeed in changing only the location and the architecture of the state hospital?" and suggests that unless we do, these would be monuments to failure. We can ask ourselves a similar question about special education. Are we merely adding more of the same in additional classrooms or are we looking for more suitable school programs? Are we looking at programs in terms of services or are we looking at programs in terms of administrative format? In some plans in our area of the country, it appears that a total redeployment of special personnel will be needed.[1]

Hobb's next issue is that the mental health specialist "must be trained in ways to multiply his effectiveness by working through other less extensively and expensively trained people." Thus, the more highly trained person will have to guide and cooperate with those with limited training in order to meet the manpower shortage. Hobbs even gives the figure that each one of us should multiply his effectiveness by a factor of six through working through other people. This raises some very interesting problems for those of us in education. How are we going to relate to the sub-specialities? We are going to expect them to be sort of educational chambermaids, doing the dirty work while we do the exciting work. This will hit at the very core of our professional concepts. The basic issue of this sharing is the end of the sacred and profane in education just as it has finally come to be understood relative to the concept of therapy. Educators chafed and groaned under the old style psychiatric dominance. Yet we can ask whether or not we, in our relationships, will be able to accept others on a co-equal basis. Basically, teaching is a King of the Hill operation where each person operates in his own fashion. For example, it has been found difficult to develop team operations of co-equals even among trained teachers. Most of the teams end with one dominant and one submissive individual. If this point of Hobbs' is taken seriously and we follow through, can we admit that there is somewhat less magic and somewhat more hard work and somewhat less specialization and somewhat more humaneness needed to accomplish some of the things that we are trying to do? It will mean less charisma and more time investment as an essential ingredient. We will have to become afraid of green thumb selfblooming expertise. It will be interesting to see whether or not we can treat our assistant personnel and sub-specialities as co-equals or will we follow what has happened to us. It becomes almost a matter of how to make others into effective team workers. For example, one teacher had older sixth grade poor to fair readers tutoring first grade very poor readers. Each of the older children worked with one of the younger children. All of this was under the teacher's guidance with coaching and materials being antecedent. She said there was a question as to whether the older or younger children benefitted more since it was obviously very important to the self-concepts and self-esteem of the older children. Or to take a more extreme example, can we accept delinquents helping potentially delinquent younger boys in programs designed to prevent delinquency? Are we ready for this sector of the mental health approach?

In one of the studies where co-teachers of less training were put in with regular teachers, it became clear that the regular teachers could not really tolerate anyone else in the room at the same time even if it was to be helpful to the children. Our problem really is how to locate less trained personnel and then to work with them to enhance their mental health functioning. How can we use lay-expertise? There is even a real question as to whether or not we have found ways to consult with our own peers and teachers to bring the mental health concepts which we believe are vital into a more active involvement with the total schooling.

Hobbs' next point is that the new mental health worker will shift toward working through the existing social institutions rather than building all new institutions. He says, and again I quote, "He will need to be adept at institution building, at social intervention, at the ordering of individual and community resources in the interest of mental health." For special education this means that we must become aware of the social system of the school to say nothing of the community at large. We must learn how to understand the values and hidden agendas (such as the overall school attitude toward special education which we have called the hospitality index). We must know better the impact of our school practices regarding evaluation, processes of grouping, and how specialists work. We certainly must understand the power structure. We must understand what the influence of "down-town" is. In a recent meeting of teachers, more time was spent in irritation about the system, the authorities in the system and other personnel than in discussing the work with the disturbed children themselves! We are sometimes using more energy in protesting about the system than we are in creative activity with our charges. The basic issue then is, are we going to become students of social systems and social institutions within which the innovation and changes must take place if the new mental health revolution is to be successful?

Hobbs next points out that mental health professors will have to accentuate prevention and put more emphasis on training with regard to the problems of children and early disorders. This emphasis on prevention is a matter about which we can also be thoughtful in special education. One of the evident concerns of master teachers who have been in the field quite awhile is that they are tired of being on the clean-up squad after catastrophes. They are interested in more preventive work. They are interested in working with younger children. The problem is, do we know enough about how to translate our efforts into prevention rather than restoration?

Hobbs goes on to point out that there is a continual obsolescence to our knowledge which makes it necessary to continue study and be a learner so that we can keep up with the vanguard of our field. But he adds one more point of particular concern to special education. It is a matter of goals and purposes. He says, and I use his words, "The therapeutic relationship whether between two people or in a broader social effort is at heart an ethical enterprise, with respect to both method and outcome." The suggestion he makes is that we are going to become more efficient in influencing human behavior, and this means that we must be more concerned about goals than we have been. In special education, we have to raise questions about our goals. Are they realistic? Are they even spelled out? Are we trying to accomplish things that are impossible? Is it cure or limited change? In a recent study of post-adolescent youngsters, it became clear that almost any goal outside of continual institutionalization for many of them was out of the question. What do we do about those after treatment fails, and those with a limited prognosis and little hope? Are we willing to change the very nature of the institutions themselves to give them a better life-long opportunity? It is also true that we haven't even thought about the personality characteristics which a youngster will need for survival in the generations to come. Most of us are still using our own as the base line, and these are outmoded.

There are some other concepts not included in the article quoted which are most important in understanding the third mental health revolution. A few of these we wish to discuss now. One of the leaders of the new revolution is Caplan at Harvard. Caplan says that we should use life's stress points for creative intervention. He talks about crisis intervention and immediate involvement. He speaks of the use of the naturalistic life space and interventions in the normal course of living. Actually, as I have suggested in another paper, the very nature of a crisis is far more complicated, psychologically speaking than one might think. But the point is, have we accepted new dimensions and have we changed our modes of intervention to fit this concept of Caplan's? Behavior is of the essence as a point of departure rather than the intra-psychic processes, though appreciation of this is still necessary. But what is important in the intra-psychic will be revealed in the behavior. Of course, again, we can get so involved with this that we forget the constant need to know intra-psychic aspects in order to interpret behavior and make meaningful observations. At the same time there are particular new skills that are involved in the life stress or crisis intervention point of view. For example, there is life space interviewing. There is the use of the on-the-line worker. Caplan makes many suggestions of ways to bring mental health to the firing line through an involvement with life's stress points. Most of us in special education dealing with the emotionally disturbed have a long way to go before we tool up to take advantage of these action concepts in the classes and programs. We spend more time avoiding crises than using them.

Another major concept in the third mental health revolution is that of comprehensive treatment. What this suggests is that a child should have what he needs rather than that the child should get what we have. We often think doing one proper thing is enough. Many of our programs are almost failures. They are 60 per cent passing programs. They would not pass any Regent's examination. Questions about where a child will finally fit into society are evaded. Few children have single problems and yet we give them single remedial programs. We need more studies of what we are not doing as well as braggadocio studies of miracles we have achieved. In our own examination of special classes, it became clear that very few of the children in these classes have anywhere near the kind of help which their difficulties indicate and which the people who are running the programs suggest as necessary. The service would not pass. This may be why many children are not helped enough. Adequate programming is expensive. Shockingly expensive. But we cannot shut our eyes and pretend. We often act embarrassed when we ask for what is needed because of the expense. Perhaps we should be ashamed of being ashamed.

Another aspect in the modern mental health revolution is the concept of milieu. Everybody has a milieu, but everybody who talks about a therapeutic milieu does not necessarily have one. The term is now so popular that no one would run an institution without implying milieu treatment. Redl has discussed in detail the nature and difficulties of accomplishing a total positive mental health milieu. Most of us are having a great deal of difficulty cleaning up the contemporary milieu and making it really a treatment milieu. All aspects of the child's life have to be considered in such a treatment program. We must learn to understand the field of forces on the child in a group life of the institution. We need to offer help wherever problems are found in the total social living. There is no place for a scapegoat in the staff or rejecting various personnel in the total milieu or for status reasons. In our own studies of children in various activities of the milieu it has been impressive how differently they behave from one place to another. For example, whether they are in a situation like a cookout, at the waterfront or in the crafts shop makes a great difference, as groups have shown. This suggests that you won't be able to tell they were the same children or the leaders the same persons. This is the use of sociological forces in our work. It doesn't mean we give up the intra-psychic but it means that we do pay attention to the sociological phenomena in the field of forces.

Another aspect of the mental health revolution

is the activist concept. It means that those of us in this business will have to expand the perimeters of our action. Most or many of the problems of children have extra class complexity. We cannot sit waiting for the mental health problems to come to us anymore. We must go where the problems are. We must make our interventions wherever they are needed. The sacred rites become less important than the fact of involvement. Some of the modern attempts to actually live in a home and plan changes with parents are examples of the extension of the approach. The account of Red-Wig Therapy,[2] the story of Shapiro, the New York principal, in the *New Yorker* magazine illustrates reaching out. Our local teachers in Headstart who are activating parents are further examples. These activist special educators upset the establishment no end. There is a real split within all the mental health professions between those who stand on ceremony and those who believe in going where the problem is. Becoming active in the whole life of the community is necessary as well as trying to resolve the conflicts of distraught individuals wherever they may be. The old style helping professions fear this and are content to sit in an office or in a restricted confine and do their business there. The mental health revolution suggests that the activist concept is extremely important.

Now, I want to speak of what I consider as a pseudo revolution. This is the great deal of energy which is continually expended to conduct a burial. Apparently the burial fails. This is a burial of the "medical model." It is like the movie *The Wrong Box*, where the supposed dead arose on the spot. The question is, what should we be burying? Accompanied by somber music and hostile delight we give the model burial. In most of our professional meetings at least one session is devoted to this macabre, well attended process. There is less attention to what will take its place. Many are content with the half model operant design to put in its place. Others would put in the "no-model model," doing whatever seems expedient. A lot of us are fixated on the learning problem model. The fact is, children do not fit models. As was indicated, they are multiply handicapped. If we go in for modeling, whatever the style, we can name the child and deposit him. Fortunate is he with one difficulty only, since there may be a model program for him but the multiply handicapped gets left out. What trips him up and gets him the attention of educators may not be his real problem. He may be tripped up by a low score on an intelligence test, but his real problem may be quite another, in the emotional area, for example. One wonders why we are so anxious to have

a name like the "learning problems" in place of the medical diagnostic categories. I find them equally misleading and equally helpful.

I wonder if it is not an attempt to reduce complexity even though this cannot really be done. Or to imply, as the name indicates, the response that we should make on a more or less automatic basis. Or do we just wish to compete with the medics in naming? While their language has not been particularly useful, one wonders whether ours will be much better. Names do not solutions make and using a name as an explanation or a symptom as a diagnosis will get us noplace. In this new matter of learning problems, a learning problem or learning disability is still a symptom and naming a learning problem does not tell us what to do. There are many patterns. For example, reading disability ranges from perceptual, deprivation and disturbance to the fact that a child may have anxiety or even a role of an unlearner. Maybe he has simply not been motivated at to learn this skill. Others with this symptom have ego lacunae, their major effort is verbal and they put forth no real learning effort. What we do in treatment follows the diagnosis and not the name. Perhaps we can find a better employment for our time than to go to the funeral held for the medical pressure group.

Another area of importance today in the mental health revolution is the concept of treating the pupil at home. This is like President Johnson's "going back to the farm" speech. Treatment is thought best in the child's own room or maybe eventually in the womb. There is no question but that we should try to get treatment as close as we can to the problem. This may be in the home or it may be in the regular classroom. We were told that such treatment would be cheaper and we could soon close our institutions. Our evidence from some studies in Michigan is that we will still need a gamut of services. It would be just as bad to have no hospitals as to advocate hospitalization for all children. It is the *inappropriate* use of what we have and the overload on services not equipped to do the job that they are asked to do which is the problem. As we watch the development of the new mental health concepts, we must be wary of this idea that everything can be treated in the home just as we should be wary of the idea that nothing can be treated in the home and all children need institutionalization. But it does portend a far greater emphasis on non-special class special education. Have we thought of how to do this?

In conclusion, it seems important to me to ask ourselves the question of whether or not we can get back to the essential aspects of our work. Can we keep the fundamental conditions before us? It is not a matter of administrative design, of classes versus crisis teachers, of tutoring versus classes. The real issue is the actual impact of *whatever* design we choose on the individual child. We can ask ourselves two basic questions. One, are we concerned with the whole child in all his aspects? It is not just his arithmetic or his spelling. It is all of him. This defines our role. And this diffuses it. Even when parts of the responsibility for the pupil are shared by other professionals, whatever we do is specifically in the context of the total child.

Second, and corollary to this, is the question: Are we aiming for the maximum individualization in our classes? We do this by differential diagnosis, looking at all of the factors. Are we looking at his learning modes? If we don't know all about him, we often know nothing. Piecemeal predictions cast in terms of prognosis will get us nowhere. The day of generalization or short cuts is over. Our question is, how unique and how specific is our planning for each child and on what is it based? We must think in terms of all areas of the milieu in which the child lives and here we mean his milieu, whether he is institutionalized or not. The challenge is to discover how we can cultivate the intensity and variety of programs needed to meet the individual differences we find in these children. Called by whatever name we want, whether learning disabilities or a psychiatric category, they are disturbed children. They may find assistance through a group therapy program, a big brother movement, Ojemann's program, course work, a special class or what have you.

The third revolution in mental health is exciting, but it is also frightening. Those of us who are working with the educational phase, as members of the team, must keep up with the major emphases and translate these into practice for our domain in the challenging times just ahead.

Article Footnotes

---

1. See Morse in Peter Knoblock (Ed.), *Second Annual Conference on the Education of Emotionally Disturbed*, Syracuse University Press, 1966.

2. Morse in Peter Knoblock (Ed.), *Educational Programming for Emotionally Disturbed Children: The Decade Ahead*, Syracuse University Press, 1965.

We can and must improve the ways we help disturbed children to mental health. As we observe the change from classic pathologies to drugs, alienation, and aggression (the new social pathologies), it is clear that the potential of education is becoming more important as a basic mental health force. However, education alone cannot compensate for unhygienic societal conditions. Our new ecological understanding shows the critical part played by poverty, racism, and national policies based upon superficial values imparted to the young. Mental health consists of the ability to hope and the ability to deal with reality. Still, education has a substantial role to play in bringing mental health to disturbed children. Schools must become as concerned with emotional maturing as with intellectual stimulation, as concerned with the self-concept as with the achievement test scores. This has been clearly stated by Jones in his exciting work, *Fantasy and Feeling in Education* (New York University Press, 1968). He claims that we cannot depend on secondary prevention or rehabilitation, but must devise processes to integrate feeling as well as thinking into education. Jones sees himself as doing for affective education what Bruner has done for cognitive education. Many of the proposals for special programs and ecological adjustments in schools, will lead in such a direction.[30]

When one examines the special role of education in work with disturbed pupils the problem becomes how to keep a balance between change and conservation of useful past insights.

Discouragement with the methods they have tried in the past has caused many to adopt any new method proposed. We have seen this happen before. Psychotherapy will help everyone and everything. Drugs will empty the hospitals and calm the classrooms. Operant conditioning will rehabilitate the autistic. We have used valid techniques in inappropriate places, over-used some techniques, and then criticized them for failing. But after the frenzy, what basic gains will be made?

Far more diversity in procedures will be available for those who work with disturbed children. All the techniques reviewed have use but in selective fashion. A technique will be chosen by astute diagnostic attention to the child and his ecology. Interventions will become selective and parsimonious. The hard work of differential diagnosis is second only to the exhausting work of rehabilitation efforts.

We see too that, in the diffusion of the term "therapy," education is finding increased importance, but certain educators, often with a minimum of experience with seriously disturbed children, appear to believe they eliminate deviant behavior by new verbalisms. Mental health is not achieved until the many aspects of life are in tune, as the ecological emphasis of education and therapy has pointed out. Unless a child can master what are for him reasonable educational tasks, he cannot be well. Often, basic restoration has been achieved through educational success alone. Later this educational success evolves to finding a position in society. A child cannot be considered on the way to mental health unless he becomes as self-sufficient as is possible in the adult world. Some will be able to reenter normal society. Others will need sheltered workshops and group living with built-in support. The task of education is to prepare them, whether the individual is in a public school class or a state psychiatric unit. To know about one's world, one's feelings, to be able to interact socially, to master skills—so much hinges on a flexible approach to education. Schooling—if it moves away from the prosaic and routine—will have more and more to do with the rehabilitation. Teachers, as Fenichel so well illustrated, are most important.

Although education will assume a larger role, the multi-disciplinary approach is just as necessary. Who should have the responsibility for setting the risk on a potential homicidal or suicidal adolescent? Are teachers able to take over all therapy, make a complicated diagnosis, decide to use drugs? When reasonable ecological restructuring in the classroom is all the help a child needs, the educator may work alone or with minimal consultive planning. However, the need for joint efforts is clear to anyone who has worked, year after year, with very disturbed youngsters. The helping professions have finally recognized that skill and potential for assisting children are maximized when they work together as equals.

As we move ahead, the designs for offering educational assistance will be more and more varied. Interesting experiments are being conducted in all types of helping designs. The crisis teacher, the individualized learning center, the resource room, group counseling and many other designs have been discussed. As most disturbed children are still in regular classes, the new styles of direct assistance and parallel work with regular classroom teachers will become more important. Drastic changes in educational content, mores, and administration will be required.

Finally, evaluation is always related to program purposes and goals, and in efforts to help the disturbed child we are in the midst of a professional re-evaluation and revolution.[31] New standards for practice are emerging.[32][33] Of course, it is easy to have a field day criticizing past practice (such as the "homes for the little wanderers") from our much "enlightened" vantage point, but we should recognize that the same will be done someday with our best. It is also possible to make blanket indictments against classes or institutional treatment without the slightest sophistication regarding the complexity of the issues, as was pointed out earlier in this section. And although it is easier to point a finger than to find a feasible solution, we must read the critics as we search for new insights and higher goals, even if their so-called "proof" is often inadequate.

The fact of the matter is we still have not clarified the process of acculturation for the normal child, the degrees of freedom for individuals, or the range of viable life-styles in a democracy. Because of these questions, we are even more in doubt when it comes to the so-called "disturbed" child. Intervention techniques are poorly understood. Because of the nature of child development itself, and the historical assumption of adult prerogatives, our problem is most difficult.[34] There are some who see every adult relationship with a youngster as *ipso facto* repressive; they advocate that adult interaction be replaced with the tyranny of immaturity, so little is their understanding of the reciprocal nature of human development.

The legal process is actively attempting to define the rights and protections of the disturbed child as well as the adult. Unfortunately, the child care professions fell so far behind that they now must listen to the law to abide by the child's rights even if in the process the child loses needed protection. As always, delinquents will be the most maligned because their behavior produces the greatest public fear-reaction, and they have no organized parent lobby.

As we move into a new age of treatment in which the nature of the healthy person has been considerably redefined and the modes of assistance have become expanded and less ritualistic, how can the professional keep abreast? There are actually several steps which one can take. First, one can continually deepen one's understanding and judgment to better apply a critical sense to the options. Second, one can participate in movements, both ad hoc and sustained, which are taking a stand for better care of the disturbed child. Sometimes it means applying pressure from the inside to make our organizations active. It may require our money and time. Mandatory legislation is a promise, not a program: what about appropriations and high standards for actual programs? What about increasing the total spectrum of services for the disturbed, ranging from prevention to after-care? To counter professional demoralization one must become involved.

Finally, there is self-evaluation. Of course, we are not child-beaters nor are we given to vicious abuse of those under our care. But each one of us must evaluate his own practice against the highest of standards. Have I escaped the human issue through relying on rules and regu-lations? Have I used my ability to maximize the sense of freedom possible for my children? Have I supported their rights with myself as well as with others? Have I tried something that I believed was right even if it involved some risk? Evaluation begins at home. In the last analysis, it is the teacher and others relating directly with children who must usher in the new day. The creative forces must focus here to help those on the line provide a more authentic human experience for the disturbed child.

Chapter 7 Footnotes

1. **W.C. Rhodes and H. Sabin,** A Study of Child Variance Vol. 3: Service Delivery System (Ann Arbor: Institute for the Study of Retardation and Related Disabilities, 1974).

2. **Nicholas Hobbs,** ed., Issues in the Classification of Children (San Francisco: Jossey-Bass, 1974), p. 119.

3. See Schizophrenia Bulletin 8 (Spring 1974).

4. **James M. Kauffman and Clayton D. Lewis,** eds., Teaching Children with Behavior Disorders (Columbus, Ohio: Charles E. Merrill Publishing, 1974), chapter 8.

5   **D.L. MacMillan,** "Special Education for the Mildly Retarded: Savant," Focus on Exceptional Children vol. 2, no. 9, (1971): 1—11.

6. **D. Kendall,** "Toward Integration," Special Education in Canada (November 1971): 3—16.

7. **C.D. Catterall,** "Taxonomy of Prescriptive Interventions," Journal of School Psychology 8 (1970): 5—12.

8. **W.C. Morse, J. Schnertfeger, and D. Golden,** An Evaluative Approach to the Training of Teachers of Disturbed Preschool Children (Ann Arbor, Mich.: School of Education, University of Michigan, 1973).

9. **Harvey Clarizio,** "Stability of Deviant Behavior Through Time," Mental Hygiene, vol. 52, no. 2 (April 1968): 228—293.

10. **D. Morris, E. Soroker, and G. Burrus,** "Follow-Up Studies of Shy Withdrawn Children: Evaluation of Later Adjustment," American Journal of Orthopsychiatry, 24 (1954): 734—754.

11. **M. Zax** et al., "Follow-Up Study of Children Identified Early as Emotionally Disturbed," Journal of Consulting and Clinical Psychology, vol. 32, no. 4 (August 1968): 369—374.

12. **J.P. Glavin,** "Persistence of Behavior Disorders in Public School Children," mimeographed (Temple University).

13. **L. Kohlberg, J. LaCrosse, and D. Ricks,** "The Predictability of Adult Mental Health from Childhood Behavior," in Manual of Child Psychopathology, ed. Benjamin B. Wolman (New York: McGraw-Hill, 1972), pp. 1217—1287.

14   **M.B. Rawson,** Developmental Dyslexia; Adult Accomplishments of Dyslexia Boys, (Baltimore: Johns Hopkins Press, 1968).

15. **H. Nichol,** "Children with Learning Disabilities Referred to Psychiatrists: A Follow-up Study," Journal of Learning Disabilities, vol. 7, no. 2 (1974): 64—122.

16. **N.F. Watt** et al., "School Adjustment and Behavior of Children Hospitalized for Schizophrenia as Adults," American Journal of Orthopsychiatry, vol. 40, no. 2 (1970): 637—657.

17. **W.M. Ahlstrom and R.J. Havighurst,** 400 Losers (San Francisco: Jossey-Bass, 1971).

18. **Charles H. King,** "The Ego and the Integration of Violence in Homicidal Youth," American Journal of Orthopsychiatry, 45 (January 1975): 134—145.

19. **Michael Shepherd, Bram Oppenheim, and Sheila Mitchell,** Childhood Behavior and Mental Health (New York: Grune & Stratton, 1971).

20. **Archie J. McKinnon,** A Follow-up and Analysis of the Effects of Placement in Classes for Emotionally Disturbed Children in Elementary School (Ph.D. dissertation, University of Michigan, 1969).

21. *A Descriptive Follow-Up Study of a Public School Program for the Emotionally Disturbed* (Pontiac, Michigan: Oakland County Schools, 1969) U.S. Dept. HEW, Project No. 8-5068.

22. "Public School Special Classes for Disturbed Children," *Canadian Psychiatric Association Journal,* vol. 13, no. 4 (1968): 375–381.

23. **Frank M. Hewett, Frank D. Taylor, and Alfred A. Artuso,** "The Santa Monica Project: Evaluation of an Engineered Classroom Design with Emotionally Disturbed Children," *Exceptional Children,* vol. 35, no. 7 (March 1969): 523–529.

24. An eloquent plea for new formats is made in the conclusion of a longitudinal study of children in Onondaga County, New York, *Behavior Patterns Associated with Persistent Emotional Disturbances of School Children in Regular Classes of Elementary Grades (Albany, N.Y.: Mental Health Research Unit, N.Y. State Dept. of Mental Hygiene, December 1967).*

25. **N.C. Vacc,** ""Long-term Effects of Special Class Intervention for Emotionally Disturbed Children," *Exceptional Children,* 39 (1972): 15–23.

26. **H.C. Quay and J. Glavin,** "The Education of Behaviorally Disordered Children in the Public School Setting," Final Report Project No. 482207, HEW, U.S. Office of Education for the Handicapped (Washington, D.C.: U.S. Government Printing Office, 1970).

27. **Lisa A. Richette,** *The Throwaway Children* (New York: Dell Publishing Co., 1969).

28. **W.C. Morse,** "Classroom Disturbance: The Principal's Dilemma," (Arlington, Va.: Council for Exceptional Children, 1971).

29. **Nicholas Hobbs,** "Mental Health's Third Revolution," *American Journal of Orthopsychiatry,* 34 (October 1964): 822–833.

30. See **William C. Morse, Craig D. Finger, and George E. Gilmore,** "Innovations in School Mental Health Programs," *Mental and Physical Health Review of Education Research,* 38 (December 1968).

31. The fact that Head Start and many other programs have been faced with "accountability" pressure has resulted in many superficial efforts. Attention is finally being given to the philosophical as well as psychological issues. See **Clifton L. Anderson,** "National Educational Research Design: A Collaborative Approach" (Ph.D. dissertation, University of Michigan, 1975).

32. **Nicholas Hobbs,** *The Futures of Children* (San Francisco: Jossey-Bass, 1974).

33. **Rhodes, William C.** *A Study of Child Variance,* vol. 4, forthcoming.

34. **William C. Morse,** "Concepts Related to Diagnosis of Emotional Impairment" in *State of the Art: Diagnosis and Treatment,* Kay F. Kramer and Richard Rosonke, eds. (Des Moines: Iowa Midwestern Educational Resource Center, 1975), pp. 113–171.